Competent Communication

Communication

Second Edition

COMPETENT COMMUNICATION

Second Edition

Dan O'Hair
University of Oklahoma

Gustav W. Friedrich
University of Oklahoma

John M. Wiemann
University of California at Santa Barbara

Mary O. Wiemann
Santa Barbara City College

St. Martin's Press
New York

Sponsoring editor: Suzanne Phelps Weir
Development editor: Susan Cottenden
Managing editor: Patricia Mansfield Phelan
Project editor: Diane Schadoff
Production supervisor: Scott Lavelle
Art director: Lucy Krikorian
Text design: Patricia McFadden
Graphics: MacArt Design
Photo research: Tobi Zausner
Cover design: Patricia McFadden
Cover art: Zita Asbaghi

Library of Congress Catalog Card Number: 95-73212

Manufactured in the United States of America.
1 0 9 8 7
f   e   d   c   b

For information, write:
St. Martin's Press, Inc.
175 Fifth Avenue
New York, NY 10010

ISBN: 0-312-13857-1

ILLUSTRATION CREDITS

Pages 3, 193, 297, and 391, C. Simonds: Adapted from "Video Guide to accompany *Competent Communication*"
Page 4, Don Klumpp/Image Bank
Page 7, Karen Kasmauski/Woodfin Camp & Associates
Page 11, Leif Skoogfors/Woodfin Camp & Associates
Page 18, (top) Esbin-Anderson/The Image Works; **(left)** Bob Daemmrich/The Image Works; **(right)** Focus on Sports
Pages 32 and 60, Shotgun/The Stock Market
Page 51, Jacques M. Chenet/Woodfin Camp & Associates
Page 62, Focus on Sports
Page 64, David De Lossy/The Image Bank
Page 78, James Wilson/Woodfin Camp & Associates
Page 94, Bob Daemmrich/Stock Boston
Page 100, Brian Yarvin/The Image Works

Acknowledgments and copyrights are continued at the back of the book on the pages following the index, which constitute an extension of the copyright page.

ABOUT THE ▲UTHORS ·········

Dan O'Hair

is Professor and Chair of the Department of Communication at the University of Oklahoma. He has also taught at Texas Christian University, New Mexico State University, and Texas Tech University. He is co-author or co-editor of six communication texts and scholarly volumes and has published more than forty research articles and chapters in dozens of communication, psychology, and health journals and books. He is a frequent presenter at national and international communication conferences, is on the editorial boards of various communication journals, and has served on numerous committees and task forces for regional and national communication associations.

Gustav W. Friedrich

is Professor in the Department of Communication at the University of Oklahoma. He previously taught at Purdue University and the University of Nebraska. He has published widely in the professional communication journals and is editor or co-author of seven books. He has received several university and professional awards for both teaching and research. He has served on numerous committees for state, regional, national, and international professional communication organizations and as president of the Central States Communication Association and the Speech Communication Association.

John M. Wiemann

is Vice Chancellor, Institutional Advancement, and Professor of Communication and Asian American Studies at the University of California, Santa Barbara. He has co-edited the Sage Annual Reviews of Communication Research series and special issues of *Communication Research* and *American Behavioral Scientist*. He is author or co-author of seven books and has published more than fifty research papers and book chapters in communication, psychology, speech and hearing, and education. He is a recipient of the Speech Communication Association's Woolbert Research Award (1991) for his communication competence research and has been a W. K. Kellogg Foundation National Fellow and a Fulbright-Hays Senior Research Scholar at the University of Bristol, England.

Mary O. Wiemann

is Assistant Professor and Chairperson of the Department of Communication at Santa Barbara City College. A longtime educator of beginning college students, she contributes a strong teaching perspective to this book. She has written communication manuals for student use at many levels as well as instructor's manuals in the areas of nonverbal communication and interpersonal communication. A recipient of awards for outstanding teaching, she has developed a communication laboratory with audiovisual and computer support and has directed classroom research projects in the community college setting.

CONTENTS IN BRIEF

CONTENTS

**PART 1
BASIC COMMUNICATION
PROCESSES 2**

Chapter 4   Language and Communication   94

PART 2
INTERPERSONAL
COMMUNICATION   192
....

Chapter 8   **Managing Conflict in Interpersonal Relationships   228**

Chapter 9   **Principles of Competent Interviewing   260**

PART 3 GROUP AND ORGANIZATIONAL COMMUNICATION 296

<table>
<tr><td>Chapter 12</td><td>Communicating in
Organizations 356</td></tr>
</table>

PART 4
PUBLIC
COMMUNICATION   390

Chapter 13   Preparing and Delivering Presentations   392

PREFACE ···

We were delighted by your enthusiastic response to the first edition of **Competent Communication** and hope that the changes in the *Second Edition* will bring the text even more in line with your needs. You asked for a chapter on organizational communication, increased coverage of male and female language, and more opportunities for your students to assess their own communication and the communication of others. With these goals in mind, we prepared the *Second Edition*.

Many students recognize the value of a communication course for building skills in public speaking, but they also need to realize that even informal conversations with close friends and family can be enriched by the study of communication. Successful communication requires more than just common sense. Through competency-based instruction in communication, students learn both the theories and the applications that will help them become successful communicators.

The second edition of **Competent Communication** addresses two related pairs of concepts: *knowledge acquisition* and *skill building* to achieve *effective* and *appropriate* communication. These concepts are introduced in Chapter 1 and applied as students progress through the book. Our approach is based on a model of communicative competence that is demonstrated in a variety of relationships: interpersonal communication, small groups, organizational communication, public speaking, and mass communication.

Today, two aspects of competent communication are receiving increasing attention from communication scholars, both in the classroom and in research. These two areas of study, *ethics* and *intercultural communication*, are essential to our model and are addressed in every chapter of this text.

HIGHLIGHTS OF THE TEXT

- **Intercultural communication** coverage is integrated throughout the text and includes relationships involving people of different nationalities and ethnic backgrounds. Cultural differences between women and men and among various racial, age-based, economic, regional, and occupational cocultures are also examined. In addition, each chapter contains at least one exercise that specifically asks students to examine a situation in which intercultural communication takes place.
- **Ethical issues** are addressed in the development of various communicative skills. These issues include stereotyping, managing conflict to achieve mutually acceptable goals, and balancing persuasion and image with accuracy.
- **Our competency-based approach** promotes both knowledge acquisition and skill development, emphasizing specific strategies students can use to improve their own communication skills. It also provides a unified theme that applies to all aspects of communication and is consistently presented throughout the book.

- **Critical thinking** receives special emphasis in our discussions of audience analysis. This emphasis on audience analysis is introduced in the context of social situations, is discussed in terms of participation in group discussions, and is carried through to the more formal situations of public speaking.
- **The activities for self-analysis** provide numerous opportunities for students to examine their communication skills. By using the Self-Checks, Reality Checks, and questionnaires presented throughout the text, students are able to assess the competency of their communication as well as the ethical implications of their choices.
- **The coverage of mass communication** includes the acquisition of media skills and examines the environment and effects of mass communication. Strategies for being a critical consumer of media are also provided.
- **Current communication theory and research** grounds the text in contemporary scholarship. The text presents information in a clear, easy-to-understand manner while maintaining the level of scholarship essential for this course.
- **The model of communicative competency** links self-concept, culture, and relationship concerns in a clear, graphic presentation.
- **A case study** is presented at the conclusion of each of the four major parts of the book. Each Case Study is a detailed scenario that incorporates material from the chapters covered in that part; questions for class discussion are also included.

ORGANIZATION OF THE TEXT

Competent Communication explores the broad range of communication interactions, from intimate and enduring relationships to the world of nonpersonal communication. The text is divided into four parts: Basic Communication Processes; Interpersonal Communication; Group and Organizational Communication; and Public Speaking, which includes mass communication.

Part 1, *Basic Communication Processes,* is comprised of the first six chapters of the book, which introduce the general principles of communication. A model of competent communication is presented, and basic processes including cognitive, linguistic, nonverbal, listening, and self-development are discussed in a variety of communication contexts.

In Part 2, *Interpersonal Communication,* both social and more formal interpersonal relationships are considered. Topics discussed include the life cycle of a relationship from development through maintenance or dissolution; managing conflict, with the goal of producing mutually satisfying and constructive results; and a particular interpersonal situation, the interview, which has special practical value in preparing students for job interviews.

Part 3, *Group and Organizational Communication,* can be applied in both classroom and work situations and has a strong "real world" perspective. It moves from communication in small groups, to the role of the group leader in decision making, to organizational communication. A new chapter on organizational communication is explicitly intended to familiarize students with communication in a work context.

Part 4 takes a comprehensive look at *Public Communication*. It may be used as a resource for the public speaking component of the course or as a guide for making presentations beyond the classroom. General advice for preparing and delivering presentations is given, with special attention to informative and persuasive presentations. New to this edition are two sample Student Speeches, which demonstrate informative and persuasive presentations. Mass communication and other forms of mediated communication are approached primarily from a consumer's perspective.

FEATURES OF THE *SECOND EDITION*

Competent Communication has been thoroughly updated and revised based on comments from instructors and students. The *Second Edition* features a streamlined presentation of information so that instructors and students have the optimal amount of material in each chapter. We have also refined the presentation of the model of communication, making it more accessible to students.

- **A new chapter on Communicating in Organizations** (Chapter 12) explores the effects of new technologies on communication in organizations and discusses leadership, communication channels within organizations, and strategies for becoming a competent communicator in the workplace.
- **New Student Speeches** give students concrete models of the persuasive and informative speech. Marginal notes call attention to how the speeches follow the guidelines given in the chapter.
- **Increased coverage of male and female language** includes discussion of language content, reasons for differences, and sex roles in male and female conversation. The focus is on language in the context of actual situations.
- **An expanded emphasis on critical listening skills** stresses the process of listening critically and the rewards of developing listening competency; numerous self-assessment activities for students are included.
- **An opening vignette and closing exercise** in each chapter introduce students to a concrete situation they revisit at the end of the chapter. They are asked to analyze each situation in light of the material presented in the chapter.

STUDENT-CENTERED LEARNING

The pedagogy in *Competent Communication* is designed to help your students plan their communications, analyze their efforts, and improve their skills.

- **Objectives**   Each chapter begins with objectives that enable the reader to preview the chapter and anticipate what should be learned from it.
- **Self-Checks**   Boxed exercises interspersed throughout the text offer self-evaluation activities that build competencies or present brief case studies. Each chapter contains at least one exercise on intercultural communication and one on ethics.

- **Reality Checks**   In the margins of each chapter are thought-provoking questions designed to quickly test students' understanding of new concepts as they encounter them and to encourage them to analyze their opinions.
- **Definitions**   Throughout *Competent Communication,* new terms are introduced in **boldface type** and defined where they are introduced. Each definition is repeated in the margin for easy reference and at the end of the text in the Glossary.
- **Case Studies and Epilogues**   At the end of each part, a Case Study presents a realistic scenario to give readers practice in identifying and applying communicative competencies. There is also an Epilogue, which reviews the major topics of each part and relates them to the model of communicative competence.
- **Reviews and Suggested Readings**   Each chapter concludes with a review to reinforce the objectives and summarize the main points. Suggested Readings are provided at the end of the text for students who want to study the subject matter in greater depth.
- **Glossary**   A comprehensive glossary contains all of the **boldface** terms and concepts that are discussed in the text. In the *Second Edition,* we have added more definitions to the Glossary and indicated in which chapter each term first occurs.
- **Notes**   Recent research as well as classical studies and theories are cited throughout the text. Notes are placed at the end of the book so as to avoid disrupting the continuity of the text and yet provide references for those who wish to consult the original sources.

ADDITIONAL COMPONENTS

The *Second Edition* of **Competent Communication** is supported by a full complement of ancillaries designed to enhance competency-based learning.

INSTRUCTOR'S RESOURCE MANUAL

Written by Joan Aitken of the University of Missouri-Kansas City, the *Instructor's Resource Manual* includes support material for teaching the hybrid communication course. It includes a guide designed especially for teaching assistants and new educators of communication. Practical advice is also provided for course directors and other experienced instructors. In addition to a discussion of competency-based communication and model syllabi for semester and quarter courses, the manual includes reports from current and recent teaching assistants; they share the benefits of their experience with the book as they focus on practical problems encountered in the classroom. Chapter-by-chapter teaching notes, a broad selection of imaginative exercises emphasizing cultural and ethical issues, and other suggestions for each chapter serve as a foundation for classroom and outside activities.

Testing Options

A test-item file in the *Instructor's Resource Manual* includes short-answer and essay questions for each chapter along with an answer key. The test questions are closely correlated with the text and cross-referenced by applicable page numbers. A computerized version of the test-item file, including Micrograde, is available for both Macintosh and IBM-compatible systems.

Videotapes

Videotapes specifically designed to correlate with the text are also available. One tape examines the stages of interpersonal relationships; another covers communication in groups; and a third provides models of public speaking. The Instructor's Manual, designed by Cheri Simonds of the University of Central Oklahoma, includes additional exercises and activities and suggests ways to integrate the tapes into classroom lectures.

Transparencies

A set of twenty-five color transparencies, including diagrams from the text and additional visual presentations of important concepts, provides an enhancement to classroom lectures.

ACKNOWLEDGMENTS

For their insightful reviews of the *Second Edition*, we thank Marcia D. Dixson, Indiana University-Purdue University at Fort Wayne; Robert Dixson, St. Louis Community College at Meramec; Catherine A. Dobris, Indiana University-Purdue University at Indianapolis; Dorothy M. Filak, The University of Michigan at Flint; Rex M. Fuller, James Madison University; Susan A. Holton, Bridgewater State College; Walter G. Kirkpatrick, University of Memphis; Deborah Meisch, University of Arkansas; Donald G. Nobles, Auburn University at Montgomery; Rebecca Parker, Western Illinois University; Paula Tompkins Pribble, St. Cloud State University; Cheri Simonds, University of Central Oklahoma; Sharon Taylor, Southwestern College; Amy Thieme, Eastern Kentucky University; and David W. Worley, Indiana State University.

We would like to acknowledge the conceptual contributions offered by the following people for the *First Edition*, which were carried over into the *Second Edition*: David L. Williams, Leeza Bearden, Melissa Stone, David Worth, Karl Krayer, Carol Cawyer, Mike Chanslor, and Mark Hovind. Special thanks goes to Karl Krayer for co-authoring the new chapter on organizational communication that appears in this edition. We also want to acknowledge the help of Leeza Bearden and Sonya Hopkins for providing dozens of test questions for the Instructor's Manual, and Cheri Simonds for her help with the video scripts and accompanying exercises that she provided.

We are indebted to our editors at St. Martin's Press for their patience, encouragement, and professional advice. Suzanne Phelps Weir, our acquiring editor, Susan Cottenden, our development editor, and Diane Schadoff, our project editor, turned the manuscript into a book. We are delighted with the attractive and pedagogically enriching design created by our designer, Patricia McFadden, and we thank our production supervisor, Scott Lavelle, for overseeing the schedule and quality of the composition and printing.

Dan O'Hair
Gustav W. Friedrich
John M. Wiemann
Mary O. Wiemann

Competent Communication

Communication

Second Edition

PART ONE

Basic Communication Processes

*A*ll communication involves the basic processes of perception, language, nonverbal communication, and listening. Skills that we develop in these areas can be applied to a wide range of communication contexts—from two friends speaking, to group meetings, to public presentations, to mass communication. We need to be especially aware of our communication processes when we are engaged in intercultural communication. Communication differences based on cultural factors can make it more challenging to appropriately interpret and construct messages. When we have a full repertoire of skills available to us, we are able to select the tactics that are both appropriate and effective in our communication.

CHAPTER ONE

Communicating Competently

●BJECTIVES •••••••••••••••••••

After reading this chapter, you should be able to:

1. Describe the six characteristics of communication.

2. Explain the functional perspective of communication.

3. Apply the three general functions of communication to the relationships in which you are involved.

4. Identify the components of communication competence.

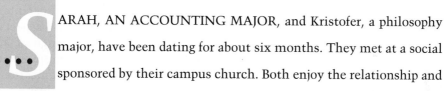

ARAH, AN ACCOUNTING MAJOR, and Kristofer, a philosophy major, have been dating for about six months. They met at a social sponsored by their campus church. Both enjoy the relationship and their time together. Recently, however, Kristofer has been dropping hints that he is increasingly uncomfortable with the amount of time Sarah spends performing her duties as president of the Undergraduate Accounting Association. Sarah has shared her feelings about this situation with you, her best friend. She knows that you are taking a communication class and asks you if you can suggest anything that might be helpful to her in her relationship with Kristofer. As you read through this chapter, think about the relevance of its content to Sarah's relationship with Kristofer. At the end of the chapter, we will return to this scenario to ask you how you might respond to Sarah's request for assistance.

Let's be clear about one thing from the very beginning: *The quality of your life depends directly on your ability to communicate!* The better you understand the communication process, the more likely you will be to use your communication skills appropriately and effectively. The more appropriate and effective you are, the more likely you will be to create satisfying, productive, meaningful (that is, competent) relationships in your personal, social, business, and public lives. We wrote this book to help you improve both your understanding of the communication process and the skills that put your understanding into action. Both are necessary for competent communication; neither is sufficient without the other.

You communicate in order to accomplish social tasks and to coordinate physical ones. In the process, you create and define relationships; you modify and dissolve relationships. And you do these things through both the content and style of your communication. Indeed, when we communicate with each other, we create ourselves and our social environment in important ways.

◆ The Nature of Communication

Given the importance of communication in our lives, most people spend surprisingly little time trying to understand it. To be sure, parents devote a great deal of effort to teaching their children the technical aspects of communication; that is, they help their children learn the language and social norms, or the general rules of politeness, that guide communication decisions. But we acquire most of what we know about communication without explicit instruction. For the most part we muddle through, learning effective and appropriate communication behavior on a trial and error basis.

The purpose of this course is to help you develop and apply a systematic, analytic understanding of communication processes. This understanding will take some of the trial and error out of your learning experiences. If you make the effort, you should become more scientific in your predictions about how your communication choices will affect others—and why their communication choices affect you as they do. In short, we believe that your ability to influence your social environment will improve as your understanding of communication increases.

Throughout this book, we will be asking you to take advantage of what you already know—your personal theories of communication. We will also ask you to question your theories and to examine them in terms of what works and what doesn't. We will ask you to test your theories against those of communication scholars. In the process, we hope you will develop an understanding of scholarly theories and learn how to apply them to everyday life.

In order to improve your own communication skills, you first need to understand the communication process. Let us now examine the characteristics basic to this process.

Understanding the communication process will help you behave appropriately and effectively in social interactions.

◆ The Six Characteristics of Communication

Communication has proved to be a rather slippery term. Since the time of Aristotle, scholars have offered various definitions of the term. All of the definitions, however, have been incomplete because they have failed to capture the richness and complexity of the communication experience. In 1976, Dance and Larson listed over 100 definitions of communication published in the previous 20 years.[1] If we attempted such a list today, we would likely double that number.

Rather than attempt another definition of communication for this book, we believe it is more useful to discuss the characteristics of communication. This approach will help you to evaluate various stimuli (messages) in your environment in terms of their communicative value. Some "messages" are more obviously communicative than others. For example, the behavior of 6-year-old Ellie sticking her tongue out at Jake is very purposeful; that of 21-year-old Sara making one-second eye contact with Alan across the room is less clear. The more ambiguous the stimulus, the more difficult it is to be certain that the message received is close to the message intended—or whether a message was intended at all.

Communication is defined by six characteristics: (1) the extent to which the code of the message is symbolic; (2) the extent to which the code is

COMMUNICATION
A process defined by six characteristics: (1) symbolic behavior; (2) the sharing of a code; (3) its tie to culture; (4) intentionality; (5) the presence of a medium; and (6) the fact that it is transactional.

shared; (3) the degree to which the message is culturally bound;[2] (4) the intentionality of the sender; (5) the presence of a medium; and (6) the extent to which the process of encoding and decoding messages is transactional. Each characteristic can be thought of as a continuum, anchored on one side by "always" or "definitely" and on the other by "never" or "definitely not." Behavior that clearly possesses all of these characteristics is communication and can be analyzed as such. Much of our behavior, however, is not so "definitely communicative," even though, in practical terms, we can and do hold people responsible for their communication. It is useful, therefore, for us to be able to analyze messages in terms of these characteristics, so that we can understand why communication problems occur and how we might solve them.

Symbolic Behavior

Behavior is symbolic when it has an arbitrary relationship to an object. The most **symbolic behavior** is language. There is no particular reason why the arbitrary transcription of the letters T-R-E-E should represent a very large variety of plant forms. But in our code, American English, it does. Every language is a code that allows those who know it to transform speech into meaningful messages.

Although spoken language is the primary form of symbolic behavior in our culture, nonverbal behavior can also be symbolic. Hand gestures, in particular, may have symbolic properties. For example, joining the thumb and forefinger in a circle while extending the other three fingers means "okay" in middle-class U.S. culture. Gestures of this sort, "autonomous gestures,"[3] operate in much the same way as language. That is to say, we do not need words to know what they mean.

We will have more to say on this subject when we discuss language and nonverbal behavior (in Chapters 4 and 5, respectively). For the moment, suffice it to say that symbols are arbitrary constructions and that they are related to the objects to which they refer. The stronger the connection between symbol and object, the clearer the intended meaning, and vice versa. Competent communicators take this relative ambiguity into consideration when they construct messages for others and interpret the messages they receive.

A Shared Code

In order for communication to take place, the participants must share the **code** (the set of symbol-meaning relationships) used to **encode** and **decode** messages. The greater the overlap, the greater the probability that one person's meanings will be similar to another's. Speaking a common language is the most obvious example of sharing a communication code, but it is not the only one. Each culture also shares *specific* meanings for gestures, graphics, and facial expressions.

Some aspects of these codes cross cultural boundaries, making them especially powerful communication vehicles. Facial expressions of surprise,

SYMBOLIC BEHAVIOR
Behavior that uses a shared symbol system.

CODE
The symbols, signals, or signs used to construct messages.

ENCODE
Mentally construct and physically produce a message.

DECODE
Physically receive a message (or other type of stimulus) and interpret and assign meaning to it.

fear, disgust, anger, happiness, and sadness seem to have universal meanings.[4] Thus, they allow people from different cultures to understand each other's most basic feelings, even though they cannot speak the same language.

The characteristic of shared codes is so obvious that people are frequently blind to its importance. We tend to assume that because people share a language code, they must necessarily also have common meanings for the symbols they use. This is clearly not the case. For example, American travelers to and from England are frequently surprised (and amused) that the same words refer to different things in the two versions of the English language. A British person in a U.S. drugstore asking for a rubber would be sent to the pharmaceutical counter for a condom rather than to the stationery aisle for an eraser. As was noted earlier, people create and negotiate meanings in the course of their interaction. A symbol can take on new meaning if at least two people agree that it will have that meaning for them. Social groups use this technique to establish their uniqueness and to create boundaries between themselves and the "outside" world.

Linked to Culture

If you've ever traveled to a different country or even through the different neighborhoods of a city, you know that communication is difficult to separate from culture. The most obvious way in which the two are related is language. People from different cultures usually speak different languages, which are usually unintelligible to "strangers." But the communication-culture relationship goes well beyond obvious language differences. For example, cultural experience and everyday life strongly influence what in the environment is important enough to name, how fine our linguistic distinctions are, and how language influences our interpretation of the world around us.[5] For example, an interior decorator may find it useful, or even necessary, to distinguish among lavender, mauve, burgundy, violet, plum, lilac, magenta, amethyst, and heliotrope. For many of us, however, these fine distinctions are unimportant; purple is purple!

We use the term **culture** to refer to the shared beliefs, values, and practices of a group of people. A group's culture includes the language or languages used by group members as well as the norms and rules about how behavior can appropriately be displayed and how it should be understood.

When we refer to people as being in the same culture, we emphasize their similarities rather than their differences. But sometimes the differences are worth noting. Thus, the term **subculture** is used to refer to groups within a larger culture that are distinguished from the rest of the population by various characteristics. For example, white Protestant males and African-American Catholic females constitute two subcultures in the United States. They are **co-cultures** of each other.

Our nonverbal behavior also is wrapped up in culture. Different cultures use and interpret time and space differently.[6] In Mediterranean cultures, for

CULTURE
The shared beliefs, values, and practices of a group of people.

SUBCULTURE
A group that is part of a larger culture but distinguished from it by various characteristics.

CO-CULTURE
One of two or more subcultures within a culture.

instance, men tend to stand very close together, frequently touching each other during conversation. In North Atlantic cultures, the appropriate conversational distance is generally about 3 feet—and, in case you hadn't noticed, men seldom touch each other during social conversation except when they shake hands in greeting.

Intentionality

INTENTIONALITY
The level of consciousness or purposefulness of a communicator in the encoding of messages.

Does a behavior have to be **intentional** to be communicative? This is a question that communication scholars frequently debate. If you see me do something or hear me say something I did not intend for you to see or hear, did I communicate with you? In other words, am I responsible to you for what I did or said in the same way as if I had intentionally formulated a message and transmitted it to you? Can you stop yourself from blushing when you don't want to blush?

Some scholars have begun to talk about two communication systems. One is characterized by behavior that is *primarily* (if not totally) symbolic and intentional and has a cognitive basis. The second system, based on emotional and physiological considerations, is characterized by a widely shared code that has few, if any, cultural boundaries and is spontaneous.[7]

The distinction between the two systems can be seen as one of *giving* information versus one of *giving off* information.[8] The practical importance of the distinction is that we tend to see a person as more accountable when he or she consciously or purposefully gives information to someone else than when the recipient gleans information from observation or overhearing.

This is not to say that information *given off* is unimportant. In fact, it may be evaluated as more honest because the person giving off the information did not have the opportunity to censor or package it. It is useful to note, however, that while some messages transmitted through the emotional communication system are highly reliable and easily interpreted (e.g., emotional displays like grief and anger), most are ambiguous and open to a variety of interpretations (What does a flushed face mean?). Generally this sort of information can be interpreted only in the light of contextual cues, and even then the validity of one's judgment is frequently open to question.

Competent communication requires a sensitivity to the fact that both your intended and unintended messages have an impact on the people around you. Keep in mind that the intended meaning (if there was one) of your behavior is not always as clearly expressed or as accurately received as you would like.

A Medium for the Message

Communication requires a medium—a vehicle to transport or carry the symbols. In face-to-face interaction, the vehicle is the air through which the sound and light waves travel. Face-to-face communication is the prototype to which other kinds of communication are usually compared. With new communication technologies becoming more accessible, distinctions between face-to-face and other methods of communication are beginning to break down.[9] Nonetheless, some medium is a prerequisite for communication to take place.

Competent relationships can be maintained through a variety of media. Long-distance relationships are becoming ever more common. As we move away from face-to-face contact and technology intervenes between us and our **audience**, the characteristics and the social impact of our messages change, sometimes in very subtle ways. With the advent of the information superhighway, which will merge television cable, telephone, and online computer services in the home, we are likely to see an increase in several types of long-distance relationships. These relationships include not only those between parents and children, siblings, and close friends, but also commuter marriages and even "telecommuting"—arrangements in which the employee is connected to the workplace by computer and audio/video media and so can go to work without leaving home. If you are or have ever been in a long-distance relationship, when did you choose to write a letter rather than use the phone? Were some types of messages in your relationship best delivered via letter? Why?

A Transactional Process

Communication is transactional; that is, two or more people exchange **sender** and **receiver** roles, and their messages are dependent on and influenced by those of their partner(s). This exchange can be immediate, as in a conversation, or delayed, as in the case of mass media messages or e-mail exchanges.

AUDIENCE

One or more people who are listening to what a person is saying and/or watching what that person is doing.

SENDER

The person, group, or organization that encodes a message or produces a stimulus.

RECEIVER

The person, group, or organization that decodes a message or other type of stimulus.

How is the responsibility for communication shared in your classes? Does it differ from class to class?

TRANSACTIONAL
PROCESS

*A process in which
two or more people
exchange speaker and
listener roles, and in
which the behavior
of each person is
dependent on and
influenced by the
behavior of the other.*

When you engage others in communication, you are attempting to influence them in some way (a point that we make in various contexts throughout this book). Equally important, but perhaps not so obvious, is the fact that you are opening yourself to influence by others. We are all involved in the **transactional process** of communication. Thus, all parties to an interaction are responsible for its outcome and have a hand in whether or not individual and relational goals are met. Whether you are talking with your significant other, a parent, a work group in a class, or the audience of a public speech, you *share* responsibility for the outcome of the interaction. The burden of responsibility is usually more or less equally distributed, depending on the communication situation. In some situations, like public speaking, the speaker tends to assume most of the responsibility and is seen as the person attempting to influence the audience. But even in this apparently lopsided situation, the audience still retains a good deal of influence. The audience's power is most obvious when applause or catcalls interrupt a speech.

We have looked at the six major characteristics of communication. Let us now turn our attention to the primary reason for constructing communicative messages in the first place: achieving satisfying relationships in which we can accomplish our personal and interpersonal goals.

*Y*our *Definition of Communication*

The six characteristics of communication can lead to different definitions of the process. Using all or some of these characteristics, construct a definition of communication that best describes your own behavior when you are communicating with others. Are there characteristics not mentioned here that you would like to use in your definition? Compare your definition with those of your classmates. Are there important differences in the definitions? How might these differences explain common communication breakdowns or misunderstandings?

◆ The Functions of Communication

FUNCTIONAL
PERSPECTIVE

*A focus on what
kinds of communi-
cation behaviors work
for people, and why
they work, in various
situations.*

Communication can be studied in a variety of ways, including structural, rhetorical, historical, and critical approaches. Each approach has its own strengths and limitations. In order to help you develop communication skills as well as knowledge about these skills, in this book we take a **functional perspective**, focusing on *what kinds of communication behaviors work* for people, and why they work, in various situations.

The Functional Perspective

A functional or pragmatic perspective presupposes that our communication is goal-directed—that we do things with some conscious or unconscious purpose in mind. Our primary goal in communicating is to have an optimal amount of influence over the people and events in our lives, or what some observers call our social environment. Communicators always exercise at least some influence on their social environment, usually more than they think. You do not need to decide to influence someone in order to do it. However, when you decide that you want to influence someone, how and when you will attempt to do so, and what you want to get from the target of your attempts, you are setting communication goals and selecting communication strategies and tactics. Your implicit concern is a functional, pragmatic one: What can I do communicationally to get what I want? What will work for me in this situation with this particular person? The same goal can be achieved in a variety of ways. Similarly, the same strategies and tactics can be used to achieve a variety of goals at different times.[10]

It is useful to distinguish between general and specific strategies and goals. General strategies and goals are abstract and not limited to specific situations or even necessarily to specific relationships. These strategies and goals are typically related to the communication process rather than the outcome and to conceptions of the self. Specific strategies and goals, as you might have guessed, are related to particular situations or relationships and tend to be outcome oriented.

The relationship between general and specific strategies and goals is somewhat fluid. Attainment of today's goal may be seen as one part of a long-term strategy in the service of higher-order goals. For example, Bill's immediate *goal* is to get an assistant manager's job in a fast-food restaurant so that he can pay his school fees, but it is also part of his long-term *strategy* for starting a career in the food-service industry. Although specific goals help us understand why a person is behaving in a particular way now, general goals are more relevant to understanding how communication works in relationships for a variety of people with a variety of specific goals. This is because general goals relate directly to the communication functions of control, affiliation, and goal achievement.

*A*chieving Communication Goals

Consider an important relationship in which you are involved. What goals do you have in that relationship? In what ways might you communicate to achieve each of those goals? How do you know when you are successful? Are some of your goals in conflict with others? How do you plan to achieve them?

A long line of research conducted in a variety of contexts, including task groups, decision-making groups, families, and social relationships, has found that communication behavior falls along three dimensions or serves three primary functions.[11] The first of these functions is almost always labeled *control*. The second has typically been termed *affiliation, empathy*, or *liking*. The third dimension has been given various names, all of which directly relate to *achieving a goal* or completing a task. These functions cannot be edited out of messages; even supposedly neutral statements say something about how you feel about the other person.

Control

Of the three primary functions of communication, control is probably the most important. It could be argued, in fact, that it *is* the most important because it seems to permeate the other functions of affiliation and goal orientation. By **control** we mean the ability of one person to influence both another person or persons and the manner in which their relationship is conducted. Let us quickly note that we are not equating control with dominance, although one person may be dominant. Nor are we using the term *control* in a negative way. Control (the influence of each partner on the other or others) is a necessary part of every relationship, including marital, boss-worker, parent-child, doctor-patient, lecturer-audience, and even friend-friend. In fact, control is a defining characteristic of every relationship.

The distribution of control is negotiated between relational partners. Distribution is important to our concept of this function because relational control is a zero-sum matter. That is to say, the more control one person has, the less the other(s) have; hence, my 60 percent control leaves you with only 40 percent. In social relationships, people expect control to be distributed approximately evenly. The exact distribution of control in interpersonal relationships is worked out communicatively—by the way people talk with each other, how they structure their conversations (including their timing), and by the content of the conversations. This negotiation takes place in all relationships, from the most informal and unstructured to the most formal and structured.

Happiness and relational satisfaction do not depend on equally distributed control; rather, they depend on the appropriate distribution and exercise of control. In many relationships, you expect, if not demand, that your partner(s) have a larger or smaller share of control than you do. Along with the control goes responsibility for the relationship and various tasks relevant to the relationship. For example, as a new employee at a bank, Manny looks to his manager, Sally, for direction and advice about how to do his job well. He expects to be told what to do and how to do it. The lopsided control distribution is appropriate and meets both Manny's and Sally's expectations of their job responsibilities. Thus, it should lead to satisfaction for both of them with regard to this aspect of their relationship. Note that their expectations for their relationship are congruent: Both expect Sally to exercise more control.

CONTROL

The ability of one person to influence another person or persons and the manner in which their relationship is conducted; one of the three primary functions of communication.

As situations become more formal and more structured, and as the number of people involved increases, there is less opportunity to negotiate control. In a public speaking situation, for example, individual members of a large audience cannot easily shift the distribution of control from the designated speaker to themselves. Heckling the speaker can be seen as an attempt to accomplish such a shift. Television viewers try to exercise control over stations and networks by participating in viewer surveys, writing letters, and watching or not watching particular shows. Viewers can also organize into groups in an effort to influence television programming.

Affiliation

By **affiliation**, the second primary function, we mean the affect, or feelings, one has for another or others along a love-hate continuum. Unlike control, affiliation is not distributed in a zero-sum fashion; all parties to a relationship can have a high level of affiliation (in everyday, lay terms, they love each other). In other words, in our social relationships we expect our partners to feel about the same amount of affiliation for us as we do for them. The more intimate and personal the relationship, the more we expect this to be the case. But, of course, not all partners have the same feelings, whether positive or negative, about each other all the time. Thus we specify that it is the *expression* of affiliation that must be negotiated. At times you might want to hide your feelings for another person because you find it desirable or strategic to do so. For example, you might not want to show your feelings about a potential dating partner until you find out whether that person is interested in you.

> AFFILIATION
> *Feelings for another, ranging from love (high positive affiliation) to hate (high negative affiliation): one of the three primary functions of communication.*

Goal Achievement

The third primary function of communication, **goal achievement**, refers to focusing attention on the task at hand in order to achieve one's goal. Communication that is highly goal or task oriented focuses on getting the job done. In unstructured social relationships, it is useful to think of maintenance of the relationship as the goal toward which both parties should be oriented. In more formal situations, the goal may include completing an interview or participating in a public speaking event.

Like the previous two functions, the task or goal to which communication partners are to be oriented can be negotiated. The task agreed upon during a meeting or get-together can shift during the course of the meeting. For example, a department meeting called by the manager to discuss the production schedule can become a forum for employees to voice their complaints about having to work overtime. Furthermore, groups often have competing tasks, and they have to deal with the allocation of time and attention to each of them. For example, students who are assigned to do a group project often have to allocate their time between "being friends" and "getting the project completed/getting a good grade." If you have had this experience, you know what we're talking about, and you understand that sometimes it is very difficult to accomplish both tasks in a satisfactory manner.

> GOAL ACHIEVEMENT
> *Focusing attention on the task at hand in order to achieve a goal; one of the three primary functions of communication. Also called* task orientation.

This discussion of functions leads us now to questions of evaluating communication behavior. How do we determine whether we are successful communicators? How do we know whether we are meeting our goals, and what we should do if we think we are not? In an attempt to provide answers to such questions, we next turn our attention to the characteristics of relationships and successful communication.

◆ Communication Relationships

RELATIONSHIP

The interdependence of two or more people in order to achieve some goal.

COMMUNICATION RELATIONSHIP

An interdependence of two or more people which is based on symbolic exchange.

DYAD

A pair of individuals maintaining a relationship.

A **relationship** is the interconnection or interdependence of two (or more) people in order to achieve some goal. A **communication relationship** is one in which the interdependence is based on symbolic exchange. If this definition leads you to think that you begin and end several communication relationships each day, you are correct. But since minimal relationships (those that last only momentarily and have little consequence for you) are usually not very interesting, we will confine our discussion to relationships that are meaningful for the participants over a period of time. We will talk about informal social relationships, such as close friendships, as well as more formal, structured ones. Some relationships (e.g., parent-child, husband-wife) have both formal and informal aspects.

Although the remainder of this chapter focuses primarily on informal relationships between pairs of people, or **dyads**, the discussion applies equally well to a variety of relationships, many of which are discussed in subsequent chapters—for example, speaker-audience.

We also want to point out that social and task groups and cultures have relationships with each other. That is, when someone communicates as a member of a specific social group rather than as an individual, when speaking with nongroup (outgroup) members, we can say that the two groups have a relationship. During labor negotiations, representatives from management and a union speak to each other as members of their respective groups, not as individuals who might even know each other personally. This line of thinking leads to concepts such as "race relations" or relationships between national governments. It is interesting that *individual* members of groups can have good relationships with one another while their groups may not. In Northern Ireland, for example, Eileen and Moiré may be personal friends, but the Catholic religious community to which Eileen belongs is at extreme odds with Moiré's Protestant community. The same kinds of variables that characterize interpersonal relationships can be extrapolated to describe social and cultural group relationships. For the moment, let's turn our attention to informal interpersonal relationships composed of two people.

By adopting the relationship as our unit of analysis, we are not discounting the important characteristics of the people who make up the relationship. Obviously, individuals embark on relationships with their self-concepts, personal experiences, preferred styles of communicating and thinking (cognitive processing), individual goals, and the like. All of these characteristics

*C*ommunicating Your Feelings ✔

Call to mind two different types of relationships in which you have been involved that have undergone change (for example, with a parent and with a romantic partner). As each relationship changed, how did your way of expressing affiliation change? Did you use different strategies or tactics for expressing your feelings in the different relationships? Are there some relationships in which you could not (or cannot) communicate your feelings about the other person? Why?

profoundly influence how they will communicate in any given conversation or relationship.

Although individuals are not lost in relationships, the influence of their partners usually leads to changes in the participants. The more important the relationship, the more influence the individuals will have on their partners and, thus, the more susceptible each is to change. This is especially the case if the participants in the relationship like each other or if one has a lot of status or desirable qualities in the eyes of the other(s). As romantic partners become more involved and committed, for example, they usually adapt to one another, taking on similar habits, mannerisms, and attitudes. This adaptation is a consequence of the influence or control the partners have over each other. A manager may have a similar effect on employees, with the employees coming to see the business world—and talk about it—in much the same way as the boss does. In hostile relationships, the partners may change in ways that make them more distinct from each other.

◆ Successful Communication

Our references to goals, strategies, influence, control, and the like indicate concern about the "success" of our attempts at communication. The issue of successful communication is so complex that we spend the rest of this book discussing it. But it is important to remember that success is typically a subjective experience and can be evaluated only against some sort of criteria applied in a particular context.

Two approaches can be taken to assess successful communication: analysis of outcomes or analysis of process. In everyday life, both are important.

An **outcome** has to do with the product of an interchange. For example, in a negotiation, the outcome may be "getting what I want." In many contexts, outcome analysis tends to focus on winning and losing and shows little concern about how the outcome was achieved.

Process measures of success have to do with how an episode is accomplished. What is said and how it is said take on greater significance, although outcomes still play a role in a process analysis.

OUTCOME

The product or end state of a communication encounter or series of encounters.

PROCESS

The manner in which a communication encounter is conducted.

The principles of competent communication apply no matter how many partners are in the relationship or how long the relationship lasts.

From the process perspective, it is better to optimize outcomes for both partners than to maximize outcomes for one. This way of thinking has led pop psychologists to write books about resolving conflict by "fighting fair."[12] More to our point, a process orientation considers strategies, general skills, and specific messages. Negotiations place greater emphasis on accomplishing your goals in light of your relationship with your partner and your partner's goals than on winning as much as you can.

We prefer the process to the outcomes approach when we are trying to understand communication success. One of the best ways to assess success from this perspective is to look at mutual satisfaction. Sometimes winning isn't the most important thing—especially when long-term relationships are involved! Geoff may win most of the arguments he has with Betsy, but she increasingly sees him as stubborn and uncaring—a view that may eventually cause her to leave him.

Behavior is both *appropriate* and *effective* when it serves to optimize outcomes for both partners, rather than maximize outcomes for one partner at the expense of the other, while generally leading to mutual satisfaction.[13]

Appropriate Behavior

Behavior is *appropriate* when it meets the expectations of (1) one's specific communication partner, (2) other people in one's immediate presence, and (3) the demands of the situation. In almost all situations, cultural norms and rules set the standards for expectations. The more intimate you are with your partner, the more likely some idiosyncratic expectations will influence what you judge to be appropriate or inappropriate, but cultural norms are always in the background. The expectations generated by different people and

---

*U*nderstanding Communication Norms

The purpose of this exercise is to help you better understand (1) the nature of communication rules and norms and (2) the problems that "strangers" to a culture encounter.

Many rules and norms are peculiar to one or a few cultures. They are observed unself-consciously by members of the culture and are not thought about until they are ignored or broken. That is, you take the rules and norms of your culture for granted, you typically follow them, and you expect your partners to follow them. But when you move from one culture (or from one sub- or co-culture) to another, rules that were taken for granted and behaviors that were automatic may become the source of interpersonal difficulties.

Observation of communication patterns: Spend 15 to 30 minutes in a familiar environment (preferably your home or dorm) observing the communication behaviors and patterns of those around you from the perspective of a visitor from a different culture. Do not take anything for granted. Do not indicate to your subjects that you are observing their behavior. Conduct your observations with respect for your subjects.

Record the results of your observations, paying special attention to how you understood what was appropriate behavior. What rules and norms can you list? How did you identify these rules and norms? Do they apply to more than one "culture" (that is, are they peculiar to the context you observed or can they be generalized to other, similar contexts)?

How does your experience compare with those of your classmates? Were conflicting or different norms "discovered" by different people from either the same or different "cultures"? How would the people around you react if you had violated these norms? How could a person from one culture best discover a rule in another culture? How can (or should) people from one culture adhere to another culture's rule when that rule violates a rule from their own culture?

situations can, of course, be in conflict with each other. Which set of expectations you choose to honor and which you decide to ignore can say a great deal about your relationship.

Even in informal, unstructured social situations, such as when you are walking in a park or at a party given by a close friend, general cultural norms (e.g., Be thoughtful of those around you) are supplemented by norms specific to that situation (e.g., Don't talk about your grades at parties). Nonetheless, these norms still provide a great deal of communicative latitude. In other words, a wide variety of communication behaviors will be considered appropriate. In informal situations, the expectations of your partner and others will be of primary importance.

As situations become more formal and more structured, what counts as appropriate gets more specific. Consider, for instance, the minimal communication latitude one has in a courtroom or a church.

Knowing what is appropriate and what is not with a wide variety of audiences and in a wide variety of situations is necessary if you are to be a successful communicator.

Effective Behavior

Communication is considered *effective* if it helps you meet your goals. This might sound obvious and straightforward, but in practice it is not always easy to know what messages will serve us in pursuit of our goals. Decisions about how to "design" your messages so that they might be most effective for a given situation or audience are further complicated by the fact that in many situations you have multiple goals.[14] For example, even though Travis might be in a conflict with Jan and wants to have the conflict resolved in his favor, he still wants Jan to continue to like him.

Some knowledge of your audience's expectations and the demands of the situation helps you decide which messages will be relatively more effective than others. In addition, knowing that you have multiple goals and prioritizing them—a task that is not always easy—also helps you construct effective messages.

Successful messages are usually, but not always, both appropriate and effective. Given your goals, the audience, and the situation, you might have to choose between messages that are primarily effective but inappropriate, and messages that are appropriate but not particularly effective. Once again, process versus outcome considerations come into play.

COMMUNICATIVE
COMPETENCE

The ability of two or more people jointly to create and maintain a mutually satisfying relationship through the construction of appropriate and effective messages.

◆ Competent Communication

Communicative competence is the ability of two or more people jointly to create and maintain a mutually satisfying relationship by constructing appropriate and effective messages. Communication is competent when it

(1) produces the optimal distribution of control, expressed affiliation, and orientation to the goal and task at hand, (2) is process oriented, and (3) is generally appropriate and effective for a given relationship.

As we have noted, messages must be interpreted in the context of relationships. Individuals, on the other hand, can be characterized by the number of skills they bring to the relationship, their knowledge of how and when to use those skills, and their motivation to do so.[15] In everyday conversation we frequently describe a highly skilled person as competent. We make the distinction between *competent* relationships and *skilled* individuals because a person does not have to possess a great many communication skills to enjoy a successful relationship. **Communication skills** are behavioral routines based on social understandings and used by communicators to achieve their goals. You may know people who have few communication skills and do not use them in a very sophisticated manner, but who nonetheless are in mutually satisfying, long-term relationships. Conversely, even the most highly skilled communicator may get involved in an unsatisfying relationship. Thus, we want to keep the communication skills and other competencies of an individual conceptually distinct from the quality of relationships. **Communication competencies** are skills and understandings that enable communication partners to exchange messages appropriately and effectively.

We evaluate communicative competence through the primary functions of communication discussed earlier: control, affiliation, and goal achievement. Competent relationships, be they interpersonal, small-group, speaker-audience, or media-audience, are marked by messages that (1) communicate an appropriate (mutually satisfying or mutually agreed upon) distribution of control, (2) express a level of affiliation that is comfortable for all participants, and (3) are consistent with both the goals of each participant and their jointly constructed relational goals.

These three dimensions allow us to describe communication in relationships in abstract terms (e.g., controlling, affiliative, goal-directed) that relate to specific message choices people make. These message choices are influenced by both audience and situation. Because this process is a complex one, to help you (and us!) put these concepts together, we have developed a model of communicative competence, to which we now turn.

The model presented in Figure 1.1 is a graphic representation of the primary aspects of communication discussed in this chapter. In this sense it is an abstraction: It omits many details for simplicity's sake, but details can be filled in when you are considering specific interactions or relationships. Even in its simplicity, the model is complex. In the pages that follow, we dissect the model into its component parts. Then, in the remainder of the book, we put the components back together in various ways.

Cultural and Relational Contexts

The context in which you communicate is important. As mentioned earlier, the context helps determine which messages are seen as appropriate and

COMMUNICATION SKILLS
Behavioral routines based on social understandings and used by communicators to achieve their goals.

COMMUNICATION COMPETENCIES
Skills and understandings that enable communication partners to exchange messages appropriately and effectively.

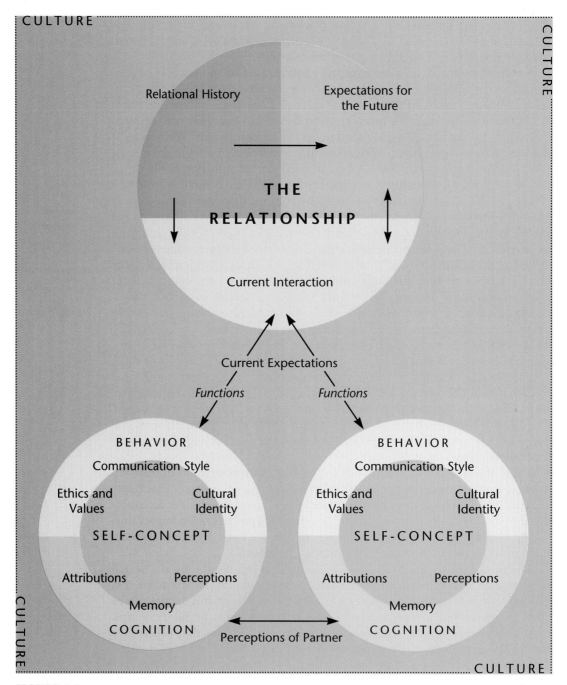

FIGURE 1.1
A model of competent communication.

Source: J. M. Wiemann & M. O. Wiemann (1992), *Interpersonal communicative competence: Listening and perceiving*, unpublished manuscript, University of California at Santa Barbara.

effective. Your social environment is the context of both your communication and your relationships. It is composed primarily of the people with whom you associate but includes nonhuman aspects, such as where you live and work, your house furnishings, your pets, and the like. In your social environment, you create meanings for people, objects, and other phenomena—meanings that distinguish these things from mere physical or biological description.

Two types of context are especially important in communication: the *cultural context* and the *relational context*.

We discover much of the richness of our social environment as we are growing up. Culture carries these rich meanings; to be socialized into one's culture is to learn how to interpret the social environment in a way that is consistent with other people in the culture. For example, Juan learns to show respect for his elders by not questioning their authority; his friends are raised that way, and their behaviors mutually reinforce respect and unquestioned control from adults. In Juan's culture, another sign of respect for older generations is that objects that have been in the family for years are passed down from generation to generation. Lana, by contrast, is raised in a social environment that encourages her to talk to and question her elders. Her friends, raised in similar fashion, mutually reinforce a different type of respect for elders, which includes frequently questioning the exercise of control. Lana treasures few old objects; her culture throws out the old and buys new things. Both Juan and Lana view their own behaviors as natural, but if each were to look at the other's behavior, it would seem very "different" and perhaps even odd or unnatural—and probably not respectful at all.

Culture allows us to take for granted the meanings of objects and relationships in our environment, which is both a blessing and a curse. On the positive side, the world is more predictable and more understandable than it otherwise would be. We generally *know* what to do and how to act because we learn what is "right" from our parents and peers. On the negative side, the communication difficulties and blind spots of those who socialize us are often reinvented in us. We may lose sight of the complexity of communication because it seems so natural—*it is so natural*. The dotted border of the model illustrates that all communication is influenced by its cultural context.

The *relational context* also has pervasive influence. It allows us to talk about generic types of relationships (between parent and child, boyfriend and girlfriend, lovers, roommates, best friends, spouses, employer and employee, work-group members, professor and class) and to generalize about communication across these types. Every aspect of our communication is evaluated in terms of the relationship we have with the person(s) with whom we are interacting.

Our messages are given meaning by our relationships. A kiss, for example, has a different meaning when bestowed on your mother than it does when shared with your lover. In one relational context, saying "Let's be friends" (e.g., when said to a new acquaintance) is an invitation to explore relational possibilities. The same phrase, when said to someone whom you've been dating for the last year, can have an entirely different meaning (as in "Let's *just* be friends," which some say is the coldest sentence in the English language!).

The Individuals

The lower half of the model of communicative competence depicts two "individuals" as circles. It is easier for us to talk about two individual persons, but it is very important to keep in mind that these "individuals" (circles) can represent small or large groups, classes of people who share an occupation or culture, and so forth. The model is designed to explain a variety of relationships, including two persons going out together, a professor lecturing to a class, a reporter interviewing a news source on television, two enemies fighting, representatives of management and labor negotiating a contract, and many other relationships. For ease of explanation, we will discuss the model in terms of two people in an informal social relationship.

Each individual comes to a new relationship as a person with a self-concept, a past, and expectations for the future—all the characteristics, in fact, that make the individual a person. Rather than getting lost in the relationship, the individual retains and maintains some sense of uniqueness even as the relationship exerts its influence and causes changes in the person. Most important here is the *self-concept*: As a person's own definition of his or her being, it is at the core of each of us.

You interpret the messages of others in light of your self-concept. That is, you actively seek out people who will confirm or support aspects of your self. You like people who like you, for example, because they tell you in many ways that they agree with you about who you are; they support you by acknowledging and supporting your self-concept.[16]

Your Ethical Standards

What ethical considerations do you think are important for competent communication? Make a list of your ethical standards (values). Are some standards more important than others? Are there some standards that apply in only one type of relationship, or that apply differently in different types of relationships? How do the two types of context—cultural and relational—influence your standards? Do your standards change as the size of the audience changes? For example, do you have different standards for yourself as a public speaker than as a student in class or as a friend?

Compare your standards to those of your classmates and discuss the similarities and differences you think are important. What might account for the differences? Can you detect cultural differences? How might these differences affect your ability to enter into a competent relationship?

Similarly, your own messages let others know who you think you are or who you would like to be. Your communication is geared toward presenting a positive self that can be supported by your relational partners. When you fail at this task—that is, when you present a self that others cannot support—they may respond negatively. When people make claims about themselves that others do not believe are true, the audience frequently evaluates these speakers negatively and lets them know how they feel. In fact, our culture has a term for one such behavior: bragging. It is clear, then, that self-concept and communication work hand in hand. Your self-concept is the product of your communication with others, but it is also the triggering mechanism for your communication.

An important part of many people's self-concept is their *cultural identity*, their view of themselves as a member of a specific culture. This identity influences the communication choices they make and how they interpret messages they receive from others. Cultural identity is reinforced by the messages people receive from those around them. Like other aspects of the self-concept, cultural identity is bound to affect how one communicates and the types of relationships one establishes.

Closely related to your self-concept are your ethics or *ethical standards*, the values you hold about what is moral and just. Your ethics influence how you evaluate your own messages and those of others in terms of appropriateness. Since communication is a powerful tool that can be used to help or hurt others, your ethics about the use of this tool are important for those in your social environment. As important as these standards are for individual and social well-being, there is agreement on only the most basic issues of communication ethics. Although there are several approaches to ethical communication, each leads to different conclusions about how to behave responsibly.[17] Even people with a comprehensive, well-articulated set of standards (which few of us have) may find that a particular context or situation makes it difficult to decide how to act most appropriately. For example, you might adhere to the ethical standard that honesty is a crucial feature of competent communication. But there might be times when complete honesty would be hurtful to your partner (or yourself). You are faced with an ethical dilemma: Do you give your honest opinion, or do you protect your partner's feelings (and possibly your relationship)?

General cognitive processing skills are also part of what people bring to relationships. **Cognitive skills** are mental capacities—the ability to think, reason, remember, and make sense of one's world.

As part of their cognitive skills, people use various cognitive processes, which are potentially important to the way they communicate. These processes include memory and perceptual and attributional biases (see Figure 1.2). *Perceptual biases* govern how one sees the world. Optimists, for example, have a perceptual bias to evaluate their experiences in positive terms. *Attributional biases* are predispositions to evaluate and assign meaning to the intentions of others and the causes of events. Relational partners also

COGNITIVE SKILLS
Mental capacities, including the ability to think, reason, remember, and make sense of one's world.

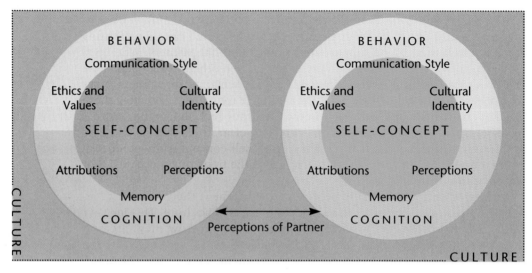

FIGURE 1.2
Each partner in a relationship has perceptions of the other, both as a partner and beyond the relationship.

have perceptions of each other that seem to be independent of the current conversation. These are relatively enduring perceptions of the partner as an individual (for example, the optimist might perceive Leah as a generous person regardless of what they are talking about at the moment).

Attributional and perceptual biases have an especially important bearing on how a person evaluates potential partners and behaves at the start of relationships, before having a great deal of information about the new partners.

BEHAVIORAL SKILLS

Communicative tools that are mastered and applied in different relational situations.

People vary in terms of both the **behavioral skills** they have mastered and the communication style in which they enact those skills.[18] The behaviors that are part of your repertoire are your tools for communicating. The more tools (skills) you have, the more likely you are to have the appropriate tool for specific relational work. As we pointed out earlier, however, the total number of skills does not determine the success of a relationship. Furthermore, the manner in which you use your skills (your style) may significantly influence the effect of your behavior. Note the difference between conversation in which the speakers smoothly take turns speaking and one in which there are abrupt interruptions between the speakers. The outcome in both exchanges may be that a different person is speaking, but the process results in different evaluations of the conversation and one's partner. Depending on the smoothness of the exchange, a partner may be considered either friendly or rude.

Interactional Goals

Both individual goals and relational goals come into play in any interaction. Our model calls attention to *current* interaction because we believe that any interaction is a microcosm of the relationship of the people interacting. This is especially clear in the case of conversation. We can learn something about a relationship by analyzing a conversation of the people involved in the relationship. The more conversations we have to analyze, the more confident we can be that we truly understand the relationship. In fact, it is through conversation or other forms of interaction, such as conducting an interview or public speaking, that relationships are defined. For example, you know you are a "student" to your professor because he or she communicates with you as you would expect a professor to communicate to a student. Thus we have current interaction in the model as part of "the relationship" (see Figure 1.3).

Your expectations for the current conversation, of course, influence the goals you set. These expectations are informed by what you know of your partner and his or her goals and expectations, the constraints the situation places on your communication options, the nature of your relationship, and so on.

It is with expectations, goals, and functions in mind that you formulate what to say in the current conversation. Similarly, you interpret what your partner says in light of these same considerations. Expectations and goals can and do change during the course of conversations, and they certainly change over the life span of a relationship. Skilled communicators are usually sensitive to these changes and can adjust their messages accordingly.

Relational History

The sum of the "objective" events and shared experiences of the relational partners is their *relational history*. This history is the essence of your current expectations and interpretation of what is going on in a current conversation. History is conceptually different from individual memory, even though history is obviously stored in memory. The reason for this concep-

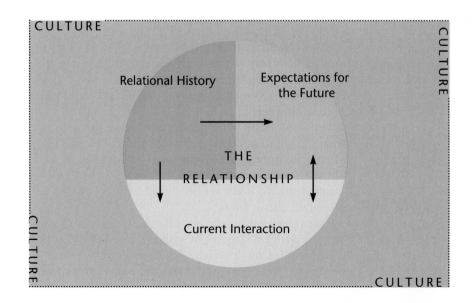

FIGURE 1.3
Each partner's understanding of the relational history and expectations for the future influence that partner's communicative behavior in the current conversation. The way these individual behaviors fit together, in turn, shapes the relationship.

tual distinction is that some things are brought into the relationship (memory) and others are created by the partners together (history). References to this common history can be important in defining a relationship, both for the participants and for the participants' associates. For example, if you and a friend went camping together and had a terrible time because of the weather, you both might develop an understanding by which any references to camping would have a negative connotation. (One of you might say, "Do you want to go to the opera with me?" The other would respond, "I'd rather go camping!"). References to your relational history indicate to you, your partner, and others that there is something special about this particular relationship and that it has some substance beyond the current interaction.

Expectations for the Future

Expectations for the future include long-term goals, both individual and relational. Expectations seem to be more closely tied to what you think your partner will do (or "outside forces" will cause to happen) than they are to what you plan for the relationship. You may want a relationship to continue (a goal), but at the same time, you may think that it won't (expectation). Again, as in the case of relational history, your understanding of the current conversation is influenced by these expectations. If you plan to marry your partner, you are likely to behave very differently in a conflict than you would if you expected to break up in the near future. Sometimes these expectations can become self-fulfilling. Denise, for example, would like to stay with her boyfriend, Ramón, but she expects him to end their relationship, so she communicates in a way that distances her from him. He interprets Denise's communication (correctly, as it turns out) as pushing him away, and thus he decides to leave. Denise has caused her expectations to be fulfilled, but her goal is not achieved.

Conclusion

The complexity of the communication process is staggering. Yet, you manage to communicate more or less successfully, day in and day out. Your experience with different types of communication situations helps you to decide how to communicate when you enter a novel one. That is, you generalize from one experience to another.

Three important dimensions along which communication episodes vary are (1) informal to formal, (2) small audiences to large audiences, and (3) familiar (known) situations to unfamiliar (unknown) situations. Because changes along these dimensions are systematic and make predictable demands on your communication abilities, we use them in this book to ease you along in your study of communication.

You spend most of your time in informal, familiar situations with small audiences. In Part 1, we start with these types of situations and examine how competent communication relationships are developed and maintained in them. In Part 2, we discuss interpersonal communication in terms of

Assessing Communicative Competence

The following questions are used by researchers to assess a person's communicative competence. You can use them to assess your perceptions of a partner's competence or to assess your self-perceptions.

Self- and partners' perceptions do not always match. Complete the scale twice—once for a partner you think is a competent or skilled communicator and once for a partner you think is not particularly competent or skilled. Be sure to keep the relationship *type* consistent (for example, evaluate a competent and an incompetent friend or boss or classmate) so that comparison of the evaluations will be consistent. If you'd like a real challenge, complete the scale a third time to assess your self-perceptions, replacing "My partner" with "I" and making other necessary changes.

Scoring: Indicate how you evaluate your partners (and yourself) on each statement using the following scale: 5 = strongly agree; 4 = agree; 3 = neutral or undecided; 2 = disagree; and 1 = strongly disagree.

Competent Partner	Incompetent Partner	Self	
			1. My partner finds it easy to get along with others.
			2. My partner can deal with others effectively.
			3. My partner generally says the right thing at the right time.
			4. My partner is easy to talk to.
			5. My partner is rewarding to talk to.
			6. My partner does not make unusual demands on her/his friends.
			7. My partner does not mind meeting strangers.

Source: Adapted from J. M. Wiemann (1977), Explication and test of a model of communicative competence, *Human Communication Research*, 3, 195–213.

relationships, conflict, and interviewing. Group and organizational communication is the focus of Part 3, which includes a chapter devoted to leadership. Finally, in Part 4, we deal with public communication, discussing presentations and mass communication.

Depending on your skills and experience and the importance of the interaction, you may need to devote more planning to prepare for larger audiences simply because it is more difficult to monitor and adapt to larger audiences than it is to one or a few partners. As a result, specific skills, together with practice using them, becomes important, although the development of "special" skills and practice is not unique to large audiences. In fact, people encounter the need to rehearse at various points in their social and work lives. The way you introduce yourself to a new employer is probably well thought out. If you are your new employer's first employee, he or she may also have done some rehearsing. Everybody likes to make a good first impression.

It is useful to remember that the same communication principles and processes that apply to informal, familiar situations apply across the board. In this book we begin with the familiar and move to the unfamiliar; as we do, formality increases and usually so does the size of the audience. Our approach, the communicative competence approach, will help you synthesize what you learn about one kind of episode and apply it to less familiar ones.

The Case of Sarah

At the beginning of this chapter you met Sarah, who is experiencing some difficulties in her relationship with Kristofer. Apparently, Kristofer believes Sarah is spending too much time on her responsibilities as president of the Undergraduate Accounting Association. She has asked you if you can help her in her relationship. Now that you have learned something about competent communication, consider how you might respond to her.

- Which of the six characteristics of communication are most relevant to Sarah's situation? Why?

- Which of the three general functions of communication is most at issue: control, affiliation, or goal achievement?

- Is it helpful for Sarah to view her problem from the perspective of communication relationships? Why or why not?

- Which components of the model of communicative competence seem most relevant to Sarah's situation? Explain.

REVIEW

- The goal of this text is to help you improve your understanding of your everyday communication experiences, your communication skills, and your effectiveness in relationships through the systematic study of communication processes.

- In this chapter we discussed the six characteristics of communication: a symbolic behavior, a shared code, a culturally bound message, the intentionality of the sender, the presence of a medium, and a transactional process.

- We examined the functions communication serves, especially control distribution, level of expressed affiliation, and goal achievement.

- We presented a model of communicative competence that relates individual communicators to functional relational concepts.

- From the perspective presented here, communication must be analyzed in the context of specific relationships, whether they be interpersonal, public, or mediated.

- The concept of communication-in-relationships is central to our approach because the relational context of an interaction forms the basis for understanding the meaning of any message. If we were to study only the individual's behaviors, removed from the relational context, we would not gain an accurate understanding of communication.

- This is the case whether the relationship is that of two people, several people in a group, a person (leader) and a group, or a speaker and a large audience. (The audience may be present in the same place as the speaker, or the communication may be mediated by some technology.)

- The relationship is the product of the communication of the people in the relationship. This is why the communication behavior of relationship participants toward each other is our unit of analysis.

- The "fit" of one partner's behavior to the other's (or others') as well as the "fit" of their goals, expectations, styles, and the like are important for successful communication relationships. The better the fit, the more competent the relationship. The more competencies you develop, the better able you will be to create a good fit with your relational partners.

CHAPTER TWO

Perception and Processing
Communication

After reading this chapter, you should be able to:

1. Explain how different factors affect your ability to process communication.

2. Discuss how memory affects communication and be able to improve your short- and long-term memory.

3. Describe the importance of attributions and the influence they have on communication processing.

4. Evaluate your reasons for using certain communication channels.

5. Recognize the importance of cultural diversity as a factor in communication.

HE 1995 WORLD SERIES, which pitted the Atlanta Braves against the Cleveland Indians, generated numerous letters to newspaper editors along the following lines:

It is unfortunate that it is only at times such as the World Series that the subject of racist symbols is given serious attention, but I was very happy to see the column against the use of Chief Wahoo. I have always felt torn between my loyalty for the Cleveland team and disgust toward its logo. Since Native Americans find the use of the nickname and its symbols offensive, they must be changed. "Redskins" may be deemed more offensive than "Indians," yet its meaning and associations are pejorative nonetheless. I applaud the efforts of the Portland *Oregonian* in refusing to identify the championship teams in any way other than Cleveland and Atlanta.

As you read through this chapter, think about the origins (and merits) of the attitudes expressed in this letter. At the end of the chapter, you will be asked for your views.

Think back to when you first decided to enroll in this communication class. What were you anticipating? Did you assume that the course would help you improve your oral and written communication? Did you expect it to examine how and why others communicate in particular ways in certain situations? You might even have anticipated that the course would address the topic of how you come to understand others. This chapter focuses on some of these issues by looking at the ways you process the communication you receive.

COMMUNICATION PROCESSING

The means by which one gathers, organizes, and evaluates received information.

Your ability to process communication goes way beyond seeing, hearing, or reading information. Actually, that is just the beginning of the process. **Communication processing** is the means by which you gather, organize, and make judgments about the information you receive. A number of questions surround communication processing, including: What information do you see, hear, or in any way receive? Why does other information get filtered out or forgotten? How do you assign meaning to the information you receive? How much information can you process? What affects your processing abilities?

In this chapter, we address these questions, and others, by focusing on the factors that most directly affect your ability to process communication: *perception, expectations, attributions, memory, cognitive complexity, cognitive load, channel capacity, culture,* and *goals.* Taken together, these elements act much like a computer does in monitoring, coordinating, and directing the operation of an automobile engine. If every part of the computer operates according to factory specifications, a car's engine should run smoothly, provided that the parts of the engine are in working order. But if one part of the computer breaks down, the entire engine is put in jeopardy. Similarly, if one of your communication processing elements breaks down, you will have little chance for competent communication.

◆ Perception

Have you ever met someone for the first time and immediately thought that you did or did not like that person? Your perception of others can create very strong feelings that develop with amazing speed. Whenever you engage in a conversation, whether it is with a longtime friend or a recent acquaintance, you will encounter numerous, specific bits of information that may influence your perception. For instance, in a leisurely walk across campus, you will likely come across at least one person to whom you say hello. Even in the briefest encounter you will receive input, including the exact words of the message, the person's tone of voice, the facial expression, and the presence or lack of eye contact. When considering the amount of information you receive in even a brief interaction, you might question how it is possible to make accurate perceptions. If you think of perception as the process of making sense of your world, you can understand the importance of perception for communication competence.

Schema Theory

Your ability to make sense out of the endless variety of inputs you receive can be explained by schema theory. Cohen explains that **schemas** are mental structures that put together individual but related bits of information.[1] These chunks of information then work together to create meaning and understanding at a more complex level. In essence, schemas help you understand how things work or anticipate how they should proceed. As you go through life, you continually discover new bits of information that combine with related information to help you structure and understand different situations.

For example, assume that during a leisurely walk across campus, you come across an acquaintance from class. When your classmate approaches and says, "Hi, how's it going?" a schema tells you that you will both exchange hellos and then, after a brief discussion of mostly nonpersonal concerns, go your separate ways. This schema assists your perception process. When you recognize one component of the schema, the entire schema is activated and you know what should follow.

Researchers Taylor and Crocker have provided more insight into the impact of schemas on your perception process.[2] They show that you develop schemas for people, roles, and events. *People schemas* allow you to recognize a few signs and then make a general assumption about an individual. You notice a few personal characteristics or a few specific actions of a person, and you use those bits of information to make a more general overall conclusion. For example, suppose that you enter a classroom on the first day of school and observe a young woman with braided black hair wearing a brightly colored outfit. She is adorned in 24-karat-gold jewelry and in the middle of her forehead is a red dot. You may assume that your new classmate is from India because you have a schema that describes the brightly colored attire as an Indian sari. The dot (*bottu*) on her forehead, along with her attire and appearance, forms your schema, although you can't be sure that she is Indian.

Role schemas allow you to develop a perception based on another's role in a group, position in a hierarchy, or occupation. You have schemas that define how a mother, father, leader, and follower should act. When someone new is presented to you as a leader, for instance, you already have some expectations about how that person should behave and what that person should do. To the extent that the leader's actions and communication conform to your schemas, you believe that person is fulfilling a leadership role.

Event schemas allow you to expect that a particular event or occurrence will proceed in a particular way. For example, a job interview will generally consist of some predictable events, such as questions about your background, qualifications, and interest in the position. Before you go into the interview, you are able to envision what is likely to happen because of your schema.

SCHEMAS

Mental structures that assemble chunks of remembered information, which in turn work together to create meaning and understanding.

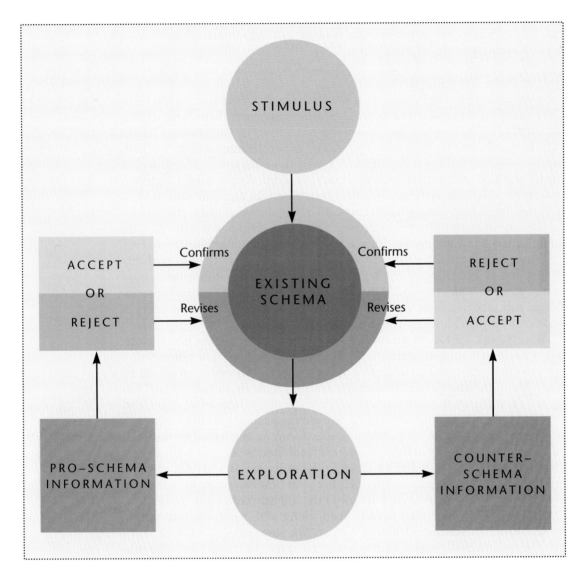

FIGURE 2.1
The schema process.

Imagine the confusion that would arise if you went into an interview and the interviewer ignored you. Such behavior certainly would not fit into your schema! Figure 2.1 demonstrates how the schema process works. The process of enacting an existing schema could occur any time a stimulus enters your awareness. A *stimulus* in this case refers to anything that your senses pick up from your world. It could simply be an idea that you have. You then take the stimulus and match it with an existing schema that best fits the information. In many cases, the existing schema will *explore* the environment (your world) for support and confirmation. If you discover this type of information, which is called *pro-schema information*, you will usually make one of two decisions. You can either accept the supporting information and confirm your existing schema or reject this pro-schema information and question whether your schema is actually valid. Why would you question and reject pro-schema information? There are lots of reasons, but the most obvious one is that you do not believe the pro-schema information as it is presented to you.

You will also encounter information that does not support your existing schema; this is referred to as *counter-schema information*. Again, you can make one of two decisions. You can accept the counter-schema information, causing you to revise your existing schema, or you can reject this information, leaving your schema intact. In many cases, when you receive messages that contradict your schema, you reject them in favor of pro-schema messages. Incorporating counter-schema messages forces you to change your existing schema, and research has shown that people will cling strongly to existing beliefs even in the face of strong evidence to the contrary.[3] If pro-schema messages are available, you generally find it much easier to attend to those messages and discount the others.

Consider the following example as an illustration of the schema process. Assume that you notice that a close friend of yours, Naomi, is acting very distant, cold, and noncommunicative (stimulus). You enact an existing schema that best fits this stimulus. You have seen Naomi act this way before, and you assume that her behavior is a result of her volatile relationship with her father (existing schema). You decide to ask her some questions (explore) to confirm your schema, and she tells you that in fact she just had a fight with her father (pro-schema information). Just as you are about to accept this information and confirm your existing schema about Naomi, her father, and her moodiness, you remember that Naomi's father has been away on a business trip for two weeks, which means that she couldn't have just had a fight with him (counter-schema information). You suspect that Naomi is lying to you, and yet you have to reject this counter-schema information because it makes you question your existing schema. The process of receiving information from the environment and proposing explanations to yourself is known as **intrapersonal communication**.

As you explore for more information, you talk to a mutual friend and learn that Naomi has been diagnosed with diabetes (counter-schema information). At first, you reject this information, but when you ask Naomi about the diagnosis, she admits she is depressed and embarrassed about her medical condition. You can now accept the counter-schema information (diabetes vs. father) and revise your old schema; you realize that Naomi can *also* act cold and distant because of her feelings about her diabetes.

The schema/perceptual process is a critical part of communication competency. In order to send and receive messages that are effective and appropriate,

INTRAPERSONAL COMMUNICATION
Messages sent and received by the self for the purpose of understanding information offered by the environment.

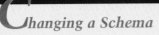

Changing a Schema

How many of your existing schemas hamper your perceptual accuracy? Are you willing to accept new information that strengthens your schemas? When was the last time one of your schemas was significantly altered? In writing, describe a recent situation that made you stop and wonder how you could have been so wrong in your understanding of another person. You may want to select a situation that involved a first date, an interaction with a person from a culture different from your own, or a conversation with a professor outside the classroom. In your description, explain how your existing schema made it difficult for you to process communication from that person.

MINDFULNESS

The process of focusing one's mind on the task at hand.

MINDLESSNESS

The process of performing behaviors or actions without being conscious of what one is doing.

How Mindful Is Your Mind?

How often do you find yourself daydreaming while someone is talking to you? Have you ever mindlessly agreed to something that you later regretted? Answering "yes" to these questions demonstrates that mindlessness can affect your communication processing and your ability to act competently.

you must be able to process information in a way that makes sense to you and at the same time reassures you that your assumptions are correct. Competence requires that we search for, objectively evaluate, and learn from information.

Mindlessness

The process of focusing one's mind on the task at hand is referred to as **mindfulness**. The use of schemas may make you a less critical processor of information by producing a state of **mindlessness**. When this occurs, you might automatically process information instead of doing an in-depth analysis of its content. The mindless processing of information might even cause you to ignore some of what you see or hear and to attend only to information previously stored in your schemas.

Roloff describes three signs of mindlessness: reduced cognitive activity, inaccurate recall, and uncritical evaluation. First, mindlessness will result in *reduced cognitive activity* (less critical thinking) when schemas take effect. In essence, when mindless processing occurs, you will simply have fewer thoughts. A second sign of mindlessness is the *inaccurate recall* of information. When asked about a particular situation, uncritical processors will recall fewer specifics than their mindful counterparts. The third sign is the *uncritical evaluation* of what is processed. The mindless processor will not question the information that is being received and will passively react to the situation.[4] In the previous example, a mindless processor might have just dismissed Naomi's behavior as moodiness and missed an opportunity to be a competent communicator and good friend.

Consider another example. You observe someone giving signs of being shy (avoiding eye contact, not attempting to talk with others), and you assume at first that this person is an introvert. The mindless processor of this information might not question why that person seems shy. There probably would be no thought as to whether those cues indicate something else, such as that person's being angry or embarrassed. The mindless observer would react only to the few cues received and not consider the situation further.

Selective Perception

The perception cycle is not a neutral, unbiased process. If a group of five people watch a televised debate between two candidates, they will likely have five different interpretations of what took place and what was important. Based on their existing schemas, one person might focus on the issue of budget deficits, another might be most concerned with foreign affairs, while a third might be intrigued only with the candidates' physical appearance. This biased nature of perception is referred to as **selective perception**.

It is easy to identify selective perception in everyday life. Simply gather a few people who have watched a late-night talk show. Ask people individually to comment on what they liked about the show, what they thought was funny, and what they thought was worthless. Write down each person's response and then share your results with them. You will likely have a few different accounts of the show.

Selective perception can be explained by the presence or absence of schemas. If the schema for a particular input is present in the receiver, he or she is more likely to pay attention to that information than is someone who does not possess the schema. However, someone who does not have an under-

SELECTIVE PERCEPTION
Biased or filtered processing of information based on strongly held attitudes, timing, or other phenomena.

Focusing on Ethics ✔

Selective perception can be deliberate. This means that communicators sometimes use their selective perception in ways that are less than innocent. You can see the ethical implications of selective perception in many professions. Journalists who work for liberal or conservative newspapers or television stations may focus on political statements and actions that best suit the needs of their stories or the political convictions of their employers. Arts and entertainment reviewers almost always have biases about certain acting, directing, or production styles and techniques. When they see a theatrical production that violates their preferences, they may selectively perceive and then report aspects of the performance that conform to their preconceived attitudes. Are these journalists and entertainment reviewers ethical in their selective perceptions? What if you attend a speech given by someone you do not like? If you focus on those aspects of the speech that strengthen your case against this person and ignore other information, are you being an ethical communication processor? How often are you faced with situations in which your selective perception may be unethical?

standing of or interest in economic matters may not attend to something a speaker says about balancing the budget or reducing the foreign trade deficit.

Selective perception can also occur when a person has the schemas to understand two competing messages but attends to one instead of the other. In these cases, the person's mind may filter the competing messages, or inputs, and attend to a particular one because it is expressed in a preferred style of language or has some preferred physical feature. Furthermore, once the mind has focused attention on a particular input, the amount of attention that can be devoted to a secondary message will be limited.

For example, during the Persian Gulf crisis of 1990–1991, then-President George Bush addressed the nation concerning the situation in the Persian Gulf and the domestic economy. Many people have schemas to comprehend both of those issues. At the time, however, many listeners did not attend to the president's discussion of the economy because the Persian Gulf situation was their primary focus. In addition, the president's remarks on the Gulf War were more dramatic and attention grabbing than his coverage of the economy.

Improvement of Perception

The following guidelines can help you improve your perception abilities and thus become a more competent communicator. First, you should always try to verify your perceptions. If you notice a classmate sitting near the back of the room who is looking from side to side during a test, your initial perception might be that this person is cheating. However, further observation may reveal that the person is simply trying to work out a stiff neck. Sometimes verifying a perception involves gathering information beyond your own observations.

Second, you should resist your natural tendency to fall back on the most obvious influence or explanation for what you observe. For example, occasionally scuffles break out among players in college and professional basketball games. Your tendency is to assume that the person who threw the first punch initiated the incident. Frequently, however, a scuffle starts when someone else says or does something that the fans do not easily perceive. In these situations, you need to ask yourself whether some information or action might have preceded what you observed. You also need to question whether you are aware of the reason that someone did or said something. Adopting this approach to verifying perceptions is difficult at first, for it is much easier to make immediate perceptions and not take the time to check their validity.

A third way to improve the accuracy of perceptions is to resist the tendency to rely completely on your very first impressions. These perceptions often lead to inaccurate conclusions. Consider this example: Todd has a tendency to stutter and to slur his words when excited. When people initially meet Todd, they assume he has a learning disability, so they talk slowly and loudly to him. Todd actually has a speech impediment, but he is of average intelligence and is not hearing impaired. Whenever possible, it is wise to delay reaction or judgment on a matter until further perceptions are made.

By now you will have concluded that the perception process is somewhat complicated. Schemas are constantly being evaluated for their accuracy. As a competent communicator, you have to be on the lookout for information that ensures that you are perceiving people, events, and issues accurately. Mindlessness and selective perception are only two of the factors affecting perceptual accuracy. In the next section, you will discover how your expectations affect your competence.

*R*ate Your Perceptual Awareness

Answer the following questions as they pertain to your perceptual attitudes and abilities. Think about how various areas of perception could be improved in your own communication behavior. Place an A in the blank if the statement is always true about you, an S if it is sometimes true, and an N if it is never true.

_____ Do you find yourself making snap judgments when it comes to personal issues?

_____ Are you too impatient to listen to all of the evidence before drawing conclusions?

_____ Do you have a tendency to weigh some types of information more heavily than others?

_____ Do you allow your personal biases to affect the conclusions you draw about people you do not understand?

_____ Are you more influenced by who a person is than by what he or she says?

_____ Do you have a tendency to ignore information that does not suit your preestablished opinion?

_____ Have you been told that your perceptions are different from those of others?

_____ Do you fail to verify your perceptions of other people?

_____ Do you attend to the most obvious influence or explanation you observe?

_____ Do you tend to rely completely on initial perceptions?

How well did you score? Did you have very many A's? If so, you may want to take stock and redirect your energies toward better perceptual awareness. If you scored mostly N's and S's, you rated yourself as an above-average perceiver. What score do you think a competent communicator should have?

◆ Expectations

Rarely, if ever, do you enter a communication situation with no thoughts or feelings as to what will or should happen. You generally have an intuitive thought or conscious desire in regard to an upcoming encounter. You might even have a strategic purpose or goal, such as a desire to change another's mind or to gain compliance with a request. Frequently, these thoughts or desires are expressed as **expectations**, and they can affect how the communication will take place. Therefore, you need to be aware of why you develop expectations and the effects they can have on communication.

Social psychologists Hilton and Darley explain that when you enter a situation with an expectation of how the encounter should progress or what the outcome should be, that expectation can affect how you process communication.[5] These expectations can lead to **self-fulfilling prophecies**. When you enter a situation with a preconceived notion about the outcome, you may attend only to the information that supports your predisposition. Think back to our discussion of schemas. Existing schemas direct you to information that confirms how you think and perceive. These schemas generate expectations, and new information that is obtained is compared against what you currently believe. Most of the expectations we generate about people are based on the norms of the groups they belong to and on their current situations. However, expectations from schema can also be generated from the unique or idiosyncratic behaviors of a particular person.[6] Our schema for that person will produce expectations for our anticipated interaction with him or her.

You can reasonably assume that if people anticipate future interaction, they will increase their communication processing efforts. The expectation of a future interaction makes the present encounter more important. Therefore, people will want to make certain that the present encounter has an outcome that is positive or in their favor. In addition, when people anticipate future interaction with others, they tend to focus more on what their partner is saying, causing better recall of the information that is exchanged.[7] There is a natural reaction to learn as much as possible about the other person. All of these concerns lead to more detailed communication processing.

Imagine yourself on the first day of a new job. You certainly expect to have future interactions with your employer and others in the workplace, so you think about the effort you will put into being a good employee and courteous co-worker. On the first day, these concerns will make you very attentive to what is going on around you and how things are explained. Three weeks later you may not listen quite as closely, but during that initial encounter you were probably processing communication at peak efficiency.

Another influence from expectations occurs when your expectations are violated.[8] When this happens, your information processing will become heightened. Although expectation violations can be positive or negative, most of the time they are negative. According to Burgoon and Walther, expectation violations are often undesirable events because they lead you to question the competence of the violator. Why would someone act in inappropriate ways that disconfirm your schema of that person? Are they immoral, inconsiderate, or just plain incompetent? With your expectations disconfirmed, you will put more effort into reevaluating what has happened to your existing schema. If a normally supportive friend of yours criticizes you in front of others, your expectations of this friend are violated. These violations may cause you to question the loyalty of your friend and the strength of your relationship, and perhaps even to question yourself.

On the other hand, some expectation violations are positive. For example, you might be pleasantly surprised by the unusually friendly behavior of an attractive acquaintance. According to Burgoon, positive violations depend on how you interpret the violation in light of social norms ("Well, I guess since we're at a party, it's okay for her to act that way"), and whether you see the unexpected behavior as a reward ("Boy, he sure smelled nice when he got close"). Perceiving this type of behavior as rewarding is often based on personal characteristics such as status, attractiveness, and reputation.

◆ Attributions

When processing communication, frequently you may try to determine why someone said something or what caused that person to act in a certain way. In other words, this person's behavior does not exactly fit your existing schema. When you look for personal characteristics to explain other peoples' behavior, you are seeking **attributions**.[9] The keys to understanding why you make attributions are *causality* and *control*. On one hand, as a communicator you make attributions to understand causes of behaviors. But with understanding comes control, and the more you make causal attributions for another's behavior, the greater your control of the situation.

When someone makes an unflattering comment, the person insulted will have a strong desire to ask or try to determine *why*.

ATTRIBUTION
A generalization that uses personal characteristics to explain communication behavior.

EMMA   Oh, you cut your hair so short! It makes your face rounder.

NANCY   (Why did Emma have to say that?) I think it looks more
         professional, and I like it.

Nancy may consider Emma jealous, envious, irate, or inconsiderate. It is important to figure out why the comment was made, for people feel a certain uneasiness about not being able to explain behavior. But if the behavior can be attributed to something (e.g., the comment was made because that person is inconsiderate), then you are put at ease because you understand the situation more fully and are in greater control.

Try to recognize how many times during a day you try to explain (understand) someone else's behavior by making attributions. You might also want to check how often you make negative and positive attributions about others. Do you tend to look for positive reasons for other people's behavior? Do you give them the benefit of the doubt, or are you more critical?

The greatest attribution pitfall you can fall into is to overemphasize the internal and underestimate the external causes of behaviors you observe. That is, when you see someone doing something wrong, you are likely to believe that person has a character flaw, and you may be less likely to attribute that person's behavior to circumstances beyond his or her control. Attribution errors of this type can be detrimental to your communication processing effectiveness.

You can prevent future problems by paying closer attention to your own attribution tendencies. When you make an attribution about someone's behavior, that attribution can affect your future encounters with that person. For example, suppose that during the first or second day of classes you observe that a classmate seems inattentive and uninterested in the lecture. Based solely on that observation, you conclude that he or she is unmotivated and irresponsible. The person, however, is actually a very good student who was feeling the effects of a 24-hour flu that day. Now suppose that during the next class period you and this student are assigned to the same group for a major course project. You will initially—and erroneously—have concerns

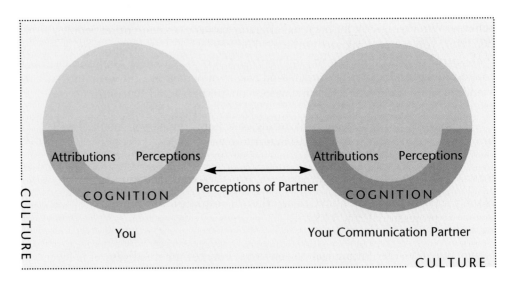

FIGURE 2.2

As the model of communicative competence demonstrates, attributions play an important role in determining your perceptions of your communication partner. They affect your impression of your partner and your own communicative behavior. These aspects of the model in turn affect the current conversation as well as your longer-term impressions of your communication partner.

about this person because of your one unverified attribution. As this example demonstrates, inaccurate attributions may cause much confusion in your social and personal relationships. (See Figure 2.2)

You can further improve your attribution abilities by becoming more patient. If you find yourself making an attribution about someone in one instance, wait for another opportunity to observe this person before committing yourself to a firm attribution. First impressions, unexplained actions, and strange behavior are not always the best evidence for making decisions about people or their communication.

◆ Memory

Memory is a necessary component in communication processing. Competent communicators are able to retrieve schemas and use them to understand the present situation. However, it is the rare person who remembers past occurrences precisely as they happened. Actually, you tend to recall past occurrences in general and adapt them to fit the present situation. Your ability to adapt information from your memory, which makes it easier to understand what others say or do, will greatly enhance communication.

The Memory Process

As researcher Loftus explains, the memory process involves three stages: *sensory register, short-term memory,* and *long-term memory.*[10] In sensory register, information enters your awareness through any of the senses (as when Javier tells you a very funny joke). The information is lost (forgotten) within a couple of seconds if it is not transferred to short-term memory. Short-term memory is an "immediate" memory that suspends information long enough for it to be used, or to permit repetition of the information and the association of related or similar items together. You can improve your short-term memory when you pay attention to the way a message is organized or think of a way to organize the information yourself. For example, without an organizing system it would be difficult to remember the names of seven people. However, it would be easier to remember their names if you thought of them in groups of males and females, by their majors, or by hair color. By finding or creating an organizational plan for remembering information that you hear, you enhance your ability to process communication.

Improvement of Long-Term Memory

Long-term memory can be improved with the use of *imagery* and *information storage*. Imagery aids memory because it allows you to associate a mental image with the information. Suppose your instructor has explained that during initial encounters between strangers, people will generally speak in short sentences, maintain appropriate distances, and not disclose personal information. In order to remember these three elements, you should picture yourself in the situation your professor has discussed. Thus, imagine yourself in a familiar place, meeting an unfamiliar person. Think about what might be said and how you would appear to a third person watching the interaction.

You can also improve your long-term memory through various information storage techniques. Perhaps the most frequently used of these techniques involves associating each letter of a word with a word in a sentence. For instance, many people learn the treble clef lines on a musical staff (EGBDF) as "Every Good Boy Does Fine." You can also improve your memory by placing bits of information into categories or related clusters and by associating the information with other things. This technique may help if you have trouble remembering people's names. When you meet someone, you can associate the person with the place where you met or the new person's job or major. Upon meeting the person a second time, you will have a greater context of information to help recall his or her name.

The ancient Greeks employed a memory system that can still be used today. The system of *loci* (places) works by associating parts of what you are remembering with parts of something that is very familiar to you. For example, you could remember a speech you have to give by associating your main points with different parts of your dorm room, apartment, or home. You could associate the introduction of your speech with walking through your front door and then proceed to associate different points of the speech with different parts of your home as you would come across them. In this way, when you give your speech, you will remember the content by visualizing yourself walking through your home. This concept shows why using analogies is an effective communication skill.

Finally, you can improve your memory by simply exaggerating the qualities of whatever it is you are trying not to forget. For example, if you have to remember to buy cheese, spaghetti, and a loaf of bread at the store, you can create a memorable little story by giving these items qualities of movement. Picture yourself making a bow and arrow out of spaghetti and then shooting a wedge of cheese through a loaf of bread. This is a silly story, and no doubt you can come up with an even more outlandish scenario. However, the fact that it is exaggerated (funny or vivid) will make it memorable. You can visualize the story of the bow and arrow and easily remember to buy the spaghetti, cheese, and bread.

◆ Cognitive Complexity and Cognitive Load

CONSTRUCTS
Mental structures that enable a person to make differentiations in judgments.

Cognitive complexity is crucial to your ability to process communication. As you grow and learn, you develop personal constructs. **Constructs** are mental structures that enable you to make judgments such as good-bad, honest-dishonest, or dominant-submissive. You develop and organize constructs to help you interpret and understand the situations you encounter.

Cognitive complexity refers to the degree to which one can perceive information in more complicated ways. Someone with a low level of cognitive complexity might refer to an argument as either good or bad. A person with a higher level of cognitive complexity would recognize that the argument may not be totally good or bad but somewhere in between and would be able to explain the issues involved. The various colors that are used in merchandising schemes can serve as an analogy. Years ago, lipstick was available only in basic colors: red, pink, and orange. Now, you can buy lipstick in hundreds of colors, including raisin rage, guava, and spicy cider. The differentiation of color has become more complex to meet the consumers' desire for greater variety and choice.

A person's level of cognitive complexity will vary on different issues. Someone might have a low level of cognitive complexity for understanding the rules and norms of interpersonal interaction. The same person, however, might be able to discuss at length the various components of personal computers. As you develop more constructs, you become more cognitively complex.

Integrative capacity is an aspect of cognitive complexity that refers to the ability to make connections between different concepts. The concern is not only with determining how good or bad something is but with how good or bad it is in comparison to a related issue or concept. For example, if you grow a healthy rose, you might look at it and conclude that your flower is quite beautiful. In this way, you have displayed some cognitive complexity regarding the rose. If you are also able to demonstrate how attractive the rose is compared to other similar roses or, better yet, to a different type of flower, then you have demonstrated integrative capacity.

The level of cognitive complexity plays an important role in communication processing. It helps you increase your ability to use information from your environment by making broader, more detailed, and more objective assessments. If you have a high level of cognitive complexity, your schema will be richer, and your attribution processes can be based on better and more meaningful information.

How can you increase your cognitive complexity? Work on making more detailed and multidimensional judgments about people and issues. In other words, develop schemas about people that include many of their attributes (friendly, intelligent, silly, quick-tempered, loyal, and so forth). To get you started, the next time you get into an argument with someone or find yourself questioning the person's character, ask yourself the following questions:

- Is this how I always think of this person? Am I in a rut?
- Is there any other possible explanation for this person's behavior?
- What are three possible reasons for my feelings?
- What is this person thinking about me at this moment?
- Am I jumping to conclusions for some reason (selfishness, jealousy)?
- How would this person feel about the way I am thinking?

COGNITIVE COMPLEXITY
The degree to which one can perceive information in more complicated and intricate ways.

INTEGRATIVE CAPACITY
The ability to make connections between different concepts; an aspect of cognitive complexity.

Coming up with answers to these questions will help you broaden your perspective and develop a more differentiated construct of the other person. You will then be able to make attributions in a more competent way.

In addition to cognitive complexity and integrative capacity, cognitive (or information) load can also affect your ability to process communication. **Cognitive load** refers to the amount of information an individual can process at one time. Just as individuals have different levels of cognitive complexity, they also differ in the amount of information they can handle simultaneously. When you are faced with an excess of information, the accuracy of your processing will decrease. Cognitive load is generally affected by environment, the individual's processing capacity, and the desire for information. If you are not really interested in a wildlife video being shown in your science course, and you are upset about your parent's illness, you will probably not be able to absorb much of the information that appears on the monitor. A member of the ecology club who has no major distractions and has equal processing capacity will probably pay more attention to the details on the video.

Correspondence bias is a general error people tend to make when experiencing cognitive overload. **Correspondence bias** occurs when a person believes that one or more actions were caused solely by another individual and disregards the possibility that other factors in the situation caused them. When you reach cognitive overload, you naturally tend to attribute too many things to a single individual or group. For example, in any given workplace a person may become swamped with a variety of tasks and decisions. When cognitive overload is reached, this person may tend to blame the boss for the workload. In so doing, the worker might overlook other factors, such as an increase in the amount of work coming into the organization, an unorganized work system, or the inefficiency of other co-workers. The level of cognitive complexity at this point is probably pretty low.

Even when you are able to manage the information load that is presented to you, it may still be easier to remember the first and last things you observe. Research into the **primacy-recency phenomenon** reveals that when

COGNITIVE LOAD
The amount of information a person can process at one time.

CORRESPONDENCE BIAS
The belief, excluding other possible factors, that another individual is the sole cause of an action or actions.

PRIMACY-RECENCY PHENOMENON
The tendency to pay close attention to initial and final inputs.

*H*ow Heavy Is Your Cognitive Load?

Take a sheet of paper or a notepad and your telephone into the room where your television is located. Call up a friend or relative while you are watching a favorite television program. If possible, get your roommate or a family member to engage you in conversation as you talk to your phone partner. As you watch television, talk on the phone, and converse, note what gets your attention the most. What do you remember the most about your cognitive ordeal? How did the person on the phone feel about your exercise?

you enter a situation and begin processing communication, you will pay closer attention to the initial inputs you receive because your attention will be primed as you enter a new situation. You are also likely to remember the last thing you see or are told. Therefore, whatever communication occurs in the middle of an overload encounter is the most likely to be forgotten.

Political speech writers take advantage of this tendency. Whenever a candidate has to talk about something that is going to be less popular than other issues, you can bet the writer will bury it in the middle of the speech. Whenever possible, candidates will try to start and end with popular comments or issues in the hopes that the unwelcome information in the middle of the speech will be forgotten.

When you feel you are experiencing communication overload, it is time to stop and reassess the situation. It is better to take the time to plan a strategy than to become overwhelmed with information. Try to prioritize your communication needs and to concentrate on the people and communication that are most critical to achieving your goals.

◆ Channels

How do you send and receive communication? Your initial answer to this question is probably "I talk and I listen." After a few more seconds you might add, "Oh, I also write and read written communication." You are beginning to identify communication channels. **Channels** are simply the vehicles or mechanisms that transmit messages from senders to receivers. The channels that come to mind first would include sound waves (oral communication) and light waves (nonverbal communication). However, you could quickly compile a list of many other frequently used communication channels. Consider, for example, the possible channels used for written communication (memos, letters), electronic communication (radio, television), and computer-transmitted communication (BITnet, Ethernet).

CHANNEL
A vehicle or mechanism that transmits a message from sender to receiver.

A variety of communication channels are capable of relaying messages, but quite often not all the choices are available to you, or those that are available may not be practical. For example, large stockbrokerage companies sometimes attempt to attract new clients by offering a satellite or teleconferencing session. During these sessions, the potential clients assemble in several locations to hear from a financial expert who is somewhere else in the country. The stockbrokers and their prospective clients might have preferred a face-to-face meeting with the expert, but for financial and other reasons, they are limited to using satellite signals or phone wires as a communication channel.

Part of your effort in processing communication involves making decisions about channels. If you love to talk on the telephone, your processing skills are likely to be directed toward that channel. You also have to process information about *why* people use certain channels. Are you curious about why some people show up unexpectedly on your doorstep without calling first? Is it because they insist on face-to-face communication? Do you wonder why some people act differently in a group than they do when they are only talking with you? Are you one of those people who refuses to leave a message on a phone answering machine?

Media Selection

Your media selection will be affected by (1) your **channel preference** and (2) media richness. Different channels are more conducive to certain communication situations. Communication traveling via light and sound waves, for instance, will permit quicker transmission and feedback and will bring people physically closer to each other. Other communication channels, such as public speaking, tend to be less interpersonal, less receiver specific, and less concerned with the receiver's immediate response. If your personality lends itself to frequent personal contact, you will likely have a channel preference for face-to-face communication. Those who are not as strongly drawn to interpersonal communication may prefer a more detached channel, such as written communication.

Another way of deciding on a communication channel is through **media richness**, which refers to the ability of a channel or medium to carry information to a receiver. Some messages are best communicated through rich media, whereas other messages are more appropriately communicated with less rich media. The following criteria can help you decide whether your message requires a rich media channel.[11]

Will the media increase the chance of immediate feedback from the receiver? Immediate feedback is an important component of media richness. When you need to gauge your receiver's level of understanding, rich media will be required.

Can the media be tailored or designed to specific targets? Tailoring or specifying a message for a particular receiver is a key element of media richness. Gossip or confidential information usually requires media that can fine-tune and tailor a message.

Can the media communicate multiple messages (visual, auditory, nonverbal)? The richest media convey meaning through numerous messages. Telephones allow you to hear a person's voice but restrict much of the nonverbal system. Letters or memos are very limited in conveying multiple communication cues. Sometimes you must be able to use as many communication signals as possible, especially when a message is sensitive or complex.

Will the media allow a diverse range of word choice? The richest media allow messages to be conveyed with a variety of words or terminology. Vulgarity and profanity are highly inappropriate in public settings. By the same token, intimate words and phrases between two people in love are best conveyed with rich media. Sensitive language usually requires a rich channel.

Rich media are effective for communicating complex messages.

According to these criteria, the richest types of media would include face-to-face speaking and telephones, which permit quick feedback, specific targets, and a wide range of word choice. The media lowest in richness are general memos, statistical reporting, and public speaking, which have slow feedback, few cues, and no specific targets.

How do you know which media to use? Rich media are most effective when messages are vague or complex. Media low in richness work best with simple messages. Approaching complex problems with less rich media will oversimplify situations because there are too few cues and too little feedback. On the other hand, using rich media for simple problems may complicate situations by presenting too many cues and too much noise and misinterpretation.[12] Most importantly, messages are best sent through multiple media.[13] For example, the best way to conclude an important telephone conversation with a colleague is to follow up with a short note.

Limits of Channel Capacity

Have you ever heard the warning about "too much of a good thing"? The same warning could apply to channels. Most people would agree that a variety of channels is beneficial, yet you need to be aware that, along with cognitive or information overload (discussed earlier in this chapter), there are limits to channel capacity. **Channel capacity** refers to the rate and amount of information that you can receive without experiencing processing errors. When you are receiving information from a single channel at a reasonable rate, you will generally be able to process the information while making adequate judgments and discriminations about the content. When you begin to receive information from two or more channels, your ability to process the content will initially increase until you reach a breaking point and your processing falters.

CHANNEL CAPACITY
The ability to process information competently via a particular communication channel or channels (e.g., face-to-face or over the telephone).

Channeling Your Communication

Communication channels are conduits for exchanging meaning with other people. Some people are prone to using particular types of channels. You may not be aware that you have a channel preference. By answering the following questions, you will be able to learn about your own channel priority system. In each of the following situations, put in the blank the letter that best represents the channel you prefer.

A = Face-to-face   D = Post-it note
B = Telephone   E = Electronic mail
C = Letter   F = Third party

_____ 1. Telling a friend that you got an A on a term paper.

_____ 2. Telling your family that you want to change your major or drop a course.

_____ 3. Telling your mate that you want to break off the relationship.

_____ 4. Telling your boss that you are quitting.

_____ 5. Chatting with an acquaintance about your career goals.

_____ 6. Objecting to some new policy at school or at work.

_____ 7. Confiding a secret.

_____ 8. Congratulating a friend on being selected for the swimming team.

_____ 9. Complaining to management about poor service at a restaurant or store.

_____ 10. Meeting a new person.

_____ 11. Informing a loved one of bad news.

_____ 12. Thanking a friend for a gift.

Look at your scores. Do you seem to prefer one channel to the others? Why? Go back to each of the questions and see whether your answers change if you ask yourself, Which channel do I prefer when I am the receiver in these situations? Do your answers change? Why or why not?

Farace, Monge, and Russell explain that certain roles require more communication flow than others.[14] As they report, a manager in charge of thirty individuals who need a great deal of attention will receive more information than a manager who deals with ten employees on a less frequent basis. You can informally examine the situations you encounter on a daily basis (home, school, work) and attempt to determine how many channels are operating and how much of a processing burden each presents. Your processing capacity will be determined by how well you use memory, attributions, and other cognitive activities. However, there is some evidence to suggest that improving your organizational and time management skills will increase your individual capacity. Finally, the desire to process communication will have some effect on how much channel capacity you might have. If you are motivated and believe the incoming information is of value, your channel capacity will increase.

◆ Culture

Recall the discussion of culture in Chapter 1. With the world becoming more culturally diverse each day, it is very important that you understand the role of culture in communication processing (see Figure 2.3). Previously, you learned that people attempt to explain human behavior through attribution; that is, when they observe a particular behavior, they usually seek a personal characteristic that they can say causes the behavior. The attribution process can play an important role when two people from different cultural backgrounds try to communicate. Obviously, people of different cultures will

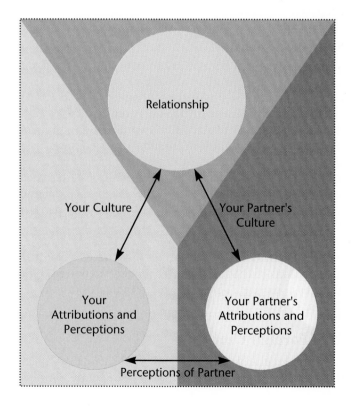

FIGURE 2.3
The model of communicative competence shows that all aspects of the communication process are contained within cultural constraints. The challenge of competent cross-cultural communication is to be willing to modify your behavior to accommodate the different expectations generated by your partner's culture and your own. At the same time, you must be careful not to make attributions based exclusively on your perceptions of your partner's culture.

CULTURAL FACTORS
Ways in which different cultural backgrounds can affect communication processing.

display behavioral and communication differences. These **cultural factors** make it necessary for individuals from both cultural backgrounds to work harder to achieve competent communication.

Once again, the biggest attribution trap is the tendency to overemphasize a person's internal responsibility for a behavior. In the case of intercultural interactions, people tend to attribute behavior to the culture and to disregard individual situational factors. Consider the following hypothetical situation. At a college in the northeast, Spanish 101 students are asked to stand up at the beginning of each semester and state in Spanish their names, hometowns, and majors. Those students with Hispanic surnames who stumble or mispronounce the information are routinely ridiculed by the Spanish instructor. This instructor assumes that all Hispanics can speak Spanish. However, the teacher is attributing characteristics to the students based on her perception of the culture and not on students' individual circumstances.

When you observe a behavioral characteristic among people from a different culture, you may fall into the trap of making the easiest assessment and decide that the behavior is culturally derived. In these situations, you have to catch yourself and remember the importance of asking if a separate factor might be responsible for the behavior. As we noted earlier in this chapter, some self-monitoring and retraining of your attribution-making tendencies might be in order.

Responsibilities of a Host Culture

Members of a host culture need to be as wary of overlooking cultural explanations for an outsider's behavior as they are of making negative attributions falsely based on cultural causes. For example, Frank recalls being in a small seminar with Akemi, a student from Japan. After several weeks, Akemi had rarely spoken and chose to sit back quietly while other members of the class became actively involved in class discussions. A few of her classmates attributed her quiet behavior to a lack of interest in the class. Eventually, Akemi explained that in Japan, students answer only direct questions from professors and otherwise rarely speak in class. Thus, rather than being uninterested in the class, she was actually just having trouble getting used to the host culture's openness in the classroom.

The *Bulletin of the Association for Business Communication*[15] reported the results of a survey that had asked 183 international students from 61 countries about their impressions of U.S. culture. Respondents reported their positive and negative impressions (see Table 2.1), which indicate some ways we might improve as a host culture.

Responsibilities of a Foreign Culture

The individual from a foreign culture is responsible for learning how people communicate in the host culture. If you are a native of the United States

TABLE 2.1 PERCEPTIONS OF U.S. CULTURE

POSITIVE IMPRESSIONS	NEGATIVE IMPRESSIONS
Educational opportunities	Rudeness
Friendly people	Weak family structure
Freedoms	Money consciousness
Career opportunities	Ethnocentricity—arrogant, snobbish people
Living conditions	Prejudice against international people
Organized and clean society	Drugs and alcohol
Lack of government red tape	Crime

Source: M. Cassady (1992), An international perspective of the United States, *Bulletin of the Association for Business Communication, 55.*

and plan to travel outside the country, you should try to learn as much as possible about the communication practices of the cultures you will visit. For example, Janet recently traveled to Pakistan to visit a close friend. In preparation for her trip, she read about the Muslim culture and her friend, who is a native of Pakistan, thoroughly explained its customs to her. But even with Janet's extensive advance preparation, she found it difficult to adjust to and communicate with the Pakistanis.

Y. Y. Kim's *Communication and Cross-Cultural Adaptation* (1988) details how to become a competent communicator in a host culture.[16] She explains that competent cross-cultural communication depends on (1) knowledge of the host communication system; (2) cognitive complexity in responding to the host environment; (3) effective co-orientation with the host culture; and (4) behavioral understanding of how people interact in the host culture. When members of a host culture remember to limit unwarranted attributions, and when those who enter the host culture work to adapt, cross-cultural communication competence can be achieved.

Initially, those seeking knowledge of a host culture's communication system should have modest expectations. When encountering a host culture for the first time, you may make oversimplifications and false generalizations. These inaccuracies can lead to miscommunication in later situations. Aside from the obvious concern of learning the host culture's language, newcomers must also study the nonverbal behaviors and communication rules. This is where Janet, the visitor to Pakistan, had difficulty. She had not fully prepared herself for the Pakistani attitudes toward women, which limit women's

Your Cultural Awareness

Have you ever visited a foreign country? Besides the language barrier, what other cross-cultural communication barriers did you experience? Was the host culture receptive to your needs?

opportunity to discuss important issues with men, and she had not anticipated a cultural belief that frowns on women openly disagreeing with men.

Oversimplifications and mistaken generalizations can test a newcomer's cognitive complexity. Although initial generalizations can be expected, a competent communicator in a new culture must learn to make complex distinctions and judgments about host culture behavior.

Along with the necessary cognitive complexity, newcomers must be able to co-orient themselves within a host culture. In other words, newcomers must be willing to accept and affirm that culture. The ultimate sign of accepting a new culture is to gain an appreciation for that culture's aesthetic and emotional drives and distinctions.

Much of this development is reflected in the newcomer's behavioral competence. Eventually, a competent communicator will learn how to blend the various verbal, nonverbal, and behavioral skills and tendencies into his or her own communicative behavior. This is the ultimate goal of a competent cross-cultural communicator.

Cultural Diversity

Culture and communication are inextricably linked. Your cultural background plays a large role when you communicate with people from other countries and when you exchange messages with culturally diverse colleagues who live and work in the United States. The basic rules of intercultural communication apply regardless of where a person resides.

What is cultural diversity? According to Loden and Rosener, cultural diversity reflects differences in age, ethnic heritage, race, physical abilities or qualities, gender, and sexual orientation. A culture that fosters diversity is "an institutional environment built on the values of fairness, diversity, mutual respect, understanding, and cooperation; where shared goals, rewards, performance standards, operating norms, and a common vision of the future guide the efforts of every employee and manager."[17]

Why is an appreciation of cultural diversity important to your communicative competence? With the face of the nation changing, the culture of the Founding Fathers—white, male, Christian, and English-speaking—is less widely accepted as the standard of normality than it was in the past. Members of this co-culture are already a minority, and although many aspects of their culture remain dominant, members of other co-cultures are asserting the equal worth of their cultural characteristics. Females, people of color, homosexuals, the elderly, people who have physical and mental challenges, non-Christians, and other groups that have long been oppressed are refusing to accept second-class status. To communicate effectively, everyone must recognize the heterogeneity of our society; members of both sexes and all ethnic, racial, and religious groups, people of all ages and abilities, must view each other without prejudice and with respect for the value of cultures other than their own.

Barriers to Competent Intercultural Communication

In the following section we discuss in turn the major barriers to competent **intercultural communication**. We also consider a variety of ways that you can face these barriers and work to overcome them.

"The belief that one's particular culture is appropriate in all situations and relevant to all others" is **cultural myopia**.[18] If you are a member of a particular cultural group and are very proud of its origin, heritage, and status, you are susceptible to cultural myopia. Problems occur when you view your cultural group as superior to other groups. You become "myopic" in your views of values, tastes, attitudes, and even communication practices. Cultural myopia is especially dangerous when members of a dominant group are unaware of, or are insensitive toward, the needs and values of members of different cultures.

Ethnocentrism is the process of valuing your own ethnic culture so much that you are comfortable only with people similar to yourself.[19] "Why aren't those people more like us? If they would only act like me, they would get the respect they want!" These are the types of comments usually made by ethnocentric individuals. Ethnocentrism is a major roadblock toward competent communication because it prevents you from understanding the expectations and goals of culturally different people. Your inability to appreciate their culture hampers competent communication. The more often you have an ethnocentric attitude when you approach a person who is culturally different from you, the less likely you are to process information about that person in a competent way.

Stereotyping is the process of organizing information about groups of people into categories so that you can generalize about their attitudes, behaviors, skills, morals, and habits. Stereotypes may be positive, negative, or neutral; they may be about a group to which you belong or one that is different from your own. In essence, you form biased schemas about particular cultural groups. As you can imagine by now, stereotypes have a powerful influence on your perceptions of other people. Stereotyping is the act of fitting individuals into an existing cultural schema.

Stereotyping is done all the time in the mass media by marketers who focus their commercials and advertisements on what are believed to be the shared values of their audience. Think of the television commercials for cereal and toys that accompany the Saturday morning cartoons, for example, or the beer commercials during sports telecasts. The advertisers are assuming certain stereotypes about their audiences.

When communicating within small groups or speaking in public, you too may be compelled to assume that the group members share some characteristics and stereotype them accordingly. But like smart advertisers, you need to realize that you cannot rely totally on stereotypes. Have you noticed how beer commercials have changed in recent years to encourage moderation in drinking and to appeal to drinkers of light beer? Had breweries been content

INTERCULTURAL COMMUNICATION
The exchange of messages by people of different cultures or subcultures.

CULTURAL MYOPIA
The belief that one's particular culture is appropriate in all situations and relevant to all others.

ETHNOCENTRISM
The process of valuing your own ethnic culture so much that you are comfortable only with people similar to yourself.

STEREOTYPING
The process of organizing information about groups of people into categories so that you can generalize about their attitudes, behaviors, skills, morals, and habits.

If You've Seen One, You've Seen 'Em All—Or Have You?

How many of your existing schemas are cultural stereotypes? Think about your views of the groups listed below. How strong are your stereotypes for these groups? What are the sources of your stereotypes? What evidence do you have that every member of a particular group acts according to your stereotype?

Mexican Americans	African Americans
Men	Women
Arabs	Redheads
Athletes	Police officers
Japanese	Jews

to accept a static, limited stereotype of their customers, they would not be aware of their market's changing values and attitudes.

The effects of stereotyping may be even more profound in interpersonal communication. Recall the last time you thought to yourself that someone was acting just as you expected a member of that individual's cultural group to act. You may have concluded that stereotyping was an efficient way of understanding this person, when in fact you limited your ability to gain information about the individual's unique qualities. You lost your chance for meaningful and competent communication.

It might help to remember that stereotyping is a *lack* of cognitive complexity and reflects a rigid, inflexible perspective. In contrast, competent communicators make judgments about people and groups that are varied, flexible, and multidimensional.

PREJUDICE

A deep-seated feeling of unkindness and ill will toward particular groups based on negative stereotypes.

Prejudice is a deep-seated feeling of unkindness and ill will toward particular groups based on negative stereotypes. These stereotypes categorize thoughts and feelings about cultural groups, leading to prejudicial attitudes. These attitudes make it easy to protect your own cultural group's attitudes and behaviors, while maliciously abusing those of other people. Sadly, prejudices often result from the insecurities and fears you have about the legitimacy or value of your cultural group. Forming prejudices is a defense mechanism against groups that threaten your (perceived) superiority. Prejudice becomes most noticeable when cultural groups assert their values and rights. It is difficult to understand why some cultural groups resent other groups' having the same rights as they themselves do. Raise this issue in class to see how other people feel.

Discrimination is the process of acting on your prejudices. Discrimination comes in many forms: speaking ill of a cultural group, refusing their members access to your own group, or denying them their basic rights and privileges. The intensity of discrimination depends on the degree of prejudice and desire for social approval. Some people are very prejudiced and do not hesitate to demonstrate their feelings. Merton calls these people "active bigots," or those who are most obvious in their discriminatory practices.[20] "All-weather liberals" are just the opposite and will actively uphold the rights of other cultural groups. Most of us fall somewhere between these two extreme positions. You may be a "timid bigot"—that is, have prejudices but not want to demonstrate discrimination because of social and legal constraints. Or maybe you're a "fair-weather liberal"—in other words, you don't have very many prejudicial attitudes toward other cultures, but at the same time you want to go along with the crowd and therefore don't always stand up for what you really believe. Some people discriminate against everyone who is not just like them, whereas others may discriminate only against one particular group. What about your discriminatory practices? What can you do about them? You can start by changing your stereotypes.

DISCRIMINATION
The process of acting on your prejudices.

Changing Stereotypes

You can change your schemas that categorize cultural groups; it is not easy to do, but it is worth the extra effort. By working to make the necessary changes, you can become a more culturally sensitive, and therefore more competent, communicator. Stereotypes can be changed in three ways.[21] One approach is to change and modify the assumptions underlying your attitudes. A second approach, and one of the simplest ways to transform stereotypes, is to concentrate on the positive qualities you notice among members of a cultural group. For example, you might notice that African Americans are very serious students, grandparents are polite to other people, and Arabs are very friendly. Making these qualities a part of your schemas about these groups will erode your negative stereotypes and build more positive ones. If you have positive stereotypes of people within a particular culture, you will probably communicate with them more pleasantly. It is important to remember, however, that positive stereotypes are not necessarily more accurate in describing an individual than negative stereotypes would be.

A third and more effective approach might be to *dismantle* broad stereotypes by recognizing the various co-cultures that exist within a cultural group. Being a member of a cultural group does not tie you to every characteristic of that group. Does being a male necessarily make Fred a chauvinistic pig? Of course not. Instead, it is more realistic to believe that he is a chauvinist if he views females as inferior and treats them as subordinate to

Successful intercultural communication with one individual can help to disintegrate the negative stereotypes you may hold of that person's culture.

males. Can we assume that because Carmen is Puerto Rican, she likes rice and beans, brightly colored clothes, and music with a Latin beat? She may have all, some, or none of these personal tastes. Reducing stereotypes to smaller, more specific schemas allows you to become more accurate in characterizing people. During the process, you are becoming more cognitively complex. You can also *disintegrate* stereotypes by perceiving culturally different people as individuals. By doing so, you begin to disassemble the stereotype, which no longer fits neatly into your perceptual process. Individuals are difficult to categorize. Think about close friends of yours. When other people ask what your friends are like, you talk about their qualities and characteristics, but you would seldom say that they are stereotypical of some group. You see your friends as individuals, and that is the best way to perceive all people. The key to disintegrating stereotypes is to emphasize the unique qualities of each person (personality, intelligence, skills, and so forth), regardless of the person's cultural background.

Embracing Differences

Every cultural group possesses admirable qualities and has special accomplishments. For example, different Latin American, African, Asian, and European cultures are each noteworthy in various respects. Understanding the different qualities of cultural groups is a fascinating process that leads to personal growth. Competent communicators view cultural diversity as an opportunity, not a handicap. Diversity gives them the chance to question old ways of thinking and to eliminate bad habits. When you embrace diversity, you are able to enrich your communication processing beyond previous levels.

◆ Goals

Communication goals also affect the success or failure of an exchange between people. They directly determine your openness to new information and also help you to process new information more competently. When an instructor announces that the upcoming lecture will be covered on the exam, students will be at their peak ability for receiving and processing the new information. Their attention becomes focused because they can visualize a goal for the information they are about to receive. A similar result is achieved when you can foresee a direct application of what is being taught. In a cardiopulmonary resuscitation (CPR) class, students are usually very attentive because they see a specific goal or use for the valuable information. Their attention to the information makes them want to rehearse the information as they hear and see it and to practice the techniques they learn. In short, communication goals enhance information processing.

Communication goals also affect how you organize information. If you listen to a friend explaining why his or her grades have dropped, your goal will affect how you organize the information. If you simply want to empathize with your friend, you might organize the information according to the reasons he or she provides (e.g., classes too difficult, too many exams at once, lack of interest). However, if your goal is to provide advice, you might organize the information in such a way as to help your friend (e.g., study tips, exam strategy, relating classes to personal interests).

Finally, communication goals affect your ability to remember new information. In general, when you have a goal for information, you tend to remember it better. Furthermore, the type of goal affects the type of information remembered. For example, suppose you listen to someone giving a speech and your goal is to form an overall general impression of his or her personality. In this instance, you would be more likely to remember statements that reflect the speaker's personality. If you were listening with no specific goal, you might instead remember specifics of the content not related to the speaker's personality.

Berger and Jordan indicate that memory also plays a role in how you try to achieve goals.[22] These researchers state that when people establish a goal, they search their long-term memory for insights into how that goal can be achieved. They go back to their long-term memory in the hopes of recalling the strategies they previously used to reach the same or a similar goal. Thus, people do not need to develop a new approach for each goal. According to Berger and Jordan, the use of previous plans results in cognitive efficiency and is much easier than constantly developing new plans for each goal.

COMMUNICATION GOAL

A desired outcome that can affect how communication takes place.

The Case of the 1995 World Series

• • • • • • • • • • At the beginning of this chapter we included a letter to a newspaper editor, which expressed opposition to the use of Native American symbols as team mascots. Viewing the letter in light of the concepts described in this chapter, consider the following questions.

- What roles do perception, expectations, and attributions play in the development of the attitudes expressed in the letter?

- How would you describe the letter in terms of cognitive complexity and cognitive load?

- Which channels of communication influenced the development of the views expressed in the letter?

- What does the letter illustrate about intercultural communication?

REVIEW

- This chapter focused on nine factors that affect your ability to process communication: perception, expectations, attributions, memory, cognitive complexity, cognitive load, channel capacity, culture, and goals.

- Perception refers to how you make sense of the world around you. Schema theory is a useful mechanism for understanding perception. Schemas are categories of information you store in your memory that are used to assimilate new information.

- Having expectations about people and communication events is a natural process. Problems occur when expectations restrict the communicator from processing information in an objective way. Expectations can also be violated, which causes communicators to question the motives or qualities of the violator and to search the environment for information to help explain the violation.

- Attributions are inferences or explanations of personal characteristics that you make based on what you observe, feel, or sense. When you observe someone communicating, you naturally tend to attribute some quality to that person. If you make generalizations about someone too hastily, however, you may perpetuate misperceptions when you communicate with that person.

- Memory guides how you select words and serves as a benchmark for selecting the appropriate communication strategy. Two types of memory are short-term and long-term memory. Committing information from short-term to long-term memory takes some effort on the part of the communicator.

- Cognitive complexity is the ability to process communication more abstractly and with more intricacy.

- Cognitive load refers to the quantity of information a communicator is able to process at any one time.

- Channel preference differs according to the person and the situation involved; some people generally prefer face-to-face communication, but others like to talk on the phone. When a channel is cluttered with noise or competing information, that channel's capacity may be stretched beyond its limits, and processing errors can occur.

- Cultural factors can have a significant impact on communication processing. In intercultural communication, there can be a tendency to attribute information to the culture rather than the individual. As a communicator, you must remain aware of the cultural factors that affect message exchange.

- Communication goals affect the success or failure of an exchange between people. Your communication goals directly affect how open you are to new information. They also help you process new information more competently. When listeners have a goal for what they are about to hear and see, they are usually more open to the information.

CHAPTER THREE

The Self and Communication

OBJECTIVES

After reading this chapter, you should be able to:

1. Describe the importance of self-concept and self-esteem to human communication.

2. Demonstrate how self-efficacy leads to communication success.

3. Discuss how self-presentation and self-disclosure affect communication competence.

4. Recognize cultural and gender differences in self-disclosure patterns.

5. Explain how feedback affects communication processes.

6. Identify various responses to communication competence assessment and how they affect the self.

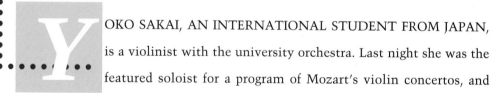

YOKO SAKAI, AN INTERNATIONAL STUDENT FROM JAPAN, is a violinist with the university orchestra. Last night she was the featured soloist for a program of Mozart's violin concertos, and this morning's student paper has published a rave review of her performance. Yoko is flushed with success as she leaves her sorority and heads to class. Yoko is a hard-working student who earns good grades (a B average), although she seems to enjoy her courses in the arts and humanities more than those in science and mathematics. Yoko's parents are both engineers, and she is in the third year of a B.A. degree program in electrical engineering. As you read through this chapter, think about how concepts concerning the "self" are relevant to Ms. Sakai. You will be asked questions about this at the end of the chapter.

Thinking about Yourself

How often do you reflect on your self-concept? What kinds of questions do you ask that reveal your understanding of your actions, abilities, goals, and other self-related matters? Do you often wish you knew more about yourself?

Acquiring the ability to understand who you are plays a large role in helping you become a competent communicator. Your view of *self* is often so biased that you misinterpret or ignore information that you need in order to communicate effectively. You can become a more competent communicator by (1) developing knowledge about self; (2) learning to communicate about who you are; (3) assessing your ability to communicate self to others; and (4) responding to feedback about your level of competence. This chapter explores how the self, your very being, is related to communication competence.

◆ The Self and Communication Competence

Few concepts in the humanities and sciences are more complicated than that of the self. To simplify our discussion of this concept, we will describe a process that is illustrated in Figure 3.1. Examine it for a moment.

At the core of this process is the self. At the center of the self are self-concept (knowing and understanding the self), self-esteem (evaluating the self), and self-efficacy (predicting success). These influence self-presentation and self-disclosure, which in turn generate feedback. The self then assesses the competence of its communication performance, and the assessment affects the self-concept, self-esteem, and self-efficacy in various ways. Ideally, the self is permeable (as demonstrated by the dotted line in Figure 3.1) so that it can learn from the feedback. The solid line on the inside of the self reflects a degree of stability. The remaining sections of this chapter provide a more thorough discussion of how this process works.

◆ Self-Concept

Think for a moment about who you are. Although you may be able to describe yourself by identifying your status as a college student, son or daughter, spouse, parent, or friend to others, there is much more to the self than just name, rank, and serial number. Numerous definitions of self-concept have been proposed, but we are partial to the idea that you learn to understand your attitudes, your personal traits, and behaviors by observing what you do, witnessing your reactions, watching others' reactions to you, and being aware of how situations can influence your behavior and feelings about life.[1]

Some writers argue that self-concept comprises many selves, each with its own framework of values, perceptions, and thoughts.[2] According to this view, you could have a separate self as student, as automobile operator, as pianist, as conversationalist, and so forth. In Chapter 1, we defined self-concept as a person's own definition of his or her being. Now we can expand that definition. **Self-concept** is your awareness and understanding of who you are as interpreted and influenced by your thoughts, actions, abilities, values, goals, and ideals, and by other people.

SELF-CONCEPT

The awareness and understanding of who one is as interpreted and influenced by one's thoughts, actions, abilities, values, goals, and ideals, and by other people.

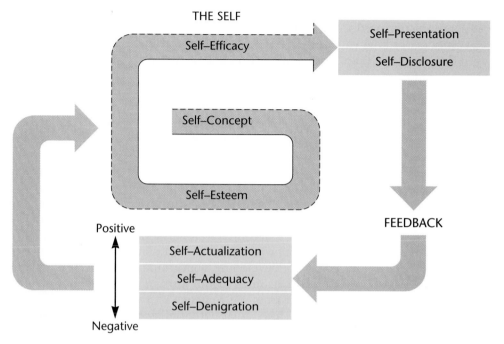

FIGURE 3.1
The self and communication competence.

Effect on Competent Communication

How does knowing about yourself affect your communication with others? From the start, you have certain views of who you are as a communicator (for any situation that involves speaking, interviewing, or just talking with others) and views of yourself in other respects that can also affect your communication. For example, if you feel strongly about the issue of the homeless, you are more likely to communicate in ways that support your viewpoint. You may think of yourself as an effective communicator when it comes to that topic. Moreover, self-concept can be a powerful influence on your communication processes; specifically, it can affect how apprehensive you get in certain communication situations,[3] whether or not you are willing to interact with others,[4] or how you approach someone with a request (e.g., whether you are meek and timid or strong and confident). The self has a strong influence on your attitude toward communication. Think about people you know who take great pride in their ability to communicate. Do these people place themselves in situations where they are able to use those skills? Do you know other people who have a less favorable concept of their communication skills and who prefer to stand back while others communicate?

The self influences communication in other ways. In the last chapter you learned how important cognitive processes are to communication. The self influences many of the mental operations that eventually affect your communication with others. In other words, your perception of others is the product of how you view yourself.[5] If certain attributes about self, such as honesty or wit, are important to you, you will also see them as important traits for other people. If you think that using profanity makes you appear cheap and vulgar, you are likely to think the same of others when they use such language. As you make decisions about your communication, your self-concept influences how you perceive the communication of others.

Although self-concept strongly influences communication, the reverse is also true. When you interact with other people, you get impressions from them that reveal how they evaluate you as a person and as a communicator. If someone you value daydreams as you tell her about your plans for the future, you are likely to think that she is not interested in you or that she finds your conversational skills lacking. Many researchers and writers in the area of self-concept identify social interaction as a key to developing one's self-concept. Communicating with others provides both direct and indirect evidence that you can use for developing, confirming, or disconfirming your self-concept. *Direct evidence* comes in the form of compliments, insults, support, or derogation. For example, if someone important to you, such as a professor, tells you that you have great potential as a manager because you possess excellent interviewing skills, you make this information part of your self-concept. *Indirect evidence* that influences your self-concept might be manifested through innuendo, gossip, subtle nonverbal cues, or by a lack of communication. For instance, if you ask someone to evaluate your promise as a public speaker and he changes the subject or looks a bit pained, you will probably get the impression that you are not yet a competent public speaker.

Schemas and Communication

One approach to viewing the self is the *self-schema theory*, as popularized by Markus. This theory states that the various pieces of information that you attribute to self are organized into separate structures or frameworks. These frameworks, or self-schemas, help you get a sense of who you are, guide your actions, and facilitate the acquisition and storage of new information as it pertains to self. According to Markus, **self-schemas** are "cognitive generalizations about the self, derived from past experience, that organize and guide the processing of self-related information contained in the individual's social experience."[6]

Since schema theory was discussed in the last chapter, the focus of this discussion is on how self-schemas and communication are related. You may begin by imagining your various self-schemas as boxes of information that you absorb from your social world. Included in these boxes are facts, data, examples, experiences, and even feelings associated with particular situations. For example, you probably have a schema (or box of information) that contains your views of self in terms of romantic love. This box will be much

SELF-SCHEMAS

Structures composed of the various pieces of information that a person attributes to self. They help that person develop a sense of self, guide the person's actions, and facilitate the acquisition and storage of new information as it pertains to self.

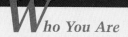**ho You Are**

Take out a sheet of paper and entitle it "This Is Who I Am!" Write a brief autobiography of yourself concentrating on your attitudes, behaviors, lifestyle, values, and beliefs. Once you have finished, ask three people who know you very well to comment on your autobiography. Ask them to judge its accuracy, honesty, clarity, and comprehensiveness. They should be encouraged to provide any important details that you left out. Comment in writing on your reactions to these people's observations. Bring this assignment to class for discussion.

larger and more varied for some people than for others. It may contain perceptions about romance that you acquired through books, movies, or stories from other people. Your own romantic experiences may shape this schema in ways that are different from those of other people (see Figure 3.2). In addition, you may adjust your own schema based on others' views and experiences. However, the stronger your schema for this topic, the less likely you are to allow its modification by new information. This last point is important. As Berger points out, the more entrenched or specifically defined the self-schema, the more likely it is that you will (1) collect information that is consistent with your preestablished views, (2) process and recall relevant information more quickly, and (3) perform communication behavior that is consistent with your self-schema.[7] To extend our example a bit further, if people have a generally negative view of romantic love, they are more likely to resist information that portrays this type of love as blissful and less likely to make this information part of their own schemas.

Some topics hold very little relevance for people and would not qualify as strong or clearly defined schemas. Your schemas for interviewing, working in groups, or public speaking, for example, may be only partially developed as a result of limited knowledge or experience. On the other hand, suppose you gave a campaign speech for someone running for office at your school a few years back; you received a nice round of applause, and your candidate won the election. In this instance, your self-schema for public speaking still may be only partially developed, but it is likely to be positive. You would therefore be receptive to new information about this topic. In fact, you might even seek out college courses such as this one in order to further develop your existing self-schema on public speaking. The information you receive may confirm or disconfirm your existing opinions, and you may seek additional information in order to expand your self-knowledge. You can therefore view a self-schema as a frame of reference whereby you organize knowledge you have in a certain area at a particular time.[8] Each of the self-schemas you hold in your consciousness provides you with a road map, recipe book, or checklist for communicating with other people about specific topics.

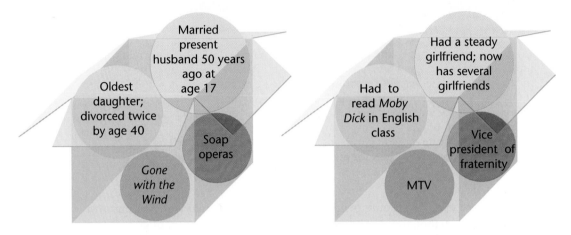

FIGURE 3.2

Self-schemas are affected by communication. Here are two individuals' self-schemas for romantic love, represented as boxes containing pieces of information from various sources in their respective social worlds. For simplicity, only a few examples of information are shown. Using these representations, one could begin to describe these two individuals and their self-schemas for romantic love.

Telling Jokes

Do you admire people who can tell one good joke after another? People who receive positive reactions to their jokes have an organizational framework for hearing and telling them. People whose jokes fall flat hold a very different schema about joke telling. Describe your self-schema for joke telling. How does it compare to your classmates' evaluation of your joke telling?

The following two examples illustrate how communication and self-schemas are linked.[9] The first example involves nonverbal communication. According to self-schema theory, a person whose self-schema is consistent with the demands of a particular situation is more likely to exhibit competent nonverbal behavior. In other words, when your view of self corresponds to what is expected of you as a communicator, you are more likely to avoid speech errors, hesitation pauses, and nonfluencies. Take the example of someone who maintains a self-schema of being good at deceiving others and doesn't feel much guilt about lying. When put into a situation requiring either truth or deception, such a person may choose lying (if it seems justified) and pull it off more skillfully than someone whose self-schema is focused on "truthfulness always."

The second example linking self-schema and communication is that of persuasion. Research demonstrates that persuasive messages containing viewpoints, information, or tactics compatible with a receiver's self-schema will be more persuasive than messages inconsistent with the schema.[10] A person with a strong religious self-schema will be more susceptible to persuasive messages that contain some appeal to spiritual values. People with strong altruistic self-schemas will be more easily persuaded to give to a charity than those without such altruistic schemas.

◆ Self-Esteem

Self-esteem usually refers to how someone thinks of himself or herself. It is essentially a set of attitudes that people hold about their feelings, thoughts, abilities, skills, behavior, and beliefs. Although self-concept and self-esteem are often equated, self-concept is generally thought to refer to *knowledge* about self whereas self-esteem is defined as how people *feel* about what they know.

SELF-ESTEEM

A set of attitudes that one holds about one's feelings, thoughts, abilities, skills, behavior, and beliefs.

*Y*our Self-Esteem Inventory

The following items should help you determine your level of self-esteem. Answer each of the questions as sincerely and honestly as you can. Use a 5-point scale for your answers: 5 = strongly agree; 4 = agree; 3 = neutral; 2 = disagree; and 1 = strongly disagree.

_____ 1. I am a very happy person.

_____ 2. I am smarter than the average person.

_____ 3. I enjoy being sensitive to other people.

_____ 4. I am a very honest person.

_____ 5. I wish I were better looking than I am.

_____ 6. I am proud of my accomplishments.

_____ 7. I can be trusted with sensitive information.

_____ 8. I communicate better than most people.

_____ 9. I am a great listener.

_____ 10. I am seldom shy in social gatherings.

_____ 11. I am mature for my age.

_____ 12. I wish I weren't so lazy.

_____ 13. I wish my friends and family trusted me more.

_____ 14. I really like myself.

_____ 15. Most people hold me in high regard.

Add up your scores on items 1–4, 6–11, and 14–15. Now reverse the scoring on items 5, 12, and 13 (5 = 1, 4 = 2, 2 = 4, 1 = 5). Finally, add these scores to the sum you calculated from the previous items.

If you scored 15–34, your self-esteem is pretty low for a college student. If you scored 35–55, you have average self-esteem. If you scored 56–75, you have high self-esteem. How do you feel about your scores? What could you do to improve your self-esteem?

Source: Scale partially adapted from J. S. Fleming & D. J. Whalen (1990), The personal and academic self-concept inventory: Factor structure and gender differences in high school and college samples, *Educational and Psychological Measurement, 50,* 957–967.

Of course, self-esteem depends on self-concept: If people do not know themselves, it is difficult to have an attitude about self. Therefore, many researchers believe that the self-concept is formed first, after which attitudes develop.

Attitudes toward Self

Your attitudes toward yourself are what make up self-esteem. These attitudes should be based on accurate information that comes from your self-concept. Campbell believes that some people have low self-esteem, or a poor view of self, because of their lack of knowledge or because of their mistrust of the knowledge they do possess. For example, you may feel that you are an effective listener, but you can't be sure of that attribution because you feel anxiety in some listening situations. Similarly, low self-esteem may result from an inconsistent view of self.[11] Some people who think they possess shortcomings or negative traits may prefer to ignore them so that these traits will not affect their more enduring self-esteem. We do not recommend that you use this self-delusionary tactic, but you should recognize the reasons for it.

You have probably noticed that people with high self-esteem have confidence in what they do, how they think, and how they perform. These individuals, realizing that they are responsible for their own destiny, are better able to incorporate successful ventures and performances into their self-concept. People with low self-esteem are particularly sensitive to how others view them. Because they have less confidence in their abilities and skills, they are more likely to maximize weaknesses instead of focusing on strong points; to believe negative information about self; to attempt to lower other people's expectations about their potential performance; and to communicate less confidence about future performances.[12] Negative attitudes about ability can lead to poor performance, which can then strengthen negative attitudes about ability. Like a dog chasing its tail, low self-esteem is an unproductive enterprise.

Self-Certainty

We have already noted that low self-esteem can result from an uncertain self-concept. Baumgardner proposes an idea that speaks to the concept of **self-certainty** or to a strong sense of identity.[13] Self-certainty is composed of strong self-attributes or ideas about self that are unaffected by adverse or competing information. It can be seen as a measure of confidence that you have in your view of the self. People with high degrees of self-certainty will be more likely to understand themselves and their abilities in various communication situations.

Self-certainty can lead to successful outcomes for three reasons.[14] First, if you are certain that you can perform a task well—say, leading and conducting group meetings—you will have more confidence going into those situations and be more likely to give a good performance. Second, when you are certain about your skills, you are more likely to seek out those situations that are conducive to bringing out your competence. In this example, you

SELF-CERTAINTY

A strong sense of identity; composed of strong self-attributes or ideas about self that are unaffected by adverse or competing information.

may search for opportunities that allow you to emerge as a group leader. Third, self-certainty is not necessarily tied to high self-esteem. It pertains to negative self-esteem as well; that is, you may feel certain that you are a poor conversationalist. In this case, you might avoid situations in which you would perform poorly and therefore would not have to endure the confirmation of negative attributes. According to Baumgardner, you can gain control of self by using self-certainty to control situations to your advantage. Problems emerge for communicators who have not developed certainty about their abilities. Low-certainty communicators are less likely to take risks when communicating in uncertain situations.

Self-certainty gives you control over your life by helping you to search for appropriate situations and to avoid inappropriate ones. In addition, it helps improve your positive feeling for self. When you feel you have control, you are more likely to possess a positive opinion of self than if you feel not in control. In this way, self-certainty leads to positive self-esteem.[15]

How can you become more certain about your knowledge, skills, and abilities in communication situations? One way is by reading this book, doing the exercises, and following the lectures and class discussion. Another method is by periodically conducting a self-diagnosis in order to discover how certain you are about what you know and how you feel about self. Many self-diagnostic tests exist. We provide one in the Self-Check "Are You Certain?"

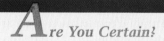

Are You Certain?

The following questions are designed to raise the certainty level of your communication skills. Although you may think you know your ability levels and have an opinion about them, you may not feel confident or certain about those abilities. When you are more certain, you can exert more control in communication situations, which in turn makes you a more successful communicator.

1. Do you know how to avoid situations that will make you feel uncomfortable?
2. Do you have concrete evidence about your ability as a listener? Public speaker? Group member? Conversationalist? Leader?
3. How can you prove that you are not successful in some communication situations?
4. What could you do to gain more certainty in some areas of your communication?
5. In what types of communication situations do you feel especially confident?
6. Overall, how would you describe yourself as a communicator?

◆ Self-Efficacy

This section explores the idea of self-efficacy as proposed by the famous psychologist Albert Bandura. **Self-efficacy** is that part of your mental and behavioral system "concerned with judgments of how well you can execute courses of action required to deal with prospective situations."[16] Whereas self-certainty is the confidence you feel about your self-concept and self-esteem, self-efficacy is the ability to *predict* actual success from your self-certainty. Two aspects of self-efficacy that are particularly important are *effort* and *coping* skills.

Effort

Your perceptions of self-efficacy guide your ultimate choice of communication situations. You are much more likely to avoid situations where you perceive low self-efficacy. Moreover, in low-efficacy situations you cannot avoid, you make less rigorous efforts than in situations where you perceive high efficacy. For example, Rebecca is 7 years old and extremely bright. She has been placed in advanced classes of reading, composition, grammar, and spelling. However, Rebecca perceives a low level of self-efficacy in math. Because of her negative attitude about her math competency, she avoids practice and will not even try to learn it. On the other hand, as a second grader she reads at the sixth-grade level and gives maximum effort to reading class and practice. In fact, Rebecca never turns down a reading challenge.

You may know people who avoid public speaking opportunities because of their low self-efficacy in this area. Even when they are forced to perform a speaking role, they will often put in only a minimum effort because they are resigned to the perception that they will not perform competently under any circumstances. In other words, they think that even a supreme effort would not convert them into competent speakers. Experienced public speaking instructors demonstrate that this perception could not be farther from the truth. Instruction added to effort can produce positive results, helping to break this cycle of low self-efficacy in communication.

Before concluding the discussion on self-efficacy and effort, we should point out that those with high efficacy may want to be careful about overconfidence. Bandura has also learned that those with very high levels of self-efficacy may withhold effort because of supreme confidence in their abilities. How many times have you seen athletes lose games or matches because their confidence was greater than their effort level? Bandura recommends that people maintain a high level of self-efficacy with just enough uncertainty to cause them to anticipate the situation accurately and prepare accordingly. Your effort must rise to the occasion no matter how confident you feel.

Coping with Stress

Self-efficacy also has an effect on your ability to cope with failure and stress. Feelings of low efficacy may cause you to dwell on your shortcomings and failures. A snowball effect occurs in that when you possess feelings of in-adequacy and then fail at some event, it takes its toll on your self-esteem, caus-ing you to experience stress and negative emotional reactions. These feelings then contribute to a lower self-esteem, which in turn lowers your self-efficacy level even further. On the other hand, individuals with high self-efficacy are less emotionally affected by failure because they usually chalk up their short-coming to a "bad day." Their feelings of positive self-efficacy can counteract the experience of a temporary failure, and short-term setbacks may make them even more determined to succeed the next time. A good approach for people with low self-efficacy is to (1) avoid situations that may cause them stress until they have begun a program of improvement in those particular areas; (2) recognize that nearly all of their skills, abilities, and knowledge can be improved with instruction and practice, especially communication skills; and (3) recognize that there is always "another day." Few people in this world fail at every attempt. Effort will lead to at least occasional successes, and these experiences must be made a part of one's self-efficacy level.

Self-efficacy is that part of the self that organizes how the self-concept and self-esteem affect communication performance. In other words, self-efficacy is the intermediary between how you think of yourself and how well you communicate with other people. The following two sections describe how the self is communicated to others. Self-presentation is an indirect ap-proach to communicating self; a more direct strategy is self-disclosure.

◆ Self-Presentation

As you have already learned, communication serves many functions. One of these functions is to let others know about your self, and a primary way of doing this is through self-presentation. **Self-presentation** is an inten-tional communication tactic designed to show elements of self for strategic purposes. For example, if you need to create an impression in others that you are competent in group communication, you may tell stories of previous in-stances of successful group work. However, not all attempts at communi-cation involve self-presentation. According to communication researchers Canary and Cody, you decide to self-present anytime your social identity is subject to evaluation by others.[17] Sometimes you know in advance that others will be evaluating elements of self (e.g., if you are conducting a group meeting). In other instances, you do not anticipate evaluation of self but may find that it happens unexpectedly (e.g., you go to a party only to find your boss there).

Just as self-presentation is affected by self-esteem, self-presentation, in turn, influences self-esteem. Self-presentation generates feedback: When per-forming, you have the opportunity to observe your own success as evaluated by you and by others. Research generally concludes that those with high self-esteem usually find their own self-presentations positive, while those with

SELF-PRESENTATION

A communication tactic intended to show elements of self for strategic purposes.

negative self-esteem are more critical of their own behavior.[18] Schlenker and his colleagues suggest that those with low self-esteem tend to take the safe path to performance, one of self-protection rather than one of self-presentation, in order to minimize losses.[19] Individuals with high self-esteem are more likely to go for the gold. On the other hand, if you have low self-esteem in a particular area, say business relationships, and you then perform quite nicely (and unexpectedly so) in your business communication, you may elevate your self-concept to a higher level. Competent self-presentation has the most impact on areas of your communication performance about which you don't have a firm self-concept. Improving self-presentation depends on your willingness to perform competently in spite of past beliefs. If you have negative self-certainty, in other words, if you are sure of a low degree of competency in a certain area, it can block your ability to believe that your communication could be enhanced.[20] You are best able to improve and enjoy your self-presentation skills when you have a high degree of self-certainty about areas in which you have performed well and an openness to change your self-concept in areas in which you have performed poorly.

High Self-Monitoring

One way of viewing self-presentation is through the self-monitoring activities of individuals. Snyder developed and popularized the concept of **self-monitoring** to account for the tendency of some people to watch their environment and others in it for cues as to how to act in particular situations. According to Snyder:

SELF-MONITORING
The tendency to watch one's environment and others in it for cues as to how to act in particular situations.

> The prototypic *high-self-monitoring individual* is one who, out of a concern for the situational and interpersonal appropriateness of his or her social behavior, is particularly sensitive to the expression and self-presentation of relevant others in social situations and uses these cues as guidelines for monitoring (that is, regulating and controlling) his or her own verbal and nonverbal self-presentation. By contrast the *low-self-monitoring individual* is not so vigilant to social information about situationally appropriate self-presentation. Neither does he or she have such well-developed repertoires of self-presentational skills.[21]

High-self-monitoring individuals try to portray themselves as "the right person at the right place at the right time." These people watch others for hints of how to be successful in social situations and attempt to emulate those verbal and nonverbal cues that seem most appropriate. You may know someone who is a high-self-monitoring communicator. During class, this person always sits in a certain strategic position, gets involved in a discussion when others do so, gestures in a similar manner to others, and, when it is time to let others talk, is very strategic with silence. Snyder terms such people "sufficiently skilled actors" who are able to implement situationally appropriate communication behaviors.[22] They consider themselves alert and flexible, ready to tackle a number of communication situations with ease.

Are you one of these sufficiently skilled communicators? Is it important that you "fit in" in each communication situation?

Low Self-Monitoring

Low-self-monitoring individuals do not see themselves and communication situations in the same way as high self-monitors do. Low self-monitors are not nearly so sensitive to situational cues that prescribe communication behavior. Rather, they communicate according to their deep-seated values or beliefs. They do not feel the need to adapt to situations or people;

Self-Monitoring Test

To test your own perceived level of self-monitoring, complete the following items, being careful to answer them as accurately and truthfully as possible. Use a 5-point scale for your answers: 5 = strongly agree; 4 = agree; 3 = neutral; 2 = disagree; and 1 = strongly disagree.

_____ 1. I am concerned about acting appropriately in social situations.

_____ 2. I find it hard to imitate the behavior of others.

_____ 3. I have good self-control of my behavior. I can play many roles.

_____ 4. I am not very good at learning what is socially appropriate in new situations.

_____ 5. I often appear to lack deep emotions.

_____ 6. In a group of people, I am rarely the center of attention.

_____ 7. I may deceive people by being friendly when I really dislike them.

_____ 8. Even if I am not enjoying myself, I often pretend to be having a good time.

_____ 9. I have good self-control of my emotional expression. I can use it to create the impression I want.

_____ 10. I can argue only for ideas that I already believe in.

_____ 11. I openly express my true feelings, attitudes, and beliefs.

_____ 12. I'm not always the person I appear to be.

Add up your scores on items 1, 3, 5, 7, 8, 9, and 12. Now reverse the scoring on items 2, 4, 6, 10, and 11 (5 = 1, 4 = 2, 2 = 4, 1 = 5). Finally, add these scores to the sum you calculated from the previous items. If you scored 43–60, you are a high self-monitor; if you scored 30–42, you are an average self-monitor; and if your score was 12–29, you are a low self-monitor.

Source: Adapted from M. Snyder (1974), Self-monitoring and expressive behavior, *Journal of Personality and Social Psychology, 30*, 526–537.

Being in a new environment or situation may promote high self-monitoring.

rather, they feel that people and situations must take them the way they are, at face value. Low self-monitors have a strong sense of self and prefer to exhibit this self when they find it appropriate. This accounts for their unwillingness to modify their behavior for a situation. If low self-monitors anticipate a communication situation that is different from their own self-presentation style, they will either avoid the situation or accept the fact that they may not be able to please all the parties involved. Tamara is a low-self-monitoring person and has a pleasant, friendly demeanor. At the same time, she is very consistent in her handling of small talk and conversation. Regardless of whether Tamara is talking with her boss, her mother, her best friend, or a group of strangers, she always limits her conversational time to just a few moments. While at the office, Tamara values her time and prefers to keep conversations short.

It would be a mistake to conclude that low self-monitors have stronger self-concepts than high self-monitors. High self-monitors may view themselves as flexible, adaptable, strategic, and situationally adept at communication. Low self-monitors may have lower self-esteem regarding some communication situations, such as public speaking. The fact of the matter is that both high and low self-monitors may have strong self-concepts because both demonstrate strength in how they deal with communication.

◆ Self-Disclosure

SELF-DISCLOSURE

Revealing information about the self to other people.

A second way in which you reveal your self-concept and self-esteem to others is through the process of self-disclosure. Simply put, **self-disclosure** is the act of revealing information about the self to other people. Some writers argue that self-disclosure must be intentional. However, sometimes you reveal information about the self unintentionally. In numerous instances in your life, you may say something to others, and then realize that you have unwittingly provided information that exposes part of your inner being. Several factors influence your patterns of self-disclosure. How much you trust someone is one factor. Others include your opinion of and relationship with your audience, the setting, cultural and co-cultural influences, the consequences resulting from what you disclose, the topic, and, of course, how and what you think of yourself. We discuss these issues in later sections of this chapter; for now it is important simply to understand that self-disclosure is a complex form of human communication.

Your ability to self-disclose competently is determined largely by what Wheeless and Grotz term the six *dimensions* of self-disclosure: amount, accuracy, honesty, depth, valence, and intentional/unintentional.[23] With regard to the first of these dimensions—*amount* of self-disclosure—how much you say to another person about yourself can greatly influence future interactions. If you self-disclose too much or too little, you may be seen as too open or too closed, depending on your audience. Some people have difficulty with those who want to tell others a lot about themselves. On the other hand, some people feel cheated when their relational partners will not self-disclose enough.

A second dimension involves the *accuracy* of self-disclosure, or the ability to represent precisely how you feel. Sometimes it may be difficult to explain exactly how you feel about yourself, and if you disclose information, you are risking inaccurate self-disclosure. The same holds true if you have a poorly developed self-concept. How can you disclose something about yourself if it is unknown even to you? Accurate self-disclosure involves knowing yourself, finding the words to express what you know, and relating the information to another person.

Self-Disclosure

Look over the questions below. Select those questions you would be willing to discuss with someone you did not know well. Which questions would you discuss with a close friend or family member?

1. How do you feel about where you live?
2. How do you prefer to spend your summers?
3. Are you sexually active?
4. How much money do you have to spend each month?
5. What do you honestly think of your spouse/boyfriend/girlfriend?
6. How do you spend your weekends?
7. What things really annoy you?
8. If you were going to brag about your best quality, what would it be?
9. Do your parents really love you? How can you tell?
10. How would you describe your personality?
11. Do you consider yourself an attractive person? If so, why? If not, why not?

Third, the *honesty* of self-disclosure can be a very important issue. It is sometimes tempting to portray yourself in a better light than you actually perceive yourself. You may know that you cannot sketch a designer outfit the way a professional designer can; or effectively juggle a career, parenthood, and a loving partnership; or run a mile as quickly as a fine athlete. However, when talking with other people who are positively disclosing their talents, you may stretch information about yourself to create a better impression.

Information about the self can be shallow or trivial, such as telling someone the name of your hairstylist, or it may contain *depth*, providing a person with private information that is buried well below the surface. Here is an example: "I know how you feel. I had a miscarriage before our son was born. Please call me when you are discharged from the hospital so we can talk." In the case of public speaking, a speaker is expected to be accurate and honest, but disclosing in-depth information about the self is considered inappropriate in most public contexts.

VALENCE
Whether the information you disclose about yourself is positive or negative.

Valence refers to whether the information that you disclose about yourself is positive or negative. You probably know people who typically reveal negative information about themselves ("I have a cyst on my bladder that will have to be removed"). Others may disclose primarily positive information ("I won $200 in the lottery last year"). Most of us disclose both positive and negative information, depending on who we are talking to. Positive information is usually reserved for people we like and for people we are trying to impress. Negative information about the self is usually reserved for people we trust. This is because negative information in the wrong hands could hurt one's pride or reputation.

Finally, self-disclosure can be viewed according to whether or not it was *intentional*. You may know people who tend to get caught up in the emotions of a communication exchange and then will say things they really do not intend ("Oh, I love you too"). Conversely, other people may feel strong emotions and want others to know their feelings—that is, they may intend to self-disclose—but may then end up not saying anything ("I just couldn't get it out").

Trust

TRUST
The belief that you can accurately predict the actions of another person.

Trust is the belief that you can accurately predict the actions of another person. It is one of the most important factors affecting the decision to self-disclose. Wheeless has studied the relationship between self-disclosure and trust and generally concludes that trust is a necessary but not sufficient condition for self-disclosing to another person.[24] Based on the other dimensions of self-disclosure we have discussed, you know that trust is not the only factor influencing your self-revelations. It is important to understand, however, that you usually have some measure of trust in a person before self-disclosure occurs.

Targeting Self-Disclosure

In the previous section we discussed some of the factors involved in self-disclosing to others. This section explores further those people who are likely

Where Does Trust Fit In?

Have people ever told you very private things about themselves that you wanted to tell others? It is tempting to repeat confidential self-disclosures. Have you ever betrayed a self-discloser's trust by repeating private and confidential information? Did the person find out? Has someone ever betrayed a confidence when you self-disclosed? How did it make you feel about that person? About your relationship? Keeping confidences is an ethical prerogative that requires a great deal of strength and trust. How easily do you trust others? How well do you think others can trust you? How highly do you value trust in your life?

targets for disclosures. There is a tendency to self-disclose to people who disclose first. In what is often referred to as reciprocity, or the *dyadic effect*,[25] people tend to exchange self-disclosure once someone gets the ball rolling. One reason for reciprocity could be an obligation factor; you feel indebted to those who reveal themselves to you. Another reason may be that you see someone's self-disclosing as an opportunity to develop a relationship with the discloser. You may also reciprocate in order to ensure that the other person does not get the upper hand or feel superior to you by revealing his or her personal thoughts ("I want this person to know I think well of myself too!").

You may also target self-disclosure to people you like.[26] Self-disclosure is an opportunity to create a certain impression in others. One way of accomplishing this is by providing people with information that is useful in building a favorable impression of you. Early in relationships, people often disclose positive information, showing themselves in a favorable light. Later on, they can increase the other persons' liking by showing that they trust them with negative information. You may self-disclose more often to people who appear to be similar to you. Research demonstrates that you are more likely to self-disclose to people in your own age group, to people who have the same status and power as you, and to those who appear to share similar personality traits.[27]

The length of relationships also influences to whom you target your self-disclosures. Interestingly, there appears to be a U-shaped curve reflecting the association between length or closeness of a relationship and self-disclosure[28] (see Figure 3.3). It is quite easy to understand that you would self-disclose to your best friends and confidants, but why might you also self-disclose to total strangers? The reason is that strangers pose no risk to you if you decide to confide in them. This is sometimes referred to as the "bus rider" syndrome: You know that strangers cannot use anything you say against you because it is unlikely you'll ever see them again. In this sense, you can actually trust them with the information. Have you ever gotten on a bus, train, or plane and found yourself listening to the life story of someone who has temporarily trusted you with this information?

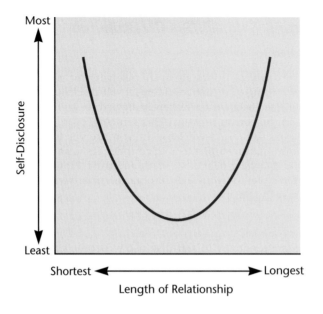

FIGURE 3.3
The U-shaped curve indicates that people are likely to self-disclose most to strangers and to close friends and least to people whose relationship with them is between these two extremes.

Reasons for Self-Disclosure

In the discussion so far, we have hinted at the reasons why you self-disclose to other people. Now let's look more closely at your possible motives or reasons; you may be surprised at some of them.

Relationship Development. Perhaps the most frequent reason for self-disclosing is to develop relationships. Have you ever tried to get to know someone better, or even to establish a more permanent relationship, without exchanging self-disclosures? It must have been a pretty difficult process! The act of revealing yourself to another person creates a special atmosphere in the relationship, which is conducive to liking and sometimes intimacy. With additional self-disclosure comes trust in the person. You are saying to this individual, "You are special" because something as risky as self-revelation is reserved for exceptional relationships. Wheeless has conducted research in this area and has determined that as two people increase their self-disclosures and as trust builds, the relationship enjoys a bonding he terms *interpersonal solidarity.*[29] Relationships built on solidarity are warmer, more sensitive, and more fulfilling than more loosely connected relationships.

Reassurance. Have you ever talked with friends who, during a conversation, "beat themselves up" to the point that you were arguing against the negative things they were saying about themselves? Self-disclosure is often used as a tactic to obtain *reassurance* or comfort from a trusted friend.[30] People may have relatively healthy self-concepts and positive self-esteem, but they may still maintain some doubts about particular areas of themselves. One way to acquire information about these doubts, in hopes of disconfirming your suspicions, is to self-disclose negative information. Some people, for example, are always worried about their personal appearance and will self-degrade to elicit reactions from their significant others:

MATT　　My hair looks terrible.

DEBBIE　　What's the matter with it?

MATT　　It's thinning, and what's left is turning gray!

DEBBIE　　I think the silver specks around your temples make you look more distinguished.

MATT　　Do you really think so?

As this conversation demonstrates, negative self-disclosure may result in reassurance or comfort.

Impression Formation. Self-disclosure is also used to make *positive impressions* on other people. When you are unfamiliar with people who appeal to you, you want to give them as good an impression of yourself as possible. Sometimes you do not or cannot wait for them to realize your talents, skills, abilities, intelligence, and other good qualities through your acts or behavior. You may have to tell them. As observed earlier, self-presentation is a communication strategy used for promoting the self to others. Frequently, you will find it necessary to promote yourself. For example, job interviews require that you demonstrate how your knowledge and skills are superior to those of other job candidates. Oral presentations, sales and marketing strategies, and public relations tactics all require that you demonstrate personal competence.

Where do you draw the line between promoting your best features and *boasting* about your positive values? Bragging and boasting serve their purposes as long as the target accepts and accommodates the self-promoter's goals, but many people are turned off by a braggart style of communication. We know from research, however, that positive self-disclosure is more favorably evaluated than negative self-revelations.[31]

Miller and her colleagues have studied the differences between positive disclosures and boasting.[32] Boasting is used to emphasize your power, status, and wealth, and how your personal qualities are better than those of other people. Positive disclosures differ from boasts in that these tactics give more credit to others for accomplishments; they are less exaggerated and more tentative; and they are perceived as more interesting, likable, honest, and attractive forms of communication. How does one decide which self-disclosure tactic to use? Bragging may be useful when a situation calls for competition and when the communicator must appear competent and successful. Positive disclosures are preferable when the communicator wants to appear socially sensitive and is more concerned about an overall positive evaluation than about competence in a particular area.

Emotional Expression. The feelings you experience in response to the thoughts and behaviors of self and others are called *emotions*. Everyone experiences emotions, though to varying degrees. How these emotions are disclosed to others also varies greatly, depending on the people, circumstances, and culture involved. You are familiar with people who are highly emotional and do not hesitate to reveal their emotions to you. Other people you know are much more reserved and restrict their emotional disclosures. Why do people differ in these respects, and what motivates them to disclose their emotions to others? Research reveals that emotional self-disclosure is a mechanism for enhancing the psychosocial development of early adolescents.[33] Exploring emotions with friends and family at an early age allows you to understand yourself and to recognize how these emotional expressions affect others' reactions to you. Your self-identity can be formed in a particular manner based on your emotional expressions. For example, gender roles are determined to some extent by the reactions you get as you express your emotions to others. In most cultures, males are not expected to disclose their emotions with the same frequency and intensity or in the same manner as females. In fact, there are often sanctions against males' disclosing their emotions:

JIM   Mom, I'm afraid of my teacher!

MOTHER   Jim, be a man! I don't want to hear you talk about your fears.

Emotional self-disclosure can be viewed according to two important dimensions: valence and intensity.[34] Emotional *valence* refers to whether emotional disclosure is positive or negative. Cultural norms seem to dictate that positive emotional self-disclosure is more socially appropriate than negative self-disclosure. In North America, most people frown on negative emotional disclosure.[35] Negative emotions are best reserved for those people you know well and trust. *Intensity* of emotional disclosure refers to the depth and strength of the emotion being expressed. Emotional intensity can be demonstrated both verbally and nonverbally. Adjectives and adverbs help you to increase the intensity of emotional disclosure: "I really, really hate being wrong." "I am extremely happy with the direction of my new career." In addition, how much you elaborate on the emotional expression and how sincere you are can reflect intensity. Nonverbally, you can signal emotional intensity by pounding your fist on a podium, gesturing flamboyantly, or using highly demonstrative facial expressions. Howell and Conway conducted a study of emotional valence and intensity and found that negative disclosures, whether intense or not, were considered more intimate than positive disclosures.[36] Apparently, when you hear negative emotions expressed, you sense that people are allowing you to see a deeper part of themselves than when positive emotions are expressed. Most people also rate highly intense positive emotional expression as intimate. Expressing jubilation or triumph in demonstrable ways reveals a deeper, more intimate side that is usually reserved for certain people. Generally, with regard to emotional self-disclosure, you must be willing to disclose how you feel to others, but at the same time you should carefully consider the target of your emotional expression.

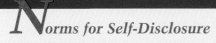orms for Self-Disclosure

Why do men and women self-disclose differently? Are these differences based on genetics or hormones? Probably not. More likely, self-disclosure differences are based on the cultural norms that guide the behavior of men and women. Think of the specific rules or suggestions that regulate how men and women should self-disclose in your culture. Do the rules change regarding self-disclosure to members of the opposite sex? To close family members versus strangers? To persons older or younger than you? To social versus business communication partners? Be ready to discuss these issues in class.

Cultural and Gender Differences

Before leaving the topic of self-disclosure, we will briefly touch on cultural and gender differences in self-disclosure patterns. We have already noted that not all cultural groups self-disclose in the same manner. People in the United States, for example, tend to express their thoughts and feelings more openly than people in other cultures. In Japan, for instance, self-disclosure is not seen as a primary means of developing relationships. In addition, the Japanese maintain relative privacy in their personal affairs. People living in Eastern European countries are also less likely to self-disclose than their Western European counterparts or people living in the United States. The Eastern European cultures tend to conceal their thoughts, feelings, and emotions in order to maintain harmonious relationships with those around them. Even within the United States, some co-cultures may be less willing to self-disclose than others.

Although much of the research on gender differences and self-disclosure suggests that women are more likely to self-disclose than men,[37] this assumption is an overgeneralization of actual communication patterns. Some studies have revealed no gender differences for self-disclosure,[38] while others have found that the two sexes have different reasons for disclosing. For example, women disclose more on the basis of liking a person, whereas men disclose on the basis of trusting.[39] Men are more likely to avoid self-disclosure in order to control the relationship, whereas women avoid self-disclosure in order to prevent hurt feelings.[40] The topics that are self-disclosed also vary between men and women. Women are more likely to discuss their feelings about women friends and spouses or lovers than men are.[41] It is important to note that the majority of these gender studies focus on white, middle-class women and men. These generalizations, therefore, are not necessarily applicable across cultures.

◆ Feedback

Information you receive about self is termed **feedback.** It comes in many forms. Some types of feedback are positive, some are ambiguous, and still

FEEDBACK
Information learned about the self that is used by the self to learn and mature.

others are negative. From Figure 3.1 (page 67) you can observe how feedback affects your competence assessment.

How you incorporate feedback into the self depends on several factors. One of the most important factors is your *sensitivity level* to feedback. Research demonstrates that some individuals are highly sensitive to feedback, whereas others are largely unaffected by such information.[42] Presumably, people who are more sensitive to feedback are susceptible and receptive to information about their abilities, knowledge, talents, and the rest. Low-sensitive people would be less responsive to such information. For example, when Joan ignores suggestions that she bathe more frequently, she is being insensitive to feedback about her personal hygiene.

Feedback is a more complicated picture than what was just painted. First, the type and source of feedback can make a big difference in how high and low sensitives view information. Edwards believes that low sensitives may be susceptible to feedback from particular sources they find worthy, such as teachers, other authority figures, parents, and best friends.[43] They have a low sensitivity to feedback because they rely on just a few sources of feedback. High sensitives, on the other hand, probably rely on many different sources. They look for feedback from parents, friends, neighbors, salesclerks, and even college professors. Furthermore, it is assumed that high sensitives have more fully developed self-schemas than low sensitives.[44] People who receive and interpret more feedback will assimilate more information about the self. The number of self-schemas will increase, resulting in a self-concept that is more vast (and probably more accurate) than that of low sensitives. Therefore, sensitivity to feedback has a positive effect on self-concept because people gain knowledge about self through this process.

What about feedback and self-esteem? When dealing with the effects of feedback on self-esteem, a larger issue than feedback sensitivity exists. The important question is: How do high- and low-self-esteem people react to feedback, regardless of their sensitivity level? There are two possible explanations. The first is termed *self-enhancing theory* and refers to the notion

*A*re You a High Sensitive or a Low Sensitive?

Stop for a moment and reflect on your sensitivity to feedback. Would you characterize yourself as a high sensitive or a low sensitive? Answer the following questions to get a better idea of your sensitivity to feedback.

1. Do you ignore what other people say when they comment on your abilities, skills, physical appearance, success level, or intelligence?
2. Do you seek out feedback from people concerning these areas of self?
3. Are you interested in learning what other people have to say about you?
4. Do you often wonder whether people really mean what they say about you?

that people with low self-esteem have a need to improve their view of self and seek information or feedback that is positive and favorable.[45] Accordingly, low-self-esteem people are more likely to "enhance" their self-esteem by attributing positive information to self ("We won the game; I guess I *am* a great softball player") and attributing negative information to other sources ("We lost; I wish the team hadn't let me down"). As a communicator, you may use self-enhancing theory to search for information that will build your self-esteem in the social skills area. How often do you seek out friends who bring out your best in communicating?

The second explanation is termed *self-consistency theory*.[46] According to this notion, people will be sensitive to information that is consistent with their existing self-esteem and resistant to information that contradicts it. From this perspective, persons with high self-esteem will react favorably to information that supports their positive view of self and ignore or disbelieve negative information. On the other hand, persons with low self-esteem will maintain consistency by accepting information that confirms their poor view of self—that is, negative information—and will react unfavorably to positive information ("I don't believe him when he says I am attractive; he just wants something from me").

Regardless of which theory is correct, Shrauger suggests six different ways of looking at the reactions or responses that people can have to feedback.[47] As you read the following list, ask yourself what reaction you usually have when hearing positive and negative feedback about yourself.

- Your initial reaction when hearing the information. Are you always optimistic? *"I can count on my leadership skills."* Pessimistic? *"I knew it wouldn't work to my advantage."*
- Your assessment of the dependability and legitimacy of the person providing the feedback. *"Does this person's opinion count?"* *"I can count on this person."*
- Whether you accept responsibility for the action or performance or attribute it to something or to others. *"I know I was wrong."* *"My boss messed up another one of my projects."*
- Whether you feel satisfied with the feedback. *"Finally my hard work paid off."* *"If only I had finished two weeks earlier."*
- Whether you change your behavior after hearing the feedback. *"This didn't work; let's try another plan."* *"I don't believe it; there must be some mistake."*
- Whether you change your self-evaluation and expectations for yourself as a result of the feedback. *"Well, this minor setback is simply an annoyance."* *"Oh, well, I'm a klutz."* *"Thank goodness I found this out in time; now I can really develop a plan."*

The next time you receive feedback, try to use this list to determine whether you are making the best use of the information for the self. The bottom line is making feedback work for you and your self.

◆ Competence Assessment

As a communicator, you are constantly assessing your competence level for signs of strengths and weaknesses. Competence assessment is especially conducted just after a communication performance, and particularly when the self has received feedback from other people (see Figure 3.4). After self-presentation or self-disclosure, you are likely to assess your level of communication competency. Your competence level may range from very positive to very negative, depending on your evaluation. You can assess or evaluate your competence at three general levels: self-actualization, self-adequacy, and self-denigration.

Self-Actualization

SELF-ACTUALIZATION
The most positive evaluation one can make about one's competence level.

The most positive evaluation you can make about your competence level is referred to as **self-actualization**—the feelings and thoughts you get when you know that you have communicated perfectly, or almost perfectly. Assessments of communication competence at this level can provide you with a sense of fulfillment, allowing you to know that you have "come into your own." Obviously, self-actualization is a desirable condition, and communicators should consider it the ultimate achievement level. It is possible, however, to feel a sense of self-actualization even when you recognize that you haven't communicated perfectly. You may understand that this is the best job you could possibly do, and that may be enough for you to enjoy a feeling of fulfillment.

Self-actualization can boost your self-esteem because of the gratifying communication performance that you assessed. Let's look at the following example. Erika went to see her friend José, to comfort him on the death of his father. Although she was nervous at first about saying the right thing, afterward, while driving home from José's house, she felt very good about the experience. In fact, Erika was quite content that she had been very supportive and comforting to José. This positive assessment of her performance added information to that part of her self-concept that holds information about comforting communication. In turn, this information led to a higher level of self-esteem. When Erika needs to be comforting in the future, her self-efficacy will be stronger.

There is a flip side to self-actualization that you should be cautious about. Carried too far, it can cause you to be smug about your communication

FIGURE 3.4
In the model of the self and communication competence, assessment usually occurs immediately after feedback is received. The assessment ranges from positive to negative.

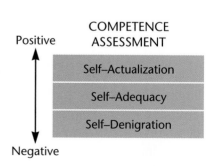

competence and become complacent about further improvement. John gave a presentation in his political science class and was very pleased with the results. His high-self-actualization led to a strong feeling of self-efficacy, a sense that "he could do no wrong." When faced with another presentation for his history class, he thought that he didn't need to prepare because he knew he was a great speaker. Unfortunately, he learned from the instructor that his poor preparation had resulted in a lackluster performance, and he was embarrassed with the results. John learned a valuable lesson. Self-actualization is a great reaction to competent communication as long as it is used to improve self-esteem and enhance self-efficacy.

Self-Adequacy

At times you may think that your communication performance was good enough to get you through a particular situation. You may think that you got your point across and made a pretty good impression on your communication partners. Although your assessments are still positive, they are less so than when you are self-actualized. When you assess your communication competence as sufficient or acceptable, you are feeling a sense of **self-adequacy**. Feelings of self-adequacy can lead you in two directions—either to contentment or to a desire for self-improvement.

First, you may think that self-adequacy may not be all that bad. In fact, if you have been working very hard to improve your public speaking abilities and you realize that you performed competently, you may feel very proud and satisfied with your newfound feeling of self-adequacy. In this case, self-adequacy is a wonderful experience. However, you probably do not want to stop at this level because most communication skills require continuous fine-tuning, and you may be surprised to learn that with a little more effort, practice, and patience, you can achieve at even higher levels of competence.

Second, you may feel that your ability to present the self needs to be extremely effective and that you need to improve your communication skills further. In this case, self-adequacy leads you to want to reach a higher level (self-actualization).

When you recognize from your competence assessment that you could communicate even better the next time around, self-improvement is a typical reaction. **Self-improvement** is a signal you send to the self indicating a desire to be even more competent in your communication, regardless of current levels. Self-improvement is a constructive reaction to competence assessment, and we encourage you to consider it as the ideal response.

In order to be constructive, self-improvement must focus on a realistic method of progress toward greater competence. First, you need to realize that although self-improvement is not an easy process, it is very gratifying. Keep the future payoff in mind as you tackle the job of enhancing your competence. Second, you need to plot or chart your current competence level relative to where you would like to be. For example, positioning your competence level on a 1 to 10 scale could be helpful in plotting a self-improvement

SELF-ADEQUACY
Assessing one's communication competence as sufficient or acceptable.

SELF-IMPROVEMENT
A signal one sends to the self indicating a desire to be a more competent communicator, regardless of current levels.

FIGURE 3.5

Self-evaluation of your communication competence must be honest and accurate if it is to help you improve. You may not start out exactly in the middle of the scale, but you should progress as you study.

path (see Figure 3.5). This method allows you to see where you are now (perhaps around 5, an average communicator), where you would like to be (8 or 9, an ideal performance), and where you will never be (1, a very poor performance). You can now focus on moving your competence level toward the ideal performance end of the scale. You can use any method for this process, but make sure that you are accurate and honest.

The next step toward self-improvement is to identify your strengths and weaknesses. Although you may enjoy several communication strengths (e.g., a strong speaking voice, effective gestures), you have to ensure that these are maintained. Don't let your strengths fade while you are working on your shortcomings. When examining your weaknesses, identify very *specific* and tangible aspects of your communication performance that can be refined. Avoid the trap of assuming that a general shortcoming can be improved. It is much easier to work on little things than it is to correct major problems.

Throughout this process you are sending feedback to the self that indicates your willingness to become more competent. In turn, this will affect your self-esteem and self-efficacy, giving you a better chance for real improvement in your communication.

Self-Denigration

SELF-DENIGRATION
The most negative assessment one can make about one's communication performance.

The most negative assessment you can make about a communication performance is **self-denigration.** The word *denigration* refers to criticizing or attacking someone or something. When you really get down on yourself for a poor communication performance, you are pursuing a course of self-denigration. Why do people do this? Self-denigration is most likely to occur when communicators place undue importance on the weaknesses or shortcomings of a performance. Sometimes self-denigration is the final step in a *self-fulfilling prophecy* ("I knew I would mess up that speech; I was just awful"). In other cases, communicators will misread the feedback in a communication situation and perceive an average or acceptable performance as poor. Because communication is easily evaluated, the tendency is to look for things that can be perceived negatively. In almost every instance, however, self-denigration is unnecessary and unwarranted, and it prevents real improvement in communication competence. One exception should be noted. Some cultures encourage their members to use self-denigration as a norm. Self-put-downs are seen as a means of respecting others and indicating that other people, God, and the environment are more important than the self. Self-denigration, therefore, can be part of a cultural fabric rather than an incompetent communication skill.

In U.S. culture, how does self-denigration act as a major roadblock to communication competency? When you attack yourself for a poor communication performance, you divert your attention away from your needs as a communicator and toward self-defeating feelings of helplessness. Blaming yourself for a poor performance can lead to self-pity, which will often feed on itself. Instead of focusing on how certain aspects of a communication performance can be improved, self-denigrating communicators choose to concentrate on the past by emphasizing the poorly executed features of a performance.

You can move past self-denigration as a competence assessment by becoming more objective about the self and the communication situation. The following steps can be very helpful in *objectifying your assessment* of your communication competence.

Remember that things are seldom as bad as you think they are. Self-denigration is a self-defeating condition that emphasizes the negative. Rarely is the situation as negative as it seems. Thoughts like "People think I'm no good because I made a lot of mistakes in my speech" are unrealistic and irrational. Instead, most people are probably thinking, "That speech was pretty good, except it could have been better organized." There is a big difference between these two perceptions.

Give yourself the benefit of the doubt. You might be surprised at how many people are willing to give others the benefit of doubt. Think about how often you are willing to cut someone some slack because you want to help them. Most people are like you. If you are in a situation where you feel a great deal of pressure to communicate well (e.g., making acquaintances, leading a group, or delivering a speech), you can expect a lot of support from people who sympathize.

Depersonalize the assessment. Self-denigration can be weakened when you move your perspective of self from the first to the third person. Taking a third-person perspective involves making your assessment as if someone else were conducting the evaluation. Third-person observers usually compare the skills of one person to those of another, and they do so objectively. Identify someone in your communication class as a source of comparison for the next assignment.

Give yourself feedback. Feedback from others is also helpful for making these comparisons. Although it is a bit more complicated, you can also become a third person by listening to yourself on audiotape or viewing your performance on videotape. You will be amazed at how much objective information this technique yields.

Defeating Self-Denigration

Why do some communicators focus on the less successful aspects of a performance instead of considering all the features involved? What are some ways to work toward establishing a more positive pattern—toward "defeating" self-denigration?

As we come to the end of this section, let's look at an example of self-denigrating behavior and how it was overcome. Claire was recently promoted to manager of the student health center on a large university campus. In spite of her outstanding qualifications, she harbored deep negative feelings about leading staff meetings. She was a great one-on-one communicator but had no confidence in herself when she needed to face a group of her peers and subordinates. Each meeting seemed to her to be a disaster because people would ask tough questions that she was unable to answer. After each meeting (performance), she would spend the rest of the day reproaching herself for her poor communication. Claire's self-denigrating tendencies led to anxiety, and she began to question her ability to lead the student health center.

Claire, then, took a course in communication confidence at her university and learned to give herself more credit for her group leadership skills. She realized that most people were supportive of her efforts and that her performances were much better than she thought. She even videotaped a meeting and actually saw that she was motivating and organizing people to do their tasks better at the health center. Her major improvement was to become more objective in her self-competence assessment. In her words, "As I learned to see myself as others saw me, I was able to improve my skills at a very rapid rate."

The Case of Yoko Sakai

At the beginning of this chapter we described Yoko Sakai, a Japanese student in the third year of an undergraduate degree program in electrical engineering. Ms. Sakai is succeeding in the program, although she appears to enjoy her arts and humanities electives more than her science and mathematics requirements. She also enjoys playing the violin in the university orchestra. Think about the relevance of the concepts in this chapter to Ms. Sakai and answer the following questions.

- What are likely to be the self-concept, self-esteem, and self-efficacy beliefs of Ms. Sakai? Why do you think so?

- What is the relevance of self-presentation and self-disclosure for Ms. Sakai?

- How do you think Ms. Sakai would assess her communication competence? How do you think she would respond to that assessment?

- What advice would you give to Ms. Sakai about using feedback to learn and mature?

REVIEW

- How you view yourself affects the way you communicate with others. Similarly, communicating with others can shape how you perceive yourself.

- Self-concept is the awareness and understanding of who you are as interpreted and influenced by your thoughts, actions, abilities, values, goals, and ideals, and by other people. Self-concept affects a number of factors influencing communication, such as memory and recall, perception, and self-evaluation.

- Self-schema theory is a way of understanding the self; it involves organizing your thoughts about self into frameworks (self-schemas) that facilitate social interaction.

- Self-esteem is an evaluation of the self-concept or how you feel about self. Self-esteem influences communication in many ways. The stronger your self-esteem, the more likely you will view communication situations as positive.

- Self-certainty refers to how strong your sense of self-identity is for a particular area. The more certain you are about areas of your self, the more likely you are to feel positive self-esteem.

- Self-efficacy is the process of predicting, on the basis of your self-concept, how successful you can be in communication situations. More positive predictions of self-efficacy should lead to more succesful communication performances.

- Self-presentation is a method of conveying your self to others. You reveal your positive traits through this process.

- Self-monitoring involves how people communicate in ways that are socially appropriate.

- Self-disclosure reveals information about the self to others; it depends on several factors, including trust, liking, length of the relationship, and gender.

- The feedback you receive about self allows you to constantly review your feelings for self, as long as you are sensitive to such information.

- After a communication performance, you will make a competence assessment. Three general levels of assessment are possible, ranging from positive to negative: self-actualization, self-adequacy, and self-denigration.

CHAPTER FOUR

Language and Communication

OBJECTIVES

After reading this chapter, you should be able to:

1. Explain how language is acquired and developed.

2. Distinguish acquiring language from acquiring communication.

3. Apply the five functional communication competencies to communication behavior.

4. Use the triangle of meaning and the abstraction ladder to explain how language interacts with thought.

5. Recognize how culture and context affect language.

6. Identify language variations related to gender and sex roles.

7. Describe how language communicates information about relationships, control, and affiliation.

AMY AND DONALD'S STORY, adapted from Deborah Tannen's book, *Talking from 9 to 5* (Morrow, 1994), is as follows:

Amy was a manager with a problem: She had just read Donald's report which was woefully inadequate. She faced the unsavory task of telling him to redo it. She made sure to soften the blow by telling him everything about his report that was good before explaining what needed to be done to make it acceptable. Thanks to her sensitivity in starting with praise, Donald seemed to understand what was needed. But when the revised report appeared on her desk, Amy was shocked. Donald had made only superficial changes. The next meeting with him did not go well. He was incensed that she was now telling him his report was not acceptable and accused her of having misled him.

In this chapter we explore the acquisition of language, its use in interacting with others, and the influence of culture on our thoughts and language. As you read, consider why it was possible for Donald to misinterpret Amy's initial praise. We will return to this scenario at the end of the chapter.

Language is a symbol system used to think about and communicate experiences and feelings. It is the meaning people attach to language that gives language its power. The communication adage is, "Meanings are in people, not in the words themselves."

Of course, communication is never pure language. A number of nonverbal behaviors accompany language—pauses, stutters, the tone and volume of the voice, the speed at which someone speaks, the accents one uses, the gestures made while speaking, and many other body movements. Those forms of nonverbal communication are studied in depth in Chapter 5. But as you read Chapter 4, it is important to understand that language does not occur in isolation—that nonverbal behaviors, especially those associated with the voice, always accompany speech. Our goal in this chapter is to examine the way we extract meaning from language. Here we set the foundation for understanding the interplay of both verbal and nonverbal communication by focusing on language itself.

◆ Language Acquisition

The first word you spoke as a child was probably greeted with much celebration by parents and family. No doubt, many phone calls were made to announce your accomplishment to anyone who would listen, and that first word may have been recorded in a "baby book." You were simply amazing, and you were encouraged to produce more words.

Many researchers, as well as laypeople, have been acutely interested in the way children acquire language. From the early work of the psychologist Piaget,[1] who studied his own two children in great detail, to the more recent and comprehensive summaries of research by Wood,[2] people have been fascinated with a child's acquisition of language and have debated how it occurs. Research shows that children isolated from human language communities do not develop language on their own.[3] So, how do people acquire language?

Here are some basic questions: Do you have to be able to think about something before you name it? Do you have to engage in nonverbal behaviors (such as pointing) before you produce a word, or does language come before thought or nonverbal behaviors? How do children learn to respond? Perhaps they don't, and the response is just innate, preprogrammed. There are five views of language acquisition that seek to answer these questions: nature, nurture, cognition, interaction, and homology.

Nature

Some people argue that the infant's response is built in, that language is *species-specific*.[4] That is, according to the **nature approach**, children are equipped with specific clues to the structures of language because of their genetic makeup. They point out that all children acquire language at about the same age, just as they acquire certain physical skills.

Scholars who argue that language is innate point out that language acquisition parallels the development of coordination in young children (see Table 4.1). Because most children acquire language similarly within these age categories, the nature theorists argue that language must be built into our genetic code.

Nurture

Other researchers believe that children learn language through *imitation and reinforcement.* The **nurture approach** views environmental factors as the most important determinants of language acquisition.[5] As children are stimulated by their parents, siblings, and other caregivers, they respond by imitating what they have seen and heard. The responses that others make to them reinforce their communication, and thus they continue to learn.

From this perspective, children strive to produce early sounds that are like the adult speech they hear. They listen to older children talking and try to mimic them. From the positive responses they get from family and peers (reinforcement) they receive the motivation to continue their efforts at imitation.

NURTURE APPROACH
An approach to language acquisition which holds that language is acquired because of the language environment surrounding a person.

TABLE 4.1 LANGUAGE DEVELOPMENT

AGE	LANGUAGE BEHAVIOR
4 months	Children coo and chuckle when people play with them.
6–9 months	Children babble ("gagagaga," "mamamama").
12–18 months	Children use a few words and follow simple commands like "no," "stop," or "come here."
18–21 months	Children form 2- or 3-word sentences and understand simple questions.
24–27 months	Children use their 300- to 400-word vocabularies to form short sentences.
30–33 months	Children sound more adultlike as they form 3- and 4-word sentences from their increased vocabularies.
36–39 months	Children talk in well-developed sentences, applying rules of grammar; others can usually understand them.

Source: Adapted from B. S. Wood (1981), *Children and communication: Verbal and nonverbal language development* (2nd ed.) (Englewood Cliffs, NJ: Prentice-Hall), pp. 27–29.

Cognition

Another argument is that thinking must precede language. According to the **cognitive approach**, certain thinking abilities, such as causality and intentionality, are precursors to language development. Thus a child must develop certain thinking patterns before producing language.

Piaget studied children's thinking patterns, inferring from their behavior (including language) what their thinking patterns are. His stages of thinking are important because they link thought and language.

Stage 1, from birth to 2 years of age, is a time of identifying the main features of the child's environment—air, water, and food, for example. Children learn that a toy hidden behind the sofa still exists even though it is not visible. Thinking about objects precedes naming them. Once acquired, the "name" of an object can be applied in multiple situations. A child at Stage 1 will say *water* for the liquid in the cup, on the floor, in the tub, or down the drain.

Stage 2, occurring from about ages 2 through 7, is a time of processing the elementary concepts of time, space, and causality. Children think about time passing before talking about being late or early. They conceptualize distance before talking about inches or miles and grapple with cause and effect before producing language that accepts responsibility for having broken the living-room lamp.

Stage 3, ages 7 to 11, is the stage of understanding complex relationships, such as the conservation of volume and weight. Observations of liquids and solids could produce language about them. Observations about human relationships could also produce explanations of "why" so-and-so likes or hates someone else.

Not until age 11 or beyond, says Piaget, do children develop the ability to make complex inferences, go through logical propositions, and make hypotheses. In Stage 4, the child could make a case for being allowed to stay up longer, or for buying that video game or CD *now*, instead of waiting until later, when it might be sold out or more expensive.

Interaction

Another group supports the **interactionist model** of language acquisition. Interactionists emphasize the social aspects of language acquisition. They believe that the richness and quality of interaction are the primary determinants of the quality and rapidity of communication acquisition. They point out that if you grow up in a communication-rich environment, you acquire language quickly; you develop skills that you can practice. Table 4.2 on page 99 gives a time frame for the development of these communication skills.

The more the various types of communication interactions are repeated, and the greater varieties of language used, the more developed the child becomes. Perhaps you have even known parents who, in addition to vocalizing all the time to create a language-rich environment, write labels for objects in the house to hasten their child's development of language skills.

TABLE 4.2 DEVELOPMENT OF COMMUNICATION SKILLS	
AGE	COMMUNICATION BEHAVIOR
birth–15 months	*Interpersonal Communication*
	Uses primarily one-to-one communication
	Uses primarily nonverbal communication (sounds, facial expression, touch)
	Learns times for interaction/withdrawal
	Engages in game playing and cooperative activities
4 months–3 years	*Communication Effects*
	Participates in interactive routines (turn-taking)
	Alters messages to accomplish goals
	Acquires linguistic communication (from single words to complex sentences)
3–5 years	*Communication Strategies*
	Uses wide range of communication behaviors to adapt to different situations (e.g., uses politeness conventions, asks questions)
	Initiates and sustains conversations
5 years and up	*Communication Monitoring*
	Checks for message accuracy and adequacy
	Comments about conversations ("talk about talk")

Source: Adapted from B. Haslett & A. Alexander (1988), Developing communication skills. In R. P. Hawkins, J. M. Wiemann, & S. Pingree (Eds.), *Advancing communication science: Merging mass and interpersonal processes* (Newbury Park, CA: Sage), p. 229.

There is some value in each of these four approaches. Obviously, those who believe language is innate are at the opposite end of the scale from those who believe language is solely the result of environment. But each of these approaches contains some truth, and some value is to be gained from considering all of them together, as the homology model does.

Homology

Researcher Bates has proposed what is called a **homology model** of language acquisition.[6] The term *homology*, when applied to behaviors, means that behaviors have a shared structural base. According to Bates, "there is a Great Borrowing going on,"[7] in which language, thought, and social interaction enable the production of one another, often simultaneously.

Language is seen to develop on a parallel course with some cognitive capacities, to follow certain others, and to constitute the building blocks of

HOMOLOGY MODEL

A model of language acquisition which holds that thinking, coordination, and language capabilities develop simultaneously.

Reading to a child regularly from the time the child is an infant is one way to provide a language-rich environment.

future thought. Social interaction may be the necessary environment in which language develops; at the same time, social interaction may be seen as the *result* of language acquisition.

Bates points out that certain precursors to the production of language are known to exist and that language development is related to the development of gestures in young children. She maintains that communicative pointing is the best predictor of the beginnings of language production.[8] For example, many toddlers would at least gesture toward the cookie jar before attempting to say the word *cookie*. Later on, a child would gesture toward him- or herself before producing "Me want cookie." Bates argues that this latter accomplishment is significant in that it distances the person from the object (i.e., the child from the cookie), illustrating more complex thought and language.

Over a period of time, then, a child goes from stretching arms upward, to vocalizing sounds ("uh, uh") while stretching arms upward, to saying "up" while stretching arms upward, to saying, "Daddy, up!" to saying "Daddy, please pick me up." Many years later, the child says, "Daddy, pick me up around the corner from the movie theater so my friends won't see you."

Understanding language acquisition is important for a number of reasons. As parents, teachers, and relatives of young children, we need to help them develop language; we need to be patient as their learning goes on and to realize the frustrations they may encounter. We also need to encourage both the simple and complex forms of language and to help children learn in a fun,

Reflections on Language Acquisition

Which approach to language acquisition do you think makes the most sense? How would you encourage language acquisition in children around you?

creative, and positive way. The acquisition of language is crucial to the development of communication skills. Understanding language acquisition is important for adults, too. Being aware of language development helps us adapt our own communication to the language level of a child or an adult.

◆ Communication Acquisition

Competent communicators need to acquire not only language but also communication.

When you learn language, you are learning isolated words and grammar, but when you acquire communication, you are learning how to use the entire symbol systems of a culture appropriately, how to construct meaningful messages. Communication is competent when meaningful messages are created that are appropriate and effective. Thus the real emphasis in language acquisition is communication acquisition.

Communication acquisition, then, requires not only that people learn language but also that they decide how to use that language to accomplish goals. Chapter 1 pointed out that communication is functional when it accomplishes goals for the participants. As you acquire communication skills, you are learning how language and other behaviors *function*, how they work for you.

Researcher Wood cites five basic functional *communication competencies* that children acquire as they move toward adulthood. They develop these competencies concurrently; that is, they acquire aspects of one at the same time as they acquire aspects of others. These competencies develop as children interact with family and peers, and as they process the media, especially television, which give them a broader picture of the social world. The five functional competencies are controlling, feeling, informing, imagining, and ritualizing.

Controlling

A child learns to use language to control self, others, and the environment. The appropriate use of language can make children appear "cute" or "smart," giving them influence. At age 2, some children attempt to control their parents; "no" seems to be their favorite word. Or a child may scream, "I *won't* do it!" in front of an audience to intimidate parents. Although these sound like negative examples, control is actually a neutral term; it may be positive or negative. Learning how to control (influence) others is a crucial social skill.

A child of 3 or 4 can boss other children around, give orders, or gain compliance through quiet words and smiles. A 4-year-old can request action from peers or adults.

Older children bargain ("I'll eat my peas if I can have ice cream") or manipulate ("You're the best, Mom—can I stay up just a little longer to finish watching this movie?"). And by the time children reach age 16, most learn how to get the car from their parents, encourage their friends to go to the movie they want to see, or convince a romantic interest to go out with them.

Feeling

As with many of these functional competencies, effectively expressing emotions is not easy. We cry or laugh in the early stages. Children as young as 3 or 4 can say, "I'm sad." Children have to learn how to express liking, love, respect, empathy, hostility, pride—a complex set of emotions.

Children sometimes express feeling by comforting someone else ("I'll be quiet while you rest your headache, Aunt June"). And Wood points out that third and fourth graders routinely use threats, bribes, insults, and praise as ways of trying to express their feelings.[9]

Teens spend hours talking about who likes whom and how much, about how they resent or care for their parents, or about how they "love" or "hate" school or some other person.

As an adult, you are sometimes chided for not having acquired the ability to express your feelings appropriately. "You never tell me how you really *feel*," a loved one may say. What you may have learned is that expressing feelings is not always a good idea, so you don't express a feeling, judging it to be inappropriate, or at least risky, for a given situation.

In a small-group setting, you might have to express your feelings of frustration to other group members or your feelings of relief and happiness once a group project is completed. In business, you might save your company a lot of money by effectively explaining your fears and hesitancy about a proposal to your vice president. In a speech, you'll be more persuasive if you can effectively express your passion for a cause or your admiration for a person.

Informing

Giving people information that they can understand is an important skill to acquire. And understanding the messages of others is an equally important skill.

Anyone who has ever tried to get a young child to "Tell me where it hurts" realizes how difficult it may be for the child to inform you in an understandable way. If "everywhere" is the answer you get, you have difficulty pinpointing the problem. Of course you try to use your adult skills, questioning more effectively to get at the source of the problem.

Questioning and describing are important aspects of this functional competency. Parents and teachers may ask children of 6 or 7 to repeat directions to their school or their home. They are encouraged to produce questions they would ask if they were lost ("May I use the telephone?" "How do I get to State Street?"). Older children develop complex vocabularies for describing action; they can give details about the behaviors of all their classmates at the school dance.

At the adult level, this functional competency exhibits itself in very important ways. For example, if you miss a class lecture, you seek out someone who can give you the lecture notes. Then, you ask sufficient questions

"ALL HE THINKS ABOUT IS THAT STUPID BALL."

Without language, informing others and obtaining information from them would be very difficult.

to clarify the material you don't understand. In this way, your questioning skills often enhance your classmate's descriptive skills. Effective informing skills are also vital when you give a speech; you must choose powerful language to get your points across, but you must be careful not to use language that might offend anyone in your audience. Throughout adulthood, the functional competency of informing remains crucial.

Imagining

Probably the most complex functional competency is imagining. It is the ability to think, to play, to be creative in communication. Children pretend to do something or to be someone (a superhero, a cartoon character, a person from a movie). They also role-play ("You be the bad guy, and I'll be the good guy"). They use images, creating glorious sets in their minds for the dramas they enact. They are spaceship captains or graceful and famous dancers.

Imagining in the adult world is the source of new theories, complex solutions, crazy jokes, and pleasurable plans. On the job, it is the ability to use language to convey to your co-workers your vision for the company. In public speaking, imagining may create hypothetical examples to engage an audience. In a debate, imagining skills enable you to think ahead of your opponent, to put words to each side of an argument, and to use language in ways that are logical and convincing.

An architect must use language, as well as blueprints and models, to explain the images the building will evoke. The comic chooses language that calls up vivid, funny images in the mind of the audience. Plan a trip or party with your friends, and you'll realize the language competency needed to communicate your image to them.

Observing Functional Competencies

From memories of your own childhood or by observing children, list some of the language behaviors that are used to control, feel, inform, imagine, and ritualize. What are some adult examples of the five functional competencies?

Ritualizing

The fifth, and final, functional competency involves learning the rules for managing conversations and relationships. Learning to say "hi" or "bye-bye" or "please" means internalizing early politeness conventions.

You usually get immediate rewards if you manage conversations well, and thus you feel involved with others. Early peek-a-boo games may teach the beginnings of turn-taking in conversations, followed later by how to introduce others and yourself. Teasing, joke telling, and even gossiping may be early lessons in how to manage relationships.

In adulthood, ritualizing effectively means you say and do the "right" thing at weddings, funerals, dinners, dates, athletic events, and other social gatherings. Rituals may be as formal as the highly prescribed Japanese tea ceremony (where every nonverbal movement and nuance is also important) or as informal as the party organized with your friends to watch the Super Bowl.

The five functional competencies of controlling, informing, feeling, imagining, and ritualizing are thus important aspects of communication development. Learning how to make language and other behaviors work together helps you function effectively.

◆ Language and Thought

A family is sitting in church on Easter Sunday; their particularly angelic-looking 18-month-old is toddling among the chairs. When he becomes noisy and knocks over a chair, his mother picks him up. He yells, "F— you!" loudly enough for about fifty people to hear him over the sounds of the service. An embarrassed father carries him out.

This child has certainly acquired language. It is doubtful that he knows the true meaning of his words, and he certainly has not developed the ability to adapt language use to situation. He may have known what he was doing (using language to express anger or frustration), but for this toddler the words have no meaning in and of themselves. He is oblivious to the church communication norm that cursing is not appropriate.

SEMANTICS

The meaning created between communicators by language and thought.

PRAGMATICS

The appropriate use of language in context; requires mastery of communication rules, not merely language rules.

Semantics refers to the meaning that words have for people, either because of their definitions or because of their use in a sentence's structure (their *syntax*). Semantics involves the relationship between symbols and objects, people and concepts. The toddler in the preceding example understood the relationship between the words he used and the concept of being unhappy; he was unhappy being pulled away from making lots of fun noise, so he uttered the same words he had probably heard family members use when they were unhappy with someone or something. He may have also observed strong responses from others to that word.

What the toddler had not learned was **pragmatics**, the ability to use the symbol systems of a culture appropriately. He may have gotten a few laughs by saying his words in front of his family at home, but he didn't realize that the "culture" of church made his words inappropriate. (Some would argue that they are inappropriate in many other, if not all, circumstances.)

When you acquire language, you are learning semantics, but when you learn how to use the verbal symbols of a culture appropriately, you are learning pragmatics. People communicate competently when they adapt their verbal tools—symbols—to the situation and the attendant people. This is not always an easy thing to do.

Words have both **denotative** and **connotative** meanings. The denotative meaning of a word is its dictionary definition; words like *church* or *computer* have clear descriptions listed in the dictionary for all to see. What is not so easy to see about words is their connotative meaning—the emotional or attitudinal response people have to words.

The word *church* in the dictionary may be "a building for public worship" (denotative), but people may have very different connotative meanings for it. Some may have positive responses to the word because they associate it with spirituality and rituals that bring them great personal joy. Others may feel negatively toward the word *church*, regarding it as a silly and meaningless place.

Obviously, choosing words carefully is important. You not only have to share the denotative meanings of words (using a six-syllable word that no one understands will not create meaning very effectively), but you also have to be aware of the many possible connotative meanings for any words you use.

Thinking about how to use language appropriately—developing the ability to choose effective words or to censor oneself at times—is part of competent communication.

The Triangle of Meaning

It is our *thoughts* that link **symbols** to an actual person, object, or concept. The "triangle of meaning," a classic representation of this process, explains how we know what a particular word or sentence means.[10] Figure 4.1 on page 106 shows how symbols, thoughts, and their referents are related. An example will make this easier to understand.

A mother says to her son, a college student, "I want you to meet a lovely young woman who is the daughter of your dad's business partner." Her words constitute the symbol—the description of the referent—shown in the lower left corner of the triangle.

The person, the woman he is supposed to meet, is the **referent**—as seen in the lower right corner.

The upper corner of the triangle is the *thought* or **reference**—the son's musings to himself or imagining what the woman would look like.

The dotted line between symbol and referent shows that there is no direct connection between the words and the objects they represent. If the son's roommate said, "You've gotta meet this dynamite babe who's my lab partner," how would the son know his roommate was talking about the same woman his mother wanted him to meet? The symbols (and the person who uses them) call up very different images.

DENOTATIVE MEANING
The dictionary definition of a word.

CONNOTATIVE MEANING
The emotional or attitudinal response people have to words.

SYMBOL
A sign (usually a word) used to describe a person, idea, or thing (a referent).

REFERENT
The actual person or thing that a symbol or symbols represent.

REFERENCE
The thoughts that occur in a person when symbols are used or referents encountered.

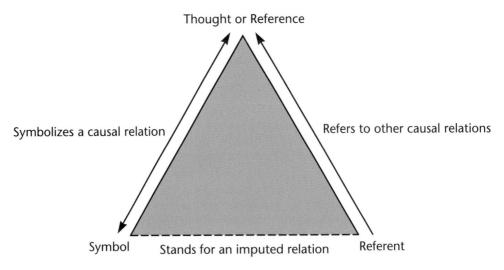

FIGURE 4.1
The triangle of meaning.

The two-way arrow between symbol and thought illustrates that the use of symbols can cause thoughts or that thoughts can result in symbols being used. The one-way arrow between referent and thought illustrates that the object, person, or concept—the referent—*can* cause thoughts.

The triangle of meaning shows that language affects thought. You can stimulate different thought processes by the words you use. Calling someone a "sweetie" and calling someone a "slug" cause different thought processes in both yourself and your listeners. Calling a boss "unreasonable" as opposed to "strict" affects the thought responses.

*R*estricted Language

Some people are unable to express their thoughts fully through language. A stroke may affect the ability to speak without interfering with thought processes. A cruel disease may likewise affect the ability to produce language. For example, people with amyotrophic lateral sclerosis (Lou Gehrig's disease) think like others, but they slowly lose their ability to control their muscles, including those that create speech.

Talk with someone who has (or has had) restricted speech. What strategies does (did) this person employ to make the most of the language use he or she does (did) have? Do (did) others respond to this person differently—for example, by acting as if the person's thoughts were restricted, too?

Special computers offer the promise of some help for people with language restrictions. Research advances continue to be made in this area.

Language can also cause misinterpretation. Saying someone lives in the "big house" may mean to one listener that the person lives in a mansion; to another, in the big apartment house—or to another, perhaps a correctional facility!

The Abstraction Ladder

Language operates at many levels of abstraction. You can speak about virtually anyone or anything in a very specific way or a very general way. You can talk so broadly that no one knows what you are talking about ("Life is so complex; you never know if you can trust people"), or you can speak so specifically that people may think you are keeping notes for a court case against them ("I saw you at 10:32 P.M. on Friday, January 29, at the right-hand corner table of Harry's Bar with a 6-foot, brown-haired man wearing black jeans, boots, and a powder-blue T-shirt").

Hayakawa has illustrated the way words can be used to describe the specific versus the general in what is termed the **abstraction ladder**[11] (see Figure 4.2 on p. 108). The top rungs of the ladder are high-level abstractions; the lower down the ladder you go, the more specific the language becomes. High-level abstractions may also be evaluative ("You jerk"), whereas low-level abstractions are usually more descriptive ("I didn't like it when you told my father I'd run out of gas"). Low-level abstractions may also involve counting things ("You've been *five* minutes late to work *three* times this week"), or dating ("Last *Saturday* you told me you'd pay me $50 by *October 5.*"). High-level abstractions may have multiple meanings ("Don't treat me like *that*"), while low-level abstractions limit the possible interpretations ("I'd prefer to order my own dinner").

In competent communication, the parties try to choose the appropriate level of abstraction. It should be higher in some circumstances and lower in others. Determining the appropriate level of abstraction involves considering yourself, your audience, and the situation.

When considering your own goals for a situation, you may decide to use high abstractions to group people or concepts together ("my classmates"), to avoid confrontation or evaluation ("I was out"), or to provide a generality that you think someone can identify with ("I've been there").

When you consider the person(s) you are talking to, you ask yourself whether they are likely to be offended by specifics ("You put one too many garlic cloves in the sauce"); whether past encounters have led you to believe that they will listen better to high or to low abstractions; and whether they are feeling defensive (in which case you may want to avoid words that would make them more so).

You also consider the situation or context. In giving a speech, you may often use high abstractions to get people to identify with your position ("Everyone here loves freedom"), but you might also use low abstractions in the form of statistics to justify a major point ("Handguns kill 65,000 people in this country every year"). If you are talking with defensive employees, you may have to use high abstractions to compliment them and show them how

ABSTRACTION LADDER
An illustration of how words can be used to describe topics ranging from the general to the specific.

HIGHER ABSTRACTIONS

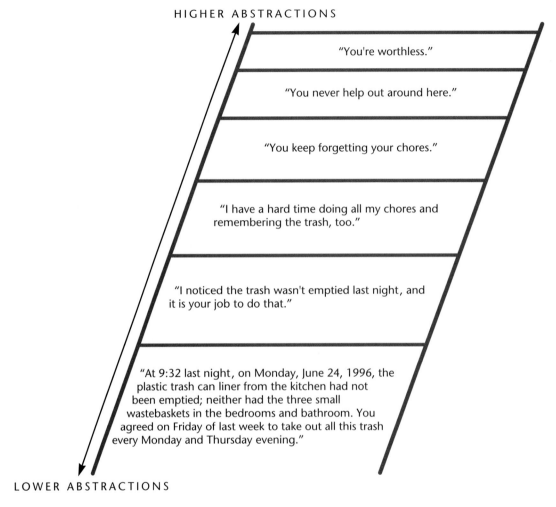

"You're worthless."

"You never help out around here."

"You keep forgetting your chores."

"I have a hard time doing all my chores and remembering the trash, too."

"I noticed the trash wasn't emptied last night, and it is your job to do that."

"At 9:32 last night, on Monday, June 24, 1996, the plastic trash can liner from the kitchen had not been emptied; neither had the three small wastebaskets in the bedrooms and bathroom. You agreed on Friday of last week to take out all this trash every Monday and Thursday evening."

LOWER ABSTRACTIONS

FIGURE 4.2
An abstraction ladder.

much they are valued ("You are such great workers") but use low abstractions to give them specific instructions about how to correct the errors they have made ("This report will be much better if you go back and put in the sub-titles I've asked for and run it through the spellchecker"). Skilled communi-cators know how and when to move up and down the abstraction ladder.

People often use high-level abstractions to avoid the pain of specifics. "I'm sorry for your loss" (high) may be more sensitive than "I'm sorry your little brown cocker spaniel was run over by the blue Nissan Pulsar" (low). The politician says, "We should guarantee the personal freedoms of every citizen" (high) to avoid offending some (and losing their votes) by saying, "I think you should be able to carry a handgun if you want" (low).

Lower-level abstractions are usually clearer; they help you understand more precisely what people mean. While "Get something interesting at the video store" (high) allows a wide range of choices, saying, "I'd like to watch a mystery movie tonight" (lower) is more likely to get you something you'll appreciate. Asking for a specific movie (lower still) will ensure your satisfaction with the choice.

Some situations call for the use of both high- and low-level abstractions. Others demand a medium level of language abstraction. At still other times, your ethical sense will tell you what type of language is appropriate. The other person, the situation, and your own goals for the interaction will determine the most effective level of abstraction.

*D*etermining Appropriate Levels of Abstraction

Reword the following high- and low-level abstractions to achieve what you think is the appropriate level of abstraction.

Situation	*Rewording to appropriate level*
You tell your employee, "Do a good job this time."	
You invite friends to "bring something" and "come over."	
You tell your roommate, "I told you eight times in October and seven times in November to take out the trash."	
You tell the new office worker, "Take a 20-gallon black plastic bag from the second left shelf in storeroom 5, place a wire tie from the shelf in your pocket, and empty the trash cans in offices 101 through 127 into the plastic bag. Twist it at the top and twist the wire tie from your pocket around it. Put the bag in the third blue trash can at the bottom of the northeast stairwell."	

◆ Language and Culture

The culture you are raised in influences your thoughts and your language. How you talk and what you think about are influenced by the culture and its language. It is difficult to say whether culture shapes language or language shapes culture. Perhaps a parallel of the homology language acquisition model might apply here. Perhaps there is another "great borrowing" going on, in which you simultaneously learn your culture through language, reshape your culture by the language choices you make (and create), and simply reflect your culture by the language you use.

The Sapir/Whorf Hypothesis

The Sapir/Whorf hypothesis claims that language determines thought.[12] According to this hypothesis, if a culture does not speak about something and has no words for something, that culture will have few thoughts about that thing or concept. Cultures without a future tense would thus harbor individuals with little concept of working for something that they could acquire next year. Cultures with only present tense verbs focus almost exclusively on the moment at hand. A person from a culture with fifty different words for *snow* would clearly attend to many more details about the "white fluffy stuff" than a person from the desert. The Quechua Indians of Peru have more words for potatoes than Eskimos have for snow; they certainly have different thought processes because of this extensive language about one food item. In very practical terms, language used in the home, classroom, or workplace will determine what people think about. For example, the family that discusses politics at dinner has heightened awareness of and thoughts about the political process.

High- and Low-Context Cultures

Culture can influence language use in another important way. Intercultural reseacher Gudykunst points out that some cultures use language that is very *indirect*; they are sensitive to situational factors, preferring to observe those factors rather than comment on each one.[13] Japan is a high-context culture; if a Japanese person disagrees with someone, he or she usually says nothing, and the person disagreed with must look for cues of disagreement in the context. These clues may include the amount of time that passes before a response, the nonverbal behaviors that occur or don't occur, or the situation in which the interaction takes place. Thus a **high-context culture** is also more likely to attribute your behavior to factors related to the situation, rather than to your personality. In other words, people in a high-context culture would not assume you were rude because you said nothing; they would be more likely to think that you didn't respond because the situation called for restraint and politeness.

HIGH-CONTEXT
CULTURE

A culture that avoids the use of direct language, relying more on context to convey meaning.

A **low-context culture**, on the other hand, uses very *direct* language. A low-context disagreement would be expressed directly and clearly to the person: "I don't think you are right about the health care plan, Jane." An individual would tend to find explanations for behavior in the person ("She's so uninformed"). The United States and Canada are such low-context cultures. In these countries, it would seem normal for someone to say, "Alex, I need a list of twenty items for the Allan project from you by 5 P.M. today." Someone from a high-context culture would more likely say, "We are starting the project," and would assume that you would have the list ready in time because you understand the situation as the speaker does.

If you did not get the list completed on time, the low-context culture would blame it on your laziness or incompetence, whereas the high-context culture would blame it on situational constraints, such as there being too many things going on for you to finish.

The way these culture types reduce *uncertainty* may also cause problems interculturally. Whenever you meet someone new, you try various uses of language to reduce the uncertainty of the situation—to know more about the other person so you will know how to act.

People from low-context cultures will normally try to reduce uncertainty by asking about the other's attitudes, feelings, and beliefs, whereas people from high-context cultures will ask about the other's status and background. This high-context strategy for reducing uncertainty is very practical, especially in cultures that have different ways of speaking to people who are seen as superior, equal, or inferior. In these cultures, uncertainty reduction involves knowing how to talk to others according to their status.

But if you are from a low-context culture and someone asks you about your position, your age, and employer (in an effort to know "how" to address you), you will probably think the person rude. Similarly, low-context questions about a high-context person's feelings are seen as equally rude.

Whatever culture you are raised in, context is important to understanding what language to use. In a multicultural society (as the United States is becoming more and more), it is important to realize that language that is "straightforward" to some is probably "invasive" to others.

Language and Your Culture

To what extent does your language use reflect your culture? Do you adapt your language use when you are with people from different cultural backgrounds? To what extent is it necessary to adapt language use in the multicultural society in which we live?

LOW-CONTEXT CULTURE

A culture that relies more on the use of direct language than on the nuances of context to impart meaning.

*C*ross-Cultural Language Use ✔

Interview someone from another culture about his or her language use. Be particularly aware of comparisons and contrasts but also find similarities to your own use of language. People usually notice differences, but they often fail to notice how much they have in common. Note your findings about direct and indirect language, uncertainty reduction, and the use of high versus low language. Report your findings to your classmates and engage them in a discussion of language use from culture to culture.

◆ Language and Context

Language is sometimes referred to as something that occurs on its own; in fact, it seems to take on a life of its own in the study of grammar and sentence construction. But studying the production of language solely from grammatical rules is not really a communicative approach; it takes social context as a given and separates language from its social uses. If you don't consider context, communication is no longer the real subject; to ignore context is to omit the social world in which you live.

Sometimes people act as if language could communicate without context. They might say whatever comes to mind without considering who is around, where they are, or the effect their words may produce. But competent language does not operate that way. There are three main ways in which language and context are related: Language reflects, builds on, and determines context.

Language Reflects Context

The situation in which language is spoken determines that language. Thus, you will choose certain types of language for different situations or different people.

Most people change their language at least a little when they talk to their grandparents. You talk differently to a person who is interviewing you for a job than you do to the people you go out with on Friday night. Depending on the situation you are in and the people you are with, you can select from among various categories of language behaviors, called **speech repertoires**.

Speech repertoires are the "files" of your language possibilities; they are the types of language you can choose from to meet the demands of a situation. The authors of your text talk differently with their children than they do with their students; they have different speech repertoires for talking with their parents than they do for talking with their colleagues.

High and Low Language. Regardless of whether you belong to a high-context or low-context culture, you probably have both high and low language use within that culture. **High language**—the more formal, polite, or "mainstream" language—is used for business, in public, and even in the classroom. **Low language** is reserved for home and everyday activities. Many people are able to "switch codes" by using multiple languages or dialects to bridge the gap or establish rapport among various groups of people. This is especially apparent in bilingual communities, as people actually switch the language they use to reflect the context. For example, in the United States many people speak English at work and another language (e.g., Spanish, Italian, Mandarin) at home.[14]

Euphemisms. Some communication contexts reflect a preference for *euphemisms*, words that substitute an inoffensive term for one considered offensive. The medical context is one with many euphemisms. A surgeon makes an "incision" rather than "cuts you open." You go to the "procedure center" to have an "injection" rather than to the "shot office" to let the

SPEECH REPERTOIRES
The possibilities communicators have for language use in any given situation, based on their experiences, cognitions, and acquired skills.

HIGH LANGUAGE
The language used in the more formal contexts of a person's life, such as work.

LOW LANGUAGE
The relaxed language usually used in the home or with close friends.

doctor stick a needle into you. The funeral business is also a rich source of euphemisms, with terms like "slumber room."

In-Group/Out-Group Distinctions. The ability to "talk like us" often determines whether one is accepted into a group. Speech repertoires are important in the secret passwords of childhood play and the "cool" language of teen groups. As adults, being able to speak the language of a job marks one as an in-group member. One who knows about computers ("You need more RAM in order to run Microsoft Word and PageMaker at the same time") and can understand the acronyms ("At the SCA meeting we'll discuss ICC") used in the workplace is on the way to being an in-group member.

The language used for in-group members versus out-group members differs at times. Some research indicates that members of a gender in-group will use more abstract language about a gender out-group.[15] Thus, if females are talking with other females about males, they will be more likely to use generalizations about them than about other females. The same applies to males' discussions. This is perhaps the source of stereotyping statements like "Men are so insensitive" or "Women are so emotional."

The young and the elderly are often the target of language aimed at making in-group and out-group distinctions. "Those silly, reckless kids" and "Those terrible elderly drivers" are attempts to stereotype the young and the elderly and to exclude them from the in-group. Patronizing language (talking down to members of a particular group) is sometimes aimed at these groups, but it also comes from them ("You're a bunch of party animals" or "When you grow up, you'll understand"). Patronizing language is valued negatively by the recipients, no matter what their age group.[16]

Language Builds on Context

People share an array of assumptions on which language choice is based. When you get to know a little about another person, you discover which

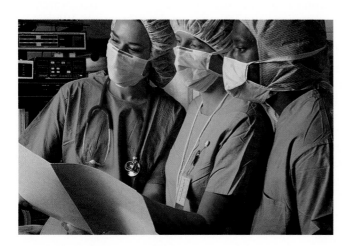

The technical language of a profession enables its practitioners to communicate with each other effectively. What social function does such specialized language serve?

*T*he Ethics of In-Group Language Use

What is your attitude concerning the ethics of using language to prevent outsiders from participating in a communication interaction? For example, consider parents who spell words when conversing within earshot of their preschool-age children or immigrants who speak a particular language when they want to discuss a private matter in the presence of others who don't speak the language. Or think of tourists in a foreign country who use their native language to make comments critical of their host country. Have you ever been involved in a situation in which language was used this way? Were you included in or excluded from the conversation? Is such behavior ethical? Does your answer depend on the situation? Does it depend on whether you are included or excluded? Considering this issue will help you understand how your values affect your communicative competence.

speech repertoires are appropriate. As you become acquainted, however, fewer questions are needed. You each develop an array of assumptions about the other. There is a shared knowledge of the social context and thus much less need to ask, "What do you mean?"

Social context also influences how people like to be addressed ("Don't call me Johnny in front of people outside of the family" or "I prefer to be referred to as 'black' rather than 'African American' "). From the earliest stages of your language development, you become aware of words that others will find offensive ("Don't say 'it sucks' in front of Grandma") and what words please others ("I really liked your calling me the manager in the meeting today").

Your development of social context also contributes to your self-confidence and reduces your feelings of uncertainty. You develop internalized assumptions about appropriate communication and times to speak or not. This awareness helps you both in group situations and among your close associates. When you sense that others will disapprove if you say something, you don't say anything.

At other times, deception may be your motivation not to speak. You might let your partner be happy with an assumption about where you were, whom you were with, or what you were doing. You may employ the "let it pass" rule purposefully to let your partner "misunderstand."

Mostly the "let it pass" rule indicates that you know someone quite well, that you are taking more for granted in conversation. Suppose one of your friends says, "Let's get tickets for the concert." You don't say, "You mean *us* go *together?*" You assume he or she doesn't mean you'll go separately and sit on opposite sides. When the "let it pass" rule is suspended, it is an indication of a "problem" in the relationship. If you say, "What do you mean, us go on a *date?*" the context needs some clarification. As language builds on context, context becomes a resource for constructing meaning.

Language Determines Context

We may create a context by the language we use.

Language is rarely neutral. Sexist language is an example. Use of the word *chick* for a woman implies far more than her gender. Many women today object to being called *girl* for reasons similar to those that black men have for objecting to being called *boy*. Attempts to rid the language of sexist terms (chairman, foreman) indicate that language determines context.

Some campuses have "fighting words" that are recognized as causing problems between genders or ethnic groups; using those words in certain ways can leave a person open to legal action.

The use of high language mentioned earlier may define you as fitting into the workplace and thus determine your context. Using language that is more formal and that is grammatically correct identifies you as a member of the group and sets expectations for the rest of the interaction.

Using formal address often determines context. If one of the authors tells her students, "Call me Mary," one context is created. If she says, "I'm Professor Wiemann," they have a different set of expectations about how the context will be managed and, thus, how they should behave and speak.

Using "baby talk" with children defines them as inferiors not capable of creating accurate representations of sounds.

"Political correctness" is an important concept today. Referring to persons as "physically challenged" instead of "handicapped" determines the way we approach them and the way they feel about themselves, so that a context of greater equality is established. Many people need to be made aware of the terms they use that are offensive or demeaning to others. One segment of the television comedy *Seinfeld* illustrated how using terms like "Indian giver" can be very offensive to an American Indian. The show also pointed out that the sensitivity can be carried too far; instead of telling his date that he had made a "reservation" for dinner, Seinfeld told her he had made an "appointment" for them.

You can often determine context by the kind of language used. How you feel about an interaction is also language-linked. In interpersonal relationships, there is a whole set of language considerations associated with initiating, maintaining, and terminating relationships.

◆ Male and Female Language

It is very popular today to claim that the language of men and women is entirely different. Some differences give talk show hosts and writers a chance to capitalize on the popular belief that men and women are from different "planets" and completely miss one another's meanings when they talk. This belief is much stronger than actual research findings indicate.[17] In actuality, decades of research into the language of women and men reveal both differences and similarities.[18]

Conversation Content

Some speech repertoires are reserved for members of our own gender. Females talking together use more language about relationships (e.g., family, close friends, health), while males use more language about doing things (e.g., sports, music, business).[19] So, we can sometimes determine the gender of the participants from the content of the conversation. Within the context of a same-sex conversation, there are few language problems. But when men and women engage in conversation with each other, each gender sometimes complains about the other. Women criticize men for talking about business or the news while ignoring relational issues (feelings, how people are getting along); women report enjoying, even *needing*, the sharing of feelings. Men criticize women for talking about "trivial" topics like who attended the meeting and how each person talked to the other (relational issues) while paying too little attention to getting things done; men report enjoying the ease and fast pace of all-male conversations.

Amount of Talk and Verbal Fillers. Despite the popular belief that women talk more than men, most studies find that men talk more than women or that there is no significant difference in how much men and women talk. Neither sex has been found to consistently use more verbal fillers (words or phrases that fill silences without having literal meaning, such as "well," "you know," or "OK") or vocalized pauses ("um," "er," or "ah," which help the speaker hold the floor.) Vocalized pauses are often thought to indicate uncertainty, so they would be more common when persons of either gender feel unsure of themselves or the situation.

Intensifiers. When you say *"terribly* cute," *"so* sorry," or *"quite* happy," you have increased the intensity of cute, sorry, and happy. It is consistently found that women do this more than men, perhaps because they attempt to be more expressive of their feelings.

Agreement. While it makes sense that women, who are socialized to pay attention to relationship maintenance, would engage in more agreement than men, it is difficult to find consistent data on this subject. Agreement involves straightforward statements like "that's right" or more subtle ones that "go along" with what another person has said. Depending on what people are trying to accomplish (establishing a new relationship versus conflict resolution, for example), either gender might engage in agreement. At times, people may engage in agreement just to get someone to be quiet ("Yeah, yeah, OK").

Control and Affiliation

Language is very important in achieving the interactional goals discussed in Chapter 1. Language helps define power, or who has more or less control in the relationship, and what the level of affection or affiliation is. Interruptions, questions and tag questions, hedges/qualifiers, justifiers, and disclaimers are types of language that contribute to these definitions.

Interruptions. Male speakers are thought to interrupt others in conversation more than female speakers do, but the situation and the status of the speakers are probably better predictors of interruptions than is gender.[20] For example, female professors could be expected to interrupt male students more often than those male students interrupt them. When status and situation are neutral, men interrupt more or there is no significant difference between men and women.

Questions and Tag Questions. In some situations, women have been found to do more questioning than men. This asking for information or opinions is often considered part of the relationship maintenance that women have been socialized to perform. Seen this way, the asking of questions functions to continue the conversation, fill in gaps, and bring others into the interaction. Tag questions are a different type of language style; they are interrogatives tacked onto a declarative or imperative sentence, such as, "This is a great book, *isn't it?*" They tend to dilute the force of a statement. "She seemed really angry, *didn't she?*" is less powerful than "She seemed really angry." Again, some studies show that women use more tag questions than men, but other studies indicate no significant difference between the sexes. Tag questions demonstrate a lack of power, since the persons using tag questions sound solicitous of another's opinion and not very sure of themselves.

Hedges/Qualifiers. Both sexes have been found to use words that qualify or soften the force of a statement. "I *guess* it would be OK" or "I'm *sort of* upset by all of this" do not sound as powerful as "It's OK" or "I'm upset." Using hedges and qualifiers in a business meeting would probably not be very effective, but *not* using them in an intimate exchange of feelings and opinions with your best friend might be equally ineffective. Sometimes we appear more open to the other persons' ideas if we use language that doesn't sound so definitive. A popular idea is that women use more hedges, but situation and status are more reliable indicators than gender.

Justifiers. Giving reasons for a declarative sentence ("I think that's right and *three of my professors agree*" or "I'm going to give him the points *because it's only fair*") may be seen as signs of uncertainty—indicating less power—or as indicators of involvement. A recent study finds that women use justifiers and agreement more than men do. [21]

Disclaimers. Language that sounds hesitant is usually perceived as less powerful. Disclaimers in conversation ("This probably doesn't mean anything, but . . ." or "I'm not really sure of this, but . . .") discount what you are about to say. Women are thought to use this type of language more than men. Disclaimers may indicate uncertainty (either with the topic or with the person you are addressing), but they may also serve to head off conflict. "This probably sounds silly, but . . ." is a disclaimer that either gender may use to prepare a partner to hear something unpleasant or contentious.[22]

In using powerful language, both men and women define the level of control in the relationship. They often use *less* controlling language to express affection, thus defining the affiliation level in the relationship. In other words, using hedges or disclaimers may be a way to show less control and at the same time indirectly express affection.

Roles, Culture, and Gender in Conversation

The roles people play and the culture in which they grow up (or find themselves) have powerful influences on their language.[23] While many people consider the different language styles women use as weak, their ability to change their language use to fit the situation may ultimately be more powerful. Women *adapt* their language use to situations more than men do, using powerful language when necessary and less powerful language in less demanding situations. In other words, a female lawyer uses language as powerful as male lawyers when practicing law, but she uses less powerful language when talking with female friends about their children.

We have already noted that the jobs people hold influence the language they use. Listen to male nursery school teachers talk on the same "power" level as their female colleagues, and you'll see that men can also adapt their language use. Many male managers today have been encouraged to use more affiliative language when they are dealing with their employees' personal problems.

In general, the language you use reflects the context you are in. Females and males adapt their language use to same-sex versus mixed-sex situations; women may use more emotional and affiliative language with other women, while men may be more direct with other men. References to "girl talk" and "guy talk" are more than casual teasings; the ability to fit into a gender group often depends on your ability to adjust your language to meet the demands of the group. Both genders adapt language use to reflect their occupations or their roles in society.[24] A successful male manager will use affiliative language when developing relationships in the workplace; a successful female manager will use direct language to clarify instructions connected with an important task. Whether male or female, a competent communicator must develop the ability to use both affiliative and powerful language in effective and appropriate ways.

Your culture or co-culture may also determine your need for powerful or powerless language. Contrast the image of the strong African-American woman (involving very powerful language) with that of the competent Asian American woman (usually involving more affiliative language). These women may use language differently to be competent in their particular co-cultures—and both may adapt their language usage outside their ethnic communities.[25]

There are differences in the language styles of men and women, and we tend to note the differences more than the many similarities. Role, status, culture, and occupation are predictors of some differences. But both men and women adapt their language usage to the situation, and most try to communicate effectively with one another in a variety of contexts by adapting their language usage to the person and the situation as competent communicators do. Men and women should be encouraged to improve their communication with each other, but they do not come from different "language planets."

◆ The Language of Relationships

The role of language in interpersonal relationships includes defining the relationship, expressing the level of commitment, and achieving influence or control over one's relational partner.

Relationship Definition

Language helps define relationships. The English language is better at defining some relationships than others. For example, it is fairly easy to label your mother, father, sister, brother, aunt, uncle, grandfather, grandmother, son, daughter—your closest blood relations—as you introduce any of these people to others.

If you say "I'd like you to meet my boss, Mr. Ramiro Sanchez," you are describing the status and professional relationship that you have. The introduction sets the stage for how people are to be treated and what further communication might go on.

Introducing someone as a stepbrother, however, can require more explanation than a person wants to give. So it may be preferable to introduce him as a brother, without bothering to produce the complex relational definitions. You might introduce a co-worker who has a slightly higher or lower status than you by saying, "Rosalinda and I work together," to avoid implications of superiority or inferiority.

Just as the English language presents few options for defining work relationships, it also lacks a very developed language system for defining the complex relationships involving friends and romantic partners. Besides the terms *husband* and *wife* and *friend* and *best friend,* we have very few terms to describe the various levels of intimacy that we have with friends and romantic partners.[26]

A first romantic interest may occur around the age of 10 or 12. At some point, such relationships evolve from "this girl I know" to "Amber and I are going out." Preteens may not really be "going out." More likely they walk around school together, hold hands, or sneak kisses. Maybe they meet after school secretly, but what they mostly do is talk on the telephone. English does not have terminology that can really describe this relationship clearly.

In high school, were you "going out" with someone or "seeing each other"? Maybe you actually *did* "go out." By the time you're a teenager, at least you feel more comfortable about introducing someone as your boyfriend or girlfriend. By age 30, however, referring to the person you have been living with for 2 years as "my girlfriend" or "my boyfriend" somehow doesn't adequately describe the relationship.

Romantic Labels

How do you label your romantic partner? Do you have no words or many to describe "where you stand" with each other? Do you label your partner differently to different people (family, friends, co-workers)? Do you have pet names for each other? How does your labeling of each other affect your understanding of the relationship? Answering these questions can help you understand both the influence and the limitations of language in defining relationships.

One practical result of the lack of terms for relationships is that this permits people to keep the level of commitment unsaid. Some commitment negotiation goes on when you move from "going out" to "living together" or becoming "engaged." Language then becomes more specific as to what is expected and how the future is to be.

In some circles, invitations to parties indicate that you and your "significant other" are invited. Others include your "spouse-like other." There is obvious strain in trying to define relationships.

The language of "disengagement" is not much clearer. English uses the terms *ex-wife* and *ex-boyfriend*, but there are many levels to those relationships, too. Some involve a lot of hostility, some involve redefinition as friends, and some involve amicable arrangements for certain behaviors such as shared custody of children.

The Language of Intimacy and Distance

In spite of language's limited ability to define relationships, you can observe language *in* relationships for clues to the levels of commitment. Knapp observes that language use helps people understand what is going on at various stages of relationships.[27]

Levels of Self-Disclosure. In the early stages of your relationships, language is very general. You usually do not verbally disagree with others, and you spend most of your time trying to find out things you and your partner have in common ("You like basketball? I *love* to watch the Lakers"). You may share a lot of biographical information, and you usually stick to "safe" topics, engaging in the small talk of not-so-intimate relationships.

Telling people about yourself and finding out about them occurs at all levels of building relationships. The more intimate the level of your relationship, the more intimate are the revelations that usually occur. Speaking about intense feelings or opinions does not normally occur in beginning relationships. Your thoughts and feelings—more intimate disclosures about self—are reserved for relationships that have a base of trust.

If you are unsure of the other, or if you are trying to put more distance in your relationship, you will generally disclose less. When this happens, the language of experimentation, of finding out about the other and revealing yourself, is shut down. You revert to the more general language of beginning relationships.

Inclusion and Exclusion. As relationships become more intimate, the language of inclusion begins. "We like Chinese food" indicates that one person feels free to speak for another. This language of inclusion makes extensive use of "we" and "us" language. Talking about the other and self increases ("Leticia and I always rent videos on Friday night"). The use of pet names ("honey," "snookums") usually occurs, as well as sarcasm or teasing. This language of *affiliation* defines the relationship to those within it as well as to those outside of it. (You may at times feel embarrassed or repelled by hearing some of the intimate terms people call one another.)

R*elational Language Detective*

Become a "relational language detective" for a few hours. While pretending to study, take notes, or watch television, write down the terms that your family members or roommates use to talk to one another. Note terms of affection, powerful/powerless language use, and amounts of self-disclosure. Also note any "in" language—language use that is unique to your family or group of friends and that outsiders might not understand. Note the ways people tease one another or complain about one another. Note the forms of address. Prepare a summary of your notes for class discussion.

When you establish a relationship, you know enough about the other so that your language use is less restricted. The language of intimate relationships may "sound bad" to outsiders. Partners who have developed habits of teasing each other or who give "friendly digs" at the other may have their own language of inclusion. Calling your brother "Snake" may sound degrading to those outside the family, but family members know it is a name of affection recalling a shared experience.

Relationships that are becoming less intimate reverse the "we" talk of past involvements. The language of differentiation relies more heavily on the use of "I" and "you" ("I like sushi, but you never want to eat it" or "He always wants to watch television, but I like to go out dancing"). Partners cease using pet names or telling inside jokes. Exclusionary talk becomes the norm.

Future Talk. Intimate relationships use language that implies future commitment ("Where shall we spend the holiday next year?"). Planning goes on, and decisions are made jointly. "Maybe in a few years we can afford a bigger house" makes use of "we" language as well as future planning.

Mutual understandings guide language use. It is possible to say, "Let's get the families together for a big barbeque" because the parties assume they will be together in the future and that they have some claim on each other's future.

If people in a relationship are disengaging, they will often talk around important topics—like the status of their own relationship. They maintain a stony silence, or they fill the silences with "empty talk" or "safe talk" about topics that don't involve the relationship.

The Language of Control

Competent relationships involve mutual influence. As we indicated in Chapter 1, relationships work out many different ways of balancing control or influence.

Asking another for favors indicates a more intimate relationship, but it is also a control move: You are trying to get the other to do something for you. Interrupting another or changing the subject of a conversation is also a control attempt. In such instances, the role of control is obvious.

The use of control is not always so obvious. Refusing to talk about something the other wants to talk about can appear to be trivial but is actually a very influential move. Cajoling, or "sweet talk," may persuade the other to do what you want even though it doesn't seem very forceful on the surface. In competent relationships, language that seems less powerful may actually contribute to the competence of the relationship. Using hesitant language with your partner may be a way of *accommodating*.

People use a wide variety of language strategies to define themselves and their relationships, to create intimacy and distance, and to negotiate levels of control. The language being used can give clues to the intimacy of a relationship and to where the partners "stand" with one another. The language can express liking, love, and respect—or dislike, hate, and disrespect. The language can say, "Let's be best friends" or "Let's give it a rest for a while." The language can define us as friends, business partners, family, enemies, past lovers, or former neighbors. The labels you use for your partner are language clues to your relationship, but so are the topics you discuss or don't, the depth of your conversations, and the things you don't say at all.

The Case of Amy and Donald

At the beginning of this chapter we encountered an example of miscommunication. Manager Amy had attempted to be diplomatic while telling Donald that his final report was inadequate and needed to be redone. Donald interpreted her diplomacy as an endorsement of the basic soundness of his report. What have you learned in this chapter that might help explain this incident of miscommunication?

• Which of the five functional competencies of communication are illustrated by this incident?

• What concepts concerned with language and thought can be used to illuminate the case of Amy and Donald?

• What levels of abstraction were used by Amy? How do you think she could have used more specific or more general language to improve her effectiveness?

• In what ways did culture and context influence this interaction? Do you believe that gender was a factor as well?

• How might you describe this incident from the perspective of the language of relationships (defining the relationship, expressing the level of commitment, and achieving influence or control over one's relational partner)?

REVIEW

- Language is acquired through a complex process of thinking and developing your biological potential. Although all children acquire language at about the same time (according to the nature theory), there are many variations in language use and complexity. A language-rich environment probably contributes to language development.

- In practice, language is probably acquired as you develop thinking, coordination, and your social relationships simultaneously. The homology model of language acquisition takes all of these aspects into account.

- As you acquire language, you also learn how to use it appropriately. You develop the basic functional communication competencies of controlling, feeling, informing, imagining, and ritualizing.

- Semantics illustrates how language and thought are related. The use of language by one person does not necessarily call up the original image in another. Highly abstract language creates many opportunities for misinterpretation between communicators. Lower abstractions, more specific language, leaves less room for misinterpretation. Finding the appropriate level of abstraction in language use is important to competent communication.

- Culture is an important influence on the use of language. The ways in which cultures talk or don't talk about certain things create many words for those things—or very few. The directness or indirectness of language is culturally linked, as is the way in which cultures reduce uncertainty through language use.

- Context is an important aspect of understanding language. Language reflects the context in which it is used, builds on that context, and in many instances, determines the context of the relationship.

- Men and women use different language styles in certain circumstances. But they have many similarities in language use, too. Status, roles, culture, context, and occupation are more significant determinants of language usage than is gender.

- You can understand relationships better by looking at the language that defines and builds them. You name your relationships as friends or lovers, as co-workers or enemies. Within those relationships, you send messages of liking or hating, influence or powerlessness, and inclusion or exclusion.

- Communicating competently requires that you understand the many uses of language and how to adapt them appropriately to your various communication situations.

Nonverbal
Communication

●BJECTIVES

After reading this chapter, you should be able to:

1. Describe the importance of nonverbal communication in your personal and professional life.

2. Distinguish among the various nonverbal codes (appearance, eye behavior, touch, etc.).

3. Discuss the effects of culture, context, and situation on nonverbal communication competence.

4. Explain the functions of nonverbal communication.

5. Describe how culture affects nonverbal communication.

DIE AND JOHN HAVE DECIDED TO MARRY. They will have a traditional wedding, primarily to please Edie's family, after which they will settle in Dallas. Edie was raised in a large Catholic, Italian-American family where affection is openly expressed. Her mother takes care of the home and the children; her father is a marketing executive. John is an only child whose parents are divorced. He admires his mother because she raised him without much help from his father. Edie was immediately attracted to John because of the way in which he showed respect for her intelligence and abilities. John believes Edie brings out the best in him. At times, however, he finds her openness a little overwhelming.

In this chapter the focus is on the nature and functions of nonverbal communication. As you read the chapter, ask yourself how the topics being discussed might impact the developing relationship between Edie and John. We will return to this scenario at the end of the chapter.

NONVERBAL
COMMUNICATION

*The process of
signaling meaning
through behavior that
does not involve the
content of spoken
words.*

You probably have some idea of what constitutes nonverbal communication, but it is hard to define. Even among communication experts, any consensus that does exist boils down to two convictions: (1) that nonverbal communication involves behavior rather than the content of spoken words, and (2) that meaning is attributed to the behavior. Therefore, **nonverbal communication** is the process of signaling meaning through behavior that does not involve the content of spoken words. Nonverbal communication consists of messages (intentional or unintentional) that are encoded and decoded with meaning and that serve specific functions. Because virtually every behavior can be interpreted as having meaning, you are continually communicating. A sigh, a nod, and a tapping foot can all convey meaning.

◆ The Impact of Nonverbal Communication

Nonverbal communication affects every facet of your life—relationships, social interactions, and careers. In fact, nonverbal behaviors are often better indicators of true thoughts and feelings than is spoken language. This makes relationships especially vulnerable to nonverbal communication. For example, maintaining a well-timed silence or avoiding touch with another can signify the beginning of the end of a relationship. On the other hand, smiling and open arms can lead to intimacy.[1]

Socially, nonverbal communication can direct interaction and determine future encounters with others. For instance, interruptions during a conversation are perceived negatively, and the interrupters are viewed as less than competent.[2] If you are at a party and interrupt a small circle of people talking, you may be seen as self-centered and overbearing, and this may cause people to avoid you in the future. If, however, you enter the conversation at the signal of another, by eye contact or someone pointing at you, you will be perceived as interesting and friendly, and others will want to talk with you further.

Nonverbal behaviors also influence the success of your career. In a 1991 study of business organizations, 94 percent of the respondents rated nonverbal communication in the business world as either fairly or very important.[3] This suggests that nonverbal behaviors can either help or hinder your growth in the professional arena. If you show up at work dressed in jeans and a T-shirt, yawn during business meetings, and display stress-related behaviors (biting your nails), you will probably be passed over for that promotion!

◆ Origins

How do people know that laughing is associated with pleasure, frowning with sadness, or foot tapping with impatience? Why do some people shake hands upon introduction while others bow? Why do some people find stares so uncomfortable? Two primary perspectives can answer these questions:

Phylogeny posits that human behavior is innate and the result of evolution; **ontogeny** views behavior as shaped by social and cultural expectations.

One of the earliest supporters of phylogeny was Charles Darwin, who believed that facial expressions were survival mechanisms that evolved in much the same way as other physical characteristics. Later research conducted by Eibl-Eibesfeldt substantiated this hypothesis. After extensive observation of blind and deaf children, who could not be influenced by the facial expressions of others, Eibl-Eibesfeldt noted that a number of facial expressions were common among the children and concluded that primary emotions are expressed by inborn facial expressions.[4] These primary emotions are sadness, anger, disgust, fear, interest, surprise, and happiness. Further studies conducted by Ekman and his colleagues proved that these basic facial expressions may be considered universal.[5]

Proponents of the other perspective, ontogeny, assert that nonverbal behavior is learned and developed throughout childhood according to social and cultural norms. Research studies conducted by Michael and Willis,[6] which traced how children interpreted gestures, showed an increased recognition ability in older children. Golomb found that physical attractiveness is perceived by children as young as age 3.[7] One study discovered that by kindergarten age, children have developed perceptions of stereotypical traits associated with body type.[8] Children understand the appropriate use of space around the third grade.[9]

Both of these perspectives, phylogeny and ontogeny, can improve your understanding of nonverbal communication. You are probably born with some nonverbal behaviors, and you learn others through your social and cultural interactions. Although you can recognize primary emotions through facial expressions, other nonverbal behaviors are expressed through subtle cues that are socially or culturally learned.

◆ Codes

Although nonverbal codes are not as sophisticated as those of *Star Trek* or as secretive as those in a James Bond movie, the codes of nonverbal communication, as with any other coding system, are the means by which messages are sent and received. Simply put, these are the types of behavior that produce potential messages. In order to better understand the meaning of a message, it is important to know the codes used in communicating messages. Nonverbal behavior can be classified into the following categories: appearance and artifacts; gestures and body movements; facial expressions; eye behavior; paralanguage; touch; the use of space; time orientations; and scents and smells.

Appearance and Artifacts

People are judgmental creatures. Whether subconsciously or deliberately, they make judgments based on appearance. Most people are aware of the

PHYLOGENY
The evolutionary development of a species over time (as distinguished from the development of individual members of that species).

ONTOGENY
The course of development of an individual organism (as distinguished from the development of a species over time).

Nature or Nurture? Expressing Emotions

The seven primary emotions are identified in this chapter. Make a list of other emotions and, for each one, indicate whether you were born with the ability to express the emotion or learned nonverbal behavior to express it. What does this list tell you about your ability to interpret nonverbal expressions of emotion by other people?

significance of attractiveness; it's why, collectively, billions of dollars are spent every year on designer clothes, haircuts, makeup, and even plastic surgery. Indeed, society accords attractive people certain advantages. For instance, attractive students receive more interaction from their teachers;[10] attractive defendants are more likely to be found innocent in a court of law;[11] "good-looking" people have a three to four times greater chance of being hired;[12] and attractiveness is the predominant factor in dating behavior.[13] Appearance affects not only perceptions of attractiveness but also judgments about a person's background, character, personality, status, and future behavior.[14] These perceptions are inferred from body shape and size, facial features, skin color, and clothing.

Body shape has been categorized into three types: **endomorphic**, which is rounded (oval or pear-shaped and often heavy); **mesomorphic**, which is triangular (broad shoulders and slim waist); and **ectomorphic**, which is straight (thin and bony with little muscle tone). The culture determines the "ideal" body type. Some cultures favor endomorphic body types, while others prefer mesomorphic or ectomorphic. Attitudes about attractiveness can change with the times. If you were to look through fashion magazines from 30 or 40 years ago, you would notice that the models appearing in those publications were not as thin or as tall as today's models.

Generally, people attach certain personality traits to body types—such as viewing rotund people as happy—but they tend to make character judgments based on facial features. For example, people tend to see dishonesty in small, close-set eyes, innocence in dimples, and maturity in gray hair.

In an ideal world, there would be no reason to discuss perceptions based on skin color. Unfortunately, however, you are already quite familiar with the racial stereotypes in U.S. culture based solely on skin color. This kind of prejudice exists in most cultures, although the attributions given to a particular color can be radically different. Do you think skin color is important in South Africa? What about in France (or in Algeria), England (or in the Commonwealth nations), or Germany? Of course it is. Competent communicators must be aware not only of their own biases but also of others' prejudices.

We have thus far discussed those aspects of appearance that are largely innate and unchangeable: body build, facial features, and skin color. What you wear, however, is one element of appearance that is under your control. Clothing deliberately communicates sociocultural messages from the sender about status, economic level, social background, goals, and satisfaction.[15] The image you promote through dress can affect getting a promising job or advancing your career. Many businesses expect their employees' dress to complement the image of the company.[16] Clothing also communicates social intent. Clothing that conforms to current styles and trends can increase your popularity.[17] Dress can also send messages of power and status. More formal attire and uniforms, for example, are perceived as status symbols.[18] Extensive research by Aiken,[19] and later by Rosenfeld and Plax,[20] was conducted to determine the link between clothing selections and personality

 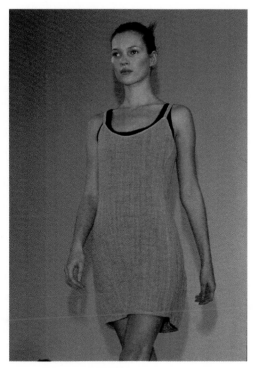

The "ideal" body type changes over time, as these celebrities, past and present, demonstrate. The voluptuous movie star Marilyn Monroe was an ideal type in the 1950s. Kate Moss, a fashion model of the 1990s, exemplifies a slender "waif" image.

traits. These researchers found that choice of clothing, or **clothing orientation**, was linked to personality traits. Rosenfeld and Plax looked at four clothing orientations: clothing consciousness, exhibitionism, practicality, and designer. People with a high *clothing consciousness* orientation believed it was important for others always to notice what they wore. Those scoring high in the second orientation, *exhibitionism*, approved of themselves' and others' wearing "skimpy" clothing. People with a high *practicality* orientation were more concerned with the practicality of clothing than with its beauty. Finally, scoring high in the fourth orientation, *designer*, were those people who would love to be clothes designers. This study established an association between the characteristics of individuals and their preferences for particular clothing.

CLOTHING
ORIENTATION
Clothing preferences.

Closely related to clothing is the use of **artifacts**, or accessories used for decoration or identification. Jewelry, glasses, hats, badges, tattoos, purses, and briefcases are all personal artifacts. Through artifacts, you can communicate your self-image, affiliation, and social attitudes, as revealed in the following story.

ARTIFACT
An accessory used for decoration or identification.

*S*elf-Description Test

Fill in each blank with a word from the suggested list following each statement. For each blank, three in each statement, you may select any word from the list of adjectives that is directly below that statement. An exact word to fit you may not be in the list, but select the adjectives that seem to fit most closely the way you are.

1. Most of the time I feel _____ , _____ , and _____ .

calm	relaxed	complacent	anxious
confident	reserved	cheerful	tense
energetic	contented	impulsive	self-conscious

2. When I study or work, I seem to be _____ , _____ , and _____ .

efficient	sluggish	precise	enthusiastic
competitive	determined	reflective	leisurely
thoughtful	placid	meticulous	cooperative

3. Socially, I am _____ , _____ , and _____ .

outgoing	considerate	argumentative	friendly
awkward	shy	tolerant	affected
talkative	gentle-tempered	soft-tempered	hot-tempered

4. Other people consider me rather _____ , _____ , and _____ .

generous	optimistic	sensitive	adventurous
affectionate	kind	withdrawn	reckless
cautious	dominant	detached	dependent

The table below has three columns of these same adjectives used in the preceding questions. Place a check mark beside each adjective you chose earlier on the test. After checking the adjectives, add the number of checks for each column and place the totals in the blanks underneath the column heads. Your three totals should add up to 12.

ENDOMORPHIC	MESOMORPHIC	ECTOMORPHIC
affected	adventurous	anxious
affectionate	argumentative	awkward
calm	cheerful	cautious
complacent	competitive	considerate
contented	confident	detached
cooperative	determined	gentle-tempered
dependent	dominant	meticulous
friendly	efficient	precise
generous	energetic	reflective
kind	enthusiastic	reserved
leisurely	hot-tempered	self-conscious
placid	impulsive	sensitive
relaxed	optimistic	shy
sluggish	outgoing	tense
soft-tempered	reckless	thoughtful
tolerant	talkative	withdrawn
TOTAL:	TOTAL:	TOTAL:

From these three numbers, you can now determine your general temperament or psychological type. If you chose 2 adjectives from the endomorphic list, 7 from the mesomorphic list, and 3 from the ectomorphic list, your score would be 2/7/3. The highest of the three numbers indicates the body type most often associated with your psychological characteristics; in this case, you would be likely to have a mesomorphic body. Research suggests that your body shape corresponds to how you describe yourself psychologically. Did your choice of adjectives correlate with your body type? Is it a mistake to develop stereotypes based on how someone looks?

Source: Adapted from J. B. Cortes & F. M. Gatti (1965), Physique and self-description of temperament, *Journal of Consulting Psychology, 29,* 432–439.© by American Psychological Association.

KINESICS

The communicative ability of gestures and body movements.

EMBLEM

A movement or gesture that has a direct verbal translation.

ILLUSTRATOR

A movement or gesture that accompanies and illustrates a verbal message.

REGULATOR

A movement or gesture that regulates conversation.

ADAPTER

A movement or gesture that satisfies some physical or psychological need.

AFFECT DISPLAY

An unintentional movement or expression that conveys a mood or emotional state.

Recently, Ruth went to the artists' sale at the community center. After admiring a painting for quite some time, she asked about the price of it. "Fourteen hundred," the artist answered. Ruth took out her checkbook. "Okay," she said, "I'll take it." While she was writing the check, the artist, in an attempt to make conversation, casually remarked, "You're not like most people who come through here; most of them try to 'Jew' me down, and I really hate that!" Ruth looked up, her face turning red, tore up her check, and snapped, "You, sir, have just lost a sale!" With storm in her eyes, she abruptly turned and vanished into the crowd. The artist had not noticed the communicative artifact: Around Ruth's neck, at the end of a long chain, was a star of David. Ruth was Jewish. Several other customers who overheard the exchange also left.

Gestures and Body Movements

The nonverbal behavior code with which you are probably the most familiar is kinesics. Sometimes called "body language," **kinesics** refers to the way gestures and body movements send messages. There are five categories of kinesic behavior: emblems, illustrators, regulators, adapters, and affect displays.[21] First, **emblems** are movements and gestures that have a direct verbal translation, and these movements are known to a specific group or culture. The sender intentionally displays emblems to replace words. Examples include the hitchhiker's thumb, the two-finger victory sign, and a wave of the hand to say hello. Examine the list of cultures in Table 5.1 for their distinctive methods of greeting others.

The second type, **illustrators**, accompany verbal messages and illustrate what is being said. They are usually intentional by the sender and cannot normally be interpreted without the use of words. Holding your hands a foot apart while saying, "The fish was this big!" is an example of an illustrator.

Regulators, the third kind of kinesic behavior, are used to regulate conversations. Examples include raising your hand, lifting your head, or raising your eyebrows to gain the floor during a conversation. Leaning back and lowering your voice help to signal that you want to relinquish the conversation floor.

The fourth type, **adapters**, are behaviors exhibited to satisfy some physical or psychological need. Physical adapters include rubbing your eyes when tired and shifting positions in a chair after sitting for a long time. Psychological adapters are used for emotional release and include twisting your hair and biting your nails when you're nervous. Adapters are not conscious behaviors; they are used in response to heightened emotional arousal.[22]

Affect displays, the last category, are used to indicate emotional or affective state. They convey mood and reactions. These are usually unintentional movements that reflect the sender's true emotions. An example is slumping in a chair, indicating fatigue or boredom, or a sad face reflecting problems in your life.

Paying respect, communicating greetings, and meeting people do not always begin with the firm handshake typical of Western cultures. Cultures from around the world use different kinesic (and sometimes touching) behavior as a greeting.

TABLE 5.1 GREETINGS FROM AROUND THE WORLD: CULTURAL DIFFERENCES IN SAYING "HELLO"	
CULTURE	DESCRIPTION
Japan	The bow—bending forward and down at the waist.
India	*Namaste*—placing hands at the chest in a praying position and bowing slightly.
Thailand	*Wai*—same as *namaste* (India).
Middle East	*Salaam*, used primarily among the older generation. Right hand moves upward, touching first the heart, then the forehead, and then moving up into the air.
Maori tribespeople (New Zealand) and Eskimos	Rubbing noses.
East African tribes	Spitting at each other's feet.
Tibetan tribesmen	Sticking out their tongues at each other.
Bolivia	Handshake accompanied by a hearty clap on the back.
Russia	Friends begin with a handshake and move to a "bear hug."
Latin America	*Abrazo*—embracing with both arms.

Source: Data from R. E. Axtell (1991), *Gestures: The do's and taboos of body language around the world* (New York: John Wiley & Sons).

Kinesics is influenced by individual communicator styles.[23] The *assertive* communicator is active in maintaining the attention and interest of others. Assertive communicators are commonly perceived as dominant and independent, and they use frequent and dynamic gestures and movements. The *responsive* communicator projects understanding, sympathy, warmth, and friendliness. This style demonstrates immediate and open body positions. The *versatile* communicator adapts to the behavior of the other. A person who uses this style is flexible in behavior and adapts body movements to complement the situation and the other interactant.

Facial Expressions

Although facial expressions are the primary nonverbal codes we use to display emotions, they can be problematic because of their complexity. The human face is capable of producing over 1000 different expressions.[24] Nonetheless, different facial expressions are associated with different emotions, and

Assertive, Responsive, or Versatile?

From the communicator styles mentioned above, choose the most effective one for each of the following occupations: classroom instructor, minister, sales clerk, public speaker, personnel director, concert performer, school counselor.

these emotions are displayed by distinct areas of the face. Happiness is shown in the cheeks/mouth and eye/eyelid areas; sadness and fear are conveyed in the eye/eyelid area; surprise is portrayed in the cheek/mouth, eye/eyelid, and brow/forehead areas. Anger is not easily noticeable unless two or more areas of the face are used for its expression. Although anger is difficult to recognize from facial expressions, other emotional states are clearly apparent.[25]

One expression that has been given particular attention by researchers is the smile. Ekman and Friesen have classified smiles into three types: felt, false, and miserable.[26] *Felt smiles* are automatic reflexes to positive emotions, such as happiness or delight.

False smiles are used to portray positive emotions that aren't actually felt. There are three kinds of false smiles: *phony smiles*, used when no emotions are felt; *masking smiles*, used to cover up negative emotions; and *dampened smiles*, used to conceal positive emotions.

Miserable smiles are responses to negative emotions, with no attempt made to conceal unhappiness. Felt and miserable smiles are true reflections of emotions, whereas false smiles conceal emotions.

False smiles are just one of the many ways that people control their facial behavior. When people manipulate their facial expressions, they are using facial management techniques. The four most commonly employed techniques are **intensification**, or exaggerating what you feel (e.g., when you exaggerate surprise about the birthday gift from your parents even though you found it hidden in the closet a week earlier); **deintensification**, or downplaying what is felt (e.g., withholding tears at a sad movie even though you want to cry); **neutralization**, or eliminating all expression of emotion (e.g., when a paramedic remains expressionless at the scene of a car accident so the injured will stay calm); and **masking**, or replacing an expression that shows true feeling with one that is deemed appropriate (e.g., congratulating a new bride with a smile even though you dislike her new husband intensely).[27] The primary emotions can be concealed by facial management techniques, and social norms help you determine which techniques are appropriate to which situations.

Consider the following scenario: Every Saturday night after the restaurant where he works closes, Anthony invites his co-workers over to his house for a quarter ante poker game. Each hand has a $5 limit, so Anthony feels comfortable (guilt-free) winning. Anthony's poker buddies have trouble reading his facial expressions because these rarely show any emotion (excitement, disappointment, etc.). Anthony is using facial management to *neutralize* his expression so that his companions will have trouble guessing whether he holds a strong or a weak hand of cards.

Eye Behavior

If you ever get bored and need something to perk you up, try this experiment—provided you are in a familiar environment such as work or school.[28]

INTENSIFICATION
The facial management technique of exaggerating what is felt.

DEINTENSIFICATION
The facial management technique of downplaying what is felt.

NEUTRALIZATION
The facial management technique of eliminating all expression of emotion.

MASKING
The facial management technique of replacing an expression that shows true feeling with one that is deemed appropriate for a particular situation.

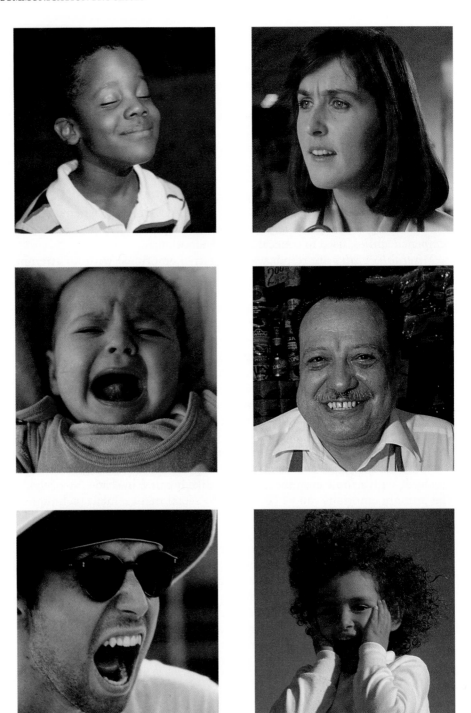

What is your interpretation of the emotions of each of these people? What areas of their faces are most significant in expressing the emotion?

Step onto a crowded elevator and instead of facing the door, face the people and keep your eyes on them. Don't speak; just look. To the people on the elevator, a 30-second ride will seem like an eternity! They will begin to squirm with uneasiness as they feel your eyes scrutinize them. Once you look down, their discomfort will begin to subside. This is the power of oculesics.

Oculesics refers to eye behavior and plays an important role in communication. Eye contact with another person commands involvement. Even when you pass strangers and make eye contact, you are connected to that person, albeit remotely. It can also stimulate arousal, either positive or negative. You can probably remember as a child receiving "looks" from your parents that communicated a specific meaning and emotion to you—eye contact that sent messages of "Be careful" or "You're in trouble when we get home." Even now, you communicate with friends in much the same way. Imagine meeting a classmate as you walk with your best friend. With eye contact, you could communicate to your friend such messages as "Can you believe that outfit?" or "Hurry, I don't want him to see me!"

OCULESICS
Communicative eye behavior.

The eye area is one of the least controllable regions of your face, and as a result, your eyes can expose your emotional state. There is a significant change in the eyes with surprise and fear, but only a little change with happiness and disgust.[29] Interpersonal encounters usually begin with eye contact to signal interest, and in Western cultures, increased eye contact with a speaker indicates interest and attention. The type and amount of eye contact can reveal the nature and stage of a relationship as well as status. If you think about it, the amount of eye contact you make with others is indicative of how much you like them.

From a general perspective, eye behavior can serve six important communicative functions.[30] The eyes can (1) influence attitude change and persuasion; (2) indicate degrees of attentiveness, interest, and arousal; (3) express emotions; (4) regulate interaction; (5) indicate power and status; and (6) form impressions in others.

You can think of eye behavior from the perspectives of mutual gaze, gaze aversion, and gaze omission. *Mutual gaze* involves two people looking in the direction of each other; that is, they share mutual eye contact. Mutual gaze is used for a number of reasons, such as ensuring someone is listening, flirting, and establishing a connection with someone.

When only one person is attempting to make eye contact, *gaze aversion* has occurred. An intentional behavior to turn one's gaze away from another person, gaze aversion is often used to signal disinterest in a person or topic or to signal the end of a conversation.

Gaze omission is similar to gaze aversion in that one person does not make eye contact with another. The difference is that the avoidance of eye contact is unintentional. For some reason, the attempt by someone to make contact has gone unnoticed. Of course, the factor of intentionality makes these two behaviors extremely difficult to interpret. As a result, it is easy to misunderstand someone's eye behavior. When was the last time you avoided eye contact with someone else? What was your motivation?

Staring is one aspect of eye behavior that has negative connotations; by most standards, it is considered rude and socially unacceptable. Staring is regarded as an invasion of privacy or a threat to the individual. At the onset of a relationship, it may indicate interest, but most of the time, it is perceived negatively. How do you feel when you are being stared at? Flattered? Annoyed? Anxious? What do you do about it?

Paralanguage

PARALANGUAGE

The communicative value of vocal behavior; the meaning of how something is said.

VOICE QUALITIES

The vocal cues of tempo; resonance; rhythm, articulation, pitch, and glottis control; and pitch range.

VOCALIZATION

A vocal cue that does not have the structure of language.

VOCAL CHARACTERIZER

A sound that conveys the emotional or physical state of the speaker.

VOCAL QUALIFIER

A vocal cue that qualifies or regulates a verbal message.

VOCAL SEGREGATE

A sound with a connotative meaning.

Paralanguage refers to *how* something is said, not *what* is said. To illustrate this point, try saying "great" to convey these messages: disappointment, excitement, congratulations, and disgust. The word (what you said) didn't change, but the voice characteristics (how you said it) changed. People make judgments about personal characteristics (age, gender, status, etc.), emotional states, and attraction on the basis of vocal cues. Vocal cues also influence persuasion and aid comprehension.[31]

Trager, an early researcher in paralanguage, classified paralinguistic activity into several categories. Of these categories, the one that is most closely related to communication competence is voice qualities.[32] **Voice qualities** encompass pitch range (actual range of pitch), vocal lip control (the degree of hoarseness in a voice), glottis control (sharp or smooth transitions in pitch), articulation control (precise or slurred speech), rhythm control (level of smoothness), resonance (thickness or thinness of tone), pitch control (the ability to vary range of pitches), and tempo (rate of speed of speech).[33]

Trager also mentions another type of paralanguage, **vocalizations**, or vocal cues outside language structure. There are three types of vocalizations: vocal characterizers, vocal qualifiers, and vocal segregates. **Vocal characterizers** include sounds such as laughing, crying, giggling, moaning, sighing, and yawning. Vocal characterizers give information about the speaker's emotional or physical state. **Vocal qualifiers** are cues that provide variety within a specific utterance. This category includes intensity (loudness or softness), pitch height (high or low), extent (duration of sound), and rate. Vocal qualifiers indicate emotional states and are used to add emphasis to meaning, as in the utterance "There *is* no Tooth Fairy." For example, an uneven rhythm (shakiness in the voice) and a fast tempo (rate) might indicate nervousness, and little resonance (thinness in voice) and slurred speech (articulation control) might signal fatigue. Vocalizations that are used in place of words and have connotative meaning are **vocal segregates**. These include "uh-huh" (yes), "shhh" (be quiet), and "uh-uh" (no). Filler sounds like "er" or "ah" are also considered segregates.

One interesting perspective on paralanguage is Giles's speech accommodation theory. Giles believes that people change their vocal patterns in respect to another's (i.e., *accommodate* the person) in order to obtain a desired response from that person. Changing vocal patterns can affect social inclusion, maintain group identity, or even increase distance between interactants.[34] The cues used to achieve a desired response from another are accent, speech rate, utterance duration (how long people speak), and pause duration. The changes made in vocal cues to increase similarity in vocal patterns can facilitate perceptions of liking and attraction; the changes made in vocal cues to become dissimilar with the other's vocal patterns can produce negative perceptions or distance. Stop for a moment and think about a business acquaintance, such as a boss or co-worker, whose relationship is important to you. Have you ever noticed how you "accommodate" this person's vocal patterns? Are you aware of how the two of you may use accommodating vocal styles in order to seem similar and therefore more attractive to each other?

Touch

Tactile communication, or **haptics**, refers to touching behavior. Touch is one of the most fundamental types of communication. It is the first communication experienced in life. As a newborn, you get your first information about yourself, others, and your environment from touching. Touch is powerful communication and provides meaning when words often fail. A father's loving touch soothes a crying baby; a handshake thanks a public speaker; a supportive pat on the back bolsters the confidence of the unsure. Although people have different perceptions of touch and some are more accepting of it than others, it is a primary means of communication and fulfills a basic human need.

One classification system for touch is Heslin's intimacy continuum.[35] This continuum defines the uses of touch based on the relationship between the interactants. Heslin divides the uses of touch into five types: functional-professional, social-polite, friendship-warmth, love-intimacy, and sexual arousal. The first type of touch, *functional-professional*, refers to touching that is used to perform a job. This type of touch is a necessary accompaniment to the completion of the job and is used without interpersonal involvement. Physicians, dentists, and hairstylists use this type of touch in the course of their work.

The next type of touch, *social-polite*, is used as a social function and is restricted by the social rules of the culture. Although it is more interpersonal than functional-professional touch is, social-polite touch is used in a social role. The goal of this sort of touch is a polite acknowledgment of the other person. A handshake between American men and a kiss between Arabic men are examples of this type of touching.

The third kind of touching, *friendship-warmth*, conveys liking and affection between people who know each other. Because it is used in interpersonal relationships, it is often difficult to interpret and frequently confused with intimacy. Back-patting and hugging are messages of affection and friendship, but not necessarily love.

HAPTICS
Touching behavior.

TABLE 5.2 HOW PEOPLE TOUCH

TYPE OF CONTACT	PURPOSE	INTIMACY TYPE
Handshake	Forming relational ties.	Social-polite
Body-guide	Touching is a substitute for pointing.	Social-polite
Pat	A congratulatory gesture but sometimes meant as a condescending or sexual one.	Social-polite or sexual-arousal
Arm-link	Used for support or to indicate a close relationship.	Friendship-warmth
Shoulder embrace	Signifies friendship; can also signify romantic connectiveness.	Friendship-warmth
Full embrace	This gesture shows emotional response or relational closeness.	Friendship-warmth
Hand-in-hand	With adults, the gesture suggests equality within the relationship.	Friendship-warmth
Mock attack	An aggressive behavior performed in a non-aggressive manner, such as a pinch meant to convey playfulness.	Friendship-warmth
Waist embrace	Indicates intimacy.	Love-intimacy
Kiss	Signals a degree of closeness or the desire for closeness.	Love-intimacy or sexual-arousal
Hand-to-head	Shows a trusting and intimate relationship.	Love-intimacy
Head-to-head	Usually agreed upon by a couple as a means to close themselves off from the rest of the world.	Love-intimacy
Caress	Normally used by romantic partners; signals intimacy.	Love-intimacy or sexual-arousal
Body support	Touching used as physical support.	Love-intimacy

The fourth category, *love-intimacy*, is used by lovers and spouses to communicate love and closeness. Kissing, embracing, and caressing are examples of love-intimacy touches. Although this type of touch is intimate, it does not necessarily involve sexual activity. In fact, this type of haptic communication may be used by parents and children and other relatives.

Sexual-arousal touch is the fifth type of touching. Sexual touch is an intense form of touch and plays an important part in intimate relationships. However, sexual-arousal touch is also used in nonintimate relationships and should not be equated with intimacy. The whole notion of one-night stands serves as a reminder that sexually charged tactile communication does not have to involve relational intimacy.

Another classification system for touch distinguishes among the different kinds of body contact. Morris separates body contact into fourteen primary types.[36] Although Morris's system is different from Heslin's intimacy continuum, each of these body-contact types can be associated with Heslin's continuum for the use of touch. Handshakes, body-guides, and pats usually serve social-polite functions. The arm-link, the shoulder embrace, the full embrace, the hand-in-hand, and the mock attack demonstrate friendship-warmth. Love-intimacy touches include the waist embrace, the kiss, the hand-to-head, the head-to-head, the caress, and the body support. Table 5.2 identifies Morris's primary types of body contact along Heslin's intimacy continuum.

Touching can communicate a variety of messages. Although not all people interpret touch in the same way, it allows people to communicate emotion—and the intensity of that emotion—more effectively. You are more likely to touch someone you like than someone you dislike. In fact, withholding touch can communicate negative emotions, while using touch can increase interpersonal attraction and positive perceptions. An exception to this is the *touch avoider*, a person who generally finds touching annoying. This person finds touching discomforting and will recoil from touch. Numerous studies indicate that the touch avoider was taught as a child to associate touching with "not nice" or "bad" behavior and has continued the "nontouching" into adulthood.[37] Studies have found that nontouchers report more anxiety and tension in their lives, less satisfaction with their bodies, and more suspicion of others. Nontouchers are less sociable and more rigid in their beliefs than people who use touch.[38] Touch can have positive or negative effects; it conditions your perceptions and the perceptions of others.

Preferences for touch are also linked to culture. Some cultures depend on touch as an important form of communication, whereas other cultures are less touch sensitive or even tend to avoid touch. For example, Latin American, Mediterranean, and Eastern European cultures rely on touch much more than do Scandinavian and some North American cultures. Which subcultures within the United States are more dependent on touch as a form of communication? Which are less dependent on touch?

What Is Your Touch Index?

What type of touch "index" do you have? Are you repelled by touches from strangers? What about touches from elderly people? Children? Members of the opposite sex? Does it depend on the situation? How so?

Space

Proxemics refers to how you use and communicate with space. One area of proxemics is **personal space**, the space around your body to which you attach ownership. Cultural norms and personal feelings about space will affect your choices about the use of this space.

Hall devised a system of identification for the space used, or spatial zones, based on the type of interpersonal relationship (see Figure 5.1).[39] Hall categorizes spatial zones as

- Intimate (0–18 in.)
- Personal (18 in.–4 ft.)
- Social (4–12 ft.)
- Public (12 ft. and beyond)

The *intimate zone* is reserved for lovers, very close friends, and family members; the *personal zone* is used for close friends and relatives; the *social zone* for professional interactions, such as business transactions or teacher-student conferences, and for casual talks; and the *public zone* for keeping distance between the interactants, such as concert performers with their audience.

Your personal space needs may vary from these general guidelines, but how you feel about allowing another person to be in one of your spaces really depends on who that other person is. Some families are close and use intimate and personal zones exclusively; other families are uncomfortable with that much closeness. Different cultures around the world vary a great deal in their preferences for proxemic closeness. Arab cultures, for example, encourage very close proxemics so that sight, smell, and touch are heightened for communicators.

Although the use of personal space is individualized, some generalizations are possible. Harper and his colleagues found that some personality characteristics influence the use of space.[40] Extroverts require less space than introverts, and highly anxious persons and shy persons prefer greater distances. People with a high need for affiliation or for control will narrow the distance between themselves and others. After researching deviant populations (criminal, schizophrenic, disruptive, and violent individuals), Malandro and Barker discovered that members of these deviant populations require more space and that they depend on that space as a means of protection.[41] In other words, the space requirements for deviants are unusually large for the social norms of the interaction. Regardless of the participants, the spatial distance between communicators must be mutually determined. Concerns for privacy, intimacy, dominance, and status all govern how people position themselves during interactions.[42]

Territoriality is another concept of proxemics. **Territoriality** is the claiming of an area, with or without legal basis, and is most commonly established through continuous occupation of that area. Territories are claimed, staked,

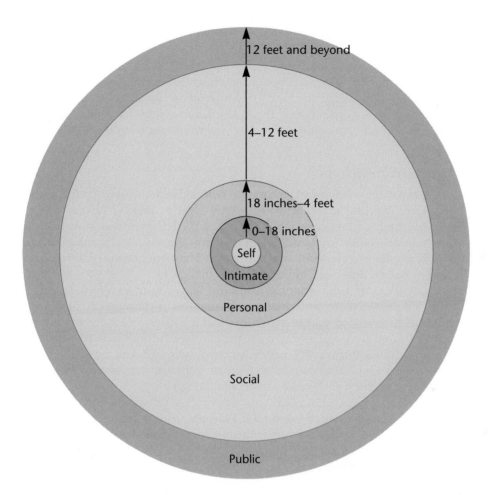

12 feet and beyond

4–12 feet

18 inches–4 feet

0–18 inches

Self

Intimate

Personal

Social

Public

FIGURE 5.1
The four zones of personal space described by Hall indicate ranges that apply across cultures.

and defended by the individuals who occupy them. Some territories that easily come to mind are your home, your car, and your office. But territories also encompass implied ownership of space, such as a favorite living-room chair, a seat in a classroom, a parking space, a "usual" table in a restaurant, or a frequented spot on the beach. When territoriality is encroached upon, it will be defended by its owner, and this defense will utilize nonverbal behavior. The behaviors used in defense are *withdrawal* (retreat from the invader), *insulation* (gestures and body movements to block the invader), and *turf defense* (fighting).

How you arrange objects within your *environment* also communicates a message. In an office, for example, your placement of your desk and chairs conveys your degree of approachability. Objects placed between you and another will inhibit communication and suggest status differential. In addition, seating arrangements imply dominance and subordination. Riess and Rosenfeld found that people choose seats in a group situation to reflect their desires to lead, to avoid interaction, or to show attraction to another. In their study, those who wanted to lead chose seats in a head position; those who wished to avoid interaction chose seats the furthest from others; and those who wanted to show attraction chose seats close to the person whom they found attractive.[43] If you think about some of your own seating choices, you will probably remember making them with a specific reason in mind.

Time Orientations

"Time's up!" "I don't have time." "Where did the time go?" All of these utterances express the importance of time. Clearly, time is a primary force in your life, and it controls much of what you do. How you use your time and how you feel about time send strong nonverbal messages. **Chronemics** refers to how people perceive and structure time. **Time orientations** fall into three categories: psychological, biological, and cultural.

Psychological time orientation is the way you perceive or feel about time. There are three principal applications of psychological time orientation: *Past-oriented* people assign particular value to past events; *present-oriented* people live and work for the present; and *future-oriented* people live and work for the future.[44] A person's orientation will determine the importance that person ascribes to conversation content, the length of the interaction, the urgency of the interaction, and punctuality.[45]

Differences in psychological time orientation can create communication problems. A past-oriented person, for example, will not value punctuality as highly as people of the other orientations might. A present-oriented person will work toward shorter interactions. In each case, the result can be feelings of irritation and impatience that will hinder communication. For example, a past-oriented instructor who keeps a present-oriented student waiting for a scheduled appointment may hinder open or effective communication.

Biological time orientation is determined by biological cycles. This is your "biological clock." It determines when you are most active, both physically and mentally. People who are at their best in the morning are referred to as "sparrows"; those who are at their best in the late afternoon and evening are considered "owls."[46] Biological time affects how you perceive others and how they perceive you and can thus be a source of communication problems. A cheerful sparrow in the morning will perceive an owl's lack of attention negatively, whereas the owl will perceive the sparrow's tiredness in the afternoon in an unfavorable way.

Cultural time orientation is the way a culture uses time. Hall proposes that three time systems operate in any culture: technical (scientific measurement), formal (the culture's system of measuring time), and informal (the casual time of a culture).[47] Formal time involves the way a culture measures, values, and uses time. The phrase "time is money," used extensively in Western cultures, indicates how people value time. Informal time involves

CHRONEMICS

The communicative ability of the use of time.

TIME ORIENTATION

Time preferences that may be psychologically, biologically, or culturally based.

What Time Do You Have?

Which type of psychological time orientation do you have? Do you live in the past, present, or future? Does your time orientation depend on the situation? How so? How does your orientation affect communication with others?

punctuality and duration. For example, most Western cultures find it extremely rude to be late, but in most Latin cultures lateness is the norm. Hall further divides the informal use of time into two types—*monochronic*, which means doing one thing at a time, and *polychronic*, which means doing several things at a time.[48] This, too, varies with culture. Which of these two types of informal time do you believe U.S. culture uses?

Scents and Smells

The perception of scents and smells is referred to as **olfactics**. Although smell is one of the primary senses, it is one of the least researched codes of nonverbal communication. Nonetheless, scents and smells can produce strong reactions and can add intensity to positive or negative perceptions. Consider how bleach stings the eyes and forces people to retreat from the odor. Consider, too, how the aroma of fresh-baked bread brings a pleasant smile. In much the same way, personal scents and smells affect interactions. Offensive odors will increase the distance between interactants and shorten the time of the interaction. Pleasant smells will increase communication with another.[49] Body scents and smells in the environment communicate things to us about others. Our judgments about other people may be influenced by the odors those people allow in their environment.

Attractiveness is associated with scent. Those who smell attractive and pleasing will receive more attention and touch.[50] Not all people prefer the same scents, however. The norms of the culture provide guidelines for distinguishing between offensive and pleasant scents and smells. Western cultures, for example, consider body odor offensive, but many other cultures prefer the natural body scents to perfume. Extremely strong scents, such as those of heavy fragrances, copiously applied perfume, hair spray, and hair permanents, are offensive to most people and can shorten the interactions between people. Other offensive odors include the smell of smoke on clothes and bad breath. Offensive scents are perceived negatively and will often determine whether an interaction is initiated, continued, or terminated.

◆ The Relationship between Nonverbal and Verbal Communication

Nonverbal behavior uses codes to form messages. Even though the different types of nonverbal behavior can communicate meaning by themselves, they are rarely used alone. Rather, they work in conjunction with verbal behavior to form a complete message, or message system.

Nonverbal messages have specific operations within this message system. Ekman defines the functions of nonverbal messages when integrated with verbal communication as complementing, contradicting, repeating, regulating, substituting, and accenting.[51] **Complementing** behavior clarifies the meaning of the verbal message, such as giving a pat on the back while saying

---

The Sweet Smell of Success

What smell(s) do you like most in members of the opposite sex? How about members of the same sex? Why do some real estate agents place cinnamon sticks in a preheated oven before potential clients arrive to view a house on the market?

OLFACTICS
The communicative characteristics of smells.

COMPLEMENTING
Nonverbal behavior that clarifies the meaning of a verbal message.

CONTRADICTING

Nonverbal behavior that conveys a meaning opposite to that of the sender's verbal message.

REPEATING

Nonverbal behavior that mirrors the accompanying verbal message.

REGULATING

Nonverbal behavior that is used to coordinate verbal interaction.

SUBSTITUTING

Nonverbal behavior that replaces the use of words.

ACCENTING

Nonverbal behavior that emphasizes the accompanying verbal message.

"Good job." **Contradicting** behavior indicates the opposite of the verbal message, such as saying "I'll miss you" while smiling and skipping off. **Repeating** behavior is nonverbal behavior that mirrors the verbal message, such as holding up three fingers while saying "three." **Regulating** behavior is used to coordinate verbal interaction, as when one looks directly at another person to signal, "Don't give away the upcoming surprise party." **Substituting** is used to replace words, such as a traffic police officer's outstretched, open hand substituting for the word *stop*. **Accenting** emphasizes the verbal message; someone who pounds his or her fist on the table while saying "no" is engaged in accenting. These functions help to integrate nonverbal behavior and verbal utterances into a complete message system.

◆ Competence Factors

Nonverbal communication constantly (and dramatically) undergoes change, reversal, and modification. The way you perceive and interpret nonverbal behavior is influenced by culture, context, and situation. In order to be a competent communicator, you must be aware of these factors.

Culture

The well-known story of a past president is a good demonstration of why culture is such an important factor to consider in nonverbal communication. In the late 1950s, then-Vice President Richard Nixon made a goodwill tour of Latin America, where there was already a feeling of hostility toward the United States. Of course, the press followed his tour. On one of his stops, Nixon stepped off his airplane and, smiling, gestured with the A-OK sign to the waiting crowd. The crowd booed. The next day, photographs of Nixon and his gesture appeared on the front page of major newspapers. Nixon had made headline news—not for his accomplishments on the tour but for his gesture. In that culture, Nixon's gesture had a completely different meaning; it meant "Screw you!" Days of delicate diplomacy were undone by two seconds of nonverbal behavior![52]

All nonverbal communication is influenced by culture. Social norms are established by cultures, and these norms greatly affect the perceptions of nonverbal behavior. Obviously, gestures have different meanings in different cultures. But the other nonverbal codes are also influenced by culture. Although the expression of primary emotions is universally recognized, how, when, and where these emotions can be displayed are guided by the social rules of the culture. For example, the Japanese are conditioned to mask emotion. Eye behavior also takes different forms; Americans and Canadians use eye contact as a form of acknowledgment or politeness in greeting, but in other cultures, such as those of Nigeria and Puerto Rico, this is often considered disrespectful. Because attractiveness is determined by social norms, appearance preferences change from culture to culture. Anyone who does not fit the physical

"Apparently I have done something to upset you."

Placement of objects within the environment can communicate a strong non-verbal message about approachability.

norms of a culture may have trouble communicating in that culture. Touch is a relevant form of communication in any culture, but again, social norms control where, when, and how touching should occur. British culture is a noncontact culture, whereas French culture is high contact. Proxemics also vary widely among cultures. Arabs and Italians require very close proximity when interacting; Americans place themselves farther apart. The value and use of time differs as well. Polychronic cultures, like those of Latin America, may find the North American monochronic cultures extremely irritating.[53]

Context and Situation

Think about your favorite professor and hold the image of that person in your mind. In the classroom, you have a certain rapport with this professor. Your communication with that person is defined by the classroom setting. Now imagine that you see this same professor at a local restaurant. Your communication would change because you see the professor in a different context. **Context** is the physical and psychological setting of an interaction.

CONTEXT
The physical and psychological setting of an interaction.

Context determines the rules of behavior and the roles people must play. Two of the primary factors involved in context are the public-private dimension and the informal-formal dimension. The *public-private dimension* refers to the degree to which the context is public or private. The invasion of privacy (physically or psychologically) solicits reduced smiles and other adapters such as restless body movements, leaning backward, gaze aversion, and vocal tension. You will be perceived negatively if you interfere with the private context of another.

The *informal-formal dimension* refers to whether the setting is personal or impersonal. This dimension involves various rules of behavior; it also includes social skills. You would be expected to know the social rules governing a formal dinner, a wedding, a funeral, and so on. The formality of a setting can be recognized by the environment, seating arrangements, punctuality expected, absence of touch, and attire.[54]

Once again, think about seeing your favorite professor in the restaurant. Along with the context, the situation would influence your communication. If the professor was having a birthday party with a group of loud, boisterous friends, you might wave in greeting, raise your glass in a toast, or display exaggerated expressions of surprise. But your behavior would change markedly if your professor was enjoying a quiet, intimate dinner.

SITUATION

A sequence of events that has a unifying goal.

The **situation** is a sequence of events that has some unifying goal. How you behave depends on the situation. Situations can be evaluated according to the dimensions of emotional responses:

- *Pleasure-displeasure* The extent to which you feel happy, satisfied, sad, or annoyed

- *Dominance-submissiveness* The extent to which you feel important and in control, or weak and restricted

- *Arousal-nonarousal* The extent to which you feel active, stimulated, responsive, sluggish, or inattentive[55]

These dimensions are used to judge social situations. For example, in your favorite class you might be alert and responsive (arousal-nonarousal) and contented (pleasure-displeasure) but restricted (dominance-submissiveness). You would modify your nonverbal behavior to accommodate the situation. Rather than waving, you would raise your hand, and you would not raise your coffee cup to toast the professor! The same dimensions affect the appraisal of other social situations.

◆ Functions

As you know from Chapter 1, functions are the purposes or outcomes of communication. Nonverbal communication accomplishes a variety of functions, namely, relationship management, interaction management, social influence, deception, and self-promotion.

Relationship Management

Relationships are delicate and fragile bonds, and as such they are always susceptible to destruction. For this reason, it is important to know how nonverbal communication functions to manage relationships. Nonverbal behaviors affect the depth (or felt closeness) of a relationship, establish partner support, and control conflict. As one study showed, there is a relationship between certain nonverbal behaviors and relational message themes.[56] Personal space was the most important cue in revealing intentions. Intimacy is expressed by close personal distance, direct eye contact, leaning forward, smiling, and touch. The absence of touch, a lack of smiling, and a backward leaning demonstrate detachment. Nonverbal cues can also convey a *desire* for intimacy.[57] For example, personal proximity and touches such as the kiss, caress, and waist embrace are usually associated with intimate relationships, so using these behaviors can convey to another a desire for intimacy.

Another factor influencing nonverbal communication and relationships is liking. Change your mental image of the professor in the restaurant to an image of a professor whom you don't particularly like. As liking changes, the relationship changes, and thus communication changes. Less eye contact, smaller gestures, and greater distance indicate less liking, whereas more eye contact, less distance, more touching (perhaps a handshake), and longer interaction are indicative of liking. Your relationships to others are not defined simply by liking, however; they can also be defined by status, gender, or age. These relational dimensions have a strong impact on nonverbal communication. Status differences, for example, are communicated through nonverbal behavior. Clothing is a symbol of status and can convey socioeconomic status and satisfaction. The higher-status person has a more relaxed posture, expresses emotions through facial expressions more freely, has more and better space, initiates touch, and often abuses time (see Table 5.3 on p. 150).

Gender is another way in which relationships are defined, and each gender has some unique characteristics of nonverbal communication. Differences might include the following: Men require more space, women establish more eye contact, men use more gestures, women smile more, men touch more, and women speak more softly.[58] The differences in liking, status, gender, age, and stage of a relationship play an important role in determining what nonverbal behaviors are displayed and how those behaviors will be interpreted.

Interaction Management

The nonverbal behaviors people use to manage interactions are so ingrained that most of the time we are not conscious of their existence. However, nonverbal cues are vital in the management of greetings, conversations, and departures.

Greetings signal the beginning of an interaction. Nonverbal behaviors during greetings can establish status differences, intimacy levels, or attitudes. Goffman proposed an attenuation rule, which states that the emotional

Greetings!

What is the strangest greeting you have ever received? Was touch involved? How did you react?

TABLE 5.3 STATUS INDICATORS	
POWER AND HIGH-STATUS INDICATORS	POWERLESSNESS AND LOW-STATUS INDICATORS
Relaxed posture and body position	Erect and rigid posture and body position
Less attentive to others	More attentive to others
More expansiveness	More restrictiveness
Seated position	Standing position
Dark, conservative suit	Light suit or strange clothing
Tall stature	Short stature
More access to space	Less access to space
Finger pointing	Receipt of finger pointing
Less direct body orientation	More direct orientation toward superiors
Closed arm position	Open body orientation
Giving less/receiving more eye gaze	Receiving less/giving more eye gaze
Sarcastic smiling/laughing	Respectful smiling/laughing
Touches others more/touched less by others	Touches others less/touched more by others
Makes others wait	Waits for others (superiors)
Determines meeting time and length	Told of meeting time and length
More flexible time schedule	Rigorous and strict time schedule
Expensive office furniture	Economical office furniture
Larger office in nicer and more private location	Office location dependent on job duties

Source: Adapted from D. O'Hair, G. W. Friedrich, & L. D. Shauer (1995), *Strategic communication in business and the professions* (2nd ed.) (Boston: Houghton Mifflin), p. 132.

intensity of a greeting with another will gradually subside with continual contact.[59] Greetings can be complicated. Kendon and Ferber describe six stages of greetings: (1) sighting, orientation, and initiation of approach (acknowledgment of the other's presence); (2) the distant salutation (a wave); (3) the head dip (lowered head); (4) approach (eye contact and open body position); (5) the final approach (less than 10 feet, mutual gaze, and smiling); and (6) close salutation (verbalizations, such as "Hi!").[60]

TABLE 5.4 NONVERBAL COMMUNICATION AND MANAGEMENT OF TURN-TAKING		
TURN-TAKING FUNCTION	**DESCRIPTION**	**NONVERBAL BEHAVIORS**
Turn yielding	Giving up the floor	Extended pauses and gazes
Turn maintaining	Maintaining control of the floor	Touching, filled pauses
Turn requesting	Requesting the floor	Rapid nods, vocalizations
Turn denying	Denying control of the floor	Silence, avoidance of eye contact

Greetings are normally initiated by a vertical or sideways motion of the head accompanied by eye contact and smiling. Smiling indicates a positive mood, and eye contact conveys the willingness to communicate. Body movement and gestures are also used extensively in greetings.

Greetings can then lead to conversation. Nonverbal **turn-taking behaviors** are employed during conversation to ensure speaking turns. Nonverbal cues are used to display our intentions (see Table 5.4). The exchange of turns during a conversation is a mutual process between speaker and listener, and the nonverbal cues facilitate the turn-taking sequence. Nonverbal behaviors can also alter the conversational topic. The listener's restlessness, shown by shifting or looking away and fidgeting, will convey his or her boredom with the topic.[61]

Nonverbal cues are also used to terminate interactions. Leave-taking behaviors include looking at one's watch, rapid head nods, increased body motion, and the production of sound, such as tapping one's fingers on the desk.[62]

Social Influence

Whether you are selling a product, asking a friend for money, or proposing marriage to your lover, you are engaged in persuasion, or social influence. **Social influence** occurs when one person's actions cause changes in another's thoughts and behaviors.[63] Nonverbal behaviors add power to persuasion. Whereas cues used in the other functions are often unintentional, behaviors used in social influence are intentional. Communicators select their behaviors to influence others. Nonverbal messages that project images of power, authority, and credibility add to the communicator's persuasiveness. Dress can depict authority and credibility; proper attire for the

TURN-TAKING BEHAVIORS

Nonverbal cues used during conversation to ensure speaking turns; include turn yielding, turn maintaining, turn requesting, and turn denying.

SOCIAL INFLUENCE

A process in which one person's actions cause changes in another's thoughts and behaviors.

situation produces positive perceptions of authority. In most cases, lavish dress will generate feelings of distrust. Physical appearance is manipulated to achieve attractiveness, for attractive people are generally better persuaders. Other behaviors that affect positive perceptions of credibility are similar voice qualities, direct eye contact, and open body orientations. Cues that increase affiliation and liking can also aid in social influence. Behaviors that increase liking include increased eye contact, the use of gestures, and increased smiling. However, a constant smile is viewed as insincere.[64]

In interpersonal relationships, communicators employ behaviors that reciprocate (via similar patterns) or compensate (via opposite patterns) the nonverbal cues of the other in order to change the other's behavior.[65] The Burgoon study found that persuasiveness is most directly affected by the following nonverbal behaviors:[66]

- *Vocal pleasantness* Vocal fluency, pitch variety, vocal clarity
- *Kinesic/proxemic immediacy* Eye contact, moderate proximity, smiling/facial pleasantness
- *Kinesic dominance* Facial expressiveness, illustrators
- *Kinesic relaxation* Self-adapters, object adapters, body tension, random trunk and limb movement

Deception

One of the striking differences between a cat and a lie is that a cat only has nine lives.

—Mark Twain

Everyone has experienced deception. It would be nearly impossible to find someone who has neither lied nor been lied to. Although it has negative connotations, deception constitutes a major portion of communication. In fact, depending on which survey you consult, most people will admit that they have lied in the last few months.[67] Several nonverbal behaviors have been identified with deception. A change in the amount of eye contact is one indication. You are usually aware of how much someone you know makes eye contact with you while talking. If the acquaintance's eye behavior changes, it could be an indication of deception. Avoiding eye contact by looking down or away has been associated with lying. Similarly suspect is staring behavior: Liars may consciously try to control detection of deception by virtually never breaking eye contact.[68] Deceivers engage in more leg and foot movements and shift posture more than honest people do. Liars tend to tap their feet nervously, swing their legs, or squirm in their chairs. Stress-related behaviors are another indication of deception.[69]

One of the best identifiers of a liar is voice pitch; vocal pitch has a tendency to rise when one is telling a lie, and it is not easily controlled by the deceiver.[70] Another physical characteristic that the deceiver cannot control is pupil dilation; the pupils have been found to dilate during lying.[71] Other nonverbal cues that have been consistently linked with deceivers are blinking, speech errors and hesitations (stammering, problems with pronunciation, unusually long pauses between words or sentences), and channel discrepancies. A **channel discrepancy** is the use of two or more channels to send contradictory or inconsistent messages. Examples include saying "I'm not nervous" while one's hands are shaking, and saying "I love you" with a smirk on one's face. When faced with channel discrepancies, most people believe the nonverbal rather than the verbal cues.

CHANNEL
DISCREPANCY
The use of two or more channels to send contradictory messages.

The deceiver's cues are affected by his or her personality, motivation, planning, and age. Nonverbal behaviors vary according to whether the deceiver has prepared a lie or is relating a spontaneous lie. The deceiver who is delivering prepared lies will show greater anxiety, arousal, and stress because the deceiver has had time to worry about the outcome of the lie. O'Hair, Cody, and McLaughlin found that deceivers in prepared lies answered questions more quickly, nodded more, smiled less, and displayed more body adapters than did truth-tellers. The *prepared lies* are usually short because the deceiver does not want to reveal too much information. *Spontaneous lies*, produced on short notice, will solicit nonverbal behaviors such as rubbing and scratching. When a deceiver falsifies information (lying about factual data), more head movements can occur.[72]

Deceivers are often aware of the nonverbal behaviors associated with lying and may try to mask these behaviors. The cues thought to be indicative of lying are leg and foot movements, illustrators, adapters, and postural shifts. In an attempt to reduce these cues, the deceiver may become abnormally rigid or stiff. Therefore, sometimes the best evidence of deception is not an increase or decrease of nonverbal behaviors but a deviation from the deceiver's normal behavior.

Forming Impressions

You may have been told since childhood that inner beauty has more value than physical beauty, that goodness is in the heart, and that it is what's inside that counts. But judgments and inferences are made at the beginning of a relationship or interaction, not after many detailed encounters. In fact, if you make a negative first impression, more than likely you will not have the chance to reveal your inner beauty. Thus, impressions play a significant role in how you relate to others, and nonverbal behavior is the predominant influence on the formation of impressions. The following principles control how you form impressions:[73]

Deception Cues

What has your experience taught you to be reliable "cues" of deception? Do you know some people who express consistent nonverbal cues when you think they are lying? What about you? What cues do you communicate when you tell a lie?

• You develop evaluations of others based on limited external information. Lack of personal information about another and the uncertainty of the situation cause you to form opinions.[74]

- Impressions are based partly on the stereotypes you hold. Common stereotypes include those based on skin color, hair, body shape and size, and age. Stereotypical traits are preconceived by the interactants.
- First impressions are often based on outward appearance, since physical appearance information is readily available.
- Initial impressions form a baseline of comparison for subsequent impressions and judgments and may affect future interactions.

Impressions consist of judgments you make on three levels: physical, sociocultural, and psychological. Physical judgments consist of evaluations about age, gender, and body shape and size. These judgments are readily noticeable, though not always completely accurate. This category does not include personality traits or character judgments but rather demographic information (male or female, general age, etc.). Appearance and vocal cues are the most important influence on these judgments.

Sociocultural judgments are made about socioeconomic status, residence, occupation, education, and group membership. Clothing is a symbol of status, and perceptions of success and education are based on dress. A person dressed in a business suit will be perceived as having more status than someone in jeans. In addition, hairstyle is associated with success. Short hair is viewed as professional for both men and women and is associated with intelligence and corporate status.[75] Dress and artifacts, whether they be T-shirts or rosary beads, also designate group membership.

Psychological judgments are judgments of personality, character, and mood. Physical features are exceptionally vulnerable to these inferences, and most stereotypes are derived from the psychological judgments of physical features. Character analyses based on skin color, body shape and size, hair color, and age are commonplace—thus the frequent stereotyping of redheads as hot-tempered, heavy people as lazy, and elderly people as slow-witted.

*E*thics and the Real You

What are the ethics involved in trying to create an impression that is not really "you"? How many of the behaviors just discussed do you use to get people to think positively of you? How successful have you been in creating positive impressions of yourself? Do you worry that giving a false impression will come back to haunt you later? Think of some examples in which other people have managed their nonverbal behaviors to create a false positive impression. What is your opinion of these people?

Vocal qualities are also stereotyped: Soft-spoken people may be viewed as passive, breathiness as sexy, and people with orotund voices as lively and gregarious. Even if they are inaccurate, such perceptions may affect interactions. For example, a business executive who has a small body frame may not be perceived as powerful in a meeting; an anchor who is soft-spoken on the evening news may not be perceived as credible; and an elderly public speaker may be perceived as boring.

Managing behavior so that others will have positive impressions is called impression management, or **self-promotion**. Several techniques can be employed to increase the formation of positive impressions. These behaviors include smiling, mutual gaze, increased gestures, relaxed body positions, leaning forward, head nods, variations in vocal pitch and range, close proximity, and increased touch.[76]

SELF-PROMOTION
Presentation of the self in a way that will create a favorable impression in others.

◆ Competent Nonverbal Communication

Nonverbal communication affects every interaction, every relationship, and every dimension of your life. It can destroy careers (e.g., when a businessperson touches a colleague inappropriately), elevate relationships (e.g., when congratulations are expressed by a handshake or a pat on the back), or determine future interactions (e.g., when an appropriate greeting is used in a foreign culture). As a competent communicator, you must remain aware of how nonverbal communication manages relationships, controls interactions, persuades, deceives, and forms impressions. You should take into consideration all the variables that can modify the message: culture, context, situation, and the relational dimension. Admittedly, this is an overwhelming task, but before you leave this chapter grumbling with frustration, remember the skills you have already developed. You can recognize the primary emotions, and you know, at least in your own culture, the socially acceptable behavioral rules. You now have the knowledge you need to enhance those skills and to understand their underlying implications.

One ingredient not mentioned previously is as much a part of nonverbal communication as any other factor—individuality. Nonverbal behavior is not always transmitted by the same channels, received with the intended message, or sent with explicit meaning. Individuals differ in the codes they use, how they use them, and the messages they apply to them. The variety of messages and ways to communicate those messages are infinite. That is one of the fascinating aspects of nonverbal communication. Individual differences, preferences, and variations of behavior should be enjoyed. An appreciation of nonverbal behaviors that are culturally different from our own enriches our communication experience and enhances our competence. The competent communicator recognizes the importance of individual expression.

The Case of Edie and John

At the beginning of this chapter we met Edie and John, a young couple anticipating marriage. They come from somewhat different family backgrounds—Edie from a large Catholic, Italian-American family where her mother worked at home; John from a home where he was raised as an only child by his divorced mother. Consider the following questions as you reflect on this couple and the content of the chapter.

• How important will nonverbal communication be for the development of their relationship? Why do you think so?

• Which of the nonverbal codes are likely to be most important? Least important? Why?

• How do you think the functions of nonverbal communication (e.g., relationship management, interaction management) will develop for Edie and John?

• Which of the nonverbal functions do you think will pose the greatest challenge to the couple? Which the least?

REVIEW

• Nonverbal communication is a system of codes used to send messages. Two perspectives suggest that these messages are developed from innate and learned behaviors.

• The nonverbal codes used to send and receive messages include appearance and artifacts, gestures and body movements, facial expressions and eye behavior, paralanguage, touch, space, time orientation, and scents and smells.

• Perceptions of personality traits are often linked to body type, clothing orientation, and artifacts. Kinesic behavior includes emblems, illustrators, regulators, adapters, and affect displays.

• Facial expressions and eye behavior primarily convey emotional states. Paralanguage includes voice qualities and vocalizations.

• The types of touch include functional-professional, social-polite, friendship-warmth, love-intimacy, and sexual-arousal.

• Proxemics includes personal space and territoriality. There are three categories for time orientation: psychological, biological, and cultural.

• Scents and smells are associated with perceptions. These nonverbal cues are affected by and changed according to culture, context, and situation.

• The functions, or outcomes, of nonverbal communication include relational management, interaction management, social influence, deception, and forming impressions. Nonverbal codes work in conjunction with each other to serve these functions.

• Relationship management illustrates messages regarding intimacy or status. Intimacy is expressed by less personal distance, direct eye contact, smiling, and touch. Status can be conveyed through clothing, open body position, access to space, and use of time.

• Interaction functions regulate greetings and turn-taking in conversations. Cues that increase immediacy and liking, such as increased eye contact, gestures, and attractiveness, aid in social influence.

• Deception can be detected by a change in eye contact, a higher voice pitch, pupil dilation, and stress-related behaviors.

• Self-promotion includes first impressions and impression management. Impressions consist of judgments on physical, sociocultural, and psychological levels.

• Nonverbal cues affect how you will be perceived by others. However, individual preferences and diversity in nonverbal messages should be appreciated as they are part of what makes each person unique.

Developing
Listening Skills

After reading this chapter, you should be able to:

1. Define the process of listening.

2. Explain the costs of ineffective listening and the rewards of competent listening.

3. Describe the four functions of listening.

4. List the components involved in managing listening skills.

5. Discuss the effects of context on listening competence.

6. Describe how listeners can adjust to speakers.

7. Identify the steps involved in critical listening.

8. Explain how interactive listening is critical to competent listening.

SHEILA GREENSTEIN, born and raised in New York, is a new student at the University of Missouri's School of Journalism. In her first semester at UM, she applied for and was chosen to be a reporter for the student paper. Her editor has asked her to report on a university-sponsored speech by Black Nationalist Louis Farrakhan, the organizer of the Million Man March, which occurred in 1995 in Washington, D.C. Ms. Greenstein believes that Mr. Farrakhan is anti-Semitic and a purveyor of hate speech. She has reluctantly agreed to report on the event, but she does not know how she will be able to maintain "objectivity".

As you read this chapter, consider the relevance of its content to Sheila's task. We will return to this scenario at the end of the chapter.

◆ Listening: The Least Developed Communication Skill

Most people think that they are adequate listeners. Consequently, the improvement of listening is a low priority. In reality, however, most of us are ineffective listeners. This chapter describes the basic skills of effective listening and presents techniques you can use to build more effective listening skills.

A Definition of Listening

LISTENING

The process of recognizing, understanding, and accurately interpreting the messages communicated by others.

Many definitions have been proposed for the term **listening.** This book approaches listening from a competency perspective. Listening is the process of recognizing, understanding, and accurately interpreting the messages communicated by others. Competent listening involves a complex process of cognitive, behavioral, and affective skills. It is much more than just hearing words. A framework for competent listening is developed in later sections to demonstrate how important listening is to your well-being.

One way to describe the listening process is to examine how frequently you actually listen. Research studies report that high school and college students spend from 42 to 54 percent of their waking hours listening.[1] Research surveys of Fortune 500 company personnel reveal that listening is one of the most important skills that a college graduate can possess. If you think about it, the time you spend listening to your professors, other students, family members, friends, radio, and television consumes a very large part of your day. Listening could even be your most common activity.

Some people consider listening a passive activity that simply "happens to them." These are often the same people who must have information and instructions repeated to them.

In 1957, Ralph Nichols, one of the pioneers of listening research, reported in *Nation's Business* that the average businessperson listened at only a 25 percent efficiency rate. Recent surveys of top U.S. companies report that listening efficiency rates are still low. Most of these studies have focused on informational listening, but the emotional aspect of messages is also often ignored. Stewart suggests that listeners are oblivious to almost 100 percent of the feelings communicated in messages and that they ignore or misunderstand 75 percent of the informational content. [2]

The Costs of Ineffective Listening

In this chapter, we can only begin to describe the great costs that result from ineffective listening. Judges grieve about the injustices perpetrated on the judicial system when jurors or lawyers do not listen well. Businesspeople are outraged by the economic costs associated with listening errors. And patients constantly complain about the poor listening habits of physicians.

Ineffective listening does exact many costs; understanding the nature of these costs will help you to develop more effective listening skills. **Listening costs** take many forms, but they have been categorized in four areas: economic, physical, emotional, and psychological.

Economic and Physical Costs. You may know of an instance in which an unsuspecting, poor listener agreed to purchase a condominium share on a payout plan of 5 years. This person had no intention of becoming involved with a profit-sharing investment but made the commitment because of poor listening habits. This kind of business mistake can be very expensive. One source has estimated that businesses lose millions of dollars each year because of listening mistakes alone.[3] These costs take the form of repeated or duplicated tasks, missed opportunities, lost clients, botched orders, misunderstood instructions, and missed appointments.

The physical costs associated with poor listening can create significant problems. When tasks must be repeated or redone, fatigue can take its toll on an ineffective listener. Listening errors can also have serious immediate effects. For example, a mother was nervous that her daughter was very ill from influenza. When the physician prescribed a liquid antibiotic at a dosage of "one ounce to be taken four times a day," the mother thought she heard "four ounces once a day." When her daughter developed complications from the overdose, the mother realized that her listening error had created a physical cost.

Emotional and Psychological Costs. Have you ever been frustrated with someone for not listening carefully to you? Frustrations are one of the most common emotional costs associated with incompetent listening. "Why do I waste my time if he is not going to listen?" "Why bother trying to explain myself if she ignores what I say?" In addition to frustration, poor listeners can annoy and anger those around them. A clerical worker was fired when he failed to respond to an order by an angry superior.

One of the costliest results of poor listening is the effect it has on self-concept. If you find that you often make mistakes, cause errors, and create problems for yourself and other people, you may begin to question your value, without even knowing why. Whether or not you actually recognize it as your problem, the costs associated with ineffective listening will lower your self-image.

The Rewards of Competent Listening

So far, a dreary picture has been painted of how ineffective listening can cause you grief. Just the opposite is true of effective, competent listening. The **listening rewards** that come to competent listeners are many; we will briefly discuss three broad categories of benefits.

How Are Your Listening Skills?

Have you been charged a fee or gotten a bad grade because you missed important information? Have you misunderstood something to such a degree that only upon reflection did you realize the opportunity you missed? These are the kinds of questions you must ask yourself in order to determine whether you need to improve your listening skills.

LISTENING COSTS
Direct and indirect penalties associated with poor listening; can be economic, physical, emotional, or psychological.

LISTENING REWARDS
Benefits of competent listening, such as saving time, enhanced relationships, and professional advancement.

Frustrations are one of the most common emotional costs associated with incompetent listening.

Time Benefits. Competent listeners save a great deal of time and can lead more productive lives. When you listen competently to someone giving you directions to a hotel to attend a meeting, you do not have to go early to make sure that you can find the place. Or, if someone tells you about a shortcut in registering for classes, you can save time enrolling in school. Businesspeople save themselves and their companies time when they act quickly and accurately on information presented to them. Time is a non-renewable resource, and good listening helps you to make the most of it.

Relationship Benefits. One of the skills that people in healthy and committed relationships most often praise in their partners is sensitive listening. Strong interpersonal relationships are built on competent listening. For example, when one partner self-discloses to the other, competent listening facilitates an appropriate response. When one person in a relationship needs empathy from the other, competent listening supplies this important need. Competent listeners become trusted friends and enjoy a variety of relationships.

MIRIAM   I get nervous and tongue-tied every time I audition for a new part in front of an unfamiliar director.

NORA   You know, I've been a struggling actress for 10 years, and there's no simple remedy.

MIRIAM   Are you telling me this feeling of anxiety never ceases?

NORA   Well, confidence and practice help. I'm free this evening, if you'd like to review your lines.

As you noticed from the preceding interaction, Nora not only listened as a friend, but she also provided supportive statements to Miriam, a sure sign of effective listening.

Professional Benefits. We have already mentioned some of the economic and professional costs associated with poor listening. On the positive side of this process, competent listening is valued and rewarded professionally. In the business world, good listeners are seen as alert, confident, mature, and judicious—qualities that can result in professional rewards. A successful businessman explained to one of the authors of this book why he has repeatedly promoted a particular young manager ahead of her older, more experienced colleagues. "Denise makes me realize that she is absorbing everything I have to say. I never worry about her leaving my office with a misunderstanding." In today's fiercely competitive economic and financial climate, competent listening is one of the advantages that can give individuals and companies the edge. Listening to clients, customers, suppliers, subordinates, co-workers, managers, and economic advisors is required of everyone.

◆ The Functions of Listening

Listening needs vary. In some situations, you need to listen for information; in others, you must listen for ideas, uderstanding, emotions, or enjoyment. In other words, you don't listen the same way in every situation. Rather, you listen according to your needs. Four types of **listening functions** are the focus of this section.[4]

Comprehensive Listening

The type of listening used to undertand the message of another person is **comprehensive listening**. It is basic to your existence because you could not accomplish very much if you did not understand the information, ideas, and opinions communicated by other people. You use comprehensive listening a great deal in class as you try to understand what the instructor is presenting. A person giving you directions, someone providing instructions, or an individual recounting an experience all require comprehensive listening. It is one of the most important listening skills.

Empathic Listening

Listening to people with openness, sensitivity, and caring constitutes **empathic listening**. If you listen with empathy, you are attempting to know how the other person feels at the time. This type of listening can provide emotional support for someone in need, so it sometimes functions as therapy. Empathic listening can also serve to comfort a person when disaster or disappointment has struck, as when you are sensitive to a friend's story of a failing grade. People in love engage in empathic listening when they are exchanging deep thoughts about their relationship. They want each other to understand the feelings involved. Empathic listening makes life more satisfying for many people.

A Listening Balance Sheet

Form a group in your communication class and brainstorm about personal examples when (1) poor listening caused costs, and (2) competent listening produced rewards. Discuss with your group how some of the skills involved in the competent listening examples could be used to improve the outcomes in the poor listening examples.

LISTENING FUNCTIONS
Different types of listening that satisfy different needs.

COMPREHENSIVE LISTENING
Listening in order to understand the message of another person.

EMPATHIC LISTENING
Listening to people with an open, sensitive, and caring ear.

Critical Listening

CRITICAL LISTENING

Listening in order to evaluate or analyze information, evidence, ideas, or opinions.

When you listen in order to evaluate or analyze information, evidence, ideas, or opinions, you are engaged in **critical listening.** Critical listening involves making a judgment about the nature of a message. You may hear something on television that you find difficult to believe, or you may listen to a political speaker on the radio and suspect that the person is just trying to win votes. These are examples of critical listening. You may even find classroom material to be suspicious. If you listen with an evaluative posture, you are listening critically. This type of listening is very valuable when you cannot take a message at face value.

Appreciative Listening

APPRECIATIVE LISTENING

Listening in order to appreciate the sounds received by one's listening mechanism.

The fourth fuction of listening involves listening enjoyment. **Appreciative listening** is used when your goal is simply to appreciate the sounds that your listening mechanism receives. Listening to music, poetry, narrations, comedy routines, plays, movies, or television shows for sheer enjoyment would qualify as appreciative listening situations. Some people find this type of listening so important that they actually schedule time to do it. Appreciative listening can help to relieve stress, unclutter the mind, and refresh the senses. Some doctors think that playing soft music while patients wait for

---

*F*ocusing on Ethics

We all encounter situations in which one type of listening function turns into another during the course of a conversation. Assume the role of a woman whose friend is telling her about a problem that she has. You will probably be listening at the empathic level, because you want to provide comfort and sympathy for your friend. Obviously, she is expecting you to listen empathically. However, as you listen to the friend talk about how her ex-husband has been telling stories about her love affairs to the judge who can adjust child-support payments, you begin to shift your listening to a critical function. This shift occurs because you know that your friend did indeed cheat on her husband while they were married. In fact, she had an affair with someone you occasionally dated, and you have never forgotten this fact. You eventually realize that you have almost shifted into an appreciative listening mode, thinking that your friend probably deserves her fate. Of course, your friend did not expect you to listen critically or appreciatively to her problem. Is it ethical to use listening functions that are different from what the speaker is expecting?

TABLE 6.1 FUNCTIONS OF LISTENING

TYPE	DESCRIPTION	STRATEGIES
Comprehensive	Listening to understand, learn, realize, or recognize.	Listen for main ideas or details; listen for organizational pattern; take speaker's perspective; use memory effectively.
Empathic	Listening to provide therapy, comfort, and sympathy.	Focus on speaker's perspective; give supportive and understanding feedback; show caring; demonstrate patience; avoid judgment; focus on speaker's goal.
Critical	Listening to judge, analyze, or evaluate.	Determine speaker's goal; evaluate source of message; question logic, reasoning, and evidence of message.
Appreciative	Listening for enjoyment of what is being presented.	Remove physical and time distractions; know more about source (e.g., artist, composer); explore new appreciative listening opportunities.

appointments helps to relax them. Table 6.1 lists the four listening functions, accompanied by descriptions of each and of ways they can best be applied.

◆ Develop Competent Listening Skills

Improving listening competency is a process. It begins with a commitment to become a more effective listener and extends to developing the listening skills needed to achieve that goal.

In order to become a more competent listener, you must make a *commitment* to improve. This requires making an adjustment in your attitudes. You should not be satisfied with your current listening abilities. Remember the rewards associated with competent listening (and the costs related to poor listening).

Most people are not interested in a mediocre life. They want good friends, a loving family, and a rewarding career. All of these goals are within your reach when you make a commitment to improve your listening skills.

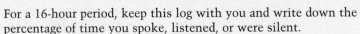

*Y*our Communication Log

For a 16-hour period, keep this log with you and write down the percentage of time you spoke, listened, or were silent.

Time	Activity	% Time Speaking	% Time Listening	% Time Silent
8:00 A.M.				
9:00				
10:00				
11:00				
12:00 noon				
1:00 P.M.				
2:00				
3:00				
4:00				
5:00				
6:00				
7:00				
8:00				
9:00				
10:00				
11:00				
12:00 midnight				

Adjust Your Listening/Speaking Ratio

One of the oldest and most frequently recommended suggestions for improving listening is to stop talking. Of course, this is easier said than done, especially when you have important things to say. It is recommended that you assess your listening-to-talking ratio to see if you talk excessively. You can do this by keeping a communication log that tracks the time you speak and listen. After completing the log, ask yourself the following questions: Were you surprised at your ratio? During what activities did you notice that you needed to listen more than you did? Are there times when you are listening and you should, instead, be providing information or opinions? The log is an excellent tool for profiling when and where you do most of your talking and listening. It is a barometer of who you are as a communicator.

If you find that your speaking-to-listening ratio is too high on the speaking side, there are a couple of things you can do. First, stop talking! Just don't say as much as you normally would. You will be surprised at how much you can learn by remaining silent. Second, maybe the time you spend talking can be better used asking questions, giving support, and providing clarification, all of which increase your chances for listening.

A Process for Improvement

To become a better listener, you must realize that listening is a communication skill, and communication skills are mastered by study, concentration, and practice. This chapter will provide you with a basis for starting that training.

It is also critical to understand that listening is more than just hearing. Hearing is an audiological sequence that involves mostly involuntary physiological processes, much like breathing or the senses of sight and smell. Your capacity for hearing is only part of your ability to listen. There are many audible sounds that you hear, but listening to them is a different story. The point is, you must have good hearing to listen effectively, but hearing is only the beginning of the process.

The good news about listening is that it is a skill that can be improved. Now that you have made the commitment to improve your listening, here is a framework that will help you. This framework involves a five-step process leading to the goal of competent listening:

- Manage your skills.
- Manage the context.
- Adjust to the speaker.
- Listen critically.
- Listen interactively.

The remainder of the chapter will discuss this five-step process in detail.

◆ Manage Your Skills

Assess Your Listening Self-Concept

As you recall from the model of competent communication, self-concept is an important aspect of communication. How you think of yourself affects your motivations, goals, attitudes, and even skills. Some people have a clear

Your Listening Self-Concept

This exercise is designed to help you assess your listening self-concept. In answering the questions, remember to trust your initial reactions because only by doing so can you evaluate yourself accurately.

For each statement, determine whether you strongly agree (SA), agree (A), don't know or have no opinion (?), disagree (D), or strongly disagree (SD), and check the appropriate box.

Question	SA	A	?	D	SD	Score
1. I interrupt others too frequently.						
2. I am not able to respond effectively to others' messages.						
3. I am effective at showing others that I understand what they are saying.						
4. I get apathetic when boring people talk to me.						
5. Sometimes I expect too much of myself when listening to others.						
6. My mind wanders when people talk to me.						
7. I am easily distracted by extraneous sounds when I listen to others.						
8. I am effective at asking questions when I think I don't understand someone.						
9. I maintain good eye contact when I listen to others.						
10. Sometimes I have to have information repeated to me.						
11. I have been told that I am a good listener.						
12. I am comfortable listening to other people's problems.						

idea of their own listening skills; other people don't give listening much thought at all. Obviously, the **listening self-concept** varies from person to person. Those who think they listen poorly may actually have average listening skills, while those who believe they listen well may possess only moderate skills.

LISTENING SELF-CONCEPT

The image one has of oneself as a listener.

Question	SA	A	?	D	SD	Score
13. I can immediately grasp the main point or idea that a speaker is trying to make.						
14. I have good hearing.						
15. It is sometimes difficult for me to understand someone when other people are talking at the same time.						
16. I am often overconfident of my listening abilities.						
17. I have a good memory for what people have said.						
18. I consider myself to be an effective listener.						
19. I can tell when people are listening carefully to what I am saying.						
20. I am a much better listener in some situations than in others.						
					Total Score:	

Scoring: Place the score for each item in the right-hand box labeled *Score.* For items 1, 2, 4, 5, 6, 7, 10, 15, and 16, use the following scale: SA = 1; A = 2; ? = 3; D = 4; and SD = 5. For items 3, 8, 9, 11, 12, 13, 14, 17, 18, 19, and 20, use the following scale: SA = 5; A = 4; ? = 3; D = 2; and SD = 1.

Add up all of the scores and write the total score in the box provided. The higher your score, the higher your listening self-concept. If you scored between 50 and 70, you have an average listening self-concept. If you scored above this (70–100), you have a favorable listening self-concept. If you scored below this (20–50), you have an unfavorable listening self-concept. You can improve a low listening self-concept through work and practice that focus on developing your potential as a listener. The rest of this chapter can help you achieve this goal.

LISTENING
SELF-ASSESSMENT
*The evaluation of
one's own listening
abilities and skills.*

We should point out that self-concept is only one aspect of **listening self-assessment**, that is, evaluating your overall listening competence. Your actual listening skills may exceed or not measure up to your evaluation of yourself as a listener.

Recognize Your Listening Barriers

LISTENING BARRIERS
*Factors that interfere
with competent
listening, such
as boredom, day-
dreaming, over-
confidence, laziness,
apprehension, and
defensiveness.*

Many people have **listening barriers** that they would like to change, while others have poor listening habits that they do not even recognize. Jill often finds herself inattentive when she thinks she already has enough information. Yoko, on the other hand, thinks that her greatest barrier to competent listening is being distracted by thoughts of other conversations. Fernando's ego is so large that he perceives himself as a totally competent listener!

Listening habits become so routine that they often operate below the level of consciousness. When this happens, the best way to change undesirable habits is to recognize them. This section discusses some of the more common listening barriers that plague college students. Do you have some of these habits?

Boredom and Daydreaming. In some situations you think that listening is a waste of your time. It may be that you have underestimated your expectations, or you may not think that a particular listening situation is worth the effort. Neglect can also result from a preoccupation with other listening situations. When this happens, you are likely to listen only halfheartedly or to ignore the person altogether. How many times have you said to yourself, "Oh, I really don't want to listen to that man. He is so boring." How often have you remarked to yourself, "Uh, they are not going over that information again, are they?" There are many times when you simply have no interest in the speaker or the topic. The problem with this attitude is that neglected listening situations are lost opportunities. When you find yourself becoming apathetic about a listening situation, remember that you can always learn *something* by listening and that the effort expended is not going to be overwhelming.

Psychological distractions are usually categorized as *daydreaming*. There are valid reasons to daydream. For example, psychological distractions can give your consciousness time to recoup. However, when you daydream during lectures, discussions, or conversations, you can miss out on a lot of useful information. Put these distractions off until an appropriate time and reward your good listening behavior with a wonderful daydream.

Expectations and Reality

Think about yourself as a communicator. How do your communication experiences compare to your expectations of how they will turn out? Are you usually right or wrong about the outcomes? Why?

Overconfidence and Laziness. Sometimes your expectations can cause you to be overconfident about certain listening situations. Overconfidence comes in the forms of poor preparation and planning, expecting too little from speakers, ignoring important information, and exhibiting an arrogant attitude. Overconfidence can lead to laziness and some unexpected listening problems.

Think about this incident: Randall walked into a business meeting certain that he knew everything that was going to be said. As he confidently sat through the meeting only half listening, several of his co-workers and his boss began asking him questions that he was unprepared to answer. Randall had to admit that he hadn't anticipated their questions, and he felt very foolish. Overconfidence can lead to unpleasant surprises that could be avoided.

Apprehension. In many situations, you may be apprehensive about listening. **Listening apprehension** is a state of uneasiness, anxiety, fear, or dread associated with a listening opportunity. Going to a job interview, being called in for a reprimand, having to listen to someone else's problems, listening to highly detailed or statistical information, listening to people with heavy accents—all are likely to trigger listening apprehension. The problem with listening apprehension is that it can affect your ability to concentrate on what is said or affect your memory of what was said.

> LISTENING
> APPREHENSION
> *A state of uneasiness, anxiety, fear, or dread associated with a listening opportunity.*

What do you think about your own listening apprehension? You may have a better idea after you complete the Self-Check on page 172. If you have a moderate to high score, you probably experience some apprehension in listening situations. Try these two things to reduce the effects of your apprehension: (1) Concentrate on the speaker's ideas and minimize thoughts about your nervousness by using your energy to understand the message; and (2) if you experience physical tension, relieve your apprehension by taking a few slow, deep breaths and by tensing and relaxing muscle groups that feel tight. You will notice a refreshed sensation that can relax you during tense listening situations, thus helping you become a more competent listener.

Defensiveness. Many people feel defensive when criticized by others and dislike feeling threatened by other people. Becoming defensive affects your listening in two ways. First, you become preoccupied with determining the other person's motive for attacking you or your group. This is true whether or not there is an actual personal attack. Think about the last time you became defensive. Didn't you spend a large amount of time thinking about *why* the speaker would criticize or threaten you? You probably missed much of what the person was saying because you were preoccupied with these thoughts or with your counterattacks. You can stem your defensive tendencies by pursuing the following steps:

1. Hear the speaker out. You do not want to rush into an argument without knowing your opponent's position. Wait for the speaker to finish before devising your own arguments.

2. While listening to the speaker, consider the person's motives for saying what is being said. You may have done something that the speaker is reacting to; you might be the cause. Be careful, however, not to become preoccupied with the person's motives.

3. Take a deep breath and smile slightly at the speaker. Your disarming behavior may be enough to force the speaker to speak more reasonably.

Your Listening Apprehension

Wheeless has developed a test that identifies listening areas that make some people apprehensive. Some of these areas are listed below. Answer the following questions to get an idea of your listening apprehension level.

Score your answers to the following questions according to whether you strongly agree (1), agree (2), are undecided (3), disagree (4), or strongly disagree (5).

_____ 1. I am not afraid to listen as a member of an audience.

_____ 2. I feel relaxed when I am listening to new ideas.

_____ 3. I generally feel rattled when others are speaking to me.

_____ 4. I often feel uncomfortable when I am listening to others.

_____ 5. I often have difficulty concentrating on what is being said.

_____ 6. I look for opportunities to listen to new ideas.

_____ 7. Receiving new information makes me nervous.

_____ 8. I have no difficulty concentrating on instructions given to me.

_____ 9. People who try to change my mind make me anxious.

_____ 10. I always feel relaxed when listening to others.

Scoring: Add up your scores for items 1, 2, 6, 8, and 10. Now add up your scores for items 3, 4, 5, 7, and 9. Subtract the total of the second set of answers from the first total to get a composite score. If your final score is positive, you have a tendency toward receiver apprehension; the higher the score, the more apprehension you report. If your final score is negative, you have little or no apprehension.

Source: Adapted from L. R. Wheeless (1975), An investigation of receiver apprehension and social context dimensions of communication apprehension, *Speech Teacher, 24,* 261–268.

4. After the speaker finishes, paraphrase what you think was said and ask if you understood the message correctly. You will be surprised how often a speaker on the offensive will back away from an aggressive stance when confronted with an attempt at understanding.

Set Listening Goals

LISTENING GOALS
Specific plans or objectives for listening.

The previous section discussed ways to recognize and overcome listening barriers. In this section, you will learn the value of setting **listening goals**, which are essential for listening effectively. Here are four steps to follow when you are setting listening goals.

Determine Needs. Do you ever think about your listening needs? Sometimes you may take a listening situation for granted and expect that you will listen

Political speeches demand critical listening.

effectively without anticipating your needs. That is when trouble can appear. One of the best methods of determining your needs is to assess what you *have* to get out of the situation, what you *expect* to get out of the situation, and what you *hope* to get out of the situation.

- Think about your obligations. What *must* you know, understand, feel, or react to in this situation? What issues, events, or people require you to listen effectively? Make a list of goals ("I need to know her 4-day flight schedule").

- List related results that you *expect* to get from the situation. These are the events or results that should happen with conscientious listening ("I think that I will understand why she wanted to go on this business trip").

- Write down some results that you *hope* will happen in this situation ("I hope she tells me why she got mad at me yesterday"). Now that you know your needs, you are ready to continue the goal-setting process.

Set Performance Standards to Meet Needs. Football teams, debate squads, orchestras, and fund-raisers all set performance standards to assess whether their goals are actually met. In a specific listening situation, you could list a set of factors that must be accomplished to satisfy your goal: "I will know all of the main points presented by the guest speaker in class today." Performance standards help you to know if you are on track with your listening goals. Write down some standards for your own listening situations.

State the Goal as an Action. The next step in this process is to state the goal in a way that encourages action. Look at the needs you identified and the standards you set, and then develop an action statement incorporating those components into a goal. From the preceding business-trip example, you could make a goal statement that goes something like this: "I will ask her to give me three reasons why this trip was more important than others." This type of goal statement considers the need, sets a standard, and is action-oriented. Develop a goal statement for yourself.

Develop Steps for Assessing Goal Attainment. The last step in this process is to develop a plan for assessing your goal attainment. This assessment must be accomplished during the listening situation and after it is over. Reflecting on the situation afterward provides an excellent chance for you to see how well you listened. It is also crucial to do some analysis while you are listening so that you can take corrective action if you are not meeting your needs. The following example demonstrates how all four steps work together in goal-setting.

Need   "I need to know her 4-day flight schedule."

Performance standard   "I will determine her arrival and departure times for each city she's visiting on her trip."

Action statement (goal)   "Before I call her, I will make a list of all the cities and establish 'arrival' and 'departure' columns for each city, so that when I talk to her I can simply fill in the blanks. I will take careful notes when she tells me about her itinerary."

Assessing goal achievement   "Before we get off the phone, I will review my notes carefully to make sure I got all the information."

◆ Manage the Context

In the preceding part of the chapter, you learned how to manage your listening skills. Effective and appropriate listening also involves managing the *communication context*. From a listening perspective, context includes the setting, culture, and third parties.

The Setting: Place, Emotion, and Time

The *place* in which you listen probably has a greater impact on your ability to listen effectively than you realize. Your classrooms vary in their acoustics, a lunchroom can produce a lot of ambient noise, and some theaters have poor audio systems. It is important that you take such factors into consideration. If you know the room will be cold, dress appropriately. If it will be a crowded auditorium and you are claustrophobic, go early and sit on the aisle. If you are going to a group meeting and you have trouble hearing when others are talking at the same time, sit next to the leader so that you will be able to hear most of the messages. Take the time to anticipate the physical setting and prepare accordingly.

Another aspect of the setting involves your feelings or *emotions.* When was the last time you were unable to listen effectively because of the emotional tension in the atmosphere? Much too often people are caught up in the emotionality of a situation or setting and become distracted. Emotions can also generate thoughts unrelated to the issues at hand. One way to fight such distractions is to allow the emotions to heighten your concentration level. Athletes are proficient at channeling their excess emotional energy into energy that can be used in their sports. You can channel your emotions into a more focused concentration on the speaker and the message.

Time is another important part of the setting. Time can be your listening ally or enemy. Ignoring the impact of time is one of the mistakes people make with their listening. If you get into a time bind, you are less likely to listen effectively than if you have ample time to listen. Sometimes having too much time on your hands also leads to ineffective listening. Time is a part of the setting that dictates the magnitude of communication opportunities. Your listening has to adjust to the temporal constraints if you are to benefit fully from the situation. Some people are better listeners when time is short. Others function better when they have ample time to digest the information slowly, carefully, and methodically.

Cultural Factors

How often have you noticed that your listening was compromised because the speaker "didn't speak your language"? Cultural factors include listening barriers that embrace all variations of language. Many cultures in the United States communicate in ways that may be difficult for you to understand. When you interact with someone who speaks a different language, it will obviously be very difficult to decipher what is being said. Cultural problems still occur, however, when people speak the same language but differ in how they use it. Slang, jargon, euphemisms, and connotative meanings can all cause listening problems. Although jargon can be efficient for those who are familiar with it, listening to and understanding jargon are difficult for those outside of the culture. The language of the medical care community is a prime illustration of the cultural language barrier jargon can cause.

How do you usually communicate with people of different cultures? Here are some suggestions that can help you. *First, make an effort to learn or to recognize the cultural background of the communicator.* If the person has a different ethnic background from yours, try to learn about the speaker's heritage so that you can understand his or her perspective. If the person is a devout member of a particular religious organization, keep this in mind as you listen, recognizing that beliefs can be a major factor in communication. *Second, reveal your cultural needs to the speaker.* Many speakers do not pay enough attention to the cultural needs of the listener. If you find that cultural differences are preventing good communication, tell the speaker ("Hey,

I don't think we are in sync here—can you say that again, more slowly, please?"). *Third, adjust to differences.* Ask more questions if necessary, but make a special effort to recognize the difficulties associated with intercultural communication. Ask the speaker to work with you in making the cultural differences understandable and enjoyable.

Third Parties

Another factor to consider when managing the context is how other people influence either your listening or someone else's speaking. Recall the last time you were talking to another student and someone you both knew joined the conversation. Did you become distracted by this person's presence? For example, some listeners may feel that third parties are *intruding* on their time with the speaker and may become distracted with those thoughts. Others may feel more pressure when a third person or other people join a conversation, and this stress distracts them from listening effectively. Still others may think that they have to impress the third party and begin preparing what to say instead of listening to the speaker. There are some instances, however, when a third party may enhance your listening. A new person may actually help you to focus on everything that is said. The best advice is to remain aware that third parties can influence your listening and to use that influence as a listening enhancement rather than a listening distraction. For instance, you can follow up with third parties to determine how much they got out of the speaker's message. Other people may catch things that you miss, and you can use their insights to improve your own listening accuracy.

◆ Adjust to the Speaker

This section focuses on the person or persons who are speaking during a listening situation. It is your job as a listener to ascertain the goals and motivations of the speaker. As you will see, you sometimes have to adjust your listening skills to the speaker in order to accomplish your goals.

Relational History

You will recall from the competence model in Chapter 1 that relational history affects your communication choices. Relational history also affects how you listen to someone else. If you are listening to someone who once reneged on a promise similar to what he or she is promising now ("Oh, don't worry, I'll pay you back"), you may not have much faith in what the speaker is saying. You may even ignore the rest of the message. Many issues can affect relational history: Hurt feelings, trust, intimacy, lying, affection, and loyalty are just some of the dynamics. To use relational history effectively as a listener, you need to follow through on four important steps. *First, objectively assess how the relational history with the other person affects your attitude toward him or her.* How has the past influenced your feelings toward this person? Do you consider this person a friend, enemy, acquaintance, colleague, or something else? *Second, avoid positive and negative biases that may exist as a result of the relational history.* There is a tendency to skew information in the direction of how one feels about a person. If you like certain people, you may tend to overlook their mistakes and to exaggerate their strengths. The opposite is generally the case for people you dislike. These types of biases can create listening deficiencies.

Goals and Expectations

Listening is enhanced if you can determine what a speaker is expecting from you, the listener, and from the communication situation. The following example illustrates this point. The instructor in Math 1212 was conducting a review for the final exam. Stacy went to the review because she was not doing well in the class. Even though she brought her textbook, she didn't prepare for the review, or have any real expectations about it. At the review, the instructor asked if the students had any specific problems with the course. Some students did, and the instructor addressed those problems, reminded everyone of the time and place of the exam, and dismissed the class. Stacy left the review disappointed because she got nothing useful out of it. Had she anticipated that the instructor was expecting students to be prepared for the review, Stacy could have brought up points that concerned her and would have benefited from the review.

How can you determine a communicator's expectations? First, reflect on the nature of the situation itself. Does the situation require an active role on the part of the listener? Large audiences do not require such participation, but small groups do. What about the speaker's track record? Is the speaker someone who usually does most of the talking and expects you to passively take in what is said? Or does the speaker usually ask for input so that you have to be ready to respond? What do you think the speaker will expect you to get out of the situation? Will the speaker try to persuade you (as a politician might do), to instruct or inform you (as a teacher might do), or to seek support and friendship (as a roommate might do)? Will you have to follow up on any of the information you receive? You should also consider the other listeners in the situation. Will the speaker expect more of them than of you? Attempting to figure out the speaker's expectations is a necessary step in improving your listening skills. Even if your expectations are wrong, you will be in a better position to respond than if you had no expectations at all (see Table 6.2 on p. 178).

Communication Style

Communication style is an overall characterization people make of a communicator. It includes vocal characteristics, word choice, and impression formation.

Vocal Characteristics. Vocal characteristics influence your listening in several ways. Voice qualities such as pitch and throaty, breathy, or nasal-sounding tones can have their own meaning for the listener. Sharon Stone has a breathy

COMMUNICATION STYLE

An overall characterization consisting of a communicator's vocal characteristics, word choice, and impression formation.

TABLE 6.2 GOALS AND MOTIVES OF COMMUNICATORS		
SPEAKER'S GOAL	WHAT TO EXPECT	LISTENING FUNCTION
Inform	Information, facts, opinions, advice, data, news	Comprehensive, critical
Persuade	Compliance gaining, compliance resisting, influence on attitudes and opinions	Comprehensive, critical
Inquire	Questions, examination, interrogation, probing, scrutiny, analysis, request	Comprehensive, critical
Entertain	Amusement, humor	Appreciative, empathic
Confront	Criticism, reprimand, setting straight	Comprehensive, critical
Seek support	Requests for sympathy, empathy, moral support, understanding	Empathic

voice, which helps to identify her as an alluring actress. It is sometimes easy to stereotype people according to their voice qualities. However, people can be fooled by voice qualities, which can lead to listening trouble. Remain wary of labeling people just because of the way their voices sound. The same is true of *accent*, which refers to how people pronounce words. People for whom English is a second language may speak it with an identifiable Spanish, Eastern European, or Chinese accent. Sometimes listeners become so preoccupied with an accent that they don't pay attention to what is being said.

Speech errors can also cause listeners to miss something that is said. Speech errors include silent pauses (gaps in talking), filled pauses ("uh," "um," "like"), and mispronounced words. When you interact with someone who makes a number of speech errors, you must guard against judging the person's content too quickly. In between the errors is information that you may need. As a listener, you have a responsibility to make sense of the broken language. You can do this by focusing on the main part of the message and by asking questions if you are unsure of the meaning.

Word Choice. The influence of word choice on listening is a rather broad subject. Obviously, some words are more easily comprehended than others, and some are more easily distracting than others. We will limit our discussion to words that may create special problems for listeners.

Each generation produces words that are unique to its values and lifestyle. During the 1940s, teenagers used connotative words that were modern at the time (*23-skidoo, zoot suit, hooch*), and in the late 1960s they used jargon (*booze, boogie, cool, out-of-sight*) that is still in use today. Think about the newer words or phrases you use with friends. Do the people you know understand all the new words? Do you? What about jargon, or in-group language? Physicians (*stat, cauterize*), accountants (*zero-base budgeting*), carpenters (*sharp-shooter*), and even college professors (*walk, dead-day*) use specialized language as part of their in-group communication systems. As a listener, it is important that you correctly identify the meanings of new words as they are used.

Words that are perceived as *vulgar* or *profane* can distract listeners. Such words can alienate people who would otherwise be interested in what is being said. What is your first reaction when you hear vulgarity and profanity? How do you cope with it if it really bothers you? Sometimes you may need to ignore the vulgarity because the speaker has information you must obtain.

Pointed words or phrases can also distract listeners. These are word choices that a speaker uses to command, instruct, intimidate, or criticize a listener. "Do it my way, or else." "You're not very good at that, are you?" When pointed words are directed at you, you may become defensive, or you may become preoccupied by the person's apparent rudeness. You may also miss other parts of the message because you are trying to figure out why the speaker is being so rude or blunt. Again, it is important to ignore the pointed language and to concentrate on the information you need.

This is particularly difficult to do when the pointed language is sexist, racist, or ageist. In some cases, for example, a speaker who uses sexist language may be trying to convey a message of chauvinism. In other cases, a speaker may not intend sexism but may use sexist language out of ignorance. Regardless of the language used or the speaker's motivation, your primary task as a listener is to understand the message.

Impression Formation. People always form impressions about speakers. You may find some speakers dull, some exciting, others interesting, and so on. The general effect that a communicator has on a listener is called **impression formation**. You form a general impression based on each speaker's verbal and nonverbal styles.

Some communication styles are more likely to enhance listening than are others. You need to decide which impressions create the most difficulty and then develop techniques for overcoming any listening problems. Think about the mannerisms that irritate you the most when people speak to you. Are the irritating speakers too loud or too soft-spoken? Too laid-back or too intense? Do boisterous speakers make you nervous? Think about the styles that are the most problematic and ask yourself why these affect your listening. Most likely you are being distracted by the *way* people are communicating. The next time you encounter an irritating communication style, ignore everything about the speaker except the message; you will be surprised by how much you can learn. With practice, you will be able not only to listen competently to the verbal message but also to desensitize yourself to the irritations of an aggravating communication style.

IMPRESSION FORMATION
The general effect that a communicator has on a listener.

Your Response to Speakers' Styles

Do you prefer to listen to some speaking styles rather than others? The following questions should help you focus on how a speaker's style can affect your competence as a listener. There is no scale for scoring your answers to this Self-Check, but your responses should make you aware of the factors that may interfere with your listening.

1. Are you more attentive to a speaker who is animated and dramatic or one who does not use gestures much?
2. Do you find yourself being overly critical when someone uses fill-ins? Incorrect grammar?
3. Are you impressed—favorably or unfavorably—by a speaker who occasionally uses foreign words? Does your reaction depend on the language used?
4. Are you impressed—favorably or unfavorably—by foreign or regional accents that are different from your own? What is your favorite accent? Your least favorite accent?
5. What words or categories of words (for example, curse words, slang, or technical jargon) bother you? Are these words always offensive, or are they more acceptable when some speakers use them than when other speakers do? How can you maintain your own standards for choosing appropriate words and, at the same time, listen competently to speakers who violate your standards?

MAIN POINT
The thesis of a speaker's message; a key to understanding and remembering the message.

What's the Main Point?

Often, determining the main point of a speaker's message is the most difficult thing to do when listening. Try practicing this in class. Be alert to the unifying structure of the lecture. As each point is made, try to determine how it fits into the lecture. Try to anticipate the direction the lecture will go. This will improve your listening skills both in and out of the classroom.

◆ Listen Critically

The fourth step in becoming a competent listener involves critical listening. *Critical listening* includes (1) determining the speaker's main point, (2) focusing your energy on listening, (3) critically decoding nonverbal cues, and (4) using your memory effectively. When you employ these tactics, you will be a much better listener.

Determine the Thesis or Main Point

One of the most widely suggested tips for effective listening is understanding the **main point** or thesis of a speaker's message. The proverbial question "What's the bottom line?" is appropriate here. What is the most important thing that the speaker wants you to get from the message? Determining the thesis of a message is not always easy, especially if the speaker is not a skilled communicator. Speakers can ramble, go off on tangents, lose a train of thought, or have no clear thesis at all. Here are some strategies to help you identify the main point in a message. *First, watch for verbal identifiers or phrases that clue you in on the main point.* "What I am trying to say. . ." "The issue is . . ." "Look, I know that . . ." "Okay, here's the deal . . ." When you hear one of these identifiers, it is likely to preview the main point of the message, so pay careful attention. *Second, watch for a more direct eye gaze.* Speakers are more likely to look at you when they are trying to make an important point. *Third, develop a mental outline of the speaker's message.* Think about the points the speaker is making and prioritize the major ones. *Finally, if you are in doubt about the main point, ask the speaker for clarification.* "Are you saying that. . . ?" "Am I to understand that . . . ?" "Could you give an example of what you mean?" Once the main point is established, it is easier to incorporate the rest of the information from a message.

Focus Your Efforts

In order to listen critically, it is necessary to focus your efforts on the task. You can do this in three ways: by storing up energy, concentrating, and avoiding distractions.

The first step involves *storing up energy* for the job ahead. Listening requires cognitive, physical, and emotional energy. With a limited supply, it is best to store your energy for the most important listening situations. One way to do this is by secluding yourself from others when you need a listening break. Another method is to schedule slack times right before important listening tasks. Both of these approaches give you a chance to catch your breath and collect your thoughts. You can also generate energy or at least store what is left by using muscle relaxation and deep-breathing exercises.

Concentration is another key to focusing on the listening task. By now you are probably an expert at concentrating on a task when it really counts. Taking exams, giving a presentation, and keeping calm while disciplining children all require concentration. Using concentration skills during listening is not very different.

Focusing your efforts is also made easier by *avoiding distractions*. Table 6.3 on page 182 organizes distractions into three categories: psychological, emotional, and physical. As you look at the table, note the examples and suggestions for reducing each type of distraction. What other distractions hinder your listening? Suggest ways to reduce the influence of these distractions.

Critically Decode Nonverbal Cues

Listening with your ears is only part of the process. As we discussed in Chapter 5, much of the message is communicated via nonverbal channels. A key to competent listening is to monitor critically the **nonverbal cues** and to decode them accurately. You can then determine whether the nonverbal cues support, amplify, illustrate, or contradict what the speaker is saying verbally. Remember the importance of expectations. Paying attention to a speaker's nonverbal behavior can provide impressions of his or her mood, which are helpful in anticipating the nature of the message. It is difficult to quantify the contribution that nonverbal behavior makes to your listening, but you know it is significant.

From the preceding chapter, you are already sensitive to the impact of nonverbal communication. This section provides additional suggestions to improve your nonverbal listening. *First, form an overall impression of the speaker from*

Follow the Nonverbal Cues

List five people whose nonverbal behaviors have helped you to listen better. Beside each name, list the speaker's most noteworthy helpful behaviors. Do you use these nonverbal skills when speaking? Your instructor may list these behaviors on the board to stimulate class discussion.

NONVERBAL CUES
Nonverbal behaviors that allow listeners to better understand a verbal message; also, behaviors that listeners use to show the speaker that they understand the message.

TABLE 6.3 AVOIDING LISTENING DISTRACTIONS		
CATEGORY	EXAMPLES	REDUCING DISTRACTIONS
Psychological	Perception of a higher listening priority	Decide which is more important.
	Preoccupation with other thoughts	Make a note to yourself to focus on the preoccupation later.
Emotional	Hurt feelings	Save the self-pity and anger for another time.
	Emotional triggers	Delay judgment about something said in an emotional tone.
Physical	Fatigue	Redirect energy for listening or postpone listening until rejuvenated.
	Illness	Make speaker aware of special circumstances. Postpone listening.

nonverbal mannerisms. Do they suggest happiness, sadness, confusion, or anger? Consistently test your accuracy by confirming or disconfirming your original impression. *Second, watch for subtleties in the speaker's nonverbal behavior.* Even though many people are sophisticated in hiding their feelings, some cue usually "leaks" out, revealing the speaker's true feelings. Subtle cues could include less or more body orientation, less or more eye gaze, the presence of adapters, or even abnormal vocal tones. *Third, inquire about inconsistencies when you observe them.* Tell speakers if they are communicating one thing verbally and quite another thing nonverbally. When confronted with the problem, speakers may be able to resolve the inconsistency.

Use Your Memory Effectively

Making sense of a message is an important part of critical listening. Remembering that message is just as important. Recall from Chapter 2 that when you process information, you store this information in short-term memory for a few seconds until long-term memory is ready to take over. Sometimes long-term memory is not engaged, and that is when you forget something you have heard. To make your short-term memory more effective, double-check your perceptual awareness. Are you hearing and seeing what you should? Do you have any immediate concerns or questions as the speaker communicates? Is the message important enough to transfer to long-term memory? After all, not everything you hear is worth remembering. You must prioritize your listening alternatives.

Once you commit yourself to remembering what someone says, you use long-term memory efficiently. To do so, you sometimes use an intermediate memory system called **rehearsal**. Rehearsal is a temporary storage area that

REHEARSAL

A temporary storage area that processes information directed from short-term memory to long-term memory.

processes information directed from short-term memory to long-term memory. People's names, phone numbers, addresses, and even flight times are bits of information that often spend time in the rehearsal area of memory.

Some researchers recommend that you use *visual imagery* to help you remember what is said.[5] Visual imagery involves producing vivid mental images that can be associated with verbal messages. For example, if your roommate asks you to pick up his or her laundry when you are running your own errands, you might envision what the cleaner's building looks like, including the sign out front, so that you will remember to include that stop in your errands. Some students may associate the face of a favorite musician with each of their major assignments in class. The association does not have to be direct; rather, it serves as a memory trigger for specific items.

◆ Listen Interactively

The final step in the listening process involves learning to listen interactively. The following story illustrates the importance of such interaction. Dominique is a friendly but quiet person who seldom reacts to things people say. Though an attentive listener, she fails to nod, shake her head, or exhibit any facial expressions when others talk. A classmate and acquaintance, Vicki, once told her, "You know, Dominique, when I talk to you I am never quite sure whether you understand what I'm saying. You never give me any feedback." Dominique seemed very surprised that Vicki felt it necessary to receive feedback. Vicki continued, "It seems that I have to explain a lot more to you because I don't know whether you're following me."

Dominique is an individual who does not respond to speakers with nonverbal cues. It doesn't mean that she is not listening. But it does mean that the people she talks with may perceive her as incompetent, lazy, uncaring, or bored with them. Conversational rules dictate that people should give appropriate nonverbal or verbal cues to speakers to regulate their talk. Besides improving speakers' confidence in their listeners, interactive cues can save listeners time, because speakers won't have to repeat or embellish to get their points across. When you can influence a speaker to perform more efficiently, you will automatically become a more competent listener. That is why this stage is *interactive.* Listeners play an important role in creating competent communication between the two interactants. There are three strategies that may help you become a more interactive listener: nonverbal facilitation, verbal reinforcers, and questioning techniques.

Nonverbal Facilitation

Eye gaze is an important nonverbal cue because it is a very obvious indicator of interest. When you look at the other person, you gain valuable nonverbal information. If you look down or away, you can give the speaker the impression that you would rather be elsewhere. The speaker may form this impression whether or not it is your intention. You might then lose valuable information if the person decides to cut off the conversation because of a perceived lack of interest on your part. Dominique was not being an interactive listener when she failed to provide nonverbal cues to Vicki. Think about your own eye gaze patterns during listening. Do you normally look at people when they talk? When do you look elsewhere and why?

Facial expressions are another form of interactive cue that facilitates other people's speaking. Timely expressions greatly aid the speaker in reading the listener. For example, frowning is an effective way to signal confusion, disagreement, or fear; smiling indicates enjoyment and agreement; and a widening of the eyes can communicate surprise or disbelief. When you use these expressions strategically and judiciously, the speaker can more accurately read your nonverbal cues and communicate with you in a more competent manner.

When you want to signal that you are listening carefully, how do you adjust your body orientation? You may give the speaker a full and direct body orientation. You may also lean forward, possibly putting your hand or elbows on your knees. Body orientation is one of the most pronounced cues that a listener can use. If you are tired of listening to a speaker, what body orientation strategy is best? Turning the body laterally directs your nonverbal attention away from the speaker and gives an impression of disinterest. Standing up may indicate your interest in changing topics or moving the conversation to a new location. All of these nonverbal cues help to facilitate speaker communication.

VERBAL REINFORCERS
Short verbal cues used by listeners to coordinate speaker–listener communication.

Verbal Reinforcers

Dominique also neglected to provide **verbal reinforcers**. Verbal reinforcers are short, quick words or sounds that express agreement, disagreement, confusion, surprise, or other listener's reactions. Think of verbal reinforcers such as "yeah," "uh huh," "umm," "uh uh," "ahhh," or even laughter.

Interactive listening is an important technique in psychotherapy. As a layperson, you can use this skill by empathic listening.

Verbal reinforcers are especially important when you are talking on the telephone because visual nonverbal cues are useless. Howard was negotiating a contract on the phone with a person who did not provide verbal reinforcers at any point during the negotiation process. Thus Howard became suspicious that the other person either was being cagey by not responding, as a strategy to keep him off balance, or was an incompetent listener. Howard chose the latter and began to ask the listener some questions. "Are you still there?" "Do you understand the terms?" "Are you able to provide these services?" "Will you agree to the time frame I discussed?" The listener answered all of the questions affirmatively. In this case, the listener's lack of verbal reinforcement created difficulties that Howard had to rectify.

Questioning Techniques

Dominique could also have been a more interactive listener if she had used effective **questioning techniques**. Questions from the listener serve two functions. *First, questions signal that listening is occurring.* If you are asking questions, the speaker knows that you are tuned in and interested, and this gives the speaker some needed confidence. *Second, questions can actually help the speaker become more effective by getting to the points that will do the listener the most good.* Consider the following example.

MR. HENSLEY   I have your career assessment test results back.

LENA   Were there any job areas that I excelled in?

MR. HENSLEY   Yes, quite a few. You are definitely a "people person," and you scored high in the health care profession.

LENA   Well, that's nice, but I was considering attending a business college and earning a court reporter certificate. Did I show any promise in that field?

MR. HENSLEY   Listen, with your eagerness to learn and focused direction, you could one day be a judge!

In this case, Mr. Hensley gave Lena the encouragement she was seeking, and he also opened her eyes to aim even higher. As this example illustrates, questions can be used to encourage more information from the speaker, to verify points of view, or to clarify issues.

As the final step to competent listening, interactive listening creates mutual participation between you and the speaker. Your listening behavior is no longer passive; it is dynamic and engaged. Do not hesitate to use nonverbal cues, verbal reinforcers, and questions to ensure a high level of interactive listening.

By now you know that you and other communicators are co-creators in competent listening. As you recall from the competence model, communicators must recognize how their relationship is mutually dependent and strive toward a mutual understanding of the issues they communicate.

QUESTIONING TECHNIQUES
Inquiries that a listener can make to coordinate what the speaker is saying with what the listener is hearing.

Sound Bites

Watch a news or public television program that presents competing points of view. Make notes about how well the speakers listen to each other's arguments. What do they focus on? From what you have read in the chapter, how could their listening be improved?

The Case of Sheila Greenstein

At the beginning of this chapter you met Sheila Greenstein, a reporter assigned to cover the speech of Black Nationalist Louis Farrakhan. Sheila, although agreeing to report on the speech, believes Farrakhan to be a hate monger. Think about the relevance of the concepts in this chapter to Sheila as you answer the following questions.

- Which of the listening barriers and habits discussed in the chapter are applicable to this scenario?

- Identify possible examples of the three categories of distractions (physical, emotional, and psychological) that Sheila might face in this situation.

- Is Sheila's task best described as comprehensive, empathic, critical, or appreciative listening? Why?

- Which of this chapter's suggestions for improving critical listening skills do you think Sheila would find most useful? Why?

REVIEW

- Listening involves cognitive and behavioral skills that you must work at in order to increase your competence level.

- There are four major functions of listening: comprehensive listening, empathic listening, critical listening, and appreciative listening.

- This chapter presents a framework for becoming a better listener. The five steps to competent listening are a guide you can enact anytime you face listening opportunities.

- The first step toward competent listening is managing your skills. First, assess your listening self-concept. Next, determine your actual listening efficiency. Listening tests can give you an idea of your strengths and weaknesses. This leads to an assessment of listening barriers. Are you bored, anxious, or defensive when some people speak? Understanding goal-setting completes Step 1 of this process.

- Step 2 in this process is managing the context. The listening context includes the setting, cultural factors, and third parties. The setting is a composite of place, emotion, and time. All of these factors have their own influence on the listening context. Cultural factors are important as well. Being sensitive to and respecting one another's cultural background are prerequisites for competent listening. Third parties influence a listening situation. Sometimes this is an advantage. In other instances, third-party influences may hinder your listening and you must take steps to avoid any distractions they create.

- Step 3 involves adjusting to the speaker. Relational history and a speaker's expectations are important elements. Because many speakers do not adjust to their listeners, it is your job as a listener to adjust to them as best you can. Understanding a speaker's communication style involves accurately interpreting vocal characteristics, remaining objective about a speaker's word choice, and understanding how a speaker's style can form particular impressions on you as a listener.

- Listening critically is Step 4 in this framework. To listen critically, first you must determine the main point of the message. Next, you must focus your efforts on the listening task. Besides its importance in decoding the verbal message, critical listening requires recognizing and understanding the speaker's nonverbal cues. In order to use the information communicated by the speaker, you must also use your memory effectively.

- Step 5, listening interactively, involves facilitating the speaker's communication so that his or her messages are easier for you to understand. One way to help speakers understand your level of listening competency is to provide appropriate nonverbal cues. Verbal reinforcers can let the speaker know that the listener agrees, understands, or is confused by the message. Questions will keep the speaker on track or provide clarification or verification of information in the message.

CASE STUDY 1

The Case of the Communication Class

In the following case study, several people are at the beginning of their relationships with one another. As with all new relationships, these people have the opportunity to construct relationships that are satisfying and productive for them and their partners. The decisions each makes about what to say and how to say it are crucial. How well do the interactants succeed, in your opinion?

During the first week of class, the professor of the Introduction to Communication course gave an in-class assignment. Students were to give impromptu speeches of approximately 1 to 2 minutes in which they were to (1) identify an issue of importance to many and (2) link that issue to themselves personally. The professor indicated that this assignment would raise issues for the rest of the term and would let students get to know one another a little.

The 5 minutes the students were given to prepare these speeches seemed too short to most of them. Leah and Tom looked at each other, rolling their eyes; both said they were "blanked" on what to talk about. Corlynne and Travis were jotting down ideas and smiling as they wrote. Louis looked nervously around the room, imagining he was the only one who had nothing to say. Alicia looked over at her friend's paper, thinking she might "piggyback" off the friend's idea. Hallmein felt catatonic; he just knew he would not be able to speak well, especially in English, his second language. At the end of 5 minutes, despite the protests and groaning, most of the students had a skeleton plan of what they would say.

Bashar spoke about the campaign to get people to use condoms. He said he thought it was "lame" because condoms hadn't been successful at preventing his girlfriend of 2 years from getting pregnant; he was sure condoms were not any better at guarding against AIDS or other sexually transmitted diseases.

Julie spoke about animal rights activists. She said she was against terrible tests and inhumane conditions for animals but thought the activists too often went overboard. She cited the time when her mother, wearing a fur coat her husband had given her for an anniversary, had had blood thrown on her.

Bud spoke about gun control. He said that there were a lot of problems with guns but that in his opinion criminals would get guns no matter what controls were established. He thought it was not right to restrict the right of responsible citizens to own guns. He said he and his brothers had grown up in Texas using guns to hunt or kill snakes or other animals that came close to the house. He cited the Constitution's reference to "the right to bear arms."

The professor asked for comments on the speeches that had been given so far. How were class members responding to the speeches, the topics, and the persons delivering them?

Naro said he was uncomfortable about the condom speech. In his native Japan, it was not appropriate to talk about such personal things in front of people. Other class members asked him whether condoms were advertised and sold in Japan. "Yes," he responded, "condoms are advertised; but many people look away from those ads, thinking them rude or in poor taste. He would not talk about a condom ad with his mother, for example. He also said that, because condom use wasn't considered very "manly," condoms were not as popular in Japan as he believed they were in the United States. Leticia wanted to know whether Naro would consider using condoms, but the professor intervened before Naro could reply, indicating that it was time to share reactions to some of the other speeches.

Gretchen said that, while she didn't want to criticize Bashar, his use of the term *lame* offended her. She added that the label was common usage and not meant to hurt anyone, but that her older brother, who had lost his leg from the knee down, objected to being called lame. She thought that everyone needed to have more sensitivity to language.

Brad agreed. A number of the speakers, he said, addressed the class members as "guys" and "girls." Many of the women he knew objected to being called "girls" but wouldn't say anything because they were afraid of being labeled "strident feminists."

"I liked the fact that a few of our speakers today weren't afraid to take what's viewed as an unpopular stance," said Kate. She cited Julie's story about her mother's fur coat and Bud's attitude toward guns. "I learned something about these people today," Kate added. "I admire their willingness to take a position, even if I don't agree with them."

The professor agreed and pointed out that many of the topics brought up that day, such as immigration, could be discussed in greater depth in the weeks to come. "Sounds like we've got an interesting group of people with some important things to say in this class—looks like a good term ahead."

Discussion Questions

1. Recall the model of communicative competence described in Chapter 1. What elements of that model were at work here? What factors helped communication be more effective? Less effective?
2. How did thinking about self affect the communication of the students in this class? How might the criticisms that some students directed at their classmates affect the self-concepts of the speakers? The future self-presentations of the speakers?
3. What do you think about the use of "politically correct" language? Do you think your classmates agree with you? Were the people in this case study out of line in their use of certain terms—or did some people overreact?
4. How might the nonverbal aspects of message presentation change the "meaning" of what the speakers said?
5. Did the fact that this discussion was held in a classroom affect what was said and how it was taken? Explain.
6. How would you rate the respondents as listeners? Identify comments that showed competent or incompetent listening.

EPIL●GUE 1

Communication Competence as a Goal for Social Interaction

The purpose of this epilogue, and those at the end of subsequent parts, is to pull together concepts covered in each chapter within the part, relate them to one another, and show how each contributes to competent communication.

The systematic study of communication has a long history. Throughout that history, there has been a common rationale for trying to understand and improve people's ability to communicate: the enhancement of the general well-being of society. Aristotle taught rhetoric to the men of ancient Athens so that they might more effectively participate in public debates about how the city-state was governed. This concern with public welfare and how communication affected society was one reason why public speaking was taught in the first American universities. A similar concern for the public's welfare was the reason for adding professional journalism courses to university curricula at the beginning of the twentieth century. The sensationalist excesses of the "penny press" led people to see the need for newspeople who were trained in both the technical aspects of reporting and the ethical responsibilities of journalists in a free society.

Organizational communication, as it is studied and practiced today, grew out of attempts to create optimal work conditions for the factory workforce during World War II. This workforce was for the first time largely female because so many men were on the battlefront, and old-line managers were not sure how to motivate their new employees. Efforts to learn about management and moti-

vation turned into concerns for the quality of the work environment—the "human relations" approach.

The communication discipline is still concerned with promoting the common good. In this book we highlight ethical considerations that should go hand in hand with competent communication. Your personal values, as well as your culture's values, provide guidance about the appropriate construction of your messages and how to critically analyze the messages directed toward you.

In Part 1, we present a model of communicative competence and discuss basic communication processes that operate in a variety of contexts. The concepts apply to the full range of communication situations: two friends speaking informally, communication in groups large and small, formal presentations by one person to a large audience, and mass communication.

The processes discussed—are best understood in an informal interpersonal context. Once you understand these concepts, you can apply them to less familiar contexts, such as interviews, group projects, working in organizations, and giving speeches to large audiences.

Competent communication occurs when it is both *appropriate* to your partners and the situation and *effective* in meeting your goals and those of your fellow communicators. It is important to remember that people with few communication skills—because of social or physical difficulties—can and do and have competent relationships. This is a crucial point in a multicultural environment, where what counts as an important skill in one culture might be irrelevant or even rude in another.

People are competent or skilled communicators to the extent that they can both process (receive and interpret) and create messages that are directed toward achieving their goals. As we pointed out in Chapter 2, message processing involves perception and attribution, as well as memory, expectations, and complexity. Attribution and perception skills are dynamic and easy to change because, in most instances, they involve active attention.

You now know that you can also develop your memory, increase your cognitive complexity, and fine-tune your expectations. In fact, the more important a relationship is to you, the more likely you are to work on these aspects. As you develop your cognitive skills, you will become a more desirable communication partner. It is likely you will also enter into competent relationships with more people.

As we discuss in Chapter 3, communication with other people, especially those who are important to you, is crucial to the development and maintenance of your own and their self-concepts and self-esteem. From this view, you know yourself as an individual only because of the way you relate to others!

Your self-concept has many facets, and not all facets are exposed or made public to all of your partners. You may want to disclose some attributes—such as honesty or assertiveness—in all of your communication encounters. Some attributes will be part of only your social relationships, whereas others may be reserved for business relationships.

The message processing skills you bring into an interaction guide you in deciding how to communicate in a specific context or relationship. These cognitive skills might be called message design skills: your use of language (Chapter 4), nonverbal behavior (Chapter 5), and listening (Chapter 6).

In face-to-face situations, such as social conversations or interviews, monitoring your partners is relatively easy. The larger the group—the greater the distance between you and them—the more difficult this becomes. Another factor—adjusting the message to suit the audience—is not always possible or desirable. Human resources interviewers, for example, may have certain questions they must ask all job applicants, even though these questions are threatening to some people. "Have you ever been fired from a job?" is such a question.

What's important here from a *theoretical* view is that individuals bring a self to their communication encounters and to their relationships. They communicate in a way that is in line with their expectations, their own goals, and what they believe to be the goals of their partners. In a competent relationship, the goals of both parties will more or less be met or revised, at least over time. A definition of the relationship will emerge in terms of control (how much influence each party can legitimately exert) and the level of affiliation (degrees of liking, love, or respect). These aspects of the relationship will be open to negotiation from time to time as people make changes in their lives or change how they feel about each other.

In *practical* terms, this means that you approach communication encounters with a preferred way of doing things, although you have to adjust depending on whom you're talking with and what you're trying to accomplish. You are concerned at some level with how much your partners like you and with who is in control of the encounter and, ultimately, the relationship. From the standpoint of ethics, you are concerned about the effects of your communication on both yourself and your partners. The theoretical view tells you how to behave in the practical situation.

Putting It Together. A competent relationship is one in which the communication is mutually satisfying to all parties in the relationship. This evaluation applies to relationships of all types, from intimate, to corporate, to public.

In this part of the book we have discussed the basic process of communication—how people attend to and process messages and the effects that messages have on the way people think about themselves, language, nonverbal behavior, and listening. The better you understand this complex process, the more likely your relationships will go the way you want them to.

Interpersonal Communication

Since we all participate in interpersonal relationships, we cannot avoid communicating with other people. Sometimes that communication is successful, and sometimes it is not. Often, our success or failure depends on how well we understand the dynamics of interpersonal relationships. As we become aware of the factors that influence relationships, we are better able to develop, maintain, or terminate relationships in our own lives. In addition, we are able to develop the social skills needed in formal as well as informal contexts.

Video Action!

"Communicating in Interpersonal Relationships" provides examples of relationship phases, competent conflict management, and the factors that influence every phase of a relationship through the use of voice-over, graphics, model building, and scenarios. The video should help you in the step-by-step process of learning to communicate competently.

Steps toward Competent Communication

- Identify the goals people have as they develop relationships.
- Explain the information-seeking strategies people use to reduce uncertainty in relationships.
- Assess the rewards and costs of relationships.
- Distinguish between productive and destructive conflict.
- Describe the factors that lead to relational decline.
- Identify the phases of interpersonal relationships.

For Discussion after the Video

Why do some relationships fail while others intensify? How can we improve our current relationships by applying communication theories?

How do you decide to initiate an interpersonal relationship? What should you *not* talk about in the initiation phase of a relationship?

From your own experience, provide an example of a productive conflict and a destructive conflict. What factors contributed to making these situations productive or destructive?

How do the dynamics of a relationship change when people of different cultures are involved? How can issues of language, eye contact, touch, world views, and values affect an intercultural relationship?

What ethical issues should you consider in interpersonal relationships?

CHAPTER SEVEN

Developing and Maintaining Relationships

●BJECTIVES

After reading this chapter, you should be able to:

1. Identify the goals and motivations people have in developing relationships.

2. Describe how expectations affect communication in interpersonal relationships.

3. Explain how relational knowledge affects interpersonal communication.

4. Explain the costs and rewards of relationships.

5. List three strategies that people use to reduce uncertainty about their relational partners.

6. Discuss the various stages of relational development.

7. Describe six characteristics of friendship.

8. Identify at least three ways to improve family relationships.

BRUCE IS AN AMERICAN student who is spending his junior year as an exchange student at the London School of Economics, where he will study economics and political science. He is from Minnesota, and he recently completed 2 years as an economics major at the University of Minnesota. Bruce's interests are his Macintosh computer and sports, especially soccer. His roommate for the year is Saleh, who is also a new exchange student. Saleh's home is in Riyadh, Saudi Arabia's royal capital and largest city, located in the east central part of the Arabian peninsula. Saleh will also study economics and political science. His outside interests include both sports and the arts, especially classical music and theater. As you read through this chapter, consider how its content might apply to the situation of Bruce and Saleh.

As you may recall from the model of communicative competence, relationships play a central role in determining the type of communication that is most effective and appropriate. In turn, competent **interpersonal communication** permits more meaningful relationships to develop. Each of you is involved in a number of relationships of different levels of importance. There is no guaranteed plan for a perfect relationship. However, by understanding how relationships form and disengage and what components make up a relationship, you may better understand your own relationships.

◆ Relational Knowledge

Relational knowledge is the information you gain through your experiences in relationships. This knowledge greatly influences your behavior, communication style, perceptions, and self-concept. As your relationships grow and develop, you begin to form theories about how others will act, feel, and think in response to your actions. As you recall from Chapter 2, these hypotheses are referred to as *schemas*, and they guide your processing of information. **Relational schemas** are the bits and pieces of information that you use to interpret the messages you receive in a relationship.[1] Jay has never had a serious girlfriend and considers himself unlucky in love. Whenever Jay has attempted a serious relationship, he has been told that he is immature, insensitive, and incapable of maintaining an adult relationship. Jay and Lesley have gone out a few times, but Jay will not pursue a serious relationship with Lesley because he fears rejection. Jay's previous experiences have formed a schema that stops him from initiating any serious relationship.

Relational history also plays an important role in relational knowledge. **Relational history** is the set of thoughts, perceptions, and impressions you have formed about current or previous relational partners. If you hold positive views about a former partner and later run into that person again, you will react differently than if your history were more negative. For example, Isabella has always focused on what she wants in life. She has worked in the county hospital since her volunteering days during high school and has become very knowledgeable in her field. Louise, the head nurse in pediatrics, first met Isabella as a candy striper and knows that Isabella recently obtained an LVN (licensed vocational nurse) degree. Louise's relational history of Isabella helped Louise nominate Isabella for the RN (registered nurse) college scholarship. As this example shows, remembering things about a relational partner contributes to your overall impression, adding to your relational schema about that person.

◆ Goals and Motivations for Relationship Development

Why do you enter into relationships with certain individuals and not with others? The goals and motivations behind the initiation and development of relationships vary. Expectations play a big role in why you enter into

---

INTERPERSONAL COMMUNICATION

The process of two or three people exchanging messages in order to share meaning, create understanding, and develop relationships.

RELATIONAL SCHEMAS

Information used to interpret messages received in a relationship.

RELATIONAL HISTORY

The sum of the "objective" events in a relationship and the shared experiences of relational partners; also, the set of thoughts, perceptions, and impressions one has formed about one's previous relational partners.

relationships, why you have relationships with certain people, and why some relationships continue to develop while others do not. However, there are yet other influences that lead you to form relationships.

Interpersonal Attraction

What attracts you to certain individuals? Their looks? Their personality? Their sense of humor? Why is it that two people who are very similar may not be attractive to each other? It is not always easy to explain why some people are attracted to others. Two people might be attracted to the same individual for completely different reasons. For instance, Jeremy and Connie both met Shellee at a community Fourth of July picnic. Both were attracted to her because of a "special quality" they saw in her. To Jeremy, Shellee was special because she had lived in Colón, Panama, where he had grown up. In contrast, the special quality that Connie admired was Shellee's satirical sense of humor.

Physical attractiveness is a special kind of interpersonal attraction. Western society places great emphasis on having a pleasant physical appearance. Of course, looks aren't everything, but they do play an important role in attracting others, especially in the early stages of a relationship. In fact, keeping up your physical appearance by eating healthful foods, working out, and getting adequate sleep has become an obsession in the 1990s. What is more, television and fashion magazines keep you up to date on current styles so that your clothing can always be "in." Plastic surgery and cosmetic dental work, once options chosen mainly by the wealthy, are now widely used to achieve the look people want.

Physical Proximity

Long-distance relationships are difficult to maintain simply because of lack of proximity. Although some would argue that "absence makes the heart grow fonder," it can also be said, "out of sight, out of mind." Julie and Moya had a relationship that seemed very successful. They were good friends and had many similar interests. When Moya graduated and moved away, however, the relationship quickly diminished. At first, the two would talk almost every day, but after only a few weeks they became involved in their own activities and their talks grew less frequent. Eventually, they spoke every once in a while but not on a regular basis. As so often happens, they made new friends and entered into new relationships.

Julie and Moya's story is possible in all types of relationships, including friendships, work relationships, and romantic relationships. The simple fact is that people who have frequent, regular contact are more likely to develop and maintain a relationship than are individuals who see one another less regularly. As proof, think for a moment about your current relationships. How many of these formed because of frequent contact? No doubt, you will find that you formed most of your relationships with roommates, classmates, teammates, co-workers, and neighbors because of frequent interaction.

Alleviating Loneliness

What Stimulates You about Relationships?

How do you feel when someone you don't know well takes a special interest in you? Is intellectual, emotional, or physical stimulation most important to you? How does your need for stimulation change as your relationships develop and grow?

Humans feel a natural need for companionship. Between 10 and 20 percent of the population is estimated to experience chronic loneliness, which can result in severe psychological problems.[2] Such problems as anxiety, stress, depression, alcoholism, drug abuse, and poor health have all been tied to loneliness. Most people, however, are lonely only from time to time, and that is when they seek out relationships with other people. A person who feels lonely tends to see a relationship as a logical answer to the problem. A relationship can act as a security blanket, helping to ward off the chill of loneliness. Do you know people who form friendships for no apparent reason other than to escape loneliness?

Stimulation

People have an innate need for stimulation, as is readily evident in the popularity of television and movies. The interaction between two people, however, provides a unique kind of stimulation because it occurs on a personal level. This stimulation is intellectual as well as emotional and physical.

At an *intellectual level*, stimulation has many guises. For example, it stems from conversations about topics of shared interest, especially current events, movies, books, and societal issues. Such conversations help people explore issues and formulate their opinions about them. On a different level, because people have *emotions*, they naturally feel a need for emotional stimulation. This need is best filled by a person who can mutually benefit from emotional gratification. The bond created between two people in a relationship, then, provides an opportunity for them to express their emotions.

Physical stimulation is yet another form. Humans love to touch and be touched. You probably know people who touch while they talk or kiss and hug "hello" and "goodbye" after every encounter. Physical stimulation can

Relational partners can provide intellectual, emotional, and physical stimulation for each other.

be a pleasurable, healthy, and natural part of relationships—as long as it does not interfere with other relational goals.

Achieving Goals

Some people enter into relationships to achieve certain goals. For example, if you have dreamed all your life about doing public service work overseas, you might seek relationships with influential people in that field. Similarly, if you are looking to advance your career, you might try to develop relationships with your superiors and co-workers. Often, your initial motivation for developing a relationship with a particular individual is to see what that person can do for you or how he or she can help you. Of course, the other person will have goals that may or may not be compatible with your own. Therefore, the negotiation of mutual or compatible goals is an important process in relationships.

Goals and Motivations in Intercultural Relationships

Are your relationships with people from other cultures and co-cultures different from your intracultural relationships? Consider two of your important relationships—both business or both social—for comparison, one with a partner from a culture other than yours and one with a partner from your own culture. For each relationship, answer the following questions; then compare your answers for the two relationships.

1. What were your goals and motivations in developing the relationship?
2. What did you believe to be the goals and motivations of your partner?
3. Did your goals and motivations seem compatible with your partner's? What factors led you to choose this partner?
4. Describe your relationship now. Has it developed as you expected? Did you encounter any obstacles? If so, how did you and your partner respond? Describe your progress toward achieving your goals. Describe how your goals and motivations have changed, if at all, as the relationship has developed.

From your answers to these questions, you can make some observations about the role of cultural differences in your relationships. Are cultural differences an important factor in relational development? Research shows that people do not view the relationship process any differently simply because a person is from another culture.* Rather, the main issue is how *similar* the other person seems to you. Intercultural relationships are as strongly grounded in perceived similarity as are intracultural relationships.

*W. B. Gudykunst (1985), An exploratory comparison of close intracultural and intercultural friendships, *Communication Quarterly*, 33, 270–283.

◆ Expectations

Recall from Chapter 1 that the model of communicative competence gives expectations a central position in forming the proper messages. How much do your expectations affect your relationships? Whenever people enter into a relationship, they form ideas as to what they think will or should happen. As the relationship develops, these ideas will change and some new ideas may form. Expectations have a way of influencing how people act and feel toward others. You may form expectations not only about the individual with whom you have a relationship but also about the relationship itself.

Expectations about Relationships

Many people have idealistic notions about relationships. "Once I have this friend," or "once I get married, I'll have it made". It is not unusual to develop expectations about relationships without having particular individuals in mind. Even before relationships begin, you form expectations about future partners. Friends, families, novels, and the media offer many models for you to choose from. Some people may prefer relationships that are intense but last only a short period of time, whereas others prefer intellectual, long-lasting relationships. Every person has strong individual expectations based on relational knowledge and personal tastes and preferences.

Expectations about Relational Partners

When you meet people for the first time, it does not take long for your initial impression to be set in stone, and only after a great deal of interaction will your initial opinion change. When people meet for the first time, they form expectations about each other, as David and Anthony did.

DAVID   When I first met Anthony, I thought he seemed a little conservative and straitlaced. He acted as if going out and having a good time were against the law. He seemed to think that I was wild and out of control. Little did I know that we would become best friends just a short time later.

ANTHONY   I thought David was a real jerk the first time I met him. He seemed so full of himself and acted as if his only goal in life was to go out and get drunk every night. I never would have believed it if someone had told me that we would become friends.

Unrealistic expectations can create problems in a relationship. Unrealistic expectations may arise because of what society says is important in a relationship. Society can give the impression that in a "good" relationship conflict will not arise.

How realistic is this couple?

JOANNIE   Being in love means we'll never fight.

STEPHEN   I know, it's great. You know I'll never make you mad.

*W*hat Are Your Expectations for Relationships?

Do you expect romantic relationships to be long and meaningful? Do you tolerate the idea of short, relatively meaningless relationships? Have you started a relationship knowing that it would probably end in hurt feelings? How would you characterize the ideal relationship? How do your expectations influence your communication? Can you explain how relational expectations affect the communicative competence model?

Unrealistic expectations produce a great deal of unnecessary stress because such expectations are hardly ever met. As a result, people sometimes dismiss relationships that might have ultimately been beneficial.

Realistic expectations can help prevent the development of potentially unsuccessful relationships. Yasar has a strong Muslim background and considers religion an important part of his life. Rachel is Jewish and has had very little exposure to the Muslim religion. The two are considering dating, but Yasar thinks that their religious differences are too great to overcome. He feels that Rachel will never be able to meet his expectations concerning religion. Yasar's expectations have prevented him from entering into a relationship that would probably not succeed.

Violated Expectations

The following story shows what can happen when one person in a relationship does not adhere to the expectations of the other. Roberto and Carol had been dating for two months, seeing each other every Friday and Saturday night and on Wednesday afternoons. Although they had occasionally discussed dating each other exclusively, they had not made a formal agreement to that effect. Roberto went out of town for several days and told Carol that he did not expect to return until after the weekend. But Roberto finished his trip early and arrived back in town on Friday night. On his way home, he decided to go by Carol's house to ask her out for Saturday night. He was stunned to learn that Carol was entertaining another man at her house. Roberto had formed certain expectations about his relationship with Carol, and now those expectations had, in essence, been violated. He was hurt and sad that Carol would "cheat on him."

Was Carol wrong to violate Roberto's expectations? What do you do if things do not turn out as you had hoped they would? Why are some people willing to ignore some expectancy violations, whereas others deal with unmet expectations severely? The difference probably has to do with the kind of relationship and the individuals involved. The more important a relationship or individual is to you, the more you will allow violations. You may think that maintaining a relationship with an individual is more

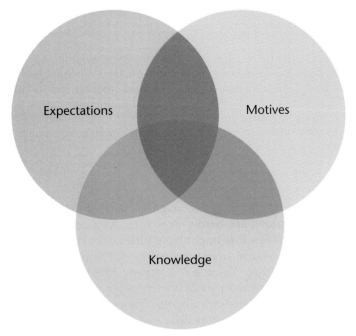

FIGURE 7.1
Knowledge, motives, and expectations affect one another as a relationship develops.

important than having your expectations met, or perhaps you may alter your expectations. Many people enter into relationships expecting a fairy-tale ending, but they soon realize that life seldom follows that kind of story line. To continue a relationship, then, you generally have to revise your expectations. Or, you may discover that the relationship or person is less important than your expectations.

Knowledge, Motives, and Expectations

When you consider knowledge, motives, and expectations together, it becomes clearer how relationships begin, develop, grow, and maybe even dete-riorate (see Figure 7.1). You initiate a relationship because of your goals and motives (loneliness, stimulation, etc.), and then you form expectations about the person and the relationship based on your level of relational knowledge. This knowledge changes as you interact with your partner and your inter-actions modify your expectations, which in turn affect your motives for being in the relationship. Relationships are highly dynamic, requiring a continuous assessment of these three elements. As you study the process of relationship development, you will gain a better understanding of the dynamic and evolv-ing nature of these elements.

How Do You Handle Expectations?

When was the last time someone violated your relational expectations? Were you too optimistic in your predictions? Too pessimistic? How do you avoid making expectations that are too high or too low?

*D*etermining Your Own List of Costs and Rewards

Consider the following list of traits and behaviors and decide which are most important to you as relational rewards and costs. Write "R1" in the blank for items that you consider primary (very important) rewards, "R2" for those you view as secondary rewards (nice to have), and "R3" for rewards that are relatively unimportant to you. Write "C1" before items that you consider primary (very important) costs, "C2" before those you view as secondary costs, and "C3" before costs that are relatively unimportant to you.

_____ Laughs at my jokes

_____ Is affectionate

_____ Is physically attractive

_____ Fits in with my friends

_____ Fits in with my family

_____ Tells inappropriate jokes

_____ Refuses to share emotions

_____ Ignores my feelings

_____ Is career oriented

_____ Wears clothes I dislike

_____ Has views about religion different from mine

_____ Has views about children similar to mine

_____ Has an exciting personality

Do you notice a pattern? Are traits or behaviors in certain areas (e.g., appearance, emotional expressiveness) particularly important to you?

◆ Costs and Rewards

Every relationship produces advantages and disadvantages for the relational partners. In a widely cited book, *Social Penetration Theory*, Altman and Taylor suggest that relationships begin, develop, grow, and deteriorate based on the rewards and costs that come from the interaction of the two relational partners.[3] *Rewards* are those relational elements that you feel good about, whereas *costs* are those that annoy you. For example, negative expectancy violations are costs, and warm companionship is a reward. When people believe the rewards outweigh the costs, they will most likely find the relationship beneficial and will work to make sure it continues. A person who thinks that the costs are greater than the rewards will most likely not attempt to develop that particular relationship.

EXTRINSIC REWARDS
Benefits gained from association with another person, including new opportunities and contacts.

INSTRUMENTAL REWARDS
Rewards that relational partners give to each other, including material benefits.

INTRINSIC REWARDS
Benefits that result from an exchange of intimacy.

Three categories of rewards are available to relational partners. **Extrinsic rewards** are gained purely from association with another person. These types of rewards range from new opportunities, to "contacts" that may later be useful, to a perceived higher social status. A struggling actor trying to become a star may become involved with a director in show business who can help his career. **Instrumental rewards** are those that relational partners give to one another—for example, a basic exchange of goods for services. Two people may decide to live together because one can provide appliances and furniture and the other can provide a steady income to pay the rent. **Intrinsic rewards** result from an exchange of intimacy.[4] People looking for these types of rewards are interested in each other for personal reasons. For example, two people who are working out at the local gym may be physically attracted to each other. They may meet later for drinks and eventually develop an intimate relationship.

◆ Strategies for Reducing Uncertainty

According to the uncertainty reduction theory developed by Berger and Calabrese, when two people meet, their main focus is on decreasing the uncertainty that lies between them.[5] Early in a relationship, uncertainty acts as a double-edged sword, creating both excitement and frustration. In a new romantic relationship, for example, the excitement comes from the mystery, which pumps your heart a little harder, stirs the butterflies in your stomach, and moistens your palms. The frustrations stem from expectancy violations, hurt feelings, and insecurity. In any type of relationship, three factors explain your motivation for reducing uncertainty. First, if you believe that developing a relationship with a particular person will benefit you in some way, you will be more motivated to secure a level of certainty with that person. Second, if you believe that you will have frequent contact with that person in the future, you will want to reduce any uncertainty you may have. Finally, if the person acts in a manner that is unexpected or not considered "normal," you will want to reduce uncertainty to help you better understand his or her behavior.

The best way to reduce uncertainty is to obtain information about a person that is unique to that individual. In this way, you will know that person at a more intimate level. Uncertainty reduction allows you to predict your relational partners with more accuracy, which in turn makes you feel more comfortable in developing your relationships even further. You will never know everything about your partner. But the more you understand, the more likely you will be able to have a fulfilling relationship with that person.

How do you reduce this uncertainty? As with many things in your life, when you are uncertain you seek information. Once you have sufficient information about your partner, you will be able to make educated predictions about that person. Predictions help you determine what the partner will say and how he or she will react or feel in particular situations. From the beginning stages of a relationship, partners make predictions about one another and the relationship. As the partners get to know each other—as there is less uncertainty between the two—their predictions will more often be correct. Information-seeking behaviors can take three forms: monitoring, proactive, and indirect.

Monitoring Strategies

When Rob wants to learn more about Deanne, he takes advantage of an opportunity to observe her as she talks with her friends in the hallway before class. He learns that she laughs frequently, that she likes to touch her friends on the shoulder when she is talking to them, and that her friends like her a lot. This type of information seeking, monitoring, is useful to Rob because it allows him to observe Deanne in her everyday settings and to obtain knowledge about her as a potential relational partner. Of course, watching Deanne talking to friends gives Rob only a small picture of what she is really like, so he may want to observe her in different settings. If he knows that she attends the public relations club, for example, he may go to one of their meetings to see Deanne in action again. Monitoring strategies allow you to observe people as they communicate with others. Do they seem like people you would want to know better? Is their behavior like that of people you enjoy being with?

Sometimes just observing others as they go about their business does not give you all the information you need. You may want to see people in situations that interest you. Rob, for instance, may want to know how Deanne would act around his friends, so he asks her out and they go to a party where his friends will be. In this way, he can monitor her behavior in a situation that is important to him.

Proactive Strategies

Proactive strategies let you obtain information about a person more directly. Rob is acquainted with one of Deanne's friends, Eduardo, and calls him up to ask some questions about Deanne. Rob finds out that Deanne is not dating anyone exclusively right now, that she loves Mexican food, and that she goes to aerobics classes on Monday and Wednesday afternoons. Of course, Rob is aware that Eduardo might tell Deanne that he called and asked about her, but Rob thinks it is worth the risk. Besides, he reasons, it wouldn't hurt for Deanne to learn of his interest in her from a third party.

A more forthright method is direct questioning of the person you are interested in. Sometimes referred to as *interactive strategy*, this technique increases your chances of learning what you really want to know about a person and shows the person you are interested. Both purposes increase your opportunities to reduce uncertainty.

ROB   [Talking with Deanne in the student union] Are you going to stay in Seattle after you graduate?

DEANNE   [Thinking, "Hmm, he must really be interested in me"] I really haven't decided yet. The job market looks pretty bleak. What about you?

ROB   [Thinking, "Good, she wants to know about me too"] Well, I'm hoping my uncle can use me at his firm. Have you thought about graduate school?

DEANNE   Yeah, but I'll have to retake the GRE to get into grad school here.

Obviously, direct questioning is helpful in reducing uncertainty, but it also entails risks. If you ask questions that are forward or inappropriate, you may do more harm than good.

ROB   Do you plan to have kids after you marry?

DEANNE   [Thinking, "Hey, slow down, Speedy"] I don't know. Hey, isn't that Richard over there? I need to talk to him. See you later.

An even riskier proactive strategy is self-disclosure. As you recall from Chapter 3, self-disclosure is revealing personal information that would otherwise remain hidden from others. How does self-disclosure function as information seeking? Quite often, recipients of self-disclosure counter with personal information of their own, either out of a sense of obligation or because they see this as an opportunity to exchange information. The risk comes when self-disclosure is not reciprocated. If you self-disclose and the other person elects not to reciprocate, that individual has an information advantage over you. On the other hand, self-disclosure is an excellent way for two people to reduce uncertainty, for it is one of the most direct means of exchanging information.

ROB   I've always felt uncomfortable about long-term relationships.

DEANNE   Really? Me, too. Although I'm willing to give the right person a chance to change my mind.

Indirect Strategies

When monitoring strategies cannot provide specific information and proactive strategies are too direct or risky, a third alternative is available: indirect strategies. These techniques can help you obtain information from a relational partner without directly asking for it. They are used when issues are too sensitive to bring into the open or when the relationship may not be ready for a full-blown discussion of some topics.

Secret tests is an indirect strategy used in learning about your partner that involves searching for information in a roundabout manner. This approach is especially useful when you are trying to determine what a partner thinks about the relationship. Examples are *jealousy* tests (making a partner jealous to see his or her reaction), *self-putdowns* (making self-deprecating remarks in the hope that your partner will correct you), and *forced choice* (giving the partner an ultimatum to decide between you and someone else).[6] Yvonne and Igor have been dating for about 3 months and seem to be developing a good relationship. They have not talked yet about the relationship or their feelings for each other. Yvonne is beginning to wonder whether Igor has serious plans for their relationship or if he is just having fun but not taking the relationship as seriously as she is. When they go to a party one night, Yvonne spends a great deal of time talking to Jack. She stands close to him and touches him several times as she speaks to him. While talking with Jack, Yvonne is constantly observing Igor to see his reaction to her behavior. This is an example of a jealousy test; it serves to decrease the uncertainty the partners might have about one another. Once uncertainty is reduced, they can make better predictions as to what the other will do, say, think, and feel.

◆ Stages of a Relationship

How do relationships develop? Although each relationship is unique, most relationships go through certain stages. These stages are graphically presented in the model of relational development, Figure 7.2 on page 208. Expectations, motives, and relational knowledge constitute one part of the model. As you know, these elements affect the relational partners' perceptions of each other and the relationship. Changes in any of these elements can significantly affect what happens to a relationship. Rewards and costs also play a role in the process. If rewards exceed costs, you are more likely to proceed in a relationship; if costs overwhelm rewards, relational decline can result. Uncertainty reduction is a key feature of this model because gaining information about a relational partner will affect expectations, motives, and knowledge as well as costs and rewards.

Examine Figure 7.2 carefully. As you will see, there are six possible stages of relational development. It is important to note that not all relationships experience each of these stages, particularly the last two, decline and exit. Assume that all relationships start with an initial stage. Many will proceed to an exploratory phase; some of these relationships will go on to intensification, and some of those will become stable. If at any point in the process costs exceed rewards, relational decline may result. If relational partners are willing to work at the relationship, repair strategies may be attempted, moving the relationship back to one of its previous stages. If relational decline has reached a "point of no return," termination strategies may be used to exit the relationship altogether.[7] We will now discuss the six stages in some detail.

The Initial Stage

When you begin a relationship, you are probably uncertain about your potential partner. Your expectations and knowledge are based on general information gained from the partner's appearance, demeanor, and behavior.

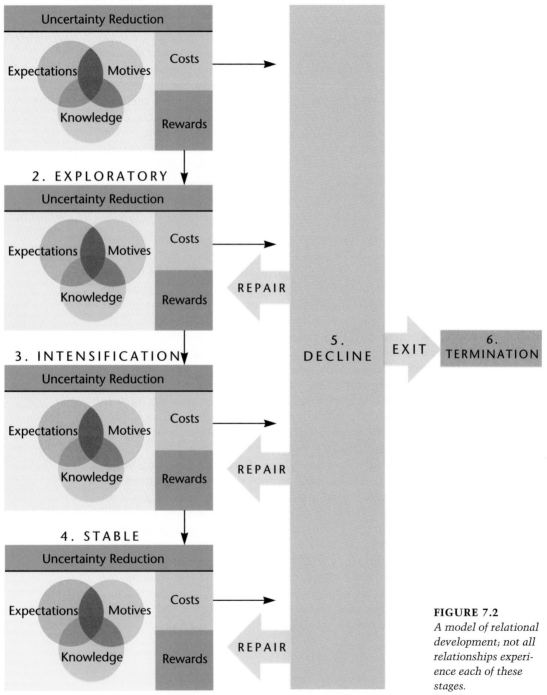

FIGURE 7.2
A model of relational development; not all relationships experience each of these stages.

After some contact with the person, you may begin to form impressions that confirm or modify your knowledge, expectations, and motives for being in the relationship. Positive impressions (assessments) translate into rewards, whereas negative impressions are perceived as costs. If costs seem to outweigh rewards, the relationship will probably end at this point. If enough rewards are present, the relationship will move to the exploratory stage.

The Exploratory Stage

The exploratory stage, true to its name, involves a great deal of information seeking. It assumes that both relational partners want to reduce uncertainty. Monitoring, proactive, and indirect strategies are used in this stage, so that enough relational knowledge is accumulated to make further assessments. In the exploratory stage, relational partners are still hesitant to delve into highly intimate topics; they are still testing the relationship. As information is exchanged, expectations, knowledge, and motives are reassessed, and rewards and costs are reexamined. If costs exceed rewards, relational decline is likely; if rewards are abundant, the next stage further intensifies the relationship.

The Intensification Stage

By the time relational partners reach this stage, they have made an investment in each other and can afford to intensify their relationship. This is especially evident in the means they use to reduce uncertainty further. Instead of seeking personal information about each other, the partners are more likely to focus on the relationship. This is especially true if the relationship is a romantic one. Intensification reflects a desire to move the relationship to a new level. Both relational partners realize that their expectations, motives, and knowledge are different from those in the earlier stages, so they assess rewards and costs along new lines. For example, two friends who are intensifying their relationship will know not to hold unrealistic expectations because their relational knowledge has grown. They may even develop new motives for being in the relationship. In the earlier stages, they may have valued companionship, but now they value their partner's trust more than anything else. Rewards and costs may change as well. It is in the intensification stage that relational intimacy or closeness may be felt for the first time.

The Stable Stage

By the time partners have reached the stable stage, their relationship is no longer volatile or temporary. Relational partners now have a great deal of knowledge about one another, their expectations are accurate and realistic, and they feel comfortable with their motives for being in the relationship. Uncertainty reduction is not a major issue in this phase unless events in the lives of the relational partners change. Perceptions of rewards and costs become more stable, providing a measure of predictability in the relationship. This is not to

cathy®   **by Cathy Guisewite**

How can you recognize the exploratory stage of a relationship?

say that relationships don't continue to evolve, for in order for relationships to enjoy stability, they must continue to interest the partners.

Wilmot characterizes stable relationships in the following three ways: "(a) relationships stabilize because the participants reach some minimal agreement on what they want from the relationship, (b) relationships can stabilize at differing levels of intimacy, and (c) a stabilized relationship still has areas of change occurring in it."[8] The concept of intimacy is worth considering in more detail.

Intimacy is a special aspect of relational development that is found in the stable phase.[9] **Intimacy** is a deep understanding of another person and is one of the highest levels that a relationship can aspire to. One popular misconception about intimacy is that it is usually sexual. On the contrary, intimacy is not restricted to romantic relationships. As noted earlier, it can occur between parent and child, best friends, and colleagues; even adversaries can enjoy intimacy if they have a deep understanding of one another.

Once partners have achieved a satisfactory level of intimacy, they must continuously work to sustain that intimacy. Many strategies can be used to maintain intimacy, but this section suggests the following ones.

Reciprocal self-disclosure and trust If individuals think that they can completely trust their partners and their partners have complete trust in them, then they are more likely to self-disclose private and personal matters and create a greater sense of intimacy. Marissa thinks that Natalie trusts her because whenever she discloses something personal, Natalie responds and often follows up with a self-disclosure of her own.

Supportive interchanges If you feel confident that your partner supports you 100 percent, you will most likely feel a greater closeness or intimacy. In order to give supportive interchanges, you should be aware

---

INTIMACY

A deep understanding of another person; one of the highest levels that a relationship can aspire to.

of your partner's successes and improvements, give frequent approval of his or her activities, and avoid expressing disapproval.[10]

Commitment talk Relationships sustain intimacy when the partners feel an involvement and use commitment talk. The rejection of competitors, a willingness to resolve any problems in order to maintain the relationship, and an acceptance of personal responsibility for the relationship are just some of the ways that partners exchange commitment talk.[11]

Enchantment People can deliberately be enchanting in order to sustain intimacy. In the beginning, relationships are exciting and full of surprises. Later, this newness can wear off and leave the partners feeling as though every day were the same. To help maintain intimacy, partners can be playful, mysterious, or unpredictable. Intimacy is unique in each relationship, and how you and your partner sustain intimacy is also unique. No matter which strategies you use, you should remember that an intimate relationship requires continuous maintenance.

A Definition of Love. Love expresses a wide range of feelings, from deep passion for another person to great fondness for a favorite dessert. Saying "I love you" seems to have lost some of its emphasis and does not appear to have the definite meaning it once did.

Love generally involves an exclusive kind of relationship. The relationship of people who claim to be "in love" is supposed to be different from any other relationship either might have. Love has been described as a permanent

The pressure on young adults to find a romantic partner remains a strong force in contemporary society.

LOVE

A deep affection for and attraction to another person; generally involves a relationship that is more exclusive than friendship.

relationship with deep emotional ties—one that is passionate and intense. However, that is the fairy-tale version. For this section, we define **love** as a deep affection for and attraction to another person.

Types of Love. Have you ever thought that love can be different for different people? Do you experience different types of love depending on who the person is? The Canadian psychologist J. A. Lee conducted extensive research with the goal of placing different types of love into categories.[12] His research, which involved hundreds of people, revealed six different types of love.

> *Eros—beauty and sexuality* Sex is the most important aspect of erotic love. This type of relationship is quite intense, both emotionally and physically. The focus is on beauty and attractiveness more than on qualities such as intelligence and sense of humor.
>
> *Ludus—entertainment and excitement* Ludus means *play* in Latin, and the ludic lover views love as a game. Ludic love does not require great commitment or feeling, for it lacks passion and intensity. It lasts only as long as the partners find each other entertaining or fun. When things begin to dull, new partners are found. The casual dating of many different people is a prime example of ludus.
>
> *Storge—peacefulness and slowness* Storge is a type of love that lacks passion and excitement. It develops over an extended period of time and often begins in friendship. Storgic lovers may have difficulty pinpointing the precise moment when they knew they were in love. For them, falling in love was a gradual process; they didn't realize it had happened until much later. Storgic lovers often share common interests and activities but rarely disclose any feelings about their relationship.
>
> *Pragma—practicality and tradition* In Greek, *pragma* means *life work*. Pragmatic lovers are extremely logical and practical in seeking a companion. They want a long-term relationship with an individual who shares their goals in life. If a person wants a relationship that does not require much time or effort, then he or she will search for a mate who is looking for the same things. Pragmatic relationships seem to last longer than any of the others, perhaps because both parties enter with realistic expectations—"with open eyes."
>
> *Mania—elation and depression* This is the love that is often referred to as "romantic love." It exhibits extreme feelings, ranging from high excitement and passion to deep depression. Manic lovers are often so concerned with the thought of losing their mate that they are unable to enjoy the relationship. Mania love is characteristically intense, obsessive, desperate, and painful. Manic relationships often appear out of control; the partners act impulsively and often get hurt. Mania love is full of excitement and intensity, but it reaches a peak and then quickly fades away.
>
> *Agape—compassion and selflessness* In this type of love, the individual gives willingly and expects nothing in return. This type of lover can

care for others without close ties; a deep relationship is not necessary for agapic love to develop. The agapic lover always wants the other to be happy, even if it results in his or her own pain or unhappiness.

No map of the road of love has ever been prepared; only trial and error, along with the passing of time and experience, will help you in your love relationships. Nonetheless, Goss and O'Hair give several helpful hints on how you may establish *effective love*.[13]

1. Develop insight into and empathy for a partner's concept of love.

2. Analyze your own and your partner's expectations of love.

3. Accept the fact that, even though two people have different concepts of love, neither owns the truth.

4. Be flexible. Adapt the way you show love to meet a partner's image of loving behavior.

5. Recall what you said or did to show loving feelings in the early stages of the relationship.

6. Notice what your partner does to make you feel loved.

Paths to Stable Relationships. Maintaining successful relationships requires a great deal of effort. Partners must gain an understanding of their individual relationship, work within its limits, and utilize its strengths. You can try to achieve stable relationships by adopting the following behaviors.

Be understanding. Try to understand how your partner views the world. Empathize with his or her fears, pain, and dreams. It is important to be supportive. Do not judge these concerns. Aim only to understand in order to communicate more effectively with your partner. Show that you care.

Reveal your feelings. Reveal yourself cautiously. It may be detrimental to self-disclose too much. Knowledge of past acts or certain feelings may harm the relationship if disclosed at the wrong time. Consider how the knowledge will affect your partner's actions and feelings; use good judgment. Still, self-disclosure is an essential part of a relationship. It strengthens the bond between relational partners.

Be flexible. Recognize that people and relationships naturally change and that these changes must be handled. Often, conscious change is necessary on the part of one or both of the relational partners. Thus, an understanding that change is natural and essential is crucial.

Be accommodating. Conflict naturally occurs. Relational partners who accept this reality and proceed in conflict situations with the right intentions will benefit greatly. Proceed with the goal of reaching a compromise instead of winning the argument; otherwise, one or both partners may get hurt. Conflict can be healthy, but when approached incorrectly it can be very detrimental.

Don't demand too much. Be realistic in your expectations of your partner and of the relationship. Do not compare your relationship with other

Thinking about Love

How many times have you experienced the types of love outlined here? Can you add any new categories? Is love always different for every person, or are some qualities common to many types of love? If so, what are some of these qualities?

*L*ove on the Move

Joyce and Jim, who were introduced by common friends, have been dating for 6 months. Joyce has told Jim on several occasions that she loves him and wants them to be together forever. Jim is thrilled to hear this and always reciprocates Joyce's sentiments and feelings. The fact of the matter is that, although Joyce does love Jim, she knows full well that her career will cause her to move soon. Jim owns a thriving business in the community where they both live, and all of his family, including his ex-wife and three children, live near him. Joyce knows that Jim would never move with her. Even though she knows they will break up in a few months, Joyce continues to discuss their future, including marriage, with Jim. Joyce fears that Jim would look elsewhere for a relationship if he knew about her impending move, and she wants to maintain the relationship as long as she is in town.

Is Joyce using unethical communication to maintain her relationship with Jim? If so, does the fact that she really loves him make her behavior less unethical? Would it be unethical for Jim to find another relationship if he thought Joyce were moving? Should ethics always come before love?

relationships that you perceive to be better than your own. Actually, most relationships experience the same kinds of trouble that your own does. Therefore, do not set your expectations too high.

The Decline Stage

Relationship decline, the erosion that occurs over time to some relationships, has several causes. Although no two relationships are the same, the causes of relationship decline share some similarities. As you observed in Figure 7.2, relational decline results when costs exceed rewards and relational partners put less effort into the relationship. Three factors in the costs/rewards evaluation typically lead to relational decline: (1) uncertainty events, (2) unmet expectations, and (3) interference (family, work, timing, money, etc.).

UNCERTAINTY EVENTS

Events that cause uncertainty in a relationship (e.g., a competing relationship, an unexplained loss of closeness, deception, or an unexplained change in the personality of one partner).

Uncertainty Events. Events or behavioral patterns that cause uncertainty in a relationship are called **uncertainty events**. Uncertainty events leave one or both partners wondering about the cause of the events and their significance for the relationship. Planalp and Honeycutt studied these events and found several factors that cause uncertainty in a relationship:[14]

- Competing relationships, either dating relationships or platonic ones
- An unexplained loss of closeness
- A change in sexual behavior

• Deception or betrayal of confidence

• An unexplained change in personality or values

These events or changes may be sudden and very noticeable, or they may be subtle and escape immediate attention.

Unmet Expectations. The way two people interact is greatly influenced by their expectations for the relationship and their perceptions of each other's expectations. These expectations range from where the relationship is going in general to very specific expectations about how the other person will react to a certain situation.

Dissatisfaction with a relationship often begins when a gap forms between a person's expectations about a relationship and the actual course the relationship is taking. This is often the result of differences between the partners' respective expectations. Susannah and Jiro were friends for 2 years while they were business majors at the same university. Upon graduation, Susannah went to work at a stock brokerage. When another job opened at the firm, Jiro expressed interest in it to Susannah. Although she encouraged Jiro to apply, Susannah felt uneasy mixing friendship and work and did not recommend Jiro for the position. Jiro expected Susannah, as a friend, to help him get the job. When she went against Jiro's expectations, he decided to end their friendship.

Interference. Many obstacles may crop up in a relationship, interfering with its growth. Timing, third-party relationships, the family or friends of one partner, and problems with work or money can all contribute to the decline of a relationship.

The amount of involvement within a particular relationship can influence the timing of the breakup. The great majority of relational breakups (71.1 percent) occur during the spring and summer months, from April to September. Research has also found that the degree of involvement in the relationship plays a part in determining when to end it.[15] Relational partners who were more emotionally involved broke up during the school year, while less involved partners ended their relationship during vacation time.

Often a relationship fails to meet a person's needs, and when this happens, that person may seek fulfillment outside of the relationship. A third party may not necessarily be a competing romantic interest; it may be a friend or family member. Whoever it is, however, that person fulfills a need that the relational partner cannot, making the presence of the partner unnecessary. When Natalie refused to go to the golf course with Carl while he played, Carl invited another friend, Katherine, to play. The two enjoyed playing golf together, and their golf games soon became a regular occurrence. Although Natalie herself was responsible for this situation, she became extremely jealous of Carl and Katherine's relationship. When she told Carl that she did not think it was right for him to play golf with another woman instead of his girlfriend, Carl did not understand why Natalie was so upset. After all, his relationship with Katherine was strictly

Causes of Unmet Expectations

Unmet expectations can result from personality differences, uncompromising attitudes, differing levels of sexual attraction and enjoyment, or lost romance. What other causes can you cite?

platonic, and he had asked Natalie to play golf before he had ever contacted Katherine. Although the relationship between Carl and Katherine was a friendship based on a hobby both enjoyed, Natalie found this third-party relationship threatening.

Often problems develop within a relationship because of differences between one partner and the family or friends of the other partner. These problems often result from personal differences or differences in value systems, leading to disapproval shown by the family or friends of the relational partner. This may cause problems as the partner "caught in the middle" tries to reconcile the competing views and decide what to do. When Rosa and Charles announced that they were getting married, their families were pleased. Rosa's Mexican heritage taught her that the groom's family was responsible for the bulk of the wedding expenses, whereas Charles's American culture led him to believe that the bride's family carried the load. As plans for the wedding began to take shape, each family had its own ideas of exactly how everything should be and who should bear most of the costs. Both Rosa and Charles felt caught between the two families. When the disagreement between the families continued, Rosa and Charles decided to elope. They felt that was the only way their relationship could survive the family interference.

Problems associated with work occur on many levels. Two of the most common complaints made about relational partners are that they spend too much time at work or "bring the office home." At issue here is time spent on one's job in proportion to time spent with the relational partner or family. A perception that more time is spent on one's job may lead to the belief that the job is more important than the partner or family.

Work also causes problems when it clashes with expectations and values. Career-oriented females with children may be viewed as neglectful and uncaring, whereas career-focused males with children are seen as ambitious providers. There are many opinions about quality time versus quantity of time. One question that is often raised about this issue is: How many professionals say on their death beds, "I wish I'd worked more!"?

Money is a major issue in most relationships. DeVito notes that one-fourth to one-third of all couples rank it among their most troublesome problems. He also states that it is the close connection between money and power that makes it such a thorny issue. For example, the person who makes more money usually has the final say about the purchase of expensive items and about many other financial decisions. Money also causes problems because couples naturally argue about how it is to be spent in general. Another reason why money may contribute to difficulties is that the partners often view money differently because of upbringing, spending habits, and gender.[16]

Relational Repair

The warning signs of a relationship in decline are often pretty obvious. An argument may get out of hand or a situation may cause misunderstandings that could have been corrected. One person may feel that not enough effort has been exerted; or the partners may simply "give up." Whatever the

Why do you think financial problems are frequently a cause of relational decline?

reason for the decline, some people will have a desire to repair the relationship. Duck suggests the following repair tactics:[17]

- Improve communication.
- Bring out the partner's positive side.
- Focus on the positive aspects of the relationship.
- Reinterpret the behavior of the partner as positive and well intentioned.
- Reduce negativity toward the partner and adopt a more balanced view.
- Reevaluate the attractiveness and unattractiveness of alternative relationships and alternative partners.
- Enlist the support of others in order to hold the relationship together.

In order to repair their relationship, partners have to decrease the amount of disagreement in their interactions. They must focus on the relationship itself and not on the source of a particular argument. Next, the partners may need to improve the quality of their communication. Some relational partners need to work on their listening skills and strive to understand the other person's perspective. Like all communication, thinking about what you are about to say is also very important because words spoken harshly are not easily forgotten. Another repair tactic is for the relational partners to display the attractive qualities that sparked the relationship in the first place. The partners may also try to increase their intimacy, by making more self-disclosures and spending quality time with one another.[18]

Applying the Model of Relational Development

Find a married couple whom you know, but are not related to, and ask them to describe how their relationship developed. Show the couple the model of relational development (Figure 7.2) and ask them how relevant the model is to their relationship.

Repair tactics used during the final stages of termination will most likely involve one of three approaches: the use of persons outside the relationship to help hold the relationship together; social support from friends; and an accounting to others of why the relationship ended.

The Termination Stage

Every relationship is influenced by unique situations and circumstances, but it is still possible to make some generalizations. Davis identifies two general reasons for terminating relationships.[19]

The first reason he notes is *passing away*, which is characterized by the gradual fading of a relationship. The relationship loses its vitality perhaps because of another intimate or because of jealousy over the time one partner spends in activities not associated with the other partner. Also, the time available for interaction may have decreased. As a result, communication and intimacy may have declined, leading to a separation of attitudes between the partners. A relationship may also pass away because the partners simply do not continue making the effort needed to maintain an intimate relationship. This leads to a stagnant relationship and a decrease in communication.

Davis also identifies the situation of *sudden death*, which refers to an unexpected ending that comes suddenly. Here the partners may terminate a relationship that one or both of them have desired to end for some time. Feelings that were once present may have died. Nonetheless, the partners may have continued the relationship because of circumstances external to the relationship, such as the years invested together or the presence of children.

If only one partner wishes to terminate a relationship, he or she may suddenly act on this desire after a long period of uncertainty. The partner seeking an end to the relationship may previously have allowed it to drag on in response to alternating good and bad phases or to the efforts of the other partner to maintain the relationship. Whatever the reason, the dissatisfied partner, once resolved to terminate the relationship, will do so quickly and "move on."

Sudden relationship death may also occur when one partner, perceiving that a relationship is moving too fast, requests a slowdown. If this request is not met, the person may react by terminating the relationship altogether. A relationship may also be ended by isolated occurrences, such as a single argument that goes too far or a unique misunderstanding that ends an otherwise smoothly running relationship. Finally, a partner may violate some implicit or explicit rule of interaction that both had adopted earlier. For example, one partner decides not to attend an official holiday celebration with the partner's family, instead opting to visit a childhood friend in another state. This action may cause the other partner to be angry enough to end the relationship.

Strategies for Terminating a Relationship. As we mentioned earlier, the circumstances present in each relationship are different; accordingly, termination strategies also vary. Several common methods of terminating romantic relationships are listed in Table 7.1. Which of these strategies have worked for

TABLE 7.1 ROMANTIC RELATIONAL
TERMINATION STRATEGIES

STRATEGY	TACTICS	EXAMPLE
Positive-tone messages	Fairness	"It wouldn't be right to go on acting like we're in love when I know I am not!"
	Compromise	"I still care about you. We can still see each other occasionally."
	Fatalism	"Destiny would never let us go on for very long in this relationship."
Deescalation	Promise of friendship	"We can still be friends."
	Implied possible reconciliation	"We need time alone; maybe that will rekindle our feelings for each other."
	Blaming relationship	"It's not your fault, but this relationship is bogging us down."
	Appeal to independence	"We don't need to be tied down right now."
Withdrawal/ avoidance	Avoid contact with the person as much as possible.	"I don't think I'll be able to see you this weekend."
Justification	Emphasize positive consequences of disengaging	"It's better for you and me to see other people since we've changed so much."
	Emphasize negative consequences of not disengaging	"We will miss too many opportunities if we don't see other people."
Negative identity management	Emphasize enjoyment of life	"Life is too short to spend with just one person right now."
	Nonnegotiation	"I need to see other people— period!"

Source: Adapted from D. J. Canary & M. J. Cody (1994), *Interpersonal communication: A goals-based approach* (New York: St. Martin's Press), pp. 266–268.

you in the past? How could you use some of these strategies more effectively in the future?

Effects of Termination. The termination of serious or lengthy relationships can be both traumatic and stressful. A great deal of research has been done on the tactics individuals use to cope with a breakup. Harvey, Orbuch, and Weber, for example, have devised a model that focuses on psychological needs, communication, and post-termination mental health.[20] According to this model, after a traumatic experience, individuals experience a natural need to explain fully what happened. Months or even years may be needed to complete this process because so much information, so many details, and so much potential for second-guessing have built up. This accounting process consists of forming a detailed, coherent story about the relationship, what happened, when, why, and with what consequences. In addition, emotional consequences must be dealt with when a relationship is terminated. Both partners will experience some type of emotion in regard to the ending of their relationship. Feelings of distress, unhappiness, and disappointment are common. The relational partner who initiated the breakup may experience guilt, while the other partner may feel angry and depressed.

Reconciliation

Reconciliation is a repair strategy that goes the extra mile. It signals that one relational partner wants to rekindle an extinguished relationship. Reconciling a relationship entails a lot of risk because the other person may have no interest in a "second chance." It takes a lot of guts and initiative for someone to risk another dose of rejection and humiliation. Nonetheless, some people will launch headfirst into a series of strategies designed to rejuvenate a relationship. Other people may carefully consider the options available and construct a message that will appeal to an ex-partner.

Relationships that are begun anew may turn out in several different ways. The relationship may be strengthened by the termination and subsequent reconciliation. In this case, the partners are sure of their goals for the relationship and their feelings about each other. In other cases, old issues may not be settled and may resurface, causing the same troubles or resulting in intensified disagreement and strife. There is no way to say with any certainty how a reconciliation attempt will turn out.

◆ Types of Relationships

There are as many different types of relationships as there are individuals who make up these relationships. Some common relationships are those between co-workers, between doctors and patients, and between salespeople and clients. However, this section is concerned primarily with two important types: friendship and family.

Friendship

Friendship is a relationship between two or more people that is perceived as mutually satisfying, productive, and beneficial. Everyone has a personal opinion as to what important qualities a friend should have.

FRIENDSHIP

A relationship between two or more people that is perceived as mutually satisfying, productive, and beneficial.

Characteristics of Friendship. In spite of individual differences as to what constitutes friendship, agreement seems to have been reached on six characteristics: availability, caring, honesty, confidentiality, loyalty, and empathy.[21]

What good would a friend be who was never available to spend time with you? People want friends to make time for them and be accessible. If the parties in a relationship seldom interact with each other, the relationship often deteriorates or loses its closeness. Do your close friends make time for you even when they are busy? You may often make friends through your activities, classes, or work. You want to have common interests and activities with your friends. What would two people do together if they had absolutely nothing in common? Usually, these shared activities mean the difference between being acquaintances and being friends.

You want your friends to care about you. Even if something in your life is of no great importance to them, you want and expect them to care about what happens because it's important to you. Your friends do not have to agree with the choices or events in your life, but they need to care about them. If an individual were to ignore you, have no regard for your feelings, and genuinely seem not to care about what happened to you, you would not identify that person as your friend.

Honesty is a virtue that is vital in all relationships. You want your friends to be open and honest with you. When a relational partner deceives you, the deception tends to decrease the degree of closeness that the two of you shared. Sometimes your friends may have to be "brutally honest" and tell you things that you would rather not hear. You have to accept this honesty as constructive criticism and remember that, although you may not like what you are hearing, you may need to hear it and hearing it from a friend may actually be best.

You want confidentiality from your friends. In other words, you want to be sure that what you disclose to your friends will not end up in the *National Inquirer* tomorrow. What you share with your friends may seem meaningless and trivial to them but may be extremely personal to you. You want to be able to trust your friends and know that they will not share your deepest, darkest secrets with others.

A friend who can be loyal in even the worst of times is a lifelong friend. Have you ever had a friend who was extremely nice and supportive to your face, but the minute you left the room tore you and your reputation to shreds? A true friend is one who is loyal and would never allow others to degrade you without standing up for you or at least letting it be known that he or she did not agree with what was being said.

You expect some degree of empathy from your friends. **Empathy** is the understanding one has of another's experience. You want your friends to be able to see particular circumstances as you do and perhaps walk in your shoes. Even if they have never shared the same experiences, you expect friends to try to empathize with you.

In 1979, *Psychology Today* conducted a survey that confirmed these friendship qualities.[22] When the respondents were asked what they felt was

EMPATHY

The understanding one has of another's experience.

the most important quality in a friend, the most often mentioned quality was that of keeping confidences. Trust seemed to be a major issue in all friendships. Along with trust came loyalty; people want to believe that their friends will stick by them come what may. The importance of warmth and affection rounded out the top three qualities mentioned.

Types of Friendship. Even though the six characteristics we have discussed may seem to apply to all friendships, it is important to understand that there are different types of friendship. Reisman identifies three types: reciprocity, receptivity, and association.[23]

RECIPROCITY
A type of friendship that involves self-surrender, loyalty, mutual respect, affection, and support, and in which the partners give and take equally and share responsibility for maintaining the relationship.

Reciprocity is an ideal type of friendship in that it is composed of characteristics such as self-surrender, loyalty, mutual respect, affection, and support. Each individual in a reciprocal friendship equally gives and takes, and each person shares the responsibility of maintaining the relationship. Mike and Russell have been best friends as long as they can remember. The two met when they were in first grade and eventually ended up sharing an apartment together. They help one another in any way they can, and they find spending time with one another to be enjoyable and beneficial. They feel they can trust one another, and they are always comfortable when they are together. Clearly, Mike and Russell's friendship is one of reciprocity.

RECEPTIVITY
A type of friendship in which one partner is the primary giver and the other is the primary taker.

In **receptivity** there is a definite imbalance in the giving and taking, with one partner being the primary giver and the other the primary taker. However, this is not always a bad arrangement. The needs of each person can be met through the particular roles played. This type of friendship often develops between individuals of different status, as the following example illustrates. Dan is a teaching assistant for a class that Mark is taking. Mark is on the baseball team, and traveling causes him to miss several classes. Mark must meet with Dan every time he misses a class to get the information he needs, and through their frequent meetings the two have become friends. Mark is using Dan's access to information, and Dan is not receiving anything comparable from Mark in return, yet they still value each other's friendship.

ASSOCIATION
A type of friendship that develops through frequent contact; more an acquaintance than a true friendship.

Association might be seen as a relationship with an acquaintance rather than as a true friendship. An associative friendship is most likely to develop between people who have frequent contact, such as co-workers, classmates, or neighbors. Holly and Susan are in three classes together, and throughout the semester the two have become friends. Even though they do not do anything together outside class, they still consider each other friends.

Family

Whom do you consider your family? Whether it's your immediate family of father, mother, sisters, and brothers, or perhaps a more extended family including your grandparents, aunts, uncles, and cousins, you have relational and blood ties to other people whom you call family. Although families at times can be major sources of stress and difficulty, they can also provide some of your greatest joys. Definitions of family range anywhere from all the people living in the same household to all those claiming descent from the same ancestor. For the purposes of this section, Nass and McDonald's definition is used.[24] They define a **family** as "a social group having specified roles and statuses (e.g., husband, wife, father, mother, son, daughter) with ties of blood, marriage, or adoption who usually share a common residence and cooperate economically."

Family members do a number of things that require competent communication. Since families provide much of the nurturing humans require in life, many of the family members' interactions are in support of one another. Healthy families strive for effective communication in ensuring mental, intellectual, and emotional growth; promoting family ties; and helping each other to succeed in their goals. It is through communication that families generate their strengths. The following section outlines the communication functions of family members.[25]

Functions of Families. At the time of birth, a human infant is unable to care for him- or herself; a family is needed to ensure the infant's survival. The family fulfills needs such as food, shelter, clothing, and basic caretaking. Without the family, infants and most young children would be helpless. Older family members also require care. As more people live longer, their need for daily care increases. Whether older adults live within the household of an offspring, as in an extended family, or live elsewhere, their care usually falls to the family. Competent communication may be more difficult with older adults, but it is still very important at this stage of family development.

Long before children enter school, they begin to learn important basic lessons. They learn about the differences between humans and animals, honesty and dishonesty, niceness and meanness, and so on. The family helps children to discover what is appropriate behavior. Many of the beliefs and values you hold are shaped and influenced by your family through a process

FAMILY
A social group whose members are related by blood, marriage, or adoption; have specified roles (e.g., husband, wife, son, mother) and statuses; and usually share a common residence and cooperate economically.

The family is the first and most important agent for developing a person's values, beliefs, and customs.

✔

*F*amily Functions in the Media and Your Life

Watch a recent movie or an episode of a television program depicting a family. You can even select one of your favorite sitcom programs. List the various functions the "media family" demonstrates. How effective are the members' communication styles in serving the family functions? Now describe how your own family performs these same functions. Is the media family unrealistic in its portrayal of family life? What lessons can be learned from the media about communicating effectively within families?

of observation and cultivation. Younger family members watch parents and older siblings as they interact with others in various contexts, learning how to handle themselves and other people in social situations. Family members encourage social skills in younger children through instructive and corrective communication practices.

Many families engage in activities that they enjoy doing together. Sports, working in the yard, or just lounging together on a lazy Sunday afternoon provide recreational opportunities for family members. Recreation also gives family members a chance to interact with one another in different contexts. For example, watching an otherwise quiet son become enthusiastic and cheer at a football game reveals a communication style seldom seen by his family members. Finally, recreational time can greatly influence the closeness of the family.

The family is the medium through which family customs or basic cultural guidelines can be passed from one generation to the next. Children learn different ideas from a variety of sources—games, books, television, and the like—but the family can be helpful in explaining these ideas and introducing different concepts. Children tend to imitate their parents and other family members; many children will arrange their homes like the one they grew up in, buy the same brands their parents did, or even vote for the same political candidates. When family members tell stories about their parents, grandparents, and great grandparents, younger members get a sense of history and pride about the family lineage and want to help perpetuate family strength. In this way, transmission becomes an important communication function for many families.

Improving Family Relations. Just about every family could improve the relationships among its members. Today, families face a host of communication challenges as they attempt to succeed in their busy lives. It takes a great deal of effort to ensure that family members use their relationships to maximum benefit. Here are several recommendations that will help enrich family relationships through competent communication.

Put yourself in their place. To understand what family members are feeling or experiencing, you must show some degree of empathy, not just sympathy. Try to grasp how others feel, even if your own experiences are different.

Let others know how you feel. Family members must be able to tell or show one another how they are feeling. If one member is hurt and angry about something that happened at school, the others will not know exactly what is wrong unless they are told. If the hurt individual keeps this feeling to him- or herself and just acts mad and upset, others may perceive that this anger is directed toward something they did. It is important to allow others to know what is happening.

Be flexible. Relationships are constantly developing and moving from one stage to another, and relationships within a family are no exception. As each member grows and develops, so will the relationships with others. For example, a daughter in a family may be extremely close to her father at the age of 10, but at the age of 16 she may become significantly closer to her mother. The parents must recognize this change as normal and must not see it as a failing on their part.

Fight fairly. Conflict is present in all relationships and sometimes more so in families. Family members need to learn how to fight fairly without unnecessarily hurting the feelings of someone who does not deserve it. Fighting fairly means listening to the other person and at least attempting to understand the other person's point of view. Fighting fairly also means that family members do not hit below the belt or gang up on one another. Families must recognize the importance of compromise and understand that there does not always have to be a definite winner and loser.

Give as much as you take. Individuals need to recognize when they are demanding too much of the other members of the family. Everyone has times when they are allowed to take more than they are giving, but there are also times when people must give more than they take. Be reasonable. Remember, how would you like it if other family members made excessive demands on you?

◆ Competent Relationships

Many experts on television and in self-help books seem to think that there is a simple formula for producing a long and happy relationship. As any happy couple will tell you, however, their relationship took a lot of time and understanding to build. One popular analogy is that a relationship is like a house that you must build from the ground up. A solid foundation is required for a solid, secure house, just as a solid foundation is needed for a solid, lasting relationship. A competent relationship is based on three main components: the characteristics of each relational partner, the relationship itself, and each partner's own relational history.

According to the model of communicative competence, each relational partner brings a unique set of personal characteristics to a relationship, including behaviors, communication styles, values, cultural identity, perceptions, memories, and attributions. Although each partner must contribute to the relationship in these areas, each must also continue to develop these same areas in his or her own self-concept and perceptions of the world. From these perceptions, you can develop realistic expectations of your partner, your relationship, and yourself in the relationship. These perceptions and values, then, are the tools that help make the relationship work.

Two types of expectations are inherent in every relationship: current expectations and future expectations. *Current expectations* and goals are often developed through daily interactions and conversations with relational partners. In contrast, expectations for the future are not discussed on a daily basis. Often *future expectations* are considered internally and given a great deal of thought before they are actually stated. The expression of expectations can give the relationship a clearer direction and set of goals, assuming both partners agree on the direction to take.

Each individual also brings his or her own relational history into the relationship. This can be both a benefit and a hindrance. Although you should learn from your mistakes, you may often find yourself dwelling on the past and concentrating too much on not repeating the mistakes you made in a previous relationship rather than enjoying the current relationship as it develops.

Every component that has been mentioned is greatly influenced by the culture in which it exists: A culture or society establishes the "dos and don'ts." The culture sets up the standards of what a "normal" relationship should be like, and often, if a relationship does not fit into society's mold, the partners may feel it is unsuccessful.

The Case of Bruce and Saleh

At the beginning of this chapter we met Bruce and Saleh, two new foreign exchange students at the London School of Economics who will be roommates for the year. Bruce is American and Saleh is from Saudi Arabia. Think about their relationship from the perspective of this chapter as you consider the following questions.

- Which of the goals and motivations for relationship development are likely to be most relevant?

- Are expectations likely to play a major role in the development of Bruce and Saleh's relationship? Explain.

- What strategies for reducing uncertainty would you recommend to them?

- What stages of relationship would you predict for Bruce and Saleh?

- What type of friendship do you think will develop between them? What might be some characteristics of their friendship?

REVIEW

This chapter focuses on developing, maintaining, and repairing or possibly ending relationships with other people.

- Relational knowledge, goals and motivations, and relational expectations are the preliminary processes that determine how and why people develop relationships.

- The influences in forming relationships are interpersonal attraction, physical proximity, alleviation of loneliness, stimulation, and achievement of goals.

- Rewards are those aspects of a relationship that are valued. Three categories of rewards are extrinsic, instrumental, and intrinsic.

- If costs, or burdens to a relationship, exceed rewards, the relationship will not develop and be maintained as well as one that enjoys a higher percentage of rewards.

- Uncertainty reduction helps relational partners understand one another better. You can reduce uncertainty through monitoring, proactive, and indirect strategies.

- As you reduce uncertainty, your ability to predict your relational partner is enhanced, facilitating the development of intimacy.

- The model of interpersonal relationship development was proposed to explain the stages that relationships can go through.

- Relationships begin in the initiation stage, when acquaintances are formed. Subsequent stages of development are the exploratory, intensification, and stable phases, all of which are dependent on uncertainty reduction and assessments of rewards and costs.

- As a relationship develops, evaluations and modifications are made by relational partners in the areas of relational knowledge, motives and goals, and expectations. As these change with time and relational maturity, so too can costs and rewards change. If a relationship declines and cannot be repaired, termination strategies may be used to exit the relationship.

- Friendships and families are important types of relationships. Friendships include a number of qualities, such as availability, caring, honesty, confidentiality, loyalty, and empathy.

- Families serve several important social and communication functions, including provision of care, socialization, recreational needs, and transmission of culture.

CHAPTER EIGHT

Managing Conflict in Interpersonal Relationships

●BJECTIVES

After reading this chapter, you should be able to:

1. Identify four conditions that produce interpersonal conflict.

2. List four reasons why conflict is an inevitable and healthy communication strategy.

3. Describe the six stages of the model for conflict management.

4. Explain how you can develop a more competent conflict management style by using the model.

 OLANDA, AGE 15, AND NIKKI, 10, belong to a stepfamily. Their mom recently married a man with three children, 14, 12, and 9. In their former arrangements, the man's three children had a baby-sitter, whereas Rolanda and Nikki depended on each other, with Rolanda acting as the baby-sitter. Thus, it was Rolanda's task to make sure the house remained neat while her mom was gone. This expectation, while unspoken, still remains. However, when Rolanda asks her step-siblings to pick up their coats and put them away, she is met with hostile name-calling. They say that she doesn't have the right to tell them what to do, and they do not comply with her requests. Nikki, who formerly listened to Rolanda, is starting to imitate the other children. As a result, when the adults come home the house is messy. All of the kids complain that Rolands is too bossy.

As you read through this chapter, think about the relevance of its content to Rolanda's situation. At the end of the chapter, we will look at her problem again.

When two people communicate while holding different positions on an issue, conflict occurs. The goal of this chapter is to impress upon you the idea that competent interpersonal communicators *manage*, rather than minimize or eliminate, conflict in their relationships with others. You may think of managing conflict as bargaining, negotiating, debating, or arguing. This chapter emphasizes several strategies for managing conflict. Before presenting these strategies, however, we discuss how conflict is produced and why interpersonal relationships are stronger when they operate with productive conflict. First, though, conflict needs to be defined.

CONFLICT

A struggle between two or more interdependent parties who perceive incompatible goals, scarce rewards, and interference from the other party or parties in achieving their goals.

Conflict is defined by Hocker and Wilmot as "an expressed struggle between at least two interdependent parties who perceive incompatible goals, scarce rewards, and interference from the other party in achieving their goals."[1] At many times in your life, you and another person or persons will have conflicting goals, or you will face competition for scarce resources. You will even encounter people who will attempt to thwart your efforts to achieve important goals.

◆ Conditions Producing Interpersonal Conflict

If you consider all the aspects of your relationships with other people, conflict is probably the issue that you have the least positive thoughts about. After all, you may think: Who enjoys fighting and arguing? Before assuming that conflict is necessarily negative, however, you should consider why conflict occurs in relationships in the first place. In this section we discuss the reasons underlying conflict, which include incompatible goals, unrealistic expectations, differing rates of relational growth, and inaccurate perceptions and attributions.

Incompatible Goals

When two people who must coordinate activities have different ideas about an outcome or end result, conflict is likely to arise. Here's a cultural conflict example. Blas Gomez and John Anders are social coordinators for their children's eighth grade Bar-B-Que Bash. Blas, a native of Bogotá, Colombia, has one set of values about the function, and John, a native Californian, has another. Blas was raised to believe that 13-year-old students should be separated by gender, and John's North American culture encourages boys and girls of that age group to "mix and mingle."

Because of these two very different outlooks, Blas and John will likely conflict on many issues as they work together. These issues might include how to handle the segregation of genders and which group of children should enter the food line first. Whether Blas and John can manage their incompatible goals will depend on the communication strategies they use.

Unrealistic Expectations

Conflict can also arise when one or both parties in a relationship have unrealistic expectations. You may know of an instance in which a head football coach, in his first year, expected to reach the playoffs. His main assistant coach, who had been on the staff more than 10 years, considered the goal optimistic but unrealistic.

The assistant coach argued that the football team was young and inexperienced, that the players would need some time to adjust to a new strategic philosophy, and that the team had a difficult schedule. Numerous conflicts occurred all year between the two coaches because of their different expectations. While the assistant coach would push fundamentals and the mastery of basic skills, the head coach would push the execution of trick plays to ensure victory.

Differing Rates of Relational Growth

Conflict also occurs when two partners view their relationship as being at different levels of development. As an example, look at the following romantic relationship. A couple has been dating for just under 2 years. Ricky views the relationship as very serious, having developed strong feelings of love and bonding, anticipating that this is the beginning of a long and happy future together. Shawna views the relationship as primarily "fun." She thinks the couple is just dating, without a long-term commitment or strong expectations for the future.

There can be little question that these partners have progressed in the relationship very differently. You can imagine the many conflicts that will surface between them. There are likely to be disagreements about sex, gifts, attendance at family outings, labels for each other, and even what to say to others about the nature of the relationship.

Relational growth may vary between relational partners because of external factors as well. If one person decides to earn a master's degree and develops an appreciation for a specialized area, say art, the relational partner may not know how to accommodate these new needs. Other external factors can also affect relational growth differently. Maturity levels, new friends, and renewed friendships with old acquaintances can cause one partner to view the relationship in a new way.

Inaccurate Perceptions and Attributions

You have already studied the power of perception in Chapter 2. How and what you perceive frequently dictate your impressions, behaviors, and activities. If you are wrong, you are likely to invoke conflict. Consider this incident in which a supervisor, Terry, misperceived two of his newer employees, Bill and Veronica. Terry had heard reports from various people in the company who knew Bill. These reports suggested that Bill was a very bright guy. Veronica had worked in several different departments in the company before reporting to Terry and, unlike Bill, had the reputation of being slow. In actuality, these labels were not only inaccurate but also reversed. Veronica was the bright one, and Bill was slow. Can you imagine the conflicts that occurred when Terry asked Veronica a question? Rather than deliver a rapid-fire response to Terry, she paused and considered the options or implications. Terry erroneously interpreted this delay as indicative of Veronica's lack of intelligence. Incorrect perceptions about someone else's ability, personality, or behavior can produce serious conflicts because people generally are quick to defend themselves in the face of inaccuracies.

Cultural Differences in Handling Conflict

Different cultures often define and deal with conflict in different ways. Ting-Toomey suggests that high- and low-context cultures manage conflict quite differently.[2] As you recall from Chapter 4, high-context cultures are those in which communication is indirect, relies heavily on nonverbal systems, and gives a great deal of meaning to the relationships between communicators. The Japanese, African-American, and Latin American cultures are examples of high-context cultures. Low-context cultures use more explicit language, are more direct in their meanings, and stress goals and outcomes more than relationships. Examples include the German, Swedish, and English cultures. Conflict managers in high-context cultures are likely to emphasize harmonious relations rather than personal goals. They will also attempt to maintain "face" for both themselves and the other people in the conflict. Their communication style is more likely to be nonconfrontational, indirect, and concealing. Communicators in low-context cultures manage conflict more directly. They are more confrontational and more goal oriented rather than being relationally focused, and they are less concerned about "saving face." As you can probably imagine, low-context conflict is more open, volatile, and threatening than high-context conflict. Are you aware of people who live in a low-context culture but who manage conflict as if they lived in a high-context culture?

◆ Conflict as Inevitable and Healthy Communication

Regardless of how conflicts arise, relationships are stronger when conflicts are managed openly and productively. To begin the discussion of productive conflict, consider some of the assumptions people make about interpersonal conflict. List some of the words and phrases you usually associate with conflict. Does your list contain any of the following behaviors?

Heated emotions	Hot temper	Intolerance
Shouting	Red faces	Clenched fists
Uncontrolled arguing	Frustration	"In-your-face" behavior

If so, you are certainly not alone. These are the behaviors that most people commonly associate with conflict. Think of people who get defensive quickly or who "cannot take a joke" or who take everything "too seriously." Those who act in these ways are prime candidates for unproductive conflict.

The point to stress here is that, although these behaviors may be associated with conflict in some relationships, they do not have to be present in all of them. You can manage conflict by engaging in it productively. *Productive conflict* is based on issues rather than on the participants' personalities. It can and should be conducted without any of the behaviors just mentioned. In fact, when such behaviors are present, the real purpose of conflict is weakened considerably. This occurs because the focus of the conflict turns to individual variables and away from actual issues. A focus on *issues* is the key to competent conflict management.

If, like many people, you have a negative attitude toward conflict, try to keep an open mind about it. Are you willing to believe that conflict can be productive rather than destructive? To do so, you need to consider the positive outcomes that can result when people disagree and argue. There are several advantages to conflict: decision making, enjoyment of conflict, relational growth, and saving time.

Decision Making

The primary positive outcome of productive conflict is a better decision. When two people get together and fully debate an issue, the chance is far greater that a quality decision will be made. Why? Because conflict provides an arena in which ideas can be tested. Proposed solutions that are logical, workable, economical, and reasonable will stand up during the course of an argument; weaker solutions are likely to be exposed during debate as flawed.

Jack and Bonita have been renting a duplex for the last 5 years of their 7-year marriage. Jack believes it is now time for the couple to purchase a small home and begin to reap the rewards of that housing investment. If Bonita wants to avoid conflict, she will respond simply "Sure" or "Let's do it."

To be productive, conflict must focus on issues rather than personalities.

However, this may result in the couple's making a bad decision. In a discussion with Jack, Bonita points out that they have only a limited amount of money in reserve, which the required down payment would significantly diminish; that interest rates are higher now than they are projected to be in the future; that at this time they cannot afford a large enough house; and that the current housing market is to a seller's, not a buyer's, advantage. Through debate, argument, and conflict, Jack and Bonita finally decide that they will wait 2 years to purchase a home and that they will put $300 per month in a special savings account earmarked for that purpose. Only through conflict did the flaws in Jack's original proposal emerge. He certainly is glad Bonita spoke up.

Conflict is the essence of decision-making meetings. This is true whether the meeting involves boss-employee, husband-wife, doctor-patient, or any other type of relationship. In fact, if two people who meet to make an important decision are unwilling to engage in conflict or at least consider opposing views, they should not be meeting in the first place. One person should simply have made the decision individually. In strong relationships, the participants introduce and use conflict as a means of reaching satisfying decisions.

Enjoyment of Conflict

In order to believe that conflict can be productive rather than destructive, you have to actively engage in it. Do you have a friend with whom you really enjoy sitting down and debating a topic? That's great. There is no greater intellectual exercise than exploring and testing ideas with another person. If you are interested in politics, discuss your party's philosophies with one of your friends who is a staunch supporter of the opposition. Through this exchange of conflict, you can have fun and learn a great deal. The key to success in doing this is to avoid taking your partner's arguments personally.

You might even think of conflict as a sport in which ideas, rather than a ball, are tossed between the participants. A healthy attitude toward conflict is marked by a special kind of enjoyment that is created when two participants share ideas.

Relational Growth

Conflict helps a relationship develop. As two people begin to explore issues together, trust and respect are fostered. For example, Isaac didn't like the way Mary shopped for groceries. He always thought she spent too much. Mary had always believed that quality products simply cost more. When Isaac confronted Mary on the issue and they discussed it, Mary's respect and attraction for Isaac increased dramatically. Mary's desires to please herself and her partner were virtually equal, and Isaac's concern helped build a communication style they had not previously explored. They were pleased to discover that there were ways that both of them could be satisfied. The relationship seemed to come alive in ways that would never have occurred without conflict. As a result, the couple began to talk about and work through more issues than ever before. Rather than having a relationship in which either partner suppressed feelings, anger, or resentment, the couple became much more open, which led to a stronger, healthier union.

Saving Time

You may think that you save time when you reach a decision without questioning, arguing, or debating. That is certainly true. Meetings in which conflict is suppressed or avoided are shorter than those in which conflict is encouraged and allowed to run its course. Unfortunately, many decisions made in the absence of conflict are poor and require much more time later to correct. Had the time been taken at the outset to make a proper decision through productive conflict, less time would have been spent in the long term.

Several years ago, in a major company, a decision was reached to radically alter the way presentations were made to major customers and suppliers. For years, the accepted style was to present information on slides, using two screens, projecting one image to the left of the speaker and a separate image on the screen to the right. One day, a top executive made a unilateral decision that henceforth all presentations would be given using only one screen and one projected image at a time.

After the order was implemented, problems cropped up immediately. Speakers who had used the old style for years had great difficulty adapting to the new technique. Standard presentations that were established for the two-screen method had to be reorganized to fit the new format. Even the seating arrangements for large meetings had to be altered so that everyone could see a single screen. After the new method had been in use for about 18 months, a task force was created to review the decision. When the committee recommended a return to the old format, everyone accepted the idea. Permanent presentations that had been created in this interim period had to be reorganized. Managers who had joined the company in the last year and a half had to undergo special training to learn the old two-screen format. Obviously, much time and effort could have been saved had the task force met at the outset to study the issue. Through productive conflict, debate, and argument, the group could have uncovered the flaws in the proposed one-screen design.

What Kinds of Conflict Have You Experienced?

1. What was your best conflict experience? Your worst? Why?
2. Have you ever experienced a conflict owing to different cultural ideas? How did you handle it? What would you do differently in the future?
3. Do you find yourself having more conflicts with people of the same or the opposite sex? Do you keep special concerns in mind during a conflict with a person of the opposite sex?
4. How do you determine whether a particular conflict is good or bad?

◆ A Model of Competent Conflict Management

Competent, productive conflict can be divided into six distinct phases. Following these phases will help you to operate rationally rather than emotionally. Moreover, you will be more likely to approach the topic proactively rather than reactively. Finally, and most important, you will focus the conflict on the issue and not on the other person. The remainder of this chapter examines these six phases: prelude, assessment, engagement, action, decision, and reflection (see Figure 8.1).

Prelude

Conflict does not simply "happen." As you have seen, conflict has many sources. In addition, you and your conflict partners bring your own personality traits, tendencies, predispositions, and conflict styles to conflict episodes. You also cannot forget that conflict takes place within a relational context. The status of a relationship is a very important factor that affects many conflict behaviors. In short, the first phase of conflict actually begins before any words are spoken.

Traits. Several traits (argumentativeness, verbal aggressiveness, and anxiety) play a key role in conflict situations. **Traits** refer to individual characteristics that typically do not vary from situation to situation; they are either physical (e.g., height, weight, eyesight) or psychological (e.g., open-mindedness, friendliness, intelligence).

In several studies, Infante and a number of his colleagues have linked personality and attempts to persuade others. One of the personality traits they have studied is **argumentativeness**. People who are highly argumentative typically do the following three things:

- Recognize issues that are "ripe" for controversy
- Take positions on those issues and provide evidence and reasoning to support their positions
- Refute others' positions if these are counter to their own

The more an individual uses these three behaviors, the more argumentative the person is. Conversely, the less someone engages in these behaviors, the less argumentative he or she is.

This trait is issue-focused, not person-focused. As a result, individuals who enjoy arguing or debating with others on issues are also likely to be favorably disposed to productive conflict. Argumentativeness is thus a positive trait for individuals to exhibit in conflict situations.

In contrast, **verbal aggressiveness** is a negative trait in conflict situations. People who are verbally aggressive focus their arguments on individuals in addition to, or instead of, issues.

When you are in a conflict situation with a person who is verbally aggressive, you typically encounter undesirable behaviors, especially name-calling,

---

TRAITS

Individual physical and psychological characteristics that typically do not vary from situation to situation.

ARGUMENTATIVE-NESS

A conflict style that seeks out controversial issues and revels in debating them.

VERBAL AGGRESSIVENESS

A conflict style that involves attacking the other party's self-concept.

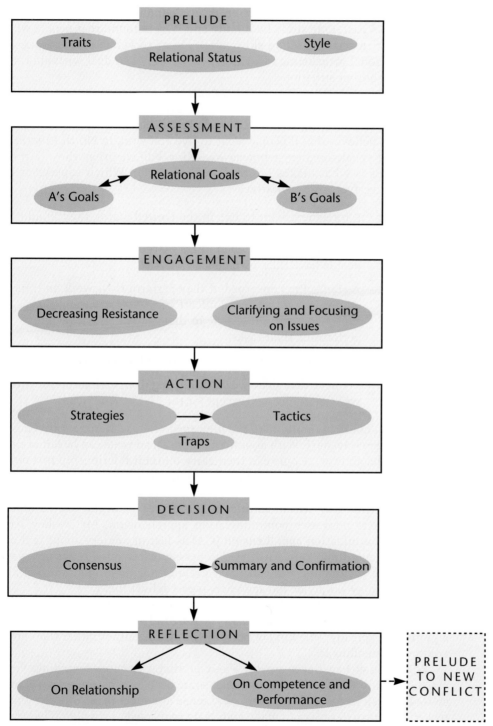

FIGURE 8.1
A model of competent conflict management.

"mudslinging," or the reintroduction of downgrading examples from the relationship's past. One study by Infante and Wigely found that people who are deficient in argumentative skills often resort to verbal aggressiveness, because personal attacks may be the only way they can deal with another person in a conflict situation.[3]

To help you see the difference between argumentativeness and verbal aggressiveness, suppose that two supervisors are discussing whether or not only English should be spoken in the workplace. They have opposing views: Ms. Sanders believes that if people want to live and work in North America, they should speak English, whereas Ms. King believes that the mixture of ethnicities is what makes North America unique. Which supervisor is verbally aggressive? Argumentative?

Ms. Sanders   If foreigners want to live in the United States, they should speak my language. I want to know if they're talking and laughing about me when I pass by them. It's like these people have their own code.

Ms. King   As far as I'm concerned, if they perform their work on time and we're able to communicate in a work situation, they can speak, sing, or whistle in their native tongues while performing their tasks.

Ms. Sanders   Well, you must be an anti-American foreigner lover.

Ms. King   I believe that since we all originated from various continents, we're all foreigners, except for the Native Americans.

People in conflict should take the high road and use argumentativeness instead of aggressiveness. With argumentativeness, an issue can be left at the conflict table, and two people can then carry on their relationship in a normal manner. A relationship may be harmed, however, if verbal aggressiveness is used.

Another trait that affects conflict is the degree to which one or more of the partners possesses communication apprehension. McCroskey has defined **communication apprehension (CA)** as fear or anxiety about real or anticipated communication with another person or persons.[4] A partner may possess good arguments, rational data, exceptional reasoning, and strong stances, but may simply be too apprehensive to deliver them.

Another type of anxiety that can affect conflict is the degree to which one partner believes that the relationship is too frail to withstand excessive argument. Typically, this kind of person will avoid conflict rather than provoking or extending it.

When you do experience anxiety about conflict, there are a few things you can do to minimize its effects. First, take some deep breaths and revive yourself with fresh oxygen. Next, alternately tense and relax those muscles that feel stiff from anxiety. Try to make your body as relaxed as possible. The next

COMMUNICATION APPREHENSION (CA)

Fear or anxiety associated with real or anticipated communication with another person or persons.

*H*itting Above and Below the Belt

The concepts of argumentativeness and verbal aggressiveness are important to the study of conflict management because the first is more likely to produce positive consequences than the second. Examine the items below and mark each one according to how you feel about most conflicts (1 = true; 2 = undecided; 3 = false).

_____ 1. Arguing over controversial issues improves my intelligence.

_____ 2. I really come down hard on people if they don't see things my way.

_____ 3. I am good about not losing my temper during conflict situations.

_____ 4. Some people need to be insulted if they are to see reason.

_____ 5. I prefer being with people who disagree with me.

_____ 6. It is exhilarating to get into a good conflict.

_____ 7. I have the ability to do well in conflict situations.

_____ 8. It is not hard for me to go for the jugular if a person really deserves it.

_____ 9. I know how to construct effective arguments that can change people's minds.

_____ 10. I avoid getting into conflicts with people who know how to argue well.

_____ 11. I know how to find other people's personal weaknesses.

Scoring: Add your scores for items 1, 3, 5, 6, 7, and 9. Reverse your scores for the following items: 2, 4, 8, 10, 11 (1 = 3; 3 = 1). After converting the numbers, add all of these scores to your previous total. If you scored between 11 and 18, you are prone to argumentativeness. If you scored between 26 and 33, you are likely to be verbally aggressive when you are in conflict situations. If you scored between 19 and 25, you are probably neither very argumentative nor very aggressive.

Source: Adapted from D. Infante (1988), *Arguing constructively* (Prospect Heights, IL: Waveland Press).

step is to view your conflict with another person as an opportunity and not as a threat. Certainly, there are going to be some tough moments during a bona fide conflict, but handling these situations will develop your confidence for future conflicts. Recognizing conflict as a communication opportunity, rather than as a personal sacrifice, will go a long way toward minimizing your fears. Finally, understand that you are going to win some conflicts and that you are going to lose others. There is no disgrace in realizing that you can sometimes be wrong. As long as you view conflict productively, losing to a conflict partner may actually increase that person's opinion of you. People who lose in a conflict competently and graciously are some of the most admired people in the world.

Relational Status. A major factor that can produce profound differences in conflict is the status of a relationship. In the last chapter, we made a distinction between how relational partners perceive each other and how they perceive the "relationship." It is important to consider the relationship factor because relationships change as a result of how conflict is handled. As you refine your relational schemas about another person, you gain a greater understanding of three factors involving conflict and relationships: valence, stability, and power.

Valence refers to the feelings of satisfaction with the communication that takes place in a relationship. When the partners in a relationship are satisfied and pleased with their interaction, the communication has a positive valence. Conversely, if the interaction produces dissatisfaction and displeasure, communication has a negative valence.

Three different pairs of valences are possible in a relationship, and conflict is affected differently by each (see Figure 8.2). One possibility is that both participants are dissatisfied with the communication that takes place in the relationship. In this kind of context, conflict is likely to fare very poorly. Because the partners do not even enjoy talking with each other under nonargumentative or nonconfrontive circumstances, the topics on which they have conflict are not likely to produce enjoyment either.

Second, when one participant is happy with the communication in the relationship and the other is not, any conflict that occurs is either going to help strengthen the bonds between the two (as in the case of Isaac's dissatisfaction with Mary's shopping habits, which was discussed earlier) or weaken

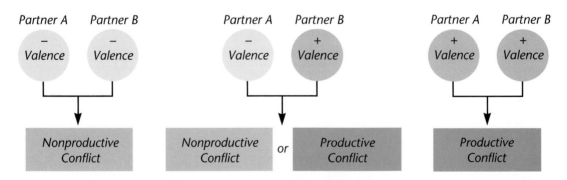

FIGURE 8.2
A positive valence in a communication partner's satisfaction with the relationship contributes to productive conflict, and a negative valence promotes nonproductive conflict.

the ties between them. It is not always easy to know another person's attitude about his or her relationship with you. Sometimes you have to guess, but it is important to understand that varying relational views produce different conflict patterns. A conflict partner unconcerned about relational consequences will fight more aggressively than someone who cares about the relationship.

Third, when both partners are pleased with the communication between them, valence is at its highest and productive conflict has an excellent chance of succeeding. Liking someone helps to reduce the possibility of verbal aggressiveness and to promote instances of beneficial argumentation. It is understandable that you want to be careful about these types of relationships, but you should take one caution here. You do not want to be so over-protective of a particular relationship that you avoid conflict in order to preserve your relational status. Productive conflict management is an essential part of all relationships, even the good ones.

Stability is measured by the degree to which a relationship experiences "peaks and valleys." All relationships have good times and bad times. The more consistent a relationship is, the more stability it has. Over time, unstable relationships tend to disintegrate. Usually one or both partners tire of the unpredictability that accompanies unstable relationships. Of course, people hope that relationships will stabilize on the positive side.

The implication for conflict is that stable relationships provide the best context for productive argument. When a relationship is typically consistent in its experiences, and the partners are consistent in their reactions to each other's communication, productive conflict can thrive. When a relationship is virtually unpredictable, who knows what impact the conflict will have? On one day, conflict over spending money could result in the planning of a budget and a commitment by both partners to stick with it. Yet on another day, conflict on the same topic could result in an eruption of emotion and tension, including such remarks as "If you don't like the way I spend our money, then I'll just spend *my* money the way I want to." The best course of action is to determine what the relational status is at a particular time and then decide if conflict is the best communication strategy. Sometimes it is best to put off conflict until the right moment.

The distribution of power in a relationship also affects conflict. When one partner has power over another, the kind of conflict is likely to be very different from the conflict between equals. Consider, for example, the case of the boss and the employees in any business. Because the boss has the responsibility for hiring employees, setting salaries, determining schedules, and assigning tasks, he or she has considerable power over employees. Invariably, you will find that employees initiate less conflict with the boss than the boss does with the employees. You will also find that employees are likely to agree with their boss most of the time. To behave differently could produce undesirable outcomes for the employees.

Conversely, consider conflict between peers. Look at the example of two employees who work for the same boss. Because they have equal status, there is very little that one partner can "hold" over the other. As a result, both partners are likely to initiate conflict at about the same rate. The refutation, argument, debate, and questioning that take place will probably be much more open and profound. Consent will occur because one partner is convinced of an argument, not because the other has power.

Power is not limited to simple hierarchical differences. In many relationships, people have power because you give it to them. Therefore, any person who controls resources that you desire has power over you. This is true whether the partner controls money you want, equipment you want to borrow, or even sex. Conflict with a person who holds power over you for any reason will likely be very different from conflict situations in which power is equal.

Style. Every individual who engages in conflict prefers certain behaviors over others. These preferences define your *style*.

Five conflict styles are assessed by the Thomas-Kilmann Conflict Management of Differences (MODE) survey.[5] These styles vary according to the degree to which an individual is assertive or cooperative (see Figure 8.3). **Assertiveness** is defined as emphasizing your own concerns and taking action to achieve your goals; **cooperativeness** is defined as emphasizing the other's concerns and working toward shared goals. The five styles are:

ASSERTIVENESS
A conflict style that emphasizes personal concerns.

COOPERATIVENESS
A conflict style that emphasizes the other's concerns.

Collaborating—highly assertive and cooperative
Compromising—moderately assertive and cooperative
Competing—assertive and uncooperative
Accommodating—unassertive and cooperative
Avoiding—unassertive and uncooperative

Assertiveness

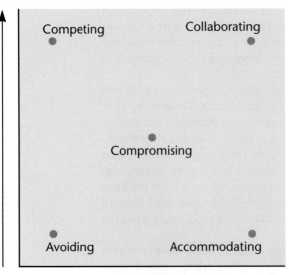

FIGURE 8.3

The Thomas-Kilmann Conflict Management of Differences (MODE) survey identifies five styles according to their degrees of assertiveness and cooperativeness.

Although you may vary your conflict style for some people and some topics, for the most part people's styles are fairly consistent. The biggest factor that produces a change in style is probably the degree to which a topic or person is important to you. You may find, for example, that you behave differently in conflicts that arise about where you should live once you graduate versus what kind of movie you should attend. You may also find that you behave differently in conflicts with your best friend than you do with your boss. Nonetheless, most people have the same predispositions or tendencies toward conflict regardless of the topic or person involved.

The Self-Check "Evaluating Conflict Styles" asks about matching conflict styles. The idea is not that conflict styles need to be identical, but that perhaps certain styles match the people, issues, relationships, and goals involved. Is it possible to have a productive conflict if one participant uses a competing style and another seems to be avoiding conflict? Can conflict be managed if one person is accommodating and the other collaborates? The answers to these questions depend on many of the factors we have already discussed. Consider these issues of style when you confront conflict situations.

Assessment

In the second phase of conflict management, you must decide what you want out of the conflict. Is your own goal the more important of the two? Or is your partner's goal more important? Are the goals of the relationship more important than the personal goals of either participant? Questions such as these must be resolved before any communication can take place in a conflict situation.

Before engaging in communication during a conflict situation, competent participants conduct a thorough assessment of their own needs and those that they believe are important to their partner. In public speaking, speakers must analyze the audience and make certain adjustments based on whom they are addressing. Failure to do so may prove disastrous for the speakers. This same assessment should be performed prior to a conflict situation with

How Assertive and Cooperative Are You?

List the names of five people you know and the topics about which you typically engage in conflict with them. Are the conflicts gender related, socioeconomically based, or focused on cultural differences? Does your style differ depending on the person or topic? How and why?

*E*valuating Conflict Styles

Think about the conflict styles of some people you know. Do you carefully consider a person's style when he or she is having a conflict with you? When you engage in conflict with certain people, do they seem to use the same style each time? Do their styles vary depending on whether they are in conflict with their mother or father? Brothers or sisters? Mate or best friend? Do particular issues cause people to use a particular conflict style? Which conflict styles really drive you up the wall? Is there any way to change someone's style to suit your own? Do styles have to match?

a partner. Let us now look at some items (personal goals, the other's goals, relational goals, and "win-win" as the ultimate goal) that should be assessed.

Personal Goals. Your own goals and objectives are very important in any conflict situation; without them, you would not have any stake in the discussion. There are several questions that you should consider in advance. For example: When you enter into the conflict, what are you likely to gain? To lose? What do you desire as an outcome? How important is that outcome to you? What positions do you plan to advance during the discussion? Can you substantiate your positions?

The Other's Goals. You are not the only one who has goals and objectives in a conflict situation; your partner has them too. Unless you consider what these goals and objectives are, you are likely to be unsuccessful in influencing your partner. What is your partner's probable reaction to the conflict? How do your partner's interests differ from your own? What issue do you think is most important to your partner? What kind of experiences or background does the partner bring to this situation?

Relational Goals. Conflict does not take place in a vacuum. Whatever happens through conflict affects a relationship. As you know, a relationship may grow stronger if the conflict is productive. If the conflict is personal instead of issue-based, the relationship may be adversely affected.

Before beginning a conversation that involves conflict, participants should consider the effect the argument or debate is likely to have on their relationship. Has this issue been discussed before? If so, what has been discussed and how? Is there any new information? If not, how much do you need to educate your partner prior to the discussion?

Is the topic one in which your partner's ego is heavily involved? Is your partner more knowledgeable about the issue than you are? What adjustments might you need to make in order to convince your partner that your position is the better one for the relationship?

"Win-Win" as the Ultimate Goal. The best reason to engage in conflict is to allow both participants to gain something from the discussion. When this occurs, the conflict has been successful. This is called "win-win" and refers to the idea that *both* parties can meet their own goals and those for their relationship from the conflict situation.

The win-win philosophy of conflict means that you not only look out for yourself during an argument but that you also monitor the role and status of the other party. This ensures that both of you receive substantive outcomes from your efforts in the conversation.

Engagement

In the third phase of conflict, engagement, the partners create a context for conflict. The physical location of a conflict as well as each participant's psychological readiness are very important. In many cases, one partner must

Major and Minor Conflicts

How do conflicts involving personal values and goals (attending religious services, raising children) differ from conflicts about trivial matters (which television program to watch, what route to take home)?

actually entice the other into engaging in conflict. During engagement, two important factors are dealt with: decreasing resistance and clarifying and focusing on issues.

Decreasing Resistance. One of the greatest barriers to productive conflict occurs when one of the partners does not want to participate in a debate. Here are some reasons why people may be reluctant to engage in conflict:

- They do not see any alternatives to a solution that seems obvious to them.
- They do not consider the issue complex enough to merit argument.
- They do not enjoy arguing or debating issues.
- They are concerned that the relationship is not strong enough to endure argument.
- They do not believe that the time or place is right for conflict.

When your partner holds one or more of these beliefs, conflict cannot take place until you convince him or her to engage in it with you. You cannot *force* anyone to argue productively with you. Attempting to do so may even result in your partner's leaving the scene. However, you can entice a partner to debate an issue with you—that is, you can make the differences seem significant, make the consequences seem important, promote different options, reassure your partner, and observe the physical environment.

Make the differences seem significant. When two or more options are possible and both parties recognize those options, one partner may believe the answer is "clear cut." In that case, that person may ask, "Why do we even need to talk about it?" We have already seen that any idea is worth testing. Testing an idea through debate, argument, questioning, and "devil's advocacy" is the best way to determine its real worth.

One of the best approaches you can use to convince your partner to argue is to make the differences seem very important. Now look at an example. Harry and Shin are planning their vacation from Des Moines, Iowa, to Providence, Rhode Island. Harry has found that there are actually two desirable routes. He tells Shin that one route would take 6 hours longer than the other. Upon hearing this, Shin proclaims, "That shorter one is what we want; no question about it." In order to entice Shin to debate the pros and cons of both routes, Harry must explain that the shorter route is all highway. They will miss much beautiful scenery and many cultural sites unless they take the longer route. "Speed or beauty? You can't have them both," Harry argues. Now that the differences between the options are clear to Shin, the debate can begin.

Make the consequences seem important. One reason why people are reluctant to engage in conflict is their attitude that "it doesn't matter" or "it doesn't make any difference." You may have felt exactly that way after just a few minutes in a conflict situation with another person.

Topics that you dismiss as unimportant are often those that come back to haunt you. Have you ever heard someone exclaim, "If only we had talked about it first." No matter what the topic, no matter how trivial it may seem to you or your partner, apply the tests of argument, debate, questioning, and devil's advocacy. A decision that seems unimportant at the moment may take on extremely important proportions later.

Promote different options. On any given topic, your partner may believe that there is only "one way" or, sometimes, "no way." In this case, you actually have to inform your partner about the possibilities *before* you can begin to argue. A few years ago, a school superintendent believed that one of the schools in the district had to be enlarged because of increasing enrollment and overcrowded classrooms. She was upset about all of the bids she had received from construction companies for the expansion. While sharing her tales of woe with a colleague, she learned that other options were available. Her friend informed her that many school districts have constructed portable classroom buildings and have placed them on school property at a fraction of the cost of expanding the size of a permanent building. After learning about this alternative, the superintendent was ready to discuss the issue with the school board.

Reassure your partner. If your partner is reluctant to engage in a conflict situation because of a personal distaste for debate or a desire to protect what he or she regards as a fragile relationship with you, a straightforward explanation of your intentions might be in order. State your desire to resolve an issue involving differences between you. Present the issue as you see it. Reassure your partner that you want to focus on the point of disagreement and not on any personal weaknesses or traits that might be detrimental to the relationship. Emphasize your respect for your partner and your desire to reach a solution that will be satisfactory for both of you. Making your case in a calm, quiet voice will demonstrate that conflict need not be hostile. Review some of the points we have discussed in this chapter so that you can convince your partner that debate can be an enjoyable experience and that positive conflict can strengthen your relationship.

Observe the physical environment. Some people are reluctant to engage in conflict because of where they are at the time. Public places, such as restaurants, bars, movie theaters, or lines at amusement parks, may call attention to the participants even if the conflict is productive and voices are kept low. Or, some confidential information may be under discussion, which should not be heard by outsiders. Both partners should be sensitive to the time and location of a conflict. If you have to move to another location in order to allow normal argument and debate, that movement should take place before the conflict begins.

Clarifying and Focusing on Issues. We have already noted that competent communicators engage in productive conflict—conflict that is based on issues and not on the personalities of the participants. One of the most important steps a communicator takes at the outset of conflict is to steer the conversation toward substantive issues. If this step does not take place, the conflict may get off to a very bad start and may never recover.

One of the best ways to safeguard the civilized tone of any encounter is to begin with statements that erase or minimize any link between the issue under discussion and the individual who is delivering a position on it. Here are some examples you might use:

- "I don't want you to take this personally. We need to talk about . . ."

- "I know that you have put a lot of time and energy into this project and that it's very important to you. But I think you should step back a little and look at this a different way."

- "You have some strong views on this matter. I respect those views, and I want to listen to what you have to say. But there are some other pieces to the puzzle that I don't think you have considered."

- "I acknowledge that I work for you and whatever you decide will stand. However, I would like to have a chance to show you some flaws that I think we can correct now, before we get too deep into this project."

Statements such as these can also be used during the course of the conversation in which the conflict takes place. They can be very important in refocusing the conflict on the issue being discussed. On some occasions you may need to be even more direct:

- "I'm sorry you are offended by what I said. I wasn't talking about you. I was talking about the position you've taken."

- "No, I would have said the same thing no matter *who* brought it up."

Competent communicators in conflict situations not only keep themselves focused on issues but also help to keep their partners focused on the subjects being discussed.

Action

The action phase includes the "how" and "what" of conflict. The "how" involves the selection of *strategies* that a communicator uses in a conflict situation. The "what" involves the *tactics*, or messages, that are used to enact the strategies. In addition, competent communicators are aware of several *traps* that can move a conflict in unproductive directions.

Strategies. We cannot emphasize enough that productive conflict is a positive enterprise for relationships. You may be thinking, How do I engage in this kind of conflict? This section discusses several strategies that you can use to engage in and manage productive conflict. One of the first determinations you need to make is to decide what is most important to you: your own goals, your partner's goals, or your relationship's goals. This decision is very important because you cannot have it all three ways. Here we focus on three options: cooperative, obstinate, and escapist.[6]

Striking the Right Balance

You have recently started a friendship, and you begin to experience a series of small conflicts. Your new friend tends to avoid confrontation and becomes passive in a conflict. You would like to discuss issues openly. What can you do to find a balance so that the blooming relationship does not suffer?

TABLE 8.1 CONFLICT STRATEGIES		
TYPE	DESCRIPTION	EXAMPLE
Cooperative	Partners work together to maximize the goals of each person and of the relationship.	"Since we both need time off, why don't I work today and you work tomorrow?"
Obstinate	Partners are self-centered and individualistic in their approach to attaining goals.	"I'm sorry, but I can't go along with any of your suggestions."
Escapist	Partners attempt to avoid conflict altogether.	"I don't want to talk about this anymore."

COOPERATIVE STRATEGIES

In a conflict, strategies that promote the objectives of the relationship rather than those of one partner or the other.

OBSTINATE STRATEGIES

In a conflict, strategies that promote the objectives of an individual rather than those of the relational partner or the relationship.

ESCAPIST STRATEGIES

In a conflict, strategies that attempt to prevent direct conflict.

Cooperative strategies are those that promote the objectives of the relationship (see Table 8.1). The important factor is not whether you win or lose but rather what is the best outcome for both partners in the relationship.

Obstinate or unyielding **strategies** promote the objectives of an individual as opposed to those of a relational partner. The impact on the relationship is not considered very important. **Escapist strategies** attempt to prevent direct conflict. In some cases, this is simply avoidance. In other cases, participants attempt to postpone conflict, change topics, or pass responsibility to other people. The objective of this strategy is simply to ensure that conflict does not take place. You will notice that these three general strategies take very different directions and are associated with different kinds of communication behaviors. Look at a simple but common example.

Suppose that Lisa and Kathy ordered only one piece of lemon meringue pie at a restaurant to eat after their dinner. If you were to go inside their minds, both Lisa and Kathy would like to eat the pie. In discussing who gets the pie, if Lisa used a *cooperative strategy*, she would probably ask Kathy, "Would you like to split the pie?" This tactic would consider the feelings of both participants. Conversely, if Lisa used an *obstinate strategy*, she might argue, "I am not on a diet, so I deserve the pie." If she used an *escapist strategy*, Lisa might simply say, "Kathy, go ahead and eat the lemon pie," even though she really wanted it.

What difference does it make whether you use one of these strategies instead of another? You get a clue from a study by Canary and Spitzberg, in which they discovered that cooperative-type strategies were more closely related to perceptions of *competence* than were the other two strategies.[7] They found that when the participants are competent in using conflict, the quality of their relationship is higher. Furthermore, their results demonstrated that when compared with other strategies, cooperative-type strategies are associated with greater perceptions of satisfaction, trust, and intimacy in a relationship.

The cooperative strategy, in which the relationship is more important than the goals of either individual, may remind you of the win-win philosophy of negotiating. From a win-win perspective, both partners in a relationship can achieve greater outcomes than either could if the individual's own goals were more important or if the other partner's goals were more important.

You may be wondering why and under what circumstances people use one of these strategies versus another. A study by Canary, Cunningham, and Cody revealed that obstinate-type strategies were often used when people were defending themselves.[8] Cooperative-type strategies were more frequently used to promote a change in a relationship. Why? Conflicts over the definition of a relationship are more likely to produce cooperative behaviors than are conflicts over the defense of a personal right.

For example, if one partner wants to define the relationship as "dating" and the other partner prefers the relationship to be "just friends," cooperative strategies are likely to be necessary to resolve the conflict. On the other hand, suppose conflict comes about because a friend has borrowed money from you, has not paid any of it back, and refuses to pay some higher interest rates that you believe are justified. This type of conflict is likely to produce obstinate or self-defending strategies.

Tactics. In the previous section, we discussed three general strategies that you can use in conflict situations. Next, we cover some specific message-based options that will help you put your strategies in motion. These options are called *tactics*. We will discuss the following tactics: probing, debating/arguing, bargaining, making threats and promises, face saving, summarizing, and compromising.

Probe for clarifications and explanations from your partner. Don't be satisfied with general positions or vague and ambiguous answers. Ask **probing** questions that force the individual to be more specific and pointed. Try to find out your partner's motivations, goals, and attitudes toward you and the conflict issue. ("What do you mean?" "Can you give me an example?" "What's at risk for me? For you?")

PROBING
In a conflict, an attempt to make a partner provide clarifications, explanations, or further information.

If you suspect that your partner is not being truthful, probing may be an appropriate tactic. You will quickly notice that increased probing for specifics can cause your partner to be less deceitful. Why? You know that unrehearsed lies can produce generalities and inconsistencies, which are often delivered with hesitations and other nonverbal behaviors that are simply not normal for that person when he or she is telling the truth.[9] In many cases, the more you probe, the less your partner has to say and the more obvious these behaviors become.

Productive conflict depends on debate and argument. Clearly, debate and argument do not mean yelling and shouting. Here are two ways you can argue and debate effectively.

First, take a *devil's advocate* position whenever possible. Before agreeing on an issue, ask what the worst-case scenario would be. A devil's advocate may bring up questions such as these:

What is the most money that could be lost?
How much time could possibly be wasted?

What is the longest distance we would have to travel?

What is the biggest safety risk we are taking by engaging in this activity?

If the answer your partner gives to these types of questions is unsatisfying to you, certainly other alternatives must be generated and explored.

Second, *argue against analogies* that the other person offers to support a position. An analogy simply indicates that what is true in one instance will be true in another. The instance or case can be time, schools, years, countries, people—just about anything. When you hear people say "It's just like . . ." or "It's no different from . . .," they are using analogies.

For productive conflict to take place, you need to demonstrate that the differences between the instances or cases that are being compared are so significant that the analogy is invalid. For example, say that two parents are arguing about whether their oldest daughter should attend a private school. The wife contends, "I went to a private school and my knowledge level moved a grade ahead of most of my friends. If Betsy goes to this private school, she should accelerate the same way." The husband can argue against the analogy by suggesting the wide differences between his wife and daughter in terms of time periods of their schooling, types of friends, development levels, particular schools available, and so on.

The same logic can be used when someone tries to compare two presidents, two time periods, two brands of fertilizer, or two airlines. Your task as an advocate of productive conflict is to demonstrate that the analogy may not be valid. In the process, you may become persuaded that the similarities between the compared instances or cases are actually quite high. If that happens, then the analogy succeeds, but it has at least been put to the test.

A word of caution is in order here. The message tactics just discussed (probing, playing devil's advocate, and resisting analogies) should be used for only one reason: to facilitate productive conflict that will result in better decisions. These tactics should not be used to harass or embarrass someone, to build ego strength, to play "one-up," or to focus on another person's personality or idiosyncrasies. Participants who do so are actually engaging in destructive, rather than productive, conflict.

When ideas and proposed solutions stand up to the tests just described, you can't be guaranteed of success, but you do know that the decisions were not arrived at hastily or without sound judgment. This is the real benefit of productive conflict.

Bargaining tactics constitute a special form of conflict. In bargaining, the partners argue for their respective positions within mutually agreed upon guidelines.[10] You are probably most familiar with the bargaining tactics used in union and labor negotiations or courtroom bargaining pleas. Each side agrees to certain rules and procedures when arguing its case. Many conflict situations that you will face may resemble bargaining sessions, and it is a good idea to become competent in bargaining tactics. Bargaining tactics are very much like the conflict strategies discussed earlier (cooperative, obstinate, and escapist strategies). The key to **bargaining** is to develop a strategy

BARGAINING

In a conflict, arguing for one's own position while expressing understanding of and sensitivity to the other party's position.

that supports a favorable position for your side while promoting the value of your adversary's point of view. Based on research findings, the following steps can lead to a successful bargaining strategy.[11]

- Begin with high but realistic offers. Starting high allows you to "give" some later.
- Present beginning offers in a cooperative manner so that adversaries know you can be reasonable.
- Clear obstacles by compromising a little on your initial offer.
- Stand your ground when you feel the opposition is taking advantage of your good faith.
- Remain committed and enthusiastic about your goals throughout the bargaining session.
- Know what you are talking about. Be well informed about your own position and your adversary's position. Don't get caught off guard by something you ought to know about.
- Let the opposition know that you understand its position and are sensitive to its needs.
- Avoid obstinate and escapist tactics unless these are absolutely necessary. Seldom do these behaviors serve a useful purpose.

Threats and promises are two interesting types of tactics in interpersonal conflict.[12] **Threats** are expressed intentions to behave in ways that are detrimental to the other party if that person does not comply with certain requests or terms. Conversely, **promises** are expressed intentions to behave in ways that are beneficial to the other party in return for compliance with certain requests or terms. The effectiveness of threats and promises depends on five factors:

Specificity The more specific the threat or promise, the more effective.
Credibility The more trustworthy and believable the threat or promise, the more effective.
Immediacy The more urgent the threat or promise, the more effective.
Equity The fairer the threat or promise, the more effective.
Climate The more cooperative the climate, the more effective the threat or promise.[13]

Threats and promises can provoke conflicts and they can resolve conflicts. Let us first look at how these tactics can *provoke conflicts.* When threatened, many people retaliate rather than consent. A promise, especially from someone who has a bad history of keeping promises, can cause all kinds of problems. For instance, how many times have you heard a dialogue such as this?

MILTON   It's no problem. If I have all the guys over to watch the game on Sunday, I'll clean up before they get here and after they leave.

LINDY   Right. Just like you said you would clean out the garage last month, fix the light in the kitchen last week, and pick up the dry cleaning this morning.

THREAT

In a conflict, an expressed intention to behave in a way that is detrimental to the other party if that party does not comply with certain requests or terms.

PROMISE

In a conflict, an expressed intention to behave in a way that is beneficial to the other party provided that party complies with certain requests or terms.

MILTON   Well, you're the one who never gets out of bed early enough on Sunday morning to get the kids ready for church. I've got to make breakfast and get the kids rounded up and dressed. Where are you?

Second, threats and promises can *resolve conflicts.* In the heat of an argument between two people, a well-placed threat may put an end to a discussion. For example, a manager may tell an employee, "Well, if you *don't* finish this project by Wednesday, I'm putting somebody else on it." Promises can have the same effect. The employee may say, "We're arguing about nothing. I promise this will get finished by Wednesday."

Face-saving messages are another tactic. How are people treated when their ideas don't win? First, Folger and Poole argue that the best solution is to create climates that avoid face saving altogether.[14] If one or more people get together in an atmosphere where the "best solution" wins, the victor is not the person but the solution. In this atmosphere, no one needs to save face.

Second, the parties should try to minimize any defensiveness or retaliation that is associated with winning or losing an argument. These responses come about because someone is concerned about having an undesirable image or making an undesirable impression.

Finally, to save face, a party must be able to have a "way out" of a position. There is no reason to devastate the other person even if you win the conflict. Instead, you can offer to support your partner in other situations.

Summarizing is one of the most useful tactics that can be used in a conflict-based conversation. Statements such as "Here's what I think we've said so far" or "What we have agreed to is" are extremely useful in keeping a discussion on track.

Summarizing gives your partner the chance to disagree, clarify a point, or amplify any part of the discussion before it moves on to another subtopic. The major advantage here is that the topic is still fresh in the participants' minds. If one partner has a different opinion, perception, or recollection of what was discussed, the best time to make a correction is right then, not 10 minutes, 1 hour, 1 week, or 6 months later.

Consider a compromise. As you read this chapter, you may have been thinking that there is a simple alternative to conflict, which is to compromise. A **compromise** can be obtained through a number of tactics, including the following:

COMPROMISE

A conflict resolution tactic that involves agreeing on a method of deciding, rather than focusing on the quality of the decision.

Averaging In conflicts over the cost of goods or services, the two parties may simply "split the difference"; for example, a compromise between $80 and $100 is $90.

Trading off Individuals may make concessions by taking the position "I'll give you this if I can get this in return."

Random selection Participants put two or more alternatives "in a hat"; each simply draws, and each has an equal chance of getting his or her way.

THE FAR SIDE   By GARY LARSON

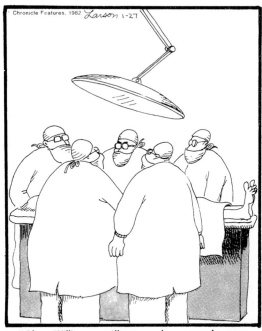

"Okay, Williams, we'll vote . . . how many here say
the heart has four chambers?"

*Majority rule is not always the
best way to make a decision.*

Voting Participants take a vote, and the majority wins. (This tactic is
applied more often in groups than in dyads.)

Compromise tactics are used so often in relationships because they are
quick and simple methods of reaching a conclusion or a result. Notice that
the focus of compromise is on reaching a quick decision by agreeing on the
method of deciding. The various methods, however, do not provide for quality checks as to whether the outcome is desirable, fair, or correct.

Settling for a compromise rather than working through issues is not the
most productive way to manage conflict in a relationship. But compromise is
helpful in certain circumstances, such as when a decision must be made
under severe time constraints. In that situation, there is no time to engage in
active debate, argument, or questioning.

You should also resort to compromise when the outcomes are relatively
unimportant to you and your partner. Why not just split the difference when
conflict is not worth the effort?

Traps. Competent communicators in conflict situations are those who avoid
or minimize falling into traps. This section discusses several traps (sidetracking, deception, and hidden agendas) that are frequently part of conversa-

SIDETRACKING

In a conflict, an attempt to move the conversation to a peripheral, often irrelevant topic.

DECEPTION

In a conflict, a partner's introduction of false data or substantiation for a general claim.

HIDDEN AGENDA

A secret goal that one partner in a conflict is pursuing under the guise of another, expressed goal.

Ethics and Traps

In which conflict situations or events would the use of traps be ethical? What ethical reasoning do you think people rely on when they use traps in conflict situations? Ask five people whom you respect to give their opinions about the ethical implications of traps.

tions involving conflict. Try as you might, you may not be able to prevent traps altogether, but you can at least be prepared for them.

Sidetracking occurs when a partner attempts to move the conversation to a peripheral topic that is often irrelevant. You will also encounter this trap when one of the participants makes a topic unnecessarily complex. Usually, a partner will revert to sidetracking when he or she is "losing" an issue and does not want to concede or modify the position. To avoid being caught in this trap, you must be firm about the focus of the conversation. Statements such as "We're not talking about that right now" can clearly signal your lack of desire to move away from the topic.

Conflict situations provide one of the "ripest" contexts for **deception**. When your partner thinks you are scrutinizing the presented ideas and feels "under fire," there is an increased chance you will hear a lie. The best opportunities for deception occur when a partner must produce data or substantiation for a general claim. Good examples include answers to questions such as "Have you ever seen that happen?" "About how much money would this take?" "Did you talk to her personally about it?"

Intuitively, you may know that your partner is lying to you. One way you can get to the truth is to avoid directly confronting your partner. If you say "You liar" or "That's just B.S." you could escalate the conflict and move it toward personalities instead of the issues. It is far better to use indirect confrontations. Hence, you might say, "If it did happen, just tell me; I really don't care, but I have to know the truth." Or you might say, "Can you think about that one more time, so we're sure that's exactly the way it really happened?" The important factor is to discover the truth, not to embarrass or confront your partner for deceiving you.

You may find that your partner has not been truthful with you about why he or she has been arguing or debating with you. We call these deceptions **hidden agendas**; your partner is using the supposed goal of the argument to score a personal gain, to secure information from you, or to achieve some other secret purpose.

You should not become paranoid about it, but you should be "on guard" about hidden agendas. When Phil Rizzuto, a veteran shortstop for the New York Yankees, was in the twilight years of his career, he was called to the general manager's office. The general manager told Rizzuto that he had to release a player and wanted to discuss some of the options with him. At first, Rizzuto was flattered. As the debate continued and the strengths and weaknesses of various players were discussed, it became clear that the general manager wanted Rizzuto to identify *himself* as the player who should be released. The general manager's hidden agenda for the conflict was to avoid having to fire Rizzuto directly by allowing him to suggest it himself.

The three traps described here have a number of ethical ramifications. Experts on ethical communication differ in their recommendations for dealing with troublesome situations. Some ethicists believe that you should act or communicate only in the most moral and ethical ways regardless of the circumstances. They advise against all of these traps—sidetracking, deception, and hidden agendas. Other ethicists take a more situational approach, advising that communicators must decide on the ethics of each situation separately. They would view sidetracking, deception, and hidden agendas as poor choices for conflict management except in certain circumstances.

Decision

The fifth phase of conflict involves agreeing on a consensus decision. In this phase, the exact agreement must be clearly summarized and reiterated to avoid all disagreement about what the final conclusion is. In some cases, the participants actually sign a contract or other formal document.

Reaching a Consensus. Once all the positions have been advanced, data have been given, and reasoning has been proposed, the participants must reach a conclusion. Reaching this decision is what the conversation that involved conflict is all about. **Consensus**, defined as a mutually satisfying agreement reached by two or more parties, is very different from compromise (whose focus is on a quick decision).

CONSENSUS
A mutually satisfying agreement reached by two or more parties.

Before the parties to a conflict "sign on the dotted line," the following three factors should be considered:

Goals Do both parties meet their goals and objectives through this decision? If not, the decision will not be the win-win outcome discussed previously.

Partner Does each partner recognize the benefits gained from the conflict? If there are any concerns, these should be pointed out before the discussion is brought to a close.

Relationship How is the relationship different as a result of the conflict? Is it stronger? Weaker? Are there topics that were alluded to but not discussed—topics that should be considered in a future conversation?

Summary and Confirmation. In some conflict situations, the parties must actually reach a formal agreement such as signing a contract or other legal document. In other situations, the outcome is far less formal. Regardless of the situation, summarizing and confirming the outcome is an extremely important step. In all conversations involving conflict, at least one of the participants should summarize the conversation. When someone says "So, our agreement is . . ." or "What we have decided to do is . . . ," then there is no room for confusion.

In some cases, one or both parties must engage in a series of follow-up steps. Even these behaviors must be agreed upon at the conclusion of a conflict-based conversation, or they may never be performed. One person may say, "So you have agreed to do these things by . . ." or "We have six steps still to take. Let me read them to be sure we agree."

Reflection

Resolution of the conflict does not mean it is over. Reflection, the sixth and final phase of productive conflict, is extremely important. It requires the participants to evaluate their behavior during the conflict situation and to assess the impact of the conflict on their relationship. The participants must consider their strengths and weaknesses in the various skills they used during the conflict situation. Furthermore, they must decide what impact the conflict has had on their feelings about the other person. In some cases the relationship is stronger, and in other cases some repair work needs to be done. The final phase of this model, then, is concerned with what happens afterward. You should look at two important factors: the relationship and the performance of communication.

Reevaluating the Relationship. Because conflict between two people takes place in a relational context, you can be assured that the relationship is different afterward. In many cases, the relationship is stronger, especially when the conflict has centered on the issues. The partners should capitalize on this advantage and find other topics or areas of concern that can be worked through together.

Sometimes conflict gets off course. Personalities may become involved, and the conflict may become destructive. If the relationship shows some "wear and tear" as a result of conflict, then several options are available to help you repair it.

- *Be open and frank with your partner about what happened.* Explain what you said and why. Ask your partner to do the same. Share your feelings and reactions about the experience with each other.

- *Agree to put the issue behind you.* Acknowledge that the topic was a difficult one for the two of you, and now that it has been discussed, it is time to go on to other things. You need not make unrealistic promises such as "This won't ever happen again." If the relationship is to continue, conflict is inevitable.

- *Focus on the process.* Explain that, although one of you is not satisfied with the outcome, the opportunity to talk and work through a problem was very worthwhile. Encourage your partner to discuss other topics with you in the same way in the near future. Suggest that you believe the relationship is actually stronger because you took the time to talk. You may be sorry about the outcome but not dissatisfied with the process.

- *Use the relational repair strategies from Chapter 7.* Remember that relationships are often in need of repair and that conflict situations can bring relational difficulties to the surface. In repairing a relationship, do not hesitate to tell your partner how you feel, demonstrate empathy for his or her feelings, tell the truth about what you are experiencing, and show that you care. You will probably find that your partner responds with some of his or her own repair strategies.

Assessing Competence and Performance. Another factor to consider after the conflict has concluded is the degree to which you performed competently as a communicator. Assess your behavior and try to discover some skills that you need to improve. For example, how well did you really *listen* to your partner? Did you *ask* your partner clear and concise questions? How *strong* were your arguments? Did your data *support* the positions you took? Were you able to *substantiate* each of your claims? Were you able to focus on *issues* instead of your partner's personality or past behavior? Did you lose your *temper* at any time?

Exactly what is competence in conflict situations? Competence in communicating was defined earlier as effectively attaining goals in a manner appropriate to the context of the relationship. The context of a relationship can be defined in many ways, including maturity of the participants, length of the relationship, status differences or similarities, and type of relationship (such as business or romantic).

Demonstrating competence in interpersonal conflict can be quite difficult. Conflict often exists because of the presence of incompatible goals. The participants must seek a successful outcome while considering each other's expectations for the relationship and the situation. Considering that most of these situations are emotion-laden, there is always the potential for inappropriate behavior.[15]

Flexibility plays an important role in keeping conflict productive and avoiding unnecessary escalation.

Focus now on one competency in productive conflict, *flexibility*. According to Folger and Poole, "In constructive conflicts, members engage in a wide variety of behaviors ranging from coercion and threat to negotiation, joking, and relaxation in order to reach a mutually acceptable solution. In contrast, parties in destructive conflicts are likely to be much less flexible because their goal is more narrowly defined; they are trying to defeat each other. . . . Neither avoidance nor hostile arguments are harmful in themselves—but rather the *inflexibility* of the parties which locks them" into escalating or avoiding conflict.[16]

Simply put, one tool that separates competent from incompetent participants in conflict is the *versatility* that each person brings to the situation. Versatile individuals, with a repertoire of all types of communication behaviors, can respond with greater flexibility than can those who typically behave in only one way.

The key to competence, however, is more than just possessing the ability to communicate in different ways. Competence requires the individual to communicate in the *appropriate* way, given situational demands. A person may be able to be sarcastic as well as serious, but how and under what circumstances these behaviors are used is the key to his or her competence. A flexible person who uses the wrong behaviors in certain circumstances is just as incompetent as an inflexible person who cannot use the behavior at all.

T he Case of Rolanda

At the beginning of this chapter, you met Rolanda, a member of a new step-family, who is having difficulty adjusting to her situation. The adults expect her to act as baby-sitter and to keep the house tidy. Her step-siblings, however, see no reason to follow her lead. Think about how this chapter applies to Rolanda's situation, and answer the following questions.

• Which of the conditions producing interpersonal conflict are most relevant to this situation?

• Describe the first phase of this conflict in terms of traits, relational status, and style.

• Which of the six stages of the chapter's model do you think will be most crucial to the successful resolution of this conflict?

• Illustrate how this family might develop a competent conflict management style by using the six stages of the chapter's model.

REVIEW

- This chapter discusses effective strategies for managing conflict in interpersonal relationships and explores four conditions under which interpersonal conflict is produced—incompatible goals, unrealistic expectations, disparate relational growth, and inaccurate perceptions.

- Accepting the fact that conflict is inevitable and healthy is the foundation for conflict management.

- Conflict can help a relationship grow, and it also helps people to make better decisions that in the long run will save time. In addition, debating a conflicting issue can be enjoyable.

- The model for competent conflict management was developed to better manage conflict that exists in interpersonal relationships.

- Conflict begins in a prelude stage before any actual words are spoken. The participants' characteristics, the relationship that provides the context, and the predispositions and tendencies people have in approaching their partners affect everything that occurs in a conflict situation.

- In the second phase, the participants must decide what they want out of the conflict and how important it is to them. Their assessment of their own goals, their partner's goals, their relational goals, and the ultimate goal of winning greatly affects how they approach the conflict situation.

- In the engagement phase of conflict, the partners create a context for conflict. This phase also involves ways in which both partners can clarify and focus on issues rather than on personalities.

- The action phase of conflict involves the "how" and "what" of conflict. The "how" involves the selection of strategies that a communicator uses in a conflict situation, and the "what" involves the tactics used to enact the strategies.

- The fifth phase of conflict involves reaching an agreement, or consensus, on the issues that have been debated. Just because the conflict has been resolved does not mean it is over.

- In the sixth phase, reflection, the participants evaluate their behavior during the conflict situation and assess the conflict's impact on their relationship.

- The key to competence is more than just possessing the ability to communicate in different ways. Competence requires the individual to communicate in the appropriate way given situational demands.

CHAPTER NINE

Principles of
Competent Interviewing

●BJECTIVES

After reading this chapter, you should be able to:

1. Distinguish interviews from noninterviews and identify the various types of interviews.

2. Describe the roles of interviewers and interviewees in the different types of interviews.

3. Explain the basic interviewing strategies, including developing clear goals, identifying potential barriers, and creating an effective structure.

4. Discuss the criteria for formulating questions in terms of type (open or closed, primary or secondary), potential impact, and sequence.

5. Specify and use an appropriate sequence of reacting moves.

6. Describe how to prepare for and participate in a screening employment interview.

 ARIBETH BERG IS A SOPHOMORE in college who is majoring in business administration. As a graded assignment for her introductory communication class, Maribeth has been asked to set up an interview with a person who (1) is engaged in professional work related to Maribeth's major and (2) does a considerable amount of interviewing. Maribeth has made an appointment by telephone to interview Jim Walsh, an insurance agent. Her task is to learn about Mr. Walsh's interviewing training (how he became a competent interviewer) and interviewing practices (the methods he uses). As you read through this chapter, think about the skills Maribeth will need in order to conduct a successful interview with Jim Walsh. At the end of the chapter, we will return to this scenario and solicit your advice.

◆ Defining the Interview

Chapter 7 identified many of the goals and motivations for initiating relationships with others: interpersonal attraction, physical proximity, alleviating loneliness, securing stimulation, and achieving goals. This chapter focuses on the last of these motivations—initiating relationships in order to achieve specific goals. Here you will understand how the resources of knowledge and skills come together in the *interview* to produce effective and appropriate communication.

Stewart and Cash describe a "situational schema" of seven goals that can be achieved by the interview.[1] Here are the goals, along with examples of each type of interview:

Information giving Teaching a friend to use a new word-processing program; helping your sister improve her backhand for racquetball

Information gathering Conducting a public opinion survey concerning student attitudes toward campus parking; asking your English professor about the career possibilities for an English major

Selection Interviewing for a part-time job at a store; meeting, as a candidate, with the selection committee charged with choosing the managing editor of the student newspaper

Problem related to the interviewee's behavior Talking with a counselor about your anxiety in regard to giving speeches; being reprimanded by your French TA for missing the midterm examination

Problem related to the interviewer's behavior Returning a defective compact disc to the retailer; asking your Chemistry instructor to reconsider the grade she has assigned to your term project

Problem solving Working on a project with a classmate in your American Government class; discussing with a friend problems you are having with your parents

Persuasion Convincing others to give blood during the campuswide Red Cross campaign; asking someone to go to a rock concert with you

INTERVIEW

A process of planned, dyadic, interactive discourse.

As these examples illustrate, every day you participate in numerous interactions that can be labeled **interviews**. Each of them involves a process of planned, dyadic, interactive discourse.[2]

Interviews are planned discourse. Each of the preceding examples has a purpose that goes beyond the establishment and development of a relationship. Although an interpersonal relationship is often an important component of an interview, at least one of the two parties (and sometimes both) has an additional predetermined reason for initiating the interview (e.g., to gather information, to inform, to persuade). Because this goal exists in advance of the interaction, it is possible (and beneficial) for at least one of the participants to plan a strategy for initiating, conducting, and concluding the interview. For example, if you intend to ask your Chemistry instructor to reconsider the grade assigned to your term project, you will have a better chance of achieving this goal if you plan what you will say ahead of time.

Interviews are dyadic discourse. Like most forms of interpersonal communication, the interview is dyadic; that is, it involves *two parties.* Although each of the two parties is typically a single person, that need not be the case. It is possible, for example, for survey researchers to conduct group interviews. It is also common for several representatives of an organization to interview job applicants in a group setting. In both cases, however, even though a number of individuals are involved, there are only two parties. Consequently, there is no one to act as a mediator or an arbiter should the two parties not agree.

Interviews are interactive discourse. Interviews involve two-way interactions in which both parties exchange speaking and listening roles. There is a heavy dependence on questions and answers, and both parties modify their verbal and nonverbal behaviors as they adapt to the ongoing process. Although most interviews occur face-to-face, interactions over the phone (or via computer) are also considered interviews.

◆ The Roles of Interviewer and Interviewee

You should now be ready to focus on some general principles that are applicable across all types of interviews. Before doing that, however, consider the role of the two parties in an interview.

For convenience, the two parties in an interview are often designated as **interviewer** and **interviewee**. Although these terms are commonly used, other labels are sometimes more precise—for example, employer/applicant, survey researcher/subject, therapist/client.

Although both parties in an interview have roles that benefit from advance preparation, it is typically the interviewer who assumes the major responsibility for the planning and success of the interview. Thus, to use two earlier examples, when teaching a friend how to use a new word-processing program, you would attempt to anticipate the best way to structure the lesson; and when attempting to convince your friends to give blood during the Red Cross campaign, you would attempt to anticipate objections and ways of countering them. In general, then, the interviewer is the person who should and does accept the major responsibility for the success of the interview. As with all general rules, however, there are exceptions. In some cases, the interviewer may wish to ask the interviewee to take over or share responsibility for taking the lead. For example, the counselor you are consulting about your anxiety may decide that the best approach is to allow you significant latitude concerning how the interview will proceed. In some situations, responsibility for planning and conducting an interview is shared. In problem-solving interviews, for example (as when you work on a project with a classmate), both parties have equal responsibility for the outcome of the interview.

Recognizing Interviews

Of the interviews you have participated in during the past week, which ones were concerned with information giving? Information gathering? Selection? A problem related to the interviewee's or interviewer's behavior? Problem solving? Persuasion? From this exercise, what have you learned about the role of interviews in your life?

INTERVIEWER

One of two parties in an interview; typically assumes the primary responsibility for the planning and success of the interview.

INTERVIEWEE

One of two parties in an interview; typically follows the lead of the interviewer during the interview.

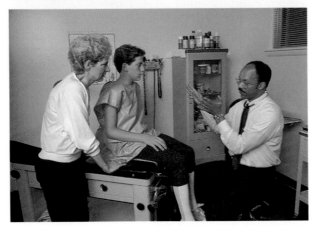

One feature that distinguishes interviews from other forms of interpersonal communication is that they have a planned purpose. How would you describe the purposes of these interviews?

In most situations, then, the interviewer sets the goals of the interview and devises a strategy to maximize the likelihood of achieving those goals. The interviewee, however, also has much to gain from anticipating what will happen in the interview. The following advice, therefore, is relevant to both parties.

◆ Basic Interviewing Strategies

There are five general guidelines for developing competence as an interviewer: (1) Keep your goal clearly in mind; (2) identify potential barriers to the achievement of that goal; (3) create an appropriate structure for the interview; (4) use effective questions to develop your structure; and (5) respond effectively during the interview.

Developing Clear Goals

You already know that an interview, by definition, is planned discourse—it has a purpose. Thus, although the establishment and development of a relationship may be important to an interview, they are secondary rather than primary goals. The primary goal is the task, and you must be careful not to focus so much or so little on the interpersonal relationship that the task doesn't get accomplished. Assume, for example, that you are the candidate meeting with the selection committee charged with choosing the managing editor of the student newspaper. On the one hand, you might focus so much on the task of getting selected that you are insensitive to the interpersonal needs of committee members. On the other hand, you might be so concerned about being perceived as a nice person that you don't do a thorough job of emphasizing your credentials for the position. The first guideline, then, is to develop a clear goal and to remind yourself of that goal as you proceed through the interview. If you are trying to gather information, put the focus on that rather than on developing and maintaining the relationship with the other party.

Identifying Potential Barriers

With a clear vision of the goal in mind, the next guideline is to focus on potential pitfalls or barriers. What issues might prevent the accomplishment of the goal? In answering this question, it is useful to consider three major factors: the interviewer, the interviewee, and the setting.

> *The interviewer* Have you prepared carefully for the interview? Have you considered potential biases, misperceptions, or preconceived notions on your part that might interfere with the achievement of your goal? Have you done your homework in terms of the topic, the interviewee, and the setting?

*A*nticipating Barriers

Bill Smith is a production supervisor who oversees a crew of twelve workers. One new employee, Sara Heap-of-Birds, has been late 3 of her first 5 days on the job. Bill has scheduled a meeting with Sara but is not sure how to communicate to her that it is unacceptable to be late to work. He has no previous experience working with Native Americans, but he once read that their attitude toward time is different from that of Anglo-Americans. What potential pitfalls or barriers should Bill anticipate? Are these barriers most likely to originate with him? With Sara? With the setting? What positive and negative influences might Bill's belief that Sara's lateness is culture-based have on the interview? What can Bill do to overcome the anticipated barriers?

The interviewee Is the interviewee both able and willing to contribute to the interviewer's goal? What are the likely attitudes of the interviewee toward the interviewer (independent of the goal)? Will these attitudes help or hinder the interview? What are the likely attitudes toward the purpose for the interview? Will these attitudes facilitate or hurt the interview? What is known about the interviewee (demographically, socially, psychologically) that could enhance or detract from the effectiveness of the interview?

The setting Is there anything in the setting that will help or hinder the interview (e.g., the time of day or week, the location of the meeting, the seating pattern)? Can any of these features be changed to make the interview more effective?

Creating an Appropriate Interview Structure

Interviews are jointly created products. Although they should be planned, they cannot be completely specified in advance. Thus, it is useful for you to anticipate the likely structural development of each interview, but participating in the actual interview requires that you adapt to the situation as it evolves.

To create a structure for an interview, think of the interview as composed of three components: the opening, the body, and the closing.

The Opening. In thinking about the best way to start an interview, you should try to put yourself in the other person's shoes. If you were a candidate interviewing for the position of managing editor of the student newspaper, what questions would be on your mind at the beginning of the interview? Although answers to this question will vary with the interview, in most situations three interrelated issues emerge:

1. *Task:* What is the nature of this interview and how will it proceed?

2. *Relationship:* Will you like and can you trust this interviewer?

3. *Motivation:* What do you hope to gain by participating in this interview?

Therefore, the interviewer's responsibility is to anticipate which, if any, of these questions are important to the interviewee and to develop a strategy for dealing with them. Assume, for example, that you are doing a telephone survey on student attitudes toward parking on campus. Will issues of task, relationship, and motivation be important to the students you intend to call? Will they want to know about the nature of the interview and how long it will take? Will they want to know something about you and how you will be using the information you gather? Will they want to know how they will benefit from participating in the interview? Assuming an affirmative answer to one or more of these questions, what can you say or do at the start of the interview that is responsive to these needs?

As you consider the unique requirements of each interview, you may find some of the following **opening techniques** helpful in providing task, relationship, or motivational support.

OPENING
TECHNIQUES

Strategies for the initial portion of an interview that deal with issues of task, relationship, and motivation.

1. A brief statement or rapid summary of a problem or need. (This technique is appropriate with an interviewee who is *vaguely* aware of the problem but is not well informed about its details.)

2. A brief explanation of how you happened to learn that a problem exists, coupled with the suggestion that the interviewee will want to discuss it. (This technique avoids the appearance of lecturing or talking down to a person and encourages a spirit of cooperative, objective discussion of a *shared* problem.)

3. The statement of an incentive (goal or outcome) that is desired by the interviewee and that may reasonably be expected *if* the proposal is accepted. (This opening is potentially the most powerful of all but is easily abused. Avoid a presentation that sounds like a high-pressure "sales pitch." Be honest and sincere.)

4. A request for the interviewee's advice or assistance with regard to a problem. (This approach is effective when it is sincere; don't use it as a slick gimmick.)

5. A reference to the known position of the interviewee regarding a situation. (This is the common-ground approach. It is an excellent one to use when the interviewee has taken a public position or has already asked you to bring in proposals, etc.)

6. Identification of the person who sent you to see the interviewee. (This opening is appropriate when the interviewee does not know you and may be wondering why you have sought out him or her. This is a good opening when the third party is respected by the interviewee.)

7. Identification of the company, organization, or group you represent. (This opening is appropriate when added prestige is needed or as an explanation of why you are there.)

8. A request for a specified, brief period of time—for example, "10 minutes of your time." (Caution! This strategy can be too apologetic and should be used only when necessary—e.g., when dealing with an impatient, irritable, or very busy interviewee.)[3]

The Body. Once you have set the stage for the interview with an appropriate opening, you need to develop an overall strategy for the body of the interview.

In a **nondirective interview**, the interviewer deliberately grants the interviewee control of the structure and pacing of the interview. Interviewers may do this for a variety of reasons: They may not have enough knowledge to effectively structure the interview; they may want to give the interviewee greater freedom to generate relevant information; or they may want to better adapt to the unique characteristics of each interviewee.

The following exchange illustrates a nondirective approach to a counseling interview between Dr. Romero, an English instructor, and Alan, a student:

NONDIRECTIVE INTERVIEW

An interview in which the interviewer grants the interviewee control of the structure and pacing of the interview.

DR. ROMERO	What goals would you like to set for yourself?
ALAN	I'd like to be a better student.
DR. ROMERO	What do you mean by that?
ALAN	I'd like to learn how to write better and get better grades in my English class.
DR. ROMERO	What do you think that would take?
ALAN	I guess I would have to manage my time a little better.
DR. ROMERO	For example?

DIRECTIVE
INTERVIEW

An interview in which the interviewer retains control of the purpose, structure, and pacing of the interview.

At the other end of the continuum is the **directive interview**. In such interviews, the interviewer retains control of the purpose, structure, and pacing of the interview. Interviewers opt to retain control for a variety of reasons: They may need to quantify the interview results in order to compare them with other interviews; they may not have the time to conduct a nondirective interview; or they may lack the training necessary to conduct a nondirective interview in a satisfactory way. Whatever the reason, when choosing the directive interview option the interviewer has four choices in terms of structure.

*S*trategies for Opening an Interview

For each of the following situations, anticipate the need to deal with the task, relationship, and motivation concerns of potential interviewees. Which of the strategies discussed in the text (alone or in combination) would be a good opening for the interview?

1. *Information giving:* You are attempting to teach a new employee your company's policy concerning how to answer the telephone.
2. *Information gathering:* A waiter at your restaurant has just resigned and you are conducting an exit interview.
3. *Selection:* You are a campus recruiter hiring people in your interviewee's area of interest.
4. *Problem related to the interviewee's behavior:* You are a counselor, and a client has come to you with a dating or relationship problem.
5. *Problem related to the interviewer's behavior:* You received a C on an essay for an English class. You think the essay deserves an A. You've scheduled an appointment to talk about the grade.
6. *Problem solving:* You and another student are getting together for the first time to talk about a joint term paper you plan to write for your introductory sociology course.
7. *Persuasion:* The customer has just walked onto your used car lot and is looking at a 1990 BMW.

The nonscheduled interview Here the interviewer prepares a guide that lists potential topics and subtopics. The topics may or may not be covered in the actual interview, and they may or may not be covered in the listed order. What actually happens in the interview depends more on the responses of the interviewee than on the interview guide. For example:

- What was your college major? (How did you choose it? If you were making the choice today, would you choose the same major? Did you consider other majors? What do you like about your major? What do you dislike about your major?)
- What is your job experience? (Which of your jobs have you enjoyed the most? Why? Which have you enjoyed least? Why? Which of your supervisors would you consider a good role model? Why?)

The moderately scheduled interview When using this option, the interviewer prepares an interview guide that includes all the major questions, with possible probe questions under each major question. Although all of the major questions are asked, the order may be varied and the probes may or may not be used. For example, consider the following approach to a counseling interview:

- What is the problem? (What is unique about the problem right now? What part of the problem can we do something about right now? What part of it do you want to work on right now?)
- How have you handled similar problems or this problem in the past? (Can you take the same approach now? Who else have you talked to about this problem? What did they say? Did you take their advice? If not, why not? If it worked before, can you do the same thing again now?)
- How can I help? (What do you want me to do?)
- Who else can be of help to you? (What about family? Friends or neighbors? Employers or teachers? Spiritual leader, physician, or counselor? Social agency, psychologist, or other specialist?)
- What do you plan to do about this problem? (When? How about tomorrow?)

The highly scheduled interview Here the interviewer prepares an interview schedule that contains all the questions that will be asked (including all probe questions), using the exact wording that will be used in each interview. Each time, exactly the same questions are given in exactly the same order. There are, however, no precoded response options. For example:

- Did you vote in the last presidential election?
- Do you intend to vote in this election?
- Have you decided which candidate you will vote for?
- If "yes," which candidate are you likely to vote for?
- If "no," if the election were held today, who would get your vote?

Surveys often take the form of highly scheduled, standardized interviews. What are the advantages of making such interviews extremely directive?

The highly scheduled, standardized interview   In this case, the interviewer prepares an interview schedule that includes all the questions to be asked in the order in which they are to be asked, with all the answer options. For example:

- Do you pay out-of-state or in-state tuition?
    _____ out-of-state; _____ in-state; _____ don't know

- Is it fair to raise out-of-state tuition at a faster rate than in-state tuition?
    _____ very fair; _____ fair; _____ not sure; _____ unfair; _____ very unfair

- How important is the issue of tuition increases to you?
    _____ very important; _____ important; _____ uncertain; _____ unimportant; _____ very unimportant

The Closing. Once the purpose of the interview has been achieved, the interviewer must consider how to bring the interaction to a satisfying close. This phase of the interview, the **closing**, is especially important in that what occurs here is likely to determine the interviewee's impression of the interview as a whole. Knapp and his colleagues studied the functions and norms involved when individuals take leave of each other.[4] Based on their review of the literature, they conclude that the termination phase of a conversation

CLOSING

The termination phase of an interview.

serves three functions: concluding, summarizing, and supporting. Thus, at this point, the interviewer needs to utilize both verbal and nonverbal strategies (1) to signal the end of the interview; (2) to review the substantive conclusions produced by the interview; and (3) to express satisfaction with the interaction and project what will happen next. The following strategies may help you achieve these purposes.

1. *Use clearinghouse questions* (e.g., "Is there anything I've missed?"). Clearinghouse questions allow you to determine whether you have covered all topics or answered all the interviewee's questions. They can be effective if you are making an honest effort to identify any questions, information, or areas of concern that have not been discussed adequately.

2. *Declare the completion of the purpose or task.* The word *well* probably brings more interviews to a close than any other phrase. When people hear it, they automatically assume the end is near and prepare for their leave-taking.

3. *Signal that time for the meeting is up.* This closing is most effective when a time limit has been announced or agreed upon in the opening of the interview. Be tactful in calling time, and try not to be too abrupt or give the impression that you are moving the interviewee along an assembly line.

4. *Explain the reason for the closing.* Tell the person why you must close the interview and be sure the justifications are real. If an interviewee thinks you are giving phony excuses, any future interactions will be strained.

5. *Express appreciation or satisfaction.* A note of appreciation or satisfaction is a common closing because interviewers usually have received something from the interview—information, help, a sale, a story, a new employee, and so on.

6. *Plan for the next meeting.* It is often appropriate to arrange the next interview or reveal what will happen next, including date, time, place, topic, content, and purpose.

7. *Summarize the interview.* A summary is a common closing for informational, appraisal, counseling, and sales interviews. Summaries may repeat important information, stages, and agreements, or verify accuracy or agreement.[5]

Using Effective Questions

In their book *The Language of the Classroom*, Bellack and colleagues describe classroom communication as a language game composed of four types of moves:[6] (1) *Structuring moves* are usually provided by the teacher and frame the classroom dialogue (e.g., "Today we will focus on the flat tax"); (2) *soliciting moves* are designed to elicit a verbal response (e.g., "Can anyone tell me who was the first person to propose a flat tax in the United States?"); (3) *responding moves* address the expectations of soliciting moves (e.g., "I think it was Steve Forbes"); and (4) *reacting moves* comment on responding moves (e.g., "No, the flat tax was proposed much earlier than 1995").

It is easy to apply these four moves to the language game of the interview. The interviewer starts with a structuring move (perhaps by talking about the purpose of the interview) and then solicits a response from the interviewee with a question. This response then serves as an opportunity for reactions by the interviewer. In this section, the focus is on the question or solicitation phase of this process. You can characterize a question in a wide variety of ways, including the latitude of response it provides an interviewee, the antecedent of the question, the question-antecedent relationship, expectations and premises implicit in the question, the content or subject matter of the question, and the vocabulary used in wording the question. Our primary concern here is with the type, impact, and sequence of questions in the interview.

Question Type. In evaluating question type, you should consider two characteristics: (1) the freedom the question grants the interviewee in terms of possible response and (2) the antecedent of the question. As labels for these two characteristics of a question, the terms *open/closed* and *primary/secondary* are used.

In some situations you should give the interviewee a great deal of flexibility in constructing a response to the question. Perhaps you are asking questions concerning a topic about which they know more than you do. Or perhaps you want to allow the interviewee to relax, and thus you ask a question for which there is no one correct answer. Or perhaps you are initiating questioning on a topic for which it is important not to bias or influence the attitudes of the interviewee. In such situations, the question should give the interviewee great freedom in terms of how to respond. That is, the interviewer should ask an **open question**. For example: "Tell me about yourself." "How do you like being a student here?" "What issues will influence your decision to vote for one of the presidential candidates?"

OPEN QUESTION
A question that gives the interviewee relative freedom in responding.

In other situations, however, the interviewer will want to give less freedom in responding. Perhaps, for example, the interviewer is conducting a survey of student attitudes toward parking on campus and wants to compare the attitudes of such groups as commuters, dormitory residents, and sorority/fraternity members. Asking open questions in such a situation would make comparisons difficult. Thus, the interviewer would be likely to ask questions at the **closed** end of the open/closed continuum.

CLOSED QUESTION
A question that gives the interviewee little or no freedom in responding.

The most closed form of a question is labeled a *bipolar* question, for which there are two possible responses—"yes" and "no." Examples of bipolar questions are "Do you normally eat breakfast?" "Do you own a car?" and "Did you vote in the last election?" Closed questions can also take the multiple-choice form: "In which college are you currently enrolled—Arts and Sciences?

Business? Education? Engineering? Fine Arts?" "What is your political party affiliation—Republican? Democrat? Independent? Other? None?"

In terms of question type, then, interviewers need to consider the advantages and disadvantages of asking questions at a particular location on the open/closed continuum. That is, they need to ask themselves: Given my particular interviewing situation, topic, and interviewee, am I better off asking a question at the open or closed end of the continuum?

A second consideration related to question form is that of question antecedent; that is, what is the relationship of this question to what has happened previously in the interview? The broad terms used to describe this relationship are primary and secondary. **Primary questions** introduce new topics; **secondary questions** seek clarification or elaboration of responses to primary questions. Thus, an interviewer might start an area of questioning by asking "What are your beliefs about the topic of abortion?" This primary question might then be followed by a number of secondary questions, such as: "Should parental notification be required for individuals of a certain age?" "What restrictions, if any, should the state be allowed to impose on the decision?"

Secondary questions can take a variety of forms; some of the more common forms are listed here.

PRIMARY QUESTION
A question that initiates a new topic.

SECONDARY QUESTION
A question that develops a topic that has already been introduced.

Clarification Directly requesting more information about a response (e.g., "Could you tell me a little more about the kind of person you would like to work for?").

Elaboration Directly requesting an extension of a response (e.g., "Are there any other features of location that you would consider important?").

Paraphrasing Putting the response in the questioner's language in an attempt to establish understanding (e.g., "Let's see if I've understood what you're saying: You consider the type of people you work with more important than salary and benefits?").

Silence Waiting without speaking for the respondent to begin or resume speaking.

Encouragement Using brief sounds and phrases that indicate attentiveness to, and interest in, what the respondent is saying (e.g., "Uh huh," "I see," "That's interesting," "Good," and "Yes, I understand").

Mirroring Repeating the response using the language used by the respondent (e.g., "You say, then, that it is important to you to be located near a university?").

Summarizing Summarizing several previous responses and seeking confirmation of the correctness of the summary (e.g., "Let's see if I've got it: Your ideal job involves an appreciative boss, supportive colleagues, interesting work, and living in a large metropolitan area?").

Clearinghouse Asking if you have elicited all the important or available information (e.g., "Have I asked everything that I should have asked?").[7]

In terms of question type, then, a single question can be (1) identified in terms of its location on a continuum from open to closed and (2) labeled as either primary or secondary. If it is a secondary question, it can be further identified as a special type of secondary question (e.g., elaboration, encouragement, mirroring). It is the interviewer's responsibility to make wise decisions in selecting open/closed and primary/secondary questions.

Question Impact. In addition to considering question type, interviewers must also consider the likely impact of a question; that is, is the interviewee likely to find the question understandable, relevant, and unbiased?

First, is the question understandable? In his book *The Art of Asking Questions*, Paine makes a number of useful suggestions for enhancing the clarity of questions.[8] He suggests, first, that the questioner start by making sure that he or she understands the issue around which the question is organized. To achieve this understanding, the questioner should ask the stock journalistic questions of who, what, when, where, and how. Second, the questioner should use a dictionary and other resources to ensure that the wording of the question is as direct and simple as possible. Third, the questioner should keep the number of words in the question in the range of twenty or fewer. Longer questions create too much ambiguity. Fourth, the questioner should phrase questions positively because negative phrasing tends to be more confusing. Thus, instead of asking "You haven't ever voted in the campus student government elections, have you?" ask, "Have you ever voted in campus student government elections?"

Second, is the question relevant? In addition to understanding the question, the interviewee should also have an answer to the question and be willing to give it. Two strategies for ensuring this are pretests and the use of filter questions. When using a pretest, the interviewer identifies a small number of individuals representative of interviewees who will eventually answer the question and asks them what they think the question means. Pretesting is also an excellent way to improve the clarity of the question. A second strategy here involves asking a **filter question** before asking the question itself. For example, an interviewer might ask "What, if anything, do you know about student government's position on the proposed new grading scale?" (a filter question) before asking, "Are you in favor of, against, or neutral toward the student government's position on the proposed new grading scale?" Both strategies, then, are ways of ensuring that the question is relevant—that the interviewee is likely to have an answer to the question and be willing to provide it.

Third, is the question unbiased? The third test of the impact of a question concerns identifying the assumptions or premises undergirding a question. The goal here is to avoid questions that unconsciously lead individuals to answer questions in a certain way. When a question suggests or implies the answer that is expected, it is called a **directed question**; that is, it directs respondents to a certain answer. Some such questions, called **leading questions**, are subtle in the direction they provide, for example, "You enjoy this class, don't you?" "Would you like to go get a cup of coffee with me?" Other directed questions are less subtle in their biasing effect: "Are you a bigot?"

FILTER QUESTION
A question designed to find out what, if anything, an interviewee knows about a particular topic.

DIRECTED QUESTION
A question that suggests or implies the answer that is expected.

LEADING QUESTION
A question that subtly suggests or implies the answer that is expected.

"When was the last time you cheated on an exam?" Both of these examples are **loaded questions**—the first is loaded with the use of an emotionally charged word (bigot), and the second is loaded because it asks two questions rather than one ("Have you ever cheated on an exam?" and "When was the last time you cheated on an exam?"). Questions that provide no hint to the interviewee concerning the expected response are labeled **neutral**. For example, "What, if anything, is your attitude toward the fraternities and sororities on this campus?"

Although generally the interviewer should ask neutral questions in an interview, there are exceptions. For example, when dealing with a topic that might threaten someone's ego, you might get a more honest response by asking a directed question that reveals that you will not be shocked by any response. Thus, under some circumstances, a loaded question such as "When was the last time you had too much to drink?" might produce a more honest response than the neutral question "Have you ever had too much to drink?" When Kinsey began to interview individuals about their sexual practices, for example, he used loaded questions such as "When was the last time you engaged in the following sexual practices?" His premise was that individuals who had not engaged in certain practices would be more than willing to tell him that fact, while individuals who had engaged in those practices would be more likely to say so when asked a loaded question that indicated he

LOADED QUESTION
A question that clearly implies or suggests the answer that is expected either by using emotional language or by asking two questions in the guise of one.

NEUTRAL QUESTION
A question that provides no clue as to the expected answer.

Sometimes the loaded question is really two questions in one.

"If elected, would you try to fool some of the people all of the time, all of the people some of the time or go for the big one: All of the people all of the time?"

would not be shocked by their answers. The key point to be made, then, is that an interviewer should know the difference between directed and neutral questions and should ask directed questions only when they are likely to serve his or her purpose.

Question Sequence. Having considered the form and potential impact of a single question on an interviewee, we will now consider some options for sequencing questions. Although a variety of formats are possible, three of the main options are the funnel, inverted funnel, and tunnel sequences.

FUNNEL SEQUENCE
A question sequence that moves from broad, open-ended questions to narrower, closed ones.

As the label **funnel sequence** implies, with this approach the interviewer starts with broad, open-ended questions and moves to narrower, more closed questions. Suppose a student is interviewing another student concerning participation in sports:

What sports, if any, do you actually participate in?
What are your experiences with racquetball?
What are your experiences with golf?
What are your experiences with running?
Which of the three sports are you best at? Worst at?
Which of the three sports do you enjoy most? Least?

INVERTED FUNNEL SEQUENCE
A question sequence that moves from narrow, closed questions to broad, open-ended ones.

The **inverted funnel sequence** starts with narrow, closed questions and moves to more open-ended questions. An example of such an approach might involve an interviewer asking a student questions about computer usage:

Do you use a PC?
Do you own your own PC? If so, what brand is it?
What kinds of software do you use?
For what major functions do you use your computer?
How did you learn to use a computer?
Is there anything else you can tell me about your use of computers?

TUNNEL SEQUENCE
A question sequence that utilizes questions at one level (i.e., either all of the questions are broad and open-ended or they are all narrow and closed).

With the **tunnel sequence**, all of the questions are at one level. A large tunnel would involve a series of broad, open-ended questions; a small tunnel (the more common form) would ask a series of narrow, closed questions. An interviewer might ask a student, for example, about participation in a variety of campus activities in the following way:

Using the following scale (VF = very frequently, F = frequently, O = occasionally, R = rarely, and N = never), indicate your participation in the following campus activities:

1. Attending sporting events (e.g., football, baseball)	VF	F	O	R	N
2. Attending cultural events (e.g., theater, art, music)	VF	F	O	R	N
3. Attending social events (e.g., parties)	VF	F	O	R	N

4. Attending academic events (e.g., lectures)	VF	F	O	R	N
5. Working for wages	VF	F	O	R	N
6. Working as a volunteer	VF	F	O	R	N

You can put together the three sequences that have been described in various combinations over the course of an interview. Say, for example, you are interviewing a political science professor concerning a research project she has recently completed on the role of hostages in international relations. You might start the interview with a funnel sequence, thus opening up avenues that you can explore with narrower secondary questions. Later in the interview, you may find it useful to develop some topics with an inverted funnel sequence as a way of focusing the professor's memory—using a series of closed questions both to jog her memory on the topic and to enhance her motivation to respond to your more open-ended questions. As the interview proceeds, you may also find uses for a tunnel sequence of questions.

In addition to these three sequences, there are other options as well. Perhaps the best known of these is the one developed by George Gallup for conducting public opinion polls aimed at determining intensity of opinions and attitudes. Labeled the **Quintamensional Plan**, it involves a five-step process:

QUINTAMENSIONAL PLAN

A five-step question sequence developed by George Gallup for use in conducting public opinion polls; involves examining awareness, uninfluenced attitudes, specific attitudes, reasoning, and intensity of feeling.

1. Awareness of the topic is ascertained by a free-answer knowledge question (also known as a *filter question*): "What, if anything, do you know about bluegrass music?"

2. Uninfluenced attitudes on the subject are developed in a free-answer question: "What is your opinion of bluegrass music?"

3. Specific attitudes are elicited through a two-way or multiple-choice question: "How frequently do you purchase bluegrass music—often, occasionally, seldom, or never?"

4. The reasoning behind the attitudes is examined via a free-answer, reason-why question: "Why do you feel this way?"

5. Intensity of feeling is examined via an intensity question: "How strongly do you feel about this—not very strongly, strongly, or very strongly?"[9]

Responding Effectively

In addition to asking good questions, interviewers need to know how to react appropriately to responses in order to further the dialogue of the interview. As we have mentioned, they need to be able to use effective "reacting" moves—that is, develop an effective **response style**. Rogers conducted a number of research studies that are helpful in thinking about this process.[10]

Rogers was interested in how people communicate with each other in face-to-face situations. One focus of his research was on the characteristic ways that one person responds to what another individual says (reacting moves). He found that 80 percent of all messages that people use can be summarized in

RESPONSE STYLE

The pattern an individual develops for using Rogers's five reacting moves: evaluative, interpretive, supportive, probing, and understanding.

five categories: evaluative, interpretive, supportive, probing, and understanding. To illustrate Rogers's categories, consider the following situation:

ANGELA   Now that you have your B.A., what do you intend to do with it?

TINA   I don't know. I got out of school last month and thought, now what? I looked for a job, but the job market is the pits. I'm thinking about working on a graduate degree, but I'm not sure I want to be in school right now—or what I'd get my degree in if I did decide to go on.

Angela, the interviewer, might respond in one of the following ways:

Evaluative response   "I find it very strange that you would even consider graduate school if you have no degree program in mind." The interviewer has made a judgment of the relative goodness, appropriateness, effectiveness, or rightness of the interviewee's response.

Interpretive response   "You're suffering from 'rejection shock.' You need to talk with a counselor." The interviewer's intent is to teach—to tell the interviewee what the response means, how she really feels. The interviewer either obviously or subtly implies what the interviewee ought to think.

Supportive response   "Boy do I know what you mean! The job market has done similar things to a lot of us these days." The interviewer's intent is to reassure, to pacify, and to reduce the interviewee's intensity of feeling. The interviewer implies that it is either appropriate or not necessary for the interviewee to feel as he or she does.

Probing response   "What graduate majors have you considered?" The interviewer's intent is to seek further information and provoke further discussion.

Understanding response   "You are worried about whether you should try to work or try to go to graduate school?" The interviewer's intent is only to make sure he or she correctly understands what the interviewee is saying.[11]

In addition to identifying the five categories, Rogers discovered that most people have a natural tendency to use evaluative and interpretive responses more frequently than the other three. In fact, he found the following order of frequency for the five categories: evaluative, interpretive, supportive, probing, and understanding.

In describing the implications of his research, Rogers suggests that our natural tendency to evaluate and interpret other people's remarks interferes with rather than enhances communication. If we were to understand, probe, and support their responses before evaluating and interpreting them, we would be more likely to comprehend what the other person was trying to say. The other person would also be more likely to find the interaction satisfying. Thus, the message of Rogers's research for the interviewer is twofold:

(1) Master the ability to use all five reacting moves and be prepared to use them; and (2) when using these moves, start with understanding, probing, and support before moving to interpretation and evaluation.

◆ The Employment Interview

The remaining pages of this chapter are devoted to a special form of interview—the selection or employment interview. For most college students, the employment interview occurs in two stages: (1) a screening interview that often takes place in the campus placement center and (2) a determinate interview that occurs on the premises of the hiring organization. The **screening interview**, from the employer's perspective, is used to screen out applicants who do not meet the job's requirements. The **determinant interview** is used to determine whether a qualified applicant should be hired. In this chapter, the primary focus is on the screening interview, although the principles discussed apply to both types of employment interviews. The employment interview is featured here for a variety of reasons: (1) It emphasizes the main functions of information giving, information gathering, and persuasion; (2) it is an interview type in which both participants are responsible for prior planning and for the success of the interview; and (3) it is an important interview that most members of society go through multiple times.

SCREENING INTERVIEW

The first stage in the employment interview process; during this stage the interviewer tries to find out whether the applicant can do the job.

DETERMINANT INTERVIEW

The second stage in the employment interview process; during this stage the interviewer decides whether or not to offer the job to the applicant.

✔ *C*onducting an Interview

Conduct an in-depth information-gathering interview and write a report (of no more than five typed pages) in which you summarize the information you received and comment on what you learned about the interview process.

The interview must last at least 2 hours; the interviewee must be a close acquaintance older than you and must have children (consider interviewing one of your parents); and the interview must cover at least two of the following topics:

1. The person's philosophy of raising children (topics such as discipline; teaching at home and at school; sex; finances; making friends; respect for authority; patriotism; character formation)
2. The person's political beliefs (political affiliation and commitment; involvement in civic affairs; involvement in government)
3. The person's religious beliefs, their effect on the person's life, and how these beliefs relate to family life
4. The person's goals in life and how the person is working to achieve these goals
5. The person's philosophy of leisure time (Ideally, how should one spend this time? In reality, how does the person spend this time?)

When we discussed the general principles of interviewing, we took the point of view of the interviewer and asked you to consider the role of the interviewee. In this section we do the reverse. We start by analyzing how an interviewee ought to prepare, and then we explore various aspects of the interview itself.

Preparing for the Interview

Prior planning from the applicant's perspective involves four interrelated tasks: (1) conducting an honest self-assessment; (2) preparing materials to be used in the process; (3) locating jobs and doing homework on the business environment and organizations; and (4) building realistic expectations about the interviewing process.

Conducting a Self-Assessment. The starting point for a job search is an honest self-assessment. Most college and university campuses have a career planning and placement center that can provide excellent assistance to students on this and the other tasks related to the employment interview. If you haven't already visited the facility on your campus, you ought to do so. You are likely to find friendly people there with good advice about what you

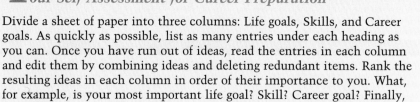

Your Self-Assessment for Career Preparation

Divide a sheet of paper into three columns: Life goals, Skills, and Career goals. As quickly as possible, list as many entries under each heading as you can. Once you have run out of ideas, read the entries in each column and edit them by combining ideas and deleting redundant items. Rank the resulting ideas in each column in order of their importance to you. What, for example, is your most important life goal? Skill? Career goal? Finally, using what you perceive to be the most important ideas in each column, create a checklist that you can use to compare job possibilities.

Here is a sample checklist:

	Company		
Life goals:	*A*	*B*	*C*
1. Get married and have a family	+	+	?
2. Retire at age 60	+	−	+
Skills:			
1. Good at oral communication	+	+	+
2. Good "people" person	+	+	+
Career goals:			
1. Live in the Dallas area	−	+	+
2. Work with interesting people	+	?	+

Note: + means that company is good for my skills/goals; − means that company is bad for my skills/goals; ? means that I am unsure whether that company is good or bad for my skills/goals.

can be doing now to prepare for the job search. It is never too early to begin the process. Campus counseling centers and the library are other resources. In addition, local bookstores typically have a section of books that provide help on such tasks as conducting self-assessment, locating jobs, preparing résumés, and conducting employment interviews. The World Wide Web is also a good source of such information.

As you engage in the process of self-assessment, you should consider three areas: (1) What are your *life goals?* What do you want to accomplish before you die? What is your life mission? (2) What are your *skills?* What things do you enjoy? What activities do you do well? (3) What are your *career goals?* Where do you wish to live and work? What will your life-style include? What income level do you need and want? What kind of work environment and level of responsibility do you want? What credentials are necessary?

Preparing a Résumé. A résumé is a printed summary of your educational and work experiences and accomplishments. It is a selling document whose sole purpose is to persuade employers to grant you an interview. It is a vehicle for making a positive first impression on potential employers. An effective résumé tells just enough about you to make employers believe that their company may need your skills and experience (see Figure 9.1, p. 282).

In thinking about putting together an effective résumé, consider the task of those who will read it. During the initial screening process, employers look at large numbers of résumés, most of which (95 to 99 percent) end up in the inactive file or the wastebasket. The conventional wisdom is that the average résumé has 45 seconds to make either a positive or a negative impression on the employer.

How do you make a positive impression? Before considering content, consider form. Although there are no hard and fast rules, there are certain biases that should only be violated for a good reason. For example, unless you are looking for a creative position in an area such as advertising or graphic design, use white, off-white, or light beige paper. If possible, limit the résumé to a single page. If you must use two pages, print it front and back to avoid the possibility of losing a page. With personal computers as widely accessible as they are, employers expect the professional look of word processing. Use a readable typeface—Palatino and Times are good choices among fonts that are readily available. Avoid any font that has a city name—for example, New York or Chicago—because they are not constructed for high-quality printing. Make the résumé attractive by using white space appropriately.

What about the content of the résumé? Once again, there are no hard and fast rules, but there are some important general principles. First, be 100 percent honest. Mention your assets rather than your liabilities, but don't falsify or embellish those assets. Second, provide a focus for your résumé. Although it might seem that nonspecific résumés might open more doors, the opposite is true. To capture the attention of an employer, the résumé should be designed with a specific employment objective in mind, and that objective should determine what is to be included and excluded. Third, while

Jane A. Doe

Current Address:	**Permanent Address:**
7001 Thistlewood, Apt. 67	339 Grant Street
Norman, OK 73072	Dallas, TX 75275
(405) 555-8884	(214) 555-3231

OBJECTIVE
To obtain an entry-level business/marketing position in an organization seeking an individual with demonstrated leadership, public speaking skills, and marketing experience

EDUCATION
University of Oklahoma, Norman, OK
Bachelor of Arts, Public Relations, May 1997, GPA 3.5/4.0

HONORS
Outstanding Young Women of America; Dean's List; Academic Scholarship; Alpha Lambda Delta (women's honorary)

ACTIVITIES
Journalism Club Secretary; Panhellenic Vice President; Varsity Debate; Delta Delta Delta Social Sorority President; Academic Programs Council

RELEVANT EXPERIENCE
June 1995–present
AT&T Marketing Division, Oklahoma City, OK
Marketing Support Assistant
*Responsible for customer support, telemarketing for new accounts, and trouble-shooting for installed firms when marketing representatives were out of the office
*Designed brochure to update client knowledge of AT&T equipment
*Presented demonstrations at executive conference in Houston, TX

Summers 1993 and 1994
Dillard's Department Store, Norman, OK
Department Supervisor
*Maintained inventory control and stock rotation
*Recognized as a member of Dillard's $100,000 club

ADDITIONAL INFORMATION
Coursework includes 16 hours of communication studies
Knowledge of Macintosh and IBM computers
Willing to travel and relocate
Hobbies include running and racquetball

REFERENCES
Available upon request

FIGURE 9.1
A well-prepared résumé is a form of competent written communication. Like speech communication, it presents its author through verbal and nonverbal means.

listing employment history and activities, use reverse chronological order—that is, list the most recent activity first and then go back in time. Fourth, when listing activities and jobs, emphasize those that relate to your job objective using action words that show results. Most young grads seeking their first full-time job have limited work experience. Include volunteer work and part-time employment, emphasizing activities that helped prepare you for the kind of work you are seeking. Wherever possible, use words such as *administered, supervised, constructed, established, coordinated, produced,* and the like. Fifth, as you list things, remember that the employer may not be familiar with abbreviations and organizations that are very familiar to you. When in doubt, spell everything out.

Given these five general principles, consider what information you will include in each of the following categories:

Name, address, etc. What will be the best way to reach you in writing? By phone? By fax? By e-mail? Will you need to include two addresses—one for campus and one for home?

Employment objective Be concise and specific. It is better to create multiple résumés than to have widely diversified objectives in the same résumé. Underneath this statement, you may wish to include information about your availability—for example, *Available July 1, 1997.*

Education In reverse chronological order (i.e., starting with the most recent), list the institutions you have attended, their locations, and the dates of attendance. Also list degrees received (or date to be received) and academic majors and areas of concentration. Awards and GPA can also be listed here if they will enhance your marketability.

Work experience As you list work experience in reverse chronological order, focus on concrete examples of achievement. Emphasize job functions rather than job titles. Remember that prospective employers read this section carefully to discover an answer to the question, How do this person's experience, abilities, and achievements relate to my organization's needs?

Student activities For employers, participation in a variety of academic, extracurricular, or social activities indicates that you are motivated and get involved. Thus, it can be beneficial to include several activities, especially if they are relevant to your career objective. Be selective in what you list and emphasize accomplishment.

Hobbies You may want to indicate some of your hobbies and extracurricular activities that reveal what you do apart from your professional life. Employers usually react positively to the opportunity to learn more about you as a "total person."

Other possibilities

Personal data It is best not to include data such as marital status, age, race, religion, and the like. Employers know that they are liable for unlawful use of such information, even if you supply it, because it might be used to discriminate.

Military status If the information is relevant, include branch of the military, dates of active duty, discharge rank, and brief description of your duties.

Publications If the information is relevant, use a standard reference form to list articles, books, convention presentations, and so on.

Professional memberships If the information is relevant, include membership, offices held, and professional certifications and/or licenses.

References Because references are almost always glowingly positive, many employers don't value them a great deal. At most, therefore, include the statement "References available upon request."

Locating Jobs. The third element of preinterview preparation involves identifying potential jobs and doing research on your field, the organizations to whom you are applying, and potential job positions.

Although there are many strategies for locating jobs, your three best sources are likely to be people you know, placement centers, and classified advertisements. The place to start is with family, friends, professors, former employers, and individuals working in your field. Let these individuals know the kind of job you are looking for and ask for suggestions. You might also make appointments with individuals who work in your field as a way of learning more about possible career opportunities and of establishing important contacts.

Placement centers are a second source of jobs. Most college campuses have a centralized placement center where recruiters from major companies come to interview potential employees. Some departments and colleges within the university provide additional services. Many professional organizations also provide resources for locating jobs. If you are unsure about the resources for your field of study, ask a faculty member who works in the area. The third source to consider is classified advertisements. In addition to your local newspaper, head over to the reading room of the library and look at the classified sections of some of the national newspapers and periodicals that emphasize your field of study. You can also "surf" the Web for appropriate listings.

Once you begin getting leads on possible jobs, learn everything you can about the potential position and the organization. Your best source for this information is likely to be your campus placement center. In addition to general reference works (e.g., *Occupational Outlook Handbook, Moody's Industrial Manual, Dictionary of Occupational Titles*), your placement center is likely to have the company's annual report, recruiting literature, and perhaps even a public relations videotape. If your placement center doesn't have these resources, call the company directly and ask for a copy of its annual report and other descriptive literature. You can also talk to current or former employees and other individuals who have relevant information. The more information you have about the company and the job you are seeking, the better you will be at answering the questions in the interviewing process. You will also be able to ask the interviewer intelligent questions.

Building Realistic Expectations. The final component of preinterview preparation involves developing realistic expectations about the interviewing process and preparing for "rejection shock."[12] It is important to remember (1) that the interviewer is interviewing many individuals for each position and (2) that his or her decisions will often be influenced more by subjective factors such as intuition, attitudes, and stereotypes of a good employee than by objective factors such as job qualifications. Thus, a job applicant is likely to face rejection numerous times during the course of a job search—because there was a better qualified applicant, because the interviewer made a mistake, or because an equally qualified candidate had an advantage (e.g., a personal contact in the company). A job candidate, therefore, needs to constantly remember that rejection is not uncommon—and that rejection is not personal but is the inevitable result of a tight job market and a less than perfect selection process. The attitude that the applicant needs to take, then, is that of the door-to-door salesperson who, knowing that she or he makes a sale at only one out of every ten homes, says: "If I get turned down at this door, it just makes it more likely that I'll make a sale at the next house." The applicant should also remember that persistence pays. If you approach the job search intelligently and persistently, you will usually get a job.

Participating in the Interview

To successfully participate in an employment interview, you must know the purpose of the interview and its likely structure; anticipate the questions the interviewer is likely to ask; and prepare questions to ask the interviewer.

Knowing the Purpose and Structure. From the perspective of the interviewer, the screening interview has three major purposes: (1) to discover if there is a potential match between the applicant and the position; (2) to build goodwill for the company or the organization; and (3) to ensure that the applicant has enough information about the company and position to make an informed decision. From the perspective of the applicant, the employment interview involves convincing the interviewer that the applicant possesses the qualifications to do an excellent job and obtaining enough information to make an informed decision, should a job be offered.

To discover whether there is a potential match between an applicant and a position, an interviewer typically explores five areas of information as they relate to the specific job: ability, desire, personality, character, and health. First, based on the résumé and the interview, the interviewer needs to discover if the applicant has the experience, education, training, intelligence, and ability to do what the job requires. Second, the interviewer needs to discover if the applicant has the desire or motivation to use those abilities to do a good job. To gather this information, the interviewer is likely to explore such things as the interviewee's record of changes in jobs, schools, majors; reasons for wanting this job; knowledge of the company; and concrete examples of prior success that indicate desire to achieve. The third area involves an assessment of the applicant's personality and how well he or she is likely to fit into the position and the company or organization. Depending on the job, this will likely involve an attempt to discover the applicant's personal goals, independence and self-reliance, imagination and creativity, and ability to manage or lead. A fourth area of judgment is that of character. What can be learned of the inter-

The employment interview involves convincing the interviewer that the applicant possesses the qualifications to do what the job requires.

viewee's personal behavior, honesty, financial responsibility, and accuracy and objectivity in reports? The final area is that of health. Is there any physical barrier that might limit the applicant's successful performance of the job?

In order to achieve the multiple purposes of the screening interview, interviewers typically use between 20 and 35 minutes to accomplish the following five functions: opening, asking questions, giving information, answering questions, and closing.

Although there are many possible approaches to the structure of an interview, the following is typical: (1) A brief opening is used to put the interviewee at ease and provide an overview of the structure of the interview. (2) This is followed by either a description of the company and the position or a series of questions that seek to gather information about the applicant's ability, desire, personality, character, and health. A major portion of the time will focus on the interviewer's asking of questions. (3) The interviewer then asks whether the interviewee has any questions. (4) The interviewer closes the interview by telling the applicant what will happen next.

Preparing Answers to the Interviewer's Questions. An important part of preparing for an employment interview is anticipating the kinds of questions you will be asked and thinking about strategies for responding to those questions. Knowing what the interviewer is looking for (ability, desire, personality, character, and health) should help you to anticipate many of the questions you will be asked. Here are frequently asked questions generated from conversations with employment interviewers and from a search of the literature.[13]

- What led you to choose your particular field (or your academic major)? What do you like about it? What don't you like about it?

- In which kinds of positions are you most interested?

- Have you had summer or other previous employment in this or a related field?

- What have you learned from your previous work experience?
- What are the most important considerations for you in choosing a job?
- What kinds of courses have you taken that you think prepared you for this occupation?
- How did you do in courses related to this job? How did you do overall in high school? In college?
- Why did you interview with our company?
- Do you have any geographical preferences about where you work?
- What do you see yourself doing five years from now? Ten years from now? What are your long-range goals?
- What percentage of your college expenses did you earn? How?
- How important is your personal life as compared to your work?
- What have you done that shows initiative and willingness to work?
- How do you spend your leisure time? What are your hobbies?
- What would you say is your strongest attribute? What is your weakest point?
- Have you ever had any problems interacting with fellow workers?
- What are your salary expectations? How much money do you want to be earning ten years from now?
- What can you contribute to our company that would make us want to hire you?
- Were you ever fired from a job? Did you ever quit a job? Why?
- Are there any questions that you want to ask?

It is a good idea to rehearse possible answers to questions like these before going into an employment interview. Ask a friend to randomly ask you the questions and then have him or her comment on your answers. Strive for answers that demonstrate your marketable skills in a direct and positive way. Interviewers are looking for results, so use stories and vignettes to provide evidence that things you have done have produced results. Although it is often uncomfortable to talk about accomplishments, in the screening interview there is no one but you who can tell the interviewer that you are able and willing to do the job well.

Several types of questions can pose special difficulties for the interviewee: illegal questions, surprise questions, and questions about weaknesses. Illegal questions are those that have no direct bearing on job performance and have the potential to lead to discrimination on the basis of race, creed, national origin, sex, handicap, and the like (e.g., "Do you have children, and if you do, what kind of child-care arrangements do you have?" "Do you have any disabilities?" "Are you married?" "This is a hectic office—can you keep up with the young people here?"). Although an organization whose employees ask illegal questions during employment interviews can be subject to a variety of legal penalties by the Equal Employment Opportunity Commission (EEOC) of the federal government, illegal questions continue to be asked and an applicant needs to consider how to answer them.

Stewart and Cash suggest five tactics you can use to respond to illegal questions: (1) Answer directly but briefly ("Do you attend church regularly?" "Yes, I do"); (2) pose a tactful inquiry ("What does your husband do?" "Why do you ask?"); (3) tactful refusal ("Do you have children?" "My family plans will not interfere with my ability to perform in this position"); (4) neutralizing ("What happens if your husband needs to relocate?" "My husband and I would discuss locational moves that either of us might have to consider in the future"); and (5) take advantage of the question ("Where were you born?" "I am quite proud that my background is Egyptian because it has helped me to deal effectively with people of various ethnic backgrounds").[14]

A second category of difficult question is the completely unanticipated "surprise" question (e.g., "Tell me a story" or "If you were an animal, what animal would it be and why?"). If this happens, don't just start talking in a rambling fashion. Instead, either ask the interviewer for additional information ("Did you have a particular kind of story in mind?") or ask for a moment or so to collect your thoughts ("That's a great question, and I've never thought about it. Can I have a minute or so to collect my thoughts?").

A third question type that can pose special difficulty is "Tell me about your weaknesses." One standard response is to talk about weaknesses that really aren't weaknesses (e.g., "I tend to be very picky when it comes to details, and I have difficulty letting go of a job until I'm sure it's right"). Another strategy is

*Q*uestionable *Questions*

How should a job applicant respond to the following questions from an interviewer? For each question, write an appropriate response for the interviewee or role-play the situation with a classmate. Be prepared to explain why your suggested response is effective and appropriate.

1. *Male employer to female applicant:* "Would you be willing to stay at the office late? It wouldn't necessarily be all work and no play."
2. *Employer to applicant who currently works for a competitor:* "What were your current employer's profits on widgets this past year?" [The information is confidential.]
3. *Employer to applicant who has a foreign name:* "You have an unusual name. Where does it come from?"
4. *Employer to applicant:* "Would you be willing to take a drug test? How about a test for HIV?"

to think about areas that you would like to develop and talk about your plans for doing so (e.g., "I've just purchased a time management utility for my computer, and I'm now working on strategies for using my time more effectively").

Preparing Questions to Ask the Interviewer. In addition to anticipating questions they might be asked, interviewees also need to prepare questions to ask the interviewer. These questions should indicate that the applicant has done solid homework and is able and willing to do a good job for the company. Instead of saying "I really don't have any questions right now" or "How much vacation will I get?" the interviewee should be prepared to ask questions such as: "I noticed in the *Wall Street Journal* that you're opening a new plant in Memphis. Do you have additional plans for expansion?" "I noticed in your annual report that you are developing a new training program. If I were hired, would I be in it?" "If you were sitting on my side of this desk, what would you say are the most attractive features of the job?"

Recognizing Inappropriate Tactics. We hope that this chapter has helped you to think about the knowledge and skills required in order to be a competent communicator in an employment interview. In closing, we would like to emphasize that, just as there are a number of tactics you can and should use to ensure that an employment interview works in your favor, there are also tactics and behaviors you should avoid. The following instances of actual interviewee behavior were documented by the personnel executives who conducted the interviews. Such behavior is almost guaranteed to work against you.

- "Said if he was hired, he'd teach me ballroom dancing at no charge, and started demonstrating."
- "She returned that afternoon asking if we could redo the entire interview."
- "Apologized for being late; said he accidentally locked his clothes in his closet."
- "Took three cellular phone calls. Said she had a similar business on the side."
- "Applicant walked in and inquired why he was here."
- "After a difficult question, she wanted to leave the room for a moment to meditate."
- "Candidate was told to take his time answering, so he began writing down each of his answers before speaking."
- "Shortly after sitting down, she brought out a line of cosmetics and started a strong sales pitch."
- "Man brought in his five children and cat."
- "Said if I hired him, I'd soon learn to regret it."
- "Wanted to borrow the fax machine to send out some personal letters."

- "Arrived with a snake around her neck. Said she took her pet everywhere."
- "Brought a mini tape recorder and said he always taped his job interviews."
- "Left his dry cleaner tag on his jacket and said he wanted to show he was a clean individual."
- "Applicant handed me an employment contract and said I'd have to sign it if he was going to be hired."
- "She sat in my chair and insisted that I sit in the interviewee's chair."
- "When asked about loyalty, showed a tattoo of his girlfriend's name."
- "Woman brought a large shopping bag of canceled checks and thumbed through them during the interview."
- "After a very long interview, he casually said he had already accepted another position."[15]

The Case of Maribeth Berg

At the beginning of this chapter you met Maribeth Berg, a college sophomore who was preparing to interview Jim Walsh, an insurance agent, concerning his interviewing training and practices. What have you learned in this chapter that might help her prepare for this task?

- What characteristics of the anticipated interaction would allow you to label it an interview? What kind of interview is it?
- What should Maribeth consider as she thinks about the goals of her interview?
- How should Maribeth begin the interview?
- Where on the directive–nondirective continuum should this interview be conducted?
- What type of closing would work best for this interview?
- What can Maribeth do to be sure her questions are clear, relevant, and unbiased? What mixture of open/closed and primary/secondary questions should she anticipate? What combination of funnel, inverted funnel, and tunnel sequences should she plan? Is the Quintamensional Plan relevant for this interview?
- As Maribeth anticipates reacting to the responding moves of Jim Walsh, what combination of evaluative, interpretive, supportive, probing, and understanding responses is likely to be most appropriate?

REVIEW

- This chapter concentrates on the most common goal-oriented form of communication—the interview.

- It is difficult to imagine going through a day without engaging in some type of interview, whether it involves information gathering, information giving, selection, a problem related to the interviewee's behavior, a problem related to the interviewer's behavior, problem solving, or persuasion.

- The key to competence in interviewing is proper preparation; five guidelines for preparing all types of interviews are: (1) Formulate a clear goal and keep it in mind; (2) identify any potential barriers to achieving that goal that may reside in you, the other participant, or the setting; (3) create an appropriate structure for the interview on a continuum that ranges from nondirective to directive and add an effective opening and closing; (4) select questions that are appropriate in terms of type (open/closed, primary/secondary), impact (understandable, relevant, unbiased), and sequence (funnel, inverted funnel, and tunnel); and (5) use reacting moves in the interview that will further your purpose (evaluative, interpretive, supportive, probing, and understanding).

- In addition to general principles, the chapter explores a special type of interview—the selection type of employment interview.

- For this interview, the applicant's preparation is very important—first to get the interview and second to succeed at it.

- In terms of getting the interview, you engage in self-assessment, prepare a résumé, locate appropriate jobs and do homework on them, and develop realistic expectations for the interview process.

- For actual participation in the interview, you should know the purpose and structure of the interview, think through appropriate responses to the interviewer's questions, and generate questions of your own for the interviewer.

CASE STUDY 2

▲
·
·
·
·

The Case of Jennifer's Problem at Work

As you read the following case study, consider how relationships are negotiated in subtle ways and the confusion and discomfort that can result when issues are not resolved.

Jennifer had been agonizing all week about whether or not to talk about her "real" communication problem in class discussion on Friday. Her communication class had a "real-life application" discussion once a week; three students were assigned a topic from the text and were asked to engage the class in meaningful discussion about relevant issues. Jennifer had been assigned the topic of communicating in work settings.

Jennifer could have talked about all sorts of issues, like interviewing for a new job, communicating with managers or peers, or communicating effectively with clients. But whenever she started thinking about how she would present any of those topics, the one thing bothering her at her own workplace made her confused and angry.

During the 6 months that Jennifer had been working at Flowers by Francis, she had become increasingly uncomfortable. The shop owner had always been very friendly to her; in fact, that had been one of the reasons why she took the job in the first place. Though the salary was not high, the work schedule allowed Jennifer to continue her classes at the university, and Francis had seemed so warm and open that she felt right at home the first day.

But Francis and his "friendliness" had become more than Jennifer expected. He asked her a lot of questions about her friends, especially the people she dated, and he had started touching her on the shoulder or the arm. Those touches seemed to last longer and longer until Jennifer became really uncomfortable. She hadn't said anything because Francis had seemed so nice at first, but she was beginning to conclude that the touches were more than just "friendly." Now Francis had started brushing against her when she stood behind the counter, even though he could have asked her to move, excused himself, or gone around another way. He also made little comments about what she wore to work every day, saying things like how her skirt really showed off her great legs. Still, Jennifer said nothing, and now she was angry at Francis and at herself for letting the situation go on so long.

Jennifer was worried about what might happen if she brought up the situation in class. Lots of people knew about Flowers by Francis; it was only a few blocks from the university. What if Francis really meant nothing and she had blown this situation out of proportion? Was she responsible for what she perceived as his sexual harassment, since she had let the "little things" pass for so long? Did she contribute to Francis's behavior when she wore shorts or short skirts to work? Did she need to be more assertive? Were others at work experiencing any problem with Francis? Would the class deride her or help her? Would the professor think she was silly and was not taking the assignment seriously? Perhaps she should just talk about effective interviewing, after all.

Discussion Questions

1. What do you think Jennifer should do about her class discussion? Should she talk about her work problem, or is class not an appropriate place for this type of discussion?
2. What is the nature or definition of the relationship from both Francis's and Jennifer's perspectives? Use the model of communicative competence to identify places where their perspectives may differ.
3. What do you think Jennifer could do, verbally and nonverbally, to help correct the problem she is experiencing at work?
4. What are the responsibilities of Francis as the manager of the shop?
5. What advice would you give Francis and Jennifer to help them communicate more effectively?
6. How might Jennifer manage the conflict that is likely to result if she confronts Francis? Should she approach him alone or should she have someone else present? How does adding another person to the relationship affect communication?
7. What conflict strategies could be used here by both Jennifer and Francis? Would face saving or compromising be appropriate? What about the threats and/or promises that may arise?
8. How widespread is the problem Jennifer is experiencing? Does it affect only women? Is the problem usually one-sided, or does it generally involve the communication behaviors of all involved?

EPIL●GUE 2

Competence in Interpersonal Communication

In Part Two we discussed the nature of interpersonal relationships and how the way you communicate in these relationships makes them more or less satisfying and productive. When you begin a relationship, you make an investment of time, energy, and self-esteem. As relationships continue, that investment can grow or shrink, depending on (1) your commitment to the other person, (2) how much you depend on your partner for important rewards, and (3) the degree to which the relationship is voluntary.

Mutual Influence in Interpersonal Relationships

In regard to this last point, completely voluntary relationships are those that you enter into willingly and that you can walk away from. Friendships are voluntary. Parent-child relationships are not. When you make a formal commitment to a partner, your relationship with that person becomes more constrained. Co-signing a lease with a roommate constrains your relationship. Getting married constrains your relationship, making it less voluntary.

This point is important because it captures the essence of relationships. When you begin a relationship, you open yourself to the influence of another; the expectation is that you will be changed by the relationship. Recall the model of communicative competence introduced in Chapter 1. People enter relationships as individuals, but as they work to negotiate control, affiliation, and goals, they are influencing and being influenced by their partners.

The more meaningful the relationship is, the more the self-concept will be affected.

The goals discussed in Chapter 7 may begin as individual motivations, but they soon become joint goals that are agreed upon by both partners. The less you have to modify your personal goals to accommodate those of your partner, the more rewarding you will think the relationship is. If one partner has to give up too much, the relationship will be costly for that person. That person will eventually either try to change the relationship or leave it.

The growth and possible decline of a relationship is directly dependent on the way you communicate with your partner. In growth stages, especially in exploratory and intensifying stages, you and your partner are frequently engaged in negotiations about the definition of the relationship. This is true for all types of relationships, whether they be romantic, supervisor-employee, or social friendships. These negotiations are about how much influence (control) each will assert over the other; how much liking each can show for the other and how that might be done; and on which goals or tasks the relationship should be focused.

Conflict in Interpersonal Relationships

Because negotiations are usually conducted in subtle ways, it is not unusual for you and your partner to experience doubt, insecurity, frustration—even anger. These feelings can produce conflict. It is important to remember that conflict is a normal part of competent relationships (see Chapter 8). The *manner* in which the conflict is conducted distinguishes competent from incompetent relationships.

Why do people in competent relationships experience conflict? As was discussed in Chapter 8, clarifying issues and relational growth are two important reasons. As you work to define your relationship with another person, you are likely to find yourself giving up some things that you like to do. For example, you may have the self-concept of a flamboyant person, but your boss expects you to be unassuming with customers. Or a prospective partner indicates that you should spend time with him if the two of you are going to "get serious." The working out of these relational details can lead to open conflict, which can be healthy for the relationship. In the course of the conflict, aspects of the relationship can get "worked out." The temporary costs associated with the conflict can lead to long-term rewards if the conflict is managed effectively and stays focused on issues.

In a relationship that has few conflicts which are productive, you probably will not look forward to conflict, but you won't be threatened by it either. If the conflicts in a relationship are unproductive and marked by personal hostility, you will be less likely to confront or be confronted by your partner until the frustration level is unbearable. In such a case, it is more difficult to make the conflict productive. Because of previous negative experiences, you may begin the conflict at a personal level and have a difficult time getting to the *issues* that promoted the conflict.

Not all conflict is about specific external issues (e.g., "always" being late). Rather, the conflict can center on uncertainties about the status of the relationship. Remember, people usually don't talk about the status of their relationships until they are at a crisis point. Conflict may be a strategy for introducing the topic of "where this relationship is going." An argument about you "always" being late might really be about what your occasional lateness says about "how you feel about me."

Of course, conflict can also lead to the termination of a relationship, which is sometimes the competent thing to do. Competent communicators get themselves out of undesirable relationships with minimal harm to their partners and themselves.

Interviewing

The final chapter of Part 2 is about interviewing. It may have seemed odd to you that interviewing was grouped with chapters about interpersonal relationships. Our reason for this organization is to make the point that competent communication applies to every kind of relationship. An interview has many of the same characteristics as social and family relationships. It is usually composed of two people who hope to establish mutually desirable relational goals and create a satisfying relationship.

There are, of course, some important differences between interviews and social relationships. Interviews are structured; there is usually a clear status difference; and there are fewer control issues to negotiate. Interviews are generally conducted by people we don't know very well, so an expression of affiliation is usually mildly positive and polite. The primary goal of the interview is almost always defined at the beginning of the meeting, but some secondary goals may need to be worked out.

It would be a mistake, however, to think that, because of the structure, there are no relational issues in interviews. Although there is a limited range of options, control, affiliation, and goal negotiation are as much a part of interviews as they are of any conversation between relational partners. In a highly structured situation—a job interview or a police interrogation, for example—the interviewee may decide to accept the relational definition imposed by the interviewer and the situation, but this is not necessarily the case.

We don't want to give you the impression that interviewing is just like chatting with one of your friends. But the same principles of communication apply to all types of relationships. If you have competent social relationships, you establish competent relationships with people in interview contexts.

PART THREE

Group and Organizational Communication

emember the adage "two heads are better than one"? We know that when two people come together to solve a problem, their combined creativity, knowledge, and experience usually make it easier for a particular task to be accomplished. Well, if "two heads are better than one," then three or more should have even greater potential. To achieve this potential, however, it is important to understand the factors involved in small-group communication. Through this understanding, we can develop the skills necessary to be competent group members—in both formal and informal groups.

Video Action!

"Communicating and Making Decisions in Groups" introduces employees of the McAluster Advertising Agency as they are beginning an advertising campaign. Listeners are advised to look at what can happen when the basic principles of communication are not applied. After demonstrating how group work can be ineffective, the video revisits the ad agency. This time, the employees attempt to exemplify effective group management and problem solving. The video should help you in the step-by-step process of learning to communicate competently.

Steps toward Competent Communication

- Identify the factors that affect the group communication process.
- Describe the role of leadership in group management.
- Explain the steps involved in effective group decision making.
- Distinguish between productive and unproductive small-group interaction.
- Evaluate individual and group performance in decision-making groups.

For Discussion after the Video

Recall a small group that you have been involved in. Describe the interaction that took place.

Give an example of how the members in your group depended on each other. For example, did the actions of one group member affect the group as a whole?

Did your group experience instances of "groupthink" in your communication? Were group members able to critically challenge ideas? Explain.

Did your group experience any conflict? If so, was it primarily issue-related or personal? How was the conflict resolved?

Did your group impose any expressed or implied norms? If so, what were they? What were the consequences if the norms were violated?

What characteristics determine whether a group is productive or unproductive? Would you describe your group as productive or unproductive? Why?

CHAPTER TEN

Communicating in
Small Groups

●BJECTIVES

After reading this chapter, you should be able to:

1. Discuss some features that distinguish groups from dyads.

2. Analyze the factors that affect individual competence in groups.

3. Describe the ways in which cohesiveness and interdependence affect group competence.

4. Show how groupthink can be minimized through productive conflict.

5. List the various ways to improve group communication.

6. Explain the four steps in effective goal setting for a group.

7. Discuss nominal group technique and self-managing teams.

 SHLEY MYERS, A SOPHOMORE majoring in computer science, is active in student government on her campus. She has recently been asked to chair a committee that will explore how to make the student union more attractive for students—especially in the evening. In appointing Ashley's committee, the dean of students sought advice from a large variety of student groups on campus and ended up with a twelve-member committee. The dean has asked the committee to meet during the fall semester and to provide a written report outlining several plans and recommending one by the end of the semester. As you read this chapter about small groups, consider how it might apply to Ashley and her committee's task. We will return to this scenario at the end of the chapter.

Groups occupy a large amount of your time and energy while you are a student, and they take up even more of your time afterward. You may participate in as many as twenty conferences or meetings a week if you decide to take a job in a large, complex organization. One estimate has suggested that 82 percent of all U.S. companies use problem-solving and decision-making groups or teams as an integral part of their operations.[1]

Learning how to communicate effectively in groups is one of the most worthwhile investments you can make. Groups are critical to your success, regardless of what kinds of activities you are involved with now or what you might undertake in the future. Groups are so important in modern organizations that they are described as the building blocks for improving effectiveness.[2] If you were the manager or owner of a small business, you would hold frequent staff meetings with your employees. You might be asked to serve on a committee in your place of worship. You may participate in a group designed to prevent crime or improve safety in your neighborhood. Undoubtedly, you will meet some new friends with whom you may go out to eat on a regular basis, thus forming a new informal group.

In short, groups are everywhere. You are part of many groups now, and your involvement in groups is likely to increase in the future. Yet, being part of these groups and working well in them are two different matters. This chapter will help you become an effective and competent communicator as a participant in groups.

◆ How Groups Differ from Dyads

As we mentioned in Chapter 1, *dyadic* communication occurs between *two* individuals. You might suspect, then, that some fundamental differences exist between communication within a group and within a dyad. These differences include the number of interactants and the complexity of the relationships, both of which will be discussed in this section.

Number of Interactants

Communication between dyads and groups differs simply because the *number* of communicators differs. As the number of participants in an interaction increases:

- *The interaction is more formal.* Participants may feel the need to obtain permission to speak; they may limit the length and frequency of their contributions so that other members will not perceive them as dominant; they may be reluctant to interrupt a speaker.

- *Each member has fewer opportunities to contribute.* Participants may want or be required by a leader to share "floor time" with other group members; time constraints can inhibit the quality and quantity of their contributions.

Much of human activity occurs in groups.

- *The communication becomes less intimate.* The greater the number of participants, the less comfortable participants feel self-disclosing or voicing controversial opinions.

- *The interaction consumes more time.* As more participants are invited to give input or to debate an idea, the interaction takes longer to complete.

Complexity of Relationships

Another factor that separates dyads from groups concerns the complexity of the relationships that are present and must be maintained. As more participants are added, the relationships become more complex. In the dyad, of course, there is only one relationship—that between person 1 and person 2.

As you can tell by examining Figure 10.1 on page 302, by adding just one person to that dyad, you now have to deal with 4 potential relationships—between persons 1 and 2; persons 1 and 3; persons 2 and 3; and persons 1, 2, and 3. In a group of four, there are 11 potential relationships; in a group of five, there are 90; and in a six-member group, there are 301 potential relationships!

As you join a group, a couple of points immediately become clear. First, you will not be able to maintain satisfactory relationships with every other

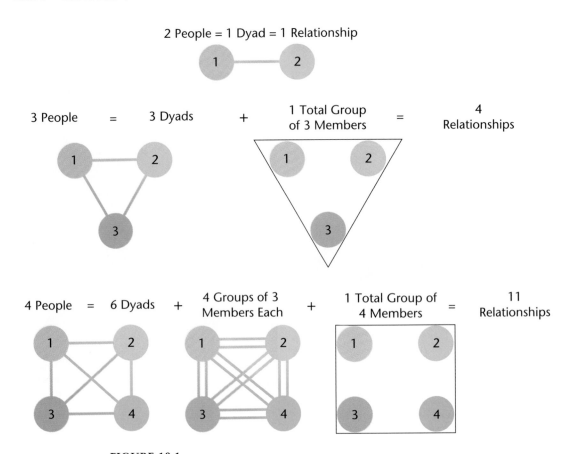

FIGURE 10.1
Each time a person is added to a group, the number of potential relationships increases substantially.

member of the group at all times. Over time, you will find evidence of mis-understanding, envy, jealousy, hatred, or possessiveness between any two or more members in the group. Group members do not usually voice these feelings in meetings; instead, they keep them inside in the hope that they will "blow over" with time. Many of these feelings result from quick judgments that are not well founded, and when people see their judgments contradicted by evidence, they often feel guilty.

Second, most groups that function over a period of time develop cliques or coalitions. **Cliques** or **coalitions** are formed by individuals who have bonded together in a group.[3] They typically sit next to each other in meetings, take breaks from meetings together, maintain contact with each other outside of meetings, act and think in similar ways, vote together, and support one another's positions.

When cliques or coalitions are present in a group, relationships become more complex because you are no longer dealing only with individuals.

CLIQUE (COALITION)
An exclusive group held together by common interests and activities.

Rather, you must maintain relationships with bonded subgroups. **Counter-coalitions**, in which persons 1 and 2 position themselves against persons 3 and 4 on an issue, can leave a fifth, "unaffiliated" participant in a very awkward position. You may be able to think of occasions when you were undecided on how to vote on a problem because you did not want to align yourself with one coalition or the other and thereby cause hurt feelings or broken relationships.

◆ Factors Affecting Individual Competence

Groups are only as good as the individuals who participate in them. Although a group is usually more effective than individuals working alone, the quality of a group's product is often determined by the competence that each person brings to a task. This section discusses several factors that affect individual competence in group activities, notably (1) critical thinking skills, (2) attributions, (3) perceptions, and (4) communication apprehension.

Critical Thinking

Critical thinking helps you view the world from a reasoned and proactive perspective. Thinking critically requires that you remain open-minded about what you perceive while you inject a healthy dose of inquiry and skepticism into your perceptions. Thus, you have to consider several different viewpoints before you are satisfied with the information you receive. Critical thinkers are always on the lookout for opinions, evidence, or facts that will lead them to accurate and responsible conclusions. This is an extremely important competency that you will want to develop as a group member.

Avoiding Traps. Critical thinkers are less likely to fall into some common traps that plague group communication. As a group member, you should be wary of certain obstacles that are more likely to arise in group communication than in dyadic interactions.[4] Some common traps to avoid are accepting communication at face value, oversimplifying issues, and making overgeneralizations and false assumptions.

During the course of group deliberation, group members come to rely on and trust one another. When time is short, the tendency is to *accept communication at face value*. This is a serious flaw of group communicators inasmuch as issues cannot be critically analyzed if communication is accepted without question. Competent communicators evaluate the worth of everything that is said based on previous discussion and information that the group knows is true. This strategy is designed not to attack others but to provide a reasoned and logical approach to analyzing what other group members say. Sometimes a simple question is enough to begin an evaluation of someone's comment or argument ("Carol, are you saying that we should just accept these preliminary figures as our data?").

COUNTERCOALITION
A relationship in which two or more people position themselves against two or more others with regard to an issue.

CRITICAL THINKING
A method of viewing the world from a reasoned and proactive perspective.

When groups deal with complex problems, they tend to *oversimplify the issues* involved. Think about the last time you and a couple of other people had to solve a problem that seemed overwhelming (e.g., travel plans, college costs, a wedding, family problems). Did you notice how some of your partners were willing to oversimplify the issue? Consider the following example in which two group members try to make recommendations about increasing cultural diversity on a college campus.

BUD   This is simply a matter of time. Once people are around other folks from different cultural groups, they will be more sensitive and less racially biased.

JAVIER Hold it, Bud! Numerous cultural groups have been mingling in the United States for hundreds of years, yet we still see racial discrimination. To say that exposure to different cultural groups will solve the problem is a gross oversimplification of the issue.

A conclusion that is taken too far is known as an *overgeneralization*. This trap occurs when one piece of data is assumed to represent all comparable data. For example, if you assume that all teenagers experiment with drugs and alcohol, you are overgeneralizing. Critical thinkers test the validity of a generalization by determining whether the basis of support is biased in any way. A valid generalization is supported by different types of evidence and does not make claims beyond a reasonable point.

Another trap that prevents effective communication is making *false assumptions*—conclusions drawn from faulty reasoning. False assumptions come primarily from inappropriate causal relationships. Inappropriate causal relationships are incorrect conclusions based on cause and effect. Sometimes people assume that because two events occurred together or are related, then one must have caused the other. For example, if all males in a class received an A for the course, you might conclude that being male "caused" the grade. However, as is true of most events, numerous factors influenced the grades, such as individual achievement, study habits, related courses, or extra credit assignments. In other words, most events are too complex to establish a single causal-effect relationship. Although it is possible that all males in the class received an A because of gender, it is more likely that individual ability and work "caused" the grades. Thinking critically in a group means looking for alternative connections or explanations when a causal connection has been suggested.

Becoming a More Critical Thinker. Improving the way you think requires that you develop specific strategies to broaden your abilities. The following strategies will help you develop your skills in critical thinking:

- *Consider multiple perspectives.* Since there is always more than one way to look at things, consider different perspectives and realize that your own perspective is subject to error.

- *Clarify values.* Determine the values that influence your judgment. Understand what your standards are and why you use them.

- *Clarify issues.* Clarify the questions you must answer or the issues with which you must deal. Formulate each issue in a clearly stated sentence.

- *Evaluate information.* Recognize the source of the information. Is it opinion, or is it based on evidence and reasoning? Examine the credibility and relevance of the information.

- *Probe.* Ask searching questions about issues. Look for underlying subjects, ideas, and specific details. Probe for reasons, causes, and alternative views.

- *Identify contradictions.* Recognize significant similarities and differences in opposing views, pinpointing contradictions between opposing arguments.

- *Consider the big picture.* Make plausible inferences and interpretations based on valid information. Explore the implications of statements and develop a fuller, more complete understanding of their meaning.

- *Pursue valid assumptions.* Avoid faulty assumptions based on inappropriate causal relationships.

- *Summarize.* Summarize relevant facts and evidence in clear, understandable statements.

- *Draw appropriate conclusions.* Generate multiple solutions and analyze the feasibility of those solutions.[5]

Attributions

When you make *attributions*, you assign reasons or causes for another's behavior. Making attributions is one of the key features of the model of communicative competence. As you know from Chapter 2, whenever you attempt to explain why someone acts in a certain way or says certain things, you make attributions. Many of your attributions are based on observations of previous behaviors and predispositions, and these can affect your ability as a competent communicator.

Many people believe that making attributions is a normal part of getting to know a person better. As you become more familiar with someone, you begin to think that you are privy to why the person behaves the way he or she does. For example, you see a friend drinking iced tea rather than a cocktail at a party. You may reason that this person is abstaining from alcohol to ensure he will feel fresh for a major presentation you know he is giving very early the next morning. You hear another friend criticize someone's lavish spending. Knowing that this friend grew up in a family with a limited income, you attribute her view to her upbringing. Note that in these two examples, more than a superficial knowledge of the individual is required.

Three variables are important in making attributions about others.[6] These variables are what you think about the other person's *intent or motivation* (internal force), *ability* (mediating force), and *environment* (external force).

Attributions and Groups

Divide into small groups during a class period and make a list of the various effects that attributions have had on groups that you have belonged to in the past. Report the findings to the class.

Now imagine that during a sorority's fund-raising committee meeting Rachel is trying to determine why someone cast a vote to approve a 25 percent increase in expenditures for promotional flyers. Rachel might reason that the individual enjoyed designing the flyers and wanted more money to increase their quality (*intent*), that this person had a good contact for printing the flyers (*ability*), and that an alumna's contributions provided the funds for their printing (*environment*).

In the small-group context, your attributions are often reactions to individual performance. People are usually interested in discovering why someone's behavior was exceptionally strong or very weak. For instance, someone may have given an outstanding report to the group, when in the past, mediocrity was expected. Another person may have failed to research an issue thoroughly before speaking on it. In the first case, you might attribute the quality report to the fact that the presenter is an expert on the topic. In the second case, family illness or time pressures may have presented major obstacles to proper research. Again, as your familiarity with other people increases, you believe you are more knowledgeable as to what made them behave the way they did.

Attributions influence your communication behavior in a group, demonstrating the adage "What you see is what you speak." If you perceive your committee chairperson as competent and intelligent, yet fiercely irritated during a meeting, you are likely to edit your comments and not antagonize this person further. If you attribute the leader's failure to stay organized and follow an agenda for a meeting to the fact that this person has flu symptoms, you may not say the negative things about the leader that you would otherwise say.

Perceptions

Group members continually form perceptions of one another. As you recall from earlier chapters, perception is the process of making sense of your world. You receive input in the form of specific bits of information, such as someone's tone of voice, facial expression, or eye contact. This input and your existing schemas influence your perception of group members and group interaction.

Perception begins with information you receive from other people. This information can be practically anything—the way people greet you, their clothing, their tone of voice, or even the way they sit in a chair. You can either observe this information yourself or hear about it from others. For instance, when you see a man walking across campus wearing a National Wildlife Federation T-shirt, you begin to form certain perceptions about his personality or his attitudes about certain topics.

Having noted another's behavior, you organize the information and try to make sense of it. In other words, you make an effort to "size" someone up. Recall from our discussion of schemas in Chapter 2 that the pieces of information work together to create meaning. You continually discover new bits of information that combine with existing schemas to help you structure and understand different situations.

To illustrate this process, use the following information about the man in the T-shirt, some of which you might have observed directly and some of which you might have learned from others:

mid-forties
slender
braided shoulder-length hair
frequently wears jeans and army fatigues
friendly smile

Do the pieces of information seem to come together to give you a total impression? Hold your answer for just a moment.

You see the man in the T-shirt again. You watch this person socialize and talk primarily with students whom you know to be biology majors. At one point he seems to be talking with them about their textbook. You perceive this person to be a faculty member of the biology department. As a result, you would probably perceive him to act and think the way most biologists act and think.

Did you also perceive the man to be an aging hippie, when you noted his age, clothing, and hair style? You may have made up your mind about him very quickly; if so, don't be alarmed. Most people form perceptions of others in a matter of seconds. For example, you drive past a 20-something-year-old male driving a shiny new BMW and think, "spoiled brat." You see a woman sitting in a corner during a talkative party and think, "shy."

Furthermore, most people think their initial perceptions are pretty accurate—yet, how easy it is to be wrong. How do you know that the BMW is his? Maybe the woman in the corner is upset or is attempting to draw attention to herself. Maybe the man in the T-shirt is a student rather than a professor. In short, you can make many interpretations of another person's behavior, but not all of them will be accurate. Although people are probably not as perceptive as they think they are, in a group context, they rarely have a chance to confirm or deny their perceptions.

Communication Apprehension

A final factor that affects an individual's competence in small groups is communication apprehension. As we mentioned in Chapter 8, *communication apprehension* may be defined as "fear or anxiety associated with real or anticipated communication with another person or persons."[7] Estimates suggest that about 20 percent of the population is highly apprehensive about communicating.[8]

Think about the times that you have been with a group and felt hesitant or apprehensive about contributing. Can you remember why you felt this way? Can you remember how you felt? Many people who are apprehensive about

What Do They Think of You?

How often do you think people have incorrect perceptions about you? For what reasons? Describe an incident in which this happened. How is your opinion of people affected when they perceive your behavior erroneously?

communicating also experience physiological reactions, such as increased heart rate, sweaty palms, quivering lips, locked knees, or an upset stomach.

Effects. Simply put, group members who are apprehensive about communicating are likely to be less effective than those who are not. Research into communication apprehension is quite extensive. Generally, highly apprehensive individuals report that this apprehension has a negative effect on many aspects of their lives.[9] Compared to those who are not apprehensive, individuals with high communication apprehension are considered less socially attractive, less competent, less sociable, less composed, and less able to lead. In addition, they are less likely to have high grades in college, to be offered interviews and jobs, or to be satisfied with their subsequent employment. However, there is no indication that they are any less intelligent.

Communication researchers McCroskey and Richmond discuss several results of communication apprehension that are specific to the small-group setting.[10] Compared to individuals who are not apprehensive, persons high in communication apprehension are seen in the following ways:

- They are perceived by other group members as being more nervous and less dominant.
- They are perceived as being less task oriented and less socially attractive (because participants are biased in favor of individuals who contribute more frequently in meetings).
- They are seldom perceived as leaders.
- They are perceived as making less valuable contributions to the group.

Assessment and Control. As you know by now, you can become a more competent communicator by assessing your current abilities and finding out where you stand. You can then move to higher levels of competence. Because apprehension can affect competence, your responses to the Self-Check "How Well Do You Interact in a Group Setting?" should be helpful to you. If you score high on this Self-Check, don't worry! Remember, you are in good company; as much as 20 percent of the general population reports the same level of apprehension as you do. You can *manage* your apprehension in a group in three ways.

First, use relaxation techniques such as breathing and muscular control. Taking a deep breath is one of the simplest relaxation tools available to you. You can take several good deep breaths during meetings, and no one will even notice. You will be much less anxious about speaking if you do this.

Second, recognize that part of your apprehension is psychological. You feel anxiety or fear because of what you *think* about the situation you are in. Often, telling yourself something like "I'll make a fool of myself if I bring up my view" produces a great deal of anxiety. Such statements are both negative and unfounded, for you have no evidence concerning whether you will or won't make a fool of yourself. If you can replace these types of statements with more realistic ones, such as "Someone here will understand

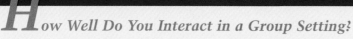

How Well Do You Interact in a Group Setting?

In order to test how apprehensive you might be in a group setting, complete the following six items, which are based on the Personal Report of Communication Apprehension (PRCA-24). Use the following scale: 1 = strongly agree; 2 = agree; 3 = undecided; 4 = disagree; and 5 = strongly disagree.

_____ 1. I do not like to participate in group discussions.

_____ 2. Generally, I feel comfortable participating in group discussions.

_____ 3. I am tense and nervous while participating in group discussions.

_____ 4. I like to get involved in group discussions.

_____ 5. I get tense and nervous when I engage in a group discussion with new people.

_____ 6. I am calm and relaxed while participating in group discussions.

Scoring: Use the following formula, in which the numbers in parentheses represent your answers to the six items. (For example, if you answered "4" for item 1, then replace the "(1)" in the formula with a 4.)

$$18 - (1) + (2) - (3) + (4) - (5) + (6)$$

A score of 24 or above indicates a high level of communication apprehension for participation in group discussions; a score of 12 or below indicates a low level of communication apprehension for this situation.

Source: Adapted from J. C. McCroskey (1982), *An introduction to rhetorical communication* (4th ed.) (Englewood Cliffs, NJ: Prentice-Hall).

and appreciate my contribution," you will have a more positive attitude and considerably less apprehension.

Third, prepare carefully for a group meeting. Organize your thoughts into notes; bring any materials needed, such as paper and pens; and summarize any data you want to share with your group. You might want to practice stating your views before the meeting, so that you will be able to explain your ideas as clearly as possible. Remember to *manage* apprehension, not *eliminate* it, because a small amount of apprehension will actually help you as a communicator.

Individual competence in group communication consists of identifying with the goals of the group and developing critical thinking skills. Individual attributions, perceptions, and apprehension also affect the individual's contribution to group communication. You can use these internal processing components competently if you maintain objectivity and pursue a healthy sense of reality.

◆ Factors Affecting Group Communication

The previous section examined factors that affect how well an *individual* contributes to the group. Now let's examine the *group's* communication by discussing factors that occur only when the group behaves as a collective unit. This section discusses (1) interdependence, (2) cohesion, (3) groupthink and productive conflict, (4) norms, and (5) group image.

Interdependence

INTERDEPENDENCE

In group relationships, how the behavior of each member affects and is affected by other members.

A key characteristic of most groups is **interdependence**. Simply put, the behavior of each member affects the behavior of every other member. In most groups today, no member exists in isolation. Many groups are organized with the goal of having their members share tasks.

In firms that emphasize production, employees frequently rotate tasks from time to time during the day. Later, we will discuss self-managing work teams, used by all types of companies, in which two or more members typically work on the same task simultaneously. Members give feedback to each other and share responsibility for their performances.

Products, services, and results from groups with high degrees of interdependence truly belong to the "group" and not to an individual. Words such as *we, us,* and *our* are frequently heard in meetings and conversations. Managers who would ordinarily blame a particular person for a problem with a product have difficulty doing so when tasks are completed interdependently. The fault and responsibility, like the credit for successes, are shared among several group members.

A good example of interdependence in groups can be found in most office units. Consider an office with one manager, one secretary, and three staff employees. If the secretary does not distribute mail to the manager and the employees, neither the customers' nor other departmental needs within the organization will be met. If the manager does not work with each employee on scheduling, the work may be distributed unevenly, overburdening one person while allowing another person to slack off. If the employees do not submit their monthly progress reports, the manager will not be able to adequately represent the department in meetings with upper management. In other words, the effectiveness and efficiency of each individual in the work group depend on the effectiveness and efficiency of each of the others.

Cohesion

COHESION

A group's ability to work as an integrated unit.

The "togetherness" of a group is called its **cohesion**. A cohesive group is a tight unit that is able to hang together in the face of opposition. Rosenfeld argues that without cohesion, "individual members are unlikely to commit themselves to the group, the task, or each other, and it is common for undesirable tasks . . . not to get done."[11]

You can determine group cohesion in two ways. First, how do the participants feel about their own membership in the group? The more that members are enthusiastic, identify with the purposes of the group, and tell outsiders about its activities, the more cohesive the group will be.

Second, how well does the group retain its members? The more that members receive satisfaction and fulfill their needs through their group participation, the more cohesive the group. Shaw provides numerous ideas about cohesiveness:

- Member satisfaction is greater in high-cohesive groups than in low-cohesive groups.
- High-cohesive groups exert greater influence over their members than do low-cohesive groups.
- Communication is more extensive and more positive in high-cohesive groups than in low-cohesive groups.
- High-cohesive groups are more effective than low-cohesive groups in achieving goals.[12]

Even the language a group uses can increase its cohesion. Baird and Weinbert argue that as groups succeed and grow, they tend to develop a unique vocabulary.[13] Over time, the words become a code that is practically impossible for an outsider to understand.

Think about how a dentist might use a unique vocabulary in her office. Rather than frightening patients by specifying the names of instruments or drugs used in her procedures, Dr. Hanna communicates to her office staff in code. An assistant may be asked to bring in a "brown 2," standing for Novocain to deaden the mouth. Similarly, "charcoal" is a term used for extraction forceps. The language used in the office among her staff, then, helps to solidify its cohesion.

Groupthink and Productive Conflict

A number of years ago, I. L. Janis coined a term to describe situations in which groups strive to reach a consensus and minimize conflict by failing to critically examine ideas, analyze proposals, or test solutions.[14] He argued that **groupthink** results from strong feelings of loyalty and unity within a group—from too much cohesion. When these feelings are stronger than the desire to evaluate alternative courses of action, a group's decision may be adversely affected. Groups that are prone to groupthink typically exhibit these behaviors:

GROUPTHINK

The tendency of group members to accept information and ideas without critical analysis.

- Participants reach outward consensus and avoid conflict so as not to hurt others' feelings, even though they may not genuinely be in agreement.
- Members who do not agree with the majority are pressured to conform.
- Disagreement, tough questions, and counterproposals are discouraged.
- More effort is spent justifying decisions than testing them.

The best way to avoid situations of groupthink is to encourage conflict in a group and use it productively. In Chapter 8, you learned that conflict is a healthy form of communication when managed properly. Conflict is just as important in group communication as it is in relationships between two people. You already know that issue-based conflict should be fostered. Groups that maximize issue-based conflict and minimize personal-based conflict are the most successful. Leaders and group members should encourage issue-based conflict and remain watchful for instances of personal attacks.

The best of all worlds occurs when group members "agree to disagree." This means that they accept the responsibilities that accompany issue-based conflict. Members know that they will be questioned, second-guessed, and required to defend their positions. They also know that they should not let any issue "slide by" without questioning, pressing other members for clarification and details, or presenting alternative ideas.

The issue of groupthink can generate several ethical considerations.[15] When groupthink causes the ideas, inquiries, and solutions of minority members to be ignored, the group may be acting in an unethical manner. All ideas are important, and the ethical group is one that searches for the best possible set of ideas. When the decision-making moment comes, only those solutions that have met the tests of critical examination and inquiry will be held as most ethical. In many cases, groupthink prevents critical inquiry. In a way, groupthink is a form of censorship because it squelches some members and their ideas. Striving for full participation by all members is a basic tenet of ethical communication.

Norms

All kinds of groups develop "sets of expectations held by group members concerning what kind of behavior or opinion is acceptable or unacceptable, good or bad, right or wrong, appropriate or inappropriate."[16] These are called group **norms**. Norms are determined by the group itself and are imposed by members on themselves and each other. Norms can be developed for just about anything a group does, and it is during the first few meetings of a group that they are developed.

Norms direct the behavior of the group as a whole and affect the conduct of individual members. For example, it may be a norm for members to arrive on time (group norm), and it may be a norm for the leader to begin discussion (individual member norm). In regard to communication, group norms can exist for (1) the kinds of topics that can be expressed in a meeting (Should nontask-related conversation be interjected? Are jokes appropriate?); (2) how long someone speaks; (3) who should speak first (Should the group sit quietly until the leader opens the meeting?); or (4) negative comments (Is it acceptable to criticize others publicly?). Group norms such as these affect the communication behavior of any group. The quality and quantity of what is said in a group are often determined by norms.

As a group member, you should be aware of the group's norms, and you should also be prepared to change them if they appear to be detrimental. For

NORMS

Expectations held by group members concerning what behaviors and opinions are acceptable in the group.

example, groups that expect one member to dominate the conversation, criticize ideas before they are analyzed and discussed, or discourage disagreement have norms that are detrimental to communication and goals. Changing the group's norms can be managed diplomatically.[17] First, you should establish yourself as a loyal member dedicated to the group. In this way, you will demonstrate that you have the group's best interest at heart. Second, you should cite specific examples of the behavior you find harmful to the group's interactions. You cannot maintain credibility with those you are persuading unless you can back up your claims with specific instances of the norm. Third, you should calmly state how the norm detracts from the goals of the group and ask for the opinions of the other members about the problem area. If the group feels that the norm is warranted, members may offer explanations, thus changing your perception, or the group may decide a change is needed. Whatever the consensus of the group members, they will appreciate your concern, and the group will not suffer undue tension.

Consider the following example. Joe was assigned to a group in his political science class that had been asked to make a class presentation on current environmental policies. The group met twice a week, at which time the members discussed the facts each had collected. The group then determined which data would be included for the presentation. At the end of each meeting, the members decided what needed to be done next and assigned specific jobs to each member. At one meeting, Joe arrived late, handed copies of his research to the other members, and announced, "This needs to go in the report. I have to go." He then left, offering no explanation to the other members. When Joe arrived for the next meeting, the group members did not give him a chance to speak, nor did they assign him another job. Joe had neglected the group norms, and the group was sanctioning him for his behavior. What norms did Joe violate?

A Cross-Cultural View of Group Norms

Not all cultures and subcultures view group norms in the same way. For example, political groups in the United States stress open participation by all members but adhere to strict parliamentary procedures when conducting official business. Japanese businesses have adopted norms whereby work groups do not recognize formal lines of authority and status during group meetings. What about gender norms? What specific norms apply to males and females as they work in groups? What about people who belong to an older generation? Do you think they prefer group norms different from those of younger people? As part of a group exercise, generate sets of norms that you believe various cultural groups prefer. Interview members of these groups to confirm your expectations. Your group should be prepared to discuss its findings in class.

Group Image

When the Chicago Bulls captured their third straight NBA championship, their players believed they were members of the greatest team in NBA history. When a high school drill team received a perfect "1000" score on its tactics competition, its members could have danced all night. These groups clearly had strong positive self-images.

A positive group image may yield several positive outcomes. First, success generates success. Having achieved one goal can motivate a group to "go for more."

Second, the group can be optimistic when facing obstacles. A group that has confidence in itself tends to minimize problems, eliminate barriers, and cope well with crises. In these cases, the members believe they cannot be defeated.

The third and final outcome is that membership in the group holds special significance. In fact, outsiders who are not part of the group frequently aspire to membership or even envy those who have it. People want to be part of groups that are doing well and that are perceived as "on the go." Many groups that achieve momentum after several successful activities find that more people want to join and participate.

Groups can be just as motivated when they are pulling themselves back up on their feet. You can probably think of a number of groups whose very survival was uncertain. If its members perceived the group's existence as worthwhile, you probably saw them "pull together" with hard work to save the group. Teamwork and cooperation are almost always at their highest when group members are in a weak position, set a high performance objective, and work feverishly to achieve that objective.

Here's one example to illustrate this notion. One very small religious organization was about to fold several years ago. The membership had dwindled, and those who remained were elderly and inactive. Even paying bills was a month-to-month struggle. Yet, because of the members' perseverance, fund-raising projects and solicited contributions helped raise the money the organization needed to meet its obligations and keep the organization afloat. No one was going to shut down *their group*; the will to survive and the members' image as a "religious organization" became important motivators.

◆ Improving Group Communication

Although communication is one of the most important functions for a group, not all of it is effective, efficient, or productive. On many occasions, group communication is of poor quality and undesirable. We now turn to a discussion of how you can enhance communication competence in a group through (1) goal setting, (2) agenda setting, (3) deliberation and participation, (4) roles, and (5) networks.

Maintaining a Group Image

Think of some groups that maintain a positive image. How did these groups develop a good image? What motivates group members to preserve a group's image? What specific things can damage a group's image?

Goal Setting

Think of the worst group meeting you have ever attended. How would you describe that meeting? Would you say it was "unorganized," "a waste of time," and "unproductive"? Did you wonder why you even spent time meeting with the group? Did you leave the meeting with a bad attitude about working with the group again in the future?

When people have these kinds of reactions, there is generally one underlying problem: the lack of a clear goal. For any organized group, members should know the answer to these questions:

For what purpose(s) does your group exist?
Do all group members understand and accept the goals? Are they committed to them?
How close is your group to achieving its goals?
How well are your group's activities or functions aligned with the goals?

Goals vary considerably depending on the type of group involved. For example, a group in one of your classes may have the simple goal of completing a 15-minute, in-class exercise and reporting the results to the rest of the class. Your volunteer group at a rape crisis center may have the goal of providing quality assistance to rape survivors. An urban beautification fund-raising committee for underprivileged families may have the goal of collecting $4,000 for neighborhood housing improvements by auctioning off a donated entertainment system.

If you have a leadership role in a group, you should be a catalyst in setting group goals. You may either set the goals yourself or work with the group in establishing goals. The second option is preferable because group members are likely to be more committed and excited about a goal that they have helped create. How can you do this?

1. *Identify the problem.* Specify what is to be accomplished or completed.

2. *Map out a strategy.* Determine the desired performance level and a means to evaluate whether the level has been attained.

3. *Set a performance goal.* Recognize the group's capabilities and limitations and establish a realistic target.

4. *Identify the resources necessary to achieve the goal.* Needed time, equipment, and money are among the important issues to consider before beginning.

5. *Obtain feedback.* Prepare to adjust directions or methods if necessary so that the group is doing its best.[18]

Your major responsibility as a leader is to keep the group "on course," assuring that its work is aligned with its goal. The more that you keep the group's goal as a benchmark from which to monitor your own activities, the better organized and the more efficient you will be.

*B*alancing Group Goals with Personal Goals

How do you balance group goals with personal goals? Think of a situation in which your personal goals were in conflict with a group's goals. Did group members try to convince you to adjust your own goals for the sake of the group? Did you attempt to change the group's goals to accommodate your own? Is it always right to subordinate personal goals to group goals or vice versa? Does it depend on the situation? As you read the following scenario, imagine yourself in the situation and consider the ethical issues involved.

At the advertising agency where you are a copy writer, you are assigned to a tobacco account. You are opposed to the advertising and promotion of smoking. The only way you can resign from the account is to resign from your job. If you stay on, how can you make a professional, conscientious effort to create effective advertising copy and still stay true to your beliefs about smoking?

As a group member, you should evaluate proposals, decisions, or other activities in light of your group's goal. You may sometimes have to resist going along with the majority or becoming emotional during a meeting. The more you use the group's goal to guide you, the more satisfied you are likely to be as a participant.

Agenda Setting

An agenda is to a group what a city map is to a tourist or a compass is to a sailor. Without these aids, people are likely to flounder aimlessly, waste time, and solve problems inefficiently. **Agendas** are more than simple outlines that a group leader follows while presiding over a meeting. Typically, at the top of an agenda is the name of the group, the meeting place, and the anticipated time span. This is followed by a list of topics and subtopics that will be covered during the meeting. Many agendas include the name of the person who is primarily responsible for each topic and a time frame for each presentation. An agenda usually looks like the model shown in Figure 10.2.

A group leader should always prepare an agenda before a meeting. This does not mean, however, that the group must adhere to it rigidly. Many group leaders distribute an agenda to participants and then ask if anyone has an item to add. During the course of a meeting, if the leader feels that a topic that is scheduled for discussion later should be dealt with at the present time, he or she can make those adjustments.

The key advantage of using an agenda is that the leader and all participants can know where the group has been and where it is going. With an agenda, it is only minimally possible that a group will omit a key discussion point. An agenda helps ensure that a meeting is orderly, efficient, and organized.

AGENDA

A sequential plan of action, usually for organizing a group meeting.

Cleveland Engineering Society

Petroleum Club, Room 224
Thursday, November 14, 1996
4:30–6:30 P.M.

I. Call to Order (1 min.)	Jane Winer, President
II. Roll Call (1 min.)	Jane Winer, President
III. Reading of Minutes (3 min.)	Ralph Sikewa, Secretary
IV. Financial Report	Barry Jefferson, Treasurer
V. Old Business	
October meeting (5 min.)	
Volunteer update (10 min.)	Viola Florez-Cantu, Volunteer Chair
VI. New Business	
December meeting (10 min.)	Randy Sato, Program Chair
Scholarship progress (10 min.)	
Christmas party (10 min.)	
Guidelines for ethics document (30 min.)	
VII. Announcements	
VIII. Adjournment	

FIGURE 10.2
A printed agenda typically follows the format of the model shown here.

Deliberation and Participation

Certainly, not all members of a group are equal; they have different backgrounds, ethnicity, experiences, education, biases, skills, competence, and interests. Therefore, to say that all members of a group should participate equally on all topics is impractical and detrimental to its effectiveness.

Yet sometimes group members do not participate when their contributions would be beneficial. Even participants who are highly qualified in a particular area sometimes choose not to do so. Why? Let's look at a few reasons for nonparticipation.

> *Apprehension* Members may experience fear or anxiety about expressing themselves in the group.
>
> *Lack of self-esteem* Members may doubt the worth of their contributions.
>
> *Dominance* Other group members may control the "floor."
>
> *Status differences* Group members who are lower in their political or hierarchical position may choose not to comment on stances taken by superiors in the group.

Research indicates that an imbalance of participation in a group will present problems. A study by Hoffman and Maier found that the solution adopted in a group is the one that receives the largest number of favorable comments.[19] Furthermore, most of those comments come from a single member! However, if the "dominating" group member has inaccurate or incomplete information or less than an optimal solution, the group may make a faulty decision.

Groups can use several techniques to encourage participation:

- *Ask "gatekeeping" questions.* By asking a member to contribute ("Carolyn, we haven't heard from you yet." "Doug, what do you think about this?"), a leader can directly influence involvement.

- *Divide participants into smaller groups for a collective response.* Group members who are reluctant to participate in the larger group can be encouraged or even obligated to provide input in a subgroup containing one or two other members. The leader may want to have each subgroup report the results of its discussion.

- *Consult the nonparticipants privately.* A leader may discover why an individual is not participating by simply remarking "You haven't said much today. Is something wrong?" This method allows the leader to identify and eliminate any obstacles to the quiet member's participation.

Roles

ROLE

In a group, the function a member performs.

Group members can have clearly identifiable roles. A person's **role** is the function that member performs in the group. Words like *leader, dominator, gatekeeper, joker,* and *analyzer* are examples of roles in a group.

Evolution of Group Roles. Roles can evolve in two ways. The first way is to consider a position in a group and think of the behaviors you expect the person filling that position to perform. For instance, if there is an elected secretary of your group, you will expect that person to attend meetings, read and take minutes, distribute correspondence, write letters, and make phone calls. You may expect a chairperson to call meetings to order, set an agenda, introduce visitors, facilitate interaction among the members, summarize the proceedings, and so forth.

Second, roles can evolve by observing someone's behavior and then placing a label on that behavior. For example, if a group member is always the first to speak on every topic, cuts others off, and uses an exorbitant amount of "floor time," you might label that person a *dominator*. Another member who is always prepared with statistics, facts, and evidence might be the *information giver*.

Types of Roles. In most groups, each member performs or contributes to two basic functions: task and personal roles.

Task roles are concerned with the accomplishment of the goals, objectives, or mission of the group. They are based on the content and substance of the group's interaction, apart from the members' personalities or personal characteristics. Elective offices in organizations and job titles in business firms indicate task roles. Here are some other examples of task roles:

Information giver Offers facts, beliefs, personal experience, or other input
Information seeker Asks for additional input or clarification of ideas or opinions that have been presented
Elaborator Offers further clarification of points, often providing information about what others have said
Initiator Helps the group get moving by proposing a solution, giving new ideas, or providing new definitions of an issue
Administrator Keeps people on track and aware of the time

Personal roles are concerned with the relationships among group members. Some people call these roles socio-emotional because they are not task related. Individuals who fill these roles help maintain the group as an operating whole. The following are a few examples of this type of role:

Harmonizer Seeks to smooth over tension in the group by settling differences among members
Gatekeeper Works to keep each member involved in a discussion by keeping communication channels open; may restrict information during periods of overload
Sensor Expresses group feelings, moods, or relationships in an effort to recognize the climate and capitalize on it

Every member in a group plays personal as well as task roles. Often, the behaviors that accompany a role are prescribed or assigned; you expect people who assume certain roles to use particular behaviors. In other cases, you learn the roles people play only by observing their behaviors.

Problems with Roles. Two kinds of problems arise concerning roles in groups. The first, *role conflict*, exists whenever competing expectations for your behavior are incompatible. A good example would be the leader of a group whose role is "friend" with many members but who must also be an "evaluator" of their performance. If you were the leader, the friendship role would

Roles in Your Group

Consider a formal or informal group in which you are active. List the members and try to identify the role of each person. You will probably find yourself using both of the methods described in the text.

Antigroup Roles

Why do you think
some people insist on
playing the more
destructive roles in a
group? What personal
communicative
competencies are
lacking in members
who assume these
roles? What is the best
method for handling
blockers, distractors,
avoiders, and
recognition seekers?

require you to be subjective and kind and to give other people the benefit of the doubt. At the same time, the evaluator role would require you to be objective, impartial, and governed by rules or policies. Experiencing role conflict is one of the most uncomfortable feelings you can have as a group member.

The second problem is the existence of *antigroup roles*. These roles consist of behaviors that attempt to satisfy individual rather than group needs, which are often irrelevant to the task at hand and are clearly not aimed at maintaining the group as a team. How many times have you seen evidence of these antigroup roles in the groups you belong to?

Blocker Indulges in negative and stubbornly resistant behavior, including disagreements and groundless opposition to ideas; reintroduces an issue after the group has rejected or bypassed it

Avoider Displays noninvolvement in the group's proceedings by such behaviors as pouting, cynicism, nonchalance, or "horseplay"

Recognition seeker Calls attention to himself or herself by behavior such as boasting, providing information about his or her qualifications, or reporting personal achievements

Distractor Goes off on tangents or tells stupid, irrelevant stories

Networks

Still another factor that has a profound effect on group interaction is its networks. **Networks** are defined as the communication patterns used within a group. In essence, you are asking questions such as "Who speaks to whom?" "How often?" and "About what?"

NETWORKS

*Communication
patterns used within
groups.*

Two key positions typically are important in describing networks in a group. The first is **centrality**, or the degree to which an individual sends and receives messages from others in the group. The most central person in the group receives and sends the highest number of messages in a given time period. You probably believe that leaders of discussion groups or managers of employee teams occupy highly centralized positions because of their status or power. If a leader calls on you to speak in a group, all communication will flow directly through that leader. Therefore, the leader occupies a highly centralized position in the group's network.

CENTRALITY

*The degree to which a
member of a group
sends and receives
messages from others
in the group.*

Another key position is **isolation**. Relative to others in the group, isolates receive and send fewer messages. You may believe that these are "thinkers" who keep their thoughts to themselves and are not very interested in socializing or interacting with others. In some groups, members are isolates because they are not liked or perceived as competent by the other participants. In other groups, isolates choose to comment very selectively. You should note that both isolation and centrality are highly dependent on the content that is being communicated (see Figure 10.3).

ISOLATION

*A position within a
group in which the
member receives
and sends fewer
messages than do
other members.*

Several types of content-based networks are possible. One type is an *innovation* network whereby participants communicate about new ideas

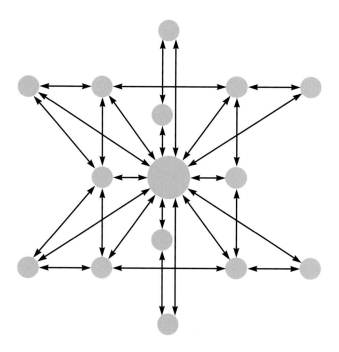

FIGURE 10.3

In a group's communication network, a position of centrality is often occupied by a manager. Isolates, on the fringe of the network, send and receive fewer messages than do other members of the group.

and directions. Another type is a *social* network in which participants discuss nonwork issues, including gossip. Still another type is a *task* network, which is defined by the job or work at hand or giving technical advice to another person.

A person can be very centralized in one network and yet be practically isolated in another. You may find many examples of this situation. Think for a moment about a group or committee of which you have been a member. Is the individual in your group who contributes and is asked the most about *task* functions the same person who also contributes the most and is asked the most about *social* activities? Probably not. You will likely find that the people who are particularly centralized in social networks are popular, outgoing, likable, and so forth. Highly centralized individuals in task networks are likely to be experienced, educated, and competent. In innovation networks, highly centralized persons are usually "insiders" with access to resources, information, and influential people.[20]

If you want to be more centralized in a group, you need to become more visible. Prepare some relevant and thought-provoking comments ahead of time. Speak up. Challenge members' ideas. Ask questions. If you first increase the number of contributions you make in a group, people will then direct comments to you as well. Depending on the quality of your contributions, you could move from an isolate to a central position rather swiftly.

We have discussed several ways that group communication can be improved. Goal setting and agenda setting are both essential. It is also important that all group members contribute through deliberation and participation. Another key is having group members assume roles that directly contribute to group competence, while minimizing roles that distract from the group's effectiveness. In addition, members need to be aware of the networks that exist so that centrality is encouraged for all group members.

◆ Special Groups and Techniques

This section discusses two special groups and their techniques. These groups meet in ways that deviate from the norm and have purposes that are different from those discussed in the earlier parts of the chapter.

The Nominal Group Technique

NOMINAL GROUP
TECHNIQUE

A process in which individuals work alone (in a group context) to produce a basis for discussion that reflects all group members' viewpoints.

Ironically, the nominal group technique is not a group process at all. Rather, the **nominal group technique** is a process used by individuals working alone in a group context (interaction among participants is not allowed). It is used to produce a *basis* for discussion that reflects the views of all the group members.

The nominal group technique can be best explained with an example. Assume that you are chairperson of a special student committee designed to recruit majors for the various departments in the School of Arts and Sciences. At an earlier meeting, an idea was proposed to conduct a 3-hour "open house," with all faculty and majors available to visit with prospective students. You and several group members are not certain this is the best course of action; therefore, as chairperson, you have decided to put the idea to a test using the nominal group technique.

To use this technique, you first ask each member to make a separate listing of the advantages and disadvantages of the proposal. After about 15 minutes, you call time. Then, by round-robin, you ask each member to contribute one of his or her advantages or disadvantages. You write each advantage and disadvantage on a flip-chart or transparency as it is mentioned, eliminating any that are repetitious. When the content of everyone's list is exhausted, you proceed to the next step.

You ask the participants to copy the master list on a sheet of paper. You then announce that, as individuals, they are to rank order each advantage and disadvantage from highest to lowest in priority. The lists are submitted to you. You might ask the group to take a break for a few minutes while you tabulate the priorities for the entire group. When the group reconvenes, you can select the top advantages and disadvantages of the issue to discuss.

Of course, "advantages/disadvantages" is only one of many possible topics for the nominal group technique. You may wish to pose a question and use the technique to brainstorm in a group. For example, you might ask, "What criteria should we use to distribute our scholarship money next year?" If this is the purpose, ideas are brainstormed, listed on a chart, prioritized, and then discussed.

Moore recommends that the nominal group technique conclude with a vote rather than a discussion.[21] He proposes that ideas be posted and then discussed or clarified among the members. After the discussion, participants select *five* ideas that are attractive to them, write them on a 3 × 5 card, and then assign a priority ranking to them. The cards are collected, rank ordered in front of the participants, and a final vote is taken for the best idea. Using e-mail capabilities, this selection of priorities can be accomplished prior to the meeting.

The nominal group technique is recommended when feelings of intimidation, domination, hesitancy, or apprehension surface in a group. Because each participant submits information simultaneously and anonymously, all input is weighted equally prior to the discussion. The technique is also useful when the group does not have a history from which to work. One study even indicated that four-person nominal groups outperformed four-person actual groups and individual groups on anagram tasks.[22]

Self-Managing Teams

One of the newest trends concerning small groups in modern organizations is the development of **self-managing teams**—teams consisting of highly skilled workers who are completely responsible for producing high-quality, finished work. Whether the work involves manufacturing, such as a mahogany china cabinet, or a service, such as a financial statement, the result is always the product of a fully integrated team. Members of the team share responsibility for each step of the process, as opposed to a single, narrow individual function, such as would be found on an assembly line.[23] According to Dumaine, one-half of surveyed Fortune 500 companies plan to implement these teams in the future.[24]

Self-managing work teams are actually an outgrowth of two major lines of thought. In the 1960s and early 1970s, *participative management* became very popular. In this style of management, supervisors would involve themselves with their subordinates in making decisions that were properly labeled group efforts. Supervisors would guide and facilitate discussions and problem-solving sessions but would not impose their decisions on the group. Rather, supervisors worked *with* their group to jointly address a problem.

In the late 1970s and early 1980s, participative management gave way to *quality circles* in many organizations. Quality circles were groups of employees from the same work area who met on a voluntary basis on company time to analyze and solve work-related problems. The meetings were led by an experienced manager, and participative decision making was used.

SELF-MANAGING TEAM

A group of highly skilled workers within a larger organization who are completely responsible for producing high-quality finished work.

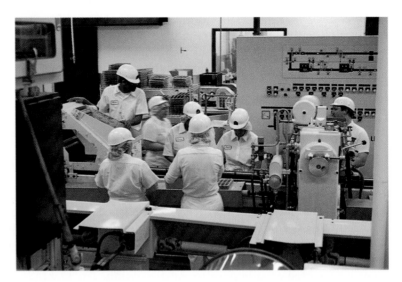

A self-managing work team within a larger organization is responsible for meeting the organization's objectives, but how the team accomplishes this is up to its members. By communicating with one another, team members determine what works best for the whole group.

Quality circles were popular because organizations were able to save large amounts of time and money by allowing employees, who were closest to and most knowledgeable about their jobs, to make recommendations on how to improve the effectiveness and efficiency of work processes. The circles would present their findings to management, who would often enthusiastically consider, endorse, and implement the ideas.

Note that in both models the supervisor is still the focus. In participative management, a supervisor guides and facilitates the meetings; and in quality circles, a supervisor leads the meetings. In self-managing work teams, however, many of the typical management functions are completely controlled by the team members. Employees who are part of these teams arrange their own schedules, buy their own equipment, and set their own standards for productivity, quality, and costs. They conduct their own peer evaluations, hire new members, and coordinate future plans with management. As a result, members have positive attitudes and are committed to the group.

While self-managing teams don't "work as they please," the organizational structure of self-managing teams encourages some of the following positive characteristics:

- A clear sense of their own separate identity
- The alignment of their activities with corporate objectives
- A sense of accountability for their activities
- Conformity to fiscal, legal, and other critical guidelines[25]

An organization's move from other organizational structures toward self-managing work teams cannot be accomplished overnight. Most organizations need approximately 24 to 42 months to fully implement self-managing teams.[26] During this time, responsibilities are gradually shifted from a manager to team members as they develop the competence to take over their new roles and responsibilities.

Perhaps the most dramatic effect of self-managing teams on the workplace is on the attitudes and skills of the workers. A competitive work environment often changes to one of cooperation. Work in isolation changes to work with others. Managers training employees changes to employees training their peers.

◆ Evaluation: Competence in Group Communication

Figure 10.4 on page 326 applies the model of competent communication to the small-group context. As you can see from the figure, individuals in a small group retain all of the characteristics they possess in a dyadic relationship (communication style, cultural identity, ethics and values, attributions, perceptions, and memory). The greatest difference, then, between dyads and small groups is the increase in the number of side interactions among dyads and cliques that occurs in a small group. Depending on group members' positions within the network, they will need to receive and send varying numbers of messages. The need to manage multiple channels of interaction calls for competent leadership skills. Thus leadership style is an important characteristic in small groups and has been added to this model. Chapter 11 is devoted to the topic of leadership in groups.

Two methods of evaluating groups are valid and helpful. First, individual member competence is evaluated by how well members accomplish their *roles*, how well they control their *apprehension* levels, how well they *participate*, and how accurate their *perceptions* and *attributions* are. In determining individual competence, it is important for members of the group to practice critical thinking skills. The best group decisions are made when members consider several different perspectives before being satisfied with the information they receive.

Second, groups can be evaluated as to how well they fulfill the functions of communication—namely, *control, affiliation,* and *goal orientation.* A group functions in a competent manner when there is general agreement by members as to the distribution of control, the amount of affiliation, and the goals of the group. Finally, competent groups are those that encourage productive conflict and critical thinking to arrive at the best decisions and minimize the extent of groupthink.

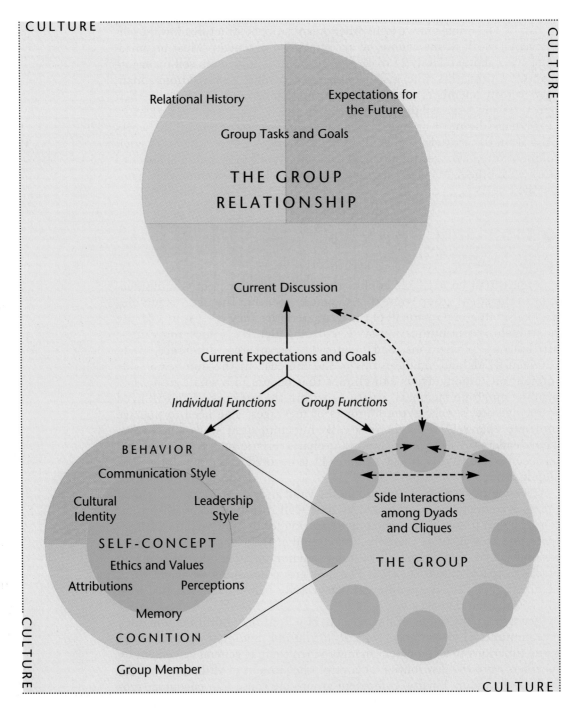

FIGURE 10.4
A model of competent communication in small groups.

Group Competence Evaluation Form

Use the following evaluation form to assess the performance of a group you belong to, using the following scoring: E = excellent performance; A = average performance; and P = poor performance.

Group Variables

_____ 1. Our group works well together as a unit.

_____ 2. Group members rely on one another for support and guidance.

_____ 3. The ability to get things done in the group is easily managed by people sharing control.

_____ 4. Our group avoids falling into a trap of jumping on the bandwagon.

_____ 5. Our group has disagreements, but they are generally productive.

_____ 6. Group members are very interested in following the rules and regulations of the group.

_____ 7. Our group thinks highly of itself and the work it does.

_____ 8. We usually set appropriate goals and accomplish them.

Individual Variables

_____ 9. Each member of the group has a special role that suits the group's needs.

_____ 10. The roles I play in the group are appropriate and effective.

_____ 11. Although I may experience anxiety or stress at times, I can usually handle it with no trouble.

_____ 12. My own participation is timely, relevant, and informative.

_____ 13. Over time, group members have developed very accurate perceptions of other group members.

_____ 14. My perceptions of other people and important issues are usually correct.

_____ 15. When members attribute behavior to others, they are usually accurate.

_____ 16. I avoid making attributions about others when I do not have all the facts.

Look at your responses. How many responses were E? A? P? A large number of A's and P's indicates areas that could use improvement. Examining strengths and weaknesses of your group and your participation in it allows you to improve your overall group communication competence.

*T*he Case of Ashley Myers

At the beginning of this chapter you learned about Ashley Myers. The dean of students has asked her to chair a committee exploring how the student union can be made more attractive for students. Reflect on Ashley's task and the content of this chapter as you consider these questions.

• How will the size of Ashley's committee (12) influence both the group process and its ultimate task?

• How will the factors affecting individual competence apply to this situation?

• What might Ashley do to encourage interdependence and cohesion and to discourage groupthink?

• How might Ashley improve group communication (e.g., through goal setting, agenda setting, etc.)?

• How might Ashley implement the nominal group technique in her task?

REVIEW

- Groups are pervasive in each individual's environment. Small groups differ from dyads in two basic ways. First, because the number of interactants is larger in a group than in a dyad, the basic qualities and characteristics of communication are affected. Second, more relationships must be maintained in a group than in a dyad.

- Several factors affect individual competence in group contexts: critical thinking skills, attributions, perceptions, and communication apprehension.

- How well an individual identifies with the purposes and goals of the group is important.

- Because "what you see is what you say," the kinds of perceptions and attributions you make in a group affect your communication.

- As a result of communication apprehension, those who are anxious are liable to be less effective, more nervous, less task oriented, and less able to lead. Individuals can mitigate their communication anxiety by using relaxation techniques, developing a positive attitude, and preparing carefully for group meetings.

- Several factors affect a group's communication as a unit. Key qualities include cohesion and interdependence among members.

- Groupthink can be a deterrent to effective decision making, but encouraging productive conflict can counteract the influence of groupthink.

- Norms also play a role in the small-group communication process.

- The three positive effects that a favorable group image can produce are success begetting success, optimism in the face of obstacles, and prestige of membership.

- When groups interact, several processes occur simultaneously—namely, goal setting, agenda setting, deliberation and participation, role enactment, and network use.

- A multistep method for setting goals includes identifying the problem and mapping out a strategy.

- Participation among group members may be increased by asking "gatekeeping" questions and removing personal identification.

- Individuals exhibit task roles, personal roles, and antigroup roles in a group.

- The two characteristics of communication networks in small groups are centrality and isolation.

- The two special groups/techniques discussed in this chapter are the nominal group technique and self-managing teams.

CHAPTER ELEVEN

Leadership and Decision Making in Groups

OBJECTIVES

After reading this chapter, you should be able to:

1. Discuss the four types of leadership.

2. Demonstrate the importance of shared leadership in groups.

3. Define competent leadership.

4. Give examples of factors that affect the decision-making process.

5. List the eight steps to effective decision making.

6. Describe the three types of groups frequently used in the business world.

7. Effectively evaluate individual and group performance in decision-making groups.

ONNIE JOHNSON, A BLACK STUDIES MAJOR, has decided to relaunch an Amnesty International chapter on campus. He is a sophomore transfer student who was very much involved in the Amnesty chapter at his former university, yet he has never held a leadership position before. The chapter at his new school died about 4 years ago when the chapter president graduated and attendance at meetings dropped off. Lonnie has circulated a petition concerning the formation of a new chapter, and he has sufficient signatures to gain the required approval from student government. As you read through this chapter, consider how its content may be relevant to the tasks faced by Lonnie. We will return to Lonnie's challenge at the end of the chapter.

Have you ever thought about the designs of conference tables? What types of decisions are made at a meeting using an oval table? What kind of leader was King Arthur, head of the knights of the round table? In corporations, why are most Japanese and American conference tables rectangular? In this chapter, we continue the discussion of groups by examining two essential dimensions of communication: group leadership and decision making. Leadership and decision making are two interrelated processes: They work together to produce valuable group outcomes. It is difficult to discuss one of these processes without discussing the other.

◆ Group Leadership

Think of the last group you were in. What was the leader like? Was he or she effective? How would you define the effective traits of this leader? Were you this leader? Over the years, countless attempts have been made to define leadership. In this section, we will review some of the basic characteristics of leadership and discuss how different styles work in different groups.

Leadership Defined

LEADERSHIP

The exercise of interpersonal influence toward the attainment of goals.

Two key terms appear in many definitions of **leadership**—*direction* and *influence*. Many people believe that a leader's primary function is to provide direction. For example, Hemphill and Coons note that leadership is the "behavior of an individual when he [or she] is directing the activities of a group toward a shared goal."[1] Stogdill suggests that leadership is the "initiation and maintenance of structure in expectation and interaction."[2] Viewed in this way, leaders structure, guide, and facilitate a group's activities and interaction in ways that will lead to a desired outcome.

Other definitions of leadership focus on influence, and scholars recognize the role of communication in influence. For example, consider these definitions of leadership:

- "Interpersonal influence, exercised in a situation, and directed, through the communication process, toward the attainment of a specified goal or goals."[3]

- "An interaction between persons in which one presents information of a sort and in such a manner that the other becomes convinced that his [or her] outcomes . . . will be improved if he [or she] behaves in the manner suggested or desired."[4]

These definitions highlight the notions that leaders have an impact on other group members and that people who can influence others become leaders. Frequently, group members are influenced by the leader's status or power. In other cases, the influence comes from the group members' admiration or respect for the leader.

Types of Leadership

Leaders of groups typically exhibit one of four decision-making styles: authoritarian, consultative, participative, or laissez-faire. Each of these styles has its own unique advantages and disadvantages.

Authoritarian leadership involves control by the leader without input from other group members. In most instances, the leader makes a decision and simply communicates it to the group. Although this style produces faster decisions, it has been shown to result in lower group member satisfaction and commitment to the task.

Authoritarian leaders (1) provide opinions and input but do not actively solicit them from members; (2) announce decisions rather than open them for discussion; (3) maximize upward and downward interaction (leader to member; member to leader) while minimizing lateral interaction (member to member); and (4) resolve conflicts when they arise. A group led by this style of leader would also have shorter meetings.

The consultative leader asks others for their opinions or ideas and then makes the decision alone after considering this input. Leaders use this style when they lack the necessary information to make an effective decision.

Subordinates often find **consultative leadership** to be a frustrating style because they see it as a facade the leader uses to make them *believe* that they are involved. In fact, they claim, very little that they suggest is ever achieved or implemented. Many subordinates wish the leader would not ask them for input in the first place! Nonetheless, leaders often use this style quite constructively to gather information and to test the waters before making a decision. This approach permits a more reasoned and educated outcome.

The **participative leadership** style is used by leaders who work together with a group in solving a problem or performing a task. The leader typically guides and facilitates but has no more influence over the outcome than does

AUTHORITARIAN LEADERSHIP

Control by a leader without input from group members.

CONSULTATIVE LEADERSHIP

Leadership that bases decisions on the opinions or ideas of group members.

PARTICIPATIVE LEADERSHIP

A leadership style that involves a leader working with other group members to achieve a desired goal.

Why is authoritarian leadership appropriate for military forces?

any other group member. Although the decisions made take longer to reach, they typically are of higher quality, result in greater satisfaction, and elicit greater commitment than do decisions made by any other leadership style.

Participative leaders (1) ask "gatekeeping" questions to involve nonparticipating members; (2) summarize discussions for group clarity; (3) give their own input and ask members for more; (4) "harmonize" discussions that may involve personal conflict; (5) announce a problem and open it for discussion rather than announce a solution; and (6) encourage all-channel participation, wherein communication flows laterally, upward, and downward.

**LAISSEZ-FAIRE
LEADERSHIP**

*A leadership style
that involves little or
no leadership per se.*

The **laissez-faire leadership** style involves little or no leadership per se. The group simply proceeds with the task. According to Bass, "The satisfaction of followers will be lower under laissez-faire leadership than under autocratic leadership if the latter is nonpunitive, appropriate for the followers' levels of competence, or in keeping with the requirements of the situation. Most often, laissez-faire leadership has been consistently found to be the least satisfying and effective management style."[5]

A laissez-faire leader is one who, according to subordinates, stays out of the way, is difficult to find when there is a problem, communicates the absolute minimum for members to do their job, and if not bothered, won't bother the group.

Most textbooks on leadership downgrade this style, although Altier has defended it.[6] Altier argues that poor problem-solving meetings are due not to a lack of leadership skills but to the person who called the meeting. As he suggests, "If the person who calls the meeting actively contributes and presents personal ideas and solutions (influenced by personal agendas

*The chief justice of
the U.S. Supreme
Court, as a "leader
among equals," is an
example of a participative leader.*

and experiences), the leader's perspectives are frequently in opposition to those of other participants. The cold, hard fact is that such a leader is often no more objective than the condemned man at a hanging."[7] Notice that *both* authoritarian and participative leaders present personal ideas and solutions. Altier argues that "a meeting leader who also participates in the content discussion fails to recognize that these two roles are contradictory and conflicting."[8]

In essence, Altier contends that a leader should not switch back and forth between the roles of participant and leader. "The leader should possess excellent process and facilitating skills; the participants should possess excellent knowledge about the problem. But the twain [two] should never meet in the leader."[9] Finally, Altier argues, "The more distant the meeting leader is, the more effective he or she can be. Only when the meeting leader possesses distance or 'stranger value' can this person hope to keep the group from falling into the 'they cannot see the forest for the trees' trap."[10] In essence, a case can be made for staying out of the way.

Once a leadership style has been established, it can be very difficult to alter, as illustrated in the following story.

The veteran manager in a large corporation attended a 3-day seminar on participative leadership during which this style was described. At the end of the seminar, he decided to give it a try. At the next staff meeting, he called everyone together, sat down, and described a problem. Instead of dictating a decision, he asked what everyone believed should be done. They sat there in silence. He asked again. Still they sat there without saying a word. He asked specific staff members. They were speechless. In their minds, they were thinking, "Has he been drinking?" "What's happened to him?"

What do you think this manager did? He went back to his authoritarian behaviors. Why? Because the group forced him to! When he tried to be participative, and the group failed to participate, he had to use authoritarian behaviors to get the job done. Thus, just because your mind is set on a particular way to behave does not always mean you will be able to do so. Circumstances may require you to employ behaviors that you had no intention of using.

Shared Leadership

Competent groups share leadership among their members. Many groups, as is well known, elect their leaders. For instance, in one large corporation, the safety board meets monthly. Each year, the board elects a chairperson, a vice-chairperson, and a secretary. In another corporation, the board leaders are appointed by an external source. At a university, the administration tells an instructor to "be in room 326 of University Hall from 1:00 to 2:00 P.M., Mondays, Wednesdays, and Fridays for Communication 211." All of these cases actually illustrate "headship" rather than "leadership." The person is in charge of the group because that person was formally placed in that position.

How many times have you seen that genuine leadership actually comes from someone other than the person who is the "head" of the group? In

---

Choosing the Right Leader

During your class session, divide into groups. Select four well-known characters from books, television, or the movies who accurately depict authoritarian, participative, consultative, and laissez-faire leaders. For each leadership style, list some types of groups (or people) for which that particular style would be appropriate.

reality, the organized manager with well-set agendas may not be nearly as useful to a group as the well-informed subordinate.

SHARED LEADERSHIP
Leadership that may emerge from any interested and talented group member, depending on the context.

A variety of situations permit **shared leadership**. Consider a city council group faced with making a difficult decision about where to build a new park and how much money to spend. The group is flooded with data; among other things, the members already have bids from contractors, maps, and expert testimonies. At some point, the members "wave a white flag." They do not need any more information. Fortunately, a group member emerges as a leader because that person can *organize* the group's information. This leader has the uncanny knack of sorting, classifying, or discarding data, and emerges as the leader because organization is what the group needs most at the present time.

Conversely, consider a task force at a department store whose responsibility is to recommend a security system to senior management. Although all members are enthusiastic about participating, only one person has insight into the store's past problems, types of systems, contact firms, and so forth. In all likelihood, this member will emerge as the group leader because she has the information the group needs at that time.

Heads of groups who encourage and facilitate shared leadership are more likely to be effective. When the talents of each individual in a group are brought out and applied, members are likely to be more motivated and the group's needs are more likely to have "all bases covered."

Many businesses and professional organizations in the United States are moving toward a shared leadership model. This means giving people who work at the lower levels of the organization decision-making and leadership responsibilities. As we saw in Chapter 10, self-managing teams are a part of this process.

Culture and Shared Leadership

How receptive to shared leadership are the various cultural groups to which you belong? Examine some of the cultures or co-cultures with which you identify—for example, your ethnic group, your gender, your religious affiliation, and your age group. On a sheet of paper, draw a horizontal line representing a continuum from authoritarian leadership at one end to shared leadership at the other. Place the leadership style common to each of your cultures/groups on the continuum. Does the style change in either direction for groups in which all the members share a cultural identity? What about groups that also include other cultures? For example, is the leadership style of groups whose members are all about the same age different from that of groups in which some members are older or younger? When you observe the leadership styles that seem most comfortable for your cultural groups, this may facilitate reaching group goals.

Competent Leadership

Our definition of leadership is consistent with the theme of this book, for it includes a component of competence. Regardless of whether one directs or influences followers, the major criterion should be *how well* the leader functions, performs, or behaves. **Competent leadership** may be authoritarian (although this is rarely the case), democratic, participative, or laissez-faire. A competent leader may share leadership in a group and ensure that his or her style is a good match for the group. The important issue is that a leader exhibit competent communication in leading the group toward desirable results.

Three factors are important for competent leadership. First, the competent leader must behave in ways that bring about desirable *outcomes*. The outcomes need not be pre-planned or even consistent with previously established goals. The outcomes must, however, be successful, productive, or beneficial for the group. Because outcomes are heavily influenced by the group process, leaders must be able to move the process toward a successful conclusion.

Second, the competent leader must behave in ways that enhance *credibility* with the group. Credibility is typically assessed through reactions to questions such as "How knowledgeable is the leader?" "How experienced is the leader?" "How believable is the leader?" or "How much do I respect the leader?" Maybe the members do not like the leader personally, but they believe nonetheless that the person is an effective leader for the group. In that case, the leader certainly has credibility.

Finally, the competent leader must *inspire* and *motivate* group members to participate. In some cases, the leader must be a cheerleader for the group. In other cases, an individual may lead by example. In still other instances, the leader may offer tangible rewards that encourage group members to try to achieve.

The three factors we have mentioned are criteria by which to assess how well or what a leader does. Competent leadership is *credible* behavior by which an individual *inspires* and *motivates* group members to achieve desirable group *outcomes* through interaction.

◆ The Complexity of Making Decisions in Groups

Making decisions with other people is a very complex process. In order to understand the process of group decision making, you need to become familiar with six concepts: (1) decision-making variables, (2) decision-making skills, (3) values and goals clarification, (4) expectations, (5) time pressures, and (6) conflict.

Decision-Making Variables

Group decisions are never made in a vacuum. No matter what topic is under discussion, several factors can influence the attitudes and behaviors of

COMPETENT LEADERSHIP
Credible behavior by which an individual inspires and motivates group members to achieve desirable group outcomes through interaction.

Seeing Yourself as a Leader

Examine again the definition of competent leadership. Can you recall examples in the past when you demonstrated the characteristics of leadership (credible behavior, inspiration and motivation of group members, and desirable outcomes)? What could you do to become more effective in demonstrating competent leadership?

individual group members, the climate of the group as a whole, and the final decision. To illustrate how multiple decision-making factors can interact with each other, consider this example.

One of the worst disasters of our time occurred as a result of poor group decision making. On January 28, 1986, the space shuttle *Challenger* exploded 92 seconds after take-off, killing all seven of its crew members. NASA officials had decided to launch the shuttle even though they had received information that cast doubt on the safety of the mission.

In an analysis of the decision making that led to this tragedy, Hirokawa, Gouran, and Martz argue that three forces influenced the faulty decision.[11] These same forces operate in practically any type of group decision making. They are *cognitive, psychological,* and *social* forces.

Cognitive Forces. Cognitive processes are mental, referring to what someone thinks, believes, or feels. They specifically involve the beliefs individuals hold and the methods they use to make decisions. They influence "the manner in which group members attend to, make sense of, and utilize available information" to make decisions.[12]

Cognitive forces include the perception, interpretation, evaluation, storage, retrieval, and integration of information input to an individual. The outcome of any group decision can be greatly affected by the way group members interpret information.

A government commission's investigation of the *Challenger* disaster found that cognitive forces had influenced the NASA officials who made the decision to launch the shuttle. The officials discounted the credibility of key negative information that was available to them at the time. The decision makers also used questionable reasoning to draw incorrect conclusions from the data. Finally, they held faulty beliefs about the shuttle system, which led them to have unwarranted confidence in its ability to launch correctly.

Psychological Forces. Psychological forces refer to the personal motives, goals, attitudes, and values of group members. In the *Challenger* example, two psychological forces influenced the participants' decision making: perceived pressure and a criterion shift.

Lower-level NASA decision makers felt pressure to reverse their earlier recommendation to postpone the launch. Initially, the group had recommended that the launch be postponed until the temperature was higher. That decision was later reversed in the face of strong opposition from higher management officials.

The decision makers also shifted the criterion for postponing the launch. Ordinarily, NASA officials employ a rule that a launch should not take place if there is any doubt of its safety. With this rule, the burden of proof is on the *safety* of the launch. In this case, officials shifted to a rule suggesting that a launch should proceed unless there is conclusive evidence that it is unsafe to do so. With this rule, the burden of proof is on the *risk* of the launch. Because risk is always harder to prove than safety, the NASA officials used an incorrect decision criterion as a basis for proceeding with the launch.

Social Forces. Social forces are communicative influences such as language use and persuasion. These forces are present whenever two or more people interact with each other. In the *Challenger* disaster, responsible engineers were unable to persuade their own management and higher NASA officials to postpone the launch. They tried, unsuccessfully, to prove that it was unsafe to launch rather than take the tactic that no data were available to prove that it was safe to launch the *Challenger*. The government commission's investigation also revealed that much ambiguous and confusing language was communicated among various officials.

How do these same forces operate in groups that you work with each day? Think about this point. Have your strongly held beliefs ever caused you to dismiss contrary information as unimportant or incorrect? Have you ever felt pressure to "go along with the crowd" as part of the decision-making process? Have you always insisted on understanding exactly what others meant before you would agree to a particular conclusion? Most people would answer "yes" to all three of these questions. In the *Challenger* disaster, the loss was greater than seven lives. What will be the cost of your group's next decision?

Decision-Making Skills

Different people, of course, have different decision-making skills. What is involved when you make any of the following decisions as an individual?

- Whether to drop or continue a course you are currently struggling in

- Whether to sacrifice now by juggling school and work in order to benefit later with a better, more rewarding job

- Whether to eat a light lunch today so that you can feast tonight without guilt at an all-you-can-eat seafood buffet

- Whether to accept a job promotion and relocate to another city

For any of these decisions—as well as other ones—you would probably use these processes: (1) Delineate the alternatives clearly; (2) decide how distinct the alternatives are; (3) analyze the "state of affairs" for each alternative; (4) determine what criteria are the most important for you in making the decision; (5) using those criteria, conduct a cost/benefit or pro/con analysis for each alternative; (6) come to a conclusion and make the decision you think is right; and (7) evaluate it later.

These same processes, and more, are present when individuals meet as a group to make a decision. Just as some people are better than others at decision making, some groups are better at it as well. In this section we will look specifically at group decision-making skills rather than the individual skills discussed in Chapter 10. We will discuss four group skills: analysis, perspective, focus, and summarizing.

Ethics and O-Rings

Many experts have characterized the *Challenger* disaster as a "communication breakdown." Several communication problems contributed to the space shuttle explosion. Besides the psychological, cognitive, and social variables at work in this situation, it has been suggested that a number of ethical communication issues were involved.* In testimony during the hearings investigating the disaster, we learned that engineers for the O-ring manufacturer, Thiokol, were very vocal in their objections to the launch of the space shuttle in cold weather. After management overruled their objections and authorized the launch, the engineers were unhappy but silent. If they really believed that people's lives would be in danger, didn't they have a moral and ethical obligation to communicate their concerns to others in positions of authority? For example, would it have been ethical for the engineers to go over their bosses' heads to even higher authorities? Would it have been ethical for the engineers to talk to the media about their fears? On the other hand, don't decision makers such as the Thiokol engineers have a moral duty to support their superiors' decisions? Going over a boss's head or leaking information to the press is a good way to get fired. Didn't the engineers have an ethical obligation to themselves and their families to keep their jobs?

*See J. A. Jaksa & M. S. Pritchard (1994), *Communication ethics: Methods of analysis* (2nd ed.) (Belmont, CA: Wadsworth).

Analysis refers to "taking apart" a problem and examining its components. When a group conducts an analysis, it probes for sources, causes, effects, and influences. Analysis mobilizes the individual skills (such as critical thinking) discussed in Chapter 10. (Analysis as part of the decision-making process is discussed later in this chapter.)

The *perspective* a group brings to a problem influences its decision-making process in several different ways. How important is the problem? How many people does it affect? How much money might a particular decision save or cost? How much time should be spent on the issues? The answers to questions such as these is what perspective is all about. Groups that put a problem in proper perspective are better at decision making than those that do not.

Can the group keep its *focus* on its task? Or does it get lured into sub-issues or topics that are irrelevant to the problem at hand? It is easier than you think to move away from the problem under discussion, especially when some group members have partisan agendas they would like to pursue. Leaders and group members must be vigilant in keeping the group focused on its primary goal.

Summarizing is very important and should occur with regularity while a group makes decisions. Summary statements allow group members to assess "where they are" on a given decision. When these statements are voiced with clarity, participants have the opportunity to confirm, correct, or clarify what has occurred up to a certain point. Some people believe that leaders should provide summaries as part of their responsibilities. This may be true, but *any* participant can attempt to summarize the discussion at any point.

Values and Goals Clarification

Before a group proceeds to make decisions, it should engage in values and goals clarification. Simply put, values help a group determine whether a decision is right or wrong; goals are the ultimate purposes for which decisions are made.

Values. The noted psychologist Rokeach defined a **value** as "an enduring belief that a specific mode of conduct or end-state or existence is personally or socially preferable to an opposite or converse mode of conduct or end-state of existence."[13] When groups express the idea that certain behaviors are right or wrong or that certain end-states are desirable or undesirable, they are operating from their values. Values significantly affect a group's decision-making process.

For example, U.S. congressional committees hold the value that democracy is preferable to dictatorship. Mothers Against Drunk Driving (MADD) has clearly sent the value-laden message that drinking alcoholic beverages before operating an automobile is very dangerous. Consumer advocacy groups suggest that safety in the manufacture of products is preferable to risk. Raters for the Motion Picture Association of America (MPAA) determine that some material may not be suitable for pre-teenagers' viewing, while other material is not suitable for anyone under age 17 to witness. Any decision made by groups such as these is strongly driven by their values.

Many groups are defined by and exist because of their values. Their participants are together because they have a common concern or interest. For example, members of the Parents and Friends of Lesbians and Gays (PFLAG) are all interested in understanding and accepting homosexual children and loved ones because they believe everyone deserves love, respect, and dignity. Other groups develop their values as they continue to interact together. If you were asked to participate on a local Teenage Pregnancy Task Force, you would surely know that everyone on that task force values the idea of "preventing kids from having kids." To find out how this value is applied to specific cases or problems, your task force would need to obtain additional values clarification.

In summary, groups make decisions that are harmonious with their values. By the same token, the processes that groups engage in while making decisions are also value-driven. Discussions of any kind are likely to be highly controlled by a group's values. Even though a group may attempt to clarify its values in advance of its meetings, leaders may need to remind the members of these values as work continues on a task.

VALUES
The enduring beliefs that individuals and groups hold about certain issues and behaviors.

Marches and civil disobedience have been the preferred modes of protest for groups that value nonviolence.

Goals. Effective groups are those whose members are working "on the same page." That is, all participants in a group envision, support, and devote their efforts to the same result or product. *Goals* are those results or products. Recall from Chapter 10 the five steps you should follow in formulating and setting effective goals. That information is relevant to this discussion.

A group's failure to clarify its goals before beginning work on a project can prove disastrous. Here is a classic example of a group that was not goal-directed. Several years ago, a university professor was working on an awards task force for a professional organization. All anyone knew about the task force was that it had been formed to make nominations and recommendations to the association's board of directors regarding individuals who should receive awards. Prior to the group's first meeting, no attempt was made to define any of the following: the kind of awards to be given, the number of people to be nominated for each award, the criteria for an award nominee, or even the date when the nominations had to be submitted for board approval. When the task force convened at the association's annual convention just 2 days before the award winners were to be announced, there was total chaos. After almost 2 hours of fruitless discussion, someone finally retrieved a copy of the association's bylaws and discovered that it contained exact titles for the awards and specific criteria for each.

You can probably think of other examples of group members disagreeing or having misperceptions about a group's task. Refer back to the Teenage Pregnancy Task Force mentioned earlier. All members of the group agreed that preventing "children from having children" was an important and worthwhile goal. As it turned out, however, the members did not agree on preventive solutions. Several members believed that abstinence was the only

Values Clarification

Rank the values in the left-hand column in their order of importance to you as an individual. Then rank the group values in the right-hand column in their order of importance to you as a group member.

INDIVIDUAL VALUES   GROUP VALUES

____ 1. Spiritual fulfillment   ____ 1. Consensus building

____ 2. World peace   ____ 2. Group productivity

____ 3. Marital bliss   ____ 3. Conflict management

____ 4. Honesty   ____ 4. Group cohesiveness

____ 5. Career achievement   ____ 5. Cordial relations among
                                             members

____ 6. Secure financial situation   ____ 6. Popularity among group
                                             members

____ 7. Professional recognition   ____ 7. Group recognition

Look at your rankings. Do you find that there are similarities in your personal values and your group values?

direction to take. Others felt that birth control devices would help deter the unwanted and unplanned pregnancies. Still others encouraged the use of educational information. Not surprisingly, the group did not reach a consensus.

Many people confuse group goals with objectives and use these two terms interchangeably. Goals are the end-states or products that a group aspires to achieve, whereas objectives are the specific and measurable *means* that lead to the goals. A series of objectives usually relate to a single goal. For example, a hospital acquisitions task force has a goal of purchasing the newest X-ray equipment for all of its examination rooms by the end of the year. This group may have several objectives that lead to that goal: (1) to have six major community corporations make donations of $5000 by June; (2) to persuade 65 percent of all employees to donate $1 from each paycheck for 6 months; (3) to make a 45 percent down payment on the equipment by September 1; and (4) to place six articles describing the project in community publications by March 3.

Expectations

Several factors determine whether a group's meeting is successful or unsuccessful. Without doubt, the expectations and goals that participants bring with them to a meeting play a major role. You are already well aware of the importance of expectations in communication. Green and Lazarus conducted a survey of over 1000 business leaders, which revealed several of the expectations held by group members and leaders.[14]

- Approximately 85 percent of the respondents expected to spend as much or more time as they currently spend in meetings 5 years hence.
- One-third of the time spent in meetings is unproductive; therefore, although the time spent in meetings is increasing, time wasted is also growing, with an estimated loss to business in excess of $40 billion.
- Ninety-seven percent of respondents believed that participants should be prepared for meetings, but only 28 percent were prepared most of the time.
- Three out of four meetings fail to end on schedule.
- Two out of three meetings fail to achieve their goals.

The many reasons for these opinions and observations are linked to individual expectations, which are so often violated, thus causing dissatisfaction with group processes.

Time Pressures

The amount of time a group has available can play a significant role in the way it makes decisions. **Time pressures** can influence two aspects of group decision making: planning and leadership styles.

TIME PRESSURES

In a group, the effects of a shortage of time on the decision-making process.

Planning. Planning and coordinating are essential activities for effective decision making. You probably know people who would "build a bridge" before they knew what river or lake it was going to cover! Similarly, groups can make decisions without engaging in proper planning and coordinating activities. Although a group might have a variety of reasons to proceed without planning and coordinating, time pressures are usually the major reason why a group fails to do so.

Consider this example. A group from a professional corporation was working on team-building processes in an outdoor simulation. The group started the activity with its twelve members standing on a wooden platform. They had one long and one short wooden plank at their disposal to assist in moving to a second platform and then to a third. Neither the participants nor the wooden planks could touch the ground; if they did so, the group would have to start over.

The simulation had two trials. In the first trial the group was given only 5 minutes to complete the task. In the second, the group had unlimited time. Not surprisingly, very little advance planning or coordinating was possible in the first trial. The group member with the loudest voice prevailed and announced the "plan" for the group to follow. The group did so, and it failed miserably. In the second trial, with plenty of time available, the group mapped out an elaborate strategy by which to complete the simulation. The participants debated and questioned each other, reevaluated ideas, and then finally reached a consensus agreement on how to proceed. The group completed the simulation successfully in only 12 minutes.

Leadership Styles. The style a group leader uses is also dependent on time. Remember the four different styles discussed earlier, each of which varies in the degree to which the leader allows group members to be involved in decision making. Allowing participation takes more time. Think about some of the reasons why a group leader may choose not to involve subordinates in decision making. One reason may be that the subordinates do not possess the knowledge or experience needed to assist in making the decision. Another may be that the subordinates do not want to participate. Yet, of all the reasons you might suggest, time pressures appear to be the most important.

Many leaders who believe in participative techniques are often forced to be authoritarian leaders simply because there is no time for the group to participate in making a particular decision. In crisis situations, participative techniques may indeed yield a better decision, but time will not permit them to be used. Consider the example of a military unit in the field of battle, with grenades and enemy fire exploding around it. There is no time for the leader to say, "What do you think we should do?" The leader must say, "Get your butt down in the ditch and don't move until I order you to!"

On the other hand, groups need not always be at the mercy of time, even in the face of strong pressures. Here are three ways that groups can work around time and produce a quality decision. First, a group may begin a discussion by taking a nonbinding straw poll. Suppose a city council is discussing whether to join a regional mass transit association. The decision must be made by the end of the meeting. The leader may begin by asking how many of the members favor the union and how many are opposed to it. A straw poll will save a group time; the group will not have to discuss items on which all participants already agree. In addition, this vote gives the group an idea of how far apart the participants are on a topic.

Second, the leader may impose time limits on certain components of a discussion. For example, one rule might be that no one speaker may have the floor for more than 5 minutes. Another might be that once a person has spoken on a topic, that person cannot contribute to the group without specific permission from the leader. Yet another might be that open discussion will take place for 60 minutes. At that time, the group will proceed to take a vote.

Third and most important, the group may not make any decision at all. No decision is often better than a bad decision. As Covey argues, "No deal basically means that if we can't find a solution that would benefit us both, we agree to disagree agreeably—No Deal. No expectations have been created, no performance contracts established."[15] Why make a bad decision that you will regret later because time pressures have forced you into it? Stop, table the discussion, or postpone reaching a conclusion.

Conflict

As you know from earlier chapters, the best decisions are usually those that have followed productive conflict. This means that clarification questions are asked, participants' ideas are challenged, counter-examples are presented, "worst-case" scenarios are considered, and proposals are reformulated. After such a process, a group can have confidence that its decision has been tested. If an idea survives these rigorous tests, it has a fighting chance to be successful when it is actually applied.

The other advantage of conflict is that group members will "own" the decision that is reached. Because they have had a part in analyzing, synthesizing, and constructing the decision, and because they have participated in its "shakedown," group members will generally agree with, adhere to, and defend the decision before others.

This explains why people prefer *consensus* decision making to majority vote. When a group takes a split-decision vote, at least one person will be dissatisfied and believe that the decision was forced. Conversely, when the participants argue about the decision and have had a chance to question and test a proposal, they will have had their "ten cents' worth" put on the table and will own part of the resulting decision. Unfortunately, time constraints may prevent a group from using the consensus method. However, it should be employed whenever possible.

◆ The Decision-Making Process

Effective groups do not make decisions arbitrarily or haphazardly.[16] Rather, they engage in very systematic processes that result in consensus decisions that all participants can understand and to which they can commit themselves. Here is an eight-step process that has worked for many groups (see Figure 11.1). For clarity, one example is used throughout this section. Pretend that you are a member of a neighborhood group that is meeting to reduce crime in the area.

Identifying the Problem

As a first step, a group must make sure that all its members are in agreement on the main problem to be solved. If the group's goal is to generate a solution, then all of its members really must understand the problem in the same way.

This step does not mean that the group simply announces the problem, then agrees on it and moves on. Thus, in the example, the simple statement, "We need to find a way to reduce crime in our neighborhood," would not be enough. Instead, this step involves gaining a thorough understanding of the problem the group is addressing.

FIGURE 11.1
The decision-making process.

The group should begin by having each participant share his or her perception of the problem. No debate or questions should be allowed until all members have had a chance to voice their perceptions. In this way, the leader will have an idea of how far apart the members are in their thinking about the problem. For example, one member might say, "We have inadequate street lighting," while another might suggest, "We do very little looking out for each other."

Next, the group should engage in an extensive analysis of the problem. The members should question each other, debate ideas, and attempt to clarify positions. They should provide philosophies, statistics, case examples, incidents, or analogies in making their analysis. During this step, the group asks questions such as, What are the origins or causes of this problem? What are the possible ramifications if the problem is not solved? What is the philosophy behind the current state of affairs? Who is affected? To what extent?

Before moving on, the leader should make sure all the participants agree on the problem. The leader should also summarize the discussion that has been held up to that point. If the members have not reached agreement, the leader should pinpoint the source of confusion and proceed to obtain a consensus.

Conducting Research

After the group has agreed on the exact problem to be solved, more information may be needed in some areas. Research may be required (1) to bridge gaps in information so that the problem can be analyzed properly; (2) to obtain clarification in order to resolve two or more inconsistent views expressed by participants; or (3) to review the historical success of a proposed solution.

In the neighborhood example, the group may not know the exact number of burglaries or the approximate dollar figures lost because of crime in the area. Some participants may want to know the actual cost of installing motion detectors on each person's property. Others may oppose that view and propose investigating the cost of hiring a private security company to patrol the neighborhood on a regular basis.

Without conducting research on these and other topics, the group operates out of ignorance or misperception. As a rule, better decisions are made when group members are armed with data and facts rather than with speculation.

Establishing Guidelines and Criteria

Once the group thoroughly understands the problem and has done sufficient research on it, the participants should discuss the criteria by which any solution they propose will be judged. This is *not* the time to propose solutions; that comes later.

In this step, the group agrees on the guidelines to be used to evaluate solutions. In the neighborhood crime example, the criteria may be requirements such as (1) a cost of under $500 per family, (2) the involvement of all families in the neighborhood, and (3) adherence to the guidelines of the city housing code.

As in step 1, group members should question each other to obtain more information or clarification. The group's goal is to reach consensus on the criteria. Although several criteria may be selected, they must be independent of each other. Before proceeding, the leader should again verify that all members agree on the criteria they will use to judge the solutions. In the event of disagreements or problems, the leader should identify the point of confusion and reopen the discussion. In order to be able to use these criteria later, the leader should record each of them on a flip-chart or blackboard.

Generating Alternatives

Unlike the previous steps, this step is actually just brainstorming. Each group member should contribute as many desirable solutions as possible, and the leader should record them as they are expressed.

This step is not interactive; that is, the group members do not now debate the worth of the proposed solutions. Each step is simply stated and recorded by the leader.

In the neighborhood crime example, you may hear proposals such as (1) install professional security equipment in each home and negotiate the purchase with group buying power; (2) close off two access roads after 11:00 P.M.; (3) have four to six residents patrol the area on foot in pairs each evening; (4) encourage each family to buy a guard dog; or (5) offer to house-sit for families who are out of town for extended periods of time.

Evaluating Alternatives

In this step, the group weighs each solution provided in the previous step against the criteria the members have agreed on earlier. It is essential at this point that the group use as much high quality information as possible, so that it can adequately consider the positive and negative qualities of the proposed alternatives. In fact, quality information may be one of the most important factors in reaching effective group decisions. Groups must be careful to weigh all evidence for all alternatives to ensure that the decisions eventually reached can be supported with good solid arguments.[17]

The leader can then announce the first proposed solution and ask the group whether the solution meets criterion number 1 and, if so, criterion number 2, and so forth, until the solution either meets *all* the criteria or is eliminated. This process should be continued until all of the solutions have been examined.

In the case of the neighborhood crime example, the leader may say, "Okay, let's look at the first proposal—that we install professional security equipment in each home and negotiate the price with our group buying power. Now, does that mesh well with our first criterion—that it cost under $500 per family?"

Selecting the Best Alternative

Once the group has arrived at a short list of alternatives, the members must select one alternative that can best fill their needs. Groups that are lucky may indeed find the perfect solution. That is, only *one* proposed solution successfully survives the evaluation. Frequently, however, one of two other things happens. Either more than one solution survives, or no solution survives. What should you do? In the first case, the group should determine whether the two or more viable solutions are mutually exclusive. Can you do both of them? If so, there is no problem, for you have two (or more) solutions that you can implement immediately. If not, pick the solution that has met the criteria most completely. This is likely to be your best solution.

In the event that no solution survives, the group must choose at least one of the previously suggested solutions—that is, the proposed solution that meets the greatest number of criteria. Although that solution may not be optimal, it is superior to any of the others.

By following this example, you can probably see that the step that establishes criteria is just as important as—if not more important than—the step that produces solutions. If the criteria are worthwhile standards, the group can feel comfortable with its solution.

Implementing the Solution

The last two steps in the decision-making process are implementing, and then evaluating, the solution reached by the group. Implementing a solution involves putting into action the ideas and decisions that the group has finalized. In some cases, this means submitting a report to a higher authority, with recommendations about how the solution can best be activated. For example, a self-directed work team in business will go through the decision-making process to arrive at a recommendation for improving some aspect of the organization. The team's recommendation is then forwarded to an executive committee, a task force, or an individual responsible for seeing that the solution is implemented in the organization.

In other cases, the group suggesting the solution is also expected to implement it. In order to do so, the group is usually expected to convert general or abstract ideas into a practical plan of action. Because most group decisions affect more people than just the group members, directions and instructions for carrying out the decision must be clear, direct, and simple. In addition, many people will want to know the reasons why a particular decision was reached. Therefore, your action plan should include some explanation of your decision and a justification for implementing it in the way you propose.

Evaluating the Results

Solutions resulting from the group decision-making process must stand the test of evaluation. Solutions are best evaluated by returning to the criteria that were established early in the process. The following questions can be helpful as you apply the group's criteria to your solution.

- Were the criteria useful and appropriate for the problem?
- How strictly were the criteria used in arriving at the solution?
- What other criteria would have been helpful in reaching a better solution?
- Does the solution have any weaknesses or disadvantages?

Real-Life Problem Solving

Select a city, state, or campus problem that is relevant to the members of the class. Divide into groups for the purpose of solving the problem using the eight-step process for decision making. As a class, discuss the solutions proposed by the various groups. Mention any notable group dynamics (conflict, consensus building, shared leadership, etc.).

Evaluating a group decision can make a good decision even better. A hard look at any result or outcome will uncover even minor shortcomings that can be eliminated before full implementation takes place. Careful scrutiny can create opportunities for precision. In addition, evaluation can help groups to improve their decision making in the future. Learning from mistakes is rarely pleasant at the time, but it can help you prevent similar problems in subsequent group work.

The steps involved in the decision-making process are a proven method of producing competent group outcomes. The sequence of steps encourages group members to think reflectively about their task. In this way, all relevant facts and opinions can be discussed and evaluated, thereby ensuring a better decision. You can also use this process for making individual decisions in your personal and professional life.

Before we move to another topic, one other important point needs to be addressed. The leader who uses these steps cannot be shy and must keep control of the group. This does not mean that the leader must be authoritarian, but he or she should stay on top of the situation. For instance, if group members start to propose solutions when they are supposed to be listing criteria, the leader should tactfully steer them back to the topic at hand. Similarly, if group members begin to debate or question a contribution that someone else makes when brainstorming is supposed to take place, the leader must restore order.

◆ Working on Committees, Task Forces, and Boards

For those of you who are planning to enter the business world, be sure that you don't underestimate the importance of this section. Your professional life will be practically synonymous with meetings, especially those of committees, task forces, and boards. Your familiarity with these professional groups will enhance your competence as a group member or leader.

Organizations typically have two types of **committees**: temporary and permanent. Temporary, or ad hoc, committees are typically assigned to perform work on a particular project that is unique and nonrecurring. Good examples include committees that plan the company picnic or raise funds for charities.

COMMITTEE
A temporary or permanent group that meets for a specific purpose.

Permanent committees usually have members who participate on a regular basis for a number of years. For example, a corporate finance committee may have six members, each appointed for a six-year term. One new member is appointed each year. In the member's sixth year, he or she serves as chairperson. After the sixth year, this person rotates off and another member joins the board.

Good examples of permanent committees in a corporation include the compensation committee, the public relations committee, the community affairs committee, and the committee that reviews employee suggestions.

Task forces are temporary groups that differ from committees in that they typically perform an investigative or research function *before* discussions are held or decisions are made. For example, a university department chairperson may appoint faculty members to a task force to decide how the curriculum should be changed in the next five years. Another task force might be formed to investigate the rising rate of teen pregnancy, the school dropout rate, and so on.

TASK FORCE
A group that researches an issue before discussions are held or decisions are made.

Members of **boards** are typically elected by a populace or appointed by someone with considerable status. For example, many large corporations have active safety boards that are charged with the review, maintenance, and enforcement of all policies and procedures related to OSHA (Occupational Safety and Hazard Administration) requirements, the driving of company vehicles, responses to workplace accidents, and worker's compensation cases. Think of your local city and school officials, who are members of a number of boards.

BOARD
An elected or appointed group that makes important decisions regarding the functioning of an organization.

Group Decision Making in Practice

Select an organization and arrange an interview with the chairperson, president, or director to determine how the various groups within the organization operate. How closely do these groups conform to the decision-making process discussed in this chapter? Report what you have learned to the class.

Positions on boards are usually prestigious and highly sought after because the members represent an elite group of well-informed, highly experienced individuals who make important decisions regarding the functioning of an organization.

◆ Evaluating Group Performance

Groups that plan to be together and meet on a regular, consistent basis should plan to evaluate their performance periodically. Without assessing where the group stands in terms of its goals, how well the group works together, or what kind of problems exist, a group will not reach its full potential.

Groups may be likened to automobiles. If either a car or a group is to run smoothly, their performance must be assessed and their components maintained. This section discusses various methods for assessing and evaluating groups.

Numerous categories, rating forms, and questionnaires have been designed to assess the strength of groups. These evaluations usually assess both groups and their individual members.

Group Evaluation

GROUP EVALUATION

An evaluation of how competently a group performs as a whole.

Kowitz and Knutson have done outstanding work on evaluating groups as a whole.[18] They divide their scheme into three dimensions for **group evaluation**: informational, procedural, and interpersonal.

Informational Dimensions. Informational dimensions are concerned with the group's designated task. According to Kowitz and Knutson, several areas may be assessed. One deals with whether or not the group is working on a task that requires interaction. If the task does not require discussion and does not need the participation of group members with diverse backgrounds and experience, or work on specialized tasks by particular people, the topic needs expansion. Alternatively, perhaps the group should drop the topic or have only one or two individuals address it.

If the task is suitable, is the group prepared for discussion? How much of the necessary research or planning is accomplished prior to the meeting? Does the group recognize the need to get more information before making a decision?

Does the group analyze the problem well? If so, is it *creative?* What is the quality of *information giving, opinion giving, evaluation and criticism, elaboration*, and *integration* among the group's members?

Procedural Dimensions. The procedural functions of a group refer to the ways in which the group coordinates its activities and communication. The key functions to be evaluated include *eliciting communication, delegating and directing action, summarizing group activity, conflict management, process evaluation*, and *tension release*. You might see a few problems regarding these areas.

One problem frequently associated with groups is the tendency of some members to talk too much while others give too little input. This problem requires a leader or other members to employ *gatekeeping*, which is an attempt to keep the lines of communication open among all group members. A leader may interrupt with a line such as, "Harry, I think we should hear from some other people on this subject."

Another problem occurs when issues that have already been decided on surface for a second time. When this happens, many members express frustration with the process. Someone may say "These are the craziest meetings" or "This is a big waste of my time." A leader or another member can use one of two options in this situation. One option is to use *summarizing*. Summarizing contributions sound like "What we've been talking about is . . ." or "So, what we seem to be saying is . . . ?" A second option is to steer the group back toward its *objectives*. The question becomes: What is the group trying to accomplish and how is the discussion at this moment helping to accomplish those objectives?

Finally, members may need to release tension at certain points during a meeting. They can do so by telling a joke or an anecdote, by letting members tell each other how they feel at a given moment, and the like. Clearly, participants may lose sight of their individual responsibilities and importance in the overall group context. Once members are reminded of what is expected of them, tension can decrease and the group can resume making progress.

Interpersonal Dimensions. In this part of the evaluation, the assessment focuses on the relationships that exist among the members while the task is being accomplished. If these relationships are strained, uncomfortable, or unpleasant, the productivity and results will be affected in negative ways. Four topics can be assessed here: *positive reinforcement, solidarity, cooperativeness*, and *respect toward others*.

As already noted, one of the most dangerous points in a meeting is reached when conflict shifts from tasks to personalities. Expressions such as "When you've been around here as long as I have, you can talk to me about it" do nothing to advance the group's work.

Individual Evaluation

Apart from examining the group as a whole, each individual participant may be evaluated. An **individual evaluation** determines how well members help the group accomplish its task and how well they perform their functions in the process. Samovar and King have created an excellent scheme for evaluating individual members as well as leaders.[19] The components that can be evaluated are as follows.

Each of the following eleven topics can be used to assess group participants: preparation, speaking, listening, open-mindedness, sensitivity to others, value of information, value of thinking, group orientation, value of procedural contributions, assistance in leadership function, and overall evaluation.

INDIVIDUAL EVALUATION

An evaluation of how competently individuals perform as members of a group.

There are eleven other topics that can be used to assess a definite or designated leader. These topics are opening the discussion, asking appropriate questions, offering reviews, clarifying ideas, encouraging critical evaluation, limiting irrelevancies, protecting minority viewpoints, remaining impartial, keeping accurate records, concluding discussion, and exerting overall leadership.

The Case of Lonnie Johnson

At the beginning of this chapter we encountered Lonnie Johnson, who is attempting to restart a dormant chapter of Amnesty International on his campus. Consider his task and the content of this chapter as you respond to the following questions.

• Which types of leadership are likely to work best for Lonnie? Why?

• How will an understanding of the components of group decision making (e.g., decision-making variables, time pressures, conflict) assist Lonnie in his task?

• In what ways might an understanding of the eight-step decision-making process help Lonnie?

• Will Lonnie be able to utilize committees, task forces, or boards in accomplishing his task?

• What will Lonnie need to know about the dimensions of group evaluation?

REVIEW

- Leadership is a vital part of competent group communication and can be defined as the exercise of interpersonal influence toward the attainment of goals.

- Several of the more common leadership styles that can be used in groups are authoritarian, consultative, participative, and laissez-faire.

- Shared leadership is important because group members who share in various leadership functions have a greater sense of ownership of the group process.

- Competent leadership should include credibility and the ability to inspire and motivate and to bring about desirable outcomes.

- Making decisions in groups is a complex process that involves cognitive, psychological, and social factors, as well as ethics.

- Decision making also involves a careful consideration of the values that individuals and the group hold. These values are the basis of the goals that are the ultimate driving force behind decision making.

- Time pressure is another consideration that must be factored into the decision-making process. Time can affect the amount of participation that can be allowed in a group, the ability to plan and coordinate, and the type of leadership required for a task.

- Groups must also be able to analyze problems effectively, develop a fruitful perspective on the problem, remain focused on the task, and be able to summarize group progress. Conflict management skills are also part of the decision-making process.

- An eight-step process allows a group to move from a state of ambiguity and uncertainty to confidence that the decision reached will produce the desired results. These steps are identifying the problem, conducting research, establishing guidelines and criteria, generating alternatives, evaluating alternatives, selecting the best alternative, and implementing and evaluating solutions.

- Finally, groups should evaluate their performance from a leadership and decision-making perspective. They must constantly evaluate their activities, output, process, and deliberations in order to ensure competence.

CHAPTER TWELVE

Communicating in Organizations

● BJECTIVES •••••••••••••••••••••••••••••••••••

After reading this chapter, you should be able to:

1. List some of the changes that have occurred in modern organizations over the last 20 years.

2. Describe the characteristics of an organizational culture.

3. Discuss the qualities of organizations as systems.

4. Describe the communication contexts in organizations.

5. Distinguish between formal and informal communication channels.

6. Explain the communication skills necessary for effective networking.

7. Recognize verbal and nonverbal behaviors that indicate sexual harassment and list the communication behaviors to deal with it.

8. Discuss the importance of negotiating and mentoring in organizations.

9. Evaluate your technological communication skills and list ways to improve them.

CHRISTOPHER HUNTER IS INTERNING in a Human Resources Department of a large bank. His boss recently returned from a business trip with a copy of TWA's *Ambassador Magazine*. It describes a 6-month training event that involved day-long seminars. "Team TWA" brought together representatives from every department—pilots, reservations agents, and ramp personnel. Employee facilitators used exercises to encourage brainstorming and to enable everyone to understand each job better. The ultimate goal of the training was to produce a renewed commitment to customer service. Christopher's boss is wondering if a similar kind of training might be worthwhile for the bank. As you read through the chapter, consider its relevance to this question. We will return to this scenario at the end of the chapter.

◆ Communication in Modern Organizations

Organizations are everywhere. Many students reading this book belong to religious organizations, political organizations, civic organizations, fraternal organizations, and business organizations. Organizations exist in order to bring people together for a common purpose so that their combined energies can be channeled into a greater good. The only way that organizations can succeed, or even exist for that matter, is through communication. Often referred to as *organizational communication*, this process involves the exchange of messages between organizational members or among members of different organizations. You will find instances of information processing, interpersonal communication, small group communication, and public speaking in most organizations. However, when these types of communication occur within a certain organizational context, different norms and rules apply than if the same communication occurred in a different context. Being a competent communicator requires that you take into consideration the organizational context.

In this chapter, you will learn about various aspects of organizational communication that will improve your chances of success. It is important for you to know about the culture of an organization and how it is structured because these aspects affect how you create and send messages. You will also become familiar with several of the most prevalent contexts in organizations, such as superior-subordinate relationships, interdepartmental relationships, and interorganizational relationships. In addition, you will learn how to use basic communication skills in the organization, including team building, networking, negotiating, and using channels and technology for greater success. However, before we discuss these issues, let's first take a look at some of the recent changes that have occurred in organizations.

Demands on Communication Today

Modern organizations make two basic demands on communication. The first demand is speed. Advances in technology allow employees in organizations to communicate more rapidly and with greater accuracy. Although employees still send an ample amount of correspondence via regular mail services, much organizational communication is accomplished via faster means.

Over the years, improved technology has made communication services more convenient and less expensive. Today, notebook computers with full capabilities weigh only a few pounds and are no larger than a clipboard. An employee can fold a cellular telephone into a shirt pocket. Fax machines are sold at practically every convenience store and shopping mall. A decade ago, the early laser printers cost more than $10,000; powerful modern models can now be purchased for less than $500.

Many of these services require a different kind of communication expertise. For example, electronic mail (e-mail) transmissions eliminate elements of nonverbal communication such as facial expressions and tone of voice,

Changing Technologies

Make a list of all the technologies you currently use—at home, school, work, or elsewhere. How different are these technologies from what you were using 5 or 10 years ago? How have these technologies changed the way you communicate? How have they changed the way others communicate with you?

that are important in face-to-face meetings. Sarcasm may be difficult to discern from sincerity. In many instances, speed requirements cause users to emphasize efficiency over effectiveness. A well thought out business letter, containing evidence or important details and using correct grammar, frequently gives way to a scribbled note suitable for faxing.

The second demand is for personal communication skills. As you know from Chapter 10, more and more organizations are introducing teamwork methods, which require employees to work together and produce joint output. Consequently, the need for strong interpersonal skills is increasing. Until recent years, most jobs in organizations were highly specialized and independent: A supervisor gave each worker a job to do and that person was responsible for its quality. Now, employees often work together to generate a product or service that belongs to no one individual. The communication skills required for teamwork include the ability to stay focused on issues; a knowledge of acceptable conversation topics and levels of self-disclosure; and flexibility and listening skills.

The use of feedback provides a good example of how important interpersonal skills have become. For years, managers have learned to give feedback that is specific, descriptive, timely, and easily understood by their employees. Today, *all* employees need these skills because in team environments, they must give feedback to each other as they perform their jobs.

Competent writing, speaking, and listening skills are in demand. Companies want employees who work well as team members and who have strong personal communication skills. Throughout this course, you have been learning how to become a competent communicator; this will be essential to your success in organizations.

What Has Happened in Organizations in the Last 20 Years?

The main reason that different types of communication skills are now required in organizations is that job requirements have changed dramatically. The company you will work for in just a few years will not be the same as it is today. Nor was it the same 20 years ago. Then, most jobs in the United States were in manufacturing. Our country was the largest and the most effective producer of consumer goods in the world, and we exported vast quantities of products to other nations. Since that time, the percentage of products and services we import from other countries has grown. Companies have also discovered that workers in low-skilled, low-technology jobs can be paid lower wages in other countries. In addition, advances in automation and computers have allowed American companies to increase output by more than 400 percent since 1947 while increasing the workforce only 17 percent.

Today, more than 78 percent of all jobs are in service industries. New jobs in industries such as health care, human services, insurance, and sales dominate the marketplace. These jobs require people to communicate regularly and accurately with one another. The 1990 U.S. Census occupational survey revealed that over a 10-year period, support occupations grew by 43 percent

What Skills Do You Look For?

What communication skills do you think are most important for clerks, receptionists, food workers, retail salespeople, and nurses? Working with your classmates, list the communication skills that you expect from people in these occupations? Do the skills vary from occupation to occupation? Are some communication skills necessary for workers in all organizations? When you encounter workers in these occupations, what percentage of them actually have the necessary skills? Which skills are strong? Which skills are often weak or lacking? How might the communication skills of these workers be improved?

and executive-managerial positions and sales jobs grew by 36 percent. Through 2005, the occupations with the fastest projected growth rates are clerks and receptionists, followed by food workers, retail salespeople, and nurses.[1] Note that all of these jobs require strong communication skills.

The composition of the workforce itself is changing and poses many communication challenges for modern employees. The number of workers 55 years of age and older will increase 38 percent between 1995 and 2005.[2] Companies are evolving from employing primarily white, Anglo-Saxon males who are younger than 50 to employing men and women of all ages from diverse ethnic backgrounds. This diversity, however, is not occurring at all levels. For example, while the number of women and minorities on the job today has increased dramatically, only 10.6 percent of all executive, managerial, and administrative positions are held by blacks and Hispanics.[3] While women account for 37 percent of the workforce,[4] they hold only 6.2 percent of director-type positions on corporate boards for American companies.[5] Another change is that organizations today fill many jobs with part-time employees. Because the cost of benefits increased more than 30 percent in just 5 years in the early 1990s, companies often avoid paying benefits altogether by filling jobs with part-time and contract workers.[6]

In many organizations today, employees receive benefits in addition to a salary, which help establish employee loyalty to the company. Numerous organizations offer on-premise day-care centers, workout facilities, and professional development opportunities. Companies want loyal employees because the organization saves money in training costs, company stability increases, and loyal employees speak well of the company, thus aiding public relations. This two-way street between loyalty and benefits has a significant impact on the communication in an organization. While many companies lay off employees with years of service or force them to take early retirement, other companies try to make the workplace an exciting and beneficial place for employees to work.

Food workers are among the labor groups with the fastest projected growth in our country through the year 2005.

Among medium and large-sized U.S. companies, 79 percent provide counseling services for employees with difficulties such as drugs, alcohol, family or marital problems, legal problems, care of elderly relatives, or AIDS.[7] Many employees also attend seminars and take advantage of other company "perks" to further their personal and professional development. Some employees perceive these benefits as marketing opportunities and make plans to leave the organization for a different job. However, only one-third of executives who take new jobs report they are still satisfied with them 2 years later. This evidence indicates that both companies and employees need to communicate their worth to each other, or face the expenses associated with employees leaving the organization.

In the last 10 years, mergers, acquisitions, and takeovers have radically altered the face of the workplace. Companies discovered that one way to increase revenue and profits was to diversify their products and services into nontraditional areas. Carbonated soft-drink companies began to bottle teas and juices; telephone companies began to make computers and to sponsor VISA and MasterCard for consumers. Indeed, all three major U.S. television networks are now owned by organizations whose traditional business is not television: The Disney Corporation bought ABC; Westinghouse purchased CBS; and General Electric owns NBC.

In the future, owners of companies will change, products and services will be transformed, organizations will hire and fire many different people, and the composition of the workforce will become more diverse. You may not be able to control these changes, but if you are a competent communicator, you will be able to adapt to them.

> ### Cultural Diversity in the Workforce ✔
>
> Consider the following example of cultural diversity in the workplace. Universal Industries is a supplier of light electronic equipment in a large city in the southwest. Leeva Wao, a 42-year-old Japanese woman, serves as director of personnel. Leeva's employees include managers Henry Tento, a 44-year-old white male who has been with Universal for 20 years; Mena Galon, a young Latino woman who was promoted at Universal last year; and George Allen, an African-American male who came to Universal from a competitor. Leeva's assistant is Luana Battinni, an Italian woman of 39. Luana uses a motorized wheelchair due to a degenerative nerve disease. The department also has a coordinator of benefits whose name is Yang Lin, a 62-year-old woman who emigrated from China in the late seventies.
>
> The diversity of Universal's Personnel Department is typical of today's workforce. Consequently, intercultural communication is a major issue within business organizations. Recall from earlier chapters some of the problems and benefits of intercultural communication. What barriers to communication (e.g., ethnocentrism, stereotyping) might arise among the employees in Universal's Personnel Department? How might Leeva Wao, as the director, help to break down these barriers? Will the employees from low-context cultures have problems communicating with their co-workers from high-context cultures? Why? What are some benefits of a multicultural Personnel Department, both for Universal Industries and for the individual employees?

◆ Looking at the Big Picture

Becoming a competent communicator in the organizational setting requires that you understand how other people in this context send messages. Depending on the size of the organization, literally hundreds of messages are sent and received in any given day. The messages that you send could be lost, ignored, or neglected if you do not have a sense of how the overall organization communicates. Therefore, seeing the big picture is essential for communication success. Two important viewpoints provide this type of understanding. In the following sections, you will learn how the culture of the organization affects communication and how applying systems theory to your organization facilitates effective communication.

The Organizational Culture

ORGANIZATIONAL CULTURE

Members' relatively stable perceptions of their organization and its norms and behaviors.

Organizational culture develops when members have relatively stable perceptions of their organization.[8] This culture emerges over time, in much the same way as the cultures of nations or ethnic groups develop. As you know, competent communication requires you to understand both the culture and the context in which you are communicating. As with other types of cultures, an organizational culture provides guidance about appropriate norms and behaviors.

In any organization, certain communication behaviors are either encouraged or discouraged. For example, some organizations develop an open culture, in which people are encouraged to question things and suggest change. Other organizations discourage communication and do not elicit new ideas. Some individuals may feel more comfortable in "closed" organizations; they come to work, do their individual jobs, and then return to their own personal lives. Other people prefer family-type organizations, in which personal and work life are closely tied together.[9] (The characteristic of openness is discussed again in the next section.)

An organization usually develops customs and rituals that contribute to its organizational culture. For example, employee award ceremonies may reinforce the values of hard work and creativity. In many companies, "dress-down Friday" allows the suit-and-tie crowd to be more casual and is often accompanied by more in-house communication, including joking and teasing. Other organizations, however, would never allow a dress-down day; their customs include a commitment to formal dress—and probably clear boundaries on many other types of communication.

Organizational culture also includes the degree to which an organization tolerates risk. Some companies reward the employee who goes out on a limb to test a new idea; others are conservative, preferring clear guidelines and policies to govern their members. An organization's tolerance for conflict is another indication of its culture. Some organizations see conflict as healthy and as part of a growth process, while others try to avoid conflict at all costs and at all levels of the organization.

Although an organizational culture develops over time, once it is formed it remains fairly constant. New members are usually assimilated into the culture, learning its values, goals, customs, and behaviors. In some organizations, however, subcultures develop, with clear—and different—views of their own. Subcultures may contest the views of the organizational culture by not cooperating with policies and procedures, not consulting with authorities, and not participating in the customs of the organization. Obviously, such actions cause conflict and division in the organization.[10] Some experts argue that certainty about an organizational culture is unlikely in today's society and that constant communication is necessary if an organization is to be effective.

They believe that there is a greater tolerance for diversity in modern organizations, and that their constant communication efforts are actually a reflection of their significant commitment to tolerate differences.[11]

Within an organizational culture, then, many communication challenges exist. Organizations involved in international business have even more challenges. Not only do they try to improve communication within their own organization, but they are likely to have to accommodate both national cultures and many different organizational cultures.

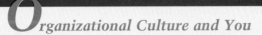

Organizational Culture and You

Discover the culture of your current workplace—or research an organization you'd like to work for. What are the customs and rituals of the organization? What is its tolerance level for conflict and risk? Is the organizational culture open or closed? What affects these aspects of the organizational culture? The area of the country it is in? The ethnic mix in the organization? Its product or service? Other factors? Compare the organizational cultures you chose to those described by others in your class. Use these descriptions to determine which types of organizations you would be most comfortable working in.

Organizations as Systems

Understanding how communication actually works in organizations is not an easy process, but viewing organizations as systems is helpful. When you study biological systems (plants, animals, etc.) you come to understand how particular plants or animals exist within larger systems and how they are affected by the environment (food, water, temperature) and other organisms. Organizations as systems are similar; they are seldom closed, that is, completely independent. Modern organizations must interact with the economy and with politics at national as well as international levels. Even small local changes may affect the organization in profound ways.

SYSTEM

A unique whole consisting of members who have relationships with one another in a particular environment.

A **system** is a unique whole that consists of the *members* who have *relationships* with one another in a particular *environment*.[12] In organizations, this means that no person can work in isolation, that no company can insulate itself from the interactions of its members, and that outside forces can change the communication processes of organizations. Examine Figure 12.1. Notice that the system is a college or university—a system you are familiar with. Some of its members shown here are faculty, students, office staff, financial aid, and the bursar, all of whom have relationships with one another. The college exists within its environment, which includes other systems that have a direct impact on it. These other systems in our example are the city and state where the college is located; the legislature, which affects tuition; part-time employers for students and positions for graduates; families who support students; and high schools that supply students. What other systems affect the college or university you attend?

There is more to systems than just members, relationships, and the environment. In order to understand organizations as systems it is important to learn about their underlying qualities or characteristics. These include *wholeness, interdependence, hierarchy, openness, adaptability, and equifinality.*[13]

WHOLENESS

A system characteristic that refers to its unique configuration; a system remains "whole" despite individual or departmental changes.

Wholeness is a characteristic that refers to a system's unique configuration. Thus, an organization is not just a collection of departments or individuals;

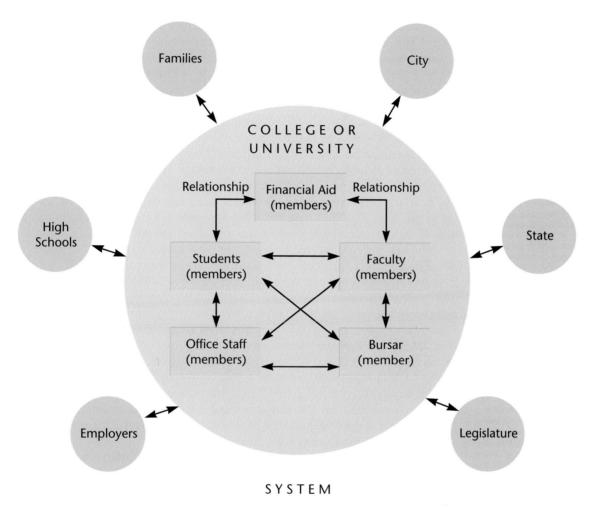

FIGURE 12.1
A college system within its larger environment.

these entities fit together in a way that makes the organization special. An organization can also be adjusted, realigned, or reconfigured and still maintain its wholeness. Departmental reorganizations or administrative shifts, for example, do not threaten the wholeness of an organization. Suppose that you work at a place we'll call Best Bank. The bank has several departments, such as loan processing, accounting, auditing, new accounts, and public relations, which collectively make up the organization. If the bank decides to separate the new accounts department into "checking accounts" and "savings accounts," the wholeness of the organization will still be intact.

As you recall from Chapter 10, *interdependence* is an important characteristic affecting group communication. Interdependence is just as important in a system. In a business organization, any hiring, firing, loss, or acquisition affects the entire system. For instance, the change in the new accounts department at Best Bank would cause changes in other departments: Auditing might set up a new bookkeeping system; administration may hire new employees; and the public relations department might devise a new advertising campaign to announce the change.

Reflecting the natural order of organisms in the world, organizations have hierarchies. A **hierarchy** is the classification of a group of people according to ability, status, function, or other criteria. Thus, individuals in a system can be identified as being related to other individuals that are above them, below them, or on the same level of hierarchy as they are. At Best Bank, for example, new account representatives work together in their department and are all on the same level of hierarchy. They report to the vice president in charge of accounts, who is above them in the organization's hierarchy.

Another important characteristic of systems is **openness**. In order to avoid becoming a "closed" system, in which the organization will collapse in on itself, a system must maintain openness by correcting any imbalances. The organization does this by using feedback to identify areas of imbalance and correcting tendencies to "topple." For example, for many years, the railroad industry was a closed system. Few new ideas flowed into the organization. Members defined themselves as being in the "railroad business," perceiving themselves to be the only game in town. When other means of transporting people and goods in a less costly and more efficient manner became available (trucks, airlines, etc.), the railroad industry went bankrupt. However, once railroad companies opened up their system to new ideas and designed new ways of generating business, their members began to redefine themselves as being in the "transportation business."

The Chrysler Corporation is another example of a failed closed system. Initially, Chrysler manufactured only large luxury cars. They were a closed system intent on doing the same thing they always did—make large cars. When gasoline prices increased to $1.00 a gallon, they still refused to make smaller, more fuel-efficient cars. Consumers began to look elsewhere to find cars that drank less gas. As a result, Chrysler went bankrupt. The "new" Chrysler Corporation is much more open to consumer needs and is a very successful open system.

The modern organization is a dynamic, changing system. In fact, change is probably the only constant of organizations. For this reason, *adaptability* is an indispensable quality; it enables a system to adjust to changes in politics, economics, individuals, or ideas. Best Bank may have divided its new accounts department because the local economy improved, producing an increase in savings accounts. Or it may have reorganized because its customers wanted two divisions, or because an employee suggested it as a more efficient way to handle accounts. Whatever the reason, Best Bank was adaptable enough to make the change.

HIERARCHY

In a system, the classification of a group of people according to ability, status, function, or other criteria.

OPENNESS

A system characteristic that refers to a system's ability to correct itself.

The final goals, or end-states, of an organization may be accomplished in any number of ways. In other words, a system is capable of generating multiple ideas and multiple behaviors for attaining its results. This characteristic is known as **equifinality**. Let's look at our example again. Best Bank is responsible for producing a profit and ensuring the security of depositors' funds. The loan processing department provides loans, the collections department receives loan payments, tellers take deposits and cash checks. Although these are multiple behaviors and are accomplished in a variety of ways, they all contribute to the final goals of the organization.

EQUIFINALITY
In a system, the characteristic that final goals may be reached in a variety of ways.

◆ Communication Contexts in Organizations

Earlier in this chapter we discussed the idea that the organizational culture provides guidance for appropriate communicative behavior. So, also, does the *context* of an interaction. Within an organization, communication is evaluated in terms of the relationships that develop at the workplace. As you know from earlier chapters, in order to become a competent communicator, you need to consider the relational contexts of your interactions. The following sections describe some of the different communication contexts that exist in organizations.

Superior-Subordinate Relationships

Communication between managers and employees still constitutes most of the work-related conversation in organizations. Even though teams are now commonplace, thus increasing the amount of employee-to-employee communication, the boss and employee still must communicate about many issues, such as the status of tasks or projects, grievances, morale, influences from other departments on a department's work, and annual performance reviews.

Interestingly, the setting, or context, in which a manager meets with an employee is critical to the communication process, the satisfaction of both participants, and the results. You are well aware of the fact that a manager and employee bring expectations and goals to a meeting and that these affect what will be said during the course of the meeting. If a manager wants to ensure that a meeting with an employee has every chance to succeed, he or she should follow these guidelines.

- Schedule adequate time for the meeting.
- Minimize distractions or interruptions, including phone calls or visitors.
- Approach the meeting with an open mind and communicate that to the employee by asking more questions and making fewer demands.
- Communicate sincerity about your desire to meet with the employee.
- Exhibit active listening skills, including nonverbal behaviors such as nodding, postural shifts, and appropriate facial expressions.

If you are the subordinate in this dyadic relationship, you can also use your communication skills to influence a positive outcome.

- Ask for a meeting time or place that will allow you to achieve your goals.

- Clarify your goals and your performance in your own mind before the meeting, so that you can represent yourself adequately to your supervisor.

- Make reasonable requests for training, advice, or resources that will enhance your performance or satisfaction.

- Exhibit active listening skills (verbal and nonverbal) to communicate your understanding of information or suggestions for improvement.

- State your commitment to the department or the organization.

Team Building and Team Leading

THEORY Z

A team management approach in which both managers and their employees participate in decision making.

Over the past years, organizations have changed from the "skilled leader" approach (Theory X) to the "skilled people" approach (Theory Y)[14] to the team management approach, known as **Theory Z**.[15] This approach requires that both the manager and the other members of the organizational group participate in management decision making—that they build teams together.

Building teams involves many of the small-group communication skills which were discussed in Chapter 10. An effective manager will build an energetic work group that produces high quality results. The group members will enjoy both their common goals and the interaction among themselves. In short, an effective team builds strong relationships while still getting the work done.

An effective manager will determine when and if team building needs to occur.[16] If a group's function can be performed better individually, if there is a history of poor relationships that would make team building difficult, or if the larger organization does not support such an approach, the manager may decide against team building.

But teams consistently outperform individuals in organizations today, so the effective manager is often a good team leader. This team leader acts as a coach, providing the vision for the team, giving it structure and organization, and helping it to remain focused. The effective coach links team efforts to those of the overall organization, so that team members understand the importance of their work within the organizational structure. The effective coach also enhances the relationships of the team members, facilitating the development of trust and supportiveness. Finally, the effective coach helps others on the team develop leadership skills themselves, thus enhancing their confidence and productivity.

When a group works exceptionally well together, it may become a self-managing team. In such a case, the manager becomes the coach "on the sidelines," providing supporting ideas and comments for the team. Regardless of the manager's particular role on the team, the effective manager needs small-group communication skills to build a highly effective, productive group.

The team management approach requires that both the manager and other members of the organizational unit participate in management decision making.

Interdepartmental and Interorganizational Relationships

Cooperation between departments is a must in modern organizations. Marketing departments must work with the sales force in order to produce proper advertising materials for the marketplace. Office Services must store and obtain sufficient computer supplies so that other departments can generate documents, correspondence, manuals, and so forth. Personnel departments must recruit the best candidates for job openings so that work in other departments may be performed properly. A company's mail room is also critical to its success. If documents and correspondence are not distributed properly and efficiently, employees may not be able to do their jobs.

Within an organization, the greatest communication issues often involve negotiating responsibility between two departments. Which department oversees what function? Which department head has the final say for approval? Is it appropriate to cross traditional departmental lines in order to accomplish work? Departments need adequate answers to such questions if they are to function effectively within the larger system.

Let us now look at the relationships between organizations. An organization uses many other organizations to conduct business. These include printers, couriers, electrical technicians, advertising agencies, groundskeepers, software developers, travel agencies, and training consultants. With today's emphasis on quality and customer service, many organizations know that in order to make money, they must take an increasing interest in the work and prosperity of the companies they serve. To accomplish this, frequent and accurate communication between organizations is essential.

No longer is it adequate for companies to offer only the "lowest price" or the "best service." They also must compete for long-term relationships with their customers who are always interested in doing business more efficiently. Communicating honest expectations and providing candid feedback are two of the most important skills in fostering these relationships. In many cases, the partnerships that organizations form between themselves make it difficult to determine which one is in fact the customer. Not too long ago, in a stunning role reversal, two advertising agencies actually fired organizations that were their clients because they no longer wished to represent those companies!

◆ Communication Skills in Organizations

In this section, you will learn how to master several communication skills that are critical for your professional success. As you have learned throughout this book, there are various channels through which to communicate. In organizations, these channels may involve many people who are superior or subordinate to you in rank and position. Thus, understanding how to handle these channels is very important. You will also learn how to use networks to your advantage. Other important communication skills to be discussed include dealing with the potential of sexual harassment, negotiating, mentoring, and using new technology.

Using Communication Channels Properly

You already know from Chapter 2 that a channel is a vehicle or mechanism for transmitting messages. In organizations, there are many such vehicles, including telephones, memos, letters, e-mail transmissions, and face-to-face conversations. We can also speak of two broad types of organizational channels: formal and informal.

FORMAL CHANNELS

The communication paths established along the hierarchical lines of an organization.

Formal channels are the communication paths established along the hierarchical lines of an organization. These paths typically come from the organizational chart of the company and involve such issues as status, authority, and power (See Figure 12.2). For example, many companies would consider a funding request memo from a sales representative to a regional vice president quite inappropriate unless the request had first received approval from a mid-level division or district sales manager. Formal communication channels also would not allow a chief executive officer to receive suggestions from entry-level employees unless the messages had first been screened by mid- and upper-level managers. As you might suspect, when you use formal communication channels, you should use formal communication methods. Thus, you would use written documentation, such as memos and letters, much more often than face-to-face conversation. In some companies, when employees write a formal memo or letter, both the sender's boss and the recipient's immediate boss must receive a copy.

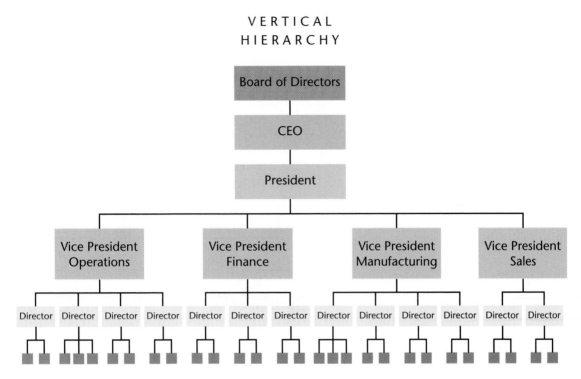

VERTICAL
HIERARCHY

FIGURE 12.2

A vertical hierarchy such as this one requires a lot of upward and downward communication along formal channels.

Informal channels refer to the "grapevine" as well as to unauthorized communication between two or more persons in an organization (See Figure 12.3 on p. 372). The grapevine is another term for "rumor mill," which is an ambiguous but accurate description in most organizations. Frequently, large numbers of employees are aware of personnel, policy, or procedural changes long before they ever appear in a memo or are announced at a meeting. Even when policies and formal lines of communication are supposed to prevent the transmission of information, those individuals who have friendships with key communicators frequently "leak" even the most confidential of information.

The key to using communication channels properly in an organization is to know what is expected. What are the norms for the organization? If formality is the rule, be clear and succinct. Be sure that the right people receive copies of your correspondence and other documents. If informality is the rule, be visible. Become known, increase your popularity, get out of your office, and get to know other people. Hang around the break room when you know key employees will be there. Stay on top of who is promoted to what job, who works for whom, and who is moving to what position in the company. Know

INFORMAL CHANNELS
The unauthorized communication paths in an organization; the "grapevine."

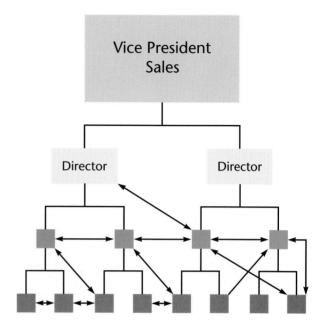

FIGURE 12.3
Informal channels allow messages to move across departments and hierarchical lines.

when and where to discuss nonwork topics such as who is getting married, who is dating whom, or what kind of car someone bought. The more you are a resource for others, the more you will be a recipient of informal news as well.

Using Communication Networks Effectively

As you recall from Chapter 10, networks are the communication patterns used within groups. In other words, networks are "who talks to whom about what" in an organization. The more "connected" an individual is to the participants in an organizational network, the more centralized he or she is. A **centralized network** is one in which a majority of the communication passes through a small number of participants, maybe even just through one person. Conversely, a **decentralized network** is one in which many participants have a number of connections to others. An example of a centralized network would be where employees in a unit interact less among themselves than with their boss, such as outside sales representatives who have most of their organizational communication with the sales manager. An example of a decentralized network would be a fast-food restaurant where employees must interact with several other employees in order to serve food products. The diagrams in Figure 12.4 illustrate the differences between these two types of network.

Research indicates that there are many advantages to being in a centralized position in a network. In general, there seem to be apparent advantages to cultivating frequent and meaningful relationships with others. Centralized persons are more likely to emerge as leaders,[17] report higher satisfaction with their tasks, have higher morale,[18] experience less job tedium and burnout,[19] and hold more favorable perceptions of their organization.[20]

CENTRALIZED NETWORK
A type of network in which a majority of the communication passes through a small number of participants.

DECENTRALIZED NETWORK
A type of network in which many participants have a number of connections to others.

Today, **networking** also refers to communicating with others outside a single organization. Defined as "simply people meeting people and profiting from the connection,"[21] networking refers to activities such as striking up conversations and exchanging business cards during airplane travel, prior to professional meetings, in churches, or in restaurant waiting areas. The key is to have people remember who you are and what services you offer.

Several skills are important for successful networking, whether this is accomplished within or outside of an organization. First, remember and use names. Associate the name with a person or object so that you may recall it easily. Second, be clever about how you describe yourself and what you do. Simply saying "I train sales managers" is not nearly as inviting as "I help companies put money in their pockets." Third, keep an eye out to help others. You never know when someone may return the favor to you. Fourth, try to get a follow-up meeting or conversation scheduled soon. Strike when the iron is hot! To call someone and say "I met you 3 months ago at a reception" does not pull nearly the same weight as "I spoke with you last night at the party." Fifth, and most important, remember that the time to build network connections is when you need them the least. Join trade associations or nonprofit organizations, go to lunch with colleagues outside your department, and attend social functions both inside and outside your typical circle of friends. If you establish these connections in advance, looking for a job or a favor will be much easier than "looking" and "building" at the same time.

> **NETWORKING**
> *Communicating with other people in order to benefit from the connection.*

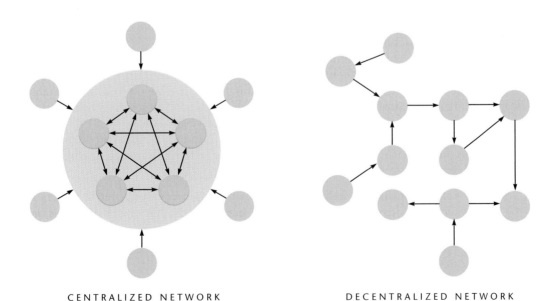

CENTRALIZED NETWORK   DECENTRALIZED NETWORK

FIGURE 12.4
Notice how centralized networks connect more people than do decentralized networks.

Responding to Sexual Harassment

SEXUAL HARASSMENT
Unwelcome sexual advances or overtures and requests for sexual favors.

Although sexual harassment appears to be a recent problem in organizations, it has actually been around a long time.[22] The Equal Employment Opportunity Commission defines **sexual harassment** as unwelcome sexual advances and requests for sexual favors. Sexual harassment is also characterized as verbal or physical conduct of a sexual nature if submission to the conduct is made a condition of employment or if the conduct creates an uncomfortable, intimidating, hostile, or offensive working environment.[23] In other words, sexual harassment is unwelcome and unsolicited behavior of a sexual nature.

Why does sexual harassment occur? Attraction is one reason. One person may become so attracted to another that status and authority are abused in order to obtain sexual satisfaction. A second cause of sexual harassment is power, which can be used to control or dominate the behavior of another. A harasser may think that he or she can wield power over another until sexual favors are delivered.

Communication is another cause of sexual harassment. You have already learned that men and women communicate differently. Females are more likely to self-disclose personal information, and some men might view such disclosures as flirting or sexual advancement. Differences in the sending and receiving of nonverbal cues can also set the stage for sexual harassment. Females often use smiles, eye contact, and touch to indicate interest in a topic or person, whereas men may use these same nonverbal behaviors as openings for sexual intimacy.[24] Some verbal and nonverbal behaviors that indicate sexual harassment are: sexist remarks, embarrassing jokes, taunting, unwelcome remarks, displaying pornographic or offensive materials or photographs, touching affectionately, and kissing.

Sexual harassment often goes unreported because there is a tendency for the victim to avoid confrontation with the perpetrator. In many instances, the victim withdraws from the situation by taking time off from work, transferring to another area, or changing jobs. Often, the victim is reluctant to press charges because the harasser has authority and status.

Sexual harassment is a degrading and dehumanizing act. You do not have to put up with it. If you think you are being sexually harassed at work, consider the following plan of action:

- If you think the behavior of another person is wrong, let that person know. Clearly and firmly tell the harasser that his or her advances are not welcome.

- Immediately report the incident to your boss or to someone in the personnel department.

- Document each incident in written form; include a description of the incident, the date, the person(s) involved, and any action you took.

- If witnesses were present, have them verify the details of the incident.

*E*thics and Sexual Harassment

Defining and identifying sexual harassment can be a problem for organizations and individuals. When do you think behavior is harassment? Is it ethical to report harassment to a supervisor without first confronting the perpetrator? Is it ethical to intervene if you are not directly involved in an incident but only witness it? If your problem concerning sexual harassment were left unresolved by your immediate supervisor, what would you do?

Negotiating

Many people think that negotiating only occurs between employees of two organizations, who must meet and mutually agree upon a price, a date, a deadline, a location, a product, or some other factor. While negotiating is involved in all of these examples, negotiating is an internal communication issue as well.

Employees regularly negotiate with their supervisors as well as with each other. Some issues that are commonly negotiated are working hours ("I want to work 9 to 6 instead of 8 to 5 because of my children"); weekend work ("I'll work on Saturday if I can have next Thursday and Friday off"); pay ("You're not worth that much money"); trading-off responsibilities ("I'll do your report if you teach my class"); vacation time ("We'll pay for your hotel room if you switch your vacation days"); or equipment ("I need my own color printer at my desk").

Negotiating in organizations involves many of the communication behaviors we have discussed in earlier chapters. Most training programs urge participants to focus on issues and to separate the problem from the person, but the negotiating process is, in fact, usually much more complicated than that. We have found that these five communication behaviors are essential to successful negotiating:

- You must listen. You must know and understand the other party's position before you can argue your own successfully.

- You must be introspective. One of the fastest ways to shut off bargaining is to speak for your partner instead of speaking for yourself.

- You must ask fact-finding questions. Try to uncover the basic who, what, when, where, and why of the other party's position or premise.

- You must communicate with an open mind. If you take a defensive, hard-line position, you will close off communication with the other party.

- You must keep your emotions in check. Rational negotiating does not need or require anger, hurt feelings, crying, or abrupt withdrawal from the situation. For specific tips on bargaining, see Chapter 8.

One major issue that many people misunderstand is the role of compromise in negotiating. While compromise is often the outcome of a negotiating session, you should not make it your objective. If your position is realistic and sound, you should argue for it and not back away until you are persuaded to do so. While many negotiators ask for more in the hope of settling for less, we do not recommend this approach. We even know of some cases in which one party set such a lofty, unrealistic goal as an outcome that the other side refused to bargain at all and cut a deal with a different group.

One alternative to compromise, however, is to brainstorm for alternate solutions that please both parties. For example, if you normally work Saturday and Sunday and want the weekend off, you might start out the bargaining session by arguing for a weekend off, validating your position with your work performance and lack of absences. During the negotiations, your supervisor suggests a compromise and offers you Saturday as a day off. If you compromise, you take Saturday off and work Sunday. If you continue to argue for the whole weekend off, you may be perceived as defensive and inflexible. However, you could suggest alternate solutions that would please both you and your supervisor, such as having a co-worker fill in for you over the weekend, or adding work hours to your other days during the week. Suggesting alternate solutions is often an effective negotiating strategy.

Mentoring

MENTOR

An experienced organization member who serves as a role model for a less experienced employee.

You are already familiar with the term *mentor*. A **mentor** is a member of the organization who is often older, experienced, and respected and who serves as a role model for a less experienced employee (protégé). Mentor-protégé relationships are beneficial to an organization because protégés can develop faster when they learn from someone who has "been there" before. The protégé benefits from this relationship by receiving support, recognition, and friendship from the mentor and through the mentor's influence with other powerful people in the organization. Mentors benefit by demonstrating that they are valuable to the organization and to new employees.

The mentor-protégé relationship depends on a mutual understanding of the roles and characteristics of the people involved. Mentors have knowledge and skills to offer, but protégés must be willing participants. For this relationship to work effectively, a mentor must be approachable, confident, and secure. A protégé must be ambitious, loyal, energetic, and open-minded.

Mentoring Stages. The mentoring relationship will usually progress through four distinct stages. These stages include initiation, cultivation, separation, and redefinition. In the *initiation* stage, the mentor and protégé begin to learn about each other. The mentor shows support by counseling and coaching. The protégé contributes to the relationship by being open to suggestions and by demonstrating loyalty to the mentor.

In the next stage, *cultivation*, the mentor and protégé begin to form an interpersonal bond. The mentor begins to protect and promote the protégé, and mutual admiration increases. Once a protégé has developed in the organization to a point where the relationship is not as important, the stage of *separation* usually begins. In this stage, the mentor and protégé drift apart, either physically or emotionally. Several factors can cause separation, but usually one of the members is transferred or promoted, or the protégé becomes increasingly independent of the mentor.

If the mentoring relationship was successful, the mentor and protégé go through a *redefinition* of their roles and the relationship. The mentor may still provide advice and expertise, but now both people see the relationship as one of equal partners, where each holds a similar position within the organization.

Finding a Mentor. If you are working in an organization and want to find an appropriate mentor, the following steps should be useful:

- Ask the Personnel or Human Resources Department about formal mentoring programs. If the organization does not have a formal program, ask your peers about previous mentor-protégé relationships or for the names of possible mentors.

- Identify people who have already followed the same career track that you are on, and determine if they would be good mentors.

- Approach someone you consider to be a good candidate for a mentor and take an interest in what that person does. Ask questions and demonstrate your enthusiasm to learn. Disclose information about yourself and your interests, and ask them for expert advice to improve your productivity.

- Build rapport with someone whom you think would be an effective mentor. Ask if he or she would like to sponsor you in a mentor-protégé relationship. Explain to the person why you think he or she would be a good mentor, and describe your qualifications as a protégé.[25]

Mastering Communication Technology

In the past 10 years, technology has advanced more rapidly than at any other time in history. These changes in technology are moving organizations in new and exciting directions. In the future, communication technology will allow you, at any time, to send and receive information from anywhere in the world. You will no longer be confined to an office as a place of work. You will use video telephones, choose from five hundred television stations, and use a video screen to read books from libraries around the world.

However, while technology has immeasurable benefits, it presents many challenges for the business communicator. These challenges come from two areas. The first challenge is to understand the rapid advancement and implementation of technologies in your organization. The second challenge is to learn to use the available technology to maximize and enhance your communication skills. This section covers some of the technology tools that will facilitate both oral and written communication.

Pagers. Pagers are simply another article of clothing for many people in business. Estimates indicate that over 31 million people carry pagers. It is quite likely that you will carry some type of pager in the future. Before, a pager was used to emit a beeping sound to alert its user to call a centralized location for a message. Now, pagers beep or vibrate to alert their users that information has been sent. For example, most pagers display telephone numbers and verbal messages that were sent from someone else.

Pagers come in a variety of shapes and sizes. There is a fountain-pen shaped unit that fits neatly in a shirt pocket and a pager in the form of a wrist watch. Some pagers hold dozens of messages; store business information like the Dow Jones industrial average; and save critical information, like the most recent weather report and winning lottery numbers.[26] Voice pagers and pagers the size of credit cards that fit into personal computers (and act like cellular modems) are coming on the market.

Telephones. Telephones are not what they used to be. Changing technology has created many new ways to use the telephone as a communication device. You are already familiar with call waiting and caller ID. The next generation of phones will sport display screens, hideaway keyboards, and magnetic card swipes. Some phones are able to act as pagers and computers; even portable phones are now capable of serving as personal computers, and Dick Tracy's wristwatch phone is now a reality.

Since you have probably been using a phone for most of your life, you may wonder why you need guidance on using the phone in organizations. Using the phone in business can be a frustrating experience if you are not knowledgeable. If you follow these steps, they will enhance your effectiveness as a communicator.

1. *Using voice mail* Many businesses have discovered that voice mail is an inexpensive and convenient way to handle messages when employees are unable to take calls. When you hear a recorded voice indicating that you can leave a message in a "mailbox," remember to state your name, position, your organization's name, the date and time you called, a brief message, your telephone number, and when you can be reached. Some people receive hundreds of voice mail messages each week; try to be succinct so that your message will receive the attention it deserves.

2. *When to call* The best time to reach people is just before lunch and just before 5:00 P.M. Many people are in their offices at those times. Remember to be sensitive of time zones.

3. *Telephone tag* Leaving messages helps to reduce telephone tag or that annoying process of people calling back and forth without reaching the desired party. When you leave messages, indicate when and where you will be and make sure you are at that number when you say you will be there.

Videoconferencing and teleconferencing can allow participants in multiple locations to meet while avoiding travel time and expenses.

Teleconferencing. When participants are unable to meet in one location, **teleconferencing** is a popular technique for conducting meetings. Teleconferencing uses telephones to link people who are in remote locations. By using speaker phones, several people in one location can speak and listen to their colleagues, who are doing the same thing at different sites. Teleconferencing is an attractive alternative to centralized meetings since both travel time and costs can be significantly reduced.

Teleconferences are most successful when certain steps are followed.[27]

1. *Before the teleconference*
   - Identify the purpose of the teleconference meeting. Let people know why you think it is necessary to hold the teleconference.
   - Identify the person who will chair the teleconference. The chair is responsible for the agenda, leading the discussion, summarizing information, and preparing the minutes of the meeting.
   - Schedule the teleconference. After you obtain desirable times from each participant, select a time that fits in with each person's schedule and confirm that time with the participants.
   - Send an agenda and resource materials to participants. Your counterparts will be better prepared for the discussion if they are given materials to review ahead of time, ideally 3 to 4 days prior to the meeting.

TELECONFERENCING
The use of telephones to link participants, so that they can speak and conduct meetings without all being at one location.

2. *During the teleconference*
   - Start on time. Teleconferences are expensive and participants' busy schedules are best accommodated with meetings that start on time.
   - Ask participants to identify themselves when they speak for the first time. It is distracting to hear someone talk without knowing who the person is. Participants then spend time trying to figure out who is talking rather than listening to what that person is saying.
   - Encourage succinct remarks. A teleconference is no place for speeches or diatribes. Ask participants to keep their remarks brief.

3. *After the teleconference*
   - Prepare and distribute minutes of the teleconference. The minutes should include a summary of the discussion, a description of any overall consensus, and a section entitled "actions agreed upon."

E-Mail. Electronic mail or e-mail is becoming a common form of personal and professional communication. E-mail is cheaper than a telephone call and faster than the postal service and, therefore, serves an important communication function when time and money are an issue. Essentially, e-mail is person-to-person communication using computers and phone lines. The Electronic Mail Association estimates that between 30 and 50 million people use e-mail and that the number is growing at more than 25 percent per year. In the United States, businesses maintain some 28 million electronic mailboxes. Every month, at Hewlett-Packard alone, 97,000 employees exchange 20 million e-mail messages in-house and 70 thousand more outside the company.

One reason that e-mail systems are so popular is that you can send memos to several colleagues at once. In addition, when you use e-mail, a record is made of the time you send your communication and the time it is received. Thus, no one can falsely accuse you of failing to send information.

You can improve your e-mail style by understanding some of the important factors regarding e-mail etiquette and politics.[28]

1. Don't flame. (A *flame* is an inflammatory remark that contains insensitive language or impetuous negative responses.)
2. Respect e-mail confidentiality.
3. Make your messages as brief as possible.
4. Eliminate sexist language from your e-mail, including masculine pronouns and gender-specific titles.
5. Be culturally aware for both U.S. and international e-mail.
6. Avoid using all capital letters or all small letters.
7. Know when not to use e-mail. If the message is very important, controversial, or confidential, consider sending a letter, using the telephone, or having a face-to-face meeting.
8. Use the SUBJECT line precisely so that it gives the reader the exact intent of your message.
9. Avoid sending copies of your message to people who do not want it.

Ethics and the New Technologies

Do the new technologies pose any ethical problems in organizations (e.g., e-mail privacy)? How might the new technologies eliminate some ethical problems?

Internet. With over 30 million users, the Internet is the largest computer network in the world. It is expected that 100 million people will be using the Internet by the year 2000. Often referred to as the "information superhighway," the Internet provides users with a vast array of options for accessing information, news, and data; it is the largest information resource in the world. According to the Internet Society, 50 percent of the Fortune 500 is on the Internet, and two-thirds of the Internet's users work for major corporations. By now, you have probably either been on the Internet or have seen a demonstration of how it works. The Internet is not just a technological fad. Because it provides such a valuable service for people who need information, the Internet will become more and more a part of our daily lives in the future.

The World Wide Web, the "Web," is a visual and graphical option on the Internet. By using special applications termed *browsers*, Web users can navigate the Internet more easily and productively. A browser can obtain the text of a Web document (referred to as a "Web page" or a "home page"), which you are able to read as incoming images, video, and audio files (see Figure 12.5 on p. 382). Links, or connections, on a Web page can lead you to other pages where related information is located. Each of these sites allows for the retrieval of text, sound bites, and even video clips. Every month, more and more business organizations are using the Web to advertise their merchandise and services.

Technology and Training

Interview an employee of an organization that does business internationally. What technologies are used for international communication? How are they used? Is training provided for the technologies? For cultural sensitivity in the use of these technologies?

*I*nternet Jargon

Because electronic communication does not allow nonverbal signals such as laughter, nodding, waving, touching, etc., acronyms or other written symbols must be used to send a complete message to a receiver. As a test of your electronic communication knowledge, match each Internet jargon term on the left with its correct meaning.

___ 1. IMHO	a. Let off a difficult assignment
___ 2. Using UPPERCASE letters	b. Denotes sarcasm
___ 3. To be "O.J.'d"	c. Laughing Out Loud
___ 4. BRB	d. In my humble opinion
___ 5. Using asterisks	e. Denotes shouting
___ 6. LOL	f. Crazy rampages caused by stress
___ 7. :)	g. Denotes smiling
___ 8. Going Postal	h. Be Right Back
___ 9. (;>)	i. Wink

FIGURE 12.5

This is the home page for a "search engine" that helps business people get information from the Internet.

Daily Picks   Web Launch

Options

- **Arts** - - *Humanities, Photography, Architecture, ...*
- **Business and Economy [Xtra!]** - - *Directory, Investments, Classifieds, ...*
- **Computers and Internet [Xtra!]** - - *Internet, WWW, Software, Multimedia, ...*
- **Education** - - *Universities, K-12, Courses, ...*
- **Entertainment [Xtra!]** - - *TV, Movies, Music, Magazines, ...*
- **Government** - - *Politics [Xtra!], Agencies, Law, Military, ...*
- **Health** - - *Medicine, Drugs, Diseases, Fitness, ...*
- **News [Xtra!]** - - *World [Xtra!], Daily, Current Events, ...*
- **Recreation and Sports [Xtra!]** - - *Sports, Games, Travel, Autos, Fishing, ...*
- **Reference** - - *Libraries, Dictionaries, Phone Numbers, ...*
- **Regional** - - *Countries, Regions, U.S. States, ...*
- **Science** - - *CS, Biology, Astronomy, Engineering, ...*
- **Social Science** - - *Anthropology, Sociology, Economics, ...*
- **Society and Culture** - - *People, Environment, Religion, ...*

[Yahoo! Surf Shop - Yahoolilgans! - Yahoo! Japan - Yahoo! Internet Life]
HTTP://WWW.YAHOO.COM

◆ Communication Competence in Organizations

Recall the model of competent communication; Figure 12.6 applies this model to organizations. As we have seen, the greatest difference between communication in dyads or small groups and communication in organizations is the *structure* of organizations. Within organizations, individuals are part of groups or teams that are organized into hierarchies; this means that some individuals or groups have more status or influence than others, but they are all interdependent. Both individuals and groups can be reconfigured (as in a department "shake up"), with the result that different individuals or groups then communicate with one another. Still, the organization persists intact. An organization has its own culture (organizational culture), which interacts with the general culture to provide a constant interchange between the outside world and the organization.

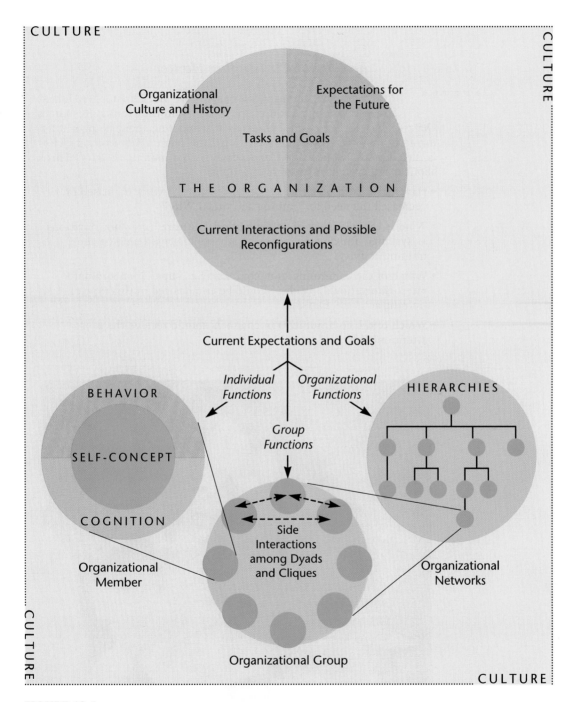

FIGURE 12.6
Model of competent communication in organizations.

*T**he Case of Christopher Hunter***

At the beginning of this chapter, we met Christopher Hunter, a communication major interning in the Human Resources Department of a large bank. His boss is wondering about doing a training activity for the bank and modeling it on Team TWA seminars. How is the content of this chapter relevant to such a training activity? Think about that as you answer these questions.

- Have changes in organizations over the past 20 years increased or decreased the need for training activities? Why?

- What is the relevance of "organizational culture" and "organizations as systems" for Christopher as he advises his boss on doing the training activity?

- Which of the communication contexts (e.g., superior-subordinate, interorganizational, dyadic) should be emphasized in this type of training activity? Explain.

- Which of the communication channels should receive the most attention? Why?

REVIEW

- Organizational communication is more complex today than in years past. Advanced technologies have created greater accuracy and speed, which require new kinds of communication expertise. The types of jobs we hold as well as changes in the composition of the workplace pose many communication challenges for modern employees.

- Within organizations, organizational cultures develop, which provide guidelines for behaviors that are either encouraged or discouraged.

- Organizations as systems include the qualities or characteristics of wholeness, interdependence, hierarchy, openness, adaptability, equifinality, and environmental interchange.

- Many communication contexts exist in the modern organization. The employee is seen as a personal resource, and managers and subordinates share responsibility for developing an effective communication environment. Team-building skills are important as are strong interdepartmental and interorganizational relationships.

- Both formal and informal communication channels exist in organizations; networks are the patterns communicators use, which may be centralized or decentralized.

- Negotiating and mentoring are important communication behaviors in organizations. Expertise in the new technologies is also required for successful communication.

▲
·
·
·
·
•

The Case of the Group Presentation

It is not easy to be an effective leader. As you read the following case study, consider the conflicting concerns this group leader faced. Note that there may have been tension between her and one of the group members concerning control distribution. The leader may have also faced a choice between keeping members happy and having the group produce a good project.

Cass was glad the group project was almost over. It had been much harder than she expected to work with five other people. At least Jared had finally cooperated with the other group members and, she had to admit, had come up with the topic for their presentation.

The professor had told the groups that they had to "teach the class something about effective communication" for their project. They would have to identify a communication problem, investigate the issues surrounding it, and then present ways of increasing communication effectiveness in that context.

Cass watched Jared summarize their presentation. "So, fighting a speeding ticket is worth all the effort you put into it," Jared said. "And, since tickets can triple your insurance premiums or get you canceled, it is well worth remembering our five basic steps for fighting back."

After applause from the class, Cass, Jared, and the other group members fielded questions from class members. Most were specific questions about how to communicate some point more effectively to the judge, the police, or the insurance company. But then Chiharo asked a very disturbing question. "What about the ethics of doing this type of thing? I mean, if you actually did speed, shouldn't you just pay for it and hope that the fine reminds you not to speed again?"

Most of the class members laughed at Chiharo's question, but Cass could see two or three faces that seemed either to agree with her or to be upset with some aspect of the presentation. One of these students, Dan, raised his hand to speak, and when the professor called on him, he started speaking softly and slowly.

"A driver speeding lost control on my family's street 5 years ago," Dan began. "He ran into a parked car near the sidewalk where my little sister and her friends were playing. The parked car was pushed into the group of children, and two of my sister's friends were severely injured. I certainly hope that speeder was unable to argue his way out of a ticket."

"Well, I'm very sorry that you and your sister and her friends had such a traumatic experience," Ron replied, "but it really was an isolated instance, you know. The majority of tickets are the result of the police harassing young drivers. They see us out having fun and target us. Every time I've been in court, it's full of young drivers who have been singled out by cops. So I think this presentation was a good one—and relevant to our communication problems with the system."

"You're exaggerating, Ron," Almarie said. "Maybe you see a lot of young drivers in court because a lot of young drivers speed. At any rate, I don't think it's right that some of us pay our tickets or go to traffic school when we get caught speeding, while other people who do the same thing or worse get off. Your group may have taught us an effective way to communicate our way out of a ticket, but I don't think that it is a very moral thing to do."

"You've brought up some interesting points," said the professor. "Should this receive an A for relevance and accuracy or an F for failing to address the possible consequences of this type of communication behavior? Should they have included an ethics section in their presentation or not done this presentation at all? Should they cite how many people are killed by speeding drivers every year, or should they not worry about that? Was this a responsible presentation?"

Discussion Questions

1. What do you think about the ethics of this presentation? Should it have been tempered by other data (such as the consequences of speeding and other traffic infractions)? Should it never have been given?
2. Can "effective" communication skills sometimes be unethical? Consider not only this case study but also instances from your life.
3. What about Ron's comments about what he perceives as police harassment? Does this real or imagined harassment justify learning how to "beat the system"?
4. What do you imagine were the dynamics of group interaction that led Cass and Jared and their group members to present this topic? Do you think any of them considered the ethical implications of the topic? Were they victims of groupthink? What factors might have influenced their project? Draw parallels with groups you have worked with.
5. If you were the professor, how much weight would you give the ethical aspect of this presentation? Should effective communication also be socially responsible?

EPIL●GUE 3

Competence in Group Communication

In this part of the book, we have moved to new, more complex levels of communication. All the basic principles of competent communication that you learned in the preceding two parts apply to groups, leadership, and organizations. But the addition of more participants to the interaction and a group leader change the way the principles work. In this epilogue, we will take a look at how basic communication principles are applied in group and organizational contexts.

Like two-person relationships, multiperson relationships are constructed and maintained by the way people in the group communicate with one another. The quality of each group member's experience is directly related to the quality of communication within the group. You are a member of many types of groups. These might include work groups; spontaneous social groups (e.g., friends who get together for dinner); structured social groups (e.g., a league softball team); members of a family; volunteer committees (e.g., a PTA); or groups of strangers who come together for a specific purpose (e.g., people on a cruise).

Despite this variety, all groups have the same characteristics as "simpler" two-person relationships. That is to say, when you are a member of a group, you will be engaged in a negotiation over the distribution of *control*, the level of *affiliation* that can appropriately be expressed, and the *tasks* and *goals* of the group and its individual members.

When you are a group member, the cognitive processes you use to plan how to communicate in a dyad are still at work. But now the difficulty of accurately perceiving and making attributions is multiplied by the number of possible relationships in the group (see Chapter 10). In addition, the group as a unit has to be dealt with independently from the individuals who make up the group. Self-presentation may become a problem in a group because you may have different relationships with different group members, each of whom may have different expectations of you.

Ethical issues often confront group members. Probably the most common issue is the need for each member to accept responsibility for the group's performance. Members must be open and honest with one another about the issues under discussion which requires (1) a focus on issues and not on personalities; (2) a climate that facilitates the expression of diverse—even unpopular—ideas; and (3) a willingness on the part of each member to object if he or she thinks the group is pursuing an improper course. A second ethical issue that group members frequently face is confidentiality. When should a group's work be secret? When should it be exposed to public scrutiny? It is important to remember that group communication must show sensitivity to a wide range of individual and collective concerns.

As we have mentioned, the introduction of an "official" leader is a significant feature that distinguishes formal group relationships from social ones. Informal groups do not always have official leaders, but most have unofficial leaders. Informal groups have the same kinds of communication concerns as do formal groups. The major difference is that informal groups have more room to negotiate group characteristics and pay more attention to the social concerns of members.

Formal Groups

When you were asked in Chapter 10 to list the groups of which you are a member, which sorts of groups—formal or informal—first came to mind? Which did you most want to learn more about? People generally think of groups as existing in a work-related context (formal groups). That is one reason why we place more emphasis on formal groups. Another is that most of you have less experience in formal groups than you do in informal ones.

The structure of formal groups limits the communication to what members see as appropriate and effective. In work groups, for example, (1) the members' hierarchical status indicates the amount of control they may exercise, and/or (2) the leader of the group is appointed by the person who forms the group. Under these circumstances, most people think the distribution of control is not an issue. Nothing could be further from the truth! In relationships control is equated with influence. *Every* member of a group has the potential to influence the group process. Although the appointed chairperson usually has a good deal of control (initially, at least), other members will inevitably begin to exercise some control.

The task/goal orientation is more obviously important in work groups than in social relationships. After all, you are in a work group to accomplish some specified goal. Even though general goals are generally determined ahead of time, group members still have to determine how to carry out their task. For example, a manager may appoint a group of employees to a task force with the general goal of "improving morale." It is left to the group members to determine how to do so.

We mention affiliation last, not because it is not important in work groups but because many people *think* it's not very important. This is the case because the emphasis in work groups is on work, not on liking one another or on friendships. In fact, friendships are often a hindrance to accomplishing work-group tasks. You probably have had the experience, however, of friendships emerging from work relationships. This isn't surprising because we tend to feel strongly about people we encounter frequently. Our point is that affiliation (and its appropriate display) is always an issue. Will members socialize with each other outside of work? Or will the group be "strictly business," with little or no contact outside of work.

The history of a group and the expectation for future interaction influence what sort of communication is considered competent. Members of a task force that will meet only a few times are less likely to spend the time and energy to forge friendships than are members of a committee that will meet regularly over a long period. In the task force, competent communication would *not* include a lot of time devoted to negotiating affiliation. In the long-term standing committee, time devoted to affiliative concerns would be time well spent.

Leadership in Groups and Teams

The complexities of communication in groups can be made more manageable by effective leadership. Good leaders work to establish competent relationships with group members. They realize that control must be distributed among group members and not just reserved for themselves. When members feel they can influence the group productively, they are more likely to take responsibility for the group product. (See the team leadership skills described in Chapter 11.) This leads to a cohesive group where personal relationships are less likely to get in the way of group performance.

Competence in Organizations

Organizations can be thought of as one large group or as many small groups comprised of many individuals. Recall the model of competent communication in organizations from Chapter 12. We saw how all of these individuals and groups function as a system. Competent organizations are able to manage levels of control and degrees of affiliation within their organizations, and they also take outside forces into account. The "culture" of the organization as well as external cultures influence the effectiveness of organizational communication.

Public Communication

When people are asked "what is your worst communication fear?" many will answer "the fear of public speaking!" Yet learning how to be an effective public speaker enhances many kinds of communication skills—interpersonal, organizational, and presentational. These skills, in turn, help us to become more successful and influential people. For example, public speaking skills help us to present our thoughts clearly and concisely. Once we are able to do this, we are perceived by others as being competent communicators and thus as more effective. Success in public speaking also leads to self-confidence, enabling us to overcome our initial fears.

Video Action!

"Competent Public Speaking: Students Show the Basics" follows a skills-oriented approach, taking you sequentially through the seven steps to effective public speaking. Examples from actual student speeches illustrate the points introduced by the narrator. The video should help you in the step-by-step process of learning to communicate competently.

Steps toward Competent Communication

- Explain the strategies for choosing a topic for a speech.
- Analyze an audience.
- Describe the specific purpose of a speech.
- Identify and organize the main points of a speech.
- Recognize the forms of support used in a speech.
- Outline a speech with an introduction, body, transitions, and conclusion.
- Analyze and evaluate the delivery of student speeches.

For Discussion after the Video

Of the seven steps discussed in the video, which one do you think is most crucial to speech preparation? Why? Which step is most difficult? Least difficult? Why?

What would happen if you skipped a step in the process? For example, how would your speech be different if you *didn't*

- analyze your audience?
- organize your main points?
- provide forms of support?

How does the process change with each new topic you decide to present?

Does the overall purpose of your presentation affect your process of speech preparation? If so, how? If not, why not?

CHAPTER THIRTEEN

Preparing and Delivering Presentations

OBJECTIVES

After reading this chapter, you should be able to:

1. Discuss the general purposes of public speaking.

2. Use a variety of techniques to select a topic for a speech.

3. Analyze audiences in terms of type, reference groups, and situational expectations.

4. Identify a specific purpose for a speech and select an organizational pattern.

5. Construct three types of speech outlines: complete sentence, topic, and a speaker's outline.

6. Compose effective introductions, transitions, and conclusions.

7. Describe four modes of delivery and how they are effective for different situations.

8. Identify potential strategies for coping with both state and trait communication apprehension.

SANDRA RAJARATNAM IS a college senior working as an intern for a computer software firm that has strained management-worker relations. Mark Acker, the human resources director, believes that his company has an unsettled corporate culture. He decides to conduct a company-wide needs assessment and involves Sandra. Using questionnaires and interviews, Sandra develops a profile of the employees. Mark has asked Sandra to make a preliminary report to him; the company's CEO, Anne Nicoterra; and the chief financial officer, Akbar Javidi, within a week.

As you read this chapter, you will learn the skills that Sandra must possess to prepare and deliver an effective speech. At the end of the chapter, we will return to this scenario and solicit your advice.

This chapter makes two major points: First, the more successful you are in life, the more likely you will be asked to give speeches—be it at a church meeting, a presentation to upper management, or at a Rotary Club dinner. Second, although speechmaking is an art that can create much anxiety and that comes naturally to few, you can improve both your comfort and skill levels for giving speeches. Barbara Ehrenreich, author and political commentator, expresses these two points forcefully:

> There are people who are not afraid of public speaking. I have met some of them and they are not psychopaths. But for the rest of us, public speaking ranks just below snake-handling among the activities we would voluntarily choose to undertake. And this is unfortunate because, while very few occupations require snake-handling in the normal course of events, a great many of them require some form of speaking, if only to plead for an alternative assignment. Rather than speak in public, many otherwise brilliant and able people consider residence in a contemplative religious order. This is not entirely necessary. I have survived it, and so can you.[1]

Ms. Ehrenreich's concerns are not unique to our times. The ability to speak clearly, eloquently, and effectively has been recognized as the hallmark of an educated person since the beginning of recorded history. Written commentary on communication goes back at least as far as the Egyptian work *Precepts of Kagemni and Ptah-Hotep* (3200–2800 B.C.).[2] The theory and practice of oral communication was also a central concern of classical Greece. The Greeks' conclusions were first systematically described by Aristotle (384–322 B.C.) in his *Rhetoric* more than 2000 years ago. In this chapter, then, we build on a long tradition as we describe the basic principles of public speaking. We cover eight tasks:

1. Understanding the nature of public speaking
2. Clarifying your purpose for speaking
3. Analyzing your audience
4. Identifying and organizing your main points
5. Providing support for your ideas
6. Outlining your speech
7. Developing an introduction, signposts and transitions, and a conclusion
8. Selecting methods and following guidelines for speech delivery

◆ The Nature of Public Speaking

What is a public speech and what are you conveying when you rise to give one? Hart, Friedrich, and Brummet answer these questions in terms of the implicit messages you send out when you address an audience.[3]

First, you communicate that you perceive that a problem exists. Here *problem* means any set of conditions that the speaker thinks requires change. The problem can be as commonplace as the annual call to rededicate ourselves to American democracy on the Fourth of July, or as controversial as a plea to nationalize the health care industry. Not all problems, of course, can be resolved through speechmaking. A single speech, for example, cannot change the eating habits of 200 million Americans. Still, when you face a group of listeners, you must have some feeling that your message can at least begin to change a situation that you consider undesirable.

Second, by deciding to address an audience, you have also reasoned that speaking intimately to a friend is not sufficient for getting the job done. Instead, you have chosen to attempt to influence a sizable portion of your social environment.

A third implicit message you send when you choose to deliver a speech is that you believe both you and the audience are capable of changing. When people gather together for the purpose of hearing public discourse, each person is making an "implicit bargain" with the speaker that goes something like this: "I'm here, and you can try to change me—but you'd better make it good!" Furthermore, the speaker and audience "agree" (except in especially turbulent times) beforehand that only symbols (as opposed to physical force) will be used in public communication surroundings. Public speaking is not, of course, a one-way street. When addressing an audience, you realize that you, too, can be affected by interaction with the audience. You may be shouted down, elected president of the organization, or encouraged to believe more strongly in your own message. Because communication outcomes are not really predictable, change is always a possibility for the speaker as well as the audience.

In summary, then, public speaking involves a situation in which you perceive that a problem exists and that overcoming the problem is worth the risk of talking simultaneously to many individuals. You also perceive that the topic is important enough to both you and your audience that you are all willing to be open to the possibilities of change.

◆ Clarifying the Purpose for Speaking

In the real world, choosing a topic and purpose for a speech is seldom a difficult task. You speak because you volunteered, or you were drafted, to speak on a topic for which your expertise is relevant to the situation at hand. For example, your boss wants you to organize the Red Cross blood drive for your unit; your candidate for student government president wants you, as campaign manager, to make the nominating speech; or you are presenting a group gift at a farewell party for a classmate who has joined the Peace Corps. This class, then, will provide you with a challenge that you will seldom face in the future—namely, finding a speech topic and purpose that fit within the constraints of an instructor-generated assignment.

General Purposes for Speeches

Your speaking assignments will fit within one of three general purposes for speeches: to inform, to persuade, or to celebrate.

To Inform. Speeches to inform try to provide audiences with information that they will find new, relevant, and useful. Such speeches can take a variety of forms. They might, for example, explain a process (e.g., how to play various styles of music on the five-string banjo, how to make a birdhouse for bats, or how a laser disc player works); describe objects or places (e.g., the Vietnam Memorial in Washington, D.C., the Black Hills of South Dakota, or roller blades); or provide definitions of things (e.g., classical music, philosophy, or communication). Speeches to inform also attempt to answer questions that we have about the world around us (e.g., What do we know about tornadoes, Lincoln's Gettysburg Address, or the differences between micro- and macroeconomics?). We discuss general principles for developing and presenting information speeches in Chapter 14.

To Persuade. Instead of describing what exists, persuasive speeches focus on building a case for what should be. Although they most frequently ask for a change in belief, attitude, or behavior (e.g., Please vote no on state question 642; boycott this store to protest its unfair labor practices; or let's consider whether it is appropriate for our government to fund art that some people consider pornographic), they can also reaffirm existing attitudes and actions (e.g., We should continue to use the existing grading structure at our university; our company should continue to sponsor a Little League team; or we should continue to ban public prayer in our nation's public schools). In Chapter 15 we elaborate on strategies that will help you build effective persuasive presentations.

To Celebrate. Ceremonial presentations use the principles of both informative and persuasive speaking for special occasions, such as introducing a speaker, accepting an honor or award, presenting a memorial, or celebrating an achievement. In the broadest sense, such presentations either demonstrate the speaker's commitment to organizational ideals or permit the speaker to articulate an organization's commitment to its ideals. Although we do not devote a separate chapter to speeches whose goal is to celebrate, the general principles we discuss are relevant to such occasions. In addition, the Suggested Readings section at the end of the book includes texts that focus on ceremonial occasions.

To Inform? To Persuade? To Celebrate?

List the public speeches that you have listened to, whether in the media or in person, in the past month. Which of them aimed to inform? To persuade? To celebrate?

Strategies for Choosing a Topic

The first consideration in selecting a topic for a speech in this class is your instructor's assignment. What is it that you are asked to do? Inform? Persuade? Celebrate? To discover this general purpose, read the speech assignment carefully. If you are in doubt, ask your instructor for clarification.

In celebrating the achievements of an individual or group, a ceremonial presentation both informs the audience of the recipient's accomplishments and persuades the audience to feel appreciation or admiration.

When you have a general purpose firmly in mind, then you can select a topic that will help you develop an effective public presentation.

In searching for a good topic, you might try three excellent strategies for generating ideas: solo brainstorming, consultation with others, and research.

Solo Brainstorming. In order to give a good speech, you must be knowledgeable about and interested in the topic. Thus, the best place to start is with your own knowledge and expertise. What experiences have you had? What do you know? What do you believe? For example, assume that the assignment requires you to give a 2- to 3-minute speech describing a place. You might begin to think about this topic in terms of your personal knowledge. What places do you know around your college or university? Your local community? Your state? The United States? Other countries? You might also ask yourself what places, in each of these settings, you would like to know. As you engage in this process, avoid evaluation (e.g., "The class won't want to know about that!"). Just write down as many ideas as you can. Evaluation comes later, when you sort through the multiple possibilities for the one topic that will become the focus of your speech.

You might also consider using the technique called *clustering.*[4] The process is somewhat similar to solo brainstorming; however, instead of resulting in a list of possibilities, clustering "spills" its ideas onto paper.

Clustering is a creative technique for identifying potential speech topics. It begins with a core idea, a nucleus word or phrase. Simply write a word in

CLUSTERING

A creative technique for identifying potential speech topics; involves writing down a core idea and all of the words, phrases, and ideas generated by it.

*C*lustering ✔

Now that you have learned about clustering, try to generate a cluster of speech topics suggested by the word *potato*. Write the word in the center of a sheet of paper and circle it. In 2 minutes, spin off as many ideas as you can. Remember, do not evaluate the ideas until your time is up. Did you come up with a topic that might be appropriate for a speech?

the center of a piece of paper and circle the word. The word can be whatever strikes you—for example, *baseball,* as in Figure 13.1.

From the nucleus word, create a web of associations. This web is a collection of ideas inspired by the nucleus word or phrase or by words spun off it. Baseball might make you think of Babe Ruth. Babe Ruth might bring to mind the Babe Ruth museum in Baltimore, which in turn might elicit thoughts of other tourist attractions in that city, and each of those thoughts might lead to other ideas. As the ideas come, write each one, circle it, and connect it to the word or phrase that inspired it.

As the process continues, you should eventually reach a point at which some concept strikes you as a good topic for a speech. To refine the topic, you can make *that* word or phrase the nucleus for a new web of associations.

One of the most important aspects of the clustering process may at first be hard to achieve: You must simply *do* it, making no judgments about the suitability of a particular association or idea. If you reach a dead end while looking at a concept, ask yourself, How does this make me feel? or What is the main thing that hits me here?

Of course, judgment eventually has to come into play. You must bring your critical abilities to bear as you evaluate potential topics and adapt them to your specific audience. The time for evaluation, however, is *after* clustering has indicated a topic, not during the clustering process.

After you have exhausted the power of your brain, it is time to turn to the second source of ideas—other people.

Consultation with Others. Friends, classmates, professors, family, and others can be an important source of topics for speeches. Not only can they help you generate speech topics that you may not have thought of ("two heads are better than one"), but they can also help you evaluate the potential value of topics for your audience. It always helps to "bounce" ideas off of other people.

Research. A third source of topics for speeches is the library—and its collection of books, journals, and other materials. Sometimes just browsing through current newspapers and periodicals will remind you of or spark your interest in a particular topic. The reference librarian can also advise you on the resources of

FIGURE 13.1
An example of a web of associations produced by clustering.

Using CD-ROM Indexes

If you have not done so recently, go to your library and ask a reference librarian whether the library provides access to any CD-ROM indexes. If it does, learn how to use one of them.

the library—including general reference guides such as the *Readers' Guide to Periodical Literature*. Increasingly, general reference indexes are available for computer searching free of charge. For example, many libraries offer free access to CD-ROM indexes such as the following:

InfoTrac Access to about 1000 popular magazines and journals

ABI Inform Business articles from over 800 business and management journals

Dissertation Abstracts Ph.D. dissertations in all subject areas since 1861

MLA Bibliography Books and journal articles in literature, language, linguistics, and folklore since 1981

SocioFile Articles, books, convention papers, and other materials in sociology since 1963

PsychLit Articles, books, convention papers, and the like in psychology since 1974

ERIC Educational Resources Information Center covering over 500 educational periodicals in addition to conference papers, speeches, monographs, research reports, bibliographies, and so forth, on educational topics

Making a Choice

You have searched for potential topics by solo brainstorming, talking with others, and visiting the library. The next task is to select the topic that best meets the following three criteria:

1. Is it a topic you are interested in and know something about?
2. Is it a good topic for the general purpose specified in the assignment?
3. Is it a topic that your audience will find worthwhile?

At this stage, it is likely that most of the potential topics on your list will at least minimally satisfy the first two criteria. You should have already chosen topics that you were interested in and informed about and that fit the general purpose of the assignment. Thus, the third criterion will probably be the most significant in selecting your final topic. Which topic is most likely to be considered worthwhile by your audience? To answer this question, you will need to engage in audience analysis.

AUDIENCE ANALYSIS
A characterization of the individuals who will listen to a speech in terms of audience type (pedestrian, passive, selected, concerted, or organized), their relevant reference groups, and their situational expectations.

◆ Audience Analysis

There are many reasons for conducting an **audience analysis**—that is, a characterization of your audience and the situation in which members find themselves. Because you are asking them to change (e.g., to learn new information; to change their attitudes, beliefs, or actions; or to recommit themselves to an organization), it is important for you to know where they are starting from both in terms of your topic and their perceptions of you as a speaker. It is also important for you to know what reasons they are likely to find compelling as motivation for changing.

Types of Audiences

How do you learn about the beliefs, attitudes, values, experiences, and needs of an audience? A good place to start is to classify the total audience in terms of its cohesiveness or togetherness. Hollingsworth uses this variable to group audiences into five types.[5]

The least cohesive group is the **pedestrian audience**—an audience of people who have no obvious connection with either the speaker or one another. For example, a fundamentalist preacher will stand on a busy street corner and attempt to attract an audience by vividly describing people's sins and their need for salvation. The speaker's first task in this and similar situations is to capture the attention of individuals who are likely to have other things on their minds.

The **passive audience** is a group that is already gathered to hear the speaker, but its motivation level is not high. When you speak in class, for example, an attendance requirement guarantees you the presence of an audience; it does not, however, guarantee that your audience will be interested in everything you have to say. Because you are addressing a passive audience whose attention you have already claimed, your first task is to sustain and direct listeners' interest.

In a **selected audience,** the speaker and audience share a common and known purpose, but they do not necessarily agree on the best way to achieve their shared goals. As Democrats or Republicans gather at their convention, for example, they agree, in general, on what will help get their party's candidates elected. Nevertheless, as they work on the party platform, many disagreements arise concerning the best approach to such issues as the economy or defense. Thus, your first task when addressing a selected audience is to channel common sources of motivation into some preconceived direction.

The **concerted audience** is quite similar to the selected audience. Its members share a need to achieve some end and are usually positively disposed toward the speaker and the topic. They are inclined to do what the speaker suggests, but they still need to be convinced. When members of the Republican Party meet to put together a party platform, they are a selected audience—they have a common goal. But different wings of the party are likely to have different concerns about what should be included in the platform—they are a concerted audience. When New York Governor George Pataki addresses the conservative wing of the party, for example, the audience is likely to be predisposed to do what he suggests. Thus, your task when addressing a concerted audience is to capitalize on the audience's predisposition to accept your ideas.

Hollingsworth's final audience type is the **organized audience**. Such audiences are completely devoted to the speaker and to the speaker's purpose. Some religious and political groups fall into this category, as do audiences who have committed themselves to a noncontroversial cause, such as honoring Julia Child on her eightieth birthday. Thus, informing and persuading organized audiences is typically less important than celebrating with them. Your main job in this instance is to specify an action and give the audience direction to carry it out.

Although identifying the type of audience you will face is an important component of audience analysis, it is only the first step. You will also need

---

PEDESTRIAN AUDIENCE

An audience of people who have come together for the moment but have no obvious connection with either the speaker or one another.

PASSIVE AUDIENCE

An audience that is gathered to hear the speaker but is not highly motivated to listen to or accept the message.

SELECTED AUDIENCE

An audience that shares the goal of the speaker but does not necessarily agree with the speaker's method for achieving the goal.

CONCERTED AUDIENCE

An audience that shares the goal of the speaker and is disposed to accept the speaker's plan of action.

ORGANIZED AUDIENCE

An audience that is completely devoted to the speaker and to the speaker's purpose.

to discover (1) your audience's attitude and knowledge about you and your topic and (2) what you will need to do to adapt your message to the audience. The most straightforward approach would seem to be to learn everything you can about each member of the audience. Unfortunately, even if you had the time and resources to accomplish this task, you would end up with an overwhelming mass of data. As an alternative, then, it is useful to cluster your audience in terms of *reference groups*; this will help you anticipate how the audience is likely to respond to you and to your message.

Reference Groups

REFERENCE GROUP

A group of people who are like a particular individual or whom that individual aspires to be like.

DEMOGRAPHIC REFERENCE GROUP

A group of people who share such traits as age, gender, and ethnicity.

VOLUNTARY REFERENCE GROUP

A group of people who have chosen to belong to a specific religious, political, social, or other group.

Reference groups are composed of persons who are like us or whom we aspire to be like. As a result, they exert significant influence on how their members are likely to respond to external stimuli, such as a speaker and a speaker's message. There are two types of reference groups: demographic and voluntary. **Demographic reference groups** are defined by qualities over which they have little control: age, gender, sexual orientation, and ethnicity. **Voluntary reference groups** include chosen membership in, for example, religious, political, and social groups—or aspiration to membership in such groups.

When a reference group is *salient* for (significant for) a situation, members will use that group to establish "acceptable" and "unacceptable" behavior. For example, membership in a sorority is likely to be more salient in the sorority house than in the classroom. By correctly identifying salient reference groups, you can use them to anticipate how an audience is likely to respond to you and your topic. Reference groups can also help you identify a set of core values which you can invoke to further the adoption of your position.

Information about salient reference groups can often be obtained informally through casual conversation, observation, and inference. It is also possible to gather this information more systematically. In your communication class, for example, you might be able to use a questionnaire to generate an audience profile. The questionnaire could focus both on salient reference groups and on the attitudes, values, experiences, and needs that will influence audience reaction to you, your topic, and your strategies for bringing about change.

✔ Your Reference Groups

Jot down a list of reference groups of which you are a member—for example, college students, your political party, your gender, your ethnic background, your living arrangement, your religious affiliation. Which of these roles are demographic and which are voluntary? Which of your reference groups do you share with members of the class? Which do you not share? How will these similarities and differences influence your choice of topics to speak on? How will they influence the approach you take to your topic?

Situational Expectations

In addition to analyzing audience cohesiveness and salient reference groups, audience analysis also involves consideration of **situational expectations**. Audiences come to public speaking situations with expectations from many sources, including the time of day, events happening in the outside world, the comfort and attractiveness of the room, and knowledge (or lack of knowledge) about the speaker or the topic. You need to know about these expectations in order to fulfill or deal with them. For every speaking situation, therefore, it is important to ask:

- Why are members of the audience here?
- What are they likely to expect to hear in this kind of situation?
- Do they have any expectations about me?
- What are they expecting to hear from me on this topic?
- Are there any features of the environment (both internal to the speaking room and external to it) that might affect audience expectations?

SITUATIONAL EXPECTATIONS
Expectations that audience members have about the speaker and the message.

◆ Identifying and Organizing Main Points

After your topic has been filtered through the three lenses of assignment relevance, speaker expertise, and audience acceptability, the topic should be summarized. This is done through a **statement of specific purpose**—a single declarative sentence that specifies what the audience is expected to know, do, believe, feel, and so on as a result of the speech. Some examples follow:

- "I want the audience to know about the history and current use of roller blades."
- "I want the audience to vote no on State Proposition 642."
- "I want the audience to understand the various meanings of the word *communication.*"
- "I want the audience to understand what AIDS is and what we need to do to combat it."
- "I want the audience to appreciate the contributions of Dorothy Day to our society."

STATEMENT OF SPECIFIC PURPOSE
A single declarative sentence that specifies what the audience is expected to know, do, believe, feel, and so on, after hearing a speech.

Identifying Main Points and Writing a Thesis Statement

With your statement of specific purpose in mind, you need to identify and organize the main points that will be used to lead the audience members to accept what you tell them. In other words, you are looking for those three to five key ideas which, if the audience understands and accepts them, will mean that you have successfully accomplished the purpose of the speech. If, for example, you want the audience to vote no on State Proposition 642, what are the three to five key points that will cause it to vote no? If you want the audience to know about the history and current use of roller blades, what are the three to five main ideas that the audience must understand and accept before it will be knowledgeable about roller blades?

Once you have identified your main points, you are ready to encapsulate your speech in the form of a **thesis statement**—a sentence that summarizes what you want the audience to get out of your speech. Whereas the specific purpose summarizes how you want your audience to *respond* to your speech (e.g., "I want the audience to vote for Jim Jones for Congress"), your thesis statement captures what you want your audience to *remember* after they have forgotten much of what you said ("I want the audience to vote for Jim Jones for Congress because he is honest, informed, and effective"). A thesis statement should be revised after you have finalized your speech because only then do you know the key elements you are using to support the goal in your specific purpose.

THESIS STATEMENT
A sentence that summarizes what you want the audience to remember from your speech.

Generating Ideas

Although generating main ideas is an art rather than a science, a systematic approach is preferable to random reflection. Using the methods of such historical figures as Aristotle and Francis Bacon, authors Wilson, Arnold, and Wertheimer recommend a **Topical System for Generating Thoughts.**[6] This approach involves using a small set of topics that identify standard ways of thinking and talking about any subject. The basic premise here is that while people can and do talk about an infinite number of subjects, the themes used to discuss them are limited—a result of shared ways of thinking about human affairs. Wilson and his colleagues have narrowed the cues to sixteen ideas that can be used to describe any subject that organizes a message. Empirical research suggests that college students who use this system are able to generate significantly more ideas than are their unaided peers. The sixteen topics are listed here:

TOPICAL SYSTEM FOR GENERATING THOUGHTS
The use of sixteen common themes for talking about any topic as a trigger for identifying ideas for inclusion in a speech.

A. Attributes commonly discussed
1. Existence or nonexistence of things
2. Degree or quantity of things, forces, and the like
3. Spatial attributes, including adjacency, distribution, and place
4. Attributes of time
5. Motion or activity
6. Form, either physical or abstract
7. Substance—physical, abstract, or psychophysical
8. Capacity to change, including predictability
9. Potency—power or energy, including capacity to further or hinder anything
10. Desirability in terms of rewards or punishments
11. Feasibility—workability or practicability

B. Basic relationships commonly asserted or argued
   1. Causality—the relation of causes to effects, effects to causes, effects to effects, adequacy of causes, and so on
   2. Correlation—coexistence or coordination of things, forces, and so on
   3. Genus-species relationships
   4. Similarity or dissimilarity
   5. Possibility or impossibility

If you supplement your results from the topical system with additional research, you are likely to wind up with dozens of potentially useful main ideas. Although it would be satisfying to be able to use all of them, doing so is not really practical—for you or for your audience. Thus, you must winnow down your ideas to a smaller number that best supports audience acceptance of your specific purpose. Although no magic number of main points works best for all occasions, for most messages it is wise to keep the number within the range of three to five.

Choosing an Organizational Pattern

You have learned how to generate ideas and how to process them through a series of three mental filters (your resources, your audience, and the occasion). The next step involves arranging those ideas in some sequence. A natural starting place is to think in terms of the logical structure of the ideas themselves. Although you can organize ideas in many ways, students of public speaking have generally identified the following five logical **organizational patterns**.

Chronological Pattern. When using this pattern, you organize the main points of the message in a time-related sequence. You might, for example, focus on the past, present, and future of calligraphy as an art form. When analyzing a process step-by-step, you are also using a chronological pattern. Thus, a message on how to use a new piece of equipment, say, a new fax machine, might be organized using a time pattern. The essence of a **chronological organizational pattern**, then, is that you describe the main points of a message forward (or backward) in a systematic fashion.

Topical Pattern. Also known as a categorical pattern, the **topical organizational pattern** organizes the main points of a message as parallel elements of the topic itself. Perhaps the most common way of organizing a presentation, the topical pattern is useful when describing components of persons, places, things, or processes. Thus, you might use it to describe the various departments within a college, the characteristics of a successful employment interview, or the reasons for giving a charitable contribution to the United Way. A secondary concern when selecting this approach is the sequencing of topics. Depending on the circumstances, this is often best handled in ascending

> **Using the Sixteen Themes**
>
> Assume that you have decided to give an informative speech on the history of modern art. Which of the sixteen themes suggest possible main topics for such a speech?

> ORGANIZATIONAL PATTERN
> *A method of arranging ideas in a logical sequence.*

> CHRONOLOGICAL ORGANIZATIONAL PATTERN
> *A pattern that presents the main points of a message in a time-related sequence.*

> TOPICAL ORGANIZATIONAL PATTERN
> *A pattern that presents the main points of a message as parallel elements of the topic itself; also known as a categorical pattern.*

or descending order—that is, according to the relative importance, familiarity, or complexity of the topics.

SPATIAL OR
GEOGRAPHICAL
ORGANIZATIONAL
PATTERN
*A pattern that
presents the main
points of a message
in terms of their
physical proximity
to or direction from
one another.*

The **spatial or geographical organizational pattern** arranges main points in terms of their physical proximity to or direction from each other (north to south, east to west, bottom to top, left to right, near to far, outside to inside, and so on). As an organizational pattern, it is most useful when explaining objects, places, or scenes in terms of their component parts. Thus, you might describe a computer keyboard, the physical layout of a media-enhanced classroom, or the Mall in Washington, D.C., using a spatial pattern of organization.

CAUSE-EFFECT
ORGANIZATIONAL
PATTERN
*A pattern that
presents the main
points of a message in
terms of cause-to-
effect or effect-to-
cause relationships.*

With the **cause-effect organizational pattern**, you attempt to organize the message around cause-to-effect or effect-to-cause relationships. That is, you might move from a discussion of the origins or causes of a phenomenon, say increases in the cost of fuel, to the eventual results or effects, such as increases in the cost of airplane tickets. Or, you could move from a description of present conditions (effects) to an identification and description of apparent causes. The choice of strategy is often based on which element—cause or effect—is more familiar to the intended audience. The cause-effect pattern of organization is especially useful when your purpose is to achieve understanding or agreement, rather than action, from the recipients of a message.

PROBLEM-SOLUTION
ORGANIZATIONAL
PATTERN
*A pattern that
presents the main
points of a message in
terms of a problem
and solutions to that
problem.*

The **problem-solution organizational pattern** involves dramatizing an obstacle and then narrowing alternative remedies to the one that you recommend. Thus, the main points of a message are organized to show that (1) there is a problem that requires a change in attitude, belief, or behavior; (2) a number of possible solutions might solve this problem; and (3) your solution is the one that will most effectively and efficiently provide a remedy. Topics that lend themselves to this pattern include a wide range of business, social, economic, and political problems for which you can propose a workable solution (e.g., proposing a new course/faculty evaluation system for the college; choosing a method for conducting job performance interviews; or suggesting a plan for reducing the national deficit). The problem-solution pattern of organization is especially useful when the purpose of a message is to generate audience action.

Having identified five potential logical patterns for organizing main ideas, we are now ready to consider how you might best enhance the credibility of these main points. What can you say or do that will help your audience understand and accept the points you wish to get across?

◆ Providing Support for Main Ideas

Before exploring the specific devices you can use to facilitate message retention and acceptance, it is helpful to regard your task as that of aiding learning. For everyone, learning is a life-long process in which experiences lead to changes. For many people, change is uncomfortable and, therefore, resisted. Even more, individuals resist *being* changed.

Applying Principles of Learning

A speaker who wants to be a change agent should try to use what is known about principles of learning. Knowles provides a useful summary in the form of **andragogy**, his term for the art and science of helping adults learn.[7] Knowles suggests that as you select supporting material to help your audience understand and accept your message—that is, learn it—you should consider the following principles:

ANDRAGOGY
The art and science of helping adults learn.

- *Individuals have different motivations for learning.* Although "What's in it for me?" and "There might be something of value that I can use" may reflect the bottom-line motivation of audience members, each person can have a different motivator. Thus, it is important to build your message on audience analysis.

- *Learning is an individual activity.* The accumulation of knowledge, skills, and attitudes is an experience that occurs within the learner and is activated by the learner. Although you can set the stage and do much to orchestrate a climate conducive to learning, learning is still an internal process.

- *Audience members have prior experience.* The more you can incorporate an audience's life experiences into the construction of a message, the more the audience can be expected to retain and use the information provided.

- *Learning results from stimulation to the senses.* An audience member will learn better when you appeal to multiple senses. Learners learn best by doing. As Confucius stated it: "I hear and I forget; I see and I remember; I do and I understand."

Using Verbal and Nonverbal Forms of Support

Within a learning framework, then, what specific verbal and nonverbal **forms of support** can you use to facilitate the retention and acceptance of a message? In the next few pages we highlight six forms of support.

FORMS OF SUPPORT
Verbal and nonverbal devices—such as language, explanations, examples, statistics, testimony, and visual aids—that can focus audience interest on the speaker's message and help the audience to understand and accept the message.

Language. Words are only arbitrary collections of letters that serve as symbols for things we wish to think and talk about (e.g., people, things, events, ideas, beliefs, or feelings). In addition to the fact that the letters B-O-O-K are an arbitrary label for what you are reading, these letters also carry with them both *denotative* and *connotative* aspects (see Chapter 4). That is, the word *book* points to or denotes an object that the dictionary describes as "a volume made up of pages fastened along one side and encased between protective covers." It also carries a connotative meaning (i.e., an attitude toward such objects) that is likely to vary from person to person. Although everyone in our culture is likely to agree that *book* denotatively means the thing you are now reading, some readers will have had mostly negative experiences with books (especially textbooks), whereas others will have had more positive experiences.

Thus, even though an audience may share a relatively common denotative meaning for a word as concrete as *book*, the wide range of connotations within an audience can make your task as a speaker quite challenging. Consequently, when you begin to think through how best to convey the main ideas of a message, it is imperative that you consider your word and language choices; the best choices will make your message relevant, clear, and unbiased for audience members. Here are some guidelines that can help a public speaker achieve this goal:

- *Public language should be personal.* Don't borrow someone else's vocabulary. Use language that *you* can use easily. Never use a word in a speech that you haven't said *out loud* previously. Practice pronouncing a new word until you make it yours.

- *Public language should be fitting.* Listen carefully to the language patterns of your listeners before you speak to them. Adjust the formality of your language to fit the situation. Resist the temptation to use a pet phrase just because you like it. Don't be flip with a serious topic or melodramatic with a light one.

- *Public language should be strategic.* Ambiguity often has its advantages, especially when you're dealing with touchy topics or hostile listeners. Try out several different ways of phrasing a volatile idea. Don't depend on the inspiration of the moment to guide your language choice. Think in advance about *what* you're going to say and *how* you're going to say it.

- *Public language should be oral.* Except in certain circumstances, manuscript speeches should be avoided. A speech is meant for the ear, not the eye. *Listen* to the words and phrases you intend to use. Put "catch phrases" in your outline rather than long, elaborate sentences. Use your voice and body to signal irony and rhetorical questions.

- *Public language should be precise.* If you're talking about bulldozers, don't call them earthmoving vehicles. Avoid jargon that is not necessary for comprehension. Define all technical terms for your listeners. Avoid vague generalities. Use concrete and specific language when providing descriptions.

- *Public language should be simple.* Use five-syllable words sparingly. Employ simple constructions (as opposed to compound or complex constructions) as often as possible. Avoid embedded clauses. Use your *voice* to emphasize a point, instead of repeating an idea several times.

- *Public language should be unaffected.* Don't seek to have your listeners remember your language. Don't get carried away with metaphors; a single simple image is always superior to several complex ones. Don't invent "cute" phrases. Euphemistic language often sounds ludicrous (e.g., referring to killing as "elimination").[8]

Explanation is the act or process of making something plain or comprehensible. It is often accomplished by a simple, concise exposition that sets forth the relation between a whole and its parts. For instance:

> A state is one of the internally autonomous political units composing a federation under a sovereign government; for example, New York, Montana, and Alaska are states within the United States.

Explanation is also accomplished when you provide a definition. This alternative can take a variety of forms:

- Providing a *dictionary definition* (which typically involves placing the item to be defined in a category and then explaining the features that distinguish the item from all other members of the category—e.g., "*Primary* means 'first in time, order, or importance'")

- Using *synonyms* (words with approximately the same meaning—e.g., "*Mawkish* as an adjective indicates that someone or something is sentimental, maudlin, or gushy") and/or *antonyms* (words that have opposite meanings)

- Using *comparisons* (showing listeners the similarities between something unfamiliar and something familiar) and *contrasts* (supporting an idea by emphasizing the differences between two things)

- Defining by *etymology* and *history* (e.g., "*Pedagogy*, a term used to describe the art and science of teaching children, is derived from the Greek *paid* meaning 'child,' and *agogus*, meaning 'leader of'")

- Providing an *operational definition* (defining a process by describing the steps involved in that process—e.g., "To create calligraphy, you begin with a wide-nibbed pen . . .")

To be effective, explanations must be framed within the experiences of members of the audience and should not be too long or abstract.

Examples serve as illustrations, models, or instances of what is to be explained. An example can either be developed in detail (an illustration) or presented in abbreviated, undeveloped fashion (a specific instance). An illustration—an extended example presented in narrative form—can be either hypothetical (a story that could but did not happen) or factual (a story that did happen). For example, a presenter might involve the listeners in a hypothetical illustration by suggesting, "Imagine yourself getting ready to get up to give a speech. You reach into your bag for the manuscript that you carefully prepared over the course of the past week. It isn't there! You madly search through everything in the bag." Whether hypothetical or factual, an illustration should be relevant and appropriate to the audience, typical rather than exceptional, and vivid and impressive in detail.

A specific instance is an undeveloped or condensed example. Therefore, it requires listeners to recognize the names, events, or situations in the

EXPLANATION
The act or process of making something plain or comprehensible; in public speaking, a form of support that relies on exposition and definition.

EXAMPLE
In public speaking, a form of support that relies on illustrations, models, or instances of what is to be explained.

instance. If a presenter, for example, uses "President Dewey" as a specific instance of the dangers of poor sampling techniques when engaged in public opinion polling, and the audience has never heard of Thomas Dewey (Harry Truman's Republican opponent in the 1948 presidential election), this example will not make the point clear and vivid.

STATISTICS

In public speaking, a form of support that relies on collecting, organizing, and interpreting numerical data.

Statistics are used to describe the end result of collecting, organizing, and interpreting numerical data. They are especially useful when reducing large masses of information to general categories (e.g., adults who start smoking in their early teens are less likely to have quit by age 30 than those who start later: those who've quit by age 30 who (a) started before age 14 = 4.4 percent; (b) 14–16 = 9.6 percent; and (c) after 16 = 13.6 percent; when emphasizing the largeness or smallness of something (e.g., adults spend an average of 16 times as many hours selecting clothes—145.6 hours a year—as on planning for retirement—9.1 hours); or when describing indications of trends—where we've been and where we're going (e.g., according to a 1996 survey of 800 newspapers and magazines, 25 percent distribute at least part of their publication electronically, 31 percent intend to do so within 2 years; 19 percent intend to do so within 5 years; and 23 percent have no plans to do so).

When using statistics, you should be aware of two basic concerns: (1) Are the statistics accurate and unbiased? (2) Are they clear and meaningful? To address the first issue, you need to answer such questions as: Are the statistical techniques appropriate and are they appropriately used? Do the statistics cover enough cases and a sufficient length of time? Although you may not have the expertise to answer such questions, you can ask about the credibility of the source of the statistics. Do you have any reason to believe that the person or group from whom you got the statistics might be biased? Are these statistics consistent with other things you know about the situation? Addressing the second issue involves more pragmatic considerations: Can you translate difficult-to-comprehend numbers into more immediately understandable terms? How, for example, might you make the difference between 4.4 percent and 13.6 percent more vivid? How can you provide an adequate context for the data? Is it useful, for example, to put together both newspapers and magazines when exploring use of electronic publication? Is the comparison between planning for retirement and selecting clothing a fair one? Would a graph or visual aid clarify the data and statistical trends? As we will see shortly, supplementing a verbal presentation with a visual aid can greatly increase comprehension and retention.

TESTIMONY

In public speaking, a form of support that relies on using a credible person's statements to lend weight and authority to a message.

Testimony involves using a credible person's statement to lend weight and authority to aspects of your presentation. For this to happen, the person being cited must be qualified; that is, the testimony must come from a person who is perceived as an expert on *this* topic and free of bias and self-interest. Just as important as actual credentials is the perception the audience has of the source of the testimony. Is the individual known to the audience? If not, you will need to tell the audience why the individual is a good authority. If known, is the person accepted by the audience as both knowledgeable and unbiased on the topic? In short, to lend support to a message, the testimony of a source must both *be* credible and *be perceived* as credible.

Visual Aids are primarily used to enhance the clarity and credibility of a message. They can also help you control apprehension by providing a safety net in an uncertain situation.

Obtaining these advantages requires skill in selecting appropriate aids and using them well. Although many choices are available to you (e.g., actual objects, blackboard, cartoons, demonstrations, drawings, flip-charts, transparencies, graphs, maps, models, movies, people), they can be conveniently grouped into three categories:

1. The actual object or a model of it (a model airplane, a cooking demonstration)
2. Pictorial reproductions (photographs, slides, sketches, videotapes)
3. Pictorial symbols (graphs, charts, diagrams)

When selecting from among these choices, you should keep several criteria in mind:

- *Use visuals that are large enough to be seen.* When possible, this means taking a visual to the room where it will be used and making sure that it will be visible to all members of the audience. When this is not possible, you should solicit advice from people who know the setting and then make informed guesses about the potential number of listeners and average viewing distances.

- *Keep the content of visuals simple and focused.* Keep the pictorial content and the wording on a visual as uncrowded and simple as possible—avoid all unnecessary details that might send audience thoughts in unrelated directions. Rather than cluttering an aid with too much information, use multiple visuals, each containing only those features and details essential to the clarity and vividness of the point being made.

- *Prepare visuals carefully and professionally.* The design and form of a visual will be interpreted by audience members as reflecting your attitude toward them and the message topic. A sloppy visual can detract from your credibility as a presenter, regardless of the visual's content. Software programs are available for preparing simple but polished looking visuals. If you lack the artistic skills or computer literacy to prepare professional looking visuals, hire a professional to prepare them, or do not use them at all.

Up to this point in the chapter, we have discussed guidelines for creating the "body" of a message. It is now time to solidify and organize these ideas, so we turn to a discussion of the principles of outlining.

Statistics and Bias

Page through a *Newsweek, Time,* or *U.S. News and World Report* to find advertisements that use statistics. Ask: (1) Are the statistics accurate and unbiased? (2) Are they clear and meaningful? Which judgment is easier to make? What are the implications of this exercise for public speaking?

VISUAL AIDS
In public speaking, a form of support that relies on using actual objects or models, pictorial reproductions, or pictorial symbols.

Visual aids supplement the verbal content of a public speech.

◆ Outlining the Speech

OUTLINE

A visual, schematic summary of a speech that shows the order of ideas and the general relationships among them.

COMPLETE SENTENCE OUTLINE

A visual, schematic summary of a speech that allows others to understand the speaker's plan for the speech.

A speech **outline** visually displays the main points and subpoints of a speech (as well as the support for those points) in a way that helps you develop the speech and helps the audience follow it. Consider the example in Figure 13.2. This outline is an abbreviated example of a **complete sentence outline** that contains five main points (I, II, III, IV, and V) and two subpoints (A and B) that develop each of the main points. Were it the actual outline for a speech, it would also include the supporting material (e.g., examples, testimony, statistics) that you would use to illustrate and support your main and subpoints. For example, for the first main point, the outline would show exactly *how* you intend to demonstrate that the effective leader is one who searches out challenging opportunities to change, grow, innovate, and improve; the outline would include your supporting material, such as examples, illustrations, and testimony.

Note that the outline alternates numbers and letters in clearly identifiable columns. This style is known as the *Harvard style* of labeling and can accommodate as many levels as you need:

     I. Main point
       A. Subpoint
          1. Support
             a. Sub-support
                1) Sub-sub-support
                2) Sub-sub-support
             b. Sub-support
          2. Support
       B. Subpoint
    II. Main point

Thesis: Being an effective leader in any organization involves five behavioral commitments.

I. Being an effective leader involves searching for opportunities by confronting and changing the status quo.

    A. An effective leader searches out challenging opportunities to change, grow, innovate, and improve.

        1. Testimony from an acknowledged effective leader.

        2. An example of a leader who has done so.

    B. An effective leader experiments, takes risks, and learns from the accompanying mistakes.

II. Being an effective leader involves inspiring a shared vision.

    A. An effective leader envisions an uplifting and ennobling future.

    B. An effective leader enlists others in a common vision by appealing to their values, interests, hopes, and dreams.

III. Being an effective leader involves enabling others to act.

    A. An effective leader fosters collaboration by promoting cooperative goals and building trust.

    B. An effective leader strengthens people by sharing information and power and increasing followers' discretion and visibility.

IV. Being an effective leader involves modeling the way.

    A. An effective leader sets the example for others by behaving in ways that are consistent with the leader's stated values.

    B. An effective leader plans small wins that promote consistent progress and build commitment.

V. Being an effective leader involves encouraging the heart.

    A. An effective leader recognizes individual contributions to the success of every project.

    B. An effective leader celebrates team accomplishments regularly.

FIGURE 13.2
A sample Harvard-style outline.

Although Harvard-style labeling, used in the above outline, is the most common, another popular style is *legal-style* labeling:

1. First main point
    1.1. First subpoint
    1.2. Second subpoint
        1.2.1. First support
        1.2.2. Second support
2. Second main point

Heads at a particular level of an outline, whether Harvard or legal style, are of equal importance. In a Harvard-style outline, the five main points (indicated by roman numerals I, II, III, IV, and V) are the main divisions of the speech and are of equal importance. The subpoints (A and B) also designate equally important divisions of the main point to which they refer. The outline has two or more elements at any level; that is, there are two or more main points, two or more subpoints under any main point, and two or more levels of support. This is normally the case because a topic is not "divided" unless it has at least two parts. If you wish to make only one subpoint, do not show it on the outline.

Most speakers start their speech preparation with a complete sentence outline. It is easy to share such outlines with other individuals and get their reactions to the logic and organization of a speech. For this reason, most instructors ask to see a complete sentence outline. Once such an outline has been developed, however, a speaker generally finds it useful to reduce the outline to a **topic outline**, one that reduces the sentences to brief phrases or single words, or a **speaker's outline**, key words and important phrases and statistics on a 3 × 5 index card, before they speak.

◆ Developing Introductions, Transitions, and Conclusions

Having composed and outlined the message, you can now add the final ingredients—an introduction, transitions, and a conclusion.

The Introduction

In Chapter 9, we suggested that at the beginning of an interview, interviewees start with three interrelated questions for which they want answers: What is the nature of this interview and how will it proceed (a *task* issue)? Will I like and can I trust this interviewer (a *relationship* issue)? What can I hope to gain from my participation in this interview (a *motivation* issue)? An audience in a public speaking situation has similar questions: What will this speech be like? Will I like and can I trust this speaker? What can I hope to get out of listening to this speech? An **introduction** attempts to answer these questions. As you think through these questions, it is important to consider which of them require attention and how best to handle them. It may well be the case, for example, that the setting or the person introducing the speaker has already provided an overview of the speaker's message; or that the group is so fired up about the topic that providing additional motivation is not necessary; or that the speaker's credibility is so high that it does not require additional development. In situations where this is not the case (in other words, for most of your presentations in this class), you will need to allocate about 5 to 10 percent of your speaking time to answering questions of task, relationship, and motivation.

Although there is no guaranteed approach to dealing with task issues, you might consider explicitly stating the topic, thesis, title, or purpose;

TOPIC OUTLINE

A visual, schematic summary of a speech that reduces a complete sentence outline to brief phrases or single words.

SPEAKER'S OUTLINE

A visual, schematic summary of a speech that includes only key ideas that a speaker needs to remember.

INTRODUCTION

The beginning portion of a speech; typically deals with issues of task, relationship, and motivation.

previewing the structure of the message ("The three points I will develop are . . ."); or explaining why you narrowed the topic. Strategies for motivating audiences include: linking the topic and thesis to the listeners' lives; showing how the topic has, does, or will affect the audience's past, present, or future; or demonstrating how the topic is linked to a basic need or goal of the audience. Strategies for building credibility include (1) verbal strategies during the introduction, and throughout the speech, that demonstrate competence (e.g., citing highly credible individuals, placing the topic in historical context, describing your personal acquaintance with the topic) or trustworthiness (demonstrating that present behavior is consistent with past behavior, entertaining alternative points of view, making verbal and nonverbal behaviors consistent); (2) referring to the audience, setting, or occasion in complimentary fashion; and (3) using relevant humor to demonstrate that both you and your listeners laugh at the same things.

In considering these strategies and others, remember that not every situation requires attention to all three issues. Furthermore, many strategies can contribute to multiple functions. For example, a story or an analogy can address both task and motivation issues; humor can further both motivation and relationship issues. Thus, when you are developing a strategy for introducing a message, the best advice is to make the introduction as compact as possible while fulfilling the audience's expectations concerning task, relationship, and motivation.

Transitions

Transitions are used to guide an audience through your speech. They are signs that tell an audience where you are going, where you are, and where you have been. Thus, they need to be overt, clear, and frequent.

The speaker might, for example, forecast the purpose and structure of the message toward the end of the introduction ("Today, I will talk about five behaviors that characterize effective leaders. They are . . ."). As the speech proceeds, the speaker might use internal previews and summaries to review a main point and anticipate the next one ("Having described why leaders need to challenge the process, let's turn now to the need to inspire a shared vision"). The conclusion of the speech might include a final summary ("I've talked today about five behaviors that characterize effective leaders. Effective leaders . . .").

The Conclusion

A **conclusion** is used to provide a sense of closure. Although a conclusion can be done in a variety of ways, it typically involves summarizing the main points of a speech and reinforcing the importance of the message by demonstrating its potential impact. An effective way to accomplish this is by using the conclusion to elaborate on an example, illustration, or quotation that was used in the introduction.

TRANSITIONS
Verbal signs to an audience indicating where the speech is going, where it is, and where it has been.

CONCLUSION
The final portion of a speech; typically brings closure in the form of a summary and a statement of impact.

*T*he Rhetorical Jigsaw Puzzle

Each numbered item (sentence or paragraph) below is a separate unit of a speech. When put together in the right order, the items make up a complete speech. Your task is to order them so as to form the best possible speech. After you have done so, label each item according to the type of rhetorical device it represents (statement of point, subject sentence, signpost transition, summary statement, example, etc.).

1. Finally, think of the ordinary door-to-door salesperson.

2. Have you ever noticed how easy it is to do something else when the TV announcer is droning out a commercial? But what happens when the golden tongue is still? You know that the set is on, but you don't hear the announcer's voice extolling the virtues of "lavish Camay soap." So what do you do? You look at the TV screen, of course, to see what is going on.

3. Well, one way is by a brief interval of silence before and after the name of a product or sponsor.

4. The next time someone says to you, "Silence is golden," just smile and think to yourself, "You don't know how right you are!"

5. Second, let us consider television.

6. Are you aware of the methods radio announcers use to call attention to their sponsor or product?

7. Such a salesperson is one who has learned that silence is golden.

8. So you see, people in the field of selling are indeed aware that silence is golden, for they know it can mean dollars and cents in radio, in TV, and even in door-to-door selling.

9. As you see, the announcer puts a parenthesis of *silence* around the name of the product in order to catch your attention.

10. Silence is golden. That's an old cliché that you've heard many times, especially when your parents wanted to impress upon you another cliché—namely, that children should be seen and not heard.

11. First of all, take radio selling.

◆ Guidelines for Delivery

Up to this point, your focus has been on generating something to say and putting that something in the most appropriate format. Having accomplished that difficult task, you now need to think about effective approaches and strategies for presenting your message to listeners.

12. Thus, you can see that the TV salesperson has also discovered that silence can be golden.

13. The announcer doesn't say: Women-all-over-the world-are-learning-that-delicious-Wrigley's-Spearmint-gum-is-a-grand-wholesome-family treat. Instead, the speaker says: Women—all over the world—ar learning that delicious—Wrigley's Spearmint gum—is a grand—wholesome—family treat.

14. I contend, however, that silence really IS golden.

15. If salespeople are really good, they know better than to just reel off a "pitch"—they know how to listen to you.

16. And I would like to present three instances in the field of selling to prove my contention.

17. If you doubt the effectiveness of silence in TV, just try not looking at the picture and notice how irresistibly your eyes will be pulled to the screen by a few moments of silence.

18. Salespeople are willing, if necessary, to listen to all of your troubles. If you want to raise a question, they will be quiet while you do so. They will ask you a question, then be silent while you answer.

Solution to the Rhetorical Jigsaw Puzzle

10. Introduction: Attention material; 14. Introduction: Subject sentence; 16. Introduction: Purpose sentence; 11. Signpost transition; 6. See next item; 3. This and preceding item state first main point; 13. Comparison; 9. Restatement; 5. Signpost transition; 17. Statement of second main point; 2. Comparison; 12. Restatement; 1. Signpost transition; 15. Statement of third main point; 18. Examples; 7. Restatement; 8. Conclusion: Summary; 4. Conclusion: Punch line.

Source: T. Clevenger, Jr. (1963), The rhetorical jigsaw puzzle: A device for teaching certain aspects of speech composition, *Speech Teacher, 12*, 139–146. Used by permission of the Speech Communication Association.

Students of speechmaking have long debated how much emphasis should be allocated to issues of content versus issues of delivery. In fourth-century B.C. Greece, for example, the philosopher Aristotle argued that speakers ought to emphasize the logic of their messages. For Aristotle, issues of delivery, though necessary, were not very important. His contemporary Demosthenes, an orator and political leader, reached exactly the opposite conclusion. The three rules of speaking he is reported to have sworn by are delivery, delivery, and—delivery.

Variations of this argument continue to the present day. Instructors in the Aristotelian tradition put little stress on delivery other than to commend students for good eye contact, appropriate posture, and conversational delivery. Their Demosthenian counterparts, however, place a major emphasis on the components of voice and physical action that enhance or detract from a speaker's effectiveness.

Our position on this issue is that to be a competent speaker, you must emphasize both content and delivery. Although it is fundamental to have a clear and logical message to present, unless that message is presented effectively the only person who will understand and accept it is the speaker. Thus, having prepared an effective message, the speaker needs to develop effective strategies for the delivery of it. The first choice is that of *mode of delivery*. Will the speech be impromptu, extemporaneous, manuscript, or memorized?

Impromptu Speaking

IMPROMPTU SPEAKING

Speaking on the spur of the moment, without formal preparation.

Impromptu speaking is what people do all the time in informal conversations with others; that is, they speak on the spur of the moment without formal preparation. The only difference is that in a public setting the audience is larger, and often the stakes are higher. Thus, when entering into a situation where you might be called on to make an impromptu speech (e.g., attending a committee meeting where you have special expertise on the topic), do what you do for important *social* conversations (e.g., asking your parents for a special favor)—anticipate that contingency and prepare your message in advance. When advanced preparation is not possible (e.g., you are asked to answer a question or describe something on the spur of the moment), do the following:

1. Quickly think of a specific purpose (e.g., to supply needed information, to urge action, to clarify an issue, to provide humor).
2. Choose a simple organizational framework that will serve your purpose (e.g., cause-effect; problem-solution; past-present-future; advantages/disadvantages; What should we do first? Second? Third?).
3. Start with an introduction that captures attention and relates your message to the activities that preceded it.
4. Speak briefly. (If you ramble on, the audience will miss the point of your message.)
5. When in doubt, summarize. (A quick review can often restore your perspective and get you back on track.)
6. Conclude with a brief summary of your speech and say what accepting your message will produce.

Whatever you do, *don't apologize*—for your lack of preparation, your lack of information, or your lack of ability as a speaker.

Extemporaneous Speaking

Extemporaneous speaking is characterized by advance preparation of ideas and supporting material, with the precise wording to be composed at the moment of speaking. As a result, no matter how many times the speech is presented, the expression of the ideas is never exactly the same. Extemporaneous speaking has a number of important advantages: (1) It allows the speaker to adapt to unforeseen situations (e.g., by adding a reference to something that occurred in the setting and adding or deleting an argument based on audience response); (2) it promotes a more personal relationship between the speaker and the audience; and (3) it leads, with experience, to a superior delivery—greater earnestness, greater sincerity, and greater power. Because of these advantages, extemporaneous speaking is the preferred mode of speaking for most situations. When using it, a speaker starts by constructing a complete sentence outline, which is then reduced to a speaker's outline. Using the speaker's outline, the speaker rehearses the presentation in front of a mirror, an audio- or video-recorder, and/or sympathetic friends. While the speech is being delivered, the speaker watches the audience for clues about how it is being received and modifies the speech based on an interpretation of that feedback.

EXTEMPORANEOUS SPEAKING
Speaking characterized by advance preparation of ideas and supporting material, with the precise wording of the speech to be determined during the process of speaking.

Speaking from a Manuscript

Although extemporaneous is the preferred mode of delivery for most situations, some occasions require you to write out a total presentation word for word and read the resulting speech to the audience. Situations that require or encourage **manuscript speaking** are those for which precision of expression is crucial. When President Clinton makes a major policy statement on an important issue, he wants to be sure that the wording of the statement is such

MANUSCRIPT SPEAKING
Speaking from a manuscript that contains the complete presentation word for word.

Extemporaneous public speaking strengthens the relationship between the speaker and the audience.

that it will not be misunderstood. Thus, he is likely to write out that statement and read it. Manuscript speaking is also encouraged in situations that require precise timing (e.g., a 2-minute speech written for inclusion in a political commercial).

Preparing a manuscript speech involves the same process as preparing an extemporaneous speech. That is, you start with a complete sentence outline, reduce it to a speaker's outline, and rehearse from this outline. Once you have experimented with a conversational style for presenting the message, it is written down word for word and rehearsed and rewritten and rehearsed and rewritten. Once in final form, the manuscript speech is prepared for easy reading (i.e., put in a format and type size that are easy to read and marked appropriately to indicate any special emphases). When presenting a manuscript speech, you attempt to establish a level of contact with the audience that approaches that of the extemporaneous speech, including good eye contact and a conversational style of delivery.

Speaking from Memory

MEMORIZED
SPEAKING

Delivering from memory a speech that has first been written out.

Memorized speaking adds but one step to a manuscript speech: After writing out the manuscript, you memorize the speech and then deliver it from memory rather than reading it. In many situations, speakers will combine both approaches. That is, they will read parts of the manuscript and then deliver other parts of the message from memory in an apparently extemporaneous fashion. In some situations, however, speakers make the extra effort of memorizing the whole speech, especially for ceremonial speeches such as tributes and eulogies. When speakers make a special effort to memorize a speech, they also make a special effort to deliver it using a style of delivery that is as close to an extemporaneous style of delivery as possible.

Having chosen a mode of delivery, you next need to consider how to use delivery to focus attention on the message and not on you. This means delivering the message in a conversational style that the audience can both hear and understand. Such a style is best developed by observing the skills of effective speakers, learning to recognize skills and deficiencies in your own delivery, and using guided practice to improve your skills and to remedy deficiencies.

◆ Communication Apprehension

A potential barrier to effective delivery is communication apprehension. McCroskey defines *communication apprehension (CA)* as "an individual's level of fear or anxiety associated with either real or anticipated communication with another person or persons."[9] (Recall the discussion of CA in Chapter 8.)

Recognizing Communication Apprehension

Most people experience **state communication apprehension**—a situational attack of anxiety that can be greater or lesser depending on such factors as the size of your audience, how well you know the people you are talking with, how well you know your subject, and the status of the individuals you are talking with. You might, for example, feel quite relaxed when talking with a friend about a movie you saw the previous evening, but feel a sudden surge of panic when asked to describe your reaction to that same movie for a professor and your classmates in an English class. For some people, CA operates as a trait; that is, they have an enduring tendency to be apprehensive about communication in all contexts. Persons with high levels of **trait communication apprehension** do everything they can to avoid communication situations. For such individuals, the level of fear or anxiety is high whether talking with friends or strangers, interacting in small groups, or giving a public speech.

McCroskey and his colleagues have discovered that people with high levels of CA are perceived negatively by those with whom they interact. They are considered less attractive, less competent, less sociable, and less composed. In addition, academically, high levels of CA are associated with lower overall grade-point averages and lower achievement on standardized tests, even though there is no meaningful relationship between level of CA and intelligence. High CA also has important effects on employment. Not only is it less likely that such individuals will be interviewed and offered a job, but the jobs they do receive are likely to be less pleasing to them.

Whether you suffer from trait (enduring) CA or state (situational) CA, the good news is that you can control both forms. If you suspect that CA is a problem for you, ask your instructor or someone in your campus counseling center whether there are any programs on campus to help people reduce CA. Such programs are generally based on the two most common approaches for reducing high levels of CA—systematic desensitization and cognitive restructuring.

Treatments for Severe Communication Apprehension

Systematic desensitization was first used to reduce CA in 1966.[10] As a treatment package, it involves three components. The first is training in deep muscle relaxation. In this phase, the trainer may instruct the client to "tense your fist; now relax it." Second is the construction of hierarchies of CA-eliciting stimuli. The client thinks of a range of activities, from those that produce low anxiety (such as lying in bed just before going to sleep) to those that cause high anxiety (such as presenting a speech before an audience). The third component involves the graduated pairing, through imagery, of anxiety-eliciting stimuli with the relaxed state. Within each of these components many variations are possible. For example, wide variations exist

---

STATE COMMUNICATION APPREHENSION

A situational attack of anxiety that can be greater or lesser depending on such factors as knowledge of the audience and topic.

TRAIT COMMUNICATION APPREHENSION

A tendency to have fear or anxiety about communication in all contexts.

SYSTEMATIC DESENSITIZATION

A method for reducing or treating communication apprehension; involves learning deep muscle relaxation, constructing hierarchies of anxiety-provoking stimuli, and pairing relaxation with anxiety-provoking stimuli.

in the timing of both the tension and relaxation phases of training in deep muscle relaxation. A great deal of research leaves little doubt that systematic desensitization is an effective approach to treating CA.

A second common approach is **cognitive restructuring**.[11] With cognitive restructuring, anxious students are first taught to identify anxiety-producing negative statements (e.g., "I'll say something stupid") that create and enhance their CA. Once they have mastered this task, they are then taught to replace these negative statements with coping statements of three types: task statements ("Speak slowly, it helps"), context statements ("It's only a small group of students like me"), and self-evaluation statements ("This was easier than last time"). As with systematic desensitization, cognitive restructuring's effectiveness in reducing high levels of CA is demonstrated by much experimental research.

Ways of Coping with Mild Communication Apprehension

Although systematic desensitization and cognitive restructuring both reduce high levels of trait CA, neither treatment is generally necessary for individuals suffering from milder versions of state CA. Such individuals can often cope effectively with periodic bouts of elevated anxiety by remembering and applying the following advice:

COGNITIVE RESTRUCTURING

A method for reducing or treating communication apprehension; teaches individuals how to identify anxiety-producing negative statements and replace them with coping statements.

Knowing that you are prepared helps to control mild state communication apprehension. Rehearsing a public speech improves your self-confidence as well as your skill in delivering your presentation.

*P*ersonal Report of Public Speaking Anxiety

The following exercise consists of 34 statements concerning feelings about communicating with other people. Indicate the degree to which the statements apply to you by marking whether you strongly agree (SA), agree (A), are undecided (U), disagree (D), or strongly disagree (SD). Work quickly, recording just your first impressions. This exercise will be helpful to you only if you are completely honest.

1. While preparing to give a speech, I feel tense and nervous.   SA   A   U   D   SD

2. I feel tense when I see the words *speech* and *public speech* on a course outline.   SA   A   U   D   SD

3. My thoughts become confused and jumbled when I am giving a speech.   SA   A   U   D   SD

4. Right after giving a speech I feel that I have had a pleasant experience.   SA   A   U   D   SD

5. I get anxious when I think about a speech coming up.   SA   A   U   D   SD

6. I have no fear of giving a speech.   SA   A   U   D   SD

7. Although I am nervous just before starting a speech, after starting I soon settle down and feel calm and comfortable.   SA   A   U   D   SD

8. I look forward to giving a speech.   SA   A   U   D   SD

9. When the instructor announces a speaking assignment in class, I can feel myself getting tense.   SA   A   U   D   SD

10. My hands tremble when I am giving a speech.   SA   A   U   D   SD

11. I feel relaxed while giving a speech.   SA   A   U   D   SD

12. I enjoy preparing for a speech.   SA   A   U   D   SD

13. I am in constant fear of forgetting what I prepared to say.   SA   A   U   D   SD

14. I get anxious if someone asks me something about my topic that I do not know.   SA   A   U   D   SD

15. I face the prospect of giving a speech with confidence.   SA   A   U   D   SD

16. I feel that I am in complete possession of myself while giving a speech.   SA   A   U   D   SD

17. My mind is clear when I am giving a speech.   SA   A   U   D   SD

18. I do not dread giving a speech.   SA   A   U   D   SD

19. I perspire just before starting a speech.   SA   A   U   D   SD

Personal Report of Public Speaking Anxiety (Cont.)

20. My heart beats very fast just as I start a speech. SA A U D SD

21. I experience considerable anxiety while sitting in the room just before my speech starts. SA A U D SD

22. Certain parts of my body feel very tense and rigid while I am giving a speech. SA A U D SD

23. Realizing that I have only a little time left to finish my speech makes me very tense and anxious. SA A U D SD

24. While giving a speech, I know I can control my feelings of tension and stress. SA A U D SD

25. I breathe faster just before starting a speech. SA A U D SD

26. I feel comfortable and relaxed in the hour or so before giving a speech. SA A U D SD

27. I do poorly on speeches because I am anxious. SA A U D SD

28. I feel anxious when the teacher announces the date of a speaking assignment. SA A U D SD

29. When I make a mistake while giving a speech, I find it hard to concentrate on the parts that follow. SA A U D SD

1. Develop a constructive attitude toward fear and anxiety. Instead of wondering how you will get rid of these common emotions, ask yourself how you will use them. Individuals need tension—feelings of excitement and challenge—to increase their thinking ability and powers of concentration. You should therefore realize that everyone who speaks experiences some apprehension and fear before speaking and that, in fact, some measure of anxiety is necessary for you to do your best.

2. Grab every opportunity to practice and experience. Whether you are skydiving, using a new computer program, or giving a speech, knowledge of the requirements of an activity is likely to increase your comfort level. For example, you will naturally be more comfortable the tenth time you've gone scuba diving than the first time. Therefore, you should continually seek out opportunities to practice and gain experience.

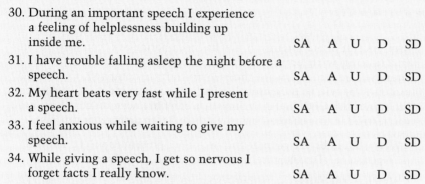

30. During an important speech I experience
a feeling of helplessness building up
inside me.   SA   A   U   D   SD

31. I have trouble falling asleep the night before a
speech.   SA   A   U   D   SD

32. My heart beats very fast while I present
a speech.   SA   A   U   D   SD

33. I feel anxious while waiting to give my
speech.   SA   A   U   D   SD

34. While giving a speech, I get so nervous I
forget facts I really know.   SA   A   U   D   SD

Scoring: For items 1, 2, 3, 5, 9, 10, 13, 14, 19, 20, 21, 22, 23, 25, 27, 28,
29, 30, 31, 32, 33, and 34, use the following scores: SA = 5, A = 4, U = 3,
D = 2, and SD = 1. For items 4, 6, 7, 8, 11, 12, 15, 16, 17, 18, 24, and 26,
use the following scores: SA = 1, A = 2, U = 3, D = 4, and SD = 5. Add up
the scores for all 34 items.

If you answered the questions honestly and your score is below 97,
you probably feel comfortable in most public speaking situations. If your
score is between 97 and 131, you need to remember and apply our five
suggestions for coping with state communication anxiety. If your score is
above 131, you may want to ask your instructor or a counselor about the
availability of systematic desensitization or cognitive restructuring to
help you cope with your anxiety.

Source: J. C. McCroskey (1970), Measures of communication-bound anxiety, *Speech
Monographs*, 37, 276–277. Used by permission of the Speech Communication Association.

3. Prepare thoroughly for each public presentation. If, when you get up
   to speak, you are worried about what you will say, how you will say
   it, and what the outcome will be, you will certainly be more anxious
   than if your only concern is about the outcome. Therefore, prepare
   your speech thoroughly and rehearse your delivery of it. Then, when
   you rise to speak, you will be able to concentrate on the outcome.

4. Concentrate on communicating with your audience. Once you get up
   to speak, focus on the question, How do I know that these individuals
   are hearing and understanding what I'm saying? If you work hard to
   observe the reactions of your audience and to adapt to them, you will
   be much too busy to worry about your anxiety or fear.

5. Remind yourself that your listeners want you to succeed. Your listeners are just like you—friendly people. Just as they want to succeed
   when they get up to speak, they want you to do well when you speak.
   Even if you do make a slip, they will understand and forgive you!

he Case of Sandra Rajaratnam

At the beginning of this chapter we met Sandra Rajaratnam, a college senior working as an intern at a computer software firm. As part of her internship, she has been poring over company records and talking with employees in an attempt to develop a profile of employee attitudes toward their work and the company. On Monday morning she will be presenting her findings to three individuals: her boss, the company's CEO, and the company's chief financial officer. What have you learned in this chapter that might help her to prepare for this task?

• What should be the general purpose of her presentation? To inform? To persuade? To celebrate? A combination of the three?

• Which of the three filters (her resources, her audience, the occasion) should be most influential in determining the specific purpose of her presentation?

• How might Sandra best go about generating and selecting main ideas for her presentation? Which patterns of organization are most likely to be useful?

• As Sandra thinks about ways of supporting her main points, will some forms of support be more important than others? What should be her concerns as she considers her alternatives?

• What should Sandra consider as she thinks about ways of introducing her presentation? What about the conclusion? Will there be any special requirements with regard to transitions?

• Which mode of delivery should Sandra use? Will any of the characteristics of effective delivery be especially crucial?

• Do you have any additional advice for Sandra?

REVIEW

- This chapter has focused on the basic principles of public speaking. You should now understand the eight tasks you face as a public speaker and some methods for completing them.

- First, understand the nature of public speaking. It takes place when you perceive that a problem exists and that overcoming that problem is worth the risk of talking to many individuals simultaneously.

- Second, identify and refine a specific reason for speaking. Determine if your purpose is to inform, to persuade, or to celebrate, then choose a topic by brainstorming, consulting with others, or doing research.

- Third, analyze your potential audience in terms of cohesiveness, reference groups, and situational expectations so you can successfully adapt your message.

- Fourth, identify the major points that form the core of your message, write a thesis statement, and choose an organizational pattern.

- Fifth, select ways to support your ideas so that they are clear and acceptable to the audience. This can be done through language, explanations, examples, statistics, testimony, and visual aids.

- Sixth, arrange your points and supporting material in the form of an outline. It is useful to start with a complete sentence outline, then simplify it to a topic outline and finally a speaker's outline.

- Seventh, make sure your speech includes an introduction, transitions to guide your audience through your talk, and a conclusion that reinforces the importance of the message.

- Eighth, choose a mode of delivery—impromptu, extemporaneous, speaking from a manuscript, or speaking from memory—that will allow you as the speaker to be responsive, conversational, direct, intelligible, and unobtrusive.

- Accomplishing this last goal may involve knowledge of communication apprehension and some methods for coping with it. In the next two chapters, we will apply these principles to two of the major tasks faced by speakers—sharing information and persuading.

CHAPTER FOURTEEN

Informative
Presentations

OBJECTIVES

After reading this chapter, you should be able to:

1. Define the term *information society* and discuss its impact on communication skills.

2. Use the eight categories of speech topics to identify potential subjects for informative speeches.

3. Explain the four types of informative speeches: descriptive, demonstration, definitional, and explanatory.

4. Describe strategies for coping with the eight most common barriers to the transmission of information.

5. Suggest guidelines for preparing and presenting effective informative speeches.

OMMY GOMEZ IS a member of the Catholic Worker Movement, a group that serves the homeless in Washington, D.C. Father Kennedy has invited Tommy to visit his class in social work at Georgetown University. Father Kennedy wants Tommy to describe the group's mission. He wants his students to learn about similarities and differences in the ways in which professional social workers and the Catholic Worker Movement view homelessness and how they think society should deal with this growing problem.

In this chapter, you will learn the skills that Tommy will need if he is to successfully present a speech to Father Kennedy's class. At the end of the chapter, we will return to this scenario and solicit your advice.

◆ The Importance of Informative Presentations

It was about 20 years ago that we began to hear the terms *information society* and the *information age*. Economists such as Fritz Machlup argued that developed countries shifted from an agricultural economy to an industrial economy during the nineteenth century.[1] After World War II (which ended in 1945), they evolved into a service economy and then, by the 1980s, an information economy. Although most of us have heard the terminology, we are perhaps still a little puzzled as to what the terms actually mean. What is the information revolution, and why should we care about it?

Postman and Weingarten use the metaphor of a clock face to help us understand the nature of the change in technology that has produced the **information society**:

> Imagine a clock face with 60 minutes on it. Let the clock stand for the time individuals have had access to writing systems. Our clock would thus represent something like 3,000 years, and each minute on our clock 50 years. On this scale, there were no significant media changes until about nine minutes ago. At that time, the printing press came into use in Western culture. About three minutes ago, the telegraph, photograph, and locomotive arrived. Two minutes ago: the telephone, rotary press, motion pictures, automobile, airplane, and radio. One minute ago, the talking picture. Television has appeared in the last ten seconds, the computer in the last second. The laser beam—perhaps the most potent medium of all—appeared only a fraction of a second ago.[2]

According to the Science Council of Canada, the pace of technological advance in recent years has been matched by its absorption into the marketplace, which is seven to ten times faster than any previous technology:

> Since 1968, the power of computers has increased 10,000 times while the price of each unit of performance has decreased 100,000 times. Stanford University economist Edward Steinmuller says that if the airlines had changed as much as computer-related technology, an airplane would now be carrying half a million passengers at 20 million miles an hour for less than a cent apiece.[3]

Accompanying these rapid changes in technology is an avalanche of information that threatens to overwhelm us. According to the *World List of Scientific Journals*, every year about 1 million articles appearing in 59,961 journals (in 65 languages) are published throughout the world. In addition, some 300,000 scientific monographs and 15,000 conference proceedings are published each year.[4]

The changes in technology and information acquisition that produced the information age have changed the workplace. According to Wallin, "Information workers today constitute the fastest growing and most highly

The terminal at a supermarket checkout counter is more than a cash register. It records and disseminates information such as the cost of each customer's order, the amount charged to a credit card, the number of units to be deducted from the store's inventory for each purchase, price changes, and total sales for the day.

compensated sector of employment in the leading industrial countries [accounting] for 50 percent of all persons employed."[5] Counted as information workers, in Wallin's scheme, are all those who produce information (such as engineers and economists), process it (such as clerks and managers), distribute it (such as teachers and journalists), and run the technical system (such as machine operators and printers).

Our growing ability to store and retrieve information is amazing—and continues to expand. A CD-ROM less than five inches in diameter can contain the equivalent of 200,000 pages of book text. By using a combination of microchip and laser technology, everything in the Library of Congress can be stored on one wall of a large living room. This ability to store information—and to move it and use it regardless of distance and time—has transformed many of our previous ways of doing things. For example, investors can access information instantly on a video display terminal, enabling them to learn current stock prices anywhere in the world. When an investor calls up a particular stock, the computer can calculate its price/earnings ratio and yield, so that the investor can make a well-informed decision. In industrial plants, computer-to-computer communication provides the capability for machinery to manufacture some products automatically, with little or no human intervention.

The ongoing transition to an economy based largely on the creation and use of information has made skillful communication the fundamental resource of our age. Individuals who know how to turn information into knowledge—by

Information Overload

Have you ever felt overwhelmed by information when learning a new job, studying for a test, or learning a new skill? What did you do to cope with this situation?

finding it, creating it, sorting it, organizing it, checking it for accuracy, and disseminating it—will continue to be hired, valued, and rewarded. Acquiring the key skills, however, is not an easy task. As Lindstrom observes:

> In a feeble effort to hold the information juggernaut at bay, you and I scan about 74 million words per year—double the volume of words in the _Encyclopedia Britannica._ We make lists, collect files, subscribe to data bases, but it's a losing battle.
>
> In his book _Information Anxiety,_ Richard Wurman explains that we are constantly in peril of falling into "the black hole between data and knowledge." At some point, like pinballs, we begin to collide with information and bounce away, without gaining anything but superficial knowledge.
>
> There is only one way to avoid falling into the black hole. We must develop systems for filtering, analyzing, and communicating information that are as powerful as the systems we have for collecting it.[6]

In a study by the National Assessment of Educational Progress, a nationally representative sample of approximately 3600 young adults (21- to 25-year-olds) were asked to complete eight speaking tasks. Their responses were tape recorded, and two trained raters listened to the tape and made judgments as to whether each response was off task, minimal, adequate, or superior. Several of the tasks asked respondents to provide information—for example, to imagine that the interviewer was new to the area and explain how to get from their present location to a nearby grocery. Do you think you could perform this task? Only 37.1 percent of the sample were rated as performing this task adequately or in a superior fashion.[7]

As this example demonstrates, there is a growing need for effective communication. In this chapter, then, we build on the fundamentals described in Chapter 13. We focus on mastering the skills necessary for capturing and presenting information to an audience in ways that are interesting, understandable, accurate, and memorable. Before explaining why this task is sometimes difficult, we will explore some of the types and forms of informative speaking.

CATEGORIES OF
SPEECH TOPICS

Eight categories that can be used to generate topics for informative speeches—people, places, things, events, processes, concepts, problems, and plans and policies.

◆ Topics for Informative Presentations

Allen and McKerrow identify eight **categories of speech topics** appropriate for informative speeches.[8] As we go through them, ask yourself three questions: (1) Do I have knowledge of or experience with a subject suggested by the category? (2) Am I interested enough to do research on a subject suggested by the topic? (3) Would my audience find a subject suggested by this category interesting and worthy of attention?

*G*enerating Speech Topics

For the category "people," jot down potential speech topics on a sheet of paper. Don't judge the topic; just list any ideas that occur to you. You can go back and sort through them later. What type of people are you most interested in? Athletes? Politicians? Artists? Businesspeople? Activists? As you read about the remaining seven categories of speech topics, repeat this activity for each category.

A good way to start selecting a topic is by following the approach in the Self-Check, "Generating Speech Topics." Complete this Self-Check for the category "people" and then use it for the other seven categories.

People

Our fascination with the lives of others, past and present, is demonstrated in many ways: biographical shelves in local bookstores; sections devoted to people in newspapers and magazines; television programs about the rich and famous (and the poor and not-so-famous); movies about politicians, athletes, movie stars, and other personalities; and a wide variety of tabloids that "reveal" the details of the lives of celebrities. Speaking about people allows us to deepen our knowledge of individuals and their achievements and to share that knowledge with our listeners. The person can be from the past (Susan B. Anthony) or present (Michael Jordan) and might have accomplishments in the realm of work, religion, entertainment, sports, art, politics, music, or some other area. In thinking about potential subjects, don't restrict yourself to famous people. Consider, for example, talking about past or present local personalities (businesspeople, professors, activists), people who do interesting things without a lot of fanfare, or other individuals whom you admire.

Places

Places you have visited or would like to visit can also serve as a topic for an informative speech. Even if you have not traveled much, you have lived somewhere and thus have natural (lakes, historic sites) or created (monuments, cities) places to talk about. Thus, in addition to places like the Grand Canyon or Buckingham Palace, you might talk about a local museum, a nature park, or bicycle trails. You might even consider talking about fictitious places, such as Lilliput and Laputa in *Gulliver's Travels*, or the islands that served as home to Scylla and Charybdis in the *Odyssey*.

Things

A third source of ideas for informative speeches consists of objects or things. Like places, things can be either natural (spiders, plants, dinosaurs) or created (CDs, roller blades, glass art). They can also be imaginary (unicorns). As you consider objects as potential speech topics, think broadly in terms of both time and setting. Things are part of the past (spinning wheels) and the present (pacemakers), and they exist in a variety of settings (work, home, religion, art, entertainment).

Events

Events are occurrences or incidents of personal or historical significance. At a personal level, you might build an informative speech around important, funny, or instructive events in your personal life—the day you went skydiving, your visit with a tax auditor, the day your first child was born, or your bar mitzvah. Our understanding of history is also shaped by events—the Civil War, the assassination of Dr. Martin Luther King, Jr., the breakup of the former Soviet Union, the discovery of penicillin. In addition to helping an audience understand the meaning of personal and historical *single* events, a speaker can also explore the social significance of *collections* of events. A speaker might, for example, talk about the role of dances for Native American tribes, Fourth of July celebrations, and weddings and funerals.

Processes

A process is a series of actions, changes, or functions that bring about a particular result. Thus, informative speeches about processes explain how something works or is accomplished. Like places and things, processes can be either natural phenomena (photosynthesis—the process by which the cells in green plants use the energy of light to synthesize carbohydrates) or created phenomena (calligraphy—the art of fine handwriting). Process speeches help an audience understand the stages or steps through which a phenomenon is produced. Potential topics for process speeches can be identified by thinking about your home life, hobbies, work experiences, and academic studies.

Concepts

People, places, things, events, and processes tend to be concrete; that is, we can readily visualize them. Concepts, on the other hand, are abstractions and are therefore more difficult for us to "see." What images come to mind, for example, when you encounter concepts like love, patriotism, and racism? The challenge of a concept speech, then, is to take a general idea, theory, or thought and make it concrete and meaningful for your audience. Although the challenge is great, many worthwhile informative speeches focus on the elucidation of a concept.

Problems

In our daily lives, we encounter personal and societal problems on a regular basis. Some of them relate to personal or psychological health (smoking, HIV/AIDS) and others to the quality of life at the level of campus, city, state, region, nation, or globe (pollution, energy shortages). Informative speeches that focus on problems help audiences to understand the symptoms, causes, and treatment of problems. Because problems frequently involve controversial issues, there is always the danger of moving from an informative purpose to a persuasive one. Thus, if you doubt your ability to describe a problem objectively, you probably should save the topic for a persuasive speech. If you have doubts, ask the advice of friends, fellow students, and/or your instructor.

Plans and Policies

Our final category for informative speeches concerns plans and policies. In such speeches, the speaker tries to help an audience understand the important dimensions of potential courses of action (e.g., passing the Equal Rights Amendment, changing the composition of the Electoral College). In such speeches, the speaker does not argue for a particular plan or policy. However, like speeches on problems, plan and policy speeches are easily turned into persuasive addresses. Thus, when in doubt, ask whether your proposed speech would be better for a persuasive speech assignment.

If you've followed our advice, at this point you will have filled a sheet of paper with a multitude of potentially good topics for an informative speech. If you need even more ideas, keep in mind the advice from Chapter 13—in searching for a good topic, use solo brainstorming or clustering, the ideas of others, and the library.

As potential topics occur to you, test each one using these criteria: (1) Is it a topic that interests you and that you have knowledge of? (2) Is it a good topic for the general purposes specified in the assignment? (3) Is it a topic that the audience will find worthwhile?

◆ Types of Informative Speeches

Once you have selected a topic for an informative speech, you can develop it in a variety of ways. In this section, we briefly describe the four major types of informative speeches.

Descriptive Speeches

Description is one of the most basic categories for presenting information. When you use it, you put into words what you have experienced with your senses. You want your audience to feel, hear, and see what you felt, heard, and saw. Making **descriptive speeches** requires that you have a clear idea of what you want to describe and why; that you emphasize important details

DESCRIPTIVE SPEECH
A speech that presents information so vividly that the audience can share the speaker's experiences.

and eliminate unimportant ones; and, most of all, that you carefully consider your audience as you think of ways to make your details vivid enough.

Following is an excerpt from a descriptive speech by Major James N. Rowe; it was delivered extemporaneously to students of the U.S. Army General Staff and Command College at Leavenworth, Kansas. Notice how he calls up details of his surroundings and his feelings as he describes his experience as an American prisoner of war in South Vietnam.

> Now, in the camp, the physical conditions in South Vietnam with the Viet Cong are primitive. I was in the U Minh Forest; the camps were temporary at best. You had two to three feet of standing water during the rainy season; in the dry season it sank out, and you were hunting for drinking water. We had two meals of rice a day, and generally we got salt and nuoc mam with them. We did get infrequent fish from the guards, but always the castoff that the guards didn't want. If we got greens, it was maybe one meal's worth every two or three months. Immediately vitamin deficiency and malnutrition were a problem. This is a thing you are going to fight the whole way through. And you are fighting on two sides. You are fighting a physical survival, and you are fighting for mental survival. The physical survival is just staying alive. We found that we had to eat a quart pan of rice each meal, two meals a day, just to stay alive. We found that [we did better] if we could put down everything we had, and I think the most difficult thing initially was the nuoc mam. It is high in protein value, but the VC don't have that much money to spend on nuoc mam. You don't get Saigon nuoc mam. Theirs is called ten-meter nuoc mam. You can smell it within ten meters, and it is either repulsive or inedible, depending on how long you have been there. But this was the type of thing you are eating for nutritional value, and not for taste. So you are fighting on that side.[9]

Demonstration Speeches

DEMONSTRATION SPEECH

A speech that uses narration and examples to describe how things happen.

Demonstration speeches use narration to answer "how" questions—how to use a communications program with a computer, how to line dance, or how to buy a used car. Giving demonstration speeches would seem to be a natural and easy task. After all, if we have figured out how things happen or work, we should be able to explain them to others! If we know how to get to the grocery store, we should be able to tell another person how to get there. Unfortunately, as you know, this is not always the case. Thus, consider the following advice as you prepare a demonstration speech. Start by identifying your audience and its level of knowledge about your topic. With a clear statement of purpose in mind, indicate the broad outline of the process and discuss the major steps in chronological order. Be sure your language is appropriate for your audience; where necessary, define terms. Do not dwell on unimportant details, and relate each major step to the whole. Occasionally, point out where you are in the process.

Demonstrating a process can convey information to your audience that is practical, interesting, or both.

The following outline of the first steps in the printmaking process of producing woodcuts illustrates a demonstration speech. You can imagine the speaker showing each step.

   A. To prepare the block
      1. Use a power sander to smooth rough, scratched, or dented boards.
      2. Lightly sandpaper the surface to ensure an even flatness.
      3. To enhance the grain quality in prints, run a wire brush over the surface in the direction of the grain.
   B. To transfer the design, use one of three methods.
      1. Coat the block with white gouache, and draw directly on it.
      2. Place carbon paper on the block, then your drawing, then tracing paper; press firmly with a pencil to draw in the main elements.
      3. Paste the drawing onto the surface of the block and cut away the white areas.
   C. To cut the block
      1. Hold the knife with your forefinger along the top of the blade to apply downward pressure, and use your other fingers as guides.
      2. Use a gouge by gently tapping it with a mallet; always direct the point of the tool away from your body.[10]

Definitional Speeches

With **definitional speeches**, speakers provide answers to "what" questions. Formal definitions—those found in dictionaries—have three parts: the name of the thing to be defined, the class to which it belongs, and the quality

DEFINITIONAL SPEECH

A speech that explains what words and/or concepts mean.

that distinguishes it from other members of its class. Thus, if we were defining *notation*, we would say that it is "a system of figures or symbols used to represent numbers, quantities, etc." Simple definitions like these, however, are often inadequate for describing complex ideas. In order for listeners to understand complex constructs, speakers need to use multiple strategies. Figures of speech—metaphors, similes, analogies, and the like—can be helpful. The speaker can compare and contrast a term with similar ones. Illustrations are also useful. Since the task is to establish a meaning the audience will understand and accept, the speaker needs to be as specific and concrete as possible.

Robert M. White, then president of the National Academy of Engineering, defined *invention* in the following excerpt from his speech "Inventors, Invention, and Innovation":

> Invention is more than the development of useful and productive devices, although these are vital for material progress. Instead, it is a manifestation of the creativity in all human activities. The invention of the Gothic arch permitted the soaring cathedrals of the Middle Ages and the Renaissance. The paintings of Monet and Pissarro brought us the glories of impressionism. Our daily lives are uplifted by the songs of Irving Berlin and the symphonies of Beethoven.
>
> In short, invention is where you find it. And so it is in industry. Whatever the function, whether in research and development, design, production, or distribution of goods and services, inventions are at the root of new products and processes and also the source of the economic success of companies. Inventions are the lifeblood coursing through the heart of industrial competitiveness.[11]

Explanatory Speeches

The basic purpose of most informative speeches is to create awareness or understanding; explanatory speeches chiefly create understanding. For example, a speech demonstrating how to fax a document creates awareness, whereas a speech explaining how fax machines work deepens understanding. **Explanatory speeches** answer the questions "Why?" or "What does that mean?" They typically deal with problems and with plans and policies. Thus, they are usually more abstract than descriptive and demonstration speeches. The challenge to the speaker is to explain a problem, action, or decision without persuading the audience.

There are at least three ways in which answers to "why" questions may be difficult for lay audiences to understand: (1) difficulty in understanding the meaning and use of a term; (2) difficulty abstracting the main points from complex information; and (3) hesitancy in grasping an implausible proposition (such as Einstein's notion that we are accelerating toward the center of the earth). The challenge for an explanatory speaker is to diagnose the principal difficulty facing the audience and to shape the speech to overcome that

EXPLANATORY SPEECH

A speech that explains the reasons underlying a problem, plan, or policy.

difficulty. The three difficulties can be overcome if speakers use elucidating, quasi-scientific, and transformative explanations.

Clarifying Concepts. If an audience's chief difficulty rests with understanding the meaning and use of a certain term, then the speaker should provide **elucidating explanations**. These explanations illuminate a concept's meaning and use. For example, speakers concerned principally with explaining concepts such as "evolution" and "municipal bond" should use elucidating explanations.

Good elucidating explanations (1) define a concept by listing each of its critical features; (2) contrast examples and nonexamples (nonexamples are instances that audiences often think are examples but are not) of the concept; and (3) present opportunities for audiences to distinguish examples from nonexamples by looking for a concept's critical features.

One effective elucidating speech explained what "science" means. The student began:

> We all know what science is. It's what Carl Sagan and Mr. Wizard do, right? Since we know, we should agree on some basic ideas. How many people think biology is a science? (Nearly all hands rise.) How many think psychology is? (A few hands rise.) How about astrology? (A few hands rise.)

This speech was effective because, after establishing that science is hard to explain, the speaker offered a definitional listing of the concept's critical features, gave an array of examples and nonexamples of science (e.g., psychology vs. astrology), and offered the audience opportunities to distinguish examples from nonexamples with a short oral quiz.

Explaining the Big Picture. If an idea is difficult chiefly because its complexity obscures its main points or the "big picture," then speakers should use a quasi-scientific explanation. Just as scientists try to develop models of the world, **quasi-scientific explanations** model or picture the key dimensions of some phenomenon for a lay audience. Speakers presenting complex topics to laypeople—topics such as how microchips work, the similarities and differences between Buddhism and Christianity, or how DNA molecules pass along genetic information—should try to use quasi-scientific explanations.

Effective quasi-scientific explanations highlight the main points with such features as titles, organizing analogies, visual aids, and signaling phrases ("The first key point is"). Good quasi-scientific explanations also connect key points by using transitional phrases such as "for example," connectives ("because"), and diagrams depicting relationships among parts.

For example, a particularly good quasi-scientific speech explained how radar works. Using an organizing analogy, the speaker said that radar works essentially the way an echo does, except that radio waves, rather than sound waves, are sent and received. The presentation was effective because consistent references to this analogy highlighted the speaker's main points.

ELUCIDATING EXPLANATION

An explanation that illuminates a concept's meaning and use.

QUASI-SCIENTIFIC EXPLANATION

An explanation that models or pictures the key dimensions of a phenomenon for a lay audience.

Types and Topics

How are the eight categories of speech topics and the four types of speeches related? That is, are speeches about people most likely to fit into one of the four types of informative speeches? How about the other seven topic categories?

TRANSFORMATIVE
EXPLANATION

*An explanation that
helps a lay audience
understand ideas that
are contrary to our
intuition.*

Challenging Intuition. Sometimes the chief source of difficulty is that the idea is contrary to what our intuition tell us. When this is the case, speakers should design their talks as **transformative explanations**. For example, the idea that when one pushes a concrete wall, that wall exerts an equal and opposite force on the pusher (Newton's Third Law of Motion) contains no difficult terms and little detail, but from a lay perspective, it just seems hard to believe. Transformative explanations are designed to help lay audiences transform their everyday "theories" about phenomena into more accepted notions.

Speakers frequently use "why" questions if an audience is predisposed to skepticism or even hostility. Thus, an important function of transformative explanations is to calm the audience by telling why a condition exists or why an action is being taken. If, for example, members of a city's board of education are fully informed about the factors that led the mayor to reduce the school budget, they are likely to be more disposed to work with the new budget than if they had not been told about the conditions that led to the cuts.

Transformative explanations are most effective when they (1) state the audience's "implicit" or "lay" theory about a phenomenon; (2) acknowledge that this theory is plausible or reasonable; (3) demonstrate its inadequacy; (4) state the speaker's explanation; and (5) demonstrate that this explanation is in some way better than the other one.[12]

Topics for informative speeches, then, can be located in eight categories: people, places, things, events, processes, concepts, problems, and plans and policies. Once a topic has been identified, it can be developed via four types of speeches: descriptive, demonstration, definitional, or explanatory.

◆ Barriers to Communicating Information

Having explored the nature of informative speaking and ways of generating topics for such speeches, we turn next to identifying the potential difficulties an informative speaker will face. Hart identifies eight of the most common **communication barriers** that speakers encounter as they begin to think about developing an informative message.[13]

COMMUNICATION
BARRIERS

*Eight dilemmas
speakers face when
they attempt to
transmit information.*

Content Barriers

The first four barriers identified by Hart have to do with the choice of information to include in an informative speech.

There is too much or not enough information. "Information overload" produces frustration as an audience feels buried by an avalanche of information and stops listening. As we stated earlier in this chapter, information must be analyzed and communicated if it is to become useful knowledge. Erring in the other direction ("information underload"), however, can produce an equally undesirable result—audience boredom. The informative

*E*thics and the "Right" Amount of Information

In deciding how much information to present, do you have an ethical responsibility to present all sides of an issue? For example, does a district attorney have a responsibility to tell a grand jury about all known facts of a case? Should a sales representative for a drug manufacturer tell doctors about the side effects of a drug? Should an army recruiter tell potential recruits about both the advantages and the disadvantages of military life? What criteria did you use to arrive at answers to these questions?

speaker must be aware of the audience's level of expertise and present enough information to challenge but not overwhelm the average member.

Information is too factual or too inferential. "Ideal" informative speakers are neither fact-spewing computers nor rambling philosophers. Rather, they know how to extend their listeners' knowledge by blending hard data and intelligent speculation. Most audiences want enough facts to support the inferences and enough inferences to answer the question "So what?" about the facts.

Information is too concrete or too abstract. Curious, searching audiences demand that speakers satisfy their needs for both concrete and abstract information. Speakers who carefully mix and match material should be able to satisfy both demands of audiences.

Information is too general or too specific. By carefully and consciously moving from the general to the specific, and back again, the speaker can introduce variety and improve the audiences' chances of seeing both the forest and the trees.

Presentational Barriers

Hart's final four barriers to communication involve the circumstances of the presentation and the speaker's style in organizing and delivering the speech.

Communication is feedback-poor or feedback-rich. Because public speaking is primarily a one-way transmission of information, the speaker must often be quite creative in finding ways to assess whether the audience is mastering the content of the presentation. Speakers can use a variety of techniques to obtain relevant feedback from an audience—for example, monitoring the reactions of one or two representative members of an audience, or reminding the audience to "Ask questions if you don't understand something." Of course, a speaker can focus so much on one or two members of an audience that the focus of the message is lost. Or one listener may

Overcoming the Barriers

As you reflect on your experience as a listener, which of the eight communication barriers do you think is (or are) the most difficult for speakers to overcome? Explain your reasoning.

interrupt with questions that are of no interest to the rest of the audience. Delayed feedback can be obtained for future use from a friend who attended the presentation or from an audio- or videotape of the presentation (focusing on the speaker and/or on the audience).

Information is presented too rapidly or too slowly. Research suggests that "normal conversational delivery" is best suited to covering material with clarity and efficiency. The important thing to remember is that both excessively rapid and inordinately slow delivery of a speech will decrease audience retention.

Information is presented too soon or too late. Fortunately, with careful preparation and the knowledge of a few elementary principles of organization, the "too soon/too late" problem is easily solved. For example, by remembering that listeners find it easier to move from the simple to the complex, from the concrete to the abstract, and from the immediate to the anticipated, you can often avoid moving into material too quickly. Similarly, by knowing that listeners have a need for pattern, chronology, and completeness, you will be reminded that information must be "packaged" for an audience to be able to absorb and retain it.

Information is presented with too much or too little intensity. When speakers get overly involved in the material being presented, the audience may feel they are more concerned about preaching than they are about sharing information. On the other hand, an audience will probably share the lack of enthusiasm of the speaker who merely goes through the motions.

◆ Guidelines for Informative Presentations

Once a topic has been selected, as you may recall from Chapter 13, the speaker has a number of tasks to perform in preparing and delivering a speech:

1. Analyzing the audience
2. Identifying and organizing main points
3. Providing support for ideas
4. Outlining the speech
5. Developing an introduction, transitions, and conclusion
6. Selecting a type of delivery and rehearsing and delivering the speech

In this section, we focus on adapting these tasks to the requirements of an informative speaker.

Adapting Your Presentation to Your Audience

In Chapter 13, we suggested an analysis of audience type, reference groups, and situational expectations as a prerequisite to developing your message. For an informative speech, ask yourself how you have adapted (or

Adjusting to Your Audience

To practice adapting an informative speech to a particular audience, consider how you would present a topic to a group that seems to have no interest in it. From the lists below, select a topic and an audience. Create a preliminary outline of the speech that includes the speech topic, a thesis statement, general and specific purposes, main points, and a list of visual aids. Show in your thesis statement, purpose statements, and main points how you will make your speech significant, meaningful, personally beneficial, useful, practical, and/or comprehensible for your audience.

Speech Topic	*Audience*
Manicuring one's nails	Auto mechanics
French cuisine	Recent immigrants from India
Writing poetry	Inner-city youth gangs
The dynamics of hang gliding	Senior citizens at a weekly meeting

Source: Based on S. D. Downey (1988), Audience analysis exercise, *The Speech Communication Teacher,* 2(2), 1–2.

can adapt) your presentation to the knowledge and interest levels of your audience. As you work through this task, consider that there are three fairly easy ways to adapt a speech to a particular audience: (1) Establish the *relevance* of the topic in the *introduction* and reiterate it in the *conclusion* of the speech; (2) adjust the *language* of the speech to fit the age, education level, and comprehension of the audience; and (3) use *examples* or *analogies* that match the interests or hobbies of the audience.

Choosing Main Points, Organizational Patterns, and Forms of Support

In Chapter 13, we used the "topical system" to identify the main points that support a specific purpose. We then placed these main points into a pattern of organization, provided support for the main points, and visually displayed the speech in the form of an outline. An alternative to the outline is Phillips's "structuring" approach, a visual presentation of the organization.[14] **Structuring** is a method of organizing messages by means of residual messages (ideas to be retained by the audience) and common patterns of message organization. After thinking about both approaches, you can decide which one works better for your purposes.

People have orderly minds. Structuring helps you organize ideas into patterns your audience can easily identify and understand. After formulating

STRUCTURING

A method of organizing messages by means of residual messages (ideas to be retained by the audience) and common patterns of message organization.

"TODAY'S RECIPE FOR WHAT I CALL 'THE ORIGIN OF LIFE,' REQUIRES A BIT OF HYDROGEN, NITROGEN, COMPOUNDS OF SULFER, CARBON, A SMATTERING OF METALS: IRON, MAGNESIUM . . . "

Analogies to subjects or ideas that are familiar to an audience can help the listeners understand information about an unfamiliar topic.

the residual message ("When I am done with my speech, I want my audience to know or believe that . . ."), choose a structure by which to organize your speech. In addition to the five patterns discussed in Chapter 13 (chronological, topical, spatial or geographical, cause-effect, and problem-solution), Phillips suggests structuring by *comparison* and by *contrast*.

The following examples, which use the general topic "cakes," are deliberately simplified to show how structuring works.

Chronological structure The speaker outlines a series of events or steps in a process; the events or steps must follow a specific order.

Residual message "When I am done with my speech, I want my audience to know that baking a cake is a simple process."

- Buy ingredients
- Mix ingredients
- Bake mixture

Topical structure Giving information is the speaker's primary goal; each of the categories must be comprised of relatively equal, nonoverlapping main points.

Residual message "When I am done with my speech, I want my audience to know that there are three superior cake mixes."

- Betty Crocker
- Pillsbury
- Duncan Hines

Preparing Contingency Plans for Public Speaking Situations

As a final step in the speech preparation process, consider how you would cope with a variety of unusual events that can confront the public speaker. Professional speakers routinely encounter situations that you, as a novice, are not likely to envision. However, if you do find yourself in an unusual situation, you cannot ignore it without endangering the effectiveness of your communication.

How would you address the following situations?

- Pillars in the room prevent some audience members from seeing the transparencies you are projecting.

- You arrive to give your speech and are asked to speak for an hour instead of 30 minutes because a second speaker has canceled.

- You take out your speaking notes but, just as you are being introduced to the audience, discover that some of the notes are missing.

- The bulb in the projector suddenly burns out, preventing you from showing your transparencies.

- Someone in the audience interrupts you to say that you are not speaking on the subject the audience has come to hear about.

- You are heckled.

- Someone in the audience begins laughing uncontrollably.

- The preceding speaker covers all of your material.

- Your introducer undermines your credibility with some caustic remarks.

- Nonverbal cues from your audience suggest that most members don't understand your supporting examples.

- An audience member challenges the statistics you have just cited.

- You can't tell whether the audience is accepting or rejecting your ideas.

- No one laughs at the joke you've just told to support a key idea.

- At the end of your speech the audience begins chanting, "Keep going!"

- Handouts are accidentally distributed ahead of schedule and the audience stops paying attention to your speech.

- The movements and facial expressions of the audience signal boredom, even though you've just begun to speak.

- A couple of audience questions can be interpreted as hints that your idea development is not sophisticated enough.

Source: Adapted from J. A. Jones (1981), Preparing contingency plans for public speaking situations, *Communication Education, 30,* 423–425.

Spatial structure The speaker describes parts of something and how they form the whole, either literally or figuratively.

Residual message "When I am done with my speech, I want my audience to know that a layer cake has four parts."

- Icing
- Layer
- Filling
- Layer

Cause-effect The speaker establishes that a relationship exists between two events or that a certain result is the product of a certain event.

Residual message "When I am done with my speech, I want my audience to know that a person who celebrates a birthday usually receives a cake."

- Cause   Birthday celebration
- Effect   Cake

Problem-solution The speaker outlines a problem, offers a feasible solution, and illustrates the advantages of the solution or how the solution solves the problem.

Residual message "When I am done with my speech, I want my audience to know that the problem associated with eating too much cake is weight gain, and that the problem can be solved through decreased cake consumption."

- Problem   Weight gain
- Solution   Decreased consumption of cake
- Advantage   Decreased weight

Comparison The speaker compares things by showing their similarities.

Residual message "When I am done with my speech, I want my audience to know that cake and pie are similar in three ways."

- Cake   Dessert; rich; baked
- Pie   Dessert; rich; baked

Contrast The speaker compares things by showing their differences.

Residual message "When I am done with my speech, I want my audience to know that cakes and poles are different in two ways."

- Cakes   Eat; batter
- Poles   Build; wood

To further develop each main point of a speech, you can use **substructuring.** Examine each main point and, on the basis of that point, choose one of the seven structures to develop your ideas, as illustrated in the following example.

Residual message "When I am done with my speech, I want my audience to know that baking a cake is a simple process."

Chronological structure: *Substructures used:*

- Buy ingredients   • Topical structure

  Solids

  Liquids

- Mix ingredients   • Chronological structure

  First do this

  Then do this

  Next do this

- Bake mixture   • Topical structure

  Baking times

  Doneness test

Polishing the Speech

Having developed a speech, you next polish it through rehearsal. This requires that the speech be ready about a week in advance to allow time to practice several times in front of a mirror or your friends. Assuming that you intend to speak extemporaneously, use the first few rehearsals to try out various phrasings of your ideas. As you start to feel comfortable with the flow of your speech, begin to work on time. Most classroom assignments will give you a range (say 5 to 7 minutes). Most often, it is wise to develop your speech with the low end of the range in mind. That is, if the range is 3 to 5 minutes, develop a speech that requires 3 minutes to deliver during practice. When you make the actual presentation, you will find that because of audience reaction, impromptu remarks, and so on, the speech will take longer than it did during rehearsal. As you reach the end of the rehearsal process, try to schedule one session in the actual room where the speech will be delivered. This will add to your comfort level and allow you to anticipate unforeseen contingencies. This is especially important if you are speaking in an unfamiliar setting or are using unfamiliar equipment, such as a microphone, an overhead projector, or a liquid crystal display (LCD) panel.

The Case of Tommy Gomez

At the beginning of this chapter we encountered Tommy Gomez, a member of the Catholic Worker Movement, whom Father Kennedy has asked to speak to his social work class at Georgetown University. Tommy's presentation will focus on the nature of the Catholic Worker Movement and its view of the societal problem of homelessness. What have you learned in this chapter that might help Tommy to prepare for his presentation?

• From which of the eight categories of speech topics should he draw his topic?

• Should his presentation be descriptive, a demonstration speech, definitional, or explanatory?

• Which of the barriers to communicating information will pose the greatest difficulty?

• What should Tommy do to analyze and adapt to his audience?

• What organizational patterns and forms of support should he use?

• What advice would you give him for practicing his presentation?

• Are there any contingency plans that he ought to formulate?

REVIEW

- Living in an *information age* means having vast quantities of data at our disposal. To take advantage of this array of facts and figures requires communication skills such as interpreting, analyzing, and transmitting information, as well as collecting it.

- There are eight categories of informative speech topics—people, places, things, events, processes, concepts, problems, and plans and policies.

- Once you have selected a topic, you can choose to develop it within four types of informative speeches: descriptive, demonstration, definitional, and explanatory.

- Common content barriers to the presentation of information include the following: too much or too little information; information that is too factual or inferential, too concrete or too abstract, too general or too specific.

- Presentational barriers include: communication that is feedback-poor or feedback-rich or information that is presented too rapidly or too slowly, too soon or too late, or with too much or too little intensity.

- Once you have determined a topic and type of informative speech, you must adapt your presentation to your audience, choose structures by which to organize your speech, and polish your speech.

- Adapting your speech to your audience includes (1) establishing the relevance of your topic, (2) adjusting the language to fit your audience, and (3) using examples or analogies that match the interests of your audience.

- You may organize your speech by structuring it according to residual messages and common patterns of message organization such as chronological, topical, spatial, cause-effect, problem-solution, comparison, or contrast.

- Finally, to present an effective speech, you should polish your speech through rehearsal and prepare contingency plans for troublesome situations that may arise.

General purpose: to inform

Specific purpose: to explain (a) the amount of nonverbal communication in baseball, (b) how nonverbal signals are used in baseball, and (c) their importance to the game.

Nonverbal Communication in the Game of Baseball

James Earley, *University of Oklahoma*

James uses his introduction to try to capture the audience's attention through the use of baseball signals. He then forecasts his three main points. Do you find his introduction interesting and informative? Why or why not?

1.   If I were to yell, "There's a long fly ball!" or "Take him deep!" or even "Give him the heater!" I'm sure that most of you would know I was about to give a speech about baseball. But if I were to give you a few signals, like: [demonstrate], I'm sure that most of you wouldn't know what I just did, and most of you wouldn't care. But if you were the runner on third base in the ninth inning of the seventh game of the World Series, those <u>exact</u> signals could mean a lot: They could mean the difference between winning the game--and being awarded a $25,000 bonus check--and losing the game and being awarded a handshake. It is the use of these nonverbal signs and signals, and how they allow baseball players and coaches to communicate with one another on the field, that I would like to focus on today. It is <u>not</u> my intention to make you all experts on the art of baseball signals. (You will not be ready for the majors after this speech.) But it <u>is</u> my intention to make you aware of the amount of nonverbal communication in baseball, to explain how the nonverbal signals are used, and to show their importance to the game.

Do you think James provides too much or too little information on the origins of baseball signals? James develops his first main point with the use of testimony. In addition to supporting his point, does the use of testimony also enhance his credibility as a speaker?

2.   Signals were not originally used in baseball. According to Tom Petroff's book <u>Baseball Signs</u>

and Signals, baseball signals began almost a century ago, when they were used by four players on the Baltimore Orioles: John McGraw, Hughey Jennings, Wilbert Robinson, and Wee Willie Keeler. At first, the signs were not liked or accepted. After the Orioles' had used those signals, the opposing manager, John Ward, said, "They weren't playing baseball; it was some new game [they] invented." Today, signals are an integral part of the game because teams use signals to encode their entire strategies. Signs are, first and foremost, a way for players to communicate with their own team members without speaking and giving their strategy away.

3.   Signs are used in virtually every aspect of the game. Signs are given to batters by the third-base coach. Signs are given to fielders by a coach in the dugout or by other fielders so the team can have a coordinated defensive strategy. Signs are given to base runners by the first- and third-base coaches so the players can be aggressive and smart on the basepaths. And most important, signs are given to pitchers. Once you get past Little League, signs are given before every pitch in every game in every league.

James provides examples showing the pervasiveness of nonverbal signs in baseball.

4.   The use of signs greatly increases the amount of strategy in the game of baseball. Because of signs, teams compete not only physically, but also mentally, with each team trying to outmaneuver the other. As Hall of Famer Keith Hernandez states in his book Pure Baseball, teams try to steal each other's signs to gain an advantage. The easiest signs to steal are the catcher's signs to the pitcher. Runners on second base will try to intercept the signs, interpret them, and signal to the batter what pitch will be coming. The signs that base coaches give are more complicated. They use an indicator when they transmit signals. For example, a base coach may give a batter signs both to bunt and to swing at a pitch, but the batter is to follow only

James uses an analogy to a children's game to explain the term indicator. Was this analogy useful?

the sign that is preceded by the indicator. This indicator confuses the opposing team in their attempts to steal the signals. This is similar to the technique used in the children's game, "Simon says." As you know, only the directions that are preceded by the proper indicator--the leader saying, "Simon says"--are to be followed.

Does James move effectively from his first main point to his second?

5.   Next, I would like to explain how baseball signals are used and take you through a hypothetical situation. I would like to start by explaining the roles of the first- and third-base coaches. These two coaches are sometimes referred to as "traffic cops." The first-base coach is responsible for some baserunning signs, and the third-base coach for baserunning and hitting signs.

After establishing the pervasiveness of nonverbal signs in baseball, James uses a hypothetical example to help the audience understand how they are used. Is this an effective form of support?

6.   Let me take you through an at-bat with Joe, to show a typical experience with signals. First, Joe comes up to the plate and looks for signals. From the third-base coach, Joe sees an indicator and the sign for a bunt; he then bunts his way to first base. Joe then watches the third-base coach again and sees an indicator, followed by a sign to steal second base, which he does. While on second, he sees the sign from the opposing catcher to the pitcher, and quickly relays the signal to his batter, letting him know what pitch will be coming. The batter hits a single, and as Joe crosses third base he is given a "go home" signal from the third-base coach. But before the play, the outfielder on the opposing team was given a sign by his coach to throw the ball to homeplate if it was hit to him. Even though the outfielder does throw the ball home, Joe is "safe!" This is yet another signal, one given by the umpire.

How effective is James's transition to his final main point?

7.   The final aspect of signals that I would like to discuss is their importance to the game. There are signals for fielding, baserunning, hitting, and pitching, all of which are extremely important. Signals give teams the opportunity to carry out their strategies, but signals can also go against a team if they are not used correctly.

8.   I would like to share with you a personal experience that demonstrates this risk. When I was a sophomore in high school, I was playing left field in a game against Yukon High School. It was the sixth inning of a very close game, and when we took the field we had a new pitcher on the mound. Yukon's best batter was at the plate. The catcher wanted an outside, low curveball and signaled this to the pitcher. The pitcher misread the sign as a call for an inside fastball, and he threw a beautiful one. Well, the batter promptly hit a two-run homer, the pitcher and the catcher started yelling at each other, and we lost the game.

To support his third, and final, point, James draws on his personal experience. Is this an effective strategy here?

9.   We tend to remember these cases of mixed up signals because they are a rare occurrence: Most of the time baseball signals are exchanged effectively. This use of signals increases the opportunities for strategy, which makes baseball more interesting--both for the fans and for the players.

10.   In conclusion, I'm sure that most of you have been to a baseball game, but did you ever notice the amount of nonverbal communication that was going on between the players and the coaches? If so, I know that you had no clue as to exactly what was being communicated, and to be quite honest with you, I can't tell you. These signs are "secret codes" that teams use and the only people who know these codes are the players and coaches. What I can tell you--again--is that signs and signals play an important role in virtually every aspect of the game. The next time you are at a baseball game, I ask you to block out all the sounds of the game and just watch the third-base coach, or the catcher, or even the second baseman. The signs you will see are not done simply because the players or the coaches are fidgety or have an itch somewhere. Rather, the signs are performed intentionally because the teams care about winning, and one way to accomplish this is through nonverbal communication.

James concludes his speech by asking his audience to apply what they have learned the next time they attend a baseball game. Will you try this?

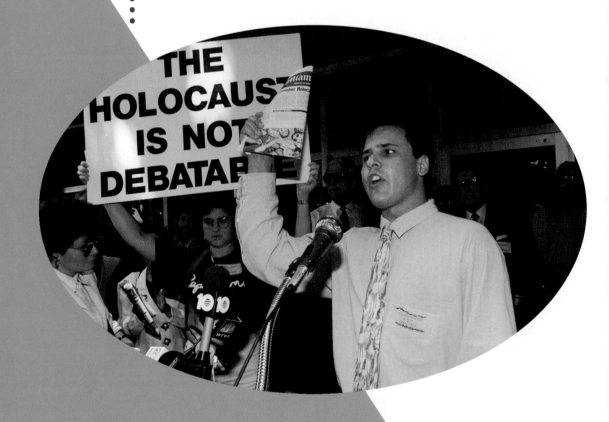

CHAPTER FIFTEEN

Persuasive
Presentations

After reading this chapter, you should be able to:

1. Explain what persuasion is and why it is important, and differentiate it from other communication purposes.

2. Give examples of four types of persuasive speeches.

3. Describe how to use the Toulmin model for displaying arguments visually.

4. Compare and contrast motivational, ethical, and logical proof.

5. Use Maslow's hierarchy to analyze an audience.

6. Identify and describe strategies for utilizing the dimensions of source credibility.

7. Discuss the impact of evidence on persuasion.

8. Describe how the Elaboration Likelihood Model can be used to plan strategies for a persuasive speech.

TEVE IS A STUDENT in a communication class much like this one. He is a religious peace activist and practices veganism, a strict form of vegetarianism. As a vegan, he avoids eating all meat and dairy products because he believes that (1) a vegetarian diet is healthier than a carnivore diet, (2) eating meat wastes God-given resources, and (3) eating meat entails violence against animals. For a persuasive speech assignment, Steve has decided to talk about veganism in order to convince other students to alter their diets.

As you read this chapter, you will learn the skills that Steve will need in order to make a successful persuasive presentation. At the end of the chapter, we will return to this scenario and solicit your advice.

◆ Persuasive Speaking, Past and Present

Speculation on how to persuade effectively was first recorded in the writings of an Egyptian sage, Ptah-Hotep (pronounced ta-ho-ta-pe), some 4500 years ago.[1] In his Maxims, Ptah-Hotep tells us that he is 110 years old, has lived through seven kings in the fifth dynasty of Egypt, and is now advising King Isesi, ruler of Upper and Lower Egypt. His counsel to the king involves five principles of effective persuasion that remain applicable today: (1) When in doubt about what to say, keep silent; (2) wait for the right moment to speak; (3) restrain passionate words; (4) speak fluently but with great deliberation; and (5) above all, keep your tongue at one with your heart so that you speak the truth.

Although the Egyptians were the first to write about persuasion, it was the Greeks (and later the Romans) who produced the first systematic accounts of the art of persuasion. Starting in the fifth century B.C., Greek philosophers/teachers began to record their observations and recommendations about how to speak effectively as a participant in the government of the city-state, in the law courts, and on ceremonial occasions. Their advice was frequently summarized within the context of five canons: *invention*—discovering the content of the message (both issues and supporting material); *arrangement*—organizing the content into introduction, narration, proof, and conclusion; *style*—wording the content in a way that meets such criteria as correctness, clarity, ornamentation, and propriety; *memory*— developing and using techniques that allow the speaker to remember the presentation after it has been prepared; and *delivery*—using voice and gestures to present a message effectively.

Greek and Roman citizens considered it important to be able to speak persuasively. When they went to the law court (as either defendant or prosecutor), they served as their own lawyers. Because anyone could prosecute and, by winning the case, receive a percentage of the fine, lawsuits were fairly common. Although they could and often did hire someone to help them prepare the case, in the courtroom these Greek and Roman citizens were on their own. The situation was similar for the assembly, the legislative branch of government. When the assembly considered such issues as war, taxes, ostracism, or the granting of citizenship, all members of the assembly were invited to participate. In addition, Greek and Roman citizens were frequently asked to speak at ceremonial occasions—funerals, births, holidays, and the like. In short, early Greece—and to a lesser extent Rome—were societies that expected all citizens to master the skills of persuasive speaking.

The circumstances have changed, but the ability to speak clearly, eloquently, and persuasively remains the hallmark of an educated member of our society. Although proportionately fewer of us argue a case in court, speak in a legislative assembly, or make ceremonial remarks, we still find many occasions to practice the important art of persuasion—at home, at church, at school, at work, with friends, in the market, or in any of the numerous contexts in which we live our lives. There are many reasons for the continuing importance of persuasion. The most central one, however,

In ancient Greece and Rome, the skills of persuasive speaking were needed to perform the duties of citizenship. In Shakespeare's play Julius Caesar, *Mark Antony's persuasive funeral oration turns his listeners against the plotters of Caesar's assassination. (This dramatic moment is shown here in a still from the 1953 movie, in which the part of Mark Antony was played by Marlon Brando.)*

results from two clashing features of our world: the continuing and ever escalating pace of change, and the general preference for a stable environment—one where people know what to do. For example, it is often easier to forgo the advanced features of a new VCR or computer program for the comfort of continuing to work with older equipment or familiar materials. In addition, individuals unable to adapt to change may find themselves ill (e.g., because they have not taken precautions against a new disease), without work (caught in an environment of downsizing), or otherwise at a disadvantage. Competent persuasive speakers can convince their listeners to share their goals, which may in turn actually affect the nature of change. If you can convince your audience to share your goals, you and your listeners can work together to cope with our rapidly changing environment.

In this chapter, therefore, we build on the previous two chapters as we focus on the special challenges of persuading an audience to accept our point of view. This chapter supplements the general principles of public speaking with more targeted advice for persuasive speaking situations. Before we proceed, however, we explore what it means to present a persuasive message. What is persuasion?

◆ Defining Persuasion

Persuasive discourse is not a pure form of discourse. It is a complex mixture of factors found in other forms of discourse and applied to uniquely persuasive ends. In other words, a persuasive speech follows the general rules of informative speaking, but it organizes arguments and information in a way that elicits a desired response from the receiver of the message.[2] To be

PERSUASION

*A conscious attempt
by one individual to
change the attitudes,
beliefs, or behavior of
another individual or
group of individuals
through the inter-
active process of
exchanging verbal
and nonverbal
messages.*

labeled persuasive, a communication situation must, at a minimum, involve a conscious attempt by one individual to change the attitudes, beliefs, or behavior of another individual or group of individuals through the transmission of some message.[3]

For our purposes, **persuasion** refers to the act of manipulating symbols in order to produce change in others.[4] For example, the desired effect of a speech on safe sex may be to encourage the audience to avoid dangerous sexual situations. In order to accomplish this outcome, an effective persuasive speaker should use examples and ideas (symbols) that convince (manipulate) the audience to alter or reevaluate its behavior.

Although many other definitions of persuasion exist, the key to understanding persuasion is knowing the five characteristics that identify persuasion as a communication event:

1. One individual (the persuader) must make a conscious, intended attempt to influence one or more other individuals.
2. The persuader generates and uses a variety of messages (both verbal and nonverbal) to accomplish this intended purpose.
3. The activity of persuasion is a process in which both the persuader and the persuadee are active participants.
4. The goal of persuasion is to change the beliefs, attitudes, or behavior of persuadees.
5. At some level, the persuadees must have a choice—that is, they must perceive that they have the option to accept or reject the persuader's message.

◆ Forms of Persuasive Speaking

As we know from Chapter 14, the task of an informative speaker is to present information in such a fashion that an audience will focus on, understand, and remember it. The persuasive speaker has yet one more task: to present a message that, if accepted, requires the audience to change beliefs, attitudes, values, or behaviors. Historically, these changes have been categorized according to four types of speeches.[5]

Propositions of Fact

**SPEECH THAT AFFIRMS
A PROPOSITION
OF FACT**

*A speech that
answers the question
"Was it/is it/will it
be true?" by making
designative claims.*

In **speeches that affirm propositions of fact**, you make and support designative claims. That is, you pose and answer the question "Was it/is it/will it be true?" The alleged fact that you want the audience to accept as true can concern an individual, an event, a process, a condition, a concept, or a policy. The following are examples of propositions that allege the existence of a fact: "The federal government has evidence that flying saucers are real."

"Workers in smoky bars and restaurants face a great risk of lung cancer."
"Your dealership will lose money on its sales of compact cars because your
inventory is too small."

Propositions of Value

Speeches that affirm propositions of value make evaluative claims. That
is, they answer the question "Of what worth is it?" In speeches of this type,
you seek to convince an audience that something meets or does not meet
a specific value standard of goodness or quality. The value standard can
be applied to an individual, an event, an object, a way of life, a process, a condition, or another value. You can urge the adoption of a new value, the adoption of a new perspective through redefining an old value, or the renewal
of commitment to an already held value. Consider the following examples: "Lee Jones is the best professor in our communication department."
"Nuclear weapons are immoral." "Organized religion has produced more
harm than good."

SPEECH THAT AFFIRMS
A PROPOSITION
OF VALUE
*A speech that
answers the question
"Of what worth is
it?" by making
evaluative claims.*

Concern about a Problem

In **speeches that create concern about a problem**, you advance definitive
claims. That is, you answer the question "What is it?" You ask an audience
to agree that specific conditions should be perceived as a problem requiring
solution. In addition to making a compelling presentation concerning the
nature of the problem, in such speeches you attempt to create concern by
showing the impact of the problem on the audience. The following are examples of propositions asserting problems: "The United States' sale of arms to
other countries is a cause for concern." "Sexual harassment is a continuing
problem on college and university campuses." "We should be concerned
about the depiction of violence on children's television shows."

SPEECH THAT
CREATES CONCERN
ABOUT A PROBLEM
*A speech that
answers the question
"What is it?" by
making definitive
claims.*

Propositions of Policy

In **speeches that affirm propositions of policy**, you make advocative claims.
That is, you answer the question "What course of action should be pursued?"
In addition to urging adoption of a new policy or course of action, you can
recommend continuing or discontinuing an existing policy or rejecting a proposed policy. Your task as the speaker is to advocate a course of action or policy as necessary and desirable (or unnecessary and undesirable). Examples
of such propositions include: "Federal regulation of the airline industry should
be reinstituted." "Gays and lesbians should have the same rights as all Americans." "Colleges and universities should not adopt speech codes."

SPEECH THAT AFFIRMS
A PROPOSITION
OF POLICY
*A speech that
answers the question
"What course of
action should be
pursued?" by making
advocative claims.*

Our fourfold category scheme is, of course, less mutually exclusive than
it would at first appear. With slight modifications, a topic in one category
could easily be made to fit another. How you shape your message is what
leads a speech to be categorized as one that affirms a fact, a value, a problem,
or a policy.

◆ Generating and Evaluating Arguments: Toulmin's Model

When you ask an audience to accept a proposition of fact, value, problem, or policy, you do so by offering good reasons—reasons that the audience will judge as either acceptable or unacceptable and hence persuasive or nonpersuasive. The analysis and terminology of English logician Stephen Toulmin provide a useful approach to generating and evaluating "good reasons."[6] As Toulmin describes it, when we give good reasons (an argument), we move from data, through a warrant, to a claim.

Claim (C) is the term Toulmin uses to describe the conclusion that you want the audience to accept. The claim might be a fact, a value, a problem, or a policy, or it might be an intermediate claim that supports your purpose. The claim is always potentially controversial and hence requires support that the audience will accept.

Data (D) answer the question "What is the support/grounding for the claim?" Data include the forms of support we described in Chapter 13: language, explanations, examples, statistics, testimony, and visuals. They can also include the credibility of the speaker or the values, motives, and beliefs of the audience.

Warrant (W) is the name Toulmin gives to the part of an argument that justifies the "jump" involved in going from accepting data to accepting a controversial claim. The warrant answers the question "How do you get from the data to the claim?" The function of the warrant is to show that the data do in fact support the claim as true or acceptable.

Toulmin diagrammed the relationship among the three foundational components of an argument as shown in Figure 15.1.

In addition to the basic triad of **Toulmin's model** (data, claim, and warrant), there is a second triad of components, any or all of which may be part of an argument. Toulmin calls these backing, rebuttal, and qualifier.

Backing (B) provides support for a warrant when listeners are not willing to accept a warrant at its face value. Support for a warrant (backing) can be a single item or an entire argument in itself complete with data and claim. In the sample argument given in Figure 15.2, it might be necessary to provide

TOULMIN'S MODEL

A method of generating, evaluating, and displaying "good reasons" for accepting a fact, value, problem, or policy in terms of a primary triad (data, warrant, claim) and a secondary triad (backing, rebuttal, qualifier).

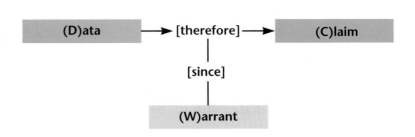

FIGURE 15.1
The three foundational components of an argument, as diagrammed by Toulmin.

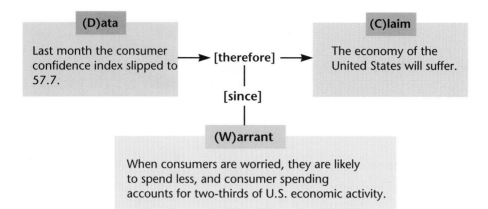

FIGURE 15.2

An example of the use of Toulmin's model.

backing in the form of statistics that demonstrate the historical relationship between consumer confidence and consumer spending.

The *rebuttal* (R) is appended to the claim and recognizes conditions under which the claim will be true or not true only in a qualified or restricted way. The rebuttal anticipates objections that an audience might advance against the claim. In the argument on consumer confidence, for example, a potential rebuttal might be: "Unless other features of the economy, such as low interest rates combined with low housing prices, lead consumers to spend in spite of their fears."

The *qualifier* (Q) expresses the degree of force that you as the speaker believe the claim to possess. When you believe the claim to be incontrovertible, no qualifier is necessary. When you do not possess this conviction, you can qualify the claim with words such as *probably, usually,* and *possibly.* The qualifier might also make specific reference to an anticipated rebuttal.

Figure 15.3 on page 462 shows the model with all six elements.

◆ Forms of Proof

Using Toulmin's model, you can think through and visually display the "good reasons" why you think your audience ought to accept your claim about a fact, value, problem, or policy. Traditionally, forms of proof have been organized into three categories. Aristotle and the ancient Greeks called them *pathos* (**motivational proof** based on the inner drives, values, or aspirations of the audience); *ethos* (**ethical proof** based on the credibility of the source of the message); and *logos* (**logical proof** based on evidence, such as statistics and examples). Using the Toulmin model, you can diagram any argument whether it is based on logical, ethical, or motivational proof. You can also use the model to anticipate objections your audience may raise (in the form of rebuttals) and think about ways of dealing with those objections (qualifiers).

MOTIVATIONAL PROOF

Proof that asks an audience to accept a claim on the grounds that the claim is consistent with listeners' needs and values.

ETHICAL PROOF

Proof that asks an audience to accept a claim because of the speaker's competence, trustworthiness, dynamism, power, goodwill, idealism, or similarity to the audience.

LOGICAL PROOF

Proof that asks an audience to accept a claim because objective evidence supports the claim.

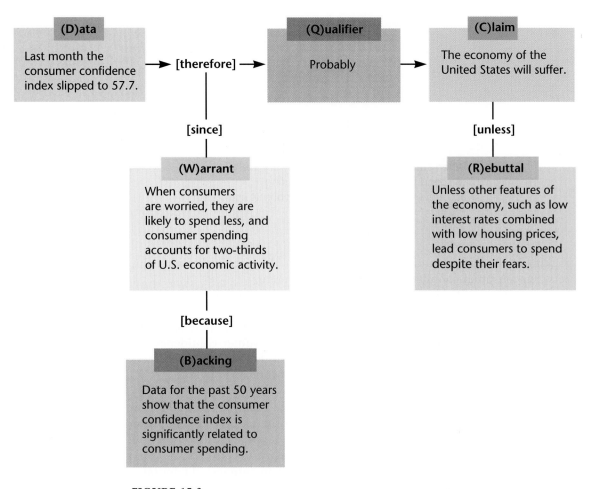

FIGURE 15.3
An example of Toulmin's model using all six elements.

Motivational Proof: Maslow's Hierarchy

At the heart of persuasion is the ability to adapt a message to the feelings, needs, and values of an audience. Helpful in this process is the work of psychologist Abraham Maslow.[7] Maslow argues that an individual's motivations, priorities, and behavior are influenced primarily by that person's needs. A need is a deficit that creates tension. Maslow identifies needs in a hierarchical structure of five categories (see Figure 15.4). From low (immature) to high (mature), they are:

1. *Physiological/survival needs*: Things you need for basic survival—air, water, food, shelter, sleep, clothing, sex, and so on.

2. *Safety needs*: Needs for security, orderliness, protective rules, and avoidance of risk. They include not only actual physical safety but safety from emotional injury as well.

3. *Belongingness/social needs*: Needs that move beyond personal needs (basic and safety) to those centered around your interactions with others. They include the desire to be accepted and liked by other people and the need for love, affection, and affiliation. These needs are normally met by family ties, friendships, and membership in work and social groups.

4. *Esteem/ego-status needs*: The need to be accepted by some group and to be recognized for achievement, mastery, competence, and so on. The need to be perceived as worthy by self and others is satisfied by special recognition, social and professional rewards, promotions, awards, power, and achievement. Unlike the previous three categories, esteem needs are not satisfied internally; they require outside feedback—that is, others must acknowledge the superior performance.

5. *Self-actualizing needs*: The highest level of needs, focusing on the need for personal development and self-fulfillment—becoming what you can become. Instead of looking for recognition of your worth from others, you seek to measure up to your own criteria for personal success. Thus, self-actualizing behaviors are growth-motivated, not deficiency-motivated. Self-actualized people accept their own and others' frailties and become what they are capable of becoming.

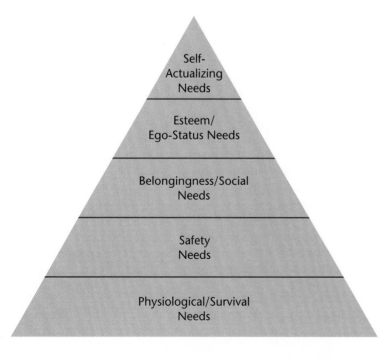

FIGURE 15.4
Maslow's hierarchy of needs.

Needs and Culture

To what degree, in your opinion, does Maslow's hierarchy transcend cultural boundaries? For example, would Americans and Asians generally rank Maslow's needs in the same order?

In Maslow's view, people have an internal need that pushes them toward self-actualization and fulfillment. However, needs are arranged in a hierarchy of importance, and behavior is always determined by the lowest category of need remaining unsatisfied. Thus, when you are truly hungry and thirsty, it is difficult to be motivated by higher-level needs. The need that is motivating, then, depends on what you already have. Needs that are not satisfied influence behavior; satisfied needs do not.

The implications of Maslow's hierarchy for persuasive speaking are straightforward. The persuasive speaker must consider the level of the hierarchy that characterizes the majority of the audience and adapt the message appropriately. For the majority of speeches in this class, the appropriate levels are likely to be those of belongingness and esteem. You should not attempt to identify the appropriate level in a hasty manner, however. Appealing to a level that is too low or too high for the majority of the audience will result in decreased audience interest and attention.

Ethical Proof

The persuasiveness of a message is commonly assumed to be influenced by the person who delivers it. Business organizations therefore spend vast amounts of money hiring people who are held in esteem by the general public to sell their products and represent their interests. For example, fundraising campaigns and membership drives list important persons on their letterheads. Even in social conversations, you may drop the names of respectable sources as you pass along rumors and gossip.

SOURCE CREDIBILITY

An audience's perception of a message source independent of that source's intent or purpose.

Students of communication, from classical to contemporary times, have devoted considerable effort to understanding this phenomenon. Their work supports our commonsense observation that **source credibility**—an audience's perception of a message source independent of that source's intent or purpose—is an important factor in whether or not listeners accept the message.

For example, in an early study, Hovland and Weiss presented identical messages on four topics (antihistamine drugs, atomic submarines, the steel shortage, and the future of movie theaters) to two groups.[8] One group was told that the author of the message was highly credible (e.g., the *New England Journal of Biology and Medicine* on antihistamine drugs); the other group was told that the source of the message was less credible (a mass-circulation monthly illustrated magazine). Opinion questionnaires were administered before, immediately after, and a month after the communication. The researchers discovered that the subjects did perceive differences in the credibility of the sources: The four high-credibility sources were judged to be trustworthy by 81 to 95 percent of the subjects, whereas the low-credibility sources were judged trustworthy by only 1 to 21 percent. The researchers also discovered that these differences in the perception of the sources produced different perceptions of the messages. Even though the messages were identical as to content, the presentations were considered to be "less fair" and the conclusions were thought to be "less justified" when the sources were of low rather than of high credibility. In addition, opinions changed more often in the desired direction when information originated from the more credible sources.

In another early study, Miller and Hewgill examined how the delivery of a speech might change an audience's perception of source credibility. Specifically, two types of vocal nonfluencies, *repetition* ("For New—uh—Newman") and *vocalized pauses* ("uh"), were considered.[9] The researchers tape-recorded nine versions of a speech given by a trained speaker who was arguing that the practice of granting scholarships to college or university students on the basis of athletic ability should be abolished. Four of the messages contained varying numbers of vocalized pauses and four contained similarly varied amounts of repetition. One version of the speech was delivered smoothly, without "uhs" or repetition. As the authors predicted, subjects who heard the professionally delivered speech rated the speaker as significantly more competent than did subjects who heard a stumbling delivery. The professional speech was also judged to be dynamic. Contrary to the authors' hypothesis, however, judgments of trustworthiness were less affected by speech errors. In fact, the most trusted versions of the speech were those containing modest levels of vocal pauses and repetition.

These two studies illustrate that, in part, an audience accepts or rejects what a speaker says on the basis of personal characteristics they perceive in the speaker; and that these perceptions are changeable—that is, credibility can be built or destroyed by what a speaker says or does.

Clearly, then, credibility is not an all or nothing proposition. In fact, numerous studies have demonstrated that individuals weigh a number of factors when they are deciding whether to believe a speaker. Although these

Martin Luther King, Jr., was one of the most persuasive speakers in U.S. history. He was highly regarded by his large following on all the dimensions of credibility.

dimensions have varied from study to study, two factors have most consistently emerged: competence and trustworthiness. They are the first two in a list of seven potential dimensions of credibility compiled by Hart, Friedrich, and Brummett. These researchers provide a number of strategies for developing each dimension.[10]

Competence. To present yourself as an authority on your topic, you should rely on the following strategies:

- *Demonstrate personal acquaintance with the topic.* It is important to let the audience know why you chose to speak on this topic—how you got involved and why you care. If the topic is something with which you are personally involved (you've done it, it's part of your job, it's your hobby, etc.), an audience is likely to accept what you say about the topic.

- *Demonstrate familiarity with the topic's special vocabulary.* An additional way to demonstrate competence is by correctly using terminology related to your topic. However, don't use jargon for the sake of jargon—and be sure to define unfamiliar terms.

- *Demonstrate familiarity with experts in the field.* Citing such authorities in support of a point is especially important if the audience perceives you as a moderate- or low-credible source. When quoting others, the more reliable your expert is, the more it will do for your own believability. Therefore, it is wise to analyze your audience carefully to discover whose opinions it values.

- *Be sure that your speech is well organized.* A well-organized message may not increase credibility, but a disorganized speech will usually decrease it. Thus, it pays to spend time organizing your speech so that your audience will find it easy to follow.

Trustworthiness. Your audience is likely to consider you reliable if you do the following:

- *If at all possible, establish verbal interaction with the audience.* This is difficult at times, but speakers who open themselves up to ongoing public scrutiny give the impression that they are sure of themselves and their positions. Listeners reason that a speaker who accepts such a challenge is one who will maintain his or her views in other communicative situations.

- *Demonstrate that your present behavior is consistent with your past behavior.* It is often good to "remind" audience members of what you have done in the past on their behalf or on behalf of the proposition you advocate.

- *Show that you can be trusted by being as explicit as possible and by entertaining other points of view.* Most listeners appreciate someone who does not waste their time. Also, it is often wise to treat both sides of an issue in order to build an image of fair-mindedness.

• *Make sure that your verbal and nonverbal behaviors are consistent.* Thousands of subtle, nonverbal cues can suggest that you do not really believe what you are saying. Because people believe that nonverbal cues are harder to fake, they tend to believe nonverbal cues more than verbal ones.

Dynamism. To appear forceful, aggressive, and emphatic, you should do the following:

• *Indicate exactly what behavioral commitments you have made to your position.* If you can show what you have done on behalf of your proposal, you are likely to be perceived as dynamic.

• *Learn to control delivery variables.* Practice your speech so that you can deliver it smoothly. Avoid speech errors such as "uh" and "er," which can call into question a speaker's dynamism.

Power. If you are in a position of power, you need not flaunt it. Here are strategies for maintaining your authority without intimidating your audience:

• *Use overt power strategies sparingly and subtly.* If you have the ability to reward and punish an audience, you do not need to mention this fact. The audience will be aware of it. When reminded of a power imbalance, an audience is likely to resent it and rebel in some fashion.

• *Indicate that the balance of power between speaker and audience will be maintained.* By this we mean that you should, if possible, indicate that you and your audience will profit equally from the interaction. In most situations, you are wise to acknowledge both what you expect to derive from the interaction and what "power" the audience itself is likely to garner.

Goodwill. To reassure your listeners about your positive attitude toward them, you should:

• *Demonstrate that your proposal will benefit the audience.* Show the audience how it will gain important rewards by accepting your position or, at least, that it will not lose by doing so.

• *Show that other groups of similar individuals have accepted your proposal.* If other groups have perceived your goodwill, this one should too.

• *Communicate genuine interest and affection.* The key word here is *genuine.* False expressions of interest and affection are often easily detected by listeners who have reason to be wary.

Strategies and Culture

Which of the strategies for building credibility are likely to be useful to audiences from all cultures? Which are likely to be effective to different degrees in different cultures?

Idealism. Present yourself as a model for your listeners by doing the following:

• *Depict yourself as being both similar to and different from your audience.* This is only one of the many dilemmas associated with building credibility. Obviously, listeners admire those who share their values, attitudes, and goals. On the other hand, unless you are somehow different from them, your listeners will have little reason to look up to you. Thus, by demonstrating that you have certain knowledge that the audience needs or that you embody certain aspirations of the audience in dramatic ways, you may be able to build an alike-but-different image of yourself.

- *Indicate what you have risked (or are willing to risk) on behalf of your proposal.* Most people, it seems, tend to believe those who have taken a stand on behalf of something they strongly believe in.

Similarity. To show that you identify with the audience, use the following strategies:

- *Provide an overt statement of agreement with the audience on at least a peripheral issue.* If you cannot agree with the audience on major issues, at least take a positive, agreeing position on a minor point. No matter who your audience is, you should be able to find some minor issue of agreement.

- *Learn to control your nonverbal behavior.* Personal appearance and demeanor, such as nuances of posture, body position, physical distance, eye contact, dress, grooming, and the like, provide audience members with cues for seeing you as similar to or different from themselves. The challenge for you as a speaker is to discover those nonverbal cues that communicate similarity to the particular audience in question.

- *Demonstrate that you represent the greatest common denominator of the audience's beliefs and values.* In public communication situations, you must be especially careful not to alienate a sizable portion of the audience. Any group of listeners usually harbors diverse and sometimes opposing viewpoints. Thus, you are wise to emphasize those aspects of your proposal that are likely to elicit the greatest amount of collective agreement.

Researchers who have studied the dimensions of credibility have found them to be relatively independent. That is, an audience's perception of a speaker on one dimension does not influence its views on the others. Thus, a speaker who is perceived as competent (knowing the subject matter) can be either trusted or not. You might consider two people—for example, your senator and a lawyer—to be equally competent, but you might trust one more than the other.

As you begin your search for credibility strategies, you need to find out what your audience currently believes about you. A good starting point is listing your assets and liabilities in relation to the seven dimensions of source credibility. As you complete the Self-Check "Are You a Credible Source?" remember that by the time you deliver your first persuasive speech in this class, you will have interacted with most of your classmates. As a result, they will have formed impressions of you. Even if they have not inter-acted directly with you, they have other sources of information on which to base credibility judgments—personal appearance and actions, reference group membership, endorsements, and so forth. What are they likely to conclude?

As you consider your options for building your credibility, think in terms of the five factors that can influence your image as you speak: source characteristics (e.g., mode of dress and fluency of delivery); message characteristics (e.g., use of evidence and language intensity); channel characteristics (e.g., visual aids and oral delivery); audience characteristics (e.g., ego involvement and identification with the speaker); and occasion characteristics (e.g., attractiveness of the setting and temperature of the room).

Logical Proof

As you may recall, in Chapter 13 we described six verbal and nonverbal devices that you can use to help an audience understand and accept your message: language, explanations, examples, statistics, testimony, and visual aids.

Evidence. Three of these devices (examples, statistics, and testimony) are especially useful as *evidence*—that is, information used as logical proof by a speaker. Evidence increases the persuasiveness of a message.[11] As you might expect, highly credible evidence sources are more persuasive than less credible ones. High-quality evidence is especially effective if the audience is unfamiliar with the subject and if the evidence is from multiple sources. Old evidence and evidence already quite familiar to the audience are not highly persuasive.

To be persuasive, you should use multiple types of evidence. Although research does not suggest that one form of evidence is superior to the others, there is some indication that examples may have greater impact than statistical evidence, perhaps because they create vivid images in the minds of receivers. Reinard suggests, however, that "although receivers may be inordinately impressed by a powerful example, persuasion is enhanced when a report is followed by a statistic that shows the example to be typical."[12]

Not all sources of information are of equal value, but how can you decide which are more credible than others? In order to evaluate sources, whether you are presenting or listening to a persuasive message, consider Andrews's criteria: Is the source reliable? Recent? Complete? Accurate?[13]

The *reliability* test holds that sources should be objective and competent. Be skeptical of sources who might have something to gain from promoting

*A*re You a Credible Source?

Imagine you are going to give a speech on a particular topic to your class or another group that you belong to. List your assets and liabilities for each of the seven dimensions of source credibility as you think they would be perceived by the group. Rank the dimensions in terms of how ethical you think it would be for you to use them.

a particular point of view. Sources should be in a position to know about the subject at hand, and they should be competent to judge or comment on the specific issue, item, or idea. The *recency* test holds that one should strive for the most up-to-date information possible. The two final tests are closely related to one another. To meet the *completeness* criterion, evidence should be based on as many sources as possible. Having multiple sources lets you test the evidence for *accuracy*. Accurate information is *redundant* and *verifiable*. In other words, a variety of sources should present similar information. You should be skeptical of the aberrant figure or idea.

Effective Use of Message Variables. Considerable research has been conducted on the effective use of certain message variables in persuasion. In reviewing these studies, O'Keefe presents the collective response of the experts to questions about how to make a message persuasive:[14]

1. *Where should a persuader put the message's most important arguments—first, last, or in the middle?* Perhaps, on average, some extremely small benefit might be obtained from placing them last, but this benefit is so small as to be negligible.

2. *Should the persuader state the point explicitly or let the receivers figure out the conclusion themselves?* Messages that include explicit conclusions or recommendations are more persuasive than messages that do not.

3. *Should a persuader ignore or answer opposing arguments?* Persuaders are well advised to present both sides of issues, even on issues unfamiliar to the audience.

Collecting and Evaluating Evidence

Imagine that you are trying to persuade your employer to buy a car of a particular make and model for employees to use for business trips. You are to make a presentation to a management committee, and you want to give the members convincing evidence for your recommendation. What sources of information (for example, people, publications, and the like) about the car might you cite? Use solo brainstorming to generate as many ideas as possible without evaluating the sources.

When you have created a list of sources, use Andrews's criteria to evaluate them. Why are the sources you rate as best likely to be credible to your audience?

Repeat this exercise for a presentation to your classmates to convince them to have an end-of-semester social dinner at a new Thai restaurant. Do some types of evidence provide especially strong support for propositions of fact? value? problem? policy?

4. *Should the speaker ask for much or for little change?* In general, it seems best to ask for a moderate amount of change. In most situations, relatively little change is obtained by asking for too little or too much. This will, however, vary with communicator credibility and receiver involvement with the issue.

5. *Are stronger fear appeals more effective than weaker ones?* Material that induces greater fear or anxiety will enhance the effectiveness of the message.

◆ A Theoretical Approach to Persuasive Effects

Now that we have explored three forms of proof (motivational, ethical, and logical), it is time to think about blending them into a persuasive message. The **Elaboration Likelihood Model (ELM)** developed by Petty, Cacioppo, and their associates is especially helpful for this process.[15]

As the name suggests, ELM addresses the probability (likelihood) that a target of persuasion will engage in elaboration—that is, give careful thought to the message being received. ELM begins with the observation that people are constantly bombarded with more messages than they can possibly process. As a result, it is necessary to develop strategies for coping—strategies that allow people to process those messages considered important and relevant, while paying less attention to messages considered insignificant.

According to ELM, messages are processed in one of two ways: the **central route**, whereby important messages are processed carefully, or the **peripheral route**, whereby less important messages receive less attention. An audience is most likely to carefully examine the information in the persuader's message, scrutinize the arguments rigorously, and think about issues not raised by the persuader under the following circumstances:

- The issue is one that the audience has encountered before.
- The audience is not distracted by other stimuli or tasks.
- The audience is interested and involved in the issue.
- The persuader uses multiple sources and arguments.
- Most members of the audience enjoy thinking about issues.

At the other end of the persuasion continuum, where an audience is less motivated and less able to elaborate on the persuasive message, lies the peripheral route to persuasion. Because the message is considered less central to an audience's concerns, the audience is less willing to take the time to do a careful analysis of the message. Instead, it is likely to use some simple decision rules to decide whether or not to accept your message. Three resources for the peripheral route are *credibility*—a belief that the message can be trusted if the source is credible, *liking*—a belief that the message can be trusted if the source is liked, and *consensus*—a belief that the message can be accepted if others accept it.

ELABORATION LIKELIHOOD MODEL (ELM)

A theory of persuasion that specifies the conditions under which an audience will process a message.

CENTRAL ROUTE TO PERSUASION

A route to persuasion in which the audience carefully considers and analyzes the content of the message in deciding whether to accept or reject it.

PERIPHERAL ROUTE TO PERSUASION

A route to persuasion in which the audience bases its decision about the message on characteristics external to the message—for example, source credibility or the reactions of other individuals.

◆ Thinking Critically about Persuasive Speeches

In an information age, being a critical thinker is growing in importance. Critical thinking is especially relevant to persuasive messages because they focus on changing audiences' attitudes, beliefs, and actions.

Thus far in this chapter, our focus has been on the task of being an effective persuasive speaker, that is, asking ourselves what we, as speakers, can do to provide our audiences with good reasons for accepting our designative, evaluative, definitive, and advocative claims. An equally important skill to be honed is the ability to think critically about the claims advanced by others in their persuasive speeches. For every speech you give in this class you may hear twenty or more speeches delivered by your classmates. You will be challenged to evaluate many other people's ideas—to think critically about what they present and to determine whether they have provided you with compelling reasons for accepting their claims.

In addition to learning about the topics of your classmates' speeches and developing your critical thinking skills, there is another payoff to this activity: Thinking critically about the persuasive strategies of your classmates can inform your decisions about which strategies to adopt and which to avoid when it is your turn to deliver a persuasive speech.

Listening Critically

How, then, does a critical thinker proceed when listening to one of the following speeches:

- A proposition of fact, making the designative claim that research on animals is unnecessary for discovering a cure for HIV/AIDS?

- A proposition of value, making the evaluative claim that abortion is immoral?

- An effort to create concern about a problem, making the definitive claim that we should be concerned about the dangers of using pesticides?

- A proposition of policy, making the advocative claim that society should make obtaining a divorce more difficult?

The starting point is to remain open-minded about what you perceive, while still injecting a healthy dose of inquiry and skepticism into your perceptions. Because values are so central to the process of persuasion, it is especially important that a critical listener remain open-minded when exploring what the speaker is asking of the audience. It is far too easy to argue with—rather than listen to and understand—a speaker who does not share your views on controversial issues such as religion, politics, or social causes. Recall the strategies for critical listening offered in Chapter 6:

1. *Determine the speaker's goal.* Step back and attempt to understand objectively the persuasive goals of the speaker. Can you figure out the speaker's specific purpose—that single declarative statement of what you, as an audience member, are expected to know, do, believe, or feel as a result of listening to the speech?

2. Evaluate the source of the message. Does the speaker have the credibility to talk about the issue? Has the speaker developed any expertise through study or experience?

3. Question the logic, reasoning, and evidence of the message. An excellent way to explore the speaker's choice of logic, reasoning, and evidence is to apply Toulmin's model, discussed earlier in this chapter: What is the conclusion you are being asked to accept? What is the support or grounding for the claim? What is the warrant for moving from the data to the claim? What is the backing for the warrant? Has the speaker acknowledged and addressed any possible objections to the claim (rebuttal)? If necessary, has the speaker qualified the claim?

Listening Critically to a Persuasive Presentation

Read the persuasive speech "A Nation of Laws" at the end of the chapter and engage in the role of critical thinker.

Thinking Critically about Your Speech

The critical thinking approach to your own speeches mirrors the process of listening critically to the persuasive message of others, and many of the questions are the same. But rather than posing these questions during the actual delivery of other speakers' presentations, you should use them to evaluate your own speech at the preparation phase. The process focuses on three sets of issues: Is my topic appropriate for me, my audience, and the occasion? Have I provided support for my topic that is reasonable, ethical, and persuasive? Will my presentation of the message help accomplish my purpose?

Let's assume that you've decided to use your speech to affirm a proposition of fact by making the designative claim that U.S. drug policy is racist. As you work at turning this specific purpose into a thesis for your speech, you need to consider each set of issues in turn.

1. *Is my topic appropriate for me, my audience, and the occasion?* What are your credentials for speaking on the topic? What is its relevance to your audience of classmates and to the occasion of a class meeting? A useful strategy here is to play the role of "devil's advocate." What response could you make, for example, if your classmates questioned your credentials? If they questioned the appropriateness of the topic?

2. *Have I provided support for my topic that is reasonable, ethical, and persuasive?* With an appropriate specific purpose and thesis in mind, you should next consider your choice of proof. You prepare to cite statistics as logical proof, after satisfying yourself that they are reliable, up-to-date, accurate, and complete. For example, your research reveals that only 13 percent of drug users are African Americans, while 35 percent of possession arrests, 55 percent of convictions, and 74 percent of

individuals sentenced are African Americans. These statistics offer dramatic, compelling support for your thesis.

In terms of ethical proof, you decide to emphasize your competence by demonstrating your extensive research on the topic. For motivational proof, you decide to emphasize the value of fairness. You decide to assume a central route to persuasion because you believe that your audience is motivated and will be engaged by this topic.

3. *Will my presentation of the message help accomplish my purpose?* Is your best choice of delivery mode impromptu speaking, extemporaneous speaking, speaking from a manuscript, or speaking from memory? Given your choice, how can you use verbal and nonverbal strategies in ways that are both persuasive and ethical?

This class should make the task of thinking critically about your persuasive messages a little easier by relating it to your evaluation of the speeches of your classmates and to the feedback you receive from your classmates and your professor.

*T*he Case of Steve

At the beginning of this chapter we met Steve, a student in a communication class much like yours who is thinking about giving a persuasive speech on veganism. What have you learned in this chapter that might help Steve prepare for his presentation?

- Is veganism a good topic for his speech? Why or why not?

- Which of the four types of persuasive speeches (fact, value, problem, policy) would you advise him to develop? Why?

- How might he use Toulmin's model to prepare for this presentation?

- Which of the audience's needs and values might Steve find most useful for his purpose? Which ones might be the most detrimental?

- Which dimensions of source credibility will be assets for Steve? Which will be liabilities? Do you have any concrete suggestions for credibility-enhancing strategies?

- Which forms of evidence are likely to be most useful? Least useful? Are there any message variables that Steve should be especially concerned about?

- Would you advise Steve to adopt a persuasive strategy based primarily on a central or a peripheral route to persuasion? Why? How should he develop his strategy?

REVIEW

- The ability to speak persuasively—which was prized by the ancient Egyptians, Greeks, and Romans—remains the hallmark of an educated member of our society. Persuasive abilities are needed to convince others to overrule their desire for a stable environment in favor of change.

- Five features define persuasion: a conscious attempt by one person to influence another; the generation of a variety of messages; active participation by both persuader and persuadee; changes in the persuadee's attitudes, beliefs, and behavior; and a perception of choice by the persuadee.

- Persuasive speeches advance four types of propositions: propositions of fact, value, concern about a problem, and policy.

- Toulmin's model can be used to generate "good reasons" for an audience to accept a speaker's proposition. In giving these reasons, the speaker moves from data to warrant to claim (sometimes adding backing, rebuttals, or qualifiers).

- Good reasons that serve as warrants fall into three categories: motivational proof, which appeals to a level of audience need characterized by Maslow's hierarchy; ethical proof, which appeals to a source's credibility; and logical proof, which appeals to evidence in the form of statistics, examples, and testimony.

- Credibility (ethical proof) is perhaps the most important factor in persuading listeners. There are seven dimensions of credibility: competence, trustworthiness, dynamism, power, goodwill, idealism, and similarity.

- A speaker can use the Elaboration Likelihood Model (ELM) to blend motivational, ethical, and logical proof into a persuasive message.

- ELM can help a speaker determine whether an audience is likely to follow the central route to persuasion (i.e., devote considerable attention to the persuader's message because the audience considers the topic important) or the peripheral route (i.e., pay less attention to a message because the audience considers the topic less important).

- Critical thinking is important both in evaluating persuasive presentations and in creating your own persuasive messages.

General purpose: to persuade

Specific purpose: to convince the audience that because the Freemen of Montana have broken our nation's laws, intervention by the federal government is warranted.

A Nation of Laws

Aaron Kallsnich, *University of Oklahoma*

Aaron uses his introduction to capture his audience's attention with a forceful statement of his philosophy: Antigovernment separatists and their law-breaking must be stopped. Is this an effective strategy? What alternate strategies might he have used?

1.   There is a new fad sweeping across America. You know what it is! It is the "We don't like the federal government or its laws, so we'll start our own nation" fad. Antigovernment separatists are popping up throughout the United States. Everyone has heard of the Branch Davidians, the Michigan Militia, and now, the Freemen of Montana. These extremist groups are willing to take lives with their ends-justifies-the-means rationale. This new fad must be stopped! Government intervention is necessary to stop such separatist groups who threaten the law-abiding majority of the United States. Today I will tell you about the laws the Freemen are breaking and the history of some of the group's members. I will also argue for government intervention to stop the Freemen.

2.   Let me begin by talking about some of the laws the Freemen have broken.

Having captured our attention, Aaron uses his first main point to develop a problem/solution format through the use of testimony. Do you find this testimony credible? Should Aaron tell us more about Wes Smith and his other sources?

3.   The Freemen of Montana, according to Wes Smith of the <u>Chicago Tribune</u>, deny the legitimacy of the U.S. government. They have refused to pay taxes, defied foreclosures, threatened public officials, and allegedly defrauded financial institutions and merchants with $19.5 million in bad checks and money orders. The Freemen occupy a 960-acre wheat farm, which they call

Justus Township, and insist they have their own laws and courts.

4.   However, the Freemen, like other antigovernment groups, do support one U.S. law. That is the right to bear arms, as found in Article 2 of the Bill of Rights. They also seem to believe that this law encompasses everything from slingshots to nuclear warheads. Some of these separatist groups are willing to use their arms against authorities and innocents alike as demonstrated by the shoot-out in Waco, Texas, and the bombing of the federal building in Oklahoma City.

Aaron links the Freemen with the Waco incident and the Oklahoma City bombing. Is this a good persuasive strategy?

5.   If you or I committed crimes such as these, we would be hauled off to jail and be hoping for a kind jury. Why should justice not be the same for members of separatist groups? These groups, however, claim that they have done nothing wrong. They claim that their own "laws" justify what they do. They don't believe in the laws of the United States, yet they want to reside here. Unfortunately for them, as federal judge Richard Kallsnick said, "this is a country of laws, not men." It is evident that the Freemen have broken many laws, and the government should step in to maintain law and order.

Aaron discounts the Freemen's justification for their actions, and he claims that they should be judged by the same laws his audience is judged by. Is this a good argument? Is it an effective appeal to his audience?

6.   Now let me give you a brief history of some individual Freemen and the specific laws they have broken.

7.   In 1982, in Jordan, Montana, Richard Clark bought a farm, but he soon was unable to pay the loan on the farm. Richard Clark fought for 12 years to keep the farm, until it was auctioned off in 1994. By that time, Clark had become well acquainted with Leroy Schweitzer and Daniel Petersen. They called themselves the Freemen and said that Clark didn't owe the government any money because the government was unconstitutional. Richard Clark's farm became the Freemen compound.

Aaron's second main point uses newspaper accounts from USA Today and the Associated Press to provide details on the history of the Freemen and the laws they have broken. Does Aaron choose details wisely? How, if at all, do the details help his audience remember his point? If you were developing this second point, would you do it differently?

8.   Leroy Schweitzer formed the Freemen of Montana in the late 1980s, and he declared it

independent of all government rules. According to Bob Twigg of <u>USA Today</u>, between August 1994 and December 1995 the group allegedly committed fraud in thirty states, handing out $19.5 million in phony checks and money orders. In late 1995, Freemen leaders Leroy Schweitzer and Daniel Petersen went into hiding in the farm compound of Justus Township in Jordan, Montana. On March 25, 1996, Schweitzer and Petersen were arrested. This prompted a standoff between the 20 Freemen members believed to be in the compound and the more than 100 FBI agents surrounding the compound. On March 30, 1996, Freemen member Richard Clark surrendered at Grass Range, Montana. Today the remaining Freemen are in the 15th day of their standoff with the FBI.

9.   According to the Associated Press, the Freemen include a hard-luck farmer swamped by debt and a mother fleeing child welfare officials, among others. The Freemen are basically outlaws banded together in Montana, hiding under the theme of self-empowerment. No one knows what the future holds in store for the Freemen.

In his last main point, Aaron invokes the general principle that we are a nation of laws. He uses this principle to support his argument that the federal government should intervene and punish the Freemen. Do you find this argument persuasive? Would you have developed the last point differently?

10.   Finally, I am going to address government intervention. We, in the United States of America, are fortunate to have the Constitution, the Bill of Rights, and other laws. We are also fortunate to have the federal government to enforce these laws. All of these elements serve to keep order in our nation. Without laws, or the enforcement of laws, there is chaos and anarchy.

11.   As long as the Freemen, or any other separatist groups, exist in the United States, they must live by the laws of the land regardless of their beliefs. If an individual citizen or separatist group breaks the laws, appropriate punishment should be meted out. The fact that the Freemen have banded together is no excuse: Criminals are criminals, and the Freemen deserve the treatment of criminals. They should be brought to justice.

12.   Some argue that the federal government should leave these groups alone. That's great! So do I! Unless, of course, they break laws, as the Freemen clearly have done. Then they should be brought to justice by the federal government. These groups require government intervention whenever they break the laws of the land!

13.   In conclusion, there are many antigovernment separatist groups forming in America. They are often militant and do not uphold the laws of the United States. The most recent group, the Freemen of Montana, are no better than outlaws. Government intervention is necessary to stop such groups when they threaten the law-abiding citizens of the United States.

14.   I do not like the idea that antigovernment groups can exist under U.S. laws. But I recognize that our laws protect all groups in America. However, when any group starts breaking laws, the government must intervene.

Does the last paragraph add to or detract from Aaron's speech? Explain.

CHAPTER SIXTEEN

Understanding and Using Mass Communication

●BJECTIVES ●

After reading this chapter, you should be able to:

1. Define *mass communication* and identify the different perspectives on the media's construction of reality.

2. Explain the types of controls placed on the media and define *gatekeeping, prior restraint,* and *FCC.*

3. Describe the characteristics of a critical consumer and use the guidelines for consuming mediated messages critically.

4. Compare and contrast five theoretical positions on media effects.

ATICE GECOL IS a Turkish student attending college in the United States. For the past few weeks she has heard and seen news reports about government elections to be held in Turkey. Many of the reports suggest that the election campaign has provoked protests, an issue of major concern for Hatice because her mother is a government official in her hometown of Izmir. She has recently received several letters from her parents, but they have mentioned nothing about the upcoming elections. Hatice is distressed because she does not know whether the reports are accurate and her parents are trying to protect her, or whether the media have sensationalized the political events in Turkey.

As you read this chapter, you will learn to evaluate mediated messages and will be exposed to guidelines that will help Hatice assess the messages the media have produced about her native country. At the end of the chapter, we will return to this scenario and solicit your advice.

◆ The Mediated Society

Most of you are daily consumers of numerous forms of mass communication. Your opinions on political issues are often based on information you have received through television and radio broadcasts or through stories printed in newspapers. You feel sympathy for the homeless and a greater respect for people with AIDS because you have been exposed to their plight through movies and newspaper coverage. Even the clothes you choose to wear, your knowledge of the latest medical breakthroughs, or the brand of toothpaste you use are often results of information provided through mass communication.

Mass communication, a term used to describe the production or transmission of messages that are received and consumed by large audiences, is a dominant force in our society. It appears in many different forms, including books like this one, magazines and newspapers, radio and television, and other mediums intended for large audiences, such as movies and videos. Mass communication is used by the **media**—organizations that create and transmit messages to the general public—to provide information about culture and society, to entertain, to persuade us to buy products or accept new ideas, and to perpetuate what McLuhan coined the "global village"—that is, a world in which millions of people feel connected to any place on the globe because of access to instant information.[1]

Currently, 98 percent of all U.S. homes are equipped with televisions and 99 percent have radios. These households access electronic information and entertainment from over 9000 radio stations and 1400 television stations. In addition, despite the pervasiveness of the electronic age, 84 percent of Americans 18 years of age and older still receive some information via newspaper readership.[2] It is no wonder, as Ruch suggests, that because of our access to information, the human knowledge base currently doubles every year.[3]

As you read this chapter, you will be exposed to ideas about the various communication mediums. You will learn the purposes of mass communication, how it affects your everyday activities, and some regulations that control its development. You will also learn ways to better process mass mediated messages. This chapter, then, seeks to increase your awareness of mass communication and to develop your skills as a critical consumer of it.

MASS COMMUNICATION
The production and transmission of messages that are received and consumed by large audiences, including various forms of printed material and messages dispersed via the airwaves or through cable networks.

MEDIA
Organizations that create and transmit informative, entertaining, or persuasive messages designed for large audiences.

The Functions of Mass Communication

The information you receive from news broadcasts or magazine articles allows you to feel connected to the fast-paced world in which you live. Mediated information serves as a barometer to measure the successes and failures of society and as a resource for making decisions. Can you imagine a presidential election without media coverage? Would you buy a car without consulting *Consumer Reports?* Thus, although critics of the mass media suggest that the information the media provide to the general public is often distorted or inadequate, the fact remains that information is a desired commodity.[4]

How representative of U.S. culture do you think the subjects and guests on morning and afternoon talk shows are?

Even forms of media designed to entertain, such as television shows like *Friends* or your favorite soap opera, offer insight into the culture in which you live. In recent years, movies such as *Splash* and *Encino Man* have depicted characters who learn English and the American way of life—however distorted their interpretations—by viewing U.S. society on television. Although these movies use unrealistic, humorous examples to portray traditional American culture, they still serve to reinforce or shape the perceptions people have about society. Thus, mass communication, though designed to inform and entertain, also functions as an avenue of instant information and persuasion.

Persuading. Some forms of persuasion that are prevalent in mass communication are obvious to even the most unsuspecting media consumer. Few people would question that the purpose of commercials for cars or fast food is to persuade. Public service announcements that discourage the use of illegal drugs or drinking and driving are also examples of obvious persuasive appeals. However, Gozzi and Haynes suggest that the mass media also use more subtle forms of persuasion because they provide the *receiver*—those who consume and use the media—with a unique and sometimes distorted definition of reality.[5] In other words, although you know that commercials are designed to sell you certain products and thus give you information that makes one product appear superior to another, you are not always aware that this same type of persuasion is used in other types of mediated messages.

For example, imagine that you are the news manager for a local television station. You have been notified that a demonstration is going on in front of an area abortion clinic. You dispatch a news crew to cover the protest and interview both the protesters against the clinic and the doctors who run it. When

*H*ow Advertising Persuades You

Select two magazine advertisements for similar products. Based on what you learned about proof in Chapter 15, evaluate the persuasive appeals used in each ad. How do the ads differ? Watch television or listen to radio commercials for the same two products. Compare and contrast the broadcast and print advertising for each product. Do certain types of persuasive arguments seem to work particularly well for selling certain products? Are the arguments valid? Credible?

the time comes to prepare the news story, decisions will have to be made concerning how the protest should be presented to the community. How much coverage—air time—will the story be given? Which excerpts from the interviews will be shown? Although you are providing the public with the news, the way in which the story is presented affects people's understanding of the event. As the news manager, you have the ability to persuade people, or at least to provide a persuasive account, of the local news. For those who watch your news broadcast, you would be creating reality.

Meeting Consumer Demand. Another perspective—one that is often supported by the media—suggests that the messages presented to the public are not a result of media bias or attempts of persuasion, but simply of supply and demand. Every year television programs are canceled because of their limited viewing audience, and it is certainly not uncommon to hear a radio announcer play listeners' requests or to find that a book you had hoped to read is no longer in print. Simply said, the media only produce the kinds of messages requested by the public.

Media organizations spend thousands of dollars annually conducting public opinion polls to determine the interests and concerns of their audiences.[6] The media must provide the information and entertainment desired by consumers in order to maintain high ratings for their programs and publications, or they will ultimately lose their audiences, advertisers, and their profits. Thus, when interviews are edited or news stories are omitted, aren't the media simply doing their job?

Providing Facts. A variation on this perspective suggests that the media present information and that consumers create reality. Graber contends that the media do not attempt to distort or bias events.[7] Instead, she proposes that it is the public's perception of information that creates bias. Individuals working in the media provide information; they compile facts and present these facts as evidence of truth. The interpretation and meaning of that information are dependent on the consumers' views of reality. For example, in the

Comparing Media Coverage

Compare and contrast how you believe CNN and MTV would cover a story about a piece of rap music that denigrates police officers. What factors would produce similarities or differences in the stories?

1992 presidential campaign, the media frequently discussed the fact that Bill Clinton had smoked marijuana as a young man. The media would argue that they did not suggest that this was bad or good, but simply provided information that the public could interpret as it wished.

Thus, when evaluating how information becomes mass communication, there are several critical questions: Who controls information? Do the media create reality? Do the media simply respond to public opinion? Or, do media interpretations depend on media consumers? Perhaps the answers lie partly in each function. Whatever your opinion, by answering these questions for yourself, you will be taking an initial step in becoming a critical consumer of mass communication.

Critical Evaluation of Mass Communication

Being a **critical consumer** means that as the user of a product—in this case, mass mediated messages—you carefully evaluate the product for its quality, worth, and usefulness. To become a critical consumer of mass communication, you must understand the dominance of mediated messages and how the media work, and have an understanding of the different perspectives used to evaluate mass media effects. The remaining pages of this chapter will be dedicated to your development as a critical consumer.

CRITICAL CONSUMER
An individual who, as the user of a product, carefully evaluates the product for its quality, worth, and usefulness. A critical consumer of the media assesses the content of mediated messages for their accuracy and reliability.

There Are Two Sides to Every Story

Based on the following information, create two news reports, each telling one side of the story.

On Thursday at 7:00 P.M., two women, Irma Lupe and Maria Ortega, were followed from the University Library to a nearby parking lot. When they arrived at their car, they immediately jumped in the car, locked the doors, and drove to the campus police station to report the incident. Police later visited the parking lot in question and interrogated a college senior, William Fernandez. Fernandez claimed that the women had left a notebook in the library and he was trying to return it when they quickly drove away. Neither Ms. Lupe nor Ms. Ortega recognized the notebook in question.

If you were reporting this incident in the campus newspaper, would you report it as a "good Samaritan" case or as a notice—especially for women—to be cautious when leaving the library? What pieces of information would affect your decision? Would your opinion be different if two men leaving the library had been followed by a woman? If so, why?

◆ Understanding the Mass Communication Environment

Before you began reading this chapter, you probably had considered the effects of mass communication on your life. Perhaps you grew up in a home where your parents or caretakers controlled the types of movies you were allowed to see or monitored the number of hours you watched television. Perhaps you were involved in a project in which mass communication was used as a resource to attract support or exposure. It is likely, however, that you were most aware of the mass media when they were absent from your life. For instance, consider the feelings of isolation you began to experience after a few days on a camping trip or when your television or radio was broken for an extended period of time.

Because everyone is constantly exposed to various forms of mass communication—from the time they are able to walk and talk and throughout adolescence and adulthood—the mass media have become a major presence in our culture, bringing their view of the world into virtually every American home. Research suggests that television viewing has dominated the family's use of leisure time for the past three decades. With the fine tuning of cable television through the use of fiber optics, there will be more programming alternatives, and television viewing will continue to increase.[8]

The Expanding Uses of Mass Communication

The expanding uses of mass communication seem to ensure its importance in the future. For example, C-SPAN (Cable-Satellite Public Affairs Network), a nonprofit cable television network created to provide unedited coverage of the U.S. political system, is being used in some college classrooms to generate discussion of political issues and ideas. Nickerson predicts that by the year 2020 our current educational system will be transformed through technological advances and the extended uses of mass communication.[9] Not only will closed circuit television—offering multiple specialized classes—be an ordinary educational resource, but also textbooks will be available on computer disks, and computer networks will allow students to access large databases such as the Library of Congress by the touch of a button. Thus, the amount of media exposure we receive will continue to be a dominant issue in our society.

Distinctive Characteristics of Mass Communication

Another factor that extends our understanding of mass communication is recognizing the differences between mass communication and communication in other contexts. Unlike face-to-face communication (such as talking to a friend or participating in a meeting at work), mass communication is best characterized as delayed communication to large groups of individuals. If you think about mass communication in terms of the model of commu-

You and the Media

Create a list of all the forms of media that you have been exposed to in the last 24 hours. Which of these information sources do you consider most credible? Least credible? Why?

nicative competence (see Figure 1.1, p. 22), the two partners are the media organization and the individuals and groups that comprise the audience. They interact as the media organization and the audience take turns sending and receiving messages.

The media create and send messages via the airwaves, or through cable networks and printed forms; messages are received without the opportunity to immediately question or paraphrase their content; and, in most instances, the ability to discern how the message was intended or interpreted is based on chance or probability. Thus, mass mediated messages differ from communication in other contexts in four primary ways: (1) the channels used, (2) the types and forms of feedback available, (3) the format of the messages, and (4) the message content.

Channels. During interpersonal, group, and organizational communication, the sender of a message generally uses a direct, person-to-person channel to communicate. Messages are interpreted and feedback is given simultaneously. Furthermore, people use their perceptions to assess the appropriateness and effectiveness of a message; they usually have the opportunity to adjust their messages or responses based on the cues received from the other participant(s). In mass communication, however, the channels for messages are more broadly diffused and are characterized by indirect, delayed, or limited feedback.[10]

Feedback. Because mass mediated messages have different objectives than the words of face-to-face interactions, feedback also serves different purposes. For instance, consider the uses of public opinion polls or market reports such as the Nielsen ratings of television programs. Although these types of feedback tell television networks whether they are receiving their share of the television viewing audience, this information is quite different from the feedback you would provide to a friend in day-to-day conversation. Unless opinions are collected systematically using appropriate research methods and sampling techniques, the results of public opinion polls and surveys to assess consumer viewpoints may be unreliable or invalid.[11] A classic example of inaccurate surveying occurred in the 1936 presidential election when a survey administered by the *Literary Digest* predicted that Republican Alf Landon would defeat Democratic incumbent Franklin D. Roosevelt in the upcoming presidential election. Ultimately, in that election, Landon received only 8 electoral votes to Roosevelt's 523. How did such an error in prediction occur? Although the survey contacted a large number of people, their names were drawn from telephone directories and automobile registrations, so that the group sampled contained a disproportionate number of wealthy people—and Republicans.[12]

Today, public opinion pollsters generally use scientific methods to obtain and collect feedback. They cannot, however, totally eliminate the communication difficulties associated with indirect, delayed, and limited feedback.

Ethical Responsibilities

Should the media's ethical responsibilities (for example, to tell the truth and to present both sides of an issue) vary more with mass media functions (for example, entertainment vs. news) or with mass media type (for example, television vs. newspapers)? Why?

Feedback that occurs after the fact or provides a partial representation of the public's ideas and opinions will continue to be a challenge to effective mass communication.

Format and Content. Mediated messages are created for large audiences and cannot rely on familiarity or history to clarify meaning. Consequently, mediated messages do not possess the spontaneity of everyday conversations; are usually scripted in order to maintain accuracy and precision; and, when carefully evaluated, may appear ambiguous. Communication for the masses must provide a middle ground—that is, a message that appeals to large numbers of different individuals.

By recognizing the differences between mass communication and person-to-person interaction, it will be easier for you to recognize and evaluate the benefits and limitations of mass mediated messages. However, your development as a critical consumer also includes understanding the controls placed on the media, which ultimately determine the mediated messages you see, read, and hear.

Regulators of Mass Media

Because U.S. society is dedicated to the ideal of freedom, the American mass media have a tremendous amount of discretion in handling and producing information. Nonetheless, there are constraining factors on the media. Some of these are official or legal regulations, whereas others have evolved because, as private businesses, the media have to operate within a capitalistic framework.

Formal Controls. One of the most basic legal considerations involving media control concerns the meaning of the phrase "Congress shall make no law . . . abridging the freedom of speech, or of the press," which appears in the First Amendment to the Constitution. Nelson, Teeter, and Le Duc note that, despite the noble intentions often ascribed to the First Amendment and the rest of the Bill of Rights, they were the result of political deal-making necessary to ratify the rest of the document.[13]

One of the main purposes of the "freedom of press" guarantee is to protect the people against prior restraint.[14] **Prior restraint** is the practice of banning certain publications before they have even been produced. It amounts to telling a publisher beforehand what it can publish rather than questioning the legality of a work after the fact. Along with any legal wranglings concerning what freedom of the press means, the electronic media are constrained by more specific governmental regulations. These media face the unique obstacle of sending their messages out over crowded airwaves. The airwaves are regulated by the Federal Communications Commission.

The **Federal Communications Commission (FCC)** was established in 1934. This regulatory agency oversees the physical resources of the media such as radio, television, wire, satellite, and cable communications. The FCC has two

PRIOR RESTRAINT

The practice of banning certain publications before they have been produced.

FEDERAL COMMUNICATIONS COMMISSION (FCC)

A regulatory agency that oversees the physical resources of the media to ensure that broadcasters use the airwaves in the public interest and that the public has access to the airwaves.

additional objectives: (1) to ensure that broadcasters use the airwaves in the public interest and (2) to make sure the public has access to the airwaves.

Although censorship by the FCC is illegal, and although recent changes in government regulations provide broadcasters with a substantial amount of freedom to broadcast information at their discretion (e.g., the Cable Communication Act of 1984 freed cable television from FCC regulation), the FCC does attempt to balance the types of programming produced by electronic media. It also supports the inclusion of controversial issues by the media and encourages a diversity of viewpoints. For instance, the FCC suggests that news stations that use editorials to present controversial issues might be well advised to present both sides of the issues.

Thus, the FCC represents a strong government control of broadcasting that the print media do not have to contend with. Broadcasters may not have to worry about official censorship by the FCC, but they do have to rely on the commission for licensing and renewal. Thus, broadcasters have to take the FCC's power into consideration as they make decisions concerning station operations. Along with the pressure felt by individual stations, the industry as a whole must respond to any broad mandates handed down by the commission.

Informal Controls. The informal controls placed on the mass media in a free society are probably more constraining than any legal regulation of these industries. As in other industries, the media must deal with structural limitations that affect how their functions are carried out. And, like any other U.S. business venture, the media have the burden of turning a profit.

Hiebert, Ungurait, and Bohn point out that much media regulation is self-imposed in order not to offend audiences or provide the government with any reason to impose restrictions.[15] A key component of self-regulation is **gatekeeping**. Because gatekeepers determine what information will be carried over mass communication channels and, conversely, what will not, they "keep the gate" on the huge amount of mass communication information available.

Although the media generally use gatekeeping so as not to offend people, some of the gatekeeping function has more to do with practical constraints of time and space. For example, no newspaper, no matter how large, has enough space to print all the possible stories of the day. Editors have to make choices as to which stories are the most important and/or entertaining. Similarly, television news directors have remarkably little time in which to provide the day's top stories. Consider how many choices must be made and how many potential stories must be eliminated in order to produce a 22-minute national news broadcast titled *World News Tonight*. Obviously, from a news standpoint it can be a very small world indeed. In the same way, entertainment programming directors must choose programs based on availability, entertainment value, and affordability.

To a certain extent, each mass medium is also constrained by unique characteristics. As Hiebert, Ungurait, and Bohn note, the newspaper cannot

GATEKEEPING
The process of regulating or determining what information will be carried over mass communication channels and what will not.

compete with radio and television in terms of speed, but its format permits better display of the news, letting the reader see on one page the most important stories. Newspapers also provide greater depth in their stories and more detailed local information. Radio is unique in that it serves a highly fragmented audience, with most stations trying to serve the needs of a homogeneous group.[16] Similar to newspapers, radio is a local medium. People listen to it to fulfill very individual needs, such as finding out what the weather will be like on a particular day. Radio listening is a secondary activity that people engage in while they are doing something else, such as driving. Television has the unique ability to combine audio, text, and moving pictures. Television news producers understandably want to highlight the visual elements in their presentations. Focusing on the visual also helps offset their inability to go into as much depth in stories as newspapers do, owing to time limitations.

The advent of cable, with its multitude of channel possibilities, has enabled television to serve more specific audiences. Because they rely on advertisers for revenue, however, broadcasters have to establish as wide an audience as possible. The need to make a profit in order to stay in business and the reliance on advertisers to do so point to a disturbing constraint on all the media.

Bagdikian argues that corporate ownership of the media and the media's reliance on mass advertising have negatively affected the information society receives.[17] Bagdikian believes that, despite corporate complaints about the media's antibusiness bias, the media have always been biased in favor of corporate America. He suggests that because of the reliance on large corporate advertisers, media content attempts to be neutral and avoids controversy so as not to offend advertisers. In other words, the media, once the watchdogs of big business, have become partners in the big business enterprise. Consequently, although the American media operate in a relatively free environment, and although many people believe that the media serve as protector or watchdog for the American public, the media's needs and objectives must be considered when evaluating the messages presented to the public.

◆ Effects of Mass Communication

DIRECT EFFECTS
MODEL
An early theory of mass communication which states that all individual members of society receive messages in the same way and that direct and uniform outcomes result.

The pervasiveness of the mass media in twentieth-century America has sparked academic researchers to study the phenomenon, often with the aim of discovering how mass communication affects society. Beginning with the study of propaganda during World War I, many theorists and researchers have tried to explain the consequences of mass media.

Direct Effects

Initially, it was believed that the media had direct effects on their audiences. Often called the hypodermic needle perspective, the **direct effects model**

By deciding what stories to cover, newscasters necessarily interpret their audiences' interests and help to shape the issues that will receive public attention. Here, a television news crew reports on efforts to repair a highway damaged by the earthquake that shook southern California in 1993.

states that all individual members of society receive mass communication messages in the same manner. The results are direct and uniform for all members of a given audience. From the direct effects' point of view, if everyone in your communication class were to watch the local news, each of you would be affected by the broadcast in the same way and the effect would be immediate.

Two-Step Flow

Later work on mass media effects dispelled the notion of uniform direct effects. McQuail and Windahl have traced this research, which produced an indirect effect or **two-step flow model** of communication.[18] According to this model, the mass media are utilized by "opinion leaders," who then disseminate information to individuals through social networks. The model recognizes the idea that the "mass media do not operate in a social vacuum but have an input into a very complex web of social relationships and compete with other sources of idea, knowledge and power."[19]

The direct effects and two-step flow theories of mass communication were relatively early attempts to explain the effects of mass communication. In the past twenty years, theories such as agenda setting, cultivation, and uses and gratifications have emerged as more probable explanations of mass communication.

Agenda Setting

Agenda setting refers to the media's ability to determine through the content of their presentations which issues or topics will be important to individual members of society. For example, if the news media highlight stories about the crime rate, then the theory of agenda setting predicts that crime will be an issue of importance to viewers. It is important to note that agenda

TWO-STEP FLOW MODEL
An early view of media effects which proposes that the mass media are used by "opinion leaders" to disseminate information to individuals through social networks.

AGENDA SETTING
The media's ability to determine, through the content of media presentations, which issues or topics will be important to individual members of society.

Agenda *Setting in Local News Reports*

While watching the evening news on one of the major television networks, create a chart of all the topics that are discussed and how many minutes/seconds are spent covering each topic. Based on your chart, what do you believe is the news agenda for the evening? In your opinion, which topics did not receive as much coverage as was required in order to understand the issue, problem, or information?

As a follow-up exercise, search for each of the news topics in the next day's newspaper. Were all the topics covered? How did coverage of the stories differ between television and the newspaper? What information, if any, is still missing from the coverage? What resources could you use to "fill in the gaps" left by media coverage?

setting is concerned primarily with the notion that the media have the power to help determine which issues are important.

Cultivation

CULTIVATION THEORY

A perspective on media effects which suggests that television is a socializing agent of culture that provides its viewers with a common world view.

Cultivation theory investigates the cultural outcomes of television exposure. As Gerbner and his colleagues suggest, "Television is a centralized system of storytelling . . . its drama, commercials, news, and other programs bring a relatively coherent world of common images and messages into every home. Television cultivates from infancy the very predispositions and preferences that used to be acquired from other primary sources."[20] Based on cultivation theory, then, television may be regarded as a socializing agent of culture that provides its viewers with a common understanding of how to view the world.[21]

Calvin and Hobbes   by Bill Watterson

Do you believe that the role of mass media should be to respond to consumer demand?

Uses and Gratifications

The **uses and gratifications theory** emphasizes the idea that the consumer is the key to understanding media effects. Consumers—those who use the media—have certain expectations concerning what mass communication is supposed to do. For example, if you believe that the evening news should provide a sports report and it does provide one, then you will evaluate the news as a positive event that meets your expectations. Thus, uses and gratifications theory suggests that you have an expectation (use) and evaluate (or are gratified by) media if this expectation is met.[22]

The five theories discussed here, though not an exhaustive list, do provide different perspectives for understanding the effects of mass communication. By considering theories such as these, it becomes possible to view and evaluate the effects of media in a critical way based on the research of experts. Thus, we become more critical and more competent consumers of the media.

> **USES AND GRATIFICATIONS THEORY**
> *A theory of media effects that emphasizes the consumer's role and expectations when evaluating the outcomes of media exposure.*

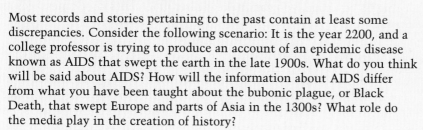

The Historical Record

Most records and stories pertaining to the past contain at least some discrepancies. Consider the following scenario: It is the year 2200, and a college professor is trying to produce an account of an epidemic disease known as AIDS that swept the earth in the late 1900s. What do you think will be said about AIDS? How will the information about AIDS differ from what you have been taught about the bubonic plague, or Black Death, that swept Europe and parts of Asia in the 1300s? What role do the media play in the creation of history?

◆ Being a Critical Consumer

Now that you are familiar with some of the basic effects of mass communication, it is time to consider some guidelines that will further your development as a critical consumer of the mass media. These guidelines include evaluating message content, being mindful, being aware of the media, and doing your homework.

Evaluating Messages

The first and perhaps most important guideline for evaluating mass communication messages is the need to *evaluate the content of the message.*

A̲re You a Critical Consumer of Advertising?

Create a list of five products that you buy regularly. How are these products sold through the media? Are you a critical consumer when buying these products? Why or why not? In what ways do you act as a critical consumer of mediated messages about these products? Is it necessary to be mindful when purchasing such everyday, relatively inexpensive items as laundry soap or pretzels?

Message content quite simply refers to what is being said or communicated. In order to effectively evaluate content, you must consider what information has been given about a topic and what information may have been omitted.

For example, people in the United States have been bombarded with information indicating that homosexual males are the group at the highest risk for AIDS. This information is true for U.S. residents but not for the world population.[23] In this country, the implication that AIDS is a "gay disease" has been very damaging to that segment of the population. By questioning the facts in mass mediated messages and by trying to fill in the gaps left by media coverage, you can make clearer judgments about messages and their meanings.

Being Mindful

A second guideline for becoming a critical consumer is related to the concept of mindfulness. *Mindfulness* refers to the withholding of immediate judgment on a message and the search for new categories, that is, new ways to interpret and assign meaning to the message. For example, a newscaster on a local television station presented a news update that went something like this: "Are children's jackets that bear the logos and names of professional football teams dangerous to your child? Tune in at 10:00 P.M. to find out more." Consider all the possible explanations of such an announcement. Is there something in the clothing dye that irritates children's skin? Are the coats a new symbol for the gangs that dominate urban schools? There are endless possibilities. However, the basis of the news story was none of these. It actually referred to a child whose coat was stolen because it was so expensive. Being mindful allows you to consider multiple possibilities about the relationship between such issues as a child's jacket and danger. It also allows you to recognize that the theft of one child's coat does not necessarily augur a crime wave or a need to panic. Mindful communication is a technique that allows you to listen to mass communication while reserving judgment and to avoid stereotyping messages that present common themes or ideas.

Media Awareness

A third guideline influencing your development as a critical consumer relates to your *awareness* of the media. Because you constantly use electronic media, you may be less sensitive to the messages you are receiving. Lack of sensitivity can affect your evaluation of mass communication messages. Often you turn on the television or radio or pick up a magazine and thumb through it, giving very little thought to the effect the information is having on you. Your cognitive processes allow you to absorb the numerous messages that bombard you and to believe they provide credible information.

The source credibility of Walter Cronkite, dubbed "the most trusted man in America" while a news anchor for CBS, is an excellent example of how cognitive processes lead to acceptance of messages sent by the media. The popular perception was that, if Walter Cronkite said something, it was true. As Jamieson suggests, you use your belief that the media are credible sources of information to draw conclusions from mediated messages.[24] In other words, you can absorb a vast amount of information without being sensitive to it and then accept it because you assume that the source of the information is credible.

Broadcasting of this amateur videotape of the beating of Rodney King by Los Angeles police officers led to the officers' arrest. The tape became the primary piece of evidence at their trial, and portions of the tape were minutely and repeatedly examined. The interpretation by the jury that the officers were not guilty of using excessive force ignited the Los Angeles riot of 1992. Live news coverage of the riot then became the subject of differing interpretations.

Doing Your Homework

The final guideline for improving your critical thinking skills requires you to *do your homework*. Frequently you hear or read information that could drastically affect your life, and yet far too often you do not question the reliability of this information. You would probably not have a heart transplant or even minor surgery without a second opinion, and you would think nothing of asking two or three people at work their opinions about a change in company policy. Mass communication must be used with the same discretion. When an issue is important to you, take the time to investigate it. Watch or listen to multiple accounts of it from different people. Compare newspaper and magazine reports to those of television and radio. When necessary, seek out less popular forms of media such as journals and government documents. The options are endless, but if you do your homework, you become a more critical consumer.

The Case of Hatice Gecol

At the beginning of this chapter, you were introduced to Hatice Gecol, a Turkish student studying in the United States. Hatice was concerned about the safety of her family because of news reports about political activities occurring in Turkey. Based on your new knowledge of mass communication, what advice would you offer Hatice? How is the gatekeeping function affecting her perceptions?

If, in a phone call to her parents, Hatice learned that protests had occurred near her home but that they had involved only small groups of picketers who wanted to register additional candidates for the elections, what theoretical perspective do you believe would best describe the media coverage? Why? How would this change in information reinforce your position as a critical consumer of mediated messages? Is it possible for you to be a competent communicator when dealing with the media?

REVIEW

- The purposes of mass communication are to inform, entertain, provide instant information, and persuade.

- Many theories have been proposed to explain mass communication. Early attempts were the direct effects and two-step flow theories. More recent theories have been agenda setting, cultivation, and uses and gratifications.

- Mass media differs from other communication in that it uses indirect channels, delayed feedback through market research or public opinion polls, and format and content that appeal to large audiences.

- Mass media is regulated through formal controls such as the Federal Communications Commission and informal controls of structural restrictions and the burden of making a profit.

- There are several guidelines that can help you improve your consumption of the media: evaluating message content, being mindful and aware of media messages, and doing your homework on issues that are important to you.

- The media will always be a dominant force in U.S. society. Everyone needs the media for information and entertainment, yet no one wants to rely on misinformation.

- In order to combat the possible negative effects of mass communication, you must develop critical thinking skills about the media and their messages, thereby becoming a more critical consumer of information.

CASE STUDY 4

The Case of Scott's Speech

In the following case study, consider how the speaker relates to his audience. Pay particular attention to the assumptions he makes about his audience's beliefs, expectations, and knowledge of his topic. Because the audience is small and knows the speaker relatively well, the matter of credibility is more complex than when the speaker and audience are more distant.

Scott Sterling had prepared his deliberative speech for weeks. His assignment was to show all sides of a controversial issue, using his research skills and speaking skills to motivate the class to consider the complexities of viewpoints involved in the issue. Scott had chosen the topic of undocumented workers in southern California by reading newspapers, magazines, and books in the library. He had interviewed a local landscaper and a local farmer who reportedly had each occasionally hired undocumented workers. Scott had also prepared appropriate visual aids and had outlined and rehearsed his points.

Scott used a number of quotations in his speech, letting the words of others show the class how different people felt about the workers. He also had quotes from a number of undocumented workers that he presented (he'd had a Spanish-speaking friend accompany him to make sure he translated their comments correctly). He thought he did a good job of representing all aspects of the issue.

After his speech, the professor conducted the usual discussion. One student, Rosalinda Flores, started yelling at Scott for saying there was a "Mexican problem" in the county. The professor and others in the class pointed out that Scott had been quoting the mayor of an adjacent city when he said that. "I don't care who said it," Rosalinda replied. "It's racist for anyone to say that kind of thing, and it's irresponsible to perpetuate that kind of misinformation. Scott's a racist or he wouldn't have slipped it in so smoothly. That plants a seed of suspicion about all of us with Mexican ancestry. It's degrading."

Scott's friend Miguel Ortega came to his defense. "Scott's not racist," Miguel said. "I've played baseball with him for years, and many different ethnic groups have been represented on our teams. Scott's always been a friend to everyone, and I've never heard him utter a bigoted word. He's never acted racist in any way."

"I think we have a number of issues going on here," the professor intervened. "One is the content and quality of this speech, including Scott's word choice. Another is the integrity of the speaker. And yet another is interpretations by different audience members. Of course, what counts as racism is also an important issue. Let's discuss each of these issues in turn."

Discussion Questions

1. Does Scott have a credibility problem? If so, on which dimension(s) of credibility? If a problem exists now, how might Scott have avoided it?

2. Is it unethical (racist, in this case) to quote someone else in the interest of giving a well-balanced presentation if the speaker believes that some audience members might consider the quotation negative? Should the speaker censor remarks or change the original words of a source so as not to offend anyone in the audience? Is it unethical to omit a potentially offensive or controversial opinion that would provide a balanced view of an issue?

3. Given an audience that is divided on a topic, is it possible for the speaker to have a competent relationship with the audience? How might such a relationship be described in terms of control, affiliation, and goals?

4. Can you, as a public speaker, reasonably expect audience members to interpret your message the same way you do? If not, why not? What strategies can you use to help them understand your interpretation? If your speech is presented as informative rather than persuasive, is it appropriate to express your opinion?

5. What does count as racist communication? Is racism in the interpretations of the audience members or in the intentions or words of the speaker?

6. How can the speaker's desire to express a position on an issue be balanced with an audience member's desire not to have an offensive position expressed at all?

7. While this speech occurred in a classroom, issues like this are often presented by the media. TV news, for example, often quotes one or two sentences of a person involved in a high profile issue. Does the media distort issues by selective quoting? Does media coverage of controversial issues inflame the situation or does the coverage contribute to a more thorough understanding by all parties involved?

EPIL●GUE 4

Competence in Public Communication

In Part 4 we move into the public arena. Although the basic characteristics of communication are the same here as they are in intimate dyads, communication in the public arena differs in several important ways from interpersonal and small-group communication.

The primary difference is that one partner takes sole responsibility for constructing the message. For convenience, we will refer to this partner as "the speaker," even though the partner may be a small group of people. Two other characteristics of public communication are that audiences are typically large and frequently anonymous. (That is, the person designing the message doesn't know the audience members personally.) Neither of these characteristics is as important as the nearly complete shift of responsibility (and therefore control) to one participant.

This is not to say that there is no negotiation of relationships in public communication; relationships are negotiated and maintained in much the same way as are friendships, work relationships, and the like. The negotiation, however, is usually indirect, with any one audience member having a difficult time influencing the speaker. The speaker, on the other hand, designs his or her message with the intent of influencing as many audience members as possible. Influence here, as in other communication contexts, refers to the ability to get your partners to do what you want them to do or feel the way you want them to feel. Thus, trying to entertain your audience is as much an influence attempt as is trying to get the audience to vote for you or buy your product.

Staying Calm and Establishing Credibility

Before we talk explicitly about how negotiations take place in public communication episodes, we want to mention that individuals bring the same cognitive and behavioral characteristics to these episodes as they do to social and business relationships. You will plan your messages and process information in the same way, although you may be more conscious in your planning of public communication. For example, you will probably write a speech and practice it before making a public presentation. But careful preparation is also common when you are about to engage in *any* type of new, important communication.

Two individual predispositions highlighted in this part of the book are communication apprehension and communicator credibility. These characteristics take on special importance in public episodes but *both* a low amount of apprehension and a reasonable amount of credibility are important in any competent relationship, be it intimate, social, or public.

It is difficult to have a competent relationship with speakers who are overly apprehensive. Because they appear to be focused on just getting the message out, you can't be sure they are paying appropriate attention to the audience—which means you, as an audience member, have little or no chance of influencing such speakers.

Similarly, credibility is an issue in all types of relationships. In those relationships in which you have firsthand knowledge of a person, you know how trustworthy your partner is. But that sort of firsthand experience is not possible in public communication, especially when the messages are mediated. If you are an audience member, you are responsible for searching for and evaluating cues of the speaker's credibility.

When you are the speaker, you must take steps to encourage your audience to see you as a person who should be listened to (see Chapter 15). Typically, this means constructing your messages in such a way that your trustworthiness, dynamism, and similarity to others are obvious to your audience. Your own ethical record plays a big role here. If your past public messages have conveyed that you can be trusted, that you check your facts, and that you respect other people, your audiences are more likely to see you as credible.

In order to build a competent public relationship, you need to see audience members as credible, too. You do this by being realistic in your influence attempts, by presenting your message in such a way that it does not compromise listeners' self-concepts (as you perceive them, at least), and by structuring your message so that it is in tune with your audience's expectations and comprehension level. The audience analysis procedures discussed in Chapter 13 are designed to help you construct your messages appropriately and effectively.

It is difficult to think about a relationship with a speaker or audience you see once or only a few times, and then usually at a distance. But, as a speaker, you do develop a limited relationship with audience members. You attempt to exercise control in the relationship by influencing them in some way and by developing a moderately positive affiliation. You want them to like you. You also want them to adopt your definition of a collective goal and the tasks necessary to meet that goal.

Affiliation at a Distance

Affiliation is typically developed by being responsive to your audience, being enthusiastic about your topics, and by expressing concern for your audience's needs and expectations.

Speakers who are mildly apprehensive may be liked by some audience members who perceive them as similar to themselves. For the most part, however, overly apprehensive speakers make the audience uncomfortable.

Negotiation between speaker and audience is usually indirect and often spread out over a period of time. In a competent speaker-audience relationship, the speaker is responsive to the audience's behaviors both before the event takes place (e.g., by learning what the audience already knows about a topic or what sort of entertainment it will like) and during the event (e.g., by changing the pace of the speech or by responding to questions). If the speaker expects to talk before the same audience on more than one occasion, this sort of negotiation can take place over time and can include feedback from the audience after the communication event is finished. For example, after hearing a political candidate's speech, audience members may call the candidate's campaign office or write a letter to the editor of the local newspaper—thus attempting to influence both the candidate and other audience members.

Because people in public relationships frequently are separated by time and space, the negotiation of the relationship lacks the precision possible in face-to-face relationships. It is difficult for a speaker to know how representative an individual response is or how much adaptation the speaker should make. These difficulties are exaggerated when the messages are mediated (see Chapter 16).

Just as speakers take on most of the control in public communication, so should they take on most of the responsibility for ensuring that the audience members find the relationship appropriate and effective. If the speaker fails to make the effort necessary to relate to the audience, the relationship will not be marked by competent communication. It will fail, like any other relationship characterized by an inappropriate distribution of control, an unsatisfactory level of affiliation, or a lack of agreement on the goals of the relationship.

Notes

CHAPTER 1
COMMUNICATING COMPETENTLY

[1] F. E. X. Dance & C. Larson (1976), *Functions of human communication: A theoretical approach*, New York: Holt, Rinehart & Winston.

[2] See M. von Cranach & I. Vine (1973), Introduction, *Social communication and movement*, New York: Academic Press, pp. 1–25.

[3] A. Kendon (1983), Gesture and speech: How they interact. In J. M. Wiemann & R. P. Harrison (Eds.), *Nonverbal interaction*, Beverly Hills, CA: Sage, pp. 13–45.

[4] P. Ekman & W. V. Friesen (1975), *Unmasking the face*, Englewood Cliffs, NJ: Prentice-Hall.

[5] B. Whorf (1956), *Language, thought, and reality*, New York: John Wiley & Sons.

[6] E. T. Hall (1959), *The silent language*, Greenwich, CT: Fawcett Publications; and E. T. Hall (1966), *The hidden dimension*, Garden City, NY: Doubleday.

[7] R. Buck (1988), Emotional education and mass media: A new view of the global village. In R. P. Hawkins, J. M. Wiemann, & S. Pingree (Eds.), *Advancing communication science: Merging mass and interpersonal processes*, Beverly Hills, CA: Sage, pp. 44–76; G. Cronkhite (1986), On the focus, scope, and coherence of the study of human symbolic activity, *Quarterly Journal of Speech*, 3, 231–243; M. T. Motley (1990), On whether one can(not) communicate: An examination via traditional communication postulates, *Western Journal of Speech Communication*, 56, 1–20.

[8] E. Goffman (1967), *Interaction ritual: Essays on face-to-face behavior*, Garden City, NY: Doubleday.

[9] S. J. Ball-Rokeach & K. Reardon (1988), Monologue, dialogue, and telelog: Comparing an emergent form of communication with traditional forms. In Hawkins et al. (Eds.), *Advancing communication science*, pp. 135–161.

[10] See R. P. Hart & D. M. Burks (1972), Rhetorical sensitivity and social interaction, *Communication Monographs*, 39, 75–91. Also see J. M. Wiemann & J. A. Daly (1994), On getting your own way. In J. A. Daly & J. M. Wiemann (Eds.), *Strategic interpersonal communication*, Hillsdale, NJ: Lawrence Erlbaum, pp. vii–xiv.

[11] See J. M. Wiemann & D. L. Krueger (1980), The language of relationships. In H. Giles, W. P. Robinson, & P. M. Smith (Eds.), *Language: Social psychological perspectives*, Oxford: Pergamon, pp. 55–62.

[12] I. J. Lynch (1985), *The language of the heart: The body's response to human dialogue*, New York: Basic Books.

[13] J. M. Wiemann (1977), Explication and test of a model of communication competence, *Human Communication Research*, 3, 195–213. Also see B. Spitzberg & W. Cupach (1984), *Interpersonal communication competence*. Newbury Park, CA: Sage.

[14] B. O'Keefe & S. A. McCormack (1987), Message design logic and message goal structure: Effects on perceptions of message quality in regulative communication situations, *Human Communication Research*, 14, 68–85. Also see D. J. Canary, M. J. Cody, & S. Smith (1994), Compliance-gaining goals: An inductive analysis of actors' goal types, strategies, and successes. In Daly & Wiemann, (Eds.), *Strategic interpersonal communication*, pp 33–90.

[15] Spitzberg & Cupach (1984)

[16] See D. Cushman & D. Cahn (1984), *Communication in interpersonal relationships*, Albany, NY: SUNY Press.

[17] R. Anderson & V. Ross (1994), *Questions of communication: A practical introduction to theory*, New York: St. Martin's Press, Chapter 10.

[18] R. Norton (1983), *Communicator style: Theory applications and measures*, Newbury Park, CA: Sage

CHAPTER 2
PERCEPTION AND PROCESSING COMMUNICATION

[1] C. E. Cohen (1981), Goals and schemata in person perception: Making sense from the stream of behavior. In N. Cantor & J. F. Kihlstrom (Eds.), *Personality, cognition, and social interaction*, Hillsdale, NJ: Lawrence Erlbaum.

[2] S. E. Taylor & J. Crocker (1981), Schematic basis of social information processing. In E. T.

Higgins, C. Herman, & M. Zanna (Eds.), *Social cognition: The Ontario Symposium on Personality and Social Psychology*, Hillsdale, NJ: Lawrence Erlbaum.

[3]M. J. Smith (1982), Cognitive schema theory and the perseverance and attenuation of unwarranted empirical beliefs, *Communication Monographs, 49*, 115–126.

[4]M. E. Roloff (1980), Self-awareness and the persuasion process: Do we really know what we are doing? In M. Roloff & G. Miller (Eds.), *Persuasion: New directions in theory and research*, Newbury Park, CA: Sage.

[5]J. H. Hilton & J. D. Darley (1991), The effects of interaction goals on person perception. In M. P. Zanna (1991), *Advances in experimental social psychology*, Vol. 24, San Diego: Academic Press; Harcourt Brace Jovanovich, pp. 236–262.

[6]J. Burgoon & J. Walther (1990), Nonverbal expectations and the evaluative consequences of violations, *Human Communication Research, 17*, 232–265.

[7]K. Kellerman (1986), Anticipation of future interaction and information exchange in initial interactions, *Human Communication Research, 13*, 41–75.

[8]Burgoon & Walther (1990).

[9]E. E. Jones (1990), *Interpersonal perception*, New York: W. H. Freeman.

[10]E. Loftus (1980), *Memory*, Reading, MA: Addison-Wesley.

[11]R. L. Daft & R. H. Lengel (1986), Organizational information requirements, media richness, and structural design, *Management Science, 32*, 554–571.

[12]R. L. Daft & R. H. Lengel (1984), Information richness: A new approach to managerial behavior and organization design, *Research in Organizational Behavior, 6*, 191–233.

[13]L. K. Trevino, R. L. Daft, & R. H. Lengel (1990), Understanding managers' media choices: A symbolic interactionist perspective. In J. Fulk & C. Steinfield (Eds.), *Organizations and communication technology*, Newbury Park, CA: Sage, pp. 71–94.

[14]R. Farace, P. Monge, & H. Russell (1977), *Communication and organizing*, New York: Random House, p. 100.

[15]M. Cassady (1992), An international perspective of the United States, *Bulletin of the Association for Business Communication, 55*, 20–26.

[16]Y. Y. Kim (1988), *Communication and cross-cultural adaptation*, Philadelphia: Multilingual Matters Ltd.

[17]M. Loden & J. B. Rosener (1991), *Workforce America! Managing employee diversity as a vital resource*, Chicago: Business One Irwin, pp. 196–197.

[18]Ibid.

[19]R. Wiseman, M. Hammer, & H. Nishida (1989), Predictors of intercultural communication competence, *International Journal of International Relations, 13*, 349–370.

[20]R. K. Merton (1957), *Social theory and social structure*, New York: Free Press.

[21]Adapted from M. Brewer & N. Miller (1988), Contact and cooperation. In P. Katz & D. Taylor (Eds.), *Eliminating racism*, New York: Plenum.

[22]C. R. Berger & J. J. Jordan (1992), Planning sources, planning difficulty and verbal fluency, *Communication Monographs, 59*, 130–149.

CHAPTER 3
THE SELF AND COMMUNICATION

[1]M. Snyder (1979), Self monitoring processes,. In L. Berkowitz (Ed.), *Advances in social psychology*, Vol. 12, New York: Academic Press, pp. 86–128.

[2]S. E. Cross & H. R. Markus (1990), The willful self, *Personality and Social Psychology Bulletin, 16*, 726–742; H. Markus (1983), Self-knowledge: An expanded view, *Journal of Personality, 51*, 543–565.

[3]J. C. McCroskey (1984), The communication apprehension perspective. In J. A. Daly & J. C. McCroskey (Eds.), *Avoiding communication: Shyness, reticence, and communication apprehension*, Beverly Hills, CA: Sage, pp. 13–38.

[4]D. Cegala (1981), Interaction involvement: A cognitive dimension of communicative competence, *Communication Education, 30*, 109–121.

[5]R. Edwards (1990), Sensitivity to feedback and the development of self, *Communication Quarterly, 38*, 101–111.

[6]H. Markus (1977), Self-schemata and processing information about the self, *Journal of Personality and Social Psychology, 35*, 64.

[7]C. Berger (1987), Self-conception and social information processing. In J. McCroskey & J. Daly (Eds.), *Personality and interpersonal communication*, Beverly Hills, CA: Sage, pp. 275–304.

[8]Markus (1983).

[9]Berger (1987).

[10]Ibid.

[11]J. D. Campbell (1990), Self-esteem and clarity of the self-concept, *Journal of Personality and Social Psychology, 59,* 538–549.

[12]B. R. Schlenker, M. F. Weigold, & J. R. Hallam (1990), Self-serving attributions in social context: Effects of self-esteem and social pressure, *Journal of Personality and Social Psychology, 58,* 855–863.

[13]Baumgardner (1990), To know oneself is to like oneself, *Journal of Personality and Social Psychology, 58,* 1062–1072.

[14]Ibid.

[15]Ibid.

[16]A. Bandura (1982), Self-efficacy mechanism in human agency, *American Psychologist, 37,* 122.

[17]D. J. Canary & M. J. Cody (1993), *Interpersonal communication: A goals-based approach,* New York: St. Martin's Press.

[18]E. E. Jones, F. Rhodewalt, S. Berglas & J. A. Skelton (1981), Effects of strategic self-presentation on subsequent self-esteem, *Journal of Personality and Social Psychology, 41,* 407–421.

[19]Schlenker et. al. (1990).

[20]Canary & Cody (1993).

[21]Snyder (1979), p. 89.

[22]Ibid., p. 94.

[23]L. R. Wheeless & J. Grotz (1976), Conceptualization and measurement of reported self-disclosure, *Human Communication Research, 2,* 338–346.

[24]L. R. Wheeless (1978), A follow-up study of the relationships among trust, disclosure, and interpersonal solidarity, *Human Communication Research, 4,* 143–157.

[25]S. M. Jourard & M. J. Landsman (1960), Cognition, cathexis, and the dyadic effect in men's self-disclosing behavior, *Merrill-Palmer Quarterly, 6,* 178–186.

[26]S. M. Jourard (1959), Self-disclosure and other-cathexis, *Journal of Abnormal and Social Psychology, 59,* 428–431.

[27]A. L. Chaikin & V. J. Derlega (1974), Liking for the norm-breaker in self-discloser, *Journal of Personality, 42,* 117–129; D. I. Slobin, S. H. Miller, & L. W. Porter (1968), Forms of address and social relations in a business organization, *Journal of Personality and Social Psychology, 8,* 289–293.

[28]W. B. Pearce & S. M. Sharp (1973), Self-disclosing communication, *Journal of Communication, 23,* 409–425.

[29]Wheeless (1978).

[30]L. C. Miller, L. L. Cooke, J. Tsang, & F. Morgan (1992), Should I brag? Nature and impact of positive boastful disclosures for women and men, *Human Communication Research, 18,* 364–399.

[31]S. J. Gilbert & D. Horstein (1975), The communication of self-disclosure: Level versus valence, *Human Communication Research, 1,* 316–322.

[32]Miller et al. (1992).

[33]D. R. Papini, F. F. Farmer, S. M. Clark, J. C. Micka, & J. K. Barnett (1990), Early adolescent age and gender differences in patterns of emotional self-disclosure to parents and friends, *Adolescence, 25,* 959–976.

[34]A. Howell & M. Conway (1990), Perceived intimacy of expressed emotion, *The Journal of Social Psychology, 130,* 467–476.

[35]S. Sommers (1984), Reported emotions and conventions of emotionality among college students, *Journal of Personality and Social Psychology, 46,* 207–215.

[36]Howell & Conway (1990).

[37]P. Himelstein & B. Lubin (1965), Attempted validation of the self-disclosure inventory by the peer nomination technique, *Journal of Psychology, 61,* 13–16; E. LeVina & J. N. Franco (1981), A reassessment of self-disclosure patterns among Anglo-Americans and Hispanics, *Journal of Counseling Psychology, 28,* 522–524; S. Petronio, J. Martin, & R. Littlefield (1984), Prerequisite conditions for self-disclosing: A gender issue, *Human Communication Research, 51,* 268–273.

[38]P. R. McCarthy & N. E. Betz (1978), Differential effects of self-disclosing versus self-involving counselor statements, *Journal of Counseling Psychology, 25,* 251–256; J. D. Blaswick & J. W. Blakwell (1977), Self-disclosure to same- and opposite-sex parents: An empirical test of insights from role theory, *Sociometry, 40,* 282–286; F. W. Vondracek & M. K, Marshall (1971), Self-disclosure and interpersonal trust: An exploratory study, *Psychological Reports, 28,* 235–240.

[39]Jourard & Landsman (1960).

[40]L. B. Rosenfeld (1979), Self-disclosure avoidance: Why am I afraid to tell you who I am? *Communication Monographs, 46,* 63–74.

[41]W. E. Snell, Jr., R. S. Miller, S. S. Belk, R. Garcia-Falconi, & J. E. Hernandez-Sanchez (1989), Men's and women's emotional disclosures: The impact of disclosure recipient, culture, and the masculine role, *Sex Roles, 21,* 467–486.

[42]Edwards (1990).

[43]Ibid.

[44]Ibid.

[45]P. D. Sweeny & L. E. Wells (1990), Reactions to feedback about performance: A test of three competing models, *Journal of Applied Social Psychology, 20*, 818–834.

[46]Ibid.

[47]J. S. Shrauger (1975), Responses to evaluation as a function of initial self-perceptions, *Psychological Bulletin, 82*, 581–596.

[48]D. G. Larson & R. L. Chastain (1990), Self-concealment: Conceptualization, measurement, and health implications, *Journal of Social and Clinical Psychology, 9*, 440.

[49]J. W. Pennebaker (1985), Traumatic experience and psychosomatic disease: Exploring the roles of behavioral inhibition, obsession, and confiding, *Canadian Psychology, 26*, 82.

[50]Larson & Chastain (1990).

CHAPTER 4
LANGUAGE AND COMMUNICATION

[1]J. Piaget (1962), *Play, dreams and imitation in childhood*, New York: W. W. Norton.

[2]B. Wood (1982), *Children and communication: Verbal and nonverbal language development* (2nd ed.), Englewood Cliffs, NJ: Prentice-Hall.

[3]For an excellent summary of animal language studies and language-deprived children, see the Verbal Communication chapter (pp. 32–64) of M. L. DeFleur, P. Kearney, & T. G. Plax (1993), *Fundamentals of human communication*, Mountain View, CA: Mayfield.

[4]N. Chomsky (1957), *Syntactic structures*, The Hague: Mouton, p. 17.

[5]B. F. Skinner (1953), *Science and human behavior*, New York: Macmillan.

[6]E. Bates (1979), *The emergence of symbols: Cognition and communication in infancy*, New York: Academic Press.

[7]Ibid, p. 6.

[8]Ibid., p. 103.

[9]Wood (1982), p. 288.

[10]C. K. Ogden & I. A. Richards (1923), *The message of meaning*, New York: Harcourt Brace Jovanovich, p. 11.

[11]S. I. Hayakawa (1964), *Language in thought and action*, New York: Harcourt Brace Jovanovich.

[12]From E. Sapir & B. Whorf (1956), The relation of habitual thought and behavior to language. In J. B. Carrol (Ed.), *Language, thought and reality*, Cambridge, MA: MIT Press.

[13]W. B. Gudykunst (1991), *Bridging differences: Effective intergroup communication*, Newbury Park, CA: Sage.

[14]V. C. Bickley (1988), Language as the bridge. In L. A. Samovar & R. E. Porter (Eds.), *Intercultural communication: A reader* (5th ed.), Belmont, CA: Wadsworth, pp. 233–243.

[15]K. Fiedler, G. Semin, & C. Finkenauer (1993), The battle of words between gender groups: A language-based approach to intergroup processes, *Human Communication Research, 19*(3), 409–441.

[16]J. Harwood, H. Giles, S. Fox, E. B. Ryan, & G. Williams (1993), Patronizing young and elderly adults: Response strategies in a community setting, *Journal of Applied Communication Research, 21*(3), 211–226.

[17]A. J. Mulac, J. M. Wiemann, S. J. Widenmann, & T. W. Gibson (1988), Male-female language differences and effects in same-sex and mixed-sex dyads: The gender-linked language effect, *Communication Monographs, 55*, 315–335.

[18]H. Giles & R. L. Street, Jr. (1985), Communication characteristics and behavior. In M. L. Knapp & G. R. Miller (Eds.), *Handbook of interpersonal communication*, Beverly Hills, CA: Sage, pp. 205–261.

[19]A. Haas & M. A. Sherman (1982), Reported topics of conversation among same-sex adults, *Communication Quarterly, 30*, 332–342.

[20]J. C. Pearson, L. H. Turner, & W. R. Todd-Mancillas (1991), *Gender and communication* (2nd ed.), Dubuque, IA: Wm. C. Brown.

[21]L. H. Turner, K. Dindia, & J. C. Pearson (Summer 1995), An investigation of male/female verbal behaviors in same-sex and mixed-sex conversations, *Communication Reports, 8*(2), 86–96.

[22]D. Borisoff & L. Merrill (1985), *The power to communicate: Gender differences as barriers*, Prospect Heights, IL: Waveland Press.

[23]W. B. Gudykunst & S. Ting-Toomey (1988), *Culture and interpersonal communication*, Newbury Park, CA: Sage.

[24]B. Bates (1988), *Communication and the sexes*, New York: Harper & Row.

[25]Gudykunst & Ting-Toomey (1988).

[26]J. J. Bradac (1983), The language of lovers, flovers and friends: Communicating in social and personal relationships. In W.P. Robinson (Ed.), *Journal of Language and Social Psychology, 2* (2, 3, 4).

[27]M. L. Knapp (1978), *Social intercourse: From greeting to goodbye*, Boston: Allyn & Bacon.

CHAPTER 5
NONVERBAL COMMUNICATION

[1]M. L. Knapp & A. L. Vangelisti (1992), *Interpersonal communication and human relationships*, Boston: Allyn & Bacon.

[2]J. K. Burgoon, D. A. Newton, J. B. Walther, & E. J. Baesler (1989), Nonverbal expectancy violations and conversational involvement, *Journal of Nonverbal Behavior, 13*(2), 97–119.

[3]G. H. Graham, J. Unrah, & P. Jennings (1991), The impact of nonverbal communication in organizations: A survey of perceptions, *Journal of Business Communication, 28*, 45–62.

[4]I. Eibl-Eibesfeldt (1973), *Social communication and movement*, New York: Academic Press.

[5]P. Ekman & W. V. Friesen (1971), Constants across cultures in the face and emotion, *Journal of Personality and Social Psychology, 17*, 124–129.

[6]G. Michael & F. N. Willis (1968), The development of gestures as a function of social class, education, and sex, *Psychological Record, 18*, 515–519.

[7]C. Golumb (1972), Evolution of the human figure in a three-dimensional medium, *Journal of Educational Psychology, 6*, 385–391.

[8]R. M. Lerner & C. Schroeder (1971), Physique identification, preference, and aversion in kindergarten children, *Development Psychology, 25*, 21–27.

[9]S. Jones & J. Aiello (1973), Proxemic behavior of black and white first- third-, and fifth-grade children, *Journal of Personality and Social Psychology, 25*, 21–27.

[10]V. P. Richmond, J. C. McCroskey, & S. K. Payne (1991), *Nonverbal behavior in interpersonal relations*, Englewood Cliffs, NJ: Prentice-Hall.

[11]M. G. Efran (1974), The effect of physical appearance on the judgment of guilt, interpersonal attraction, and severity of recommended punishment in a simulated jury task, *Journal of Research in Personality, 8*, 45–54.

[12]J. T. Molloy (1983), *Molloy's live for success*, New York: Bantam Books.

[13]E. H. Walster, E. Aronson, D. Abrahams, & L. Rohmann (1966), Importance of physical attractiveness in dating behavior, *Journal of Personality and Social Psychology, 4*, 508–516.

[14]D. Morris (1985), *Bodywatching*, New York: Crown.

[15]R. Sybers & M. E. Roach (1962), Clothing and human behavior, *Journal of Home Economics, 54*, 184–187.

[16]J. P. Davidson (1988), Shaping an image that boosts your career, *Marketing Communication, 13*, 55–56.

[17]Richmond et al. (1991), pp. 44–45.

[18]Sybers & Roach (1962).

[19]L. R. Aiken (1963), The relationship of dress to selected measures of personality in undergraduate women, *Journal of Social Psychology, 59*, 119–128.

[20]L. B. Rosenfeld & T.G. Plax (1977), Clothing as communication, *Journal of Communication, 27*, 24–31.

[21]P. Ekman & W. Friesen (1969), The repertoire of nonverbal behavior: Categories, origins, usage, and coding, *Semiotica, 1*, 49–98.

[22]B. Goss & D. O'Hair (1988), *Communicating in interpersonal relationships*, New York: Macmillan.

[23]R. Norton (1983), *Communicator style: Theory, applications, and measures*, Beverly Hills, CA: Sage.

[24]P. Ekman, W. Friesen, & R. Ellsworth (1972), *Emotion in the human face: Guidelines for research and an integration of findings*, New York: Pergamon.

[25]J. Boucher & P. Ekman (1975), Facial areas of emotional information, *Journal of Communication, 25*, 21–29.

[26]Ekman & Friesen (1971).

[27]Richmond et al, (1991), p. 81.

[28]Gallagher (Performer), M. Fowlkes, & J. Simon (Producers) (1983), *Gallagher: The maddest* [Videotape], Hollywood: Wizard of Odd & Paramount Home Videos.

[29]P. Eckman & W. V. Friesen (1975), *Unmasking the face: A guide to recognizing emotions from facial clues*, Englewood Cliffs, NJ: Prentice-Hall.

[30]D. Leathers (1986), *Successful nonverbal communication: Principles and applications*, New York: Macmillan.

[31]M. L. Knapp & J. A. Hall (1992), *Nonverbal communication in human interaction*, Fort Worth, TX: Holt, Rinehart & Winston; D. W. Addington (1968), The relationship of selected vocal characteristics to personality perception, *Speech Monographs, 35*, 492–503.

[32]G. L. Trager (1958), Paralanguage: A first approximation, *Studies in Linguistics, 13*, 1–12.

[33]Goss & O'Hair (1988).

[34]H. Giles & R. L. Street, Jr. (1985), *Handbook of interpersonal communication*, Beverly Hills, CA: Sage; W. B. Putman & R. L. Street (1984), Implications for speech accommodation theory,

International Journal of the Sociology of Language, 46, 97–114; and J. Jaffe & S. Feldstein (1970), *Rhythms of dialogue,* New York: Academic Press.

[35]R. Heslin (1974), Steps toward a taxonomy of touching. Paper presented at the Western Psychological Association Convention, Chicago.

[36]D. Morris (1977), *Manwatching,* New York: Abrams.

[37]Knapp & Hall (1992), p. 234.

[38]J. F. Anderson, P. A. Anderson, & M. W. Lustig (1987), Opposite sex touch avoidance: A national replication and extension, *Journal of Nonverbal Behavior, 11,* 89–109; J. F. Deethardt & D. G. Hines (1983), Tactile communication and personality differences, *Journal of Nonverbal Behavior, 8,* 143–156.

[39]E. Hall (1959), *The silent language,* New York: Doubleday.

[40]R. G. Harper, A. N. Wiens, & J. D. Matarazzo (1978), *Nonverbal communication: The state of the art,* New York: John Wiley & Sons.

[41]L. A. Malandro & L. Barker (1983), *Nonverbal communication,* New York: Random House.

[42]Goss & O'Hair (1988).

[43]M. Riess & P. Rosenfeld (1980), Seating preferences as nonverbal communication: A self-presentational analysis, *Journal of Applied Communications Research, 8,* 22–28.

[44]Richmond et al. (1991), pp. 190–191.

[45]J. K. Burgoon, D. B. Buller, & W. G. Woodall (1989), *Nonverbal communication: The unspoken dialogue,* New York: Harper & Row.

[46]Richmond et al. (1991), p. 195.

[47]Hall (1959).

[48]Ibid.

[49]Richmond et al. (1991), pp. 184–185.

[50]Ibid.

[51]P. Ekman (1965), Communication through nonverbal behavior: A source of information about an interpersonal relationship. In S. S. Tomkins & C. E. Izard (Eds.), *Affect, cognition, and personality,* New York: Springer-Verlag.

[52]R. E. Axtell (1991), *Gestures: The do's and taboos of body language around the world,* New York: John Wiley & Sons

[53]Richmond et al. (1991), pp. 202–203.

[54]Burgoon et al. (1989).

[55]A. Mehrabian (1972), *Nonverbal communication,* Chicago: Aldine-Atherton.

[56]Burgoon et al. (1989).

[57]Goss & O'Hair (1988).

[58]J. C. Pearson, L. H. Turner, & W. Todd-Mancillas (1985), *Gender and communication,* Dubuque, IA: Wm. C. Brown.

[59]E. Goffman (1971), Relations in public: *Microstudies of the public order,* New York: Basic Books.

[60]A. Kendon & A. Ferber (1971), A description of some human greetings. In R. P. M. Michael & J. H. Crook (Eds.), *Comparative ecology and behavior of primates,* New York: Academic Press.

[61]Burgoon et al. (1989).

[62]Ibid.

[63]Ibid.

[64]V. O'Donnell & J. Kable (1982), *Persuasion: An interactive dependency approach,* New York: Random House.

[65]Burgoon et al. (1989).

[66]J. Burgoon, T. Birk, & M. Pfau (1994), Nonverbal behaviors, persuasion, and credibility, *Human Communication Research, 17,* 140–169.

[67]See D. O'Hair & M. Cody (1994), Interpersonal deception. In W. Cupach & B. H. Spitzberg (Eds.), (1994), *The dark side of interpersonal communication,* Hillsdale, NJ: Lawrence Erlbaum.

[68]Ibid.

[69]Goss & O'Hair (1988).

[70]Burgoon et al. (1989).

[71]Goss & O'Hair (1988).

[72]D. O'Hair, M. Cody, & M. McLaughlin (1981), Prepared lies, spontaneous lies, Machiavellianism, and nonverbal communication, *Human Communication Research, 7,* 325–339.

[73]Burgoon et al. (1989).

[74]C. R. Berger & J. J. Bradac (1982), *Language and social knowledge: Uncertainty in interpersonal relations,* London: Arnold.

[75]Richmond et al. (1991), pp. 34–35.

[76]Knapp & Hall (1992), pp. 456–458.

CHAPTER 6
DEVELOPING LISTENING SKILLS

[1]M. T. Perras & A. R. Weitzel (1981), Measuring daily communication activities, *The Florida Speech Communication Journal, 9,* 19–23; C. G. Coakley & A. D. Wolvin (1990), Listening pedagogy and andragogy: The state of the art, *Journal of the International Listening Association, 4,* 33–61.

[2]J. Stewart (1986), *Bridges, not walls* (4th ed.), New York: Random House, p. 181.

[3]J. E. Goldman, In L. K. Steil, J. Summerfield, & G. de Mare (1983), *Listening: It can change your life,* New York: John Wiley & Sons, pp. 22.

[4]Wolvin & Coakley (1988); L. K. Steil, L. L. Barker, & K. W. Watson (1983), *Effective listening: Key to success*, Reading, MA: Addison-Wesley; F. I. Wolff, N. C. Marsnik, W. S. Tacey, & R. G. Nichols (1983), *Perceptive listening*, New York: Holt, Rinehart, & Winston.

[5]Gambrell & R. Bales (1987), Visual imagery: A strategy for enhancing listening, reading, and writing, *Australian Journal of Reading, 10*, 146–153.

CHAPTER 7
DEVELOPING AND MAINTAINING RELATIONSHIPS

[1]S. Planalp (1985), Relational schemata: a test of alternative forms of relational knowledge as guides to communication, *Human Communications Research, 12*(1), 3–29.

[2]R. A. Bell (1985), Conversational involvement and loneliness, *Communication Monographs, 52*, 218–235.

[3]I. Altman & D. Taylor (1973), Social penetration theory, New York: Holt, Rinehart & Winston.

[4]J. Rempel, J. Holmes, & M. Zanna (1985), Trust in close relationships, *Journal of Personality and Social Psychology, 49*, 95–112.

[5]C. Berger & R. Calabrese (1975), Some explorations in initial interaction and beyond: Toward a developmental theory of interpersonal communication, *Human Communication Research, 1*, 100.

[6]L. Baxter & W. Wilmot (1984), Secret tests: Social strategies for acquiring information about the state of the relationship, *Human Communication Research, 11*, 171–201.

[7]This model is based on the following research: G. Miller & M. Steinberg (1975), *Between people*, Palo Alto, Ca: Science Research Associates; Altman & Taylor (1973); M. L. Knapp & A. L. Vangelisti (1992), *Interpersonal communication and human relationships* (2nd ed.), Boston: Allyn & Bacon.

[8]W. Wilmot (1981), Relationship stages: Initiation and stabilization. In J. Civikly (Ed.), *Contexts of communication*, New York: Holt, Rinehart & Winston.

[9]Knapp & Vangelisti (1992).

[10]E. Goffman (1971), *Relations in public*, New York: Harper & Row.

[11]Knapp & Vangelisti (1992).

[12]J. A. Lee (1973), *The colors of love: An exploration of the ways of loving*, Don Mills, Ontario: New Press; S. S. Hendrick & C. Hendrick (1992), *Liking, loving, and relating*. Pacific Grove, CA: Brooks/Cole.

[13]B. Goss & D. O'Hair (1988), *Communicating in interpersonal relationships*, New York: Macmillan.

[14]S. Planalp & J. Honeycutt (1985), Events that increase uncertainty in personal relationships, *Human Communication Research, 11*, 593–604.

[15]C. Hill, Z. Rubion, & L. A. Peplau (1976), Breakups before marriage: The end of 103 affairs, *Journal of Social Issues, 32*, 147–168.

[16]P. Blumstein & P. Schwartz (1983), *American couples: Money, work, sex*, New York: Morrow.

[17]S. W. Duck (1984), A perspective on the repair of personal relationships: Repair of what, when? In S. W. Duck (Ed.), *Personal relationships 5: Repairing personal relationships*, New York: Macmillan.

[18]Blumstein & Schwartz (1983).

[19]M. S. Davis (1973), *Intimate relations*, New York: Free Press, pp. 245–283.

[20]J. H. Harvey, T. L. Orbuch, & A. L. Weber (1990), A social psychological model of account-making in response to severe stress, *Journal of Language and Social Psychology, 9*, 191–207; J. H. Harvey, G. Agostinelli, & A. L. Weber (1989), Account-making and the formation of expectations about close relationships, in C. Hendrick (Ed.), *Close relationships*, Newbury Park, CA: Sage; J. H. Harvey, A. L. Weber, K. S. Galvin, H. C. Huszti, & N. N. Garnick (1986), Attribution in the termination of close relationships: A special focus on the account, in R. Gilmour & S. W. Duck (Eds.), *The emerging field of personal relationships*, Hillsdale, NJ: Lawrence Erlbaum; J. H. Harvey, A. L. Weber, & T. L. Orbuch (1190), *Interpersonal accounts: A social psychological perspective*, Cambridge, MA: Basil Blackwell.

[21]J. C. Pearson & B. H. Spitzberg (1990), *Interpersonal communication: Concepts, components, and contexts* (2nd ed.), Dubuque, IA: Wm. C. Brown.

[22]M. Parlee (1979), The friendship bond, *Psychology Today, 13*(10), 43–54, 113.

[23]J. Reisman (1979), *Anatomy of friendship*, Lexington, MA: Lexis Publishers.

[24]G. D. Nass & G. W. McDonald (1982), *Marriage and the family*, New York: Random House.

[25]S. Trenholm & A. Jensen (1988), *Interpersonal communication*, Belmont, CA: Wadsworth.

CHAPTER 8
MANAGING CONFLICT IN INTERPERSONAL RELATIONSHIPS

[1]J. L. Hocker & W. Wilmot (1985), *Interpersonal conflict* (2nd ed.), Dubuque, IA: Wm. C. Brown.

[2]S. Ting-Toomey (1985), Toward a theory of conflict and culture. In W. B. Gudykunst, L. Stewart, & S. Ting-Toomey (Eds.), *Communication, culture, and organizational processes*, Beverly Hills, CA: Sage.

[3]D. Infante & C. Wigely (1986), Verbal aggressiveness: An interpersonal model and measure, *Communication Monographs, 53*, 61–69.

[4]J. C. McCroskey (1977), Oral communication apprehension: A summary of recent theory and research, *Human Communication Research, 4*, 78–96.

[5]K. W. Thomas & R. H. Kilmann (1974), *Thomas-Kilmann Conflict MODE Instrument*, Tuxedo, NY: Xiacom.

[6]These strategies summarize and categorize the many conflict strategies and tactics reported by others.

[7]D. J. Canary & B. H. Spitzberg (1989), A model of the perceived competence of conflict strategies, *Human Communication Research, 15*(4), 630–649.

[8]D. J. Canary, E. M. Cunningham, & M. J. Cody (1988), Goal types, gender and locus of control in managing interpersonal conflict, *Communication Research, 15*(4), 426–446.

[9]D. Buller & J. Burgoon (1994), Deception: Strategic and nonstrategic communication. In J. Daly & J. Wiemann (Eds.), *Strategic interpersonal communication*, Hillsdale, NJ: Lawrence Erlbaum.

[10]L. Putnam & M. Poole (1987), Conflict and negotiation. In F. Jablin et al. (Eds.), *Handbook of organizational communication*, Beverly Hills, CA: Sage.

[11]W. Donahue, M. Deiz, & M. Hamilton (1984), Coding naturalistic negotiation interaction, *Human Communication Research, 10*, 403–426.

[12]J. P. Folger & M. S. Poole (1984), *Working through conflicts: A communication perspective*, Glenview, IL: Scott, Foresman.

[13]Ibid.

[14]Ibid.

[15]Canary & Spitzberg (1989).

[16]Folger & Poole (1984).

CHAPTER 9
PRINCIPLES OF COMPETENT INTERVIEWING

[1]C. J. Stewart & W. B. Cash, Jr. (1991), *Interviewing: Principles and practices* (6th ed.), Dubuque, IA: Wm. C. Brown, p. 6.

[2]D. O'Hair & G. W. Friedrich (1992), *Strategic communication in business and the professions*, Boston: Houghton Mifflin, p. 205.

[3]Slightly modified version of R. S. Goyer & J. T. Rickey (1968), *Interviewing principles and techniques: A project text* (rev. ed.), Dubuque, IA: Wm. C. Brown, p. 10.

[4]M. L. Knapp, R. P. Hart, G. W. Friedrich, & G. M. Shulman (1973), The rhetoric of goodbye: Verbal and nonverbal correlates of human leave-taking, *Communication Monographs, 40*, 182–198.

[5]Stewart & Cash (1991), pp. 48–49.

[6]A. A. Bellack, H. M. Kleibard, R. T. Hyman, & F. L. Smith, Jr. (1967), *The language of the classroom*, New York: Teachers College Press, Columbia University, p. 4.

[7]The labels and definitions are from O'Hair & Friedrich (1992), pp. 220–221.

[8]S. L. Payne (1951), *The art of asking questions*, Princeton, NJ: Princeton University Press.

[9]G. Gallup (1947), The quintamensional plan of question design, *Public Opinion Quarterly, 11*, 385.

[10]C. R. Rogers (1951), *Client-centered therapy*, Boston: Houghton Mifflin.

[11]Paraphrased from D. W. Johnson (1972), *Reaching out: Interpersonal effectiveness and self-actualization*, Englewood Cliffs, NJ: Prentice-Hall, p. 125.

[12]J. P. Galassi & M. Galassi (1978), Preparing individuals for job interviews: Suggestions from more than 60 years of research, *Personnel and Guidance Journal, 57*, 188–192.

[13]B. Greco (1977), Recruiting and retaining high achievers, *Journal of College Placement, 37*(2), 34–40.

[14]Stewart & Cash (1991), pp. 155–156.

[15]R. Miller (1991), Personnel execs reveal the truth about job applicants, *Dallas Morning News*, January 31, p. 2D.

CHAPTER 10
COMMUNICATING IN SMALL GROUPS

[1]J. Gordon (1992), Work teams: How far have they come? *Training, 29*, 59–65.

[2]R. Y. Hirokawa & D. Gouran (1989), Facilitation of group communication: A critique of prior research and an agenda for future research, *Management Communication Quarterly, 3*, 71–92.

[3]W. W. Wilmot (1987), *Dyadic communication* (3rd ed.), New York: Random House.

[4]K. Brilhart & G. J. Galanes (1992), *Effective group discussion* (7th ed.), Dubuque, IA: Wm. C. Brown.

[5]D. O'Hair, J. S. O'Rourke, & M. J. O'Hair, (1997), *Business communication*, unpublished manuscript.

[6]H. H. Kelley (1971), The process of causal attributions, *American Psychologist, 28,* 107–128.

[7]J. C. McCroskey (1977), Oral communication apprehension: A summary of recent theory and research, *Human Communication Research, 4,* 78–96.

[8]J. C. McCroskey (1997), *An introduction to rhetorical communication* (7th ed.), Englewood Cliffs, NJ: Prentice-Hall.

[9]McCroskey (1977).

[10]J. C. McCroskey & V. P. Richmond (1988), Communication apprehension and small group communication. In R. S. Cathcart & L. A. Samovar (Eds.), *Small group communication: A reader* (5th ed.), Dubuque, IA: Wm. C. Brown, pp. 405–420.

[11]L. B. Rosenfeld (1988), Self-disclosure and small group interaction. In Cathcart & Samovar (Eds.), *Small group communication,* pp. 288–305.

[12]M. E. Shaw (1988), Group composition and group cohesiveness. In Cathcart & Samovar (Eds.), *Small group communication,* pp. 42–49.

[13]J. E. Baird, Jr. & S. Weinbert (1977), *Communication: The essence of a group synergy,* Dubuque, IA: Wm. C. Brown.

[14]I. L. Janis (1972), *Victims of groupthink,* Boston: Houghton Mifflin.

[15]J. A. Jaksa & M. S. Pritchard (1994), *Communication ethics: Methods of analysis* (2nd ed.), Belmont, CA: Wadsworth.

[16]P. H. Andrews (1988), Group conformity. In Cathcart & Samovar (Eds.), *Small group communication,* pp. 225–235.

[17]Brilhart & Galanes (1992).

[18]D. O'Hair & G. Friedrich (1992), *Strategic communication in business and the professions,* Boston: Houghton Mifflin.

[19]L. R. Hoffman & N. R. F. Maier (1964), Valence in the adoption of solutions by problem-solving groups: Concept, method, and results, *Journal of Abnormal and Social Psychology, 69,* 264–271.

[20]T. L. Albrecht & B. Hall (1991), Relational and content differences between elites and outsiders in innovation networks, *Human Communication Research, 17,* 535–561.

[21]C. M. Moore (1987), *Group techniques for idea building,* Newbury Park, CA: Sage.

[22]S. Kanekar & M. E. Rosenbaum (1972), Group performance on a multiple-solution task as a function of available time, *Psychometric Science, 27,* 331–332.

[23]J. D. Orsburn, L. Moran, E. Musselwhite, & J. H. Zenger (1990), *Self-directed work teams: The new American challenge,* Homewood, IL: Business One Irwin.

[24]B. Dumaine (1990), Who needs a boss? *Fortune, 121*(10): pp. 52–60.

[25]Orsburn et al. (1990).

[26]A. B. Cheney (1991), Self-managed work teams, *Executive Excellence, 8,* 11–12.

CHAPTER 11
LEADERSHIP AND DECISION MAKING IN GROUPS

[1]J. K. Hemphill & A. E. Coons (1957), Development of the leader behavior description questionnaire. In R. M. Stogdill & A. E. Coons (Eds.), *Leader behavior: Its description and measurement,* Columbus, OH: Bureau of Business Research, Ohio State University, p. 7.

[2]R. M. Stogdill (1974), *Handbook of leadership: A survey of the literature,* New York: Free Press, p. 411.

[3]R. Tannenbaum, I. R. Weschler, & F. Massarik (1961), *Leadership and organization,* New York: McGraw-Hill, p. 24.

[4]T. O. Jacobs (1970), *Leadership and exchange in formal organizations,* Alexandria, VA: Human Resources Research Organization, p. 232.

[5]B. M. Bass (1990), *Bass and Stogdill's handbook of leadership,* New York: Free Press, p. 546.

[6]W. J. Altier (1990), Problem-solving meetings, *Executive Excellence, 10,* 10.

[7]Ibid.

[8]Ibid.

[9]Ibid.

[10]Ibid.

[11]R. Y. Hirokawa, D. S. Gouran, & A. E. Martz (1988), Understanding the sources of faulty group decision-making: A lesson from the Challenger disaster, *Small Group Behavior, 19,* 411–433.

[12]Ibid., p. 416.

[13]M. Rokeach (1973), *The nature of human values,* New York: Free Press, p. 5.

[14]W. A. Green & H. Lazarus (1990), Are you meeting with success? *Executive Excellence, 7,* 11–12.

[15]S. R. Covey (1989), *The seven habits of highly effective people,* New York: Simon & Schuster, p. 213.

[16]J. Dewey (1933), *How we think,* Lexington, MA: D. C. Heath.

[17]R. Y. Hirokawa (1992), Communication and group decision-making efficacy. In R. S. Cathcart and

L. S. Samovar (Eds.), *Small group communication: A reader* (6th ed.), Dubuque, IA: Wm. C. Brown, pp. 165–177.

[18] A. C. Kowitz & T. J. Knutson (1980), *Decision making in small groups: The search for alternatives*, New York: Allyn & Bacon.

[19] L. A. Samovar & S. W. King (1981), *Communication and discussion in small groups*, New York: Gorsuch Scarisbrick Publishers.

CHAPTER 12
COMMUNICATING IN ORGANIZATIONS

[1] Bureau of Labor Statistics (1993), Jobs: Separating fact from fiction, *Dallas Morning News*, June 1, p. D1.

[2] S. Shellenbarger & C. Hymowitz (1994), Over the hill? As population ages, older workers clash with younger bosses, *Wall Street Journal*, June 13, pp. A1, A8.

[3] Bureau of Labor Statistics (1993).

[4] D. Kunde (1993), Looking through glass, *Dallas Morning News*, December 11, pp. F1–2.

[5] J. H. Dobrzynski (1993), The 'glass ceiling': A barrier to the boardroom, too, *Business Week*, November 22, p. 50.

[6] Bureau of Labor Statistics (1993).

[7] Helping hands (1995), *Business Week*, July 10, p. 8.

[8] S. P. Robbins (1984), *Essentials of organizational behavior*, Englewood Cliffs, NJ: Prentice-Hall.

[9] R. B. Adler (1989), *Communicating at work: Principles and practices for business and the professions* (3rd ed.), New York: Random House.

[10] P. Frost, L. Moore, M. Louis, C. Lundberg, & J. Martin (1991), *Reframing organizational culture*, Newbury Park, CA: Sage.

[11] E. M. Eisenberg & H. L. Goodall, Jr. (1993), *Organizational communication: Balancing creativity and constraint*, New York: St. Martin's Press.

[12] P. Monge (1977), The systems perspective as a theoretical basis for the study of human communication, *Communication Quarterly*, 25, 19–29.

[13] S. W. Littlejohn (1992), *Theories of human communication* (4th ed.), Belmont, CA: Wadsworth; A. D. Hall & R. E. Fagen (1968), Definition of system. In W. Buckley (Ed.), *Modern systems research for the behavioral scientist*, Chicago: Aldine.

[14] D. McGregor (1960), *The human side of enterprise*, New York: McGraw-Hill.

[15] W. G. Ouchi (1981), *Theory Z*, Reading, MA: Addison-Wesley.

[16] S. DeWine (1994), *The consultant's craft*, New York: St. Martin's Press.

[17] H. J. Leavitt (1951), Some effects of certain communication patterns on group performance, *Journal of Abnormal and Social Psychology*, 46, 38–50.

[18] M. E. Shaw (1954), Some effects of unequal distribution of information upon group performance in various communication nets, *Journal of Abnormal and Social Psychology*, 49, 547–553.

[19] T. Albrecht, K. Irey, & A. Mundy (1982), Integration in communication networks as a mediator of stress: The case of a protective services agency, *Social Work*, 27, 229–235.

[20] T. L. Albrecht, The role of communication in perceptions of organizational climate. In D. Nimmo (Ed.), *Communication Yearbook 3*, New Brunswick: NJ: Transaction Books, pp. 343–357.

[21] Baber & Wayman (Summer 1993), Your company.

[22] Adapted from D. O'Hair, J. S. O'Rourke, & M. J. O'Hair.

[23] H. Witteman, The interface between sexual harassment and organizational romance. In G. Kreps (Ed.), *Sexual harassment: Communication implications*, Cresskill, NJ: Hampton Press.

[24] This section influenced by C. Berryman-Fink, Preventing sexual harassment thorough male-female communication training. In G. Kreps (Ed.), *Sexual harassment*.

[25] K. E. Kram (1983), Phases of the mentor relationship. *Academy of Management Journal*, 12, 608–625.

[26] J. Simons (1995), Pagers send a strong message, *U.S. News and World Report*, November 27, pp. 58–59.

[27] J. S. O'Rourke (1993), Presentation delivered to the Executive Conference, Sisters of Saint Francis, Health Services, Inc., South Bend, IN.

[28] Ibid.

CHAPTER 13
PREPARING AND DELIVERING PRESENTATIONS

[1] B. Ehrenreich (1989), Public freaking, *Ms.*, September, p. 40.

[2] G. W. Gray (1945), The "Precepts of Kagemni and Ptah-Hotep," *Quarterly Journal of Speech*, 32, 446–454.

[3] R. P. Hart, G. W. Friedrich, & B. Brummet (1983), *Public Communication* (2nd ed.), New York: Harper & Row, pp. 13–15.

[4] R. E. Smith (1993), Clustering: A way to discover speech topics, *The Speech Teacher*, 7(2), 6–7.

[5]H. L. Hollingsworth (1935), *The psychology of the audience*, New York: American Book.

[6]J. F. Wilson, C. C. Arnold, & M. M. Wertheimer (1990), *Public speaking as a liberal art* (6th ed.), Boston: Allyn & Bacon, pp. 112–113.

[7]M. S. Knowles (1975). *Self-directed learning: A guide for learners and teachers*, New York: Cambridge.

[8]Hart, Friedrich, & Brummet (1983), pp. 170–171.

[9]J. C. McCroskey (1977), Oral communication apprehension: A summary of recent theory and research, *Human Communication Research, 4*, 78.

[10]G. W. Friedrich & B. Goss (1984), Systematic desensitization. In J. A. Daly & J. C. McCroskey (Eds.), *Avoiding communication: Shyness, reticence and communication apprehension*, Beverly Hills, CA: Sage, pp. 173–188.

[11]W. J. Fremouw & M. D. Scott (1979), Cognitive restructuring: An alternative method for the treatment of communication apprehension, *Communication Education, 28*, 129–133.

CHAPTER 14
INFORMATIVE PRESENTATIONS

[1]F. Machlup (1962), *The production and distribution of knowledge in the United States*, Princeton, NJ: Princeton University Press.

[2]N. Postman & C. Weingarten (1969), *Teaching as a subversive activity*, New York: Dell, p. 10.

[3]Staff (March/April, 1985), The information society, *The Royal Bank letter*, p. 1.

[4]As cited in J. Fiala (1987), Citation analysis controls the information flood, *Thermochimica Acta, 110*, 11–22.

[5]F. Wallin (March 1983), Universities for a small planet—a time to reconceptualize our role, *Change*, pp. 7–8.

[6]R. Lindstrom (February 1992), Facing facts, *Presentation Products*, p. 6.

[7]A. L. Vangelisti & J. A. Daly (1989), Correlates of speaking skills in the United States: A national assessment, *Communication Education, 38*, 132–143.

[8]R. R. Allen & R. E. McKerrow (1981), *The pragmatics of public communication* (2nd ed.), Dubuque, IA: Kendall/Hunt, pp. 106–107.

[9]R. L. Johannesen, R. R. Allen, & W. L. Linkugel (1992), *Contemporary American speeches* (7th ed.), Dubuque, IA: Kendall/Hunt, p. 52.

[10]Adapted from B. Robertson & D. Gormley (1987), *Step-by-step printing*, London: Diagram Visual Information Ltd., p. 71.

[11]Johannesen, Allen & Linkugel (1992), p. 66.

[12]K. Rowan (1990), The speech to explain difficult ideas, *The Speech Communication Teacher, 4*(4), 2–3.

[13]R. P. Hart (1975). *Lecturing as communication*, unpublished manuscript, Purdue University, Purdue Research Foundation.

[14]M. Mino (1991), Structuring: An alternative approach for developing clear organization, *The Speech Communication Teacher, 5*(2), 14–15.

CHAPTER 15
PERSUASIVE PRESENTATIONS

[1]M. V. Fox (1983), Ancient Egyptian rhetoric, *Rhetorica, 1*, 9–22.

[2]K. E. Andersen (1971), *Persuasion: Theory and practice*, Boston: Allyn & Bacon.

[3]E. P. Bettinghaus & M. J. Cody (1987), *Persuasive communication* (4th ed.), New York: Holt, Rinehart and Winston.

[4]G. Cronkhite (1969), *Persuasion: Speech and behavioral change*, Indianapolis, IN: Bobbs-Merrill.

[5]R. L. Johannesen, R. R. Allen, & W. A. Linkugel (1992), *Contemporary American speeches* (7th ed.), Dubuque, IA: Kendall/Hunt.

[6]S. Toulmin (1958), *The uses of argument*, Cambridge: Cambridge University Press. The treatment in this chapter draws from W. Brockriede & D. Ehninger (1960), Toulmin on argument: An interpretation and application, *Quarterly Journal of Speech, 46*, 44–53.

[7]See A. H. Maslow (1943), A theory of human motivation, *Psychological Review, 50*, 370–396; A. H. Maslow (1970), *Motivation and personality* (2nd ed.), New York: Harper & Row.

[8]C. I. Hovland & W. Weiss (1951), The influence of source credibility on communication effectiveness, *Public Opinion Quarterly, 15*, 635–650.

[9]G. R. Miller & M. A. Hewgill (1964), The effect of variations in nonfluency on audience ratings of source credibility, *Quarterly Journal of Speech, 50*, 36–44.

[10]R. P. Hart, G. W. Friedrich, & B. Brummett (1983), *Public Communication* (2nd ed.), New York: Harper & Row, pp. 213–217.

[11]J. C. Reinard (1988), The empirical study of the persuasive effects of evidence: The status after fifty years of research, *Human Communication Research, 15*, 3–59.

[12]Ibid., p. 25.

[13]P. B. Andrews (1985), *Basic public speaking*, New York: Harper & Row.

[14]D. J. O'Keefe (1990), *Persuasion: Theory and research*, Newbury Park, CA: Sage.

[15]R. E. Petty & J. T. Cacioppo (1986), *Communication and persuasion: Central and peripheral routes to attitudes change*, New York: Springer-Verlag.

CHAPTER 16
UNDERSTANDING AND USING MASS COMMUNICATION

[1]M. McLuhan (1964), *Understanding media*, New York: McGraw-Hill.

[2]U.S. Bureau of the Census (1993), *Statistical Abstract of the United States 1993* (113th ed.), Washington, DC.

[3]W. V. Ruch (1989), *International handbook of corporate communication*, Jefferson, NC: McFarland.

[4]S. J. Baran & D. K. Davis (1981), *Mass communication and everyday life: A perspective on theory and effects*, Belmont, CA: Wadsworth.

[5]R. Gozzi, Jr., & W. L. Haynes (1992), Electric media and electric epistemology: Empathy at a distance, *Critical Studies in Mass Communication, 9*, 217–228.

[6]E. Babbie (1990), *Survey research methods* (2nd ed.), Belmont, CA: Wadsworth.

[7]D. Graber (1989), *Mass media and American politics* (3rd ed.), Washington, DC: Congressional Quarterly Press.

[8]A. Alexander (1993), Exploring media in everyday life, *Communication Monographs, 60*, 55–61.

[9]R. S. Nickerson (1988), Technology in education in 2020: Thinking about the not-distant future. In R. Nickerson & P. Zodhiates (Eds.), *Technology in education: Looking toward 2020*, Hillsdale, NJ: Lawrence Erlbaum, pp. 1–10.

[10]This information is not intended to include messages generated through computer networks, for mediated messages are a type of interpersonal communication exchange.

[11]E. Singer & S. Presser (1989), *Survey research: A reader*, Chicago: University of Chicago Press.

[12]E. Babbie (1989), *The practice of social research* (5th ed.), Belmont, CA: Wadsworth.

[13]H. Nelson, D. Teeter, & D. Le Duc (1989), *Law of mass communications: Freedom and control of print and broadcast media* (6th ed.), Westbury, NY: The Foundation Press.

[14]Ibid.

[15]R. Hiebert, D. Ungurait, & T. Bohn (1988), *Mass media V: An introduction to modern communication*, New York: Longman.

[16]Ibid.

[17]B. Bagdikian (1990), *The media monopoly* (3rd ed.), Boston: Beacon.

[18]D. McQuail & S. Windahl (1981), *Communication models for the study of mass communications*, New York: Longman.

[19]Ibid., p. 50.

[20]G. Gerbner, L. Gross, M. Morgan, & N. Signorielli (1986), Living with television: The dynamics of the cultivation process. In J. Bryant & D. Zillmann (Eds.), *Perspectives on media effects*, Hillsdale, NJ: Lawrence Erlbaum, pp.17–40.

[21]S. Littlejohn (1989), *Theories of human communication* (3rd ed.), Belmont, CA: Wadsworth.

[22]Ibid.

[23]S. Francisco (Ed.) (1990), *AIDS: Education and prevention*, Official publication of the International Society for AIDS Education, San Francisco.

[24]K. Jamieson (1992), *Dirty politics: Deception, distraction, and democracy.* New York: Oxford University Press.

Glossary

ABSTRACTION LADDER An illustration of how words can be used to describe topics ranging from the general to the specific. (Ch. 4)

ACCENTING Nonverbal behavior that emphasizes the accompanying verbal message. (Ch. 5)

ADAPTER A movement or gesture that satisfies some physical or psychological need. (Ch. 5)

AFFECT DISPLAY An unintentional movement or expression that conveys a mood or emotional state. (Ch. 5)

AFFILIATION Feelings for another, ranging from love (high positive affiliation) to hate (high negative affiliation); one of the three primary functions of communication. (Ch. 1)

AGENDA A sequential plan of action, usually for organizing a group meeting. (Ch. 10)

AGENDA SETTING The media's ability to determine, through the content of media presentations, which issues or topics will be important to individual members of society. (Ch. 16) See also *agenda.*

ANDRAGOGY The art and science of helping adults learn. (Ch. 13)

APPRECIATIVE LISTENING Listening in order to appreciate the sounds received by one's listening mechanism. (Ch. 6)

ARGUMENTATIVENESS A conflict style that seeks out controversial issues and revels in debating them. (Ch. 8)

ARTIFACT An accessory used for decoration or identification. (Ch. 5)

ASSERTIVENESS A conflict style that emphasizes personal concerns. (Ch. 8)

ASSOCIATION A type of friendship that develops through frequent contact; more an acquaintance than a true friendship. (Ch. 7)

ATTRIBUTION A generalization that uses personal characteristics to explain communication behavior. (Ch. 2)

AUDIENCE One or more people who are listening to what a person is saying and/or watching what that person is doing. (Ch. 1)

AUDIENCE ANALYSIS A characterization of the individuals who will listen to a speech in terms of audience type (pedestrian, passive, selected, concerted, or organized), their relevant reference groups, and their situational expectations. (Ch. 13)

AUTHORITARIAN LEADERSHIP Control by a leader without input from group members. (Ch. 11)

BARGAINING In a conflict, arguing for one's own position while expressing understanding of and sensitivity to the other party's position. (Ch. 8)

BEHAVIORAL SKILLS Communicative tools that are mastered and applied in different relational situations. (Ch. 1)

BOARD An elected or appointed group that makes important decisions regarding the functioning of an organization. (Ch. 11)

CATEGORIES OF SPEECH TOPICS Eight categories that can be used to generate topics for informative speeches—people, places, things, events, processes, concepts, problems, and plans and policies. (Ch. 14)

CAUSE-EFFECT ORGANIZATIONAL PATTERN A pattern that presents the main points of a message in terms of cause-to-effect or effect-to-cause relationships. (Ch. 13)

CENTRAL ROUTE TO PERSUASION A route to persuasion in which the audience carefully considers and analyzes the content of the message in deciding whether to accept or reject it. (Ch. 15)

CENTRALITY The degree to which a member of a group sends and receives messages from others in the group. (Ch. 10)

CENTRALIZED NETWORK A type of network in which a majority of the communication passes through a small number of participants. (Ch. 12)

CHANNEL A vehicle or mechanism that transmits a message from sender to receiver. (Ch. 2) See also *formal channels; informal channels.*

CHANNEL CAPACITY The ability to process information competently via a particular communication channel or channels (e.g., face-to-face or over the telephone). (Ch. 2)

CHANNEL DISCREPANCY The use of two or more channels to send contradictory messages. (Ch. 5)

CHANNEL PREFERENCE The preference of a communicator for one type of communication channel over others. (Ch. 2)

CHRONEMICS The communicative ability of the use of time. (Ch. 5)

CHRONOLOGICAL ORGANIZATIONAL PATTERN A pattern that presents the main points of a message in a time-related sequence. (Ch. 13)

CLIQUE (COALITION) An exclusive group held together by common interests and activities. (Ch. 10)

CLOSED QUESTION A question that gives the interviewee little or no freedom in responding. (Ch. 9)

CLOSING The termination phase of an interview. (Ch. 9)

CLOTHING ORIENTATION Clothing preferences. (Ch. 5)

CLUSTERING A creative technique for identifying potential speech topics; involves writing down a core idea and all of the words, phrases, and ideas generated by it. (Ch. 13)

COALITION See *clique.*

CO-CULTURE One of two or more subcultures within a culture. (Ch. 1)

CODE The symbols, signals, or signs used to construct messages. (Ch. 1)

COGNITIVE APPROACH An approach to language acquisition which holds that certain thinking abilities must precede language development. (Ch. 4)

COGNITIVE COMPLEXITY The degree to which one can perceive information in more complicated and intricate ways. (Ch. 2)

COGNITIVE LOAD The amount of information a person can process at one time. (Ch. 2)

COGNITIVE RESTRUCTURING A method for reducing or treating communication apprehension; teaches individuals how to identify anxiety-producing negative statements and replace them with coping statements. (Ch. 13)

COGNITIVE SKILLS Mental capacities, including the ability to think, reason, remember, and make sense of one's world. (Ch. 1)

COHESION A group's ability to work as an integrated unit. (Ch. 10)

COMMITTEE A temporary or permanent group that meets for a specific purpose. (Ch. 11)

COMMUNICATION A process defined by six characteristics: (1) symbolic behavior; (2) the sharing of a code; (3) its tie to culture; (4) intentionality; (5) the presence of a medium; and (6) the fact that it is transactional. (Ch. 1)

COMMUNICATION ANXIETY See *communication apprehension.*

COMMUNICATION APPREHENSION (CA) Fear or anxiety associated with real or anticipated communication with another person or persons. (Ch. 8) See also *state communication apprehension; trait communication apprehension.*

COMMUNICATION BARRIERS Eight dilemmas speakers face when they attempt to transmit information. (Ch. 14)

COMMUNICATION COMPETENCIES Skills and understandings that enable communication partners to exchange messages appropriately and effectively. (Ch. 1)

COMMUNICATION CONTEXT   See *context*.

COMMUNICATION GOAL   A desired outcome that can affect how communication takes place. (Ch. 2)

COMMUNICATION PROCESSING   The means by which one gathers, organizes, and evaluates received information. (Ch. 2)

COMMUNICATION RELATIONSHIP   An interdependence of two or more people which is based on symbolic exchange. (Ch. 1)

COMMUNICATION SKILLS   Behavioral routines based on social understandings and used by communicators to achieve their goals. (Ch. 1)

COMMUNICATION STYLE   An overall characterization consisting of a communicator's vocal characteristics, word choice, and impression formation. (Ch. 6)

COMMUNICATIVE COMPETENCE   The ability of two or more people jointly to create and maintain a mutually satisfying relationship through the construction of appropriate and effective messages. (Ch. 1)

COMPETENCY   See *communication competencies; communicative competence*.

COMPETENT LEADERSHIP   Credible behavior by which an individual inspires and motivates group members to achieve desirable group outcomes through interaction. (Ch. 11)

COMPLEMENTING   Nonverbal behavior that clarifies the meaning of a verbal message. (Ch. 5)

COMPLETE SENTENCE OUTLINE   A visual, schematic summary of a speech that allows others to understand the speaker's plan for the speeCh. (Ch. 13)

COMPREHENSIVE LISTENING   Listening in order to understand the message of another person. (Ch. 6)

COMPROMISE   A conflict resolution tactic that involves agreeing on a method of deciding, rather than focusing on the quality of the decision. (Ch. 8)

CONCERTED AUDIENCE   An audience that shares the goal of the speaker and is disposed to accept the speaker's plan of action. (Ch. 13)

CONCLUSION   The final portion of a speech; typically brings closure in the form of a summary and a statement of impact. (Ch. 13)

CONFLICT   A struggle between two or more interdependent parties who perceive incompatible goals, scarce rewards, and interference from the other party or parties in achieving their goals. (Ch. 8)

CONNOTATIVE MEANING   The emotional or attitudinal response people have to words. (Ch. 4)

CONSENSUS   A mutually satisfying agreement reached by two or more parties. (Ch. 8)

CONSTRUCTS   Mental structures that enable a person to make differentiations in judgments. (Ch. 2)

CONSULTATIVE LEADERSHIP   Leadership that bases decisions on the opinions or ideas of group members. (Ch. 11)

CONTEXT   The physical and psychological setting of an interaction. (Ch. 5)

CONTRADICTING   Nonverbal behavior that conveys a meaning opposite to that of the sender's verbal message. (Ch. 5)

CONTROL   The ability of one person to influence another person or persons and the manner in which their relationship is conducted; one of the three primary functions of communication. (Ch. 1)

COOPERATIVE STRATEGIES   In a conflict, strategies that promote the objectives of the relationship rather than those of one partner or the other. (Ch. 8)

COOPERATIVENESS   A conflict style that emphasizes the other's concerns. (Ch. 8) See also *cooperative strategies*.

CORRESPONDENCE BIAS   The belief, excluding other possible factors, that another individual is the sole cause of an action or actions. (Ch. 2)

COUNTERCOALITION   A relationship in which two or more people position themselves against two or more others with regard to an issue. (Ch. 10)

CRITICAL CONSUMER   An individual who, as the user of a product, carefully evaluates the product for its quality, worth, and usefulness. A critical consumer of the media assesses the content of mediated messages for their accuracy and reliability. (Ch. 16)

CRITICAL LISTENING   Listening in order to evaluate or analyze information, evidence, ideas, or opinions. (Ch. 6)

CRITICAL THINKING   A method of viewing the world from a reasoned and proactive perspective. (Ch. 10)

CULTIVATION THEORY   A perspective on media effects which suggests that television is a socializing agent of culture that provides its viewers with a common world view. (Ch. 16)

CULTURAL FACTORS   Ways in which different cultural backgrounds can affect communication processing. (Ch. 2)

CULTURAL MYOPIA   The belief that one's particular culture is appropriate in all situations and relevant to all others. (Ch. 2)

CULTURE   The shared beliefs, values, and practices of a group of people. (Ch. 1)

DECENTRALIZED NETWORK   A type of network in which many participants have a number of connections to others. (Ch. 12)

DECEPTION   In a conflict, a partner's introduction of false data or substantiation for a general claim. (Ch. 8)

DECODE   Physically receive a message (or other type of stimulus) and interpret and assign meaning to it. (Ch. 1)

DEFINITIONAL SPEECH   A speech that explains what words and/or concepts mean. (Ch. 14)

DEINTENSIFICATION   The facial management technique of downplaying what is felt. (Ch. 5)

DEMOGRAPHIC REFERENCE GROUP   A group of people who share such traits as age, gender, and ethnicity. (Ch. 13)

DEMONSTRATION SPEECH   A speech that uses narration and examples to describe how things happen. (Ch. 14)

DENOTATIVE MEANING   The dictionary definition of a word. (Ch. 4)

DESCRIPTIVE SPEECH   A speech that presents information so vividly that the audience can share the speaker's experiences. (Ch. 14)

DETERMINANT INTERVIEW   The second stage in the employment interview process; during this stage the interviewer decides whether or not to offer the job to the applicant. (Ch. 9)

DIRECT EFFECTS MODEL   An early theory of mass communication which states that all individual members of society receive messages in the same way and that direct and uniform outcomes result. (Ch. 16)

DIRECTED QUESTION   A question that suggests or implies the answer that is expected. (Ch. 9)

DIRECTIVE INTERVIEW   An interview in which the interviewer retains control of the purpose, structure, and pacing of the interview. (Ch. 9)

DISCRIMINATION   The process of acting on your prejudices. (Ch. 2)

DYAD   A pair of individuals maintaining a relationship. (Ch. 1)

DYADIC RELATIONSHIP   See dyad.

ECTOMORPH   A person with a thin, angular body. (Ch. 5)

ELABORATION LIKELIHOOD MODEL (ELM) A theory of persuasion that specifies the conditions under which an audience will process a message. (Ch. 15)

ELUCIDATING EXPLANATION   An explanation that illuminates a concept's meaning and use. (Ch. 14)

EMBLEM   A movement or gesture that has a direct verbal translation. (Ch. 5)

EMPATHIC LISTENING   Listening to people with an open, sensitive, and caring ear. (Ch. 6)

EMPATHY   The understanding one has of another's experience. (Ch. 7)

ENCODE   Mentally construct and physically produce a message. (Ch. 1)

ENDOMORPH   A person with a rounded, oval, or pear-shaped and often heavy body. (Ch. 5)

EQUIFINALITY   In a system, the characteristic that final goals may be reached in a variety of ways. (Ch. 12)

ESCAPIST STRATEGIES   In a conflict, strategies that attempt to prevent direct conflict. (Ch. 8)

ETHICAL PROOF   Proof that asks an audience to accept a claim because of the speaker's competence, trustworthiness, dynamism, power, goodwill, idealism, or similarity to the audience. (Ch. 15) See also *source credibility*.

ETHNOCENTRISM   The process of valuing your own ethnic culture so much that you are comfortable only with people similar to yourself. (Ch. 2)

EXAMPLE   In public speaking, a form of support that relies on illustrations, models, or instances of what is to be explained. (Ch. 13)

EXPECTATION   An intuitive thought or conscious desire in regard to an upcoming encounter. (Ch. 2)

EXPLANATION   The act or process of making something plain or comprehensible; in public speaking, a form of support that relies on exposition and definition. (Ch. 13)

EXPLANATORY SPEECH   A speech that explains the reasons underlying a problem, plan, or policy. (Ch. 14)

EXTEMPORANEOUS SPEAKING   Speaking characterized by advance preparation of ideas and supporting material, with the precise wording of the speech to be determined during the process of speaking. (Ch. 13)

EXTRINSIC REWARDS   Benefits gained from association with another person, including new opportunities and contacts. (Ch. 7)

FAMILY   A social group whose members are related by blood, marriage, or adoption; have specified roles (e.g., husband, wife, son, mother) and statuses; and usually share a common residence and cooperate economically. (Ch. 7)

FEDERAL COMMUNICATIONS COMMISSION (FCC)   A regulatory agency that oversees the physical resources of the media to ensure that broadcasters use the airwaves in the public interest and that the public has access to the airwaves. (Ch. 16)

FEEDBACK   Information learned about the self that is used by the self to learn and mature. (Ch. 3)

FILTER QUESTION   A question designed to find out what, if anything, an interviewee knows about a particular topic. (Ch. 9)

FORMAL CHANNELS   The communication paths established along the hierarchical lines of an organization. (Ch. 12)

FORMS OF SUPPORT   Verbal and nonverbal devices—such as language, explanations, examples, statistics, testimony, and visual aids—that can focus audience interest on the speaker's message and help the audience to understand and accept the message. (Ch. 13)

FRIENDSHIP   A relationship between two or more people that is perceived as mutually satisfying, productive, and beneficial. (Ch. 7)

FUNCTIONAL PERSPECTIVE   A focus on what kinds of communication behaviors work for people, and why they work, in various situations. (Ch. 1)

FUNNEL SEQUENCE   A question sequence that moves from broad, open-ended questions to narrower, closed ones. (Ch. 9)

GATEKEEPING   The process of regulating or determining what information will be carried over mass communication channels and what will not. (Ch. 16)

GEOGRAPHICAL ORGANIZATIONAL PATTERN
See *spatial or geographical organizational pattern*.

GOAL ACHIEVEMENT   Focusing attention on the task at hand in order to achieve a goal; one of the three primary functions of communication. Also called *task orientation*. (Ch. 1)

GROUP EVALUATION   An evaluation of how competently a group performs as a whole. (Ch. 11)

GROUPTHINK   The tendency of group members to accept information and ideas without critical analysis. (Ch. 10)

HAPTICS   Touching behavior. (Ch. 5)

HIDDEN AGENDA   A secret goal that one partner in a conflict is pursuing under the guise of another, expressed goal. (Ch. 8)

HIERARCHY   In a system, the classification of a group of people according to ability, status, function, or other criteria. (Ch. 12)

HIGH LANGUAGE   The language used in the more formal contexts of a person's life, such as work. (Ch. 4)

HIGH-CONTEXT CULTURE   A culture that avoids the use of direct language, relying more on context to convey meaning. (Ch. 4)

HOMOLOGY MODEL   A model of language acquisition which holds that thinking, coordination, and language capabilities develop simultaneously. (Ch. 4)

ILLUSTRATOR   A movement or gesture that accompanies and illustrates a verbal message. (Ch. 5)

IMPRESSION FORMATION   The general effect that a communicator has on a listener. (Ch. 6)

IMPROMPTU SPEAKING   Speaking on the spur of the moment, without formal preparation. (Ch. 13)

INDIVIDUAL EVALUATION   An evaluation of how competently individuals perform as members of a group. (Ch. 11)

INFORMAL CHANNELS   The unauthorized communication paths in an organization; the "grapevine." (Ch. 12)

INFORMATION SOCIETY   Our current society, in which individuals working with information are the largest segment of the work force. (Ch. 14)

INSTRUMENTAL REWARDS   Rewards that relational partners give to each other, including material benefits. (Ch. 7)

INTEGRATIVE CAPACITY   The ability to make connections between different concepts; an aspect of cognitive complexity. (Ch. 2)

INTENSIFICATION   The facial management technique of exaggerating what is felt. (Ch. 5)

INTENTIONALITY   The level of consciousness or purposefulness of a communicator in the encoding of messages. (Ch. 1)

INTERACTIONIST MODEL   An approach to language acquisition which claims that social interaction is the most important aspect of language acquisition. (Ch. 4)

INTERCULTURAL COMMUNICATION   The exchange of messages by people of different cultures or subcultures. (Ch. 2)

INTERDEPENDENCE   In group relationships, how the behavior of each member affects and is affected by other members. (Ch. 10)

INTERPERSONAL COMMUNICATION   The process of two or three people exchanging messages in order to share meaning, create understanding, and develop relationships. (Ch. 7)

INTERVIEW   A process of planned, dyadic, interactive discourse. (Ch. 9)

INTERVIEWEE   One of two parties in an interview; typically follows the lead of the interviewer during the interview. (Ch. 9)

INTERVIEWER   One of two parties in an interview; typically assumes the primary responsibility for the planning and success of the interview. (Ch. 9)

INTIMACY   A deep understanding of another person; one of the highest levels that a relationship can aspire to. (Ch. 7)

INTRAPERSONAL COMMUNICATION   Messages sent and received by the self for the purpose of understanding information offered by the environment. (Ch. 2)

INTRINSIC REWARDS   Benefits that result from an exchange of intimacy. (Ch. 7)

INTRODUCTION   The beginning portion of a speech; typically deals with issues of task, relationship, and motivation. (Ch. 13)

INVERTED FUNNEL SEQUENCE   A question sequence that moves from narrow, closed questions to broad, open-ended ones. (Ch. 9)

ISOLATION   A position within a group in which the member receives and sends fewer messages than do other members. (Ch. 10)

KINESICS   The communicative ability of gestures and body movements. (Ch. 5)

LAISSEZ-FAIRE LEADERSHIP   A leadership style that involves little or no leadership per se. (Ch. 11)

LANGUAGE   A symbol system used to think about and communicate experiences and feelings. (Ch. 4)

LEADERSHIP   The exercise of interpersonal influence toward the attainment of goals. (Ch. 11) See also *authoritarian leadership; competent leadership; consultative leadership; laissez-faire leadership; participative leadership; shared leadership.*

LEADING QUESTION   A question that subtly suggests or implies the answer that is expected. (Ch. 9)

LISTENING   The process of recognizing, understanding, and accurately interpreting the messages communicated by others. (Ch. 6)

LISTENING APPREHENSION   A state of uneasiness, anxiety, fear, or dread associated with a listening opportunity. (Ch. 6)

LISTENING BARRIERS   Factors that interfere with competent listening, such as boredom, daydreaming, overconfidence, laziness, apprehension, and defensiveness. (Ch. 6)

LISTENING COSTS   Direct and indirect penalties associated with poor listening; can be economic, physical, emotional, or psychological. (Ch. 6)

LISTENING FUNCTIONS   Different types of listening that satisfy different needs. See *appreciative listening; comprehensive listening; critical listening; empathic listening.* (Ch. 6)

LISTENING GOALS   Specific plans or objectives for listening. (Ch. 6)

LISTENING REWARDS   Benefits of competent listening, such as saving time, enhanced relationships, and professional advancement. (Ch. 6)

LISTENING SELF-ASSESSMENT   The evaluation of one's own listening abilities and skills. (Ch. 6)

LISTENING SELF-CONCEPT   The image one has of oneself as a listener. (Ch. 6)

LOADED QUESTION   A question that clearly implies or suggests the answer that is expected either by using emotional language or by asking two questions in the guise of one. (Ch. 9)

LOGICAL PROOF   Proof that asks an audience to accept a claim because objective evidence supports the claim. (Ch. 15)

LOVE   A deep affection for and attraction to another person; generally involves a relationship that is more exclusive than friendship. (Ch. 7)

LOW LANGUAGE   The relaxed language usually used in the home or with close friends. (Ch. 4)

LOW-CONTEXT CULTURE   A culture that relies more on the use of direct language than on the nuances of context to impart meaning. (Ch. 4)

MAIN POINT   The thesis of a speaker's message; a key to understanding and remembering the message. (Ch. 6)

MANUSCRIPT SPEAKING   Speaking from a manuscript that contains the complete presentation word for word. (Ch. 13)

MASKING   The facial management technique of replacing an expression that shows true feeling with one that is deemed appropriate for a particular situation. (Ch. 5)

MASS COMMUNICATION   The production and transmission of messages that are received and consumed by large audiences, including various forms of printed material and messages dispersed via the airwaves or through cable networks. (Ch. 16)

MEDIA   Organizations that create and transmit informative, entertaining, or persuasive messages designed for large audiences. (Ch. 16)

MEDIA RICHNESS   The ability of a channel or medium to carry information to a receiver. (Ch. 2)

MEMORIZED SPEAKING   Delivering from memory a speech that has first been written out. (Ch. 13)

MENTOR   An experienced organization member who serves as a role model for a less experienced employee. (Ch. 12)

MESOMORPH   A person with a triangular and athletic body. (Ch. 5)

MINDFULNESS   The process of focusing one's mind on the task at hand. (Ch. 2)

MINDLESSNESS   The process of performing behaviors or actions without being conscious of what one is doing. (Ch. 2)

MOTIVATIONAL PROOF   Proof that asks an audience to accept a claim on the grounds that the claim is consistent with listeners' needs and values. (Ch. 15)

NATURE APPROACH   An approach to language acquisition which holds that language acquisition is an innate human developmental process and does not depend on environmental factors. (Ch. 4)

NETWORKING   Communicating with other people in order to benefit from the connection. (Ch. 12)

NETWORKS   Communication patterns used within groups. (Ch. 10) See also *centralized network; decentralized network.*

NEUTRAL QUESTION   A question that provides no clue as to the expected answer. (Ch. 9)

NEUTRALIZATION   The facial management technique of eliminating all expression of emotion. (Ch. 5)

NOMINAL GROUP TECHNIQUE   A process in which individuals work alone (in a group context) to produce a basis for discussion that reflects all group members' viewpoints. (Ch. 10)

NONDIRECTIVE INTERVIEW   An interview in which the interviewer grants the interviewee control of the structure and pacing of the interview. (Ch. 9)

NONVERBAL COMMUNICATION   The process of signaling meaning through behavior that does not involve the content of spoken words. (Ch. 5)

NONVERBAL CUES   Nonverbal behaviors that allow listeners to better understand a verbal message; also, behaviors that listeners use to show the speaker that they understand the message. (Ch. 6)

NORMS   Expectations held by group members concerning what behaviors and opinions are acceptable in the group. (Ch. 10)

NURTURE APPROACH   An approach to language acquisition which holds that language is acquired because of the language environment surrounding a person. (Ch. 4)

OBSTINATE STRATEGIES   In a conflict, strategies that promote the objectives of an individual rather than those of the relational partner or the relationship. (Ch. 8)

OCULESICS   Communicative eye behavior. (Ch. 5)

OLFACTICS   The communicative characteristics of smells. (Ch. 5)

ONTOGENY   The course of development of an individual organism (as distinguished from the development of a species over time). (Ch. 5)

OPEN QUESTION   A question that gives the interviewee relative freedom in responding. (Ch. 9)

OPENING TECHNIQUES   Strategies for the initial portion of an interview that deal with issues of task, relationship, and motivation. (Ch. 9)

OPENNESS   A system characteristic that refers to a system's ability to correct itself. (Ch. 12)

ORGANIZATIONAL CULTURE   Members' relatively stable perceptions of their organization and its norms and behaviors. (Ch. 12)

ORGANIZATIONAL PATTERN   A method of arranging ideas in a logical sequence. (Ch. 13) See also *cause-effect organizational pattern; chronological organizational pattern; problem-solution organizational pattern; spatial or geographical organizational pattern; topical organizational pattern.*

ORGANIZED AUDIENCE   An audience that is completely devoted to the speaker and to the speaker's purpose. (Ch. 13)

OUTCOME   The product or end state of a communication encounter or series of encounters. (Ch. 1)

OUTLINE   A visual, schematic summary of a speech that shows the order of ideas and the general relationships among them. (Ch. 13) See also *complete sentence outline; speaker's outline; topic outline.*

PARALANGUAGE   The communicative value of vocal behavior; the meaning of how something is said. (Ch. 5)

PARTICIPATIVE LEADERSHIP   A leadership style that involves a leader working with other group members to achieve a desired goal. (Ch. 11)

PASSIVE AUDIENCE   An audience that is gathered to hear the speaker but is not highly motivated to listen to or accept the message. (Ch. 13)

PEDESTRIAN AUDIENCE   An audience of people who have come together for the moment but have no obvious connection with either the speaker or one another. (Ch. 13)

PERIPHERAL ROUTE TO PERSUASION   A route to persuasion in which the audience bases its decision about the message on characteristics external to the message—for example, source credibility or the reactions of other individuals. (Ch. 15)

PERSONAL SPACE   The space around one's body to which one attaches ownership. (Ch. 5)

PERSUASION   A conscious attempt by one individual to change the attitudes, beliefs, or behavior of another individual or group of individuals through the interactive process of exchanging verbal and nonverbal messages. (Ch. 15)

PHYLOGENY   The evolutionary development of a species over time (as distinguished from the development of individual members of that species). (Ch. 5)

PRAGMATICS   The appropriate use of language in context; requires mastery of communication rules, not merely language rules. (Ch. 4)

PREJUDICE   A deep-seated feeling of unkindness and ill will toward particular groups based on negative stereotypes. (Ch. 2)

PRIMACY-RECENCY PHENOMENON   The tendency to pay close attention to initial and final inputs. (Ch. 2)

PRIMARY QUESTION   A question that initiates a new topic. (Ch. 9)

PRIOR RESTRAINT   The practice of banning certain publications before they have been produced. (Ch. 16)

PROBING   In a conflict, an attempt to make a partner provide clarifications, explanations, or further information. (Ch. 8)

PROBLEM-SOLUTION ORGANIZATIONAL PATTERN A pattern that presents the main points of a message in terms of a problem and solutions to that problem. (Ch. 13)

PROCESS   The manner in which a communication encounter is conducted. (Ch. 1)

PROMISE   In a conflict, an expressed intention to behave in a way that is beneficial to the other party provided that party complies with certain requests or terms. (Ch. 8)

PROXEMICS   The communicative aspects of the use of space. (Ch. 5)

QUASI-SCIENTIFIC EXPLANATION   An explanation that models or pictures the key dimensions of a phenomenon for a lay audience. (Ch. 14)

QUESTIONING TECHNIQUES   Inquiries that a listener can make to coordinate what the speaker is saying with what the listener is hearing. (Ch. 6)

QUINTAMENSIONAL PLAN   A five-step question sequence developed by George Gallup for use in conducting public opinion polls; involves examining awareness, uninfluenced attitudes, specific attitudes, reasoning, and intensity of feeling. (Ch. 9)

RECEIVER   The person, group, or organization that decodes a message or other type of stimulus. (Ch. 1)

RECEPTIVITY   A type of friendship in which one partner is the primary giver and the other is the primary taker. (Ch. 7)

RECIPROCITY   A type of friendship that involves self-surrender, loyalty, mutual respect, affection, and support, and in which the partners give and take equally and share responsibility for maintaining the relationship. (Ch. 7)

REFERENCE   The thoughts that occur in a person when symbols are used or referents encountered. (Ch. 4)

REFERENCE GROUP   A group of people who are like a particular individual or whom that individual aspires to be like. (Ch. 13) See also *demographic reference group; voluntary reference group.*

REFERENT   The actual person or thing that a symbol or symbols represent. (Ch. 4)

REGULATING   Nonverbal behavior that is used to coordinate verbal interaction. (Ch. 5) See also *regulator.*

REGULATOR   A movement or gesture that regulates conversation. (Ch. 5) See also *regulating.*

REHEARSAL   A temporary storage area that processes information directed from short-term memory to long-term memory. (Ch. 6)

RELATIONAL HISTORY   The sum of the "objective" events in a relationship and the shared experiences of relational partners; also, the set of thoughts, perceptions, and impressions one has formed about one's previous relational partners. (Ch. 7)

RELATIONAL SCHEMAS   Information used to interpret messages received in a relationship. (Ch. 7)

RELATIONSHIP   The interdependence of two or more people in order to achieve some goal. (Ch. 1)

REPEATING   Nonverbal behavior that mirrors the accompanying verbal message. (Ch. 5)

RESPONSE STYLE   The pattern an individual develops for using Rogers's five reacting moves: evaluative, interpretive, supportive, probing, and understanding. (Ch. 9)

ROLE   In a group, the function a member performs. (Ch. 10)

SCHEMA THEORY   See *schemas.*

SCHEMAS   Mental structures that assemble chunks of remembered information, which in turn work together to create meaning and understanding. (Ch. 2)

SCREENING INTERVIEW   The first stage in the employment interview process; during this stage the interviewer tries to find out whether the applicant can do the job. (Ch. 9)

SECONDARY QUESTION   A question that develops a topic that has already been introduced. (Ch. 9)

SELECTED AUDIENCE   An audience that shares the goal of the speaker but does not necessarily agree with the speaker's method for achieving the goal. (Ch. 13)

SELECTIVE PERCEPTION   Biased or filtered processing of information based on strongly held attitudes, timing, or other phenomena. (Ch. 2)

SELF-ACTUALIZATION   The most positive evaluation one can make about one's competence level. (Ch. 3)

SELF-ADEQUACY   Assessing one's communication competence as sufficent or acceptable. (Ch. 3)

SELF-CERTAINTY   A strong sense of identity; composed of strong self-attributes or ideas about self that are unaffected by adverse or competing information. (Ch. 3)

SELF-CONCEPT   The awareness and understanding of who one is as interpreted and influenced by one's thoughts, actions, abilities, values, goals, and ideals, and by other people. (Ch. 3)

SELF-DENIGRATION   The most negative assessment one can make about one's communication performance. (Ch. 3)

SELF-DISCLOSURE   Revealing information about the self to other people. (Ch. 3)

SELF-EFFICACY   The ability to predict actual success from one's self-certainty; viewing oneself and predicting how competent one can be in anticipated situations. (Ch. 3)

SELF-ESTEEM   A set of attitudes that one holds about one's feelings, thoughts, abilities, skills, behavior, and beliefs. (Ch. 3)

SELF-FULFILLING PROPHECY   A phenomenon in which behavior occurs as a result of expectations. (Ch. 2)

SELF-IMPROVEMENT   A signal one sends to the self indicating a desire to be a more competent communicator, regardless of current levels. (Ch. 3)

SELF-MANAGING TEAM   A group of highly skilled workers within a larger organization who are completely responsible for producing high-quality finished work. (Ch. 10)

SELF-MONITORING   The tendency to watch one's environment and others in it for cues as to how to act in particular situations. (Ch. 3)

SELF-PRESENTATION   A communication tactic intended to show elements of self for strategic purposes. (Ch. 3)

SELF-PROMOTION   Presentation of the self in a way that will create a favorable impression in others. (Ch. 5)

SELF-SCHEMAS   Structures composed of the various pieces of information that a person attributes to self. They help that person develop a sense of self, guide the person's actions, and facilitate the acquisition and storage of new information as it pertains to self. (Ch. 3)

SEMANTICS   The meaning created between communicators by language and thought. (Ch. 4)

SENDER   The person, group, or organization that encodes a message or produces a stimulus. (Ch. 1)

SEXUAL HARASSMENT   Unwelcome sexual advances or overtures and requests for sexual favors. (Ch. 12)

SHARED LEADERSHIP   Leadership that may emerge from any interested and talented group member, depending on the context. (Ch. 11)

SIDETRACKING   In a conflict, an attempt to move the conversation to a peripheral, often irrelevant topic. (Ch. 8)

SITUATION   A sequence of events that has a unifying goal. (Ch. 5)

SITUATIONAL EXPECTATIONS   Expectations that audience members have about the speaker and the message. (Ch. 13)

SMALL GROUP COMMUNICATION   The process of exchanging messages among a collection of people (more than four and usually not more than twenty) for the purpose of developing relationships and accomplishing goals. (Ch. 10)

SOCIAL INFLUENCE   A process in which one person's actions cause changes in another's thoughts and behaviors. (Ch. 5)

SOURCE CREDIBILITY   An audience's perception of a message source independent of that source's intent or purpose. (Ch. 15) See also *ethical proof.*

SPATIAL OR GEOGRAPHICAL ORGANIZATIONAL PATTERN   A pattern that presents the main points of a message in terms of their physical proximity to or direction from one another. (Ch. 13)

SPEAKER'S OUTLINE   A visual, schematic summary of a speech that includes only key ideas that a speaker needs to remember. (Ch. 13)

SPEECH REPERTOIRES   The possibilities communicators have for language use in any given situation, based on their experiences, cognitions, and acquired skills. (Ch. 4)

SPEECH THAT AFFIRMS A PROPOSITION OF FACT   A speech that answers the question "Was it/is it/will it be true?" by making designative claims. (Ch. 15)

SPEECH THAT AFFIRMS A PROPOSITION OF POLICY   A speech that answers the question "What course of action should be pursued?" by making advocative claims. (Ch. 15)

SPEECH THAT AFFIRMS A PROPOSITION OF VALUE   A speech that answers the question "Of what worth is it?" by making evaluative claims. (Ch. 15)

SPEECH THAT CREATES CONCERN ABOUT A PROBLEM   A speech that answers the question "What is it?" by making definitive claims. (Ch. 15)

SPEECH TOPICS   See *categories of speech topics.*

STATE COMMUNICATION APPREHENSION   A situational attack of anxiety that can be greater or lesser depending on such factors as knowledge of the audience and topic. (Ch. 13)

STATEMENT OF SPECIFIC PURPOSE   A single declarative sentence that specifies what the audience is expected to know, do, believe, feel, and so on, after hearing a speeCh. (Ch. 13)

STATISTICS   In public speaking, a form of support that relies on collecting, organizing, and interpreting numerical data. (Ch. 13)

STEREOTYPING   The process of organizing information about groups of people into categories so that you can generalize about their attitudes, behaviors, skills, morals, and habits. (Ch. 2)

STRUCTURING   A method of organizing messages by means of residual messages (ideas to be retained by the audience) and common patterns of message organization. (Ch. 14)

SUBCULTURE   A group that is part of a larger culture but distinguished from it by various characteristics. (Ch. 1)

SUBSTITUTING   Nonverbal behavior that replaces the use of words. (Ch. 5)

SYMBOL   A sign (usually a word) used to describe a person, idea, or thing (a referent). (Ch. 4)

SYMBOLIC BEHAVIOR   Behavior that uses a shared symbol system. (Ch. 1)

SYSTEM   A unique whole consisting of members who have relationships with one another in a particular environment. (Ch. 12)

SYSTEMATIC DESENSITIZATION   A method for reducing or treating communication apprehension; involves learning deep muscle relaxation, constructing hierarchies of anxiety-provoking stimuli, and pairing relaxation with anxiety-provoking stimuli. (Ch. 13)

TASK FORCE   A group that researches an issue before discussions are held or decisions are made. (Ch. 11)

TASK ORIENTATION   See *goal achievement.*

TELECONFERENCING   The use of telephones to link participants, so that they can speak and conduct meetings without all being at one location. (Ch. 12)

TERRITORIALITY   The claiming of an area, with or without a legal basis. (Ch. 5)

TESTIMONY   In public speaking, a form of support that relies on using a credible person's statements to lend weight and authority to a message. (Ch. 13)

THEORY Z   A team management approach in which both managers and their employees participate in decision making. (Ch. 12)

THESIS STATEMENT   A sentence that summarizes what you want the audience to remember from your speeCh. (Ch. 13)

THREAT   In a conflict, an expressed intention to behave in a way that is detrimental to the other party if that party does not comply with certain requests or terms. (Ch. 8)

TIME ORGANIZATIONAL PATTERN   See *chronological organizational pattern.*

TIME ORIENTATION   Time preferences that may be psychologically, biologically, or culturally based. (Ch. 5)

TIME PRESSURES   In a group, the effects of a shortage of time on the decision-making process. (Ch. 11)

TOPIC OUTLINE   A visual, schematic summary of a speech that reduces a complete sentence outline to brief phrases or single words. (Ch. 13)

TOPICAL ORGANIZATIONAL PATTERN   A pattern that presents the main points of a message as parallel elements of the topic itself; also known as a *categorical pattern.* (Ch. 13)

TOPICAL SYSTEM FOR GENERATING THOUGHTS   The use of sixteen common themes for talking about any topic as a trigger for identifying ideas for inclusion in a speech. (Ch. 13)

TOULMIN'S MODEL   A method of generating, evaluating, and displaying "good reasons" for accepting a fact, value, problem, or policy in terms of a primary triad (data, warrant, claim) and a secondary triad (backing, rebuttal, qualifier). (Ch. 15)

TRAIT COMMUNICATION APPREHENSION   A tendency to have fear or anxiety about communication in all contexts. (Ch. 13)

TRAITS   Individual physical and psychological characteristics that typically do not vary from situation to situation. (Ch. 8)

TRANSACTIONAL PROCESS   A process in which two or more people exchange speaker and listener roles, and in which the behavior of each person is dependent on and influenced by the behavior of the other. (Ch. 1)

TRANSFORMATIVE EXPLANATION   An explanation that helps a lay audience understand ideas that are contrary to our intuition. (Ch. 14)

TRANSITIONS   Verbal signs to an audience indicating where the speech is going, where it is, and where it has been. (Ch. 13)

TRUST   The belief that you can accurately predict the actions of another person. (Ch. 3)

TUNNEL SEQUENCE   A question sequence that utilizes questions at one level (i.e., either all of the questions are broad and open-ended or they are all narrow and closed). (Ch. 9)

TURN-TAKING BEHAVIORS   Nonverbal cues used during conversation to ensure speaking turns; include turn yielding, turn maintaining, turn requesting, and turn denying. (Ch. 5)

TWO-STEP FLOW MODEL   An early view of media effects which proposes that the mass media are used by "opinion leaders" to disseminate information to individuals through social networks. (Ch. 16)

UNCERTAINTY EVENTS   Events that cause uncertainty in a relationship (e.g., a competing relationship, an unexplained loss of closeness, deception, or an unexplained change in the personality of one partner). (Ch. 7)

USES AND GRATIFICATIONS THEORY   A theory of media effects that emphasizes the consumer's role and expectations when evaluating the outcomes of media exposure. (Ch. 16)

VALENCE   Whether the information you disclose about yourself is positive or negative. (Ch. 3)

VALUES   The enduring beliefs that individuals and groups hold about certain issues and behaviors. (Ch. 11)

VERBAL AGGRESSIVENESS   A conflict style that involves attacking the other party's self-concept. (Ch. 8)

VERBAL REINFORCERS   Short verbal cues used by listeners to coordinate speaker-listener communication. (Ch. 6)

VISUAL AIDS   In public speaking, a form of support that relies on using actual objects or models, pictorial reproductions, or pictorial symbols. (Ch. 13)

VOCAL CHARACTERIZER   A sound that conveys the emotional or physical state of the speaker. (Ch. 5)

VOCAL QUALIFIER   A vocal cue that qualifies or regulates a verbal message. (Ch. 5)

VOCAL SEGREGATE   A sound with a connotative meaning. (Ch. 5)

VOCALIZATION   A vocal cue that does not have the structure of language. (Ch. 5) See *vocal characterizer; vocal qualifier; vocal segregate.*

VOICE QUALITIES   The vocal cues of tempo; resonance; rhythm, articulation, pitch, and glottis control; and pitch range. (Ch. 5)

VOLUNTARY REFERENCE GROUP   A group of people who have chosen to belong to a specific religious, political, social, or other group. (Ch. 13)

WHOLENESS   A system characteristic that refers to its unique configuration; a system remains "whole" despite individual or departmental changes. (Ch. 12)

SUGGESTED READINGS

Chapter 1

Coupland, N., Giles, H., & Wiemann, J. M. (Eds.). (1991). *"Miscommunication" and problematic talk*. Newbury Park, CA: Sage.

Grove, T. G. (1991). *Dyadic interaction*. Dubuque, IA: Brown.

Hecht, M., Collier, M. J., & Ribean, S. A. (1993). *African American communication*. Thousand Oaks, CA: Sage.

Knapp, M. L., & Vangelisti, A. L. (1992). *Interpersonal communication and human relationships* (2nd ed.). Boston: Allyn & Bacon.

Wiemann, J. M. (1977). Explication and test of a model of communicative competence. *Human Communication Research, 3*, 195–213.

Wiemann, J. M. & Giles, H. (1996). Interpersonal communication. In M. Hewstone, W. Stroebe & G. Stephenson (Eds.), *Introduction to social psychology* (2nd ed.). Oxford: Basil Blackwell.

Williams, F. (1992). *The new communications* (3rd ed.). Belmont, CA: Wadsworth.

Chapter 2

Carroll, J. S., & Payne, J. W. (Eds.). (1976). *Cognition and social behavior*. Hillsdale, NJ: Lawrence Erlbaum.

Cody, M. J., & McLaughlin, M. L. (1990). *Psychology of tactical communication*. London: Multilingual Matters.

Donohew, L., Sypher, H., & Higgins, E. T. (Eds.). (1988). *Communication, social cognition, and affect*. Hillsdale, NJ: Lawrence Erlbaum.

Goss, B. (1991). *Processing communication*. Prospect Heights, IL: Waveland.

Gudykunst, W. B., & Kim, Y. Y. (1997). *Communicating with strangers*. New York: McGraw-Hill.

Kim, Y. Y. (1998). *Becoming intercultural: An integrative theory of communication and cross-cultural adaptation*. Thousand Oaks, CA: Sage.

Roberts, C. V., & Watson, K. W. (1989). *Intrapersonal communication processes*. New Orleans: Spectra.

Chapter 3

Derlega, V. J., & Berg, J. H. (Eds.). (1987). *Self-disclosure: Theory, research, and therapy*. New York: Plenum.

Derlega, V. J., Metts, S., Petronio, S., & Margulis, S. T. (1993). *Self-disclosure*. Newbury Park, CA: Sage.

Jourard, S. M. (1971). *Self-disclosure: An experimental analysis of the transparent self*. New York: Wiley-Interscience.

Ross, L., & Nisbett, R. E. (1991). *The person and the situation: Perspectives of social psychology*. Philadelphia: Temple University Press.

Chapter 4

Bates, E. (1979). *The emergence of symbols: Cognition and communication in infancy*. New York: Academic Press.

Giles, H., & Robinson, W. P. (1990). *Handbook of language and social psychology*. Chichester, England: John Wiley and Sons.

Tannen, D. (1990). *You just don't understand: Women and men in conversation.* New York: Morrow.

Wood, B. (1982). *Children and communication: Verbal and nonverbal language development.* (2nd ed.). Englewood Cliffs, NJ: Prentice-Hall.

Chapter 5

Argyle, M. (1988). *Bodily communication* (2nd ed.). London: Methuen.

Burgoon, J., Buller, D., & Woodall, W. (1996). *Nonverbal communication: The unspoken dialogue.* New York: McGraw-Hill.

Feldman, R. S. (1992). *Applications of nonverbal behavioral theories and research.* Hillsdale, NJ: Lawrence Erlbaum.

Poyatos, F. (Ed.). (1988). *Cross-cultural perspectives in nonverbal communication.* Toronto: Hogrefe.

Woodall, K. (1993). *How to talk so men will listen.* Chicago: Contemporary Books.

Chapter 6

Floyd, J. J. (1985). *Listening: A practical approach.* Glenview, IL: Scott, Foresman.

Journal of the International Listening Association. See recent issues.

Steil, L. K., Barker, L. L., & Watson, K. W. (1983). *Effective listening: Key to success.* Reading, MA: Addison-Wesley.

Wolff, F. I., Marsnik, N. C., Tacey, W. S., & Nichols, R. G. (1983). *Perceptive listening.* New York: Holt, Rinehart & Winston.

Wolvin, A., & Coakley, C. G. (1992). *Listening* (4th ed.). Dubuque, IA: Wm. C. Brown.

Chapter 7

Canary, D. J., & Cody, M. J. (1994). *Interpersonal communication: A goals-based approach.* New York: St. Martin's Press.

Duck, S. W. Issues in the series *Interpersonal relationships.* Beverly Hills, CA: Sage.

Kalbfleisch, P. J. (1993). *Interpersonal communication: Evolving interpersonal relationships.* Hillsdale, NJ: Lawrence Erlbaum.

Knapp, M. L., & Miller, G. R. (1994). *Handbook of interpersonal communication* (2nd ed.). Beverly Hills, CA: Sage.

Rawlins, W. (1992). *Friendship matters.* New York: Aldine de Gauthier.

Stewart, J. (1990). *Bridges, not walls.* New York: McGraw-Hill.

Chapter 8

Bazerman, M. H., & Lewicki, R. J. (Eds.). (1983). *Negotiating in organizations.* Beverly Hills, CA: Sage.

Folger, J., & Poole, M. (1984). *Working through conflict.* Glenview, IL: Scott, Foresman.

Hocker, J., & Wilmot, W. (1993). *Interpersonal conflict* (3rd ed.). Dubuque, IA: Wm. C. Brown.

Kolb, D. M., & Bartunek, J. M. (Eds.). (1992). *Hidden conflict in organizations: Uncovering behind-the-scenes disputes.* Beverly Hills, CA: Sage.

Lulofs, R. S. (1994). *Conflict: From theory to action.* Scottsdale, AZ: Gorsuch Scarisbrick.

Putnam, L. L., & Roloff, M. E. (Eds.). (1992). *Communication and negotiation.* Beverly Hills, CA: Sage.

Sandole, D., & Sandole-Staroste, I. (Eds.). (1987). *Conflict management and problem solving: Interpersonal to international applications.* New York: New York University Press.

Stulberg, J. B. (1987). *Taking charge/managing conflict.* Lexington, MA: Lexington Books.

Chapter 9

Barbour, K., Berg, F., Eannace, M., Greene, J. R., Hessig, M. J., Papworth, M., Radin, C., Rezny, E., & Suarez, J. (1991). *The quest: A guide to the job interview*. Dubuque, IA: Kendall/Hunt.

Gorden, R. (1992). *Basic interviewing skills*. Itasca, IL: F. E. Peacock.

Hunt, G. T., & Eadie, W. F. (1987). *Interviewing: A communication approach*. New York: Holt, Rinehart & Winston.

Stewart, C. J., & Cash, W. B., Jr. (1994). *Interviewing: Principles and practices* (7th ed.). Dubuque, IA: Wm. C. Brown.

Wilson, G. L., & Goodall, H. L., Jr. (1991). *Interviewing in context*. New York: McGraw-Hill.

Chapter 10

Cathcart, R. S., & Samovar, L. A. (1988). *Small group communication: A reader* (5th ed.). Dubuque, IA: Wm. C. Brown.

Ellis, D. G., & Fisher, B. A. (1994). *Small group decision making: Communication and the group process* (4th ed.). New York: McGraw-Hill.

Moore, C. M. (1987). *Group techniques for idea building*. Newbury Park, CA: Sage.

Wellins, R. S., Byham, W. C., & Dixon, G. R. (1994). *Inside teams*. San Francisco: Jossey-Bass.

Chapter 11

Gouran, D. S. (1990). *Making decisions in groups: Choices and consequences*. Prospect Heights, IL: Waveland.

Johanson, R., Sibbet, D., Benson, S., Martin, A., Mittman, R., & Saffo, P. (1991). *Leading business teams*. Reading, MA: Addison-Wesley.

Rothwell, J. D. (1992). *In mixed company: Small group communication*. Fort Worth, TX: Harcourt Brace Jovanovich.

Whettin, D. A., & Cameron, K. S. (1993). *Developing management skills*. New York: HarperCollins.

Chapter 12

Eisenberg, E., & Goodall, H. (1993). *Organizational communication*. New York: St. Martin's Press.

Jablin, F., & Putnam, L. (Eds.). (1987). *Handbook of organizational communication*. Beverly Hills, CA: Sage.

O'Hair, D., O'Rourke, J., & O'Hair, M. (forthcoming). *Business communication*. Reading, MA: Addison-Wesley.

Chapter 13

Daly, J. A., & McCroskey, J. C. (1984). *Avoiding communication: Shyness, reticence, and communication apprehension*. Beverly Hills, CA: Sage.

Hart, R. P. (1990). *Modern rhetorical criticism*. Glenview, IL: Scott, Foresman/Little Brown.

Jamieson, K. H. (1988). *Eloquence in an electronic age*. New York: Oxford University Press.

Johannesen, R. L., Allen, R. R., & Linkugel, W. A. (1992) *Contemporary American speeches: A sourcebook of speech forms and principles* (7th ed.). Dubuque, IA: Kendall/Hunt.

Sprague, J., & Stuart, D. (1992). *The speaker's handbook* (3rd ed.). Fort Worth, TX: Harcourt Brace Jovanovich.

Chapter 14

Baird, J. E., Jr. (1974). The effects of speech summaries upon audience comprehension of expository speeches of varying quality and complexity. *Central States Speech Journal, 25*, 119–127.

Hackman, M. Z. (1988). Reactions to the use of self-disparaging humor by informative public speakers. *The Southern Speech Communication Journal, 53*, 175–183.

Petrie, C. R., Jr. (1963). Informative speaking: A summary and bibliography of related research. *Communication Monographs, 30*, 79–91.

Rowan, K. E. (1988). A contemporary theory of explanatory writing. *Written Communication, 5*, 23–56.

Spicer, C., & Bassett, R. E. (1976). The effect of organization on learning from an informative message. *The Southern Speech Communication Journal, 41*, 290–299.

Chapter 15

Larson, C. U. (1992). *Persuasion: Reception and responsibility* (6th ed.). Belmont, CA: Wadsworth.

O'Keefe, D. J. (1990). *Persuasion: Theory and research.* Newbury Park, CA: Sage.

Perloff, R. M. (1993). *The dynamics of persuasion.* Hillsdale, NJ: Lawrence Erlbaum.

Pfau, M., & Parrott, R. (1993). *Persuasive communication campaigns.* Boston: Allyn & Bacon.

Reinard, J. C. (1988). The empirical study of the persuasive effects of evidence: The status after fifty years of research. *Human Communication Research, 15*, 3–59.

Trenholm, S. (1989). *Persuasion and social influence.* Englewood Cliffs, NJ: Prentice-Hall.

Chapter 16

Alexander, A. (1993). Exploring media in everyday life. *Communication Monographs, 60*, 55–61.

Altheide, D. (1976). *Creating reality: How T.V. news distorts events.* Beverly Hills, CA: Sage.

Cantor, M., & Cantor, J. (1994). *Prime-time television.* Thousand Oaks, CA: Sage.

Fowles, J. (1994). *Why viewers watch.* Thousand Oaks, CA: Sage.

Gurvetch, M., & Kavoori, A. (1992). Television spectacles as politics. *Communication Monographs, 59*, 415–420.

INDEX

Page 103, Nick Downes: "All he thinks about is that stupid ball." Cartoon on p. 10 in *Big Science* by Nick Downes. Copyright © 1992 by Nick Downes. Reprinted by permission of the cartoonist.

Page 106, Figures 4.1: C. K. Ogden and I. A. Richards (1923), *The Meaning of Meaning* (New York: Harcourt Brace Jovanovich), p. 11.

Page 113, Will & Deni McIntyre/Photo Researchers, Inc.

Page 124, (top) Tomas D. W. Friedmann/Photo Researchers, Inc.; **(bottom left)** Jeff Greenberg/Photo Researchers, Inc.; **(bottom center)** Catherine Karnow/Woodfin Camp & Associates; **(bottom right)** Harriet Gans/The Image Works

Page 129, (left) Photofest; **(right)** Randy Brooke/Sygma

Page 133, (top left) Stephanie Maze/Woodfin Camp & Associates; **(center left)** Tomas D. W. Friedmann/Photo Researchers, Inc.; **(bottom left)** Fujifotos/The Image Works; **(top right)** Hermine Dreyfuss/Monkmeyer Press; **(bottom right)** Bettina Cirone/Photo Researchers, Inc.

Page 136, (top left) Jeff Greenberg/Photo Researchers, Inc.; **(center left)** Art Glauberman/Photo Researchers, Inc.; **(bottom left)** Topham/OB/The Image Bank; **(top right)** Harriet Gans/The Image Works; **(center right)** Catherine Karnow/Woodfin Camp & Associates; **(bottom right)** Renee Lynn/Photo Researchers, Inc.

Page 147, John McPherson. "Apparently I have done something to upset you." Cartoon featured in CLOSE TO HOME by John McPherson. Copyright © 1994 by John McPherson. All rights reserved. Reprinted with permission of Andrews and McMeel, a Universal Press Syndicate Company.

Pages 158 and 184, Will & Deni McIntyre/Photo Researchers, Inc.

Page 162, Nicole Hollander: "A baloney sandwich." Cartoon featured on p. 9 in *Never Tell Your Mother This Dream* by Nicole Hollander. Copyright © 1984, 1985 by Nicole Hollander. All rights reserved. Reprinted by permission of St. Martin's Press, Inc.

Page 173, Cynthia Johnson/Liaison

Page 186, Stephen Ferry/Gamma Liaison

Pages 194 and 198, Richard Hutchings/Photo Researchers, Inc.

Page 210, Cathy Guisewite: Cartoon featured in *Why do the right words always come out of the wrong mouth?* by Cathy Guisewite. Copyright © 1988 by Universal Press Syndicate. All rights reserved. Reprinted with permission of Andrews and McMeel, a Universal Press Syndicate Company.

Page 211, Nadine Markova/The Stock Market

Page 217, Esbin-Anderson/The Image Works

Page 223, Michal Heron/Woodfin Camp & Associates

Pages 228 and 257, Richard Hutchings/Photo Researchers, Inc.

Page 233, Alan Carey/The Image Works

Page 253, Gary Larson: "Okay, Williams, we'll vote . . . how many here say the heart has four chambers?" Cartoon from *The Far Side* by Gary Larson. Reprinted by permission of Chronicle Features, San Francisco, CA. All rights reserved.

Pages 260 and 264, (top left) Jay Freis/The Image Bank

Page 264, (bottom left) Blair Seitz/Photo Researchers, Inc.; **(right)** Mark Reinstein/The Image Works